STUDIES AND TEXTS

47

PREACHERS, FLORILEGIA AND SERMONS:

Studies on the *Manipulus florum* of Thomas of Ireland

BY

RICHARD H. ROUSE

AND

MARY A. ROUSE

PONTIFICAL INSTITUTE OF MEDIAEVAL STUDIES
TORONTO 1979

ACKNOWLEDGMENT

This book has been published with the help of a grant
from the Humanities Research Council of Canada
using funds provided by the Canada Council.

Canadian Cataloguing in Publication Data

Rouse, Richard H., 1933-
   Preachers, florilegia and sermons

(Studies and texts - Pontifical Institute of Mediaeval Studies; 47 ISSN 0082-5328)

Bibliography: p.
Includes index.
ISBN 0-88844-047-2

1. Thomas Hibernicus. Manipulus florum.
2. Preaching - History - Middle Ages, 600-1500.
I. Rouse, Mary A., 1934-   II. Title.
III. Series: Pontifical Institute of Mediaeval Studies. Studies and texts — Pontifical
Institute of Mediaeval Studies; 47.

BV4207.R68   251'.009'022   C79-094149-X

PRINTED BY UNIVERSA, WETTEREN, BELGIUM

Contents

VI

APPENDICES

Acknowledgments

This work, begun in 1963, has introduced us to subjects, places and people, some medieval, some modern, that have become the familiar world and community in which we live and work. We are happy to thank those who have helped us with this study directly or indirectly in the years since it began: Judson Allen, Marie-Thérèse d'Alverny, M.-L. Auger, L.-J. Battaillon O.P., Robert Benson, John Benton, Ludwig Bieler, Bernhard Bischoff, Leonard Boyle O.P., Carlos Contreras, Lloyd Daly, Ruth Dean, Antoine Dondaine O.P., A. I. Doyle, J. N. Garvin C.S.C., Pierre Gasnault, Jean Glénisson, R. W. Hunt, Thomas Kaeppeli O.P., N. R. Ker, Lester Little, A. C. de la Mare, Gilbert Ouy, Julian Plante, Élisabeth Pellegrin, Graham Pollard, Foster Sherwood Jr., André Vernet, Jean Vezin, Siegfried Wenzel, and Lynn T. White jr. Despite their kind assistance, errors doubtless remain, the responsibility for which naturally lies with us.

We are indebted to the staffs of the Institut de recherche et d'histoire des textes, Paris; the Département des manuscrits, Bibliothèque Nationale, Paris; Duke Humphrey's Library, Bodleian Library, Oxford; the Research Library, University of California, Los Angeles; and those of numerous other libraries in Europe and North America, for their considerate and generous response to our needs.

We are grateful to the University of California, the American Council of Learned Societies, the American Philosophical Society, the Centre national de la recherche scientifique, and the John Simon Guggenheim Memorial Foundation for the financial support that allowed us to complete this and related studies.

Introduction

The common, everyday handbooks of the later Middle Ages, ubiquitous works existing in hundreds of copies, have for the most part been bypassed by modern scholarship because they do not stand out as original thought or great literature. It is natural and generally more fruitful to single out the creative genius, to concentrate on the intellectual high points. Similarly, because of the normal tendency to deal with the substance of an author's thought or with the finished product—a *summa*, a poem, a miniature—the method by which a man worked and the handbooks or tools that he employed have remained in the shadow. Yet, obviously, we do not come to know the ordinary world of the literate populace of the thirteenth and fourteenth centuries only through a study of its extraordinary figures. Conversely, we cannot properly know the exceptional figures of late medieval thought and letters without some knowledge of the tools with which they worked, the manuals and reference books that constituted an integral part of their training and comprised ever after a portion of their intellectual equipment.

This is the study of one such ordinary book. The *Manipulus florum* contains no original thought and makes no intellectual pretensions. Yet one can scarcely deny that it is a more typical product of its age than are the works of St. Thomas. The *Manipulus* is an alphabetically-arranged topical compendium of *auctoritates*, designed for use in writing sermons. It therefore epitomizes several of the occupations and preoccupations of the thirteenth century, including the creation and development of alphabetical reference tools, a new and urgent emphasis upon the preaching ministry, and the evolution in the form and content of the sermon itself. We have, thus, considered each of these in turn and at some length, as significant elements in the thirteenth-century background to the *Manipulus florum*.

Thomas of Ireland, the author of the *Manipulus*, is, as often as not, mistaken for or conflated with one or even two other Thomases; and questions of identity aside, he is occasionally denied the authorship of the *Manipulus florum*. We have pulled together what is known about his life and other writings. In discussing the *Manipulus florum* itself, we have naturally devoted much attention to its structure and organization. Considered from these aspects, the work is unique: it is the first alphabetically-organized collection of *auctoritates patrum*, and no later collections ever

equalled it in popularity before the advent of the printing press. In terms of
its content, the *Manipulus* has its roots in widespread and sometimes unexpected places. It draws upon the classical interests of the twelfth-century
Florilegium Gallicum and *Florilegium Angelicum*, and of the library of
Richard de Fournival; the spiritual and doctrinal interests of early thirteenth-century Cistercians flow into the *Manipulus* via the *Flores paradysi*
and the *Liber exceptionum*. In turn, the *Manipulus* transmits to its own
readers not only the borrowed quotations but, inevitably, something of the
interests which determined their original selection. We have sorted out
Thomas of Ireland's sources, many of them previously unstudied, and
examined the ways in which he transformed and recast them for a vastly
wider audience.

The *Manipulus florum* was published by the university stationers. An understanding of the operation of this system of publication depends upon the
combined results of examinations of the written regulations of the medieval
book trade, of the surviving books published by the stationers, and of the
textual history of individual works produced by the trade. The *Manipulus*
lends itself to such a study because it survives in a large number of copies,
among them Thomas' donation copy for the Sorbonne, a collection of
exemplar *peciae*, and a number of manuscripts copied from this and
two other university exemplars. In addition to the some 180 surviving
manuscripts, the *Manipulus florum* underwent some 47 printings between
1483 and 1887.

As these figures imply, the work was of use to many, over a long time. It
was quoted, imitated, and cited as an authority; recommended by preachers'
manuals; employed in scholastic sermons and vernacular literature; known
to such disparate figures as William of Pagula and Petrarch. Its users saw
the *Manipulus* as a mine of authorities suitable for use in composition.
From a broader perspective, we see it as a vehicle through which the contents of its twelfth- and thirteenth-century sources were made available to a
host of later writers. For example, many of the patristic quotations in the
works of Christine de Pisan derive, via Thomas of Ireland, from the thirteenth-century library of Clairvaux as reflected in the *Liber exceptionum*.
Again, the bibliography which concludes the *Manipulus*, a list of books
nearly all of which had belonged to Richard de Fournival, is incorporated
almost entire into a list of supposedly English texts, the *Catalogus* of Henry
of Kirkestede ("Boston of Bury").

Thomas' introduction and the bibliography that he appended to the
Manipulus are edited here for the first time. We have included detailed
notices of over 180 surviving manuscripts, to show the community of texts
with which the *Manipulus* circulated, the physical form that it took, and the

geographical and chronological extent of its dissemination. The list of the authors and works cited in the *Manipulus* has been indexed in a form that can be used with any printed edition of the work.

The *Manipulus florum*, regarded in terms of both content and structure, provides insights into many aspects of the medieval world, the thoughts, ideas and movements which flowed into, around and out from this *florilegium*. Surely, many of the users of the work were much more significant figures than was Thomas of Ireland; and many of the contingent topics discussed here are of greater moment than is the *florilegium* itself. Yet, to each of them, the *Manipulus florum* has served as a key. We hope by means of this study to make that key more accessible for use by others.

Part One

The Thirteenth-Century Background

1

Thirteenth-Century Sermon Aids[1]

The *Manipulus florum* belongs to the genre of *florilegia*. Scholars tend to treat all *florilegia* as collections made for spiritual reading and moral edification, devoid of any originality. Thus H. Rochais, in describing spiritual *florilegia*, brackets the *Manipulus florum* between the *Communiloquium* of John of Wales and the anonymous *Liber Pharetrae*.[2] The *Manipulus* has little in common with either of these works, or with the spiritual *florilegium* as a type. The background of the *Manipulus florum*, instead, is to be found among the alphabetically-arranged and searchable tools which emerged in the thirteenth century. The *Manipulus florum* distinguishes itself from the typical spiritual *florilegium* on two counts: (1) The *Manipulus* was written not to be read, but to be used—that is, to be searched. The work was so constructed that its user could quickly locate quotations pertaining to virtually any moral or doctrinal topic of interest to him. (2) It was not conceived of as an end in itself, to stand in place of the whole works, but rather as a mode of approach to them. To that purpose Thomas of Ireland appended to the *Manipulus florum* a list of 400 *originalia patrum*, with their first and last lines. Therefore, while the *Manipulus* is by genre a *florilegium*, its originality lies in its purpose and in the structure invented to achieve that purpose. In order to perceive and to assess the achievement of Thomas of Ireland, we must examine the *Manipulus florum* in the context of the development of searchable tools. Certainly, the history of the origin, development and dissemination of research tools in the thirteenth century is a large topic, matter for a book in itself. We wish here, at very least, to provide sufficient background for the *Manipulus florum* that one might place it in its tradition.[3]

---

[1] This chapter has benefited from the comments and suggestions of those who have read it in draft; we wish in particular to thank M.-Th. d'Alverny, John Baldwin, Robert Benson, John Benton, R. W. Hunt, N. R. Ker, Lester Little, M. B. Parkes, Graham Pollard and Lynn T. White, jr.

[2] H. Rochais, "Florilèges spirituels," *Dictionnaire de spiritualité* 5 (1962) 446 no. 20, s.n. Thomas de Palmerstown (d. 1269).

[3] For a fuller investigation of this subject see R. H. Rouse, *The Development of Aids to Study in the Thirteenth Century*, Rosenbach Lectures in Bibliography, University of Pennsylvania, forthcoming. There is unfortunately no comprehensive discussion of this subject in

Tools such as the *Manipulus florum* begin to appear in the opening decades of the thirteenth century, and are taken for granted by Thomas of Ireland's lifetime. Between 1220 and 1306 a veritable flood of such books appeared, among them alphabetical collections of distinctions, the great concordance to the Scripture, alphabetical subject indexes to the writings of the Fathers, and location lists of books. These are works designed to be used, rather than to be read. Tools such as these are unknown in classical Antiquity. They are alien to the Hebrew and Byzantine traditions until imported from the Latins. And they emerge with striking suddenness in the West, to the point that one may say that, probably before 1220, certainly before 1190, no such tools existed; and that, after the 1280s, the dissemination and new creation of such aids to study were commonplace. Far from being a product of the printing press, they are a thirteenth-century invention.[4]

The appearance of such devices indicates a significant change in attitude toward written authority. The major works of the twelfth century, the *Gloss* on the Bible, the *Sentences* of the Lombard and the *Decretum*, represent efforts to assimilate and organize inherited written authority in systematic form. In contrast, the tools of the thirteenth century represent efforts to search written authority afresh.[5] These tools epitomize an effort to get at material, to gain access, to locate, to retrieve information. The spirit they embodied was more assertive, even aggressive, than that of the twelfth century. As Dom Wilmart remarked, at the turn of the thirteenth century "patristic antiquity is not rejected; to the contrary, it is employed with fervor, if not with the same superstitious respect.... But it is no longer merely

---

print. Studies of individual tools and techniques will be referred to in the notes as they are taken up.

    [4] The notion persists that indexes—as well as the general apparatus for finding one's way about in books—resulted from the invention of printing which, in freezing the text, would render indexing feasible. Scholars have only grudgingly admitted the existence of a primitive index here or there in the fourteenth century. See F. Witty, "Early Indexing Techniques: A Study of Several Book Indexes of the Fourteenth, Fifteenth and Early Sixteenth Centuries," *The Library Quarterly* 35 (1965) 141-148; idem, "The Beginnings of Indexing and Abstracting: Some Notes towards a History of Indexing and Abstracting in Antiquity and the Middle Ages," *The Indexer* 8 (1973) 193-198; E. H. Wilkins, "Early Alphabetical Indexes," in *The Manly Anniversary Studies in Language and Literature* (Chicago 1928) 315-322 (concerning indexes to Boccaccio): "The earliest alphabetical index of which I have knowledge is an index of the *De consolatione philosophiae* of Boethius made in 1322"; and most of all perhaps the writings of Walter Ong, s.j., for whom this is a basic factor distinguishing printed from scribal culture. See for example his *The Presence of the Word* (New Haven 1967) 85-87, and *Rhetoric, Romance and Technology* (Ithaca 1971) 277.

    [5] M. D. Chenu, *Introduction à l'étude de S. Thomas d'Aquin* (Paris 1951) 40-41; and R. W. Hunt, "Manuscripts Containing the Indexing Symbols of Robert Grosseteste," *Bodleian Library Record* 4 (1952-1953) 249-250.

reproduced; it is pressed into the service of a mode of thought which is in the process of self-renewal."[6]

This is not to say that the techniques for making tools, such as alphabetization, did not exist before 1190; there are isolated earlier examples of virtually all the devices which are used in thirteenth-century tools. Nor is it to say that no one before 1200 needed access to information. It is simply that the first half of the thirteenth century provided the proper context, the balanced mixture of ingredients—a pressing need, the techniques with which to meet the need, and the institutional framework in which to apply the techniques of tool-making.

Over a century earlier, when the Gregorian reform placed demands on inherited authority similar to those of 1190-1220, the response was remarkably different and the contrast is instructive. To counter the claims made for secular authority, the Church sought out and assembled the written authority on which its claims to primacy were based; the reformers put together the first great canon law collections. Yet the Gregorian reform produced no indexing tradition. It would seem that, at the end of the eleventh century, both the body of material dealt with and the number of people involved were small enough that a rational and increasingly well-honed classification by subject sufficed. The canonists, thus, felt no compulsion to break with the traditional aim of Christian scholarship: to discern the proper relationship of one thing to another; an index would have been an unnecessary artifice.

An exception proves the rule. The canonical collection of Cardinal Deusdedit was equipped with a primitive subject index.[7] Written between 1083 and 1087, the work is a collection of 1173 texts, each numbered as a chapter, and arranged by broad subject into four books. Deusdedit explains in the preface that he refrained from organizing each book internally by subject, lest the documents be broken up and dispersed under various topic headings. Therefore, to permit one to find a canon pertinent to a given subject, he has provided a list of subjects for each of the four books—some 800 in all—with reference by number to the proper chapter or chapters.[8] What

[6] A. Wilmart, "Les allégories sur l'écriture attribuées à Raban Maur," *Revue bénédictine* 32 (1920) 56.

[7] Regarding Deusdedit's collection see P. Fournier and G. Le Bras, *Histoire des collections canoniques en Occident* (Paris 1932) 2: 37-54. The collection itself is edited by Victor Wolf von Glanvell, *Die Kanonessammlung des Kardinals Deusdedit* (Paderborn 1905) vol. 1. We thank Robert Somerville for this reference.

[8] For example, from the *Capitula libri primi*: "Ut laicalis potestas se non interserat electioni vel promotioni pontificis. Cap. CCXLIIII; in libro III° cap. CLII, CLIII, CLIIII; in II°, cap. XXXI; in libro IIII° cap. XI, XVI, XVII, XVIII, XX' (Wolf von Glanvell 13).

looks like a standard table of contents has been transformed into a primitive
index in subject rather than alphabetical order. It is somewhat similar, in
fact, to the primitive indexes in subject order that are among the earliest of
the thirteenth-century indexes—but with this major difference, that Deusdedit's index was neither precursor nor portent. Other canonists did not
imitate his index nor improve upon his technique; the index of Cardinal
Deusdedit produced no heirs.

The historical accident that the canon lawyers faced the demand for access to written authority a century earlier than did the theologians, and thus
responded in the terms, and via the institutions, of the late eleventh century, goes far toward explaining why canon law was so resistant to the new
devices of the thirteenth century. The canon of topics and its arrangement
had been meticulously worked out between the time of Gregory VII and
Gratian; it dominated the arrangement of canon law material until the late
thirteenth-century efforts to extract the legal matter necessary for parish
priests in indexed manuals like John of Freiburg's *Summa confessorum*, and
the fourteenth-century efforts to concord canon and Roman law.

Tools used to get at information first emerge in that community which is
neither monastic nor university, but rather urban school—populated collectively or consecutively by monks, canons, seculars and friars—which
flourished from about 1175 onward at Paris and Oxford in northern
Europe. To say this does not explain the cause of their appearance, however. One associates, justifiably, the making of reference tools both with the
mendicant orders and with the formalized university structure (that is, a
university with statutes, fixed curricula, and especially organized book
production). Yet the earliest alphabetical tools antedate the arrival of the
friars, as well as the institutionalization of learning. Similarly, while some
of the earliest tools appear in Cistercian circles, it would be misleading
to consider the origin of tools as strictly an outgrowth of Cistercian
spirituality.

Instead, for the origin of tools one must look to the growing concentration upon pastoral ministry and preaching, which manifested itself in
the Church as a whole and which intimately involved the groups we have
mentioned.[9] The Cistercians were heavily committed to the new ministry in
the last decades of the twelfth century, as were the masters of theology in
the schools. The Church's concentration upon preaching and pastoral
ministry served as the impetus for the emergence and the confirmation of
the mendicant orders, as well as for the institutionalization of learning in

---

[9] See chapter 2 below.

the thirteenth century. Tools, mendicants, and (to a large degree) university are all responses to the same demand, the Church's need for a clergy properly trained and provided with the necessary books to preach and to minister to a Christian community.

I. TOOLS

The tools developed in the thirteenth and fourteenth centuries emerge in a discernible sequence. The earliest tools are those which provide access to the scriptures, namely, the alphabetical collections of biblical distinctions, and the great verbal concordance; the latter provides the basic reference system used in a large proportion of later tools—as well as a means for compiling further collections of distinctions. These scriptural tools are established works by the 1240s, when one sees the appearance of the first true alphabetical subject indexes in monastery, school and diocese. More complex *accessus* to authors, and catalogs locating books in one or more libraries, are not seen until the last third of the century, by which time the compilation and use of the concordance and the subject index and the techniques that they employ (such as alphabetical order and arabic numerals) have become commonplace to clerics, whether preacher, lawyer, doctor or administrator. Beyond this general outline a chronological or developmental approach is unrealistic, because by mid-century various tools employing a variety of techniques appear simultaneously in different locales in response to similar needs and among people who are obviously part of the same intellectual community.

A. Distinctions and Concordances

The collections of biblical distinctions which abound in western Europe from the end of the twelfth century are the earliest of all alphabetical tools aside from dictionaries.[10] Distinction collections provide one with the various figurative or symbolic meanings of a noun found in the scriptures, illustrating each meaning with a scriptural passage. Take for example a thirteenth-century distinction on *equus*:[11]

---

[10] For a fuller description of distinction collections, see R. H. and M. A. Rouse, "Biblical Distinctions in the Thirteenth Century," *Archives d'histoire doctrinale et littéraire du Moyen Age* 41 (1974) 27-37, and the bibliography cited there.

[11] On the flyleaf of Rouen Bibl. mun. MS 109 (before 1249; Jumièges): "Equus: Predicator. Iob XXXIX.e, 'Numquid prebebis equo fortitudinem, aut circumdabis collo eius hinnitum?' Glosa Gregorii hoc loco equi nomine sanctus predicator accipitur, cui dominus se dare prius fortitudinem et postmodum hinnitum asserit. Nam predicator ante fortitudinem

Horse = Preacher. Job 39: 'Hast thou given the horse strength, or encircled his neck with whinnying?' Gregory's gloss on this says that the horse means a preacher, to whom God first gives strength to conquer his own vices, and then a whinny—a voice to preach to others. Horse = Temporal dignity, as in Ecclesiastes 10: 'I have seen servants upon horses....' Horse = The easy life; thus in the Psalm: 'Be ye not as the horse or as the mule, which have no understanding.' Horse = The present age; Genesis 49: 'Dan shall be a serpent by the way ... that biteth the horse's heels so that his rider shall fall backward.'

Some distinction collections give as many as fifteen different figurative meanings, for several hundred to several thousand terms. It is the task of these tools to provide access to the scriptures, or, as Alan of Lille says, to provide a freer entrée to the sacred page: "Dignum duximus theologicorum verborum significationes distinguere, metaphorarum rationes assignare, occultas troporum positiones in lucem reducere, ut liberior ad sacram paginam pandatur introitus." [12]

Distinctions have usually been treated as tools for scholarly exegesis, and described in static terms. However, their use in the classroom must have been marginal indeed; and the notion of what comprised a *distinctio* changed markedly with time, as we shall see. This device first emerges at the end of the twelfth century, in sermons and in theology lectures. It is hard to determine which was the original matrix; but the alphabetized collections of such distinctions are, from the beginning, a biblical tool for preachers. The collections fall into two groups, those made largely for personal use, which frequently are known in only one or two manuscripts, and those which were meant to be circulated. The former—e.g., the Cistercian *Distinctiones monasticae*—are by far the most numerous. Among the latter are the *Summa Abel* of Peter the Chanter (d. 1197), and the collections of Alan of Lille (d. 1202), of Warner of Langres (d. 1202), of William de Montibus (d. 1213) and that of Peter of Capua written ca. 1220 expressly for the use of the clergy of Rome. This last is provided with systematic cross-references, in a style adapted from the glossed Bible. For alphabetical tools, Peter's is the most sophisticated such apparatus until the appearance of the *Manipulus florum* some eighty years later. In the second half of the century the most popular collections are mendicant, including those of

---

accipit, vicia in se extinguendo; demum pro erudiendis aliis vocem predicationis emittit. — Dignitas temporalis. De quo Ecclesiaste X°c, 'Vidi servos in equis ambulantes...'. —Lubrica vita. Unde in psalmo, 'Nolite fieri sicut equus et mulus quibus non est intellectus.' — Presens seculum. Gen. XLIX.e, 'Fiat Dan coluber in via ... mordens ungulas equi, ut cadet ascensor eius retro.'"

[12] Alan of Lille, *Distinctiones dictionum theologicarum*, PL 210: 688.

Maurice of Provins, Nicholas Gorran and Nicholas Biard, which were given wide circulation by the Paris stationers.

A look at contemporary sermons shows how preachers used this tool, as we shall see below. Early in the century, the commonest use is the dry recitation of three or so meanings of a word, or of several words, in the Bible text which serves as the theme of a sermon. By mid-century, preachers increasingly choose three meanings, given in a distinction, of the main word of their theme, and use these as the structure of a three-part sermon. Distinction collections themselves evolve in the same direction. The earliest are laconic in the extreme, often presented in diagrammatic form. As time passes, the individual distinctions become lengthier, with subdivisions and moralizations—in effect, the outline and scriptural basis for an entire sermon.[13] Late thirteenth-century distinction collections heavily emphasize moral topics, useful for preaching: one is less likely to find *equus* than *equitas*. By the fourteenth century, new collections of so-called distinctions incorporate *exempla*, patristic *auctoritates* and the like; they have become diffuse alphabetical compendia of *materia praedicabilis*.

The verbal concordance to the scriptures is at once an aid to study for the theology classroom, and a tool for preachers writing sermons based on *distinctiones*. This combination is fitting, since the verbal concordance was the creation of a body of scholar-preachers, the Dominicans at Saint-Jacques in Paris. The history of the verbal concordance was first investigated by Quétif and Échard.[14] Scholars since then have largely been content to quote them. A look at the manuscripts of the concordance tells a story quite different from that given in the standard contemporary treatment.[15] The first concordance was compiled at Saint-Jacques under the aegis of Hugh of Saint-Cher, and was in existence probably by 1239.[16] This pioneer work devised the reference system : each appearance of a word was indicated by book of the Bible, by the chapter divisions attributed to Stephen Langton, and by one of the seven letters A-G to indicate relative position within the chapter. The production of this lengthy work involved an impressive organization of manpower. There are, in the fifteenth-century bindings of Saint-Jacques books, four surviving cahiers of what must be the

[13] See chapter 3 below.

[14] J. Quétif and J. Échard, *Scriptores ordinis praedicatorum* (Paris 1719) 1: 203-210, 466-467, 610-611, 632.

[15] For example, H. Mangenot, "Concordance de la Bible," *Dictionnaire de la Bible* 2 (1926) 895-899.

[16] The following is expanded and documented in R. H. and M. A. Rouse, "The Verbal Concordance to the Scripture," *Archivum fratrum praedicatorum* 44 (1974) 5-30.

penultimate draft, revealing a part of their working method. Each cahier was written by a different man, who had a fixed alphabetical segment to cover, leaving blank space at the end when he completed his assignment. Corrections are noted in, making it ready for the final copy. A disadvantage of this first concordance was that it did not cite words in context. This version survives in eighteen manuscripts, of which thirteen date from the thirteenth century. A second concordance, the work of Richard of Stavensby and perhaps other English Dominicans at Saint-Jacques, provided a lengthy context for each word. This, the *Concordanciae anglicanae*, is usually treated as the main medieval concordance. It survives, however, in only seven manuscripts, evidently no two of them containing the same text; and it was clearly too cumbersome to render practical service. The need for a concordance of words-in-context was met by the third Saint-Jacques concordance, in circulation by 1286; it provides a brief four-to-seven word context for each *lemma*. This version was published by the university stationers and exists in over eighty copies. Only in the 1280s did medieval Europe finally have an effective biblical concordance.

Both the method of compilation described above and the rapid cultural assimilation of the concordance are witnessed in an early fourteenth-century moralized *exemplum* of an Anglo-Norman contemporary of Thomas of Ireland, Nicholas Bozon. Nicholas illustrates the lesson that one should be concerned with one's own faults, rather than with those of others:

> Wherefore I would that each one did as did once the brothers who compiled concordances. Each took charge of the letter that was committed to him. He who had A had nothing to do with B and he who had charge of B did not intermeddle with C, and so each letter of the ABC was delivered to different men, and each took his letter, and no one wished to interfere with the act of the other. Thereby they arrived at the noble book with which the Holy Church is much comforted.[17]

Here we see a moral lesson taught in terms of the new technology, just as pious nineteenth-century clergymen were to moralize the steam engine; and the procedure described corresponds with the physical evidence, the individual quires on which different brothers worked that are found in the Saint-Jacques bindings.

---

[17] We are grateful to M. Jean Batany for this reference. Nicholas Bozon, o.f.m., *Contes moralisés*, ed. Lucy Toulmin Smith and Paul Meyer (Paris 1889) 160; we give the text from the English translation by "J.R.", *Metaphors of Brother Bozon* (London 1913) 173-174, no. 134. Concerning Bozon see M. Amelia Klenke, o.p., "Nicholas Bozon," *Modern Language Notes* 69 (1954) 256-260, and the bibliography cited there.

In the course of the thirteenth century the concordance became the main tool for the compilation of biblical distinctions. One of the two oldest datable copies of the first Saint-Jacques concordance belonged to a parish priest who left it to Jumièges in 1249, after he had filled its flyleaves with distinctions, including the one for *equus* cited above. As we shall see below, preachers of the second half of the century used concordances to form veritable chains of scriptural *auctoritates*. By the fourteenth century, the *artes praedicandi* take it for granted that a preacher will have access to a concordance. Thomas Hibernicus assumes widespread familiarity with the concordance, using it as his standard for comparison: in describing the alphabetical arrangement of the *Manipulus florum* he explains, twice, that his work is ordered "more concordantiarum."

B. Subject Indexes

At roughly the same time that the Dominicans in Paris are completing the first verbal concordance, the alphabetical subject index appears. Early indexes are products of the same concentration on a pastoral training grounded in scripture and patristic authority that produced the distinction collections and the concordance. Eminently useful, the index as a technical device is rapidly dispersed. Numerous indexes employing a variety of techniques appear in different places almost simultaneously, the majority of them for use in composing sermons. A chronological or developmental approach to them is tenuous at present, since so few early indexes can be precisely dated. The earliest indexes were probably made at the schools in Paris, since this is where their antecedents, the distinction collection and the verbal concordance, were formed. Nevertheless, the manuscripts themselves will not permit one to distinguish between Paris proper and the communities represented by the students and masters who, collectively, comprise the Paris schools, and who carry ideas, procedures and techniques from one place to another—among them in particular a number of important Cistercian houses and the schools at Oxford. It is possible, however, from the tools themselves to see a development in techniques from non-alphabetical to alphabetical order. Among the oldest subject indexes are a number which are arranged in systematic order, and others simply in random or haphazard fashion. This sort of indexing gives way by mid-century to arrangement in alphabetical order. We shall examine indexes in the formative, one might rather say primitive, stage at the Paris schools. Then we shall see developments in indexing at three Cistercian communities, Clairvaux, Villers-en-Brabant and Bruges, and at the Oxford schools, and finally return to Paris to see the application of indexing techniques by contemporaries of Thomas of Ireland at the Sorbonne in the last decades of the thirteenth century. Each community, stimulated by the same needs, draws upon a common body of techniques developed in the production of the distinction collection and the concordance and adapts them to its own needs, giving back new techniques which will in turn be applied by others.

Among the earliest tools which one might term an index is the concordance to the Bible in subject order, or "real concordance," at one time incorrectly attributed to Antony of Padua.[18] This work, the *Concordancie morales bibliorum*, is divided into five books:

> Primus liber agit de iis que pertinent ad depravationem primi hominis, cum suis oppositis.... Secundus liber agit de iis que pertinent ad Deum, cum suis oppositis.... Tertius liber agit de iis que pertinent ad bene pugnantem et succumbentem bello spirituali, cum aliquibus oppositis.... Quartus liber agit de iis que pertinent ad perfectum virum, cum suis oppositis.... Quintus liber agit de diversis personis et quibusdam aliis que ad eos pertinent, cum aliquibus oppositis....

Each book is subdivided into from two to eight parts, and for each of these there are numerous subject headings. For the five books together there are some 550 subjects. Under each heading is a list of Bible passages pertinent to the topic, each identified by book, chapter, letter (A-G) and *lemma*—for example, "Contra peccatum simpliciter. Iob xxvi e. obstetricante manu; [etc.]." Kleinhans showed in 1931 that the work was not written by Antony of Padua (d. 1231). It must, in fact, date after the appearance of the Saint-Jacques concordance (ca. 1239), since it employs the A-G system of reference devised by the Dominicans to subdivide the chapters of the Bible. It cannot postdate it by many years, however, since the oldest manuscripts, written in the middle of the thirteenth century, are very similar in appearance to the copies of the first Saint-Jacques concordance. Oxford, Bodleian MS Can. pat. lat. 7 (SC 18993), s. xiii med., is a good example; in this manuscript the *Concordancie morales* accompanies the first Dominican concordance. While unsearchable, because of its lack of any discernible arrangement, the *Concordancie morales* nevertheless proved useful, for it survives in at least twenty-five copies dating from the thirteenth to the fifteenth century.

[18] A. Kleinhans, "De concordantiis Biblicis S. Antonio Patavino aliisque Fratribus minoribus saeculi xiii attributis," *Antonianum* 6 (1931) 273-326; and F. Stegmüller, *Repertorium biblicum medii aevi* (Madrid 1950) 2: 119-120, no. 1382. We cite the concordance from Paris, B.N. MS lat. 601 (s. xiii) and Oxford, Bodleian Library MS Can. pat. lat. 7 (s. xiii).

Two other similar tools were produced at roughly the same time. The first is the subject index compiled apparently for his own use by a former canon of Saint-Victor, Thomas of Vercelli.[19] The index no longer survives, but it is cited, according to Théry, in works which Thomas composed between 1242 and 1246 and is, hence, thought to date from the early 1240s. Théry has demonstrated from references to it in Thomas's works that it was arranged by subject as was the *Concordancie morales*. Not dissimilar from these works is the index to the scriptures in subject order compiled by the Dominicans at Saint-Jacques which survives in a Clairvaux manuscript, Troyes MS 2019 ff. 1-33ᵛ (s. xiii; Clairvaux A.64). It begins,

> Incipiunt capitula vel superscriptiones titulorum xviii numero minorum concordantiarum veteris ac novi testamenti quas ad utilitatem multorum, fratres predicatores compilaverunt. Concordantie vero iste continent xviii titulos. Qui tituli continent centum octaginta quatuor partes. Primus titulus continet tres partes et sic singuli tituli continent suas partes per ordinem. Prima pars: De primi consilii in comodo consilio et exemplo; secunda: Que dicit quod querenda sunt consortia beatorum; tercia: De eo quod toleranda sunt interdum pravorum consortia.

In the words, "The preaching friars compiled this for the use of many," we see an explicit statement of the common denominators of Dominican tools : utility, community and anonymity.

By mid-century, alphabetical subject indexes to Aristotle's *Ethics* and natural works have been compiled, as well as indexes to the Old and New Logic. There is no proof that these were made at Paris, since they are all anonymous. However, the conjunction of Aristotelian studies with indexing activity points to Paris. The discovery of these indexes was Grabmann's.[20] The oldest known manuscript containing the indexes, now MS 124 of the Seminary Library in Pisa, is a splendid example of someone's mid-thirteenth-century manual or compendium of aids to Aristotle. The volume begins with a list of incipits of the chapters of the *Ethics*, followed by an alphabetical subject index. Next are the chapter incipits and alphabetical subject index to the Old Logic (Porphyry's *Isagoge*, the *Categories*, *Periermeneias*, *Liber sex principiorum*) and to Boethius' *De divisionibus* and *De*

[19] G. Théry, "Thomas Gallus et les concordances bibliques," *Aus der Geisteswelt des Mittelalters*, Beiträge zur Philosophie und Theologie des Mittelalters, suppl. 3.1 (Munster i.W. 1935) 427-446.

[20] M. Grabmann, *Methoden und Hilfsmittel des Aristotelesstudiums im Mittelalter*, Sitzungsberichte der Bayerischen Akademie der Wissenschaften, Phil.-hist. Abt. 5 (Munich 1939) 139-149; C. H. Lohr, "Medieval Latin Aristotle Commentaries," *Traditio* 26 (1970) 156-157.

differentiis topicis; incipits and alphabetical indexes to the *Prior Analytics*, to the *Posterior Analytics*, to Plato's *Timaeus*, and to six Boethian works, including the *De consolatione philosophiae*. Next is the alphabetical index (without chapter incipits) to the *De animalibus* (Michael Scott's translation). The last item in the manuscript is the list of chapter incipits, and the lengthy alphabetical index, to Aristotle's *Libri naturales*.[21] The *tabula* to the *Ethics* is based on the old partial translations of the *Ethica nova* and *Ethica vetus*, rather than the later translation from the Greek of the whole *Nichomachean Ethics* by Robert Grosseteste ca. 1244. A relatively early date is likewise indicated by the table to the natural books, based on a mixture of translations from Greek and Arabic, pre-Moerbeke and, in Grabmann's opinion, "at, or more likely before, the middle of the thirteenth century."[22] Each reference under a given topic cites the name of the work, the number of book and chapter, and a letter of the alphabet indicating relative location within the chapter. This, of course, is the system devised by the Paris Dominicans in the 1230s for the first Biblical concordance.

The index at mid-century was no longer a novel device; a steadily increasing number of patristic authors are equipped with indexes. A good example is the index to selected works of Augustine, Jerome, Dionysius, Anselm, Bernard and others, seen in Paris B.N. MS lat. 16334 which was compiled, according to its colophon, by Robert of Paris in 1256 for Master Guy of Motun, canon of Saint-Géry in Cambrai.[23] Under some 570 topics, alphabetized by the first two letters of each word, the volume refers to work, book, and chapter, and frequently employs the A-G method of reference to subdivide chapters. It begins, "*Abraam.* Quod Saare ius erat qui peteret filium ab eo, xv de civ. Dei 4...," continuing with *ablutio, abstinencia, abyssus, accidia, acceptio personarum, accidens, Adam,* and so on. The work was acquired, doubtless soon after it was made, by Gerard of Abbeville, with whose books it passed to the Sorbonne.[24]

The techniques being developed in Paris spread almost instantaneously, being carried back by students and masters to the dioceses and religious houses from which they had come—institutions which shared with Paris not only a common personnel, but, in particular, a common commitment to the ministry of preaching. Along with the transmission, of course, came adaptation and innovation.

[21] Grabmann 124-155.
[22] Ibid. 129.
[23] C. Samaran and R. Marichal, *Catalogue des manuscrits en écriture latine portant des indications de date, de lieu ou de copiste* 3 (Paris 1974) 521; plate 47.
[24] See p. 21 below.

The Cistercians were particularly ingenious at applying notions of indexing and devising reference systems for texts that were difficult to index.[25] At Clairvaux and its daughter house Villers-en-Brabant, a mature means of indexing *florilegia* was in existence before 1246. Two such indexed *florilegia*, the *Liber exceptionum ex libris viginti trium auctorum* and a *Flores Bernardi*, are attributed to William of Montague, ninth abbot of Clairvaux (d. 1246).[26] Montague divided his *florilegia* into numbered *distinctiones*, each *distinctio* subdivided by letters of the alphabet. The divisions are arbitrary, unrelated to divisions in the text. The index, occupying twenty-three folios, contains some 2200 subjects with up to twenty-five or more references each. References provide *distinctio*, letter and lemma—for example, ABDUCERE: XIX.a *Magni*. In the late thirteenth century the system, employing three concentric and successively more explicit sequences of the alphabet (*Aaa*—main division *A*, section *a*, extract *a*), was applied to a *florilegium* of Biblical extracts at Clairvaux (Troyes MS 1037; Clairvaux A.61), a manuscript of 151 folios with an index of forty-three folios. It is also seen in Troyes MS 1692 (s. xiii; Clairvaux A.62) and Darmstadt MS 510 (s. xiii; Saint-James, Liège O.S.B.). The other major example of this system is the *Flores paradysi* produced at Villers-en-Brabant in the first half of the thirteenth century. The oldest version of this work (Brussels, Bibl. roy. MS 4785-93; Van den Gheyn 970), dating from ca. 1216-1230, bears an artificial reference system with each verso-recto opening of pages designated by letters of the alphabet (*Aa, Ab, Ac..., Ba, Bb*, etc.) and each extract in the opening designated by a single letter. The index of 450 subjects refers to opening and *sententia*—for example, *Ac.g.* In the enlarged version of the *Flores paradysi*,[27] three concentric series of alphabets replace the sequence of lettered openings. The index contains some 900 entries—chosen, the prologue states, for their usefulness in sermons. Although monastic in origin, both the *Liber exceptionum* and the *Flores paradysi* soon found their way to Paris, where they were used by Thomas of Ireland. The *Liber exceptionum* made its way to Oxford as well.[28] They are fascinating devices because, as indexes to *florilegia*, they cannot be explained in terms of an evangelical return to the whole works,

---

[25] See R. H. Rouse, "Cistercian Aids to Study in the Thirteenth Century," *Studies in Cistercian History* 2 (1976) 123-134.

[26] The *Liber exceptionum* survives in eight manuscripts of which the oldest is Troyes Bibl. mun. MS 186 (s. xiii[1]; Clairvaux L.50); the *Flores Bernardi* in two, of which the older is Troyes MS 497 (s. xiii[1]; Clairvaux H.49). Concerning William of Montague see the two notices in *Histoire littéraire de la France* 18 (Paris 1835) 149-152, 338-346.

[27] Brussels, Bibl. roy. MS 20030-32, Van den Gheyn 1508 (s. xiii[1]).

[28] These two *florilegia* are described in detail in chapter 5 below.

which has hitherto been used to account for medieval indexing. It is preaching, rather, which motivates the making of these particular tools.

Further north, the Cistercians of Ter Duinen and its daughter house Ter Doest on the outskirts of Bruges borrowed and developed their own devices for indexing.[29] The scriptorium of Ter Duinen, serving both houses, devised a method of foliation composed of letters and dots—*a* through *z*, followed by dot-*a* through dot-*z*, then *a*-dot through *z*-dot, double-dot-*a* and so on, through seventeen permutations. Despite its clumsiness, this system was methodically applied to products of this scriptorium in the first half of the thirteenth century. Lieftinck has suggested that the dotted-letter system was used because the monks still lacked a numeral system with a decimal base. At least five manuscripts from these houses have short subject indexes to their contents, with a reference to the folio (letter and dot) followed by one of the first seven letters of the alphabet to indicate vertical location on the page—this latter an adaptation of the A-G system of the Dominican concordance. A device employed by the thirteenth-century users of these indexes survives.[30] It is an 8-inch strip of parchment, serving as a bookmark, which bears a key to the sequence of alphabets: "Ut memoriter teneatur alphabetum taliter ordinatur: a .a a. :a a: ..." etc. A vertical set of letters A-G, on the other side, divides the marker into seven equal sections. The user can hold this against the edge of any quarto leaf to help him find his reference. Attached to the head of the strip is a parchment disk in a sleeve, one quarter exposed. The disk is marked at 12, 3, 6 and 9 o'clock respectively. "I prima, II secunda, III tertia, IIII quarta," for the columns left to right across the opening; one left visible the column number, when using this as a book mark. Destrez considered this and similar disks to be copyists' tools ; in the present case, at least, one could with more justification call it a reader's tool.

It is however an almost meaningless distinction to speak of Cistercian

[29] See G. I. Lieftinck, *De Librijen en scriptoria der Westvlaamse Cisterciënserabdijen Ter Duinen en Ter Doest in de 12ᵉ en 13ᵉ Eeuw...*, Mededelingen van de koninklijke Vlaamse Academie voor Wetenschappen, Letteren en schone Kunsten van België, Kl. der Let. 15, no. 2 (Brussels 1953).

[30] Concerning this and similar devices see A. Schmidt, "Mittelalterliche Lesezeichnen," *Zeitschrift für Bücherfreunde* 2.1 (1898-1899) 213-215; J. Destrez, "L'outillage des copistes du xiiiᵉ et du xivᵉ siècle," *Aus der Geisteswelt des Mittelalters* 1 (n. 19 above) 19-34 ; H. Schreiber, "Drehbare mittelalterliche Lesezeichen," *Zentralblatt für Bibliothekswesen* 56 (1939) 281-293; P. Lehmann, "Blätter, Seiten, Spalten, Zeilen," in his *Erforschung des Mittelalters* 3 (Stuttgart 1960) 55; A. C. de la Mare, *Catalogue of the Medieval Manuscripts bequeathed to the Bodleian Library, Oxford, by James R. Lyell* (Oxford 1971) pl. XXXIa; and R. B. Marks, *The Medieval Manuscript Library of the Charterhouse of St. Barbara in Cologne*, Analecta Carthusiana 21 (Salzburg 1974) 40-42, and 61 plates 1-3.

tools and university tools after the establishment of a Cistercian house of study at Paris, the College of Saint Bernard; though the foundation was confirmed in 1245, there is evidence of its quasi-official existence since the 1220s. The Cistercian use of marginal letters of the alphabet as the reference system is employed at the university, and the A-G reference system devised by the Paris Dominicans is adapted by the Cistercians of Bruges. Parisian school books flow into Cistercian libraries, to the extent of eclipsing Cistercian *scriptoria*; and the Cistercian indexed *florilegia*, from both Villers and Clairvaux, find their way to the schools in Paris and Oxford.

Evidence of the need to prepare people for the ministry is as apparent at Oxford as at Paris. Figures like William de Montibus, Alexander Neckham, Odo of Cheriton and Stephen Langton stand out among what must have been a considerable number of individuals who brought back to England interests and procedures acquired in Paris in the opening years of the thirteenth century. The schoolroom interest in preaching is witnessed in the anonymous *Moralities on the Gospels*, formerly attributed to Grosseteste.[31] The *Moralities* were probably written in the second quarter of the thirteenth century. The oldest surviving manuscript, Oxford, Lincoln College MS 79, is still written beginning on the top line in the older fashion. The work consists of moralizations of passages from the Gospels, frequently provided with illustrative *exempla*; it appears to have originated as classroom lectures. The *Moralities* are similar in nature to the didactic works written by William de Montibus and Richard of Wethringsett. They are of substantial interest to the present study because, to enhance their usability, the author arranged his text to facilitate reference and provided it with two indexes, both of which are very primitive and among the earliest examples of their kind. These survive only in Lincoln Coll. MS 79 (on ff. 1-9, both recopied on ff. 249-257^v), since its sister manuscript from which the remaining survivors descend did not have the indexes. The first index is arranged by topic in a random fashion—like the real concordance—following neither the order of the chapters in the *Moralities* nor any obvious logical schema; it begins with the topics *Superbia, Vana gloria, Ypocrisis, Humilitas, Obedientia, Timor, Ira, Discordium*, and ends with *Prelatus, Articuli fidei* (fol. 4va). There follows a second index, beginning (fol. 4va) *Arma, Aranea, Aurora, Asinus, Aloen, Auditus* and ending (fol. 9va) with *Zona*. This series, which is

---

[31] E. Dobson, *Moralities on the Gospels* (Oxford 1975), and the review by R. Rouse and S. Wenzel in *Speculum* 52 (1977) 648-652. Dobson has shown convincingly that the *Moralities* were not written by Grosseteste and that Lincoln College MS 79 stands at the head of the manuscript tradition. The work cannot, however, date from 1205-1211 as he argues, because of the presence of subject indexes.

alphabetized by first letter, consists mainly but not entirely of the names of objects, animate and inanimate, such as one might find in a collection of distinctions. None of the topics in this second index appears in the first. Reference in both indexes is made to part, chapter, and marginal index note in the text. Thus, for *Cupiditas* the first reference reads "In xxix capitulo prime partis, Cupiditas i." In part 1 chapter 29 of the *Moralities*, about midway through the chapter, there is a marginal note "Cupiditas i" (Lincoln Coll. MS 79 fol. 32ᵛ). The compiler of this double index is obviously experimenting; he has no examples to follow, and he has not yet reached a sensible solution. He shows, however, that from the earliest date preaching and tools are closely linked one to the other.

The friars at Oxford devote substantial energy and genius throughout the thirteenth century to rendering more accessible the writings of the Fathers.[32] In its origin the work has all the appearances of involving only a handful of people groping toward solutions to a difficult problem. Under Grosseteste's direction a mechanism was devised probably at Greyfriars in Oxford for indexing patristic texts, consisting of a complicated series of symbols—Greek letters, mathematical and conventional signs—which one could note in the margins of a text as one read, for eventual incorporation into a master subject index. The key to the symbols, and the start of a composite index to the scriptures and the Fathers, was discovered by Harrison Thomson in a Bible, now Lyon MS 414.[33] The table bears the rubric, "Tabula magistri Roberti Lincolniensis episcopi cum addicione fratris Ade de Marisco...." Thomson assigns the index to the period 1235-1250. The table is logically arranged under nine headings (*De Deo*, *De Verbo*, etc.), each copiously subdivided. The symbols continued to be used into the second half of the thirteenth century, and are found in the margins of seventeen manuscripts, the most recently discovered of which turned up at the Huntington Library in 1972 in a mid-thirteenth-century Bible.[34]

The Oxford Franciscans under Adam Marsh or his successor were also probably responsible for compiling the *Tabula septem custodiarum super bibliam*: a concordance to the incidental passages in the writings of the

---

[32] A good survey of this is seen in R. W. Hunt, ed., *The Coming of the Friars: A Commemorative Exhibition* (Oxford 1974).

[33] S. H. Thomson, "Grosseteste's Topical Concordance of the Bible and the Fathers," *Speculum* 9 (1934) 139-144; idem, "Grosseteste's Concordantial Signs," *Medievalia et humanistica* 9 (1955) 39-53. The manuscripts containing the symbols are discussed by Hunt, "Indexing Symbols of Robert Grosseteste," 241-255. A second version of the concordance exists in Paris, B.N. n.a.l. 540.

[34] San Marino, California, Huntington Library MS 26061. Only the Psalms bear the indexing symbols. The Book of Job is equipped with a full concordance to Gregory's *Moralia* (see below at n. 95); there is also a marginal cross-reference system for the Gospels.

Fathers, arranged according to the text of the scriptures.[35] With it, one can look up any passage in the Old and New Testaments and find in what places any one of twelve major doctors of the Church have commented upon the sense of the passage. The work, a sizable one often occupying two volumes, goes through the Bible passage by passage from Genesis to Revelation. It survives in nine English copies, but never circulated on the continent.[36]

Parallel to this activity is the work of Robert Kilwardby.[37] During his years as regent master of theology in Oxford, 1256-1261, Kilwardby produced a three-level system of providing access to the core of authority, namely (a) the *Intentiones*, chapter-by-chapter synopses of sixty-one works of Augustine, Chrysostom's *Quod nemo laeditur nisi a seipso*, Ambrose's *Hexameron*, Hugh's *Didascalicon* and the Lombard's *Sentences*; (b) an alphabetical subject index or *tabula* to each of forty-six works of Augustine, four of Anselm, Damascenus and the *Sentences*; and (c) a composite alphabetical subject concordance to major works of Augustine, Ambrose, Boethius, Isidore and Anselm, with occasional references as well to the *Historia scholastica* and the *Sentences*. Kilwardby used throughout the

---

[35] Hunt, for example, noted a passage in a letter of Adam Marsh (d. 1259) to William of Nottingham which may refer to the *Tabula*: "Ad haec de investigandis expositionibus sacrae scripturae in libris originalibus sanctorum cum eodem contuli, sicut mandastis, qui prompta devotione paratum se obtulit." See Hunt, "Indexing Symbols of Robert Grosseteste," 250 n. 2.

[36] There is as yet no published study of the *Tabula*. The manuscripts known to us are Cambridge, Peterhouse College MS 169, enlarged version (s. xv, before 1452); London, British Library MSS Harley 3858, NT only (s. xv; f. 3ᵛ, *Assignatur communi librarie Dunelmensis per dominum Johannem Welsyngton priorem* i.e., John Wessington of Durham [d. 1451]); and Royal 3 D.i (1452), copied from Peterhouse 169; Oxford, Balliol College MSS 216-217 (s. xv; ex dono William Grey 1478); Bodleian Library MS Bodley 685 (SC 2499; AD 1339; f. 117, *Iesus . Francisus*); Magdalen College MSS 78, NT only (s. xiv in.) and 150 (1449; paper); Merton College MS 205 (s. xiv); and New College MS 315, enlarged version, Gen.-Job only (s. xiv ex.). The *Tabula* also appears in the 1372 library catalog of the Austin Friars at York, ed. M. R. James, in *Fasciculus Joanni Willis Clark dictatus* (Cambridge 1909) 2-96 no. 57. Another example of indexing by means of signs distinct from that employed at Greyfriars is seen in a Bury manuscript of Robert of Cricklade, now Cambridge, Pembroke College MS 30 (s. xiii; Bury St. Edmunds R 54). The key to the signs was recently discovered by N. R. Ker among the fragments in Pembroke College MS 313, and now returned to MS 30.

[37] Concerning Kilwardby's indexes, see D. A. Callus, "The 'Tabulae super originalia patrum' of Robert Kilwardby O.P.," in *Studia medievalia in honorem ... R. J. Martin* (Bruges 1948) 85-112; idem, "New Manuscripts of Kilwardby's 'Tabulae super originalia patrum'," *Dominican Studies* 2 (1949) 38-45; idem, "The Contribution to the Study of the Fathers made by the Thirteenth-Century Oxford Schools," *Journal of Ecclesiastical History* 5 (1954) 139-148; and Thomas Kaeppeli, *Scriptores ordinis praedicatorum medii aevi* 3 (Rome forthcoming).

A-G system devised by the Dominicans at Saint-Jacques as his smallest unit of reference, which had by now become common practice. A prodigious outpouring, his works form a comprehensive introduction to the Fathers; their survival in over thirty manuscripts indicates that they were appreciated on both sides of the Channel.

As did the Cistercians and the Paris masters on the Continent, the scholars at Oxford devised their own technique of reference and indexing which they took home with them to Lincoln, Worcester or wherever. This was the device of supplying manuscripts with column and line numbers, to permit precise referral.[38] Thanks to the efforts of Pelster, Richard Hunt, Neil Ker and Graham Pollard, over a hundred such manuscripts have turned up. The columns are lettered across the opening A B C D, and the lines are numbered, usually in fives, down the center of the page. This device functioned for over 150 years: it first appears in manuscripts of the Commentary on the *Sentences* of Richard Fishacre O.P. (d. 1248);[39] and the last use noted is in a manuscript dated 1404.[40] The numbers are frequently added by early owners as an apparatus to render the text more usable. In at least two cases line numbers have been added to twelfth-century books—for the purpose of adapting an old book to the needs of early fourteenth-century parochial work.[41] Line numbering was not limited to Oxford, as Pelster thought. Oxford students carried the practice home with them when they returned to their livings and continued to apply it. It is not surprising

[38] Line numbers in Oxford books were first noticed by F. Pelster, "Das Leben und die Schriften des Oxford Dominikanerlehrers Richard Fishacre (†1248)," *Zeitschrift für katholische Theologie* 54 (1930) 517-553. See also A. G. Little and F. Pelster, *Oxford Theology and Theologians* (Oxford 1934) 61-62; and Lehmann, "Blätter, Seiten" 58-59. For additional references see N. R. Ker, *Fragments of Medieval Manuscripts used as Pastedowns in Oxford Bindings*, Oxford Bibliographical Society Publ. 5 (Oxford 1954) nos. 210, 372, 1644b, 1722, 1902a, 1943. We are indebted to the late Graham Pollard for having shared with us his unpublished notes on manuscripts with line numbers.

[39] Of the thirteen surviving copies of Fishacre, all of which are of English origin, these have line numbers: Bologna, University MS 1546 (s. xiii); Cambridge, Gonville and Caius College MS 329 (s. xiii); London, British Library MS Royal 10 B.viii; Oxford, New College MS 112 (s. xiii), with index beg. f. 322 (the index alone appears in New College MS 31); Oxford, Oriel College MS 43 (s. xiii); Paris, B.N. MS lat. 15754 (before 1272); and Vatican, Ottoboni MS lat. 294. These do not: Brescia, Queriniana MS B VI.2 (s. xiv); Cambridge, Trinity College MS 1054 ff. 1-30 (s. xiii); Naples, Bibl. naz. MS VII C.19 ff. 86-147 (s. xiii); Oxford, Balliol College MS 57 (s. xiii); Paris, B.N. MS lat. 16389 (s. xiii); and Vienna, Nat. Bibl. MS 1514 (s. xiii ex.). Regarding Fishacre see A. B. Emden, *A Biographical Register of the University of Oxford to A.D. 1500* (Oxford 1957) 685-686.

[40] Oxford, Bodleian Library Hatton MS 11 (SC 4132), *Regimen animarum*, evidently in the hand of Johannes de Clyua (?).

[41] London, British Library MS Royal 6 C.ix (s. xii), S. Bernard; London, Lambeth Palace MS 347 (s. xii), S. Jerome.

to find that many books with numbers are texts used in the administration of diocese, deanery or parish—e.g., several manuscripts of Raymond of Pennafort's *Summa* bear numbered lines.[42] The purpose of the numbers was to enable the owner to compile an index of his book, or simply to make precise references to portions of it. At least sixteen manuscripts have indexes using this system, and one[43] contains a mid-thirteenth-century description of how it is to be used. This system of reference, employed in classical texts today, never migrated to the continent, though line-numbered manuscripts (such as Gerard of Abbeville's copy of Fishacre) were carried to Paris and Bologna well before the end of the thirteenth century.

Having observed the virtually simultaneous responses to the need to render books searchable among the Cistercians and the mendicants on the Continent and at Oxford, let us return to Paris, to Thomas of Ireland's immediate background, in examining the use and the creation of indexes by scholars associated with the Sorbonne during or just before the years that Thomas of Ireland was a student there.

By the 1270s there was wholesale acceptance of the index and of reference tools in general among the masters and scholars at Paris. One could not ask for a clearer indication of this fact than the picture presented by the personal library of one Paris master, Gerard of Abbeville—a library which passed at his death (1272) to the Sorbonne.[44] Among Gerard's books are basic reference works, which one can almost call "standard" by this date: an alphabetical dictionary of terms, beginning "Abyssus...";[45] an alphabetical biblical concordance,[46] probably the first version; and two collections of biblical distinctions.[47] Among the indexes or indexed works which Gerard owned are Robert Kilwardby's massive alphabetical index to patristic writings;[48] a copy of Kilwardby's *Intentiones* to the works of St. Augustine;[49] the alphabetical index to the works of Augustine and others,

---

[42] Oxford, Bodleian Library MS Selden supra 48 (SC 3436; s. xiii²), with index on pp. 418-435; Oxford, University College MS 21 (s. xiii); and others.

[43] Oxford, New College MS 112, Fishacre (s. xiii) fol. 322.

[44] Concerning Gerard of Abbeville see P. Glorieux, *Répertoire des maîtres en théologie de Paris au xiiiᵉ siècle*, Études de philosophie médiévale 17 (Paris 1933) 1: 356-360; and P. Grand, "Le quodlibet xiv de Gérard d'Abbeville," *Archives d'histoire doctrinale et littéraire du Moyen Age* 31 (1964) 207-269.

[45] Paris, B.N. MS lat. 15983 ff. 204-208.

[46] Sorbonne 1338 catalog, XXI, 4 (ed. L. Delisle, *Cabinet des manuscrits de la Bibliothèque nationale* [Paris 1881] 3: 23).

[47] Paris, B.N. MS lat. 15569; and 1338 catalog XLI, 14, *Distinctiones Philippi cancellarii*.

[48] B.N. MS lat. 15984.

[49] B.N. MS lat. 15983 ff. 164-204.

made in 1256 by Robert of Paris,[50] which we mentioned above; a patristic *florilegium* with an alphabetical index, namely, the Cistercian *Liber exceptionum*;[51] and an alphabetical index to the *Physica, Meteorica, Parva naturalia* and *Metaphysica.*[52] In addition, Gerard owned an indexed copy of Fishacre's Commentary on the *Sentences*; this manuscript originated in Oxford, and once bore line numbers for reference and indexing purposes.[53] The elaborate alphabetical subject index of some eight folios in length was perhaps compiled by or for Gerard himself. The indexer ignored the reference apparatus already available, namely, the line numbers, since this was a practice alien to him; and he applied instead the standard Parisian system, entering letters of the alphabet in the margin and referring to these letters in the index. Gerard's private reference collection covered a wide range, from the Bible to patristics to Aristotle to the writings of a contemporary master.

With the exception of the index to Fishacre's Commentary, Gerard's subject indexes (as well as his other tools, such as the concordance) were ready-made independent tomes which he purchased. By the time of Gerard's death, as the century neared its end, a different type of indexing becomes commonplace at Paris: the personal index, drafted by the possessor of a manuscript for his private use. Scholars handled with ease the flexible reference system that one might well call the Paris method of indexing; it relied upon a combination of numbered openings and marginal letters of the alphabet. A man entered in the margins as many or as few letters as he needed to suit his purposes, and drew up a list of topic headings—with the quantity and the type of subject both determined by his interests—noting for each the location (folio number and marginal letter) of passages in his manuscript which treated the topic. The free-standing indexes, such as most of those in Gerard of Abbeville's library, provided access to monuments of tradition, such as patristic writings and the works of Aristotle. The individualized device, on the other hand, served particularly for providing access to the writings of contemporary university masters or the collected sermons of contemporary preachers—such as Gerard's index of Richard Fishacre's Commentary. Godfrey of Fontaines (d. 1306) and Peter of Limoges (d. 1307) both leave manuscripts supplied with indexes of this sort, in their own hands, among the books they bequeathed to the Sorbonne. Peter of Limoges seems to have made some sketch, however rudimentary, of an in-

[50] B.N. ms lat. 16334.
[51] B.N. ms lat. 15983 ff. 1-163ᵛ.
[52] B.N. ms lat. 16147.
[53] B.N. ms lat. 15754.

dex in each of his collections of contemporary sermons. A particularly thorough example appears in B.N. MSS lat. 16492 and 16493, a two-volume collection of sermons for which Peter created an index six folios in length; the foliation and marginal reference letters also are in Peter's hand.[54] The indexes in Godfrey's hand, in his manuscripts of the works of contemporary theologians such as St. Thomas and Henry of Ghent, were often casually inserted in whatever blank space was available, including the bottom margins of pages of text. Duin has described those in B.N. MSS lat. 15350, 15811 and 15819;[55] to these one might add Godfrey's indexes in MSS lat. 15848 (ff. 54, 190) and 16096 (f. 257). The indexing activity of these two masters is notable, because they are figures who are known and dated, and whose hands have been identified. However, they are not unique in this activity, but instead should be regarded as representative of many Parisian students and masters whose private indexes remain anonymous.

At Paris, among the Cistercians, and at Oxford, the creation of subject indexes began as a response to the need of teachers and preachers to get at material. In each community the tools and their techniques, idiosyncratic and halting at first, became more polished and self-assured as the century progressed. By the end of the thirteenth century the practical utility of the subject index is taken for granted by the literate West, no longer solely as an aid for preachers, but also in the disciplines of theology, philosophy, and both kinds of law. This acceptance is exemplified in the work of the Dominican John of Freiburg (d. 1314), writing in the last decades of the century.[56] It is no surprise, at this date, to find him producing an alphabetical table that encompassed both Raymond of Pennafort's *Summa* and William of Rennes' gloss upon it. But it is striking to see John making an alphabetical subject index as an adjunct to his own work, the *Summa confessorum* (written 1297-1298)—an index designed to accompany the work, in order to make its contents more readily accessible. This, to our knowledge, is the first instance in which a full subject index is incorporated as part of the structure of a new work.[57] Obviously, the index had become recognized as enhancing the usability of a book and, hence, its value.

[54] Peter's hand is described, with plates, by M. Mabille, "Pierre de Limoges, copiste de manuscrits," *Scriptorium* 24 (1970) 45-47, pls. 10-13; and "Pierre de Limoges et ses méthodes de travail," *Collection Latomus* 145 (1976) 244-251.

[55] J. J. Duin, "La bibliothèque philosophique de Godefroid de Fontaines," *Estudios Lullianos* 3 (1959) 24, 26, 29.

[56] Leonard E. Boyle, "The *Summa confessorum* of John of Freiburg and the Popularization of the Moral Teaching of St. Thomas...," *St. Thomas Aquinas 1274-1974: Commemorative Studies* (Toronto 1974) 2: 245-268, esp. 248-249.

[57] We know of three earlier attempts of an author to index his own work—each doubtless made from motives similar to John of Freiburg's, but composed too early to benefit from the

C. Library Catalogs

Concordances, and all the varied types of indexes, are new tools per-
forming a new function, that of aiding a search. The book list, on the contrary, is an old form; but in the thirteenth century a great deal of ingenuity
was devoted to fitting it to a new purpose. The majority of medieval book
lists, particularly prior to the thirteenth century, are inventories of property,
to be checked at intervals against extant volumes. The thirteenth century
witnesses the first catalogs whose purpose it is to help one locate books, in a
library or in a given geographical area.

Location lists in fact precede the appearance of subject catalogs, because
people were no doubt sufficiently familiar with the books of their own
house. Du Molinet in 1678 and Bellaise in 1687 describe a collection of
catalogs of Norman abbeys, Savigny, Mont-Saint-Michel, Saint-Stephen of
Caen, Bec, Jumièges and others, which they date 1210 and 1240, respectively, and which was possibly compiled at Savigny.[58] The volume no longer
survives, but Bellaise's description implies that this was a simple collection
of individual catalogs, not an integrated list.

The earliest integrated location list, and the most impressive in many
ways, is the *Registrum Anglie de libris actorum et doctorum.*[59] This is a list
of 1412 works (many with their incipits) of some 98 authors, largely
patristic. Nearly all of these works are accompanied by an indication of
their location in from one to over thirty libraries in England, Scotland and
Wales. This is done by means of arabic numerals[60] that refer to a key num-

---

advanced techniques available to John. The three are the indexes of Cardinal Deusdedit and
the anonymous author of the *Moralities on the Gospels*, discussed above at n. 7 and n. 31,
respectively; and the index made by Vincent of Beauvais for the *Speculum historiale*. The
first redaction, completed by 1244, is equipped with an alphabetical index—not to the text
of the *Speculum*, but to the proper nouns that appear in the numerous and often lengthy
chapter headings or *tituli* to the thirty books that it contains. Printed with the early editions
of the *Speculum historiale*, it still serves as a useful guide to Vincent's *Mirror*.

[58] Noted in Delisle, *Cabinet des manuscrits* (1868) 1: 527-528.

[59] M. R. James, "The List of Libraries prefixed to the Catalogue of Boston of Bury and
the Kindred Documents," *Collectanea franciscana* 2 (1922) 37-60; E. A. Savage, "Notes on
the Early Monastic Libraries of Scotland with an Account of the *Registrum librorum Angliae*
and of the *Catalogus scriptorum ecclesiae* of John Boston of the Abbey of Bury St. Edmunds," *Edinburgh Bibliographical Society* 14 (1930) 1-46, repr. as "Co-operative Bibliography in the Thirteenth and Fifteenth Centuries," in *Special Librarianship in General
Libraries* (London 1939) 285-310. The *Registrum* is to be edited by R. W. Hunt and R. A.
B. Mynors.

[60] There is also a scattering of roman numerals, referring evidently to libraries that were
afterthoughts.

bered list of 189 libraries, prefixed to the register. Although the libraries are not at all restricted to Franciscan houses, the numbered list is arranged geographically according to the Franciscan Custodies within which the institutions were located. The three surviving manuscripts date from the fifteenth century;[61] however, one can determine, from the houses on the list, that the *Registrum* was compiled sometime after 1250.

While external evidence is lacking, it is a reasonable assumption that a Franciscan project of these dimensions must have emanated from Greyfriars. Oxford, among the same circle of men who produced the *Tabula septem custodiarum* described above. Indeed, two of the surviving copies of the *Registrum* appear in codexes which contain the *Tabula* as well. It is possible that the compilation of the *Tabula* served as the impetus for the making of the *Registrum*. The *Tabula*, for each Bible passage, gave references to the works of various of the "twelve doctors," but no quotations from them. This created a problem; as one scribe wryly observed, "If you have the works of these twelve doctors, or of some of them, this present book (the *Tabula*) will be very useful to you for preaching; but if not, I don't know what good it will do you."[62] Perhaps it was this consideration that initially prompted the Franciscans at Greyfriars to compile a list of the places where an itinerant friar might find these books. At any event, once under way, the project grew beyond any such limits to become a list of the locations of a much larger number of works of a body of Christian writers many times more numerous than the *Tabula*'s original twelve. The purpose remained: to permit a friar to find, in his own neighborhood, the books that were "valde utilis ad predicandum."

The actual information about the holdings of the various institutional libraries was collected by circuit visitations. Once the data were collected, the integrated list was probably assembled at Greyfriars—in all, a remarkable feat of energy and organization. The number of people involved is not known, but this was surely a corporate effort of the Franciscan Order in England, comparable to the production of the Concordance by the Dominican Order.

Toward the end of the thirteenth century, a collection of book lists of Parisian houses was assembled in tabular form, probably by someone at the

[61] Oxford, Bodleian Library MS Tanner 165 (s. xv); Cambridge, Peterhouse College MS 169 (s. xv); and a copy of the latter in London, British Library MS Royal 3 D.i (AD 1452).

[62] British Library MS Harley 3858 f. 62: "Si hos duodecim doctores aut aliquos ex hiis habueris, valde utilis ad predicandum presens liber tibi sit; sin autem, nescio quid tibi valebit."

Sorbonne.[63] Only a fragment survives, containing the end of the list for Sainte-Geneviève and the beginning for Saint-Germain-des-Prés. The book inventories of the various houses included were transcribed (for Sainte-Geneviève it preserves part of an inventory of the 1230s or 1240s now lost) on large sheets of parchment, written on one side only. These must have been posted on a wall or door for the use of all, to permit the locating of books not available at the Sorbonne. It is one of the oldest wall catalogs to have survived.

Changes in book usage such as those we have been discussing also affected the arrangement and inventorying of books at university institutions. Book collections were traditionally kept in chests or armaria, and the books themselves were probably for the most part in the hands of members of the house. We get an indication in 1270 from Humbert of Romans that the books in the chest should be grouped by subject and that certain books should be chained for the use of all.[64] Before the turn of the century, the Sorbonne, Merton, and possibly University College Oxford have collections of codices chained on reading benches, rather than locked away inaccessible. Soon thereafter, ca. 1320, a fellow at the Sorbonne compiled a subject catalog of the hundreds of individual texts contained in the Sorbonne's 300 chained codices.[65] These steps—subject arrangement of codices, chaining of selected codices, index to the contents of a whole collection—are comparable with the production of distinction collections, concordances, indexes and location lists, and their appearance should be understood in that context. They are all intended to provide access to materials.

II. TECHNIQUES

In order to make their tools both useful and usable, their creators devised a number of new techniques, or applied old techniques to new situations, customarily in an independent and personal fashion. In considering the making of these tools, then, we must bear in mind that we are dealing not so much with technical evolution, as with a fairly mixed bag of adoption, adaptation and innovation of techniques. We have noted individual technical achievements as we went along. Here, let us consider three

[63] See R. H. Rouse, "The Early Library of the Sorbonne," *Scriptorium* 21 (1967) 69-71.

[64] Humbert of Romans, *Instructiones de officiis ordinis*, in his *Opera de vita regulari*, ed. J. J. Berthier, 2 vols. (Rome 1888-1889) 2.263.

[65] Rouse, "Early Library," 232ff.

techniques pertinent to toolmaking as a whole: 1) the development of a layout for book and page; 2) the emergence of systems of reference, including the adoption of arabic numerals; and 3) the acceptance of alphabetical order as a means of arranging words and ideas. Some of these techniques, such as the adoption of arabic numerals, have been the subject of detailed study but in isolation from a context such as ours; others, such as systems of reference, have not previously been studied at all. These topics need to be examined together, as varied aspects of a general change in approach to the written page which evolves from the end of the twelfth century and through the course of the thirteenth century.

A. Layout

The interest in getting at information—in making the contents of books more readily accessible—was responsible for certain changes in the layout of the book and the page.[66] On looking at the early manuscripts of the *Manipulus florum*, namely, those copied from *peciae*, one cannot help but appreciate the benefits of these developments; the material has been consciously arranged so as to help the user quickly find the section and the passage for which he is searching. Signposts such as running headlines, marginal letters of the alphabet designating individual extracts, marginal notation of the authors that are cited, rubrics dividing the subjects and paragraph marks distinguishing the extracts one from another, and a table of chapters all assist in this purpose. Color, size of letter and spacing are all effectively used to distinguish visually one part of the text from another and to help the user find his place. These techniques are common to books of the period 1250-1350, and particularly to stationer-produced tools such as the third version of the concordance, the layout of which is a remarkable achievement.

Our consideration of signposts is concerned not so much with their origin as with their acceptance. The importance of this distinction is seen in the manuscripts of Papias' dictionary, the *Elementarium doctrinae erudimentum*. Written in northern Italy in the middle of the eleventh century, it is the first sophisticated medieval glossary of biblical terms and a model for

---

[66] Regarding changes in the layout of the page see M. B. Parkes, "The Influence of the Concepts of *Ordinatio* and *Compilatio* on the Development of the Book," in *Medieval Learning and Literature: Essays presented to R. W. Hunt*, ed. J. J. G. Alexander and M. T. Gibson (Oxford 1976) 115-141—bearing in mind, however, that these two concepts are not responsible for changes in the development of the book but are themselves products of the same stimuli which produced the changes. If anything, the two concepts are articulated after the fact, to explain the change in attitude to the text and to deal with it in a context.

its successors, notably the dictionaries of Huguccio (1180) and of William Brito (mid-thirteenth century). In order to help readers find their way through this complicated lexicon Papias conceived a series of signposts, all of which he explained in detail in the prologue.[67] The natural breaks in alphabetic sequence were to be marked by three sizes of letters: the first word beginning with a given letter was to be marked by a large A, B, etc., in the text; each successive change in second letter (words beginning *ab*—, *ac*—, *ad*—) was to be marked in the margin by a middle-sized letter, and each change in the third letter (*aba*—, *abb*—, *abc*—) by the appropriate small letter in the margin. Genders of nouns were to be designated (*m., f., n.*), and the names of authors cited to be given in abbreviated form in the margins (Hisidorus, *hi*; Augustinus, *aug*; etc.).

Daly was quite right in noting that Papias' conception was advanced. His apparatus was in fact so far ahead of its time that the detailed instructions in the prologue were virtually disregarded in the early manuscripts of the dictionary. Such use of marginal signposts was a technique of the future, unknown, and presumably of no interest, to the idiosyncratic copyists of most early manuscripts of the dictionary. One must also take into consideration the absence of a means of uniform production from exemplars, like that which produced numerous copies of the concordance and the *Manipulus florum*, each with the same intricate layout. Papias' description of his layout begins to be heeded in practice only in the course of the thirteenth century. Paris, B.N. MS lat. 17162 (s. xiii[1]), a good example,[68] bears large, ornate majuscule initials designating each primary letter division, with smaller majuscule letters in the margins marking the second and third divisions. The thirteenth-century scribes in fact added to Papias' original scheme, by painting the letters in alternating red and blue to enhance the visual impact.[69]

It should be understood, thus, that we are dealing not so much with the invention of techniques such as the use of signposts, but rather with their consistent application, attempting to discern when they come into vogue and why. The isolated and sporadic use of most signposts can be traced back to the Carolingian or even the patristic book. In early books, however,

---

[67] Papias' introduction is edited with translation in L. W. and B. A. Daly, "Some Techniques in Medieval Latin Lexicography," *Speculum* 39 (1964) 229-239. See also L. W. Daly, "Contributions to a History of Alphabetization in Antiquity and the Middle Ages," *Collection Latomus* 90 (Brussels 1967) 71-72.

[68] We are grateful to Professor Daly for referring us to this manuscript.

[69] The failure of Papias' elaborate apparatus, due to its origin in an unreceptive chronological and institutional framework, is reminiscent of the fate of Cardinal Deusdedit's index; see above at n. 8.

these signposts were never consistently employed; and many of them dropped out of use, only to be revived in response to the needs of later scholars. It is only in the late twelfth and thirteenth centuries that such signposts become an expected, rather than an occasional, feature of the manuscript book. Out of the procedure of commenting upon a set text as the primary means of accumulating and transmitting knowledge in theology and law, there resulted the layout of the glossed page—or double-page opening—of the late twelfth century, in which virtually the whole range of signposts is adopted as a normal part of the book. It is from this time, that of the great glossed book of the late twelfth century, that such signposts are used in unbroken succession to the present.

We shall discuss here those signposts which are clearly part of the layout of the *Manipulus florum*—lists of chapters and running headlines, to organize the book; and, to organize the page, paragraph marks, use of color, marginal notation of authors quoted, and cross-references.

Lists of chapters at the beginning (or at the end, as in the *Manipulus florum*) of each book have been with us since the second or third century AD, when the texts of books of the Bible were divided into chapters.[70] The chapters were, not infrequently, listed at the head of the book. For works of the Fathers also, lists of chapters preceded the books in similar fashion. This particular finding device never fell into complete desuetude. The major change in the thirteenth century is the imposition of a chapter structure upon works which had none; and lists of the new chapter *tituli* are frequently added to older manuscripts.

Running headlines, so common in late medieval books, are occasionally seen in books before the year 800—the titles of books of the Bible are sometimes noted at the top of the page. The practice is haphazard in the Carolingian era and spotty thereafter; but it becomes *de rigueur* in the great set texts of the second half of the twelfth century, in which the section (book, chapter, etc.) of the text, as well as the author and title, appear across the top of each two-page opening: "Aug. de civ. dei .ix." The importance attached to this device in the thirteenth century is underscored by the frequency with which thirteenth-century hands have added running headlines to older books that lacked them.

Running headlines and lists of chapters gave help in finding one's way through the codex as a whole. Other devices, signposts and techniques of layout, help to organize the material on the page—or, rather, on the

---

[70] See W. H. P. Hatch, *The Principal Uncial Manuscripts of the New Testament* (Chicago 1939) 3-25; and idem, *Facsimiles and Descriptions of the Minuscule Manuscripts of the New Testament* (Cambridge 1951) 3-71.

double-page opening: such items as gradations in the size of majuscule letters, the paragraph mark, the effective use of color. Gradations in size of the
initial majuscule letter go back to the patristic book. The twelfth- and thirteenth-century departures of interest are these: the number of gradations in-
creases to three and four sizes; large initials tend to occur at the left (at the
beginning of a new line) rather than just anywhere in the line; and color,
usually alternating red and blue, is applied to add to the visual distinction
between sections of the text.

The paragraph mark undergoes a reasonably clear evolution. Paragraphi
(Γ) descend from the patristic book, in their gibbet form. They usually
bracket the chapter or paragraph number entered in the margin, and occasionally they are used to bracket or set off an insert into the text or to
distinguish the words run over from a line above into the line below. Pre-
twelfth-century paragraph marks are almost invariably written in the same
color ink as the text. The form remains the same, with the occasional addition of one or two diagonal braces to the gibbet (Γ), until the middle of
the twelfth century. At some point between 1180 and 1200 the paragraph
mark moves from the margin to the interior of the column; it assumes a
rounded and solid form in two chronological stages (Γ) (℃); and it is
painted alternately red and blue.[71] The paragraph mark has obviously been
co-opted and adapted to serve a new purpose, that of distinguishing sections, usually the smallest units, of a text one from the other.

The use of color itself in initials and paragraph marks deserves comment.
Alternating colors can effectively block off and separate sections of a text,
rendering them easily distinguishable at a distance. Surely, the university
book of the late twelfth and the thirteenth century is a highly colorful object
in comparison with the monastic schoolbook of the ninth century. The effective use of color to distinguish sections occurs at the earliest, it would
seem, in liturgical books, which are composed of different interchangeable
units and which have a structure that must be readily perceptible at a
distance. Alternating red and blue initials already appear in non-liturgical
books in a group of manuscripts written in Chartres around the middle of
the twelfth century. Paris, B.N. MS lat. 5802 is typical of these, and can be
dated before 1164, by which time it had been given to Bec by Philip of
Bayeux.[72]

[71] Note the paragraph marks in Durham Cathedral MSS A III.4 f. 4 (s. xii³), A III.17 f. 4
(s. xii⁴), and C II.1 f. 3 (s. xii⁴); shown in R. A. B. Mynors, *Durham Cathedral Manuscripts
to the End of the Twelfth Century* (Oxford 1939) no. 116 pl. 43, no. 138 pl. 48, and no.
134 pl. 47.
[72] B.N. MS lat. 5802 can be identified with no. 76 in the Bec catalog, G. Becker, ed.,
Catalogi bibliothecarum antiqui (Bonn 1885) 201.

Location of quotations from other authors and texts is accomplished in several fashions. The equivalent of quotation marks or dots in the outer margin next to the quoted passage is the oldest method; it goes back to the patristic book and carries up through the twelfth century, when it is replaced by two other methods: underscoring the quotation in red, and giving the author's name in the margin as an index reference. The practice of marginal notation of authors may go back to Bede, and it is seen in Carolingian manuscripts of his works. We saw above how Papias in the mid-eleventh century provided a list of abbreviations to be used in the margins to indicate the authors quoted in his dictionary, and how his instructions were ignored. Marginal notation of authors' names does not become common until the end of the twelfth century, when it is specifically associated with Peter Lombard's works. How best to cite authority is the subject of an interesting and extended conversation. Herbert of Bosham, in his introduction to the Lombard's gloss on the Psalter, says, "The words of the glossator [Lombard] are frequently inserted as explanations among the authentic sayings of the doctors"; and so he has carefully marked the beginnings and ends of quotations "to distinguish the commentators one from the other and also from the words of the glossator, lest one mistake Cassiodorus for Augustine or Jerome, or mistake the glossator for the commentator—a matter in which we have seen not only beginners but very learned readers fall into error."[73] The Lombard's practice of confining virtually all of his *apparatus fontium* to the margins had its drawbacks, for many scribes ignored marginalia in copying a manuscript. Therefore, Vincent of Beauvais says in 1244 that he intends to give his citations of authorship in the *Speculum historiale* "never in the margins, as they are given in the *Sentences* and [the Lombard's] glossed Psalter and Pauline epistles, but in the text itself, as they are treated in the *Decretum.*"[74] Thomas of Ireland prudently employed both methods, marginal as well as internal citation of authors, in the *Manipulus florum.*

[73] "Preterea glosatoris verbula que frequenter autenticis doctorum dictis interserit ... et presertim que exponendo interserit, notavi attente et ... signavi in margine, ne lector ... errore expositorum alicui glosatoris verba ascribat.... Verba expositorum inter se et etiam a verbis glosatoris distinxi, ne Cassiodorum pro Augustino sive Ieronimo, vel glosatorem inducas pro expositore; in quo interdum non simplices sed eruditiores etiam risimus [sic; for vidimus?] lectores errasse"; quoted from I. Brady, "The Rubrics of Peter Lombard's Sentences," *Pier Lombardo* 6 (1962) 5-25, esp. 10-11. Bosham's work on the Psalter dates from 1171-1176.

[74] "Ne facile transponerentur [nomina auctorum] de locis propriis, nequaquam in margine, sicut fit in Psalterio glosato et epistolis Pauli et in sententiis, sed inter lineas ipsas, sicut fecit Gratianus in compilatione canonum, ea inserui"; prologue, ch. 3, printed with the *Speculum naturale* (Venice 1591) fol. 1.

One final type of signpost that we wish to mention is the cross-reference. Writers always had means of referring to other parts of their works by book and chapter in the text. Formal cross-reference notes, however, in the margins or at the ends of chapters—of the type, "See also the following..."—are a development associated with the glossed book. In glossed books of the second half of the twelfth century a separate column is ruled for the marginal cross-reference, which usually takes the form, "Supra, lxix super *Exultent*." This form continues in use in the thirteenth century, and is that found, for example, in Peter of Capua's collection of distinctions. Thomas of Ireland moved his cross-references into the text at the end of each topic, no doubt a wise course given the rather poor survival rate of marginalia from one copy of a work to the next.

Tables of chapters, running headlines, gradations of letter-size, paragraph marks, purposeful use of alternating color, marginal citation of authors quoted, formal cross-references—none of these techniques was devised by the makers of thirteenth-century preaching tools. Rather, like such techniques as alphabetization and foliation, these signposts were avidly seized upon and put to effective and consistent use by the toolmakers. In time, they were taken for granted as intrinsic to the apparatus of a good book; and all of them were employed in the *Manipulus florum*.

B. Reference Symbols

Second, besides signposts and direction signals, tools of reference required a system of symbols with which to designate either portions of the text (book, chapter) or portions of the codex (folio, opening, column, line). Toolmakers were nearly unanimous in their rejection of roman numerals as being too clumsy for this purpose. Before widespread acquaintance with arabic numerals, the lack of a feasible sequence of symbols posed serious problems in the creation of a reference apparatus. The most common substitute was use of letters of the alphabet; it was possible to provide for a sequence longer than twenty-three items (folios, extracts, etc.) by repeating, with alterations in each successive alphabet—a double or triple letter-sequence, or the peculiar "dotted letters" of the Bruges Cistercians.

The interest in getting at and referring to materials was significant in hastening the acceptance of arabic numerals in the West at this time. Sarton, explaining the delay in acceptance of arabic numerals, remarks that they were "not actually needed by business..., [there was] no social need ... nor ... for a long time any scientific need, because hardly anyone realized the implications of the new symbolism."[75] In contrast, one can see that for

---

[75] George Sarton, *Introduction to the History of Science* (Baltimore 1931) 2.1: 5.

the makers of indexes and dividers of manuscripts, there was indeed a need for arabic numerals. In fact, the Cistercians with their letters and dots were obviously creating a homemade place-value numbering system, so urgent was their need. Virtually every major tool save the concordances came to employ arabic numerals. Arabic numerals are available to the West through the translations of mathematical and astronomical treatises since the mid or early twelfth century; but only in the course of the thirteenth century do they supersede roman numerals and letters of the alphabet for use in foliation; and the use of arabic numerals for line-numbering by Oxford scholars before mid-century is one of the earlier instances of routine, wholesale use. So, while historians of science shake their heads over the tardy Western acceptance of the "radically new [Arabic] arithmetic"[76] with its concept of zero, we should take note of the *ready* acceptance of the arabic numbering system by indexers, on the no-nonsense grounds that it provided a good way to find one's place.

The technical key to concordances or indexes was the method of citation or reference, dependent on how one divided one's text. Three basic systems were used. First is reference to existing divisions in the text, namely, book and chapter, at times made more precise by including the incipit of the specific portion of the chapter referred to. Second is division of the text into artificial sections (of quasi-equal length) by use of marginal letters of the alphabet. This sort of division was particularly applicable to *florilegia*, which lacked structured organization and inherent divisions of their own. Another sort of artificial or arbitrary structure for *florilegia* consisted of labeling each statement of a text in sequence with a marginal letter, to facilitate both reference and cross-reference. The *Manipulus florum* in 1306, even though it is arranged alphabetically by subject and, thus, needs no subject index, has identified each extract with a marginal letter entirely for the purpose of cross-reference—so that, for example, at the conclusion of the topic *Amicitia* one might be told to see also *Amor* d. The third method is division of the codex, according to folio or opening, page, column and line. Here we should note first, that, rather than marking folios, thirteenth-century scribes are usually designating openings (the two pages which face each other, rather than the two which, back to back, comprise the same leaf). Their mark appears on the upper outside corner of the verso; and the four columns, when designated with letters, are lettered across the top of the opening A B C D.[77] Second, and more important, the practice of foliating

[76] Ibid.

[77] The opening as a literary unit is discussed by C. A. Robson, *Maurice de Sully and the Medieval Vernacular Homily* (Oxford 1952) 14-24; and idem, "The Pecia of the Twelfth-

manuscripts and of numbering columns and lines is not simply an accidental occurrence in a vacuum, but rather the specific, direct result of a desire on the part of users of manuscripts to be able to refer to precise locations in their texts. Although arabic numerals are used for foliation with increasing frequency in the second half of the thirteenth century, the acceptance of arabic numerals did not cause or instigate the great increase in foliation—any current of causation flows in the other direction. Foliation, a rare if venerable practice, expanded suddenly because there was need. Quite apart from these three systems of division was a reference device which could be used with any of them—dividing a section of a work mentally into seven equal parts, which are designated A-G. First employed in the Dominican concordances, this technique could be used in conjunction with, for example, a chapter reference to indicate which portion of the chapter was meant—Étienne de Bourbon, Robert Kilwardby, and virtually all later indexers used the A-G system. Or one could use it, as some of the Cistercian indexers did, in conjunction with a folio and column reference, to indicate the portion of the column. In both cases, it serves as a convenient lowest unit of reference.

C. Alphabetization

As their method of organization, virtually all tools employ alphabetical order. In theory, this involved nothing more than the application of a technique already in existence; but in practice, the use of alphabetization in one circumstance had little transference value for other circumstances. First-letter alphabetization of lists of words was a Greco-Roman inheritance, as Lloyd Daly has demonstrated; and the technique was employed in the Middle Ages by, among others, the dictionary-makers, Papias, Huguccio and Brito.[78] But, we should note, they each in turn explain alphabetical arrangement, as if they assumed that the process was unfamiliar to their readers.

The medieval intellectual world was predisposed to organizing any given body of things according to their logical interrelationship. God created a harmonious universe, and its parts must have a logical and harmonious

---

Century Paris School," *Dominican Studies* 2 (1949) 267-279. There are surely exceptions to this rule; Father Boyle has noted that British Library ms Add. 30508 (ca. 1270-1280) contains a contemporary index that treats the columns as AB = recto, CD = verso of the folio. See L. E. Boyle, "The *Compilatio quinta* and the Registers of Honorius III," in *Scritti in onore di Giulio Battelli* (forthcoming).

[78] Lloyd W. Daly, "Contributions to a History of Alphabetization," and L. W. and B. A. Daly, "Some Techniques."

relationship with one another. For a writer to place things in alphabetical order was to deny this logical relationship, or to confess that he was unable to discern it. Now, obviously, for many literary forms an alphabetical arrangement is irrelevant; but those forms which might have lent themselves to alphabetization also rejected it. To put the names of a series of stones in alphabetical order would be acceptable, for no logical classification had yet been discerned; but for a *summa sententiarum* or a topical *florilegium* to discuss *Filius* before *Pater*, or *Angelus* before *Deus*, simply because the alphabet required it, would have seemed absurd. Alphabetical arrangement was in fact disparaged. Albertus Magnus illustrates this nicely: in his *De animalibus*, he apologizes for arranging his discussion of animals in alphabetical order after having previously said "hunc modum non proprium philosophie esse"—but he does so nevertheless, for the benefit of the unlearned.[79] Alphabetical arrangement was considered inappropriate to philosophy because it is the antithesis of rationally discenred relationships among things. Aside from lists of words, such as dictionaries, glossaries, herbals, lapidaries, recipes and mnemonic verses, which defy systematic organization, systematic order dominates the scene. Its hold is witnessed in the number of early indexes which are systematically rather than alphabetically arranged—such as the subject concordance formerly attributed to St. Antony of Padua, and the index to the *Moralities on the Gospels*. As keys to the contents of logically-organized works, one had a list of chapter headings; as keys to scriptural language, one searched the gloss for the purpose of concording, after having located one's word in the text itself. Both of these processes were serviceable for reading or browsing, but not for searching. However, it was some forty years after the appearance of the first alphabetical collection of biblical distinctions when the idea occurred, and spread, that alphabetization be applied to the necessary task of rendering works searchable, on a massive number of topics. Alphabetical indexes and alphabetical concordances appeared rapidly and in numbers, once transfer to the system had begun, and they supplanted their systematically arranged predecessors. But it was only after alphabetization had gained recognition and acceptance in the distinction collection, concordance and subject index that it was generally applied to the organization of materials in encyclopedias, *exempla* collections, *florilegia* and other compendia—namely, with

---

[79] Albertus Magnus, *De animalibus* lib. 23 tract. 1, in *Opera omnia*, ed. A. Borgnet (Paris 1891) 12: 433; and *De vegetalibus et plantis* lib. 6 tract. 1, *Opera* 10: 159-160; noted in L. C. Mackinney, "Medieval Medical Dictionaries and Glossaries," *Medieval and Historiographical Essays in Honor of James Westfall Thompson* (Chicago 1938) 244 n. 6.

the *Alphabetum narrationum* (1297-1308) of Arnold of Liège[80] and the *Manipulus florum* in 1306. Despite its—to us—obvious practicality, alphabetization, thus, was adopted only in stages; each time that alphabetical order was applied to a new task, it involved a fresh mental effort to cast off old modes of thought. Seen in this light, Thomas of Ireland's work must be regarded as the progenitor of alphabetical manuals. In the fourteenth century, alphabetically-arranged handbooks gain numerical parity with those systematically arranged.

III. THEORY

The tools and techniques described above reflect a basic change in attitude to the written page. This change, what one might call the intellectual context of toolmaking, is perceptible in (1) the recognition at the end of the twelfth century of the difference between reading the Fathers through extracts and reading them in the whole; (2) the effort to discern the intent of a work through its structure, and, a concomitant, the effort to provide chapter structures for works which did not have them and to improve the structure of those that did; and (3) the appearance of a distinctly utilitarian and aggressive attitude toward the book.

A. Originalia

At the university there is a clear recognition that the teaching of the Church is founded on the scriptures and the Fathers, and that the preacher must be thoroughly grounded in them. This recognition manifested itself in a focus of attention on using a text as an integral whole. Whereas in the twelfth century one might normally expect to find one or two individual patristic works in a codex, in the thirteenth we see the formation of collections of a given Father's works in a single volume, such as those assembled by Richard de Fournival.[81] B.N. MS lat. 15641, for example, containing thirty-four works of St. Ambrose, clearly represents an effort to assemble the Ambrosian corpus between two covers.

Increased emphasis upon the whole work, as opposed to excerpts, is revealed by a significant change in terminology. Geoffrey of Auxerre describes how Gilbert of Poitiers, in his defense at the consistory of Rheims

---

[80] Concerning the *Alphabetum narrationum* of Arnold of Liège see J.-Th. Welter, *L'exemplum dans la littérature religieuse et didactique du Moyen Age* (Paris 1927) 304-319; and Kaeppeli, *Scriptores* 1: 130-133.

[81] Callus, "Contribution," 145-146.

in 1148, arrived with his party bearing the *codices integri*, to the consternation of Bernard and his other accusers who were armed only with a compilation of *auctoritates* on a single sheet.[82] In the last decades of the twelfth century theologians at the schools themselves acknowledge the distinction between reading extracts and immersing themselves in the whole works, and come to consider the latter so essential that they will equate the whole works with the authority of the author's original, applying to them the term *originalia*.

Earlier in the Middle Ages one had used the phrases *originalia rescripta*, *originalia documenta*, to refer to the originals, i.e., the documents with signature and seal, issued by lay or ecclesiastical officials.[83] By 1191, Ralph Niger uses the phrase *originalia scripta* in a different sense, meaning, not the original or autograph, but the whole work of a writer rather than excerpts from his work. Niger says that, from the very brevity of the quotations in the *Gloss*, readers should understand the necessity of going back to the whole works—"intelligent ad originalia scripta fore recurrendum."[84] In Langton's usage, the word has become a noun, *originale* or *originalia*—as when he contrasts *glosa Ieronimi* with *Ieronimus in originali*, or simply *in glosa* with *in originali*.[85] Langton's and Niger's uses of *originale* in this sense are possibly the earliest examples. The change is a meaningful one, which rapidly achieves universal currency. By 1250, such phrases as *compilatio originalium, ad originalia inquirenda, legit in originali* abound. *Originalia* always means "whole works in contradistinction to excerpts or extracts"; moreover, in the use of *originale* rather than *integrum*, there is the deliberate implication that the whole works possess an authority or authenticity lacking in mere excerpts. Once the notion of whole text, and of its importance, is established, its counterpart, the index or *tabula originalium*, can emerge. This is no mere word-game; in this case at least, the thing itself does not appear before the name is coined. Both—the acceptance of the word *originale* and the creation of *tabulae originalium*—are visible signs of the new emphasis on whole works. By the beginning of the fourteenth century an alphabetized *florilegium*, the *Manipulus florum*, can claim to be an introduction to the *originalia patrum*.

[82] The texts are given in N. M. Haring, "Notes on the Council and Consistory of Rheims (1148)," *Mediaeval Studies* 28 (1966) 39-59, esp. 48-49.

[83] J. de Ghellinck, "*Originale* et *originalia*," *Archivum latinitatis medii aevi (Bulletin du Cange)* 14 (1939) 95-105.

[84] Quoted by B. Smalley, *The Study of the Bible in the Middle Ages* (Oxford 1952) 226 n. 4. Concerning Niger see G. B. Flahiff, "Ralph Niger: An Introduction to His Life and Works," *Mediaeval Studies* 2 (1940) 104-126.

[85] Smalley, *Study of the Bible*, 227 and n. 3, 228 and n. 1.

B. Divisions

In the first half of the thirteenth century, theorists of rhetoric recognized that one of the ways to perceive the intent of an author is to understand the structure and organization of his thought. Jordan of Saxony is the first to put this into words. In the introduction to his commentary (ca. 1220) on the grammar of Priscian, he says: "The 'formal cause' of this subject is both the *forma tractandi* [the form in which it treats things] and the *forma tractatus* [the form in which it has been treated].[86] The *forma tractandi* is its method of procedure.... The *forma tractatus* ... consists of the separation into books and chapters, and their order." We must not allow the strange terminology of Aristotelian "causes" to obscure the import: Jordan is implying a relationship between the flow of an author's thought and the physical divisions of the author's text. Jordan's casual acceptance of this is significant in light of the fact that earlier introductions to Priscian make no mention of book and chapter divisions when describing the author's *modus agendi*. Other commentators of the thirteenth century reiterate Jordan's observation that a description of the "form" of any work includes mention of the work's division into "books and parts and chapters." By the end of the century a commentary may go one step further: not content with merely mentioning the fact that his text is divided into parts, a commentator may go on to consider alternative schemes of division, and to indicate and explain his preference.[87]

This is the theoretical and descriptive aspect of the very practical concerns of providing (1) chapter structures to works which had none, and an improved structure for certain of those that had; and (2) introductions to the works of the Fathers in the form of chapter summaries such as we see being done at Greyfriars, Oxford and in the work of Robert Kilwardby.[88]

[86] Quoted by M. Grabmann, *Mittelalterliches Geistesleben* 3 (Munich 1956) 234. The passage is discussed by Jan Pinborg, *Die Entwicklung der Sprachtheorie im Mittelalter,* Beiträge zur Gesch. d. Phil. u. Theol. d. Mittelalters 42.2 (1967) 25-26.

[87] Introduction to an anonymous commentary on the Ciceronian *Ad Herennium* (probably French, probably s. xiii ex.), found in Milan, Bibl. Ambros. ms I 142 inf. f. 104: "Et ista est divisio superficialis et rudis est, et alia divisio fertilior et utilior...." We thank John Ward, University of Sydney, for this reference.

[88] R. W. Hunt, for example, noted that many thirteenth- and fourteenth-century manuscripts of Augustine's *De trinitate*, products of the Scholastic period in which the *De trinitate* was most intensively studied, contained not the ancient chapter divisions but the more detailed divisions into sections imposed by Robert Kilwardby. See his "Chapter Headings of Augustine *De trinitate* Ascribed to Adam Marsh," *Bodleian Library Record* 5 (1954) 63-68. Kilwardby also divided the books of the *City of God* into chapters, "ut libri huius lectioni faciliorem redderet," according to Trevet. See B. Smalley, *English Friars and Antiquity in the Early Fourteenth Century* (Oxford 1960) 62 n. 3.

Contemporary comments witness the interest at Oxford in making chapter summaries: Adam Marsh chastises his pupil Thomas of York for being slow to return the chapter summaries to Augustine's *De trinitate* that Marsh had lent him; and in another letter Adam Marsh advises Thomas that he will receive the Maimonides which he had requested and the chapter summaries, which Adam felt would help Thomas no small amount in understanding the text.[89] The earliest and best-known example of the focus on chapter structure is the new division of the scriptures into chapters, attributed to Langton, which was in existence by 1203 and which was popularized in the biblical tools produced by the Dominicans.[90] Similar in purpose is the division of the *Sentences* of Peter Lombard into distinctions, which, thanks to the work of Father Brady, we know to have been done by Alexander of Hales in the years 1223-1227.[91] These distinction-divisions were frequently added into margins of older manuscripts and were rapidly assimilated by new copies.

Three other texts which undergo a change in structure are Lactantius, Gregory the Great's *Moralia* on Job, and Glanville's *De legibus*.[92] Gregory's *Moralia* is a good example of what happens to a cumbersome work in the course of the thirteenth century.[93] Here we see theory and practice working hand in hand, altering both the structure and the format of the *Moralia* by the addition of necessary chapter divisions and appropriate signposts. The *Moralia*, in six volumes divided into thirty-five books, presented difficulties for the user. By the late twelfth century running headlines appear or begin to be added, to distinguish the books. Quotations from the Book of

---

[89] Hunt, "Manuscripts containing Indexing Symbols," 245-246.

[90] See Smalley, *Study of the Bible*, 222-224.

[91] *Magistri Petri Lombardi Sententiae in IV libris distinctae* 1.1, Spicilegium Bonaventurianum 4 (Grottaferrata 1971) 143*-144*.

[92] For example, the text of Lactantius' *Institutiones divinae* in Oxford, Bodleian Library MS Canon. pat. lat. 131, written in France probably in the third quarter of the twelfth century, has chapter divisions added in the margins by an early thirteenth-century writer. The manuscript is being studied by Braxton Ross. Concerning its date see his "*Audi Thoma ... Henriciani nota*: A French Scholar appeals to Thomas Becket?" *English Historical Review* 89 (1974) 333-338. Glanville, *On the Laws and Customs of the Realm*, written in an undivided form ca. 1187-1189, undergoes a number of revisions in the next twenty years to render it more usable. It had rubrics added at an early date, its sections were numbered, and it was then divided into *causae* and *tractatus*. This still proved cumbersome and the work was finally divided into books and chapters, primarily for the purpose of cross-reference. These revisions have all been made by ca. 1210. See G. D. G. Hall, ed., *The Treatise on the Laws and Customs of the Realm of England Commonly Called Glanvill*, Medieval Texts (London 1965) xl-lvi.

[93] N. R. Ker, "The English Manuscripts of the Moralia of Gregory the Great," in *Kunsthistorische Forschungen Otto Pächt* (Salzburg 1972) 77-89.

Job are set off in yellow, underscored, or designated with quotation marks in the margins. By the mid-thirteenth century, a chapter structure has been created. Tables of chapters begin to appear at the heads of the books, and chapter divisions are noted, or added in the margins of older manuscripts, "ut per ea diligens lector citius invenire possit sentencias quibus edificari desiderat," as the thirteenth-century writer of Eton MS 13 notes at the end of the table of chapters.[94] Since the *Moralia* is a commentary on Job, it was necessary to note the forty-two chapters of the Book of Job in the margins of the *Moralia*; and the Huntington Bible, mentioned above in connection with Grosseteste's indexing symbols, is equipped with a reverse concordance, from Job to the *Moralia*.[95] (By the fourteenth century, one has a concordance in the order of the scriptures to exegetical passages in Gregory's *Moralia*, *Pastorale* and homilies.) While the *Moralia* is not issued in pocket book format as are the scriptures, it nevertheless follows the trend toward compression, and is usually found in a single manageable volume (rather than in two or three) from the thirteenth century on. This investigation of how structure and format reflect changes in usage and interest could profitably be extended to other patristic texts.

C. Utility

In the thirteenth century we find a more utilitarian and aggressive attitude toward the written page than heretofore. Certainly the tools that we have discussed embody the concept of utility, of sheer practical usefulness. They are meant to be used, as the homely word "tool" implies—and as the prologues constantly reiterate: *ad utilitatem predicandi...*, *ad utilitatem simplicium maxime, quosdam casus utiles...*, *valde utilis ad predicandum...*, *utilem et salutarem scientiam apprehenderis....* It is less of a commonplace to note that tools are designed as well to help one use the materials to which they are keys. The notion that the Bible or the works of the Fathers are *useful* would be foreign, and likely repugnant, to monastic thought. But a preacher with sermon after sermon to prepare, a theologian wishing to argue on the basis of authority, or a writer in search of an appropriate phrase, finds this a natural mode of thought. For example, Kilwardby explains that he has indexed not only the text but also Augustine's prologues to the books of the *De trinitate*, "because they contain many useful things" (*quoniam utilia plura continent*).[96]

---

[94] Cited from Ker 83.
[95] See n. 34 above.
[96] Cited from Callus, "New Manuscripts," 43.

This utilitarian nature betokens an aggressive attitude toward the written word—an aggressiveness still conveyed in the French verb "to excerpt," *dépouiller*, meaning also "to despoil" or "to ravage." This attitude is in marked opposition to the passive or contemplative attitude characteristic of monastic use of books in the twelfth century, wherein reading is directed toward meditation.[97] Even "active" reading, being oral, is described by the word *ruminatio*. In circumstances where the scriptures were largely known by heart and each individual was a living concordance, there was little need to dismember the scriptures and rearrange the words alphabetically one after the other. Similarly, monastic collections of extracts grew out of spiritual reading. They were not arsenals for *quaestio*, *disputatio* or *praedicatio*, but instead were repositories of ascetic and mystical texts containing words "to turn over frequently in one's heart," *frequenter in corde revolvere*—since reading and prayer were neighboring points on a single continuum.

The frame of mind at the schools in the thirteenth century stands in stark contrast to this. To Hugh of Saint-Cher, "First the bow is bent in study, then the arrow is released in preaching." Thirteenth-century collections of authorities for use in preaching, such as the *Liber Pharetrae* or "The Archer's Quiver," project a combative and bellicose image. The *Pharetra*'s author, probably a Paris Franciscan working before 1264, sees the diverse authorities that he has assembled in this "quiver" as arrows to be shot at the ancient Enemy.[98] Humbert of Romans, O.P., considers that holy books are repositories of weapons with which we defend ourselves and fight against evil: "The weapons of preachers are the authorities taken from books.... Holy men in orders ought always to have about them the necessary divine books ... so that whenever they wish they can take from them spiritual weapons for attacking their enemies."[99] In similar vein, it is only in the thirteenth century that writers begin to substitute, for the rather neutral *colligere* 'to collect', the more aggressive *compilare* 'to pillage' to describe the method of composition involved in toolmaking. These tools are for mining a text, for gutting it, in search of material pertinent to questions

---

[97] Regarding monastic reading see Jean Leclercq, *The Love of Learning and the Desire for God*, trans. C. Misrahi, ed. 2 rev. (New York 1974) 18-22, 89-90.

[98] Regarding the *Liber Pharetrae* see E. Longpré, ed., *Tractatus de pace auctore fr. Gilberto de Tornaco* (Quaracchi 1925) xxiv-xxviii. The *Pharetra* is printed in *S. Bonaventurae Opera omnia*, ed. A. C. Peltier (Paris 1866) 7: 3-231.

[99] Humbert of Romans, *Expositio regulae b. Augustini* 140, "De libris divinis procurandis," in *Opera* 1: 421: "Arma praedicatorum sunt auctoritates sumptae de libris.... Debent ergo viri sancti religiosi semper habere libros divinos ubique sibi pernecessarios..., quia inde possunt quandocumque volunt arma spiritualia sumere ad inimicorum impugnationem."

that might never have occurred to its author. They were devices; and by that very nature, they were meant for use. If this use was aggressive, it is because the sermons produced from these tools were themselves aggressive in intent, meant to capture—or recapture—the faithful for God.

* * *

We have attempted here to set the *Manipulus florum* firmly in an intellectual context, examining the types of tools from which it descends and the techniques of toolmaking which Thomas of Ireland inherited. In order to understand what forces motivated Thomas, however, we must examine the question of why these tools appeared. Why, when Western religiosity and instruction had followed their course for centuries with only a minimal technical apparatus, does the thirteenth century see the creation of a multitude of reference devices and study aids? Since the *Manipulus florum* is a preaching tool, one might expect that the answer to the question will here be restricted to the needs of preachers. The fact is, however, that even for the larger picture—the explanation of the genesis of tools of all sorts, whether for preachers, writers, lawyers or what-have-you—the single most important causative factor, and certainly the earliest chronologically, is the demand for sermon material. The non-preaching tools are all slightly later than, and modeled upon, the sermon aids; initially, the creation of tools is bound up almost exclusively with the essential need to minister through preaching. The Church in the late twelfth century began to perceive the need for an increase in preaching to the laity, and throughout the thirteenth century devoted much energy and intelligence to the achievement of this goal.

2

The New Emphasis on Preaching

The Church, in the thirteenth century, changed its view on the nature and importance of preaching, and increasingly recognized the sermon as a major instrument of the Church's ministry. As a natural concomitant, there was a marked increase in preaching, especially by preachers who were school-trained and, thus, more apt to use and to devise tools.

In the twelfth century much of the preaching was monastic, preached by monks to a monastic congregation. The homily, thoughtful, usually brief, and simple in organization, was the customary vehicle of monastic preaching. Sermons to the laity were not totally lacking, of course; in particular, preaching to the lay faithful was associated with the Crusades, and with wandering evangelists such as Robert d'Arbrissel. But the ordinary parish priest was not expected, and often not competent, to prepare and deliver regular sermons. The task of routine preaching to the lay faithful was the responsibility of the bishops, who were required to preach once each Sunday. When this requirement was fulfilled, and it often was not, the result might be no more than one sermon per diocese per week. Furthermore, the location and the number of dioceses failed to keep abreast of rapid social and demographic changes in the late twelfth and early thirteenth centuries. Father Mandonnet, after noting the growth of towns and town rights, chartered communes, a wealthy bourgeoisie of merchants and artisans, and a concentration of landless working classes, remarked, "In general, given the rapid growth of civil institutions which were opening a new era [the end of the twelfth century], ecclesiastical institutions were notably out of date, fixed as they were in the forms of the feudal age."[1]

It is not to be supposed that the Church ignored the well-being of the souls in its care. Rather, the Church considered preaching largely as a missionary function, aimed at the conversion of non-believers. But for the populace of the Latin West, Christians by birth and heritage, the faith was

---

[1] Pierre Mandonnet, with M.-H. Vicaire and R. Ladner, *Saint Dominique*, 2 vols. (Paris 1938) 1: 28: "On peut dire, d'une façon générale, qu'en présence de l'évolution rapide des institutions civiles, qui ouvrent une ère nouvelle, les institutions ecclésiastiques sont en notable retard, maintenues qu'elles sont dans l'état où l'âge féodal les avait placées."

transmitted principally through the sacraments. This must have been in part
a matter of pragmatic acceptance of the composition of the parish priesthood: ordination could not confer the learning or intelligence needed to
preach, nor could it guarantee the moral probity required to teach by example; but ordination could and did make a man a priest, empowered to convey, untainted and undiminished by any personal lack of learning or
morality, the initial cleansing of baptism and the ultimate solace of final absolution and, between the two, to nourish the soul with the living Body of
Christ in the Eucharist. The hearing of sermons was not, and has never
quite become, a requirement for salvation.

However, in the late twelfth century and the early thirteenth, the Church
began to awake to the value and necessity of increased moral instruction
through preaching. Unquestionably, this was in large part a reaction to the
shock of major heresies, endemic in certain areas and threatening to become
pandemic. In addition, there seem to have been numerous wandering
preachers circulating in western Europe, not necessarily adherents of a particular heretical sect but certainly occupying an irregular position and
usually suspected of heterodox opinions or of fraudulent claims or both.
Their relatively sudden appearance in force indicates that they met a
popular need or hunger for evangelical preaching. One is not certain
whether it was in reaction against these unorthodox preachers that the
Church began to emphasize and encourage sermons by the orthodox; or
whether, in effect, the Church began in earnest to emphasize the sermon as
a vehicle for instruction simply because there was an audience receptive to
preaching.

The evidence of increased preaching in the late twelfth and early thirteenth centuries consists partly of a spate of new ecclesiastical prohibitions
of unauthorized preaching. By 1215, the Church in general council considered the problem of unauthorized wandering preachers to be sufficiently
widespread to require a general prohibition.[2] Not surprisingly, we see thereafter a great number of such ordinances promulgated throughout the
Western Church; but they appear principally among episcopal and archie-
piscopal decrees putting into force on the diocesan level the canons of
Lateran iv. However, prior to the council, and thus more clearly indicative
of local conditions, there are several instances of recorded concern. In 1184
Pope Lucius iii, presiding over the Council of Verona, anathematized all

---

[2] Fourth Lateran Council of 1215 (hereafter Lateran iv), canon 62; *Sacrorum conciliorum nova ... collectio*, ed. J. D. Mansi, 22 (Venice 1778) 1049-1051; and J. Alberigo et
al., eds., *Conciliorum oecumenicorum decreta*, rev. ed. (Basel 1962) 239-240.

who preached without specific papal or episcopal authorization.[3] The constitutions of Odo bishop of Paris (1197) enjoin each pastor actively to prevent any unauthorized persons from preaching, not merely from his pulpit but at any spot within the bounds of his parish.[4] The statutes of the First Canterbury Council, in 1213 or 1214, reveal the same concern across the Channel: they decree that no outsider is to preach unless he bears authorization from the bishop or archbishop.[5] The wording of the statute suggests that a principal concern in this instance was with wandering *quaestuarii*, alms-gatherers and relic-toters whose motives were mercenary. The *quaestuarii* are specifically mentioned in the canons issued by the papal legate Robert Courson for the diocese of Paris in 1213, and reissued by him at the Council of Rouen in the following year. The legatine statutes, now lost, from the slightly earlier Council of Rheims may also have been identical.[6] The canon in question forbids any "conductitius vel quaestuarius praedicator," or any other strangers, from preaching without the authorization of the bishop. Moreover, the canons of Paris and Rouen, and presumably Rheims, contain a further provision connected with preaching: it forbids that the preaching of any province or parish "tanquam ad firmam concedatur" to any such *quaestuarii* or other strangers. The implication that the preaching for an entire ecclesiastical province might have been "let out at farm" is striking; and it presents another gauge of the increased demand for preaching: if preaching as a business had become lucrative enough to attract large-scale frauds and swindlers, obviously there was a market, that is, people who would come, with open hands, to hear sermons.

The *quaestuarii*, since they touched the quick in draining off revenues at the local level, doubtless received as a result a disproportionate amount of attention in local Church legislation. Certainly they constituted a minor contingent among the wandering preachers of the day. There must have been numbers of devout itinerants individually moved to carry the word of God to their fellows, such as Brother Albert of Mantua who in 1204 "came to Bologna and preached there for six weeks and many were converted," otherwhiles conducting a private campaign of peace-making;[7] or such as the

---

[3] In the bull *Ad abolendam*, Mansi 22: 477: "Omnes qui vel prohibiti vel non missi, praeter authoritatem ab apostolica sede vel episcopo loci susceptam, publice vel privatim praedicare praesumpserunt ... pari vinculo perpetui anathematis innodamus."

[4] Ibid. 22: 683 no. 41.

[5] Statutes of Canterbury ɪ, canon 51; F. M. Powicke and C. R. Cheney, *Councils and Synods* (Oxford 1964) 2.1: 33-34.

[6] Concerning the legatine statutes of Courson at Paris, Rouen and Rheims see N. Paulus, *Geschichte des Ablasses im Mittelalter* (Paderborn 1923) 2: 268-269 and n.

[7] R. W. Southern, *Western Society and the Church in the Middle Ages*, Pelican History of the Church 2 (Harmondsworth 1971) 273-274. Concerning itinerant preachers of an

more exuberant "Alleluia people" reported at Parma in the 1240s by Salimbene, who were led by a simple and unlearned man belonging to no order, one Brother Benedict, complete with long black beard and short brass trumpet which "terribiliter reboabat."[8] However, at the end of the twelfth century, the group of unauthorized preachers who had the greatest impact upon the Church, and who were probably also the greatest numerically, were those composed of members of organized heretical sects, Waldenses, Humiliati, Cathars, and others upon whom the Church bestows various catchall epithets—Arians, Manichees, Patarins, and so on. Cathar preaching, at least in public, was evidently confined to those regions of southern France where the Cathars were most firmly entrenched. The preaching activities of Waldenses and Humiliati were more widely spread, geographically.[9] The heresies of Waldes in France and of the Humiliati in Italy had passed rapidly from inception to full flower within the short span of the last quarter of the century,[10] their adherents insisting from the very first upon their mission, obligation, and intention to preach. Disagreeing upon some other aspects of the *vita apostolica*, Waldenses and Humiliati were in accord upon the central issue: that preaching the divine word was an act of charity toward one's neighbor, and an act of obedience to the explicit command of Christ, "Ite, praedicate Evangelium omni creaturae" [Mark 16:15]. This was, in fact, the essence of their heresies, their insistence upon the right to preach, without the necessity of anyone's permission or license. Until their intransigent insistence, and the Church's intransigent refusal, upon this issue eventually forced them into other errors, it was solely their disobedience to Church authority in the matter of preaching, not doctrinal error, which caused the Waldenses and the Humiliati to be condemned. We know that they preached widely and were successful widely because they are widely condemned in orthodox records: from Lorraine in the north and east,

---

earlier age, see G. G. Meersseman, "Eremitismo e predicazione itinerante dei secoli xi e xii," in *L'Eremitismo in occidente nei secoli xi e xii*, Atti della seconda Settimana internazionale di Studio, Mendola ... 1962, Miscellanea del Centro di studi medioevali 4 (Milan 1965) 164-181; and Johannes von Walter, *Die ersten Wanderprediger Frankreichs*, 2 vols. (Leipzig 1903-1906).

[8] Salimbene de Adam, *Cronica*, ed. F. Bernini, Scrittori d'Italia 187 (Bari 1942) 1: 98-100.

[9] The discussion of the Waldenses and Humiliati is based upon Christine Thouzellier, *Catharisme et Valdéisme en Languedoc*, ed. 2 rev. (Paris 1969); and the articles in *Vaudois languedociens et Pauvres catholiques: Cahiers de Fanjeaux* 2 (1967). Concerning the relationships between heresy and preaching, see Ernst Werner, *Pauperes Christi* (Leipzig 1956).

[10] The Humiliati evidently contained a leavening of Henricians and Arnaldians from the previous generation; but this is a new impetus, with rather more moderate adherents.

where Waldenses are preaching and teaching the scriptures in the vernacular,[11] to Aragon in the south and west, where merely listening to a Waldensian sermon constitutes the crime of lèse-majesté,[12] to Italy, where Humiliati and Waldenses alike are anathematized in 1184.[13]

After this brief view of unauthorized preaching, let us examine the response within the framework of the Church. We are faced with two separate responses, sometimes difficult to disentangle. There is the Church's response to heretical preachers and heresy—all the condemnations, anti-heresy tracts, preaching missions and rules of Church councils, which are a fairly simple matter to substantiate. One has in addition the Church's response to the same stimuli in society, whatever they may have been, which have generated contemporaneously the heretical and unauthorized preaching movements. The extent of this latter response, of isolated and to some degree spontaneous increase in popular preaching within the framework of the Church, can only be suggested, given the present state of knowledge concerning twelfth-century preaching. Yet what bits of evidence we have seem to point in the direction of such an increase. Canonically, although preaching was permitted to those who held a *cura animarum*, it was required only of the bishop. Only in 1215, in the canons of Lateran IV, does the Church as a body see fit to direct each bishop to find others to help him with the ministry of preaching. Yet already in the late twelfth century Maurice of Sully, bishop of Paris 1160-1196, encouraged the priests in his diocese to preach daily.[14] Slightly later in England, the canons of Canterbury I (1213 or 1214) contain an implication that parish priests preached to the people at least once a week. In condemning Sunday commerce, the reason given is not drawn from the Decalogue as one might have expected, but instead is based upon the fact that it is on Sundays, above all, that a priest's parishioners ought "to hear prayers and the ecclesiastical office and God's word."[15] Furthermore, a study of the application of the Lateran IV canons in England argues convincingly that episcopal directives respecting

---

[11] Thouzellier 152-154. The investigation of the Waldenses at Metz is known primarily through Innocent III's letters: bk. 2, epp. 141, 142, 235 (PL 214: 695-698, 698-699, 793-795).

[12] Thouzellier 134-135.

[13] Council of Verona, 1184 (Mansi 22: 492-494), and the decretal *Ad abolendam* (Mansi 22: 476-478, esp. 477).

[14] R.-A. Lecoy de la Marche, *La chaire française* (Paris 1868) 23, citing Maurice's sermon in B.N. MS fr. 13314 fol. 8.

[15] Canon 57; Powicke and Cheney 35. It should be noted that, although Powicke and Cheney regard this as a reference to preaching (see their index s.v. Sermons), the words may equally well be interpreted as a reference to scripture readings.

the canon on preaching are designed, not to engender popular preaching
where none was taking place, but merely to insure that the year's cycle of
sermons—presumably numerous—should incorporate specific matters of
doctrine newly articulated by the Council.[16]

The most plentiful evidence of increased interest in preaching comes from
the Paris schools in the late twelfth to early thirteenth centuries. The
masters of theology give implicit and explicit indications that a part at least
of their task is the training of preachers. We are unable to offer conclusive
evidence that a seeming increase in training for the pulpit may not rather
reflect a general increase in the size and in the formality of structure of the
schools themselves. Perhaps, in effect, the entire scale of activity was
growing, so that one naturally finds an increased training of preachers along
with an increased training of every other sort. Nonetheless, one misses, in
the intense dialectic examination of theological problems characteristic of
the schools earlier in the century among such masters as Abelard, Robert of
Melun and Peter the Lombard, the sense of "applied theology" which
abounds in the works of late twelfth-century masters, and which is virtually
second nature to a master like Stephen Langton. Peter the Chanter, Peter of
Poitiers, Prepositinus, Alan of Lille, Langton—these masters, in teaching
theology, are consciously aware that most of their students will spend part
of their lives preaching. All five of these masters were themselves noted
preachers, at very least of sermons *ad cleros*. While there is no external
proof, internal evidence in his works makes it apparent that Alan of Lille
must at one time have exercised a *cura animarum* involving him in regular
preaching to laity.[17] He has left us many sermons. Stephen Langton, according to Matthew Paris, preached to the populace "in northern Italy, in
France..., and in parts of Flanders" in the period after 1215, when to be
sure he was no longer a master. Phyllis Roberts has rescued from obscurity
the epithet "Stephanus de Lingua-Tonante" affixed to a manuscript of
Langton's sermons.[18] But it is not merely these masters' own pulpit activity
which reveals an increased interest in preaching; their writings, and so
much as we know of their teaching, display the same concern. The Chanter,
Peter of Poitiers, Prepositinus, Alan of Lille all have left collections of
biblical *distinctiones*.[19] Though these collections may have been intended by

---

[16] D. W. Robertson, Jr., "Frequency of Preaching in Thirteenth-Century England,"
Speculum 24 (1949) 376-388.

[17] M.-Th. d'Alverny, *Alain de Lille: Textes inédits* (Paris 1965) 27, 119, 153.

[18] Phyllis Barzillay Roberts, *Stephanus de Lingua-Tonante: Studies in the Sermons of
Stephen Langton*, Pontifical Institute of Mediaeval Studies, Studies and Texts 16 (Toronto
1968); for Matthew Paris' observation see p. 18.

[19] See above, chapter 1 at n. 10, and the bibliography given there.

their authors primarily as teaching rather than preaching tools—and there is some doubt as to that assumption[20]—the utility of such works for aid in sermon composition was immediately apparent to preachers, who promptly applied the works to this end. What was so obvious to readers, or hearers, must have occurred to the authors as well; so that we assume that the masters had it in mind, as they composed these collections, to be of service to students in their future preaching. As to the purpose of Alan of Lille's *Ars praedicandi* there is no room for doubt. This work, we may observe, gives weight to the supposition that in the late twelfth century there was not merely interest, but increase of interest, in preaching. It is the first treatise to deal specifically with the practical question—How shall I preach?—since the generalized treatment of this subject by Guibert of Nogent (d. 1124), the so-called *Liber quo ordine sermo fieri debeat* prefixed to his *Moralium* on Genesis.[21] Guibert's thoughtful but brief reflections upon the difference in styles of sermons *ad cleros* and *ad populum* find as their parallel in Alan's treatise more practical advice (ch. 39 in PL), followed by the even more practical models of sermons to be preached to various audiences (soldiers, orators, princes and judges, monks, priests, married people, widows, virgins)—the first-born of a long line of collected *Sermones ad status*.[22] Alan's concern over heresy, manifest in his *Contra hereticos* and other writings, was perhaps a partial motivation for his interest in orthodox preaching.[23] Stephen Langton seems never to have written anything that might be classed as a preacher's manual or tool—although one of William de Montibus' preaching handbooks, the *Similitudinarius*, incorporated so much matter from Langton's sermons that the work is occasionally attributed to the latter.[24] In Langton's case, however, we are fortunately provided with a masterful investigation[25] of the manuscript materials, students' *reportationes*, that show us Langton in the classroom. There we find copious signs of his continued awareness that his students will, in a short time, find themselves in the pulpit. In the reports of his glosses, we

[20] Mgr. Lacombe thought that both Peter of Poitiers' and Prepositinus' *Distinctiones* on the Psalms may originally have been preached; G. Lacombe, *La vie et les œuvres de Prévostin*, Bibliothèque thomiste 11, Section historique 10 (Le Saulchoir 1927) 120-121.

[21] PL 156: 21-32.

[22] Alanus, *Summa de arte praedicatoria*, PL 210: 111-198; model *sermones ad status*, PL 210: 185-198.

[23] In the introduction to his collection of distinctions, Alan gives as one motive for his compilation the intention that heretics might not argue on the basis of false interpretation of scriptural terms: "Ne ex falsa interpretatione errorem confirmet hereticus" PL 210: 687.

[24] Roberts, *Stephanus de Lingua-Tonante*, 92-94.

[25] Beryl Smalley, *Study of the Bible in the Middle Ages*, ed. 2 rev. (Oxford 1952) 196-263.

find distinctions and *exempla*, both of which are material for sermons, and he frequently draws his students' attention to specific passages of scripture suitable for sermon themes.[26] In as explicit a statement as one could wish, he tells his students that "it is the master's duty ... to incite his promising pupils to preach." Indeed, one has found *exempla* in the glosses, a tell-tale sign of interest in preaching, since Peter the Chanter.[27] One can see, as well, concrete examples of preachers putting to practical use the teachings of the Paris masters of theology. "The famous English preacher, Odo of Cheriton, drew largely on Langton's glosses for his material."[28] Jacques de Vitry reports that the well-known popular preacher Fulk of Neuilly came to the lectures of Peter the Chanter, stylus and tablet in hand, to gather material for use in his sermons.[29]

It is plain, in fact, that the schools at Paris were not merely one center, but the primary center of a concentrated interest in and effort toward enhancing the role of the sermon in the ministry of the Church. They are the natural home of the movement, so to speak. Orthodoxy did not require simply a quantitative increase in preaching; what was wanted in addition was intelligent preaching, by trained and able preachers. The teachers, the training facilities, the methods and the instructional materials for preachers were all either to be found or being developed at the schools. Certainly the preachers who had been pupils of Langton, the Chanter, Alanus, are the sort who will use (and create) sermon tools, because they are oriented toward the use of written aids. These Paris masters accepted a responsibility, not only to their students, but to those whom their students would instruct in turn. Thus, out of this ferment at the Paris schools there emerged such programs of local renewal as that of William de Montibus, disciple of the Chanter, contemporary or nearly so of Langton and Alanus, and chancellor of Lincoln ca. 1186-1213.[30] When William was recalled from Paris to Lincoln by Bishop Hugh, he set about devising means for conveying, on a simpler level, the new ideas of sacramental and pastoral theology from Paris for the instruction of his local clergy—the *Numerale, Versarius, Speculum penitentis, Tropi* and others. In addition he compiled a number of preaching

---

[26] Ibid. 254.

[27] Ibid. 153; ibid. 256-257.

[28] Ibid. 209; see also B. Smalley, "*Exempla* in the Commentaries of Stephen Langton," *Bulletin of the John Rylands Library* 17 (1933) 121-129.

[29] Lecoy de la Marche, *La chaire française*, 299-300.

[30] See Hugh MacKinnon, "William de Montibus ...," in *Essays in Medieval History Presented to Bertie Wilkinson*, ed. T. A. Sandquist and M. R. Powicke (Toronto 1969) 32-45.

tools—a collection of distinctions, the *Similitudinarius* or collection of similitudes, the *Proverbia*—to assist the clergy of the diocese in their own programs of instruction, that is, the instruction of their parishioners in Christian faith and morals through regular preaching. William's tools are significant not only for being among the earliest of their kind but also for the use of alphabetical arrangement and numerical subdivision. And his interests were continued by one of his students, Richard of Wethringsett, who wrote a manual for parish priests that became quite as popular as William's own works. De Montibus, hence, is an important link between the Paris schoolroom and the English diocese, between Peter the Chanter whose lectures he heard and Robert Grosseteste whom he evidently taught at Lincoln.

Alongside the increased emphasis on orthodox preaching at the schools and in certain dioceses, there was a formal and directed increase in orthodox preaching resulting from the organized anti-heresy campaign waged under the immediate supervision of the papacy. We have mentioned above the mushroom growth of Waldenses and Humiliati in the late twelfth century. The ultimate origins of Cathar beliefs, and the original means and paths of their dissemination, are still matters of controversy.[31] The pertinent fact is that, as is generally agreed, the impact of this sect upon the Church as a whole dates only from the 1170s. With striking suddenness they force themselves upon the Church's attention, as two contrasting examples reveal. At the Council of Tours in 1163, presided over by Pope Alexander III, the body takes note (canon 4) of the "heresy around Toulouse, spreading to Gascony and infecting several other provinces."[32] And the canon's principal directive was that these heretics should be ostracized. It was assumed that the inconvenience of being cut off from commerce with Christians, coupled with public ecclesiastical censure, would suffice in time to cause the heresy to wither, meanwhile protecting the faithful from contamination. Sixteen years later, in canon 27 of Lateran III (1179), the Church exhorts secular powers to take up arms against the Cathars, offering a two-years' indulgence as enticement.[33] The wielders of the secular sword, it happened, were not for the moment prepared to crusade in Languedoc, thus giving the papacy time to reconsider and to adopt a less violent sort of combat, the sending of missionary preachers into the newly-discovered missionary fields of Catholic Europe.

[31] See the bibliographic survey of Ét. Delaruelle, "L'état actuel des études sur le Catharisme," in *Cathares en Languedoc: Cahiers de Fanjeaux* 3 (1968) 19-41.
[32] Mansi 21: 1177-1178. In 1163, of course, the papacy still carried the burden of schism, a fact that restricted its freedom of action.
[33] Mansi 22: 231-233.

Preaching was merely one of the many options open to and employed by the Church in resisting heresy. There are conciliar condemnations and pro-hibitions; there are pressures brought to bear, often quite effectively, upon local secular administrations to despoil and banish heretics from their midst; there are the firm measures taken by the kings of Aragon, Alphonzo II and Pedro II, in threatening heretics with physical violence (in effect, since after a certain time limit the heretics were no longer protected by the laws) or even execution, in some circumstances;[34] there are proto-inquisitorial procedures, with the odious business of rewards being offered to informers;[35] and there are, with grim finality, full-fledged crusade and long-term Inquisition. However, our interest here is focused upon anti-heretical preaching—and even so, we are not so much concerned with the effect of this preaching upon heresy, as with the bearing that anti-heretical campaigns had upon the role of preaching in the life of the Church at large.

By the 1170s, Catharism was entrenched, more or less publicly, in many parts of what is now the south of France.[36] Alexander III, relieved at last in 1177 of the encumbrance of a schism of nearly twenty years' duration, was eager to set his house in order. The catalyst—almost any would have served—was the initiative of Raymond V of Toulouse in requesting aid against the heretics from the General Chapter at Cîteaux, in the autumn of 1177. His request was more for material than spiritual aid; he wished the abbots to help him secure the armed intervention of Louis VII of France and Henry II of England. Nonetheless, it provoked the first suggestion that preaching missions should be sent, the suggestion coming from Henry II writing on behalf of both monarchs;[37] admittedly, the kings envisaged a mixed embassage, part preachers and part soldiers. The mission eventually sent by Alexander III in August-September 1178 was, in effect, just such a company. In addition to the legate, Peter of St. Chrysogonus, the group in-cluded Abbot Henry of Clairvaux, Archbishop Garin of Bourges (likewise a Cistercian), Bishop John "Belles-Mains" of Poitiers, who later retired to

---

[34] Thouzellier, *Catharisme*, 134-136.

[35] Ibid. 135; Yves Congar, "Henri de Marcy, abbé de Clairvaux, cardinal-évêque d'Albano et légat pontifical," *Analecta monastica* ser. 5, *Studia Anselmiana* 43 (1958) 20.

[36] The classic description often cited is that in Count Raymond's request of the abbot of Cîteaux in 1177: "Insuper sic in finibus nostris obscuratum est aurum, ut quasi lutum sub pedibus diaboli sternatur; quoniam et qui sacerdotio funguntur haeresis foeditate depravan-tur, et antiqua olimque veneranda ecclesiarum loca inculta jacent, diruta remanent, bap-tismus negatur, eukaristia abominatur, poenitentia parvi penditur, hominis plasmatio, carnis resurrectio, abnegando respuitur, et omnia ecclesiastica sacramenta annullantur, et, quod nefas est, duo etiam principia introducuntur." The letter is preserved in the *Chronicle* of Gervase of Canterbury, ed. William Stubbs, Rolls Series 73 (London 1879) 1: 270.

[37] Congar, "Henri de Marcy," 22 and n. 33; Thouzellier, *Catharisme*, 20.

die as a monk at Clairvaux, Archbishop Pons d'Arsac of Narbonne, Bishop Reginald of Bath and other ecclesiastics, as well as Raymond of Toulouse and other *seigneurs* and their retinue—in all, the imposing total of nearly 300 men.[38] The importance of preaching in this mission was dwarfed by other considerations, even more so than the roll of participants indicates, since the clerics themselves concentrated principally upon inquisitorial fact-finding and upon rendering judgments. Even so, the participation of Cistercians (the elect of pre-Mendicant missionaries) in a leading role is portentous for the future; and it is unlikely that Henry of Clairvaux, for all his vociferous bellicosity, would have failed to employ as well his known talent as a preacher. In 1180, Alexander sent a second mission, with Henry of Clairvaux, now Henry of Albano, himself as the legate. This second became, at Henry's instigation, more of a military expedition than the first; paradoxically, perhaps, it also leaves us more than does the first with testimony to the power of preaching (by this same Henry of Albano) in converting leading heretics, and suggests, as Congar observes, that Henry accomplished as much by his preaching as by his other activities. These two are the only attempts—half-hearted ones at best, with their focus elsewhere—at the organized use of preaching and preachers to root out heresy in Languedoc, until the pontificate of Innocent III.

Elected to the papacy at the beginning of 1198 and consecrated in February, by April 1198 Innocent III had launched the first of the preaching missions of his pontificate. The mission, destined for Languedoc, was confided to two Cistercians, one Brother Guy and, in chief place, Innocent's own confessor Rainier of Ponza. Their charge was ample—they were to act with all the authority of ecclesiastical Judges of Assizes; but also, explicitly, they were charged to preach. From this time onward, if indeed one may not date it from the earlier legatine missions of Henry of Albano in Alexander III's pontificate, Cistercians formed the elite corps of anti-heretical preachers until the arrival of Dominicans upon the scene. As others have remarked, the Cistercians were employed by the twelfth-century papacy for many of the tasks that popes of the thirteenth and later centuries would assign to the Friars. Cistercians were used as papal emissaries, as trouble-shooters,[39] as legates, as bishops particularly in difficult sees,[40] and

---

[38] Congar 19; Thouzellier 21 n. 28.

[39] E.g., Innocent III assigns three Cistercian abbots to investigate and make a final disposition of the problems of Waldenses in Metz; bk. 2 ep. 235 (PL 214: 793-795).

[40] E.g., the elevation of Fulk, abbot of Florège, to the see of Toulouse in 1206. Cf. Thouzellier 192, and the bibliography in n. 49.

as missionary preachers. Cistercians were sent to preach on the eastern
frontier with the Slavs, in Sicily, and most notably in Languedoc.

In addition to the mission of 1198-99 (followed by a non-preaching,
non-Cistercian mission in 1200), Innocent III sent to Languedoc in 1203 a
Cistercian preaching mission which continued, with later augmentations in
personnel and changes in procedure, up to and through the Albigensian
Crusade itself. Beginning with the Cistercians Pierre de Castelnau and
Raoul de Fontfroide in the fall of 1203, the mission was enlarged in 1204
to include the abbot of Cîteaux, Arnaud-Amaury, as a third legate.[41] When
Innocent gave the legates additional responsibilities at the end of 1204, he
specified in their instructions that these new tasks were not to interfere with
their commission to preach.[42] In the summer of 1206 came the chance addition, so significant in retrospect, of the Spanish bishop Diego of Osma
and Dominic, sub-prior of his cathedral chapter. The three Cistercian
legates quickly adopted Diego's impromptu inspiration that they continue
their preaching, *pauperem Christum pauperes imitantes*, not as practised
canonically by the Cistercian Order but in the most literal sense as applied
to themselves individually. Innocent III almost at once (November 1206)
perceived the genius of this suggestion and converted the experiment into a
formal papal directive, prescribing a life of poverty and humility as the style
henceforth to be followed by the missionary preachers in Languedoc. In the
spring of 1207 the size of the mission was increased severalfold by the
arrival of some dozen Cistercian abbots, each accompanied by one or two
monks; to each little team Arnaud-Amaury assigned a specific region, and
they set out on foot, these princes of the Church, temporarily assuming the
life of a poor wandering preacher as zealously as ever Waldes had done or
the Dominicans would do.

This promising attempt to demonstrate the power of popular preaching in
the face of a reluctant or hostile populace had, as we know, little time in
which to prove itself—because of unforeseen outside events, and because of
weaknesses inherent in the program itself. The unexpected death of Bishop
Diego, at the close of 1207, effectively cut off the missions' main source of
funds; since the Cistercian missionaries were living as paupers and not as
mendicants, outside support was indispensable. Furthermore, the enlistment
of so many abbots, while a dramatic gesture of Christian humility and

---

[41] Ibid. 185 n. 11, 187.

[42] Innocent III, bk. 7 ep. 166 (PL 215: 474): "Consulimus et monemus ut super negotio
vobis injuncto vehementius intendentes, non requiratis in aliis qui possint impedire commissa, ne unum quod inevitabilem necessitatem inducit per aliud quod est tolerabile impedimentum assumat."

charity, nevertheless insured that the missionaries could not long attend single-mindedly to the ministry of preaching. The abbots were torn by the pull of older duties, their material and spiritual responsibilities for their houses, and their own vows (and, often, a deeply-felt personal vocation) to the contemplative life. Certainly a basic weakness was the utterly unrealistic expectation, on the part of the pope and presumably of the Cistercians (the abbots, at least, cannot have envisaged any protracted absence from their monasteries), of a rapid reconversion of the whole province. In the fall of the same year which saw the large-scale experiment begin, Innocent III was already concluding that the results were insufficient and that the secular arm would have to intervene in force. Finally, of course, the assassination of the legate Peter of Castelnau at the beginning of 1208 effectively signaled the end of the attempt to extirpate Catharism by dint of persuasion alone. In sum, if one were to assess the total effect of the preaching missions in reconverting the Cathars, the judgment would have to be: inconclusive even in potential, negligible in accomplishment.

However, our ultimate concern is with the effect of the preaching campaign against heresy upon the role of popular preaching in the daily life of the Church. Primarily, inevitably, this means its effect upon the key figure of Innocent III. As we have observed, there is scattered evidence of encouragement to preach in various bishoprics, and a concentrated interest in the training of preachers at the University of Paris, before the papacy takes any formal step in that direction. The overwhelming need to preach, and hunger to hear, had been responsible for the emergence of unauthorized heretical preachers unable to await direction or even permission from above. The fact is elementary, however, that any broad-based new emphasis upon preaching in the Church as a whole would eventually require papal sanction and encouragement. This support Innocent III provided; and it is possible to regard his preaching missions in Languedoc as, in a certain sense, laboratory experiments in popular preaching. If we consider the alacrity with which he began to send out preachers, then we may presume that even before his election he had pondered "the problem of the ignorance of the masses. All the coercive measures already taken [in Languedoc] would remain without effect unless one first of all undertook to instruct the faithful—not simply with sermons against heresy, but with frequent and fruitful teaching, bread of the soul. The pontiff had realized the imperious human need to search for profound truth in oral explanation and discussion."[43] As Lothar of Segni, he had had ties of friendship with Stephen Langton and

[43] Thouzellier 186.

others of the masters at Paris, whose interest in preaching he must have known and shared. As pope, we see him urging individual bishops to do more preaching[44] and castigating the prelates who "fail to break the bread that the young children ask of you," so that they continued to hunger for preaching.[45] Early in his pontificate (1201-1208), beginning before his larger preaching missions were dispatched, Innocent had in effect "domesticated" or annexed as large a proportion of the Humiliati and the Waldenses as would permit themselves to be salvaged, controlling and channeling their preaching activities, in preference to suppressing those activities entirely. Humbert of Romans records an incident wherein Innocent half-recited, half-read a homily of St. Gregory, rather than preaching a sermon of his own, as a striking demonstration of the fact that even the non-gifted, incapable of composing their own sermons, could preach the sermons of the Fathers to their congregations.[46]

Innocent III's interest in and personal commitment to popular preaching existed both prior to, and outside of, the specific anti-Cathar preaching missions in Languedoc. The mixed results of these latter did not alter his eventual decision to commit the whole Church to a new emphasis on popular preaching. Evidently Innocent III was able to distinguish the value and vitality of the popular preaching from the entirely antipathetical surroundings into which his preachers had been sent. His conviction remained unaltered that sermons should be a principal vehicle of the faith, not merely in situations of conflict vis-à-vis the heretics, but universally, in defense and reinforcement of the faith. We know that his impatience in Languedoc, and his understandable outrage at the murder of his legate, never caused him to abandon his belief in the eventual efficacy of persuasion. His instigation of the Albigensian Crusade was in accord with venerable Christian beliefs, that punishment is often required to prepare sinners for repentance.[47] But all during and after the armed campaigns, Dominic and his companions with Innocent's authorization and encouragement still wandered preaching to those who were ready to hear.

The Fourth Lateran Council was convened in 1215 largely to assess the situation in Languedoc and to take measures designed both to continue to

---

[44] E.g., in a letter to the bishops of Viterbo and Orvieto in 1205; Innocent III, bk. 8 ep. 105 (PL 215: 654-657, esp. 655-656).

[45] E.g., in a letter to the archbishop of Narbonne in 1203; Innocent III, bk. 6 ep. 81 (PL 215: 84): "Et dum parvulis petentibus panem, juxta quod ad officium pertinet pastorale, non frangis..." (cf. Lamentations 4: 4).

[46] Humbert of Romans, *De eruditione praedicatorum* pt. 1, in his *Opera de vita regulari* ed. J. J. Berthier (Rome 1889) 2: 397.

[47] Expressed, for example, in Augustine's *De disciplina christiana*.

its conclusion the extermination of the Cathar heresy and to ensure, they hoped, that such an entrenched regional disaffection would never again confront the Church. It is in this context, not of attack but of active defense, "preventive medicine," that we must place canon 10 of Lateran iv:

> *De praedicatoribus instituendis.* Inter cetera quae ad salutem spectant populi Christiani, pabulum verbi Dei permaxime noscitur sibi esse necessarium, quia sicut corpus materiali, sic anima spirituali, cibo nutritur, eo quod *non in solo panem vivit homo, sed in omni verbo quod procedit de ore Dei.* Unde cum saepe contingat, quod episcopi propter occupationes multiplices, vel invaletudines corporales, aut hostiles incursus, seu occasiones alias (ne dicamus defectum scientiae, quod in eis est reprobandum omnino, nec de cetero tolerandum) per se ipsos non sufficiunt ministrare populo verbum Dei, maxime per amplas dioeceses et diffusas, generali constitutione sancimus, ut episcopi viros idoneos ad sanctae praedicationis officium salubriter exequendum assumant, potentes in opere et sermone, qui plebes sibi commissas, vice ipsorum, cum per se idem nequiverint, solicite visitantes, eas verbo aedificant et exemplo, quibus ipsi, cum indiguerint congrue necessaria ministrent, ne pro necessariorum defectu compellantur desistere ab incoepto. Unde praecipimus tam in cathedralibus, quam in aliis conventualibus ecclesiis viros idoneos ordinari, quos episcopi possint coadjutores et cooperatores habere, non solum in praedicationis officio, verum etiam in audiendis confessionibus, et poenitentiis injungendis, ac ceteris quae ad salutem pertinent animarum. Si quis autem hoc neglexerit adimplere, districtae subjaceat ultioni.[48]

In a recent essay, Father Boyle has suggested that this canon is an application at large of what Saint Dominic and his followers had achieved at Toulouse under Bishop Fulk.[49] Canon 10, in effect, is the culmination and the combination of the various spontaneous movements toward increased preaching, and of the various papal missions of preachers, witnessed by the late twelfth and the early thirteenth centuries. It gives them an official stamp of approval.

Again, though, the emphasis was not simply upon more preaching, but upon more preaching of the proper sort. The Church considered fervor in a preacher an unacceptable substitute for learning and orthodoxy.[50] Canon 62

---

[48] Quoted from Mansi 22: 998-999; see also Alberigo, *Conciliorum oecumenicorum decreta* 215-216.

[49] See L. E. Boyle, "The *Compilatio quinta.*"

[50] Cf. J. Leclercq, "Le magistère du prédicateur au xiiie siècle," *Archives d'histoire doctrinale et littéraire du Moyen Age* 15 (1946) 105-147, esp. 143-144: "Exceptionnellement, sans doute ... la sainteté charismatique ou une impulsion extraordinaire du Saint-Esprit peuvent suppléer aux études. Mais normalement, dans le gouvernement ordinaire de l'Eglise, c'est la théologie qui prépare à prêcher avec fruit."

reiterated the familiar theme, that strangers may not come in and preach, unless they bear authentic letters of permission from the bishop.[51] This was control of the personnel of preaching; but its ultimate intent, of course, was proper supervision of the content of preaching. Another canon of Lateran IV approached the same problem from the positive end: Canon 11 reiterated Lateran III's provision (slightingly observed, says canon 11 of Lateran IV) that each cathedral church, and all others that have the capacity, select a school master to teach "grammar and other things" to the clerics of this and of other churches.[52] And it adds that each metropolitan church is likewise to have a theologian to instruct the priests and others in theology, especially pastoral theology.[53] Canons 10 and 11 taken together reveal the sentiment of the Council that heresy was not merely combatted, but effectively prevented, by an increase in orthodox preaching, provided that the preachers were properly trained.

The implementation of the Council's canon on preaching appears in synodal and provincial statutes across Europe in the years that follow. A few examples will indicate the seriousness with which the bishops regarded the matter. The Council of Rouen (1223), under Archbishop Theobald, repeated almost verbatim the operative phrase of Lateran IV's canon 10: "Each bishop shall choose men fitted for the task of preaching, so that the message of holy preaching may circulate through all the dioceses."[54] In England, the provincial council held at Oxford (1222) under Stephen Langton enjoined parish priests to see to it that their parishioners receive a sufficient diet of preaching, lest the priests "be considered, quite rightly, as worthless watchdogs that will not bark."[55] And Bishop Peter des Roches, in the synodal statutes of Winchester I (ca. 1224), not only ordered his parish priests to preach often, but threatened those found negligent with suspension.[56] The statutes of the Council of Trier (1227) well exemplify the dual

[51] Mansi 22: 1049-1051.
[52] Mansi 22: 999: "... qui clericos ecclesiarum ipsarum et aliarum gratis in grammaticae facultate ac aliis instruat juxta posse."
[53] Ibid.: "Sane metropolitana ecclesia theologum nihilo minus habeat, qui sacerdotes et alios in sacra pagina doceat, et in his praesertim informet quae ad curam animarum spectare noscuntur."
[54] Ibid. 22: 1198 statute 2: "Singuli *episcopi viros idoneos ad officium praedicationis assumant*, quatenus per totos episcopatus sanctae praedicationis rota discurrat"; words in italics are taken from Lateran IV, canon 10. See also Rouen statute 10 (col. 1199).
[55] Powicke and Cheney 110, statute 15: "... ut plebes sibi commissas pabulo verbo Dei, secundum quod eis fuerit inspiratum, informare produrant, ne canes muti merito iudicentur."
[56] Ibid. 130, statute 28: "Precipimus insuper quod parochiales presbiteri proponant sepius parochianis suis verbum Dei.... Qui autem in hoc negligens inventus fuerit incontinenti ab officio suspendatur."

aim of Lateran ɪᴠ on preaching—to eliminate the preaching of error while fostering the preaching of right doctrine. Statute 7 (*De decanis*) orders that priests instruct their parishioners on the virtues and vices, the articles of faith and the Ten Commandments. However, "ignorant and inexperienced priests should by no means presume to preach to their parishioners," lest such priests become *magistri erroris*. But they should actively encourage attendance, when learned men came to preach. Most especially, the Council orders that friars, both Dominican and Franciscan, should be warmly received and treated with charity, and that "you shall lead your people to hear the word of God from them."[57] And later still, in 1238, Grosseteste proposes to give demonstration sermons to all the priests of his diocese, one deanery at a time, as an encouragement to preach and an instruction in method and content.[58]

Certainly, however, the most visible and most immediately effective indication of an increased emphasis upon preaching was the official recognition in 1216, only a year after Lateran ɪᴠ, of the Dominicans, an order uniquely devoted to preaching and determined that its preaching should be based upon sound biblical and theological training; "an order of preachers was necessarily an order of doctors."[59] The Franciscans likewise, in a manner unforeseen by St. Francis, were quickly and inevitably drawn into a preaching ministry. And the friars and the university, with that supple adaptability of which young institutions are capable, quickly joined forces, the friars making their indelible mark upon the school of theology, the university imposing its modes of thought even upon the Franciscans with little delay. In short, the thirteenth century saw the working out, in practical terms, of what was at most a diffuse notion at the end of the twelfth century: that Western "Christendom" was in fact a mission field in need of preachers, not to convert but to strengthen and maintain the faith.

[57] Mansi 23: 31-32: "De talibus [scil. viciis etc.] vero in articulis fidei et de decem praeceptis, sacerdotes subditos suos instruant, et alias illiterati et inexperti sacerdotes nullatenus populo sibi subdito praedicare praesumant, ne contingat eos fieri magistros erroris..., sed cum aliis viris literatis subditis suis contigerit praedicari, verbum Dei devote audiant ... [et] in omnibus promoveant...; item praecipimus firmiter et districte ut viros religiosos, scilicet fratres praedicatorum [*sic*] et minores, cum ad vos venerint, benigne recipiatis, et caritative pertractetis, et plebes vobis subditas ad hoc inducatis, ut ab ipsis verbum Dei audiant."

[58] Grosseteste, ep. 50; in *Roberti Grosseteste epistolae*, ed. H. R. Luard, Rolls Series 25 (London 1861) 146.

[59] Smalley, *Study of the Bible*, 268, based on Mandonnet, *Saint Dominique*, 2: 65-67. See also Mandonnet 2: 50-59, for other examples of the equation *ordo praedicatorum* equals *ordo doctorum*.

We see concrete evidence in the thirteenth century of a new attitude evolving toward the place of the sermon in the Church, as it were a theology of predication struggling to emerge. Tangible in the strictest sense are the changes in Dominican architecture which bring the preacher into closer contact with the lay congregation.[60] We also see a change in the explicit expression of the worth or value of the sermon to the Church's mission. Prior to the Fourth Lateran Council, most legislation on preaching was inhibitory; the primary emphasis was placed upon insuring that the faithful were not corrupted by error from the pulpit. Although strict control over preaching continues to attract the attention of thirteenth-century legislators, the negative attitude is accompanied by frequent positive statements of the value of sermons.[61] William of Auvergne, bishop of Paris 1228-1249, wrote that the "veritas evangelica" is committed to preachers, to guard it, to publish it abroad, and to bind it in indissoluble wedlock to human understanding.[62] Odo of Cheriton wrote, in 1224, that "the doctors of the Church are especially God's helpers, for—so it seems to me at present—a preacher whom we can hear and see does more good than an angel or archangel whom we do not see."[63] An anonymous thirteenth-century commentary stated that the preacher, because of the difficulty of his task, is endowed with a dignity the equal of the virgins and martyrs.[64] Later in the century, Humbert of Romans, Master General of the Order of Preachers, cataloged the exceedingly grave situations from which the world is saved by the office of preaching, "without which the full glory of the Kingdom of Heaven would not be consummated, hell would fill up faster, and the world would be altogether sterile; demons would dominate the earth, human hearts would not soar to heavenly hopes, the nations would not receive the Christian faith; and the Church would not have been esta-

[60] G. Meersseman, "L'architecture dominicaine au xiiiᵉ siècle: législation et pratique," *Archivum Fratrum Praedicatorum* 16 (1946) 136-190; and M. Durliat, "Le rôle des ordres mendiants dans la création de l'architecture gothique méridionale," in *La naissance et l'essor du gothique méridional au xiiiᵉ siècle: Cahiers de Fanjeaux* 9 (1974) 76ff.

[61] Jean Leclercq has assembled some of the more pointed statements on this subject, in his "Le magistère."

[62] In his *De faciebus*, prologue ; see N. Valois, *Guillaume d'Auvergne* (Paris 1880) 225 n. 1: "Veritas evangelica praedicatoribus ... est commissa, ut ipsam custodiant, ipsam in manifestum producant, ipsam denique humano intellectui matrimonio indissolubili, tanquam sponso, coniungant."

[63] From his *Sermones in Epistolas*, as contained in Lincoln Cathedral MS 11 fol. 53: "Doctores ecclesie precipue Dei sunt adiutores, quoniam plus proficit, sicud ad presens sencio, predicator quem audire et videre possumus quam angelus et archangelus quem non videmus." Quoted from A. C. Friend, "The Life and Unprinted Works of Master Odo of Cheriton," D.Phil. diss. (Oxford 1936) 73, 122.

[64] Leclercq, "Le magistère," 112.

blished, nor have prospered, nor would she stand." Moreover Humbert proved, in best scholastic fashion, that the office of preaching was apostolic, was angelic, was even divine; and, "since among the saints none are more excellent than the apostles, among the created species none more excellent than the angels, and in the universe nothing more excellent than God, how excellent is that office" which partakes of all three natures.[65] And just after the turn of the century, in 1304, Raymond Lull flatly asserts: "Preaching is the highest, the most difficult, and the noblest office."[66]

Particularly revealing as an indication of the sermon's new stature in the life of the Church is the fact that one begins, first in the thirteenth century, to ascribe to the preaching and hearing of sermons something of a sacramental nature. In practice, the papacy began very early in the century a process which integrated sermons with the sacrament of penance: the act of preaching, specifically of preaching a crusade, merits an indulgence for the preacher. The earliest instance can only be inferred, as an indirect result of the encouragement to crusade in the canons of Lateran IV, granting indulgence to any who gave aid as well as to those who actually fought, thus presumably to preachers.[67] Honorius III included preachers of the crusade in his grant of indulgences in a bull of 1218.[68] Once begun, the process was irreversible; one is reminded of R. W. Southern's evocative phrase, "inflationary spiral."[69] By the late thirteenth and on into the fourteenth century, it became a matter of course to grant indulgences for preaching, during a specified length of time, a call to crusade, or even for preaching an exhortation to the populace to pay their crusade-tithes. The amount of the indulgence varied, and frequently it was on a "piece-work" basis, for example, 100 days' indulgence for each sermon delivered. The general trend, however, was to grant indulgences of ever increasing length.[70]

Inevitably the process came to include the congregation as well. The earliest instance of this practice in fact antedates Lateran IV: in 1213, Innocent III granted indulgences of an unspecified number of days to those who came to hear sermons exhorting to crusade. Honorius III granted sometimes ten, sometimes twenty days' indulgence for the same.[71] The first

[65] Humbert of Romans, *De erud. praed.* 1, *Opera de vita regulari* 2: 378, 374.
[66] Raymond Lull, *Liber de praedicatione*, in *Raimundi Lulli Opera latina*, ed. F. Stegmüller (Palma, Majorca 1961) 3: 140: "Quoniam praedicatio est officium altissimum, arduissimum et nobilissimum, ... idcirco intendimus facere librum de praedicatione."
[67] Lateran IV canon 3; Mansi 22: 987-988.
[68] Paulus, *Geschichte des Ablasses*, 2: 42 n. 3.
[69] Southern, *Western Society*, 133, referring to the period ca. 1300-1520.
[70] Paulus 2: 43-44.
[71] Ibid. 44.

pope to employ this practice to any significant extent was Gregory IX. In addition to indulgences for hearing crusading sermons, Gregory in 1237 permitted the Dominicans preaching in Lombardy, an area perennially rife with heresy, to grant as inducement a three-years' indulgence to "omnibus qui ad praedicationem eorum accesserint in singulis stationibus viginti dies."[72] Normally the figures were considerably lower—forty days' indulgence to those who heard the sermons of missionaries in "Ruscia" (1233),[73] ten days' indulgence for those who heard missionary sermons in "Sclavonia" (1234);[74] and, in 1233, an indulgence of twenty days to all who heard three sermons in one week delivered by the Dominican John of Vicenza.[75] Again, however, as the thirteenth century progressed the figures for hearing a single sermon gradually increased—up to a year and forty days' indulgence for hearing a crusading sermon, up to 100 days' indulgence for hearing the sermons of specified preachers.[76]

It had become fairly commonplace, from as early as the patristic era, to refer to sermons as "bread"; whether or not this imagery ever had specific reference to the bread of the Eucharist, such reference is one of the implicit and ever-present allusive overtones. Although the late twelfth- and early thirteenth-century preachers thus did not originate this symbol, they frequently employed it. For example, Maurice of Sully urged his priests to preach every day, using as his text, "Give us this day our daily bread."[77] Innocent III, pitying the faithful who hungered to hear the word of God, cited the passage, "Parvuli petierunt panem...."[78] In justifying a preacher's right to preach a sermon composed by another, Humbert of Romans took as his authority the miracle of the loaves and fishes, when Christ ordered his disciples merely to distribute the bread, not to bake it themselves.[79]

However, the thirteenth century went farther than any previous age in manifest *rapprochement* of sermons and sacraments.[80] As a theoretical basis, one has for example the conclusion of Thomas Docking, the English Franciscan, in a *quaestio* ca. 1260 attempting to determine which, preaching or baptism, holds higher rank in the hierarchy of instruments of grace:

[72] Mansi 23: 75.
[73] Lucien Auvray, ed., *Les registres de Grégoire IX*, 4 vols., Bibliothèque des Écoles françaises d'Athènes et de Rome 9, ser. 2 (Paris 1890-1955) no. 1180.
[74] Ibid. no. 2127.
[75] Ibid. no. 1461.
[76] Paulus 2: 44, 2: 229.
[77] See n. 14 above.
[78] See n. 45 above.
[79] Humbert, *Opera* 2: 397.
[80] See for example Leclercq, "Le magistère," 144 and nn. 2-3.

Docking applied three criteria of comparison, and preaching prevailed over the sacrament in two of the three.[81] Humbert of Romans demonstrated that preaching is an essential adjunct to the sacraments. Under the heading "De excellentia praedicationis super alia opera," he says, "Although salvation is conferred by sacraments, yet preaching is more effective in one respect, that it moves and prepares the hearts of men. For sacraments cannot confer salvation save on those prepared to receive them."[82] Doubtless the near- or quasi-sacramental status of the sermon in the thirteenth century helped to lend credibility to the empty threats of the *quaestuarii*, who are reported in 1256 and again in 1267 to have presumed to menace the faithful with excommunication if they failed to attend the alms-beggars' sermons.[83] The most extreme claims of all are those which give the sermon precedence over the Mass. Though one is more likely to think of fifteenth-century formulations of this,[84] we see the same sentiment expressed in the thirteenth century: "We read that Christ consecrated his body, in the Last Supper, only once; but he preached frequently. Now, however, on the contrary we celebrate Mass every day, but preach seldom. Are we wiser than Christ and the Apostles? In very truth, it would be better if we preached every day."[85] It is no great step from this to the conclusion of Geiler of Keisersburg, Angelus, St. Bernardino, and others in the fifteenth century, that if one must temporarily choose between the Mass and hearing a sermon, it is wise to choose the latter.[86]

The Church's new emphasis on and elevated regard for the ministry of preaching, and the subsequent quantum increase both in the frequency with which sermons were preached and in the number of trained preachers

---

[81] Ibid. 109-111.

[82] Humbert in his "Expositione super constitutiones fratrum praedicatorum," *Opera* 2: 32: "Item licet per sacramenta salus conferatur, tamen praedicatio quodammodo efficacior est ad hoc: ipsa enim movet corda et praeparat; sacramenta vero non conferunt salutem nisi praeparatis."

[83] Paulus, *Geschichte des Ablasses* 2: 273.

[84] Such as, for example, the statement of St. Bernardino of Siena (1380-1444): "If you can do only one of these two things, hear the Mass or hear a sermon, you should rather leave the Mass than the preaching." Quoted, with other similar texts, by G. G. Coulton, *Five Centuries of Religion*, Cambridge Studies in Medieval Life and Thought (Cambridge 1923) 1: 124-125.

[85] Odo of Cheriton, in his *Sermones in Epistolas* (1224), Lincoln Cathedral MS 11 fol. 21ᵛ: "De Christo legitur quod semel in cena corpus consecratur; set frequenter predicavit. Nunc autem, econtra, singulis diebus missa celebratur, set raro predicatur. Numquid Christo et apostolis sapienciores sumus? In veritate expediret quod singulis diebus predicaretur." Quoted from Friend, "Odo of Cheriton," 73.

[86] See E. J. D. Douglass, *Justification in Late Medieval Preaching*, Studies in Medieval and Reformation Thought 1 (Leiden 1966) 86-91.

engaged in preaching them—this state of affairs goes far toward explaining the rapid creation of preaching tools, including the *Manipulus florum*. It would be difficult to name any other genre of medieval literature that consumed the "raw materials" of literary composition so rapidly as did the sermon. The demand for ready access to various sermon materials was the earliest and the most constant motive force in the creation of tools.

The increasingly important role of the sermon in the Church's ministry may of itself sufficiently account for the increase in production of preachers' tools. However, something of the pace with which these tools were produced, and much of the pattern of the creation of new types of tools, were largely determined by the evolution of sermon form from the late twelfth through the thirteenth century. In practice, the emergence of new types of tools and of new forms of sermons is a circular phenomenon: thus, to take a specific example, Thomas of Ireland provided in the *Manipulus florum* a searchable body of *auctoritates*, because preachers had begun increasingly to employ such citations; but preachers were thereafter encouraged in this practice, because of the accessibility of *auctoritates* afforded by the *Manipulus florum*. A close examination of thirteenth-century sermon form will bear out this suggestion.

3

The Evolution of Sermon-Form
in the Thirteenth Century

In considering sermons and sermon form, we need first a definition of terms, or perhaps one should call it a statement of limitations. By *sermons*, obviously we mean only those sermons which survive in written form, whether committed to writing by the preacher or "reported" by one of his auditors. Moreover, we have of necessity relied heavily upon sermons which are available in print. The effect is to eliminate all those sermons, a vast majority of the total, which were never recorded in a permanent fashion. A quite disproportionate emphasis falls upon the sermons of university masters, because theirs are the sermons which were recorded and which have been printed. Two factors diminish the handicap of this built-in bias. First, among the sermons of university masters are many which were preached *ad populum*, and some of the masters have left us as well collections of model sermons *ad varios status*: thus we are by no means bereft of examples of popular sermons. Second, more importantly, it was after all these masters and their students who created and disseminated the preachers' tools, who set the style in sermon form, who in short were at the heart of the movement to train preachers. They are in the very strictest sense the predecessors of Thomas of Ireland. A final necessary distinction: we are not considering the thought nor, in broadest terms, the style of these sermons, but rather the mechanics of expression—the form is our focus. As the various *artes praedicandi* repeatedly insist, effective preaching requires three things of the preacher: an exemplary life, a grounding in theology, and a system for putting his knowledge to practical use. The exemplary life they were normally willing to leave up to divine grace. The knowledge of what to say came from the lectures in theology. The practical business of how to say what one wished to say was the generating force behind the production of tools. Therefore the "how" and not the "what" will be the thread which we shall follow through the sermons themselves. In specific terms, then, we are considering the changes of structure and technical devices in the type of sermon which one learned how to preach at the University of Paris before the fourteenth century.

The new type of sermon, the school sermon,[1] appears as a distinct form in the second half of the twelfth century, readily distinguishable from the older style of the homilary sermon. The best introduction to this new form is a tangible example. J. P. Bonnes[2] has provided one, printing in juxtaposition two sermons based on the same theme, the first composed by Geoffrey Babion, archbishop of Bordeaux (d. 1158) and the second by Peter Comestor (d. ca. 1179); they demonstrate strikingly the change in sermon form which is in process in the late twelfth century, and they go far to demonstrate the origin of the need for sermon aids when no such lack had previously been felt. The difference in treatment can be summarized as follows.

Both sermons are addressed *ad sacerdotes*, both adopt for theme Psalm 81:1, *Deus stetit in synagoga deorum, in medio autem deos diiudicat*. Geoffrey's sermon is homilary in style. He explains that God stands in *synagoga*—that is *congregatione*—*deorum*, that is, *sacerdotum*, and judges, both directly and through the agency of his vicars the priests, the good and the bad. From this base, Geoffrey proceeds to discuss priests as judges—condemning sins, calling sinners to repentance, assessing penance and granting absolution—and priests as those who are themselves judged, and who must therefore avoid certain failings which Geoffrey describes in turn. He concludes with an exhortation that the priests correct their own faults so that they may better be able to correct the faults of their flocks. Geoffrey's sermon is almost conversational in tone, its structure being no more obtrusive than one would find in the ordinary discourse of an intelligent and learned man attempting to give a clear, thoughtful answer to a friend's question. Geoffrey laces his sermon with quotations and echoes from scripture; but it is imperative that one distinguish his practice from the use of scriptural *auctoritates*. For him, the familiar language of the Bible is "a way of thinking and a way of expressing oneself."[3] He does not cite scripture as a buttress or authority, to justify his own conclusions and assertions, but rather in the most natural fashion uses scriptural language to express his thoughts.

[1] We adopt this ungainly phrase deliberately; "scholastic sermon" has fourteenth-century connotations which we wish to avoid, and "university sermon" refers to only one sort of the sermons we consider here, the official sermon of a particular day in the university calendar.

[2] J. P. Bonnes, "Un des plus grands prédicateurs du xiie siècle: Geoffroy du Louroux, dit Geoffroy Babion," *Revue bénédictine* 56 (1945-1946) 174-215.

[3] Jean Leclercq's phrase, describing monastic use of classical quotations, is equally applicable here; see his *The Love of Learning and the Desire for God*, tr. C. Misrahi (New York 1961) 183.

Peter Comestor's sermon, in contrast, is the product of the schoolroom,[4] of a master "reading" the Sacred Page, leading his students word by word. He announces his structure at the outset: in the theme, the psalmist shows "quis est iste qui stetit et ubi stetit et ad quid stetit." Who stands? God. He continues, "Sometimes by the name *God* is meant the power of God"; and Peter quotes a passage of scripture which verifies this fact: "at other times, the justice of God" and a second biblical *auctoritas* follows; "again, the wisdom of God" and a third quotation; "and at still other times, the mercy of God" and the inevitable fourth quotation. He then summarizes the four in one sentence, and concludes by noting that it is God's justice which is the particular aspect of divinity emphasized in the theme. Next comes a consideration of *stare*; following the pattern of alternating statement and *auctoritas* set by his treatment of *Deus*, Peter finds five different types of standing—a standing of permanence, of aid, of ministry, of expectation, of manifestation—and substantiates each in turn from scripture. Then he summarizes the progress thus far: "Ecce habemus quis stetit." There is no point in following the Comestor through *ubi stetit* and *ad quid stetit*, which proceed in similar fashion.

As Peter Comestor's sermon illustrates, a school sermon is one with a deliberately obvious structure, its parts being announced clearly as an aid to the congregation so that they may follow the logic of the preacher's exposition and so that they may retain more easily the salient points of the sermon; and the preacher's conclusions are proven by *auctoritates*. Whether addressed as an argument to an audience tainted with heresy or simply directed to the faithful assembled in cathedral or parish church, the school sermon never strays far from the function of teaching. Various *artes praedicandi* reiterate this fact through the years: "Preaching is ... instruction in faith and morals, for the purpose of informing men," says Alan of Lille at the end of the twelfth century;[5] "preaching is ... a devout exposition for the orthodox enlightenment of the understanding," notes John of Wales in the second half of the thirteenth century;[6] the preacher preaches "to the glory of God and the edification of his neighbor," adds Thomas Waleys, after 1337.[7] Provided that one does not press the point too far, one might say

---

[4] One might note, all the same, that Geoffroy Babion was also a schoolmaster, of the cathedral school at Angers; see Bonnes (n. 2 above) 190-191.

[5] "Praedicatio est ... morum et fidei instructio, ... informationi hominum deserviens..."; Alan of Lille, *De arte praedicatoria*, PL 210: 112.

[6] "Predicacio est ... devota expositio, ad intellectus catholicam illustracionem..."; John of Wales, in Paris, Bibl. Maz. MS 569, cited by Étienne Gilson, *Les idées et les lettres* (Paris 1932) 97 n. 1.

[7] Th.-M. Charland, *Artes Predicandi. Contribution à l'histoire de la rhétorique au Moyen*

that in general the monastic sermon relies upon persuading its listeners by touching their emotions through rhetorical devices, while the school sermon relies on the techniques of instruction—organization, signposts, documentation and example—to teach its listeners. Each is designed to convince, but by quite different means. Of the two, the method of the schools won out, and dominated sermon form until the appearance of evangelical preaching in the fourteenth century, such as that of Eckhardt, the English and German mystics, and the *Devotio moderna*.

While the instructional function of the school sermon remained stable, the structure grew through the years, becoming increasingly logical and increasingly complex. Discussions of school sermons have not adequately demonstrated this fact. Although they often give lip service to the notion of evolution of structure, in practice most considerations of school sermons describe the genre as if it were static, having suddenly sprung forth at the end of the twelfth century neatly tailored, in advance, to the precise size and shape described by the fourteenth-century *artes praedicandi* of Robert of Basevorn and Thomas Waleys. We can examine the growth of sermon structure in light of three sermon collections representing three points in time, from 1230 to the end of the thirteenth century; all of the sermons were preached at Paris. We shall supplement them with the consideration of a few individual preachers, particularly for the years prior to the earliest collection. As we proceed, we should especially notice when certain aspects of sermon structure first become common—the protheme, the formalized infrastructure; and secondly we should observe the chronology of the employment of certain special materials, technical devices used to flesh out the bare bones of structure—*distinctiones*, *auctoritates* both biblical and patristic, *exempla*—which may suggest the use of preaching tools. Naturally such matters vary widely, as an affair of personal preference, from one preacher to another; however, by relying upon the collected sermons of numerous preachers, one can achieve something of a chronological cross-section which, it is to be hoped, will prevent one's being misled by the idiosyncratic individual.

School sermons at the end of the twelfth century and the beginning of the thirteenth seem to be still quite fluid in structure, with much of the informal sequence from one idea to another, by word association, which remind one rather of the monastic homily. Our example from Peter Comestor certainly has an overall structure, which is announced at the start and adhered to strictly. However, this sermon was chosen as an example precisely because

Age, Publications de l'Institut d'études médiévales d'Ottawa 7 (Paris 1936) 330: "... ad Dei laudem et proximi aedificationem."

it presented a clear contrast; such rigidly-controlled structure was not the rule but the exception for its time. The sermons of Alan of Lille, almost a generation later, are still entirely lacking in that feeling of an imposed framework which one finds later in the thirteenth century. A sermon on the Trinity, for example, or upon the feast of Epiphany with its three gifts, evokes from Alan an extravaganza of triplicity, each successive threesome leading to the next simply by association of thought, concluding with a threefold admonition or exhortation to his hearers. However, there is no threefold division of the sermon as a whole; roughly a half-century later, such an overall division would have been the very first step a preacher would take in constructing a sermon on either of these topics. The sermons of Alan's near-contemporary Pope Innocent III present much the same sort of structure—a sequence of lists, rather than an overall division subdivided internally.[8]

The device employed in constructing these lists in sermons at the turn of the century is the *distinctio*. As we have seen in describing sermon tools, *distinctiones* are difficult to define precisely because the men who collected and employed them perpetually altered and enlarged the meaning of the word. As an omnibus definition, let us accept that a *distinctio* provides for a given scriptural term several figurative meanings, and for each meaning provides a passage of scripture illustrating the use of the term in the given sense. The preachers we have mentioned displayed a near single-minded enthusiasm for the *distinctio*; for preaching purposes, it was the biblical *auctoritas* multiplied to the extreme. Preachers were obviously taken by the versatility of this new-found method of exegesis as applied to preaching. One can see from the analysis of the beginning of Peter Comestor's sermon that his enthusiasm for *distinctiones* was second to none. Small wonder, then, that the earliest of the preaching tools discussed above are collections of distinctions. In the sermons of Alan of Lille, for example, we can see a direct connection with such collections. His *distinctio* on the word *lectulus*[9] seems to depend upon a *distinctio* from the collection of Peter of Poitiers,[10] although the interpretations are Alan's own. M.-Th. d'Alverny has noted numerous parallels between the distinctions in Alan's sermons and in Alan's own collection—see, for example, in just a single sermon, his distinctions on the words *magus*, *intellectus*, *ratio*, *mundus*, *Epiphania*, *Theophania*, *triclinium*, all to be found as well in his collected *distinc-*

---

[8] Innocent's sermons are printed in PL 217: 309-688.
[9] *Sermo ad sacerdotes in synodo*, in M.-Th. d'Alverny, *Alain de Lille: Textes inédits* (Paris 1965) 283-287, esp. 283-284.
[10] See P. S. Moore, *The Works of Peter of Poitiers* (Notre Dame, Indiana 1936) 79-81.

tiones.[11] Even the sermons of a preacher like the Cistercian Warner of Rochefort (fl. 1180-1225) rely occasionally on *distinctiones*. We know little of Warner's connection with the Paris schools, save that he seems at least to have studied Arts there.[12] While his sermons do not have the ease of style that one associates with the homily, they are so loosely organized that one hesitates to classify them as school sermons. Yet in his sermons, too, we find *distinctiones*, including echoes of ones contained in the collection of distinctions attributed to him. See, for example, his distinction on the word *jugum*, in sermon 40: "There is a yoke of nature, of which we read, 'A heavy yoke is upon the sons of Adam' (Ecclus. 40:1). And there is a yoke of discipline, thus: 'My yoke is easy' (Matt. 11:30); and before that, he said, 'Learn of me' (Matt. 11:29). And there is a yoke of guilt, thus: 'The yoke shall be destroyed because of the oil' (Isa. 10:27)—that is, sin will give way because of the presence of the Holy Spirit. And there is a yoke of punishment, as in Isaiah: 'The yoke of his burden' (Isa. 10:27). You have overcome the yoke of burden—that is, the captivity of eternal punishment."[13]

Absent from the late twelfth and early thirteenth-century sermons in any numbers are *exempla* and patristic *auctoritates*; even the use of biblical *auctoritates* per se, to authenticate conclusions and the like (as opposed to citations which "authorize" the parts of *distinctiones*) is modest compared with later practice. This generalization encompasses a considerable variation in practice, from one sermon to the next and from one man to another— the sermon of Peter Comestor's that we examined has, for example, not a single quotation from the Fathers; Innocent's sermons also tend to do without such support, while Alan's frequently include two or three. In this respect, it is curious to contrast Alan's practice with his precepts, as contained in his *Ars praedicandi*. There he advises the use of *exempla*, in an offhand way in the last paragraph of general advice preceding his model

---

[11] d'Alverny, *Alain de Lille* 241-245 and notes.

[12] N. M. Haring, "The Liberal Arts in the Sermons of Garnier of Rochefort," *Mediaeval Studies* 30 (1968) 47-77.

[13] PL 205: 827: "Est enim jugum naturae, de quo legitur: *Grave jugum super filios Adam.* Et est jugum disciplinae, unde: *Jugum meum suave est*; et praemisit, dicens: *Discite a me.* Et est jugum culpae, unde: *Computrescet jugum a facie olei,* id est, deficiet peccatum a facie praesentiae Spiritus Sancti. Et est jugum poenae, unde Isaias: *Jugum enim oneris ejus.* Jugum oneris, id est captivitatem aeternae poenae, devicisti." Cf. the distinction collection called *Angelus,* s.v. *jugum,* PL 112: 972. The attribution of this collection to Warner is far from certain; see A. Wilmart, "Les allégories sur l'écriture attribuées à Raban Maur," *Revue bénédictine* 32 (1920) 48-50. Warner evidently used other collections of distinctions in writing sermons, possibly those of Alan, Prepositinus and Peter of Poitiers; see Haring, "Garnier of Rochefort" 59 n. 75, 60 n. 88, 74 n. 24, etc.

sermons—not one of which seems to include an *exemplum*, nor (with one exception) añ indication of a place at which a preacher might provide one of his own.[14] His collected sermons are likewise devoid of *exempla*, as we have noted. His model sermons are all provided, at the beginning, with two, three or four biblical quotations and a like number of patristic citations pertinent to the subject or the audience, followed by remarks which say, in substance, "Using these as a base, one might go on to say...." Yet, as we have said, among the sermons which he actually preached one would rarely find so many patristic *auctoritates* in an entire sermon, given in extenso (rather than in the briefly sketched form of his models). Finally, his *ars praedicandi* contains, in addition to a general warning against use of flippant or vulgar language inappropriate to the pulpit, a specific injunction against the confection of rhymes and jingles: "Praedicatio enim in se non debet habere ... rhythmorum melodias et consonantias metrorum, quae potius fiunt ad aures demulcendas quam ad animum instruendum."[15] Yet, amusingly enough, he himself is an inveterate employer of such devices, both in his model sermons and in the sermons which he preached; to take but one example, he lists four sorts of *obedientia*, and tells his listeners, "Prima est meritoria, secunda introductoria, tertia quaestuosa, quarta perniciosa. Prima est efficiens, secunda faciens, tertia deficiens, quarta inficiens."[16] In this practice he is many years ahead of his time; we will find such rhymes coming into more than occasional use only in the second half of the thirteenth century, and by the fourteenth century their employment is virtually *de rigueur* in a preacher's statement of his division of the theme.

Helinand of Froidmont (d. after 1230), a Cistercian who spent time at the schools, leaves us sermons that show how the influence of school sermon structure begins to affect the homily of the cloister. Helinand's sermons are sometimes divided,[17] sometimes only haphazardly,[18] sometimes not at all.[19] He uses *distinctiones* (e.g., on the word *verbum*, in Sermon III),[20] but only rarely. He cites patristic authorities three or four times per

---

[14] PL 210: 114, "In fine [sermonis] vero debet uti exemplis ad probandum quod intendit, quia familiaris est doctrina exemplaris." The model sermons are printed, PL 210: 114-198. Welter notes the exception, at the end of a model sermon on the topic *De contemptu mundi*: "Praedicator concludat admonitionem suam in exemplari doctrina, ostendens quomodo antiqui patres contempserint mundum," PL 210: 116. See J.-Th. Welter, *L'exemplum* (Paris 1927) 66-68.
[15] PL 210: 112.
[16] PL 210: 145.
[17] E.g., serm. I, PL 212: 481-486.
[18] E.g., serm. III, PL 212: 498-511.
[19] E.g., serm. VIII, PL 212: 544-554.
[20] PL 212: 499.

sermon, but his classical and pseudo-classical quotations are perhaps more numerous. The striking aspect of his sermons is his effective use of *exempla*, both those drawn from Antiquity and ones taken from personal experience. In this he reflects neither monastic nor university practice of his time, but simply the fact that he was an inveterate storyteller. Through excerpts in Vincent of Beauvais' *Speculum historiale*, Helinand's *exempla* were given currency in Dominican and other school circles; so that, while Helinand's monastic sermons occasionally reflected the influence of the schools—some formal structure here, a *distinctio* there—they also fed back, in the opposite direction, a treasury of stories useful for preachers talking to a new audience. In the next century, they even provide occasional fodder for the English classicizing friars.[21]

The first large collection which we shall consider is the group of sermons contained in B.N. ms nouv. acq. lat. 338, representing sermons preached in various churches in Paris during the academic year 1230-1231. There is a total of eighty-four sermons in the collection, representing at least sixteen different preachers (twenty-three sermons are anonymous), including the bishop of Paris, the chancellor of the university, secular masters, and friars of both orders. Of these, M. M. Davy has printed forty-four sermons.[22] Davy's work, particularly her long introduction, has become the accepted characterization of the early thirteenth-century school sermon; it is, however, uneven and must be used with some caution. This is true, not only of the introduction but of her presentation of the sermons themselves. Davy has seen fit to outline the structure of each sermon, in the course of which she occasionally gives the impression of a more formal structure than actually existed, and occasionally misinformation, such as the labeling of prothemes in places where there are none. The major difficulty is that, despite pro forma mention of the preaching manuals of Alan of Lille and Guibert of Nogent, she has in practice based her description of sermon structure upon the *ars praedicandi* of Thomas Waleys, who wrote over a century after these sermons were preached. Davy is, on the contrary, very good indeed when she discards preconceptions of what one ought to find and instead describes directly from the sermons themselves "les procédés qui nous ont paru les plus typiques à retenir dans notre collection."[23] She

---

[21] Robert Holcot's anecdote about Caesar, which he attributes to John of Wales, is not found in John's works; cf. B. Smalley, *English Friars and Antiquity* (Oxford 1960) 151 n. 4. Instead, the story was told by Helinand, serm. ɪv, PL 212: 519.

[22] M. M. Davy, *Les sermons universitaires parisiens de 1230-1231*, Études de philosophie médiévale 15 (Paris 1931).

[23] Ibid. 41.

discusses, with examples, a variety of methods of organization employed by her preachers, including an etymological approach, a use of dialectic, the employment of the methods and terminology of the *disputatio* and the *quaestio*, and even "sermons impossibles à cataloguer, parce que dépourvus de tout système."[24] There is little we can add to that, from the point of view of structure. It is worth noting, though, that in contrast with the turn-of-the-century sermons, many of these sermons have an overall structure, being divided into a fixed and announced number of parts, each of which may be subdivided in turn. For example, one may contrast the linear structure of Alan of Lille's sermon on the feast of Epiphany, with the symmetrical structure of the sermon of Pierre of Bar-sur-Aube on the same feast.[25] Pierre divides his sermon into three parts—the gifts Christ brings to man, the gifts man owes in return, and the special gifts owed by the religious. Each part, inevitably, is subdivided into three, symbolized in each case by gold, frankincense and myrrh. Such neatly constructed sermons are much in the minority in 1230-1231, but with the advantage of hindsight one can see that the type of structure which will prevail as the accepted mode by the end of the century has made a strong beginning.

By good fortune, the sermons of this particular year are roughly contemporary with the origin of that curious item of sermon structure, the protheme. In examining these early prothemes, one must first of all ignore Davy's indications. Here in particular Davy permitted the *dicta* of Thomas Waleys to divert her attention from the reality of the manuscript; and with little or no justification, she seized upon the first scriptural *auctoritas* that occurred after the announcement of the theme and labeled it *protheme*.[26] Instead, we should apply for ourselves the definition of a protheme: a second text, usually scriptural, allied verbally or logically to the theme itself, and serving as an introduction to remarks upon the necessity of invoking divine aid, which invocation is the purpose and termination of the protheme structure; thereupon one reiterates the theme and begins the sermon proper. Of the forty-four sermons in Davy's edition, only eight have prothemes.[27] One occurs in a sermon preached by an anonymous Franciscan; one in a sermon of Odo of Chalons, a secular but preaching at the convent of Saint-Jacques; and the other six in sermons of Dominicans. These are slender statistics, but they point in a single direction. At this time, the protheme was just

[24] Ibid. 46.

[25] Ibid. 251-257.

[26] For instance, the example which she cites in the introduction to illustrate the use of the protheme is not, in fact, a protheme; ibid. 37.

[27] The sermons on pp. 257-265; 271-276; 277-281; 281-287; 288-293; 321-327; 332-338; and 401-407.

beginning to make its appearance; and it appeared first of all in Mendicant, almost entirely Dominican, sermons. This dovetails with the fact that the earliest discussion of the protheme known to us in any *ars praedicandi* appears in the treatise of the Dominican Master-General, Humbert of Romans.[28]

In the devices employed to expand ("dilatare") these sermons of 1230-1231, a major shift has occurred since the turn of the century. The overwhelming favorite, of virtually all of these school preachers, is the scriptural *auctoritas*. Overwhelming is scarcely too strong an expression: using Davy's count of the scriptural citations found in the forty-four printed sermons,[29] one arrives at an average of thirty per sermon. We are here at the verge of the practice common to a large share of fourteenth-century sermons, of supporting every statement however banal with one, two, three or even more proofs from scripture. One even finds occasional "chains" of scriptural authority, i.e., strings of quotations tied together with a minimum of non-scriptural knots—for example, this string of passages, from a sermon by Philip, prior of Saint-Jacques:[30] "Dicit ergo, *Exiit qui seminat seminare semen suum* [Luke 8:5], et propter hoc dicit Dominus in Apocalypsi [18:4] *Exite de illa* (id est Babylone, id est mundo) *populus meus*, scilicet vos, clerici, et ne sitis participes delictorum ejus. Ecclesiasticus [13:1]: *Qui tetigerit picem, inquinabitur ab ea.* Unde Isaias LII [:11]: *Recedite, recedite! exite inde, pollutum nolite tangere: exite de medio ejus, mundamini qui fertis vasa Domini.* Hoc proprie dicitur ad clericos, de quibus dicit Apostolus: *Templum Dei sanctum est, quod estis vos* [1 Cor. 3:17]. Oportet ergo mundari et lavari a peccatis. Unde Isaias [1:16]: *Lavamini, mundi estote, auferte malum cogitationum vestrarum ab oculis meis, quiescite agere perverse, discite benefacere.*"

Davy discusses together in her introduction the citation of scriptural *auctoritates* and the citation of patristic *auctoritates*.[31] When one gets right down to numbers,[32] however, one finds ninety-nine patristic quotations—this, in comparison with 1300 biblical extracts. Moreover, some forty of these are employed in the four sermons of Master Guiard of Laon; leaving only sixty patristic excerpts to be divided with very rough equality among the remaining forty sermons. The era of the patristic quotation is not yet arrived; and *exempla* also are still extremely rare.

---

[28] Humbert of Romans, *De eruditione praedicatorum* pt. 7.45, in his *Opera de vita regulari*, ed. J. J. Berthier (Torino 1956) 2: 481-483.

[29] Davy, *Sermons universitaires* 49.

[30] Ibid. 305.

[31] Ibid. 46-52.

[32] Ibid. 50.

The surprising element in the shift of technical devices since the turn of the century is the near disappearance of the *distinctio*. One finds the traditional *distinctio* only rarely, such as those on the words *cena* and *panis* in a sermon of Philip the Chancellor on Maundy Thursday.[33] That an element central to the sermons of thirty years before has been reduced to insignificant use is perplexing in itself, but all the more so when one considers that the compilation of ever larger collections of *distinctiones* for use in preaching continued uninterrupted to the end of the thirteenth century. The solution to the puzzle is that *distinctiones*, widely available in collections, had been diverted to serve one and probably two new purposes in the 1230-1231 sermons. First, the collected *distinctiones* were probably being mined as a source for scriptural *auctoritates*. In the passage just cited, for example, the prior wished to begin his chain from the first word in his theme, *Exiit*; he could look up the word *exire* in a collection of *distinctiones* and select from among the several meanings and examples given only one, which dealt with his topic, clerics. The use of collections of *distinctiones* in this fashion is conjectural, but probable. By 1230 one had as yet no alphabetically arranged, topical collections of biblical authorities, nor even a verbal scriptural concordance; the alphabetized collections of *distinctiones* appear to be the logical source for such quotations.

One can speak with certainty concerning another and quite important new use found for *distinctiones*, because examples abound in this collection of sermons: preachers used *distinctiones*, with their several figurative meanings for a given term, to construct the divisions, i.e., the several members, of their sermons' organization. In illustrating how this was done, one should at the same time contrast the practice with that of earlier sermons, in which *distinctiones* served in lieu of structure. Peter Comestor's sermon on the passage "Deus stetit" can once more serve our turn. He takes the first word of his text and distinguishes it: sometimes by the name "God" we mean A, sometimes B, C, and D; they are illustrated respectively by passages V, X, Y and Z. Then Peter moves to the next word of his text. A contrasting example from a sermon preached in 1230 by the Dominican John of Saint-Giles shows how a distinction could be used instead to build a structure.[34] His theme is from Job, "Numquid est numerus militum ejus, et super quem non surget lumen illius?" which he divides neatly at the conjunction to form a two-part sermon. The second half is wholly built upon a distinction of the word *lumen*: "Est autem lumen gratiae, lumen rationis et

[33] Ibid. 154-160.
[34] Ibid. 272-276.

item intentionis et item fidei.'' These are the topic-headings of the four members or subdivisions of the last half of his sermon. Each, as it is considered in turn, is provided with its illustrative scriptural passage, as in a traditional distinction; but this serves merely to get the preacher into his exposition of the topic—the light of grace, the light of reason, and so on. There are numerous other examples among the Paris sermons of 1230-1231 which show the versatility of the *distinctio* as basis for part or all of the structure of a sermon—old wine in new bottles.[35]

The second annual collection to be considered preserves sermons that were delivered forty years later, the cycle for 1272-1273. They differ in many respects from the sermons that we have just discussed. To gain some insight into the changes taking place in the intervening period, let us look at two individual figures, the Franciscan doctor Saint Bonaventure (d. 1274) and the fifth Master-General of the Dominican Order, Humbert of Romans (d. 1277); their works reflect the transition from sermon forms characteristic of the beginning of the century to those characteristic of the end. Saint Bonaventure's sermons, as printed in the Quaracchi edition of his collected works, survive in varying forms including the briefest of *reportationes* and outlines; for this study we have examined only sermons surviving at or near full length.[36] An interesting aspect of this collection is that it contains, and distinguishes whenever possible, both sermons preached to exclusively clerical audiences and popular sermons, so that one may compare the effect of the audience on sermon form. For our part, we found the differences to be less than expected. The structure of the *sermones ad cleros* is more formal than that of the popular sermons, naturally. The clerical sermons frequently, though by no means always, have prothemes of considerable length—perhaps one-third to one-quarter of a column of print, in a sermon that fills from four to eight columns. His favorite structure, always clearly announced and justified by *auctoritates*, is a division into three parts, each having three subdivisions,[37] although there are numerous variations in his practice.[38] His statement of divisions is nearly always in rhyme, in double or triple rhyme if possible: a sermon on the octave of

[35] E.g., sermon divisions based on *distinctiones* of the following words: *panis*, ibid. 155-156; *furnus*, 156-158; *Antipas* (not, in this instance, an etymological consideration, but a *distinctio* of symbolic meanings), 239-241; *aurum, thus, myrrha*, 251-257; *carbunculus*, 284-285; *propheta*, 285-286; *navis*, 311-314; *aurum*, 318-319; *vas*, 319-320; again *panis*, 358-360; *Israel*, 383-386.

[36] St. Bonaventure, *Opera omnia* (Quaracchi 1901) vol. 9.

[37] E.g., ibid., sermons beginning on 171, 179, 183.

[38] E.g., ibid., sermon beginning on 30 has 3 divisions; (1) has 2 subdivisions, with 6 and 4 sub-subdivisions respectively, (2) and (3) have 4 subdivisions each.

Epiphany has as its divisions, "dulcedo benignae allocutionis, amaritudo magnae tribulationis, sollicitudo discretae inquisitionis."[39] Exceptions to this rule are rare indeed. The subdivisions, and occasionally the main divisions, of Bonaventure's sermons are largely based upon *distinctiones*, certainly to a greater extent than was the case for the average sermon in the 1230-1231 collection. As was the average (not the extreme cases) among Davy's preachers, Saint Bonaventure employs scriptural *auctoritates* to substantiate his divisions or his conclusions, but without elaborate chains of quotations. Patristic *auctoritates* are rare, *exempla* much more so.

One immediately apparent difference in Saint Bonaventure's sermons to lay audiences is the absence of prothemes, which he evidently felt unnecessary for popular sermons. In general, also, his sermons to laity seem to have been briefer than those to clerks; however, this may be a false impression, resulting from a less detailed *reportatio* of such sermons and, especially, from the fact that a large number of his recorded sermons to laity were addressed to members of the court, whose attention span seems to have been very short indeed. Yet even in these sermonettes, for example one preached "coram rege et regina Franciae et familia tota, in capella," Saint Bonaventure employed his favorite three-times-three structure, with rhymed divisions.[40] A longer sermon, preached "apud Castrum Plebis coram populo, praesente provinciali totius Thusciae," reveals a less rigid structure.[41] Using the text on the loaves and fishes as his theme, Bonaventure gives no less than seven (i.e., five plus two) different symbolic explanations of the five loaves and their two accompanying fish. What we have here, thinly disguises, is an extended *distinctio*, serving as both structure and content. There are no *exempla*, and only one quotation, from Saint Bernard. If one had anticipated finding that a thirteenth-century preacher employed *distinctiones* for sermons to the learned and *exempla* for sermons to the masses, Saint Bonaventure's practice is a chastening warning against facile generalization.

The preachers' manual of Humbert of Romans gives in passing some incidental information on sermon structure at mid-century. In considering possible stumbling blocks that might trouble a preacher in his planning of a sermon, Humbert cautions against trying to say too much, "by means of multiplying the members of sermons, *distinctiones*, *auctoritates*, reasons, *exempla* and synonyms; by means of repeating the same ideas many times; by means of making prolix prothemes; by means of expounding the same

---

[39] Ibid. 171.
[40] Ibid. 292.
[41] Ibid. 234-235.

word many times—which are very bad practice in sermons."[42] Here we
have a detailed catalog of the elements which commonly went into the composition of a sermon; Humbert implies that those he mentions are sufficiently common that one must take care not to overindulge. However, it is
merely the excess which he cautions against—note the words, *multiplicantes*, *multoties*, *prolixa*, *multipliciter*. The preacher should see to it that
whatever he says be said "sub mensura mediocri." Humbert does not express disapproval of these devices per se. In fact, in the passage which
follows he warns against neglecting one device in favor of another. Some
preachers, he says, employ only *distinctiones*, others only *exempla*; it is
preferable to include some of each, since those in the congregation who are
not persuaded by the one may on the contrary respond to the other.

Bibliothèque Nationale MS lat. 16481 contains a collection of some 216
sermons preached at Paris in the academic year 1272-1273.[43] Its existence
has been noted,[44] but the manuscript has never been the subject of a study.
MS 16481 was among the books bequeathed to the Collège de Sorbonne by
Peter of Limoges in 1306; the volume contains marginal notes in his
hand,[45] and the collection may have been compiled at his instigation. At the
head of a sermon of Giles of Orleans, beginning on fol. 38, the rubric adds,
"Et fuit sermo peroptimus, in quo fuit Magister Petrus Lemovicensis, et
notavit ibi quod modum bonum habet frater, et quod plus facit sepe modus
quam res; et quomodo de auctoritate transcurrebat, capiens quod faciebat ad
suum propositum quando tota auctoritas non faciebat." Although it does
not say so expressly, this note seems to indicate that Peter was the *rapporteur* of this sermon, at least; we noticed no other *rapporteur*'s name given
in the collection, and certainly no other such lengthy assessment. Whether
or not this is sufficient basis for considering the collection to be of Peter's
making is debatable. It is evident, either that more than one *rapporteur* took
part in recording the sermons, or that the collection stems in part from

---

[42] *De erud. praed.* pt. 1.7, "De difficultate hujus officii," *Opera de vita regulari* 2: 395:
"Sunt alii qui student ad dicendum multa: multiplicantes modo membra sermonum, modo
distinctiones, modo auctoritates, modo rationes, modo exempla, modo verba idem signi-
ficantia, modo eadem multoties repetentes, modo prolixa prothemata facientes, modo idem
verbum multipliciter exponentes: quae valde vitiosa sunt in sermonibus."

[43] This figure is taken from the marginal numbering in the manuscript.

[44] P. Glorieux, "Pour jalonner l'histoire littéraire du XIIIᵉ siècle," *Aus der Geisteswelt
des Mittelalters* 1, Beiträge zur Geschichte der Philosophie und Theologie des Mittelalters
(Münster 1935) 497, 500; idem, "Sermons universitaires parisiens de 1267-1268," *Revue
de théologie ancienne et médiévale* 16 (1949) 41; and M. Mabille, "Pierre de Limoges,
copiste de manuscrits," *Scriptorium* 24 (1970) 47.

[45] The lengthy notes on ff. 188ᵛ-193, for example, are his; cf. Mabille, "Pierre de
Limoges."

copies provided by the preachers themselves; for the rubrics, which usually record not only the occasion but the time of the sermon (*in mane* or *post prandium*), not infrequently list two sermons delivered at different Paris churches at the same time. An instance occurs in the first two sermons in the collection: fol. 3ʳ, "Sermo fratris Droconis de Provins gardiani minorum ad Sanctum Anthonium. In festo apostolorum Symonis et Iude," and fol. 3ᵛ, "Sermo fratris Egidii de Aurelianis predicatorum ad Sanctum Paulum. Eodem die et hora." Although there are obvious failures—seemingly over half of the first sermon is encompassed in the concluding "etc."—the compiler of the manuscript made an effort to include as faithful a report of the preachers' words as possible. The scribe has frequently left blanks, the length of a word or two normally, to indicate a blank in the *reportatio*.[46] Some of the blanks have later been filled in, from some source—consultation with the preacher himself or with a second *rapporteur*.[47]

An element completely lacking from the sermons of 1230-1231 in MS nouv. acq. lat. 338 abounds in this collection from 1272-1273: namely, the frequent insertion of vernacular phrases. It seems to have been almost a convention for the preacher to reiterate his theme in French; it was the scriptural point of departure, introduced by the standard phrase "Et vult tamen dicere themum in Gallice: ...." Often the French itself is not recorded, but merely the indication[48]—sometimes reduced to a formula, "Et vult tamen etc."[49] The opening words after the announcement of the theme are often "Doce genz" or "Bone gens." Otherwise the vernacular seems to be intruded without pattern—in the invitation to prayer at the end of a protheme, "Saluons la gloriese vierge Marie: Ave Maria";[50] in translation of a Latin phrase, "de tercio adventu, de la terce venue";[51] and, on many, many occasions simply in the midst of the Latin discourse. The reason for this eludes us. If these sermons were copies of texts provided by the preachers themselves, one would conclude: written in Latin, spoken in French. However, the incomplete state of some of the texts, as well as the note implying that Peter of Limoges "reported" a particular sermon (one which contains several French phrases), indicates at least a partial dependence upon *rapporteurs*, who were surely not making a simultaneous trans-

---

[46] E.g., f. 6ʳᵇ (two instances), f. 7ᵛᵇ.
[47] E.g., f. 6ᵛᵃ.
[48] E.g., f. 22ʳᵇ, French included; ff. 9ᵛᵃ, 21ʳᵇ, French omitted.
[49] E.g., f. 20ʳᵇ.
[50] F. 31ᵛᵇ.
[51] F. 38ʳᵇ.

lation as they took notes. Whatever the explanation, the presence of French—particularly of French which reiterates Latin—in these sermons likely indicates the presence of laymen as an unknown proportion of the audience. Quite apart from considerations of the language, we may be sure that some of these sermons were not so-called "university sermons," i.e., the official sermon of each Sunday and feastday which the students, especially the students of theology, were expected to attend, because of the previously noted fact that the manuscript frequently includes two sermons for the same day and hour, or one sermon marked such-and-such day "in mane" and a second, "eadem die, statim post."

The structures of the sermons of 1272-1273 offer changes, but no surprises; for they reflect further developments along lines already discernible in 1230-1231. Prothemes, for example, we saw just coming into occasional use, in the earlier collection; Saint Bonaventure's sermons included prothemes frequently, but not invariably. In MS 16481 sermons without prothemes are quite the exception. We should, no doubt, be more precise and distinguish between full-fledged prothemes, which develop a secondary scriptural text into an invitation to prayer, and simple indications of an opening invocation. There are many of the latter, reduced in this collection to a terse note: between the announcement of the theme and its reiteration appear the words, "In principio—Ave Maria." There is obviously no knowing how long or how short, how complex or how simple, the introductory remarks hidden behind this formula. We may at any rate conjecture that they were not found sufficiently interesting to be worth recording. Usually the protheme is given at length, if length is the appropriate term; for, although they could extend to as much as thirty column-lines, prothemes often filled no more than five to ten lines in these sermons all told—scripture, development, and the ultimate "Ave Maria" or "Rogabimus etc." We find here none of the overblown, hyperstructured prothemes castigated by later critics.

With regard to the structure of the sermon proper, by 1272-1273 the practice of dividing the theme overall into parts or members had clearly carried the day. One announced these overall divisions at the beginning of the sermon, though frequently the statement of divisions was preceded by a brief introduction of the theme as a whole (as well as by protheme and prayer, of course). Both the rhyming of divisions, and the urge toward symmetrical structure (i.e., the feeling that three major divisions require three subdivisions apiece) characteristic of Saint Bonaventure's sermons are absent from the collection in general, though we do not exclude the occasional occurrence of either. In MS 16481, the employment of *distinctiones* to build one's substructure is standard procedure, and by the same token the vogue of reciting *distinctiones* per se seems definitely past.

As for other technical devices in these sermons, the citations of scriptural *auctoritates* seem scarcely more numerous on average than they had been forty years earlier; there is the same sort of range, however, with an occasional lengthy string of quotations. The continuity here serves to remind us that most preachers did not have access to a biblical concordance until the appearance of the version published by the university stationers in the 1280s. Patristic *auctoritates* continue to be as rare as they were in the 1230-1231 sermon cycle. We can furnish no statistics such as Davy provided for her edition, but such is our impression from leafing through the volume. As a sampling, in the contents of ten successive sermons on fols. 24-34ᵛ, we noted the following number of patristic citations, respectively: two apiece in the first two sermons, none in the next four, then two, one, none, one—suggesting that the average was quite low.

A noteworthy change, in comparison with the earlier cycle, is that the sermons of 1272-1273 contain many more *exempla*, drawn both from literary sources ("Legitur in vita beati Bernardi...") and from life ("Audivi loqui de quodam...").[52] It is particularly interesting to observe that, not only are *exempla* more plentiful than they had been forty years before, but they are frequently singled out in this manuscript by the scribe, sometimes with the use of a paragraph mark, or at others by the label *Exemplum*. Collections of *exempla* (non-alphabetical) had begun to appear in respectable numbers in the second half of the century, but one could never have too large a stock of good stories on hand: hence the marks intended to facilitate retrieval of these from the text of the sermons. We should not overstate the case; sermons with *exempla* are still in a definite minority. But *exempla* there are, and one never need look far to find them.

The final group of sermons which we shall consider are those contained in Bibliothèque Nationale ᴍs lat. 3557. Glorieux thought this to be a sermon cycle for the year 1301-1302;[53] however, the presence in the manuscript of a sermon from an earlier collection, and of sermons attributed to Gerard of Rheims (d. between 1282 and 1290), indicates that the order of this cycle is not strictly chronological.[54] Nonetheless, in light of the preachers included here who were known to be in Paris at or just after the

---

[52] F. 26 in both cases.

[53] Glorieux, "Pour jalonner" 497-499.

[54] See T. Kaeppeli, "Praedicator Monoculus: Sermons parisiens de la fin du xiiiᵉ siècle," *Archivum Fratrum Praedicatorum* 27 (1957) 151 n. 24; R. H. Rouse, "The Early Library of the Sorbonne," *Scriptorium* 21 (1967) 62 and n. 69.

turn of the century, and in light of the attempt to compile a series *de tempore* which fit an ecclesiastical year equivalent with the calendar of 1301-02, Glorieux is probably correct in the main; we may at least assume, lacking any contrary indications, that all of the ninety-nine sermons in MS 3557 are posterior to our 1272-73 collection, with the bulk of them dating from the later end of the period 1274-1302.

As with the sermons in MS lat. 16481 from 1272-73, we can say of the later sermons in MS 3557, that the structure is the same only more so. The use of prothemes is universal; some of them begin to be quite lengthy, such as that on f. 7ᵛ, which bears the rubric *Prothema* and fills three columns. More significant is the occasional appearance of structured prothemes: that is, one divides the protheme as one does the theme, announcing and justifying one's "members."[55] We may well regard this as a sinister development, which will soon burgeon out of all proportion and produce complexities woven simply for the delight in weaving; but in the context of our particular concerns here, we must observe that the development of structured prothemes can only have increased the need for preaching aids, to lighten the preacher's ever-growing burden.

The broad outlines of the structure of the sermon proper, in MS 3557, is almost universally of the sort described later by Thomas Waleys, after 1336—an announcement of divisions, complete with supportive justification for having so divided, the justifications being composed of scriptural or patristic *auctoritates*. The physical appearance of the text demonstrates how thoroughly the technique of dividing the theme was taken for granted. Each of the parts, "Firstly..., Secondly...," etc., is singled out on the page with alternating blue and red paragraph marks; and these same divisions are indicated in the margin with the appropriate roman numerals, apparently in the same hand which has noted in the upper margin the names of preachers and occasions, along with the judgments *bonus*, *valde bonus*, and the like.

Exempla are employed at least as frequently as in the sermons of 1272-1273, and possibly more so. These also (as was sometimes the case in the earlier manuscript) are frequently singled out in the text by the notation "Exemplum," and sometimes in the margin as well. Scriptural *auctoritates* definitely have increased in number, in comparison with those in the 1272-1273 collection. The one element which represents not a gentle progression but a real innovation is the use of patristic *auctoritates*. Quotations from the fathers and doctors of the Church appear in full force, for the first time in

---

[55] E.g., ff. 64ᵛ, 82, 109.

the chronological sequence developed here. This is, of course, less true for some sermons than for others; and we can provide no comprehensive statistics for the collection as a whole. Concrete examples will best serve to indicate the contrast with earlier practice. In a sermon beginning on fol. 18, the preacher cites the following as authorities: *Augustinus ii super illud Johannis, Hugo de Sancto Victore, Dionysius de divinis nominibus, Gregorius in omelia Penth., Gregorius, Augustinus ii^a omelia, Augustinus in libello suo de disciplina christiana, Augustinus de vera religione, Gregorius in omelia Penth., Augustinus, Anselmus de similitudinibus*; two citations from the *Gloss* should perhaps be counted in the list as well. Even in a brief sermon, one folio in length (fol. 107), one finds *Gregorius in moralia, Gregorius, Jeronimus, In libro de libero arbitrio, Augustinus, Seneca, Boecius de consolatione philosophie,* and *Quidam magnus* (sic). It is easy to see how the impulsion of sermons like these, at the end of the thirteenth century or the beginning of the fourteenth, underlies Thomas of Ireland's decision to produce a useful alphabetically-arranged collection of such *auctoritates* in 1306. These patristic *auctoritates,* numerous as they were, were interspersed with the much more numerous scriptural *auctoritates*; so that we have in many of these sermons true "chains of authorities." By the time when the majority of these sermons were composed, a verbal concordance to the scripture was available through the university stationers, a factor which obviously affected the use of biblical *catenae* in sermons.

We have made this collection of sermons, dating 1274-1302, the terminus of our chronological survey. It brings us to the years in which Thomas of Ireland was compiling the *Manipulus florum*; furthermore, there seem to be no surviving manuscripts of Parisian sermon cycles from any later years. But the decision suggested by expediency is justifiable logically as well. By the beginning of the fourteenth century the school sermon has reached the limits of its useful development as a vehicle for popular preaching. Certainly there are further developments, and new departures, in the styles of sermon preached to laity; however, despite the fact that some of these were even preached by masters at the university—Meister Eckhardt is a good example—they were divorced from the didactic structure that we have called the school sermon. The vital center of innovation in sermon structure was no longer the schoolroom. On the other hand, there are certainly further developments in the structure of the school sermon, some of which have already cropped up in individual sermons; but they involve the addition of complexity for its own sake, and are not easily adaptable to popular preaching. In the fourteenth century, the university would increasingly teach preachers to preach to preachers; whereas the thirteenth-century university was still involved in teaching preachers to preach to all the faithful. Let us examine this latter generalization, to see to what extent it is defensible.

Our survey of the thirteenth-century sermons has kept us close to the page, isolating, identifying and cataloging changes, sometimes small ones, in technique. This seemed the only way to ferret out a sufficient body of evidence. The overview this provides reveals, above all, that the type of sermon evolved at the University of Paris through the course of the thirteenth century was an admirable instrument for routine preaching to laymen. This should not surprise us, in light of the needs of the Church, repeatedly expressed from the beginning of the century; however, it is surprising, because we have schooled ourselves to expect the contrary, by accepting at face value those criticisms which denigrate and ridicule the surely ridiculous and hairsplitting extremes of the mid-fourteenth century scholastic sermon, but which then falsely imply that the extremes are equivalent to the mean of all which had gone before. The sermons we have examined are not pedantic, if one uses that term in the pejorative sense of an esoteric learned coterie busily talking to itself; but they are didactic, in the best sense of the word, and deliberately so. The purpose of the sermon was to instruct one's hearers in matters of faith and morals.[56] There is a reasonable case to be made for all of the elements we have discussed, as useful mnemonic and/or instructive devices.

1. First there is the division into numbered parts. If we go back to the very earliest of the sermons we have considered, Alan of Lille's, and the still earlier one of Peter Comestor, we find an element which may serve, along with the scriptural *auctoritas*, as the touchstone of school sermons as opposed to homilies: the school preachers number things—almost one might say, they number everything. Look, for example, at the first of Alan's sermons printed by Migne:[57] "Triplex autem osculum virgo petiit...," "Hic est triplex funiculus...," "unitas claustralis ... quae in tribus consistit...," "Duo sunt ubera Sponsi...," "Tria autem sunt genera unguentorum...," "Sunt enim speculorum tria genera...." All the way through the thirteenth century "preaching by numbers" continues, with the explanation of "first..., second..., and third..." based frequently on *distinctiones.*[58] It is unnecessary to insist upon the obvious mnemonic and instructional value of the use of

---

[56] Concerning the similarities and differences between preaching and teaching, see J. Leclercq, "Le magistère du prédicateur au xiiie siècle," *Archives d'histoire doctrinale et littéraire du Moyen Age* 15 (1946) 105-147, esp. 144ff.

[57] PL 210: 197-200.

[58] Contrast this with the way numbers are occasionally employed in homilies, as exemplified by the sermons of Bernard discussed by Leclercq, *Love of Learning* 210-211.

numbers in this fashion, still practiced in the teaching and preaching of our own age, and employed in our summary here.

2. The next step was the division of the whole sermon into a few broad parts—from two to five or more, but three was the most common.[59] This practice, employed only by some of the sermons in the 1230-1231 cycle, is the favorite structure by 1272-1273 and is universally adopted by the end of the century. Regarded as a rigid mold into which all sermons must be crammed, this is a stultifying development; but as a pattern or model proposed to young preachers in need of practical examples, it is hard to fault. Because the divisions are announced in advance and reiterated in turn, it is easier for the congregation both to understand the preacher's exposition and to retain it in memory.

3. The protheme develops from the need to prepare one's hearers so that they will be receptive to prayer, as an alternative to an unexplained, pro forma invocation which does not engage their spirits. When Humbert of Romans adds, to this basic purpose, that one can also use the protheme to introduce oneself to a strange parish and to mark time until latecomers arrive,[60] his is simply the voice of common sense injecting a welcome reminder of the realities to which the ideal must accommodate itself "in the field." The protheme has made only a timid beginning by 1230-1231, not surprisingly among the Dominicans, for whom the ministry of preaching to the laity was primary. By 1272-1273 there is indication that all the sermons employed a protheme, or at least some sort of introduction or preparation for the opening prayer. The appearance by the end of the century of occasional structured prothemes, containing the germ of what later developed into elaborate sermonettes, is one of the signs that the evolution of the school sermon as a model for preaching *ad populum* has reached the limits.

4. Finally, there were the technical devices, *distinctiones*, *auctoritates*, *exempla*, the nature and role of which altered as the century proceeded. At the end of the twelfth century, *distinctiones* formed part of the matter of sermons; by the end of the thirteenth, they are used to form part of the major structure of sermons. In 1230-1231, the style of distinguishing a

---

[59] J. G. Bougerol, *Introduction à l'étude de Saint Bonaventure*, Bibliothèque de théologie, Ser. 1.2 (Tournai 1961) 194-195, links this to the Trinity; but the "rule of three" surely has older and wider literary roots. Thomas Waleys advises division into either two or three parts, without indicating a preference. Robert of Basevorn opts categorically for three, observing that some say this three-fold division derives out of reverence for the Trinity, or from other reasons, but that he personally thinks it is simply that three parts are long enough without being too long. Cf. Charland, *Artes Praedicandi* 368-369, 254.

[60] Humbert of Romans, *Opera de vita regulari* 2: 481-482.

word in all its levels of scriptural meaning is passing, by 1272-1273 it is
passé. The use of distinctions to construct appears in inverse proportions,
just beginning in 1230-1231 and in wide use forty years later. These are
not the old-style distinctions, however, restricted to the four traditional
levels of scriptural meaning, literal, allegorical, moral and anagogical. As
we have seen above, the term *distinctio* had enlarged to incorporate a
myriad of figurative meanings for a scriptural term; and even though one
was normally offered a scriptural illustration, many of these meanings had
more to do with metaphor than with exegesis. These gave the preacher a
wide latitude in developing his sermon from the words of his theme. This
was an urgent need in particular for those days in the ecclesiastical year
whose sermon-topics were quite narrowly prescribed by custom. For example, we should hate to count (and even more, to have heard) all of the Advent sermons based upon the dictum that there are three advents—in the
flesh, in the spirit of individual Christians, in the Day of Judgment. And
each year as Epiphany approached a preacher must have racked his brain
for something novel to say about gold, frankincense and myrrh. In such a
case, the more *distinctiones* to choose from, the better; they were a boon to
preacher and congregation alike.

Exempla never appear in great numbers in the sermons we have
examined, probably because the audiences were largely clerical and hence
theoretically not in need of stories to make a point, to the extent that a lay
audience might be. Nonetheless we see a progression in their use, which
follows in pace if not in numbers the growing use and availability of *exempla* described by Welter.[61] Scriptural *auctoritates* are heavily cited in the
sermons of 1230-1231 and, with the appearance of the third verbal concordance (ca. 1286), threaten to get out of hand by the end of the century.
However, *auctoritates* from the Fathers and from other ecclesiastical
authors do not begin to be included frequently in the average sermon until
the end of the century. The use of *auctoritates* had many purposes in a sermon to laymen. They gave instruction in the scriptures and in the heritage
of Christian thought which a congregation of the unlearned or unlettered
would receive in no other way. They provided interesting variety in
language from the preacher's own words. And as their name implies they
lent impressive authority to his conclusions. The practice of quoting an important person who agrees with our own assertions is still a common
element in techniques of persuasion.

Such was the school sermon at the end of the thirteenth century: still

---

[61] Welter, *L'exemplum.*

reasonable in length, with an uncluttered and deliberately obvious structure designed so that a lay audience could easily understand and even, with luck, remember for a while the preacher's message—enlivened by the inclusion of stories and quotations, not yet submerged by them. With a few notable exceptions, we have not examined the moving expressions of great preachers, but a cross-section of routine sermons of the solid journeyman preachers. They best illustrate the kind of workaday sermon that the average university-trained preacher would emit. Moreover, they best represent the mentality which needed, produced and employed sermon aids or preaching tools. These are the preachers for whom Thomas of Ireland compiled the *Manipulus florum*.

* * *

A concrete example will serve better than any summary to draw together the three streams of development examined in the preceding chapters. The *Summa Guiotina*,[62] written at the very end of the century, embodies the various elements in Thomas of Ireland's thirteenth-century background: (1) It is, most certainly, a tool for preachers—though one whose structure defies categorization. (2) It amply demonstrates the fact that, by the end of the thirteenth century, it was taken for granted that a parish priest would preach on every Sunday, every feast day, and a number of special occasions; and the *Summa*'s purpose is to help him meet these constantly recurring deadlines. (3) It confirms, as well, the picture that has emerged here of the didactic structure of the sermon at the turn of the century.

The *Summa Guiotina* is a tool by means of which a preacher could compose a sermon for any Sunday, feast day, or special occasion in the liturgical year. Completed ca. 1290-1293 by the Paris-trained Dominican Guy of Évreux, the *Summa* comprises nine parts—six of them equipped with explanatory prologues. Parts 1 and 2 consist of 66 sermons for the Sundays of the year (66, not 52, because of some duplication and because of allowance for the movable feast of Easter) and 8 sermons on "divine persons" (the Virgin, angels, etc.). These sermons are fully developed; indeed they are, deliberately, longer than one could actually preach, so that the user could abridge to suit himself. The sermons contain: (a) a biblical text or theme;

---

[62] The *Summa Guiotina* is described by P. Michaud-Quantin, "Guy d'Evreux OP, technicien du sermonnaire médiéval," *Archivum Fratrum Praedicatorum* 20 (1950) 213-233; and analyzed by J. B. Schneyer, *Repertorium der lateinischen Sermones des Mittelalters*, Beiträge zur Geschichte der Philosophie und Theologie des Mittelalters, Texte und Untersuchungen 43 (Münster i.W. 1970) 2: 319-364. For a list of surviving manuscripts see Schneyer 364-365.

(b) the "division of the theme" in three parts; (c) a protheme; and (d) a distinction on one of the key words of the biblical text. There is no attempt to shape or slant the distinction to fit the given Sunday. Each distinction is divided into four parts, each part subdivided into two or three "members." Part 3 of the *Summa* is an alphabetical index to the seventy-four key words distinguished in the seventy-four sermons (66 + 8) in parts 1 and 2, referring to the folio on which each word appears. These three parts constitute the central core of the *Summa*, and some two-thirds of its length; the remaining parts enable one to put these to use, in a variety of ways, to construct an almost infinite number of sermons. Part 4 is a list of biblical texts, from three to five for each Sunday in the liturgical year (Advent to the last Sunday after Trinity). The texts are simply listed without comment, save an indication of the word in the text on which to build a sermon. Part 5 contains the same list of texts given in part 4, but here each text is "divided" or discussed in parts, to provide an introduction for a sermon. Parts 7 and 9 are the biblical texts for saints' days; they are analogous to parts 4 and 5, that is, a simple list of texts and a list of "divided" texts. For good measure, a few texts for *sermones ad status* (to monks, to beseech rain, etc.) are included at the end. Part 8 contains four special tables of texts, to be applied by category to any saint not in the preceding lists: a table for the feast of one single martyr, another for the feast of several martyrs, a third for confessors, a fourth for virgins. And part 6 is a brief section on sermons for the dedication of a church.

The key to the working of this tool lies in the fact that *all* of the words singled out for "distinction," in however many different biblical texts in parts 4 through 9, are to be found on the list of seventy-four words arranged alphabetically in part 3. One has, in effect, a standard structure, the school sermon, provided here with interchangeable parts. Suppose, for example, that a preacher wanted a sermon for the first Sunday of Advent. He might simply take from Part 1 Guy of Évreux's own sermon for that day, abriding it to proper length. But let us assume, rather, that he wished to "put together" a sermon. He would first choose, from part 4, one of the five biblical passages listed for the first Sunday in Advent—for example, "In die honeste ambulemus" (Romans 13:13), with the note, "Let the sermon be made on *ambulare*." He would next turn to the same text in part 5, for the "division of the theme" or introduction. This is extensive, roughly one column in length, but in summary it reads like this: those of noble birth have teachers to instruct them in behavior fitting their station. We are of noble descent, being the sons of God, and Saint Paul instructs us in proper behavior, saying, "In die honeste ambulemus," which contains three admonitions: (1) That we be plentiful in good works: therefore he says *ambu-*

lemus, i.e., let us advance or move forward in our career as Christians; (2) That we be wary in our service: therefore he says *In die*, since those who walk in the light of day do not stumble and we who walk in the light of grace will avoid stumbling into sin; and (3) That we be edifying in our conversation: therefore he says *honeste*, for just as light illuminates everything it touches, so man edifies all with honest conversation. He says, therefore, "In die honeste ambulemus." (And again there is the reminder, "Sermon on *ambulare*.") Therefore, he would look up *ambulare* in the index (part 3), and find there the number of the folio on which there begins a distinction on the word *ambulare* in one of Guy's fully developed sermons in part 1 (in this case, the sermon for the Seventh Sunday after Trinity). The *distinctio* fills some three-and-a-half to four pages of script; in outline, it begins like this: "Note that, just as four things impel a man to walk (*ambulare*) physically, so these four things in a spiritual sense impel a man to 'walk' spiritually. First, a call from some worthy person. How much more promptly do we respond to a call from the king than to one from a pauper! And who more honorable, who worthier than God? Therefore when He calls you, answer the summons promptly. As it is said in 1 Thess. 2, 'Ambuletis digne Deo qui nos vocavit.' Now, by 'Ambuletis digne Deo,' the Apostle means...." Here is the pattern: a reason that causes "ambulation," interpreted both literally and spiritually; the spiritual meaning is bolstered by a Bible text which is "divided." Then on to the second, third and fourth reasons—and with this, the sermon is done. The *Summa Guiotina* would have provided an appropriate theme, an introduction, and the body of the sermon.

The range of possible variations for a saint's day is still wider than that for Sundays. To compose a sermon for the Feast of Saint Andrew, for example, a preacher might choose from part 7 one of the biblical themes listed under Saint Andrew's name, take his introduction or "division of the theme" from part 9, look up the theme's key word in the index (part 3), and find the body of his sermon, the lengthy distinction of that word, in parts 1 or 2. Or, he might instead choose a theme from the anonymous lists in part 8, under the heading "one martyr," thereafter following the established procedure for his introduction and the body of his sermon. Or, he might very well substitute from part 7 a biblical theme applicable to virtually any other apostle-saint, because these, too, are interchangeable. This tool was the ultimate in flexibility.

Guy's system inevitably fostered the preaching of very bland sermons, since none of the biblical themes, none of the theme divisions, and none of the *distinctiones* could be the least bit specific or pertinent, because they were designed to fit any number of occasions and contexts. However, for preachers with little time or little skill and an endless series of sermons to preach, the ease of composition afforded by the *Summa Guiotina* made it quite popular. This fact is demonstrated by the number of surviving manuscripts of the *Summa*—over sixty, dispersed all across the Continent and in England. The work was disseminated by the university stationers at Paris at the beginning of the fourteenth century, in at least two different editions. Complex in conception yet eminently practical, the *Summa Guiotina* exemplifies the extraordinary inventiveness devoted to tools for preachers.

Part Two

Thomas of Ireland's *Manipulus florum*

4

Thomas of Ireland

The compiler of the *Manipulus florum* is known as Thomas Hibernicus or Thomas de Hibernia.[1] His identity even today is often obscured by contradictory information. He is variously called a Franciscan and a Dominican; he is said to have spent most of his life both at Paris and at Aquila; and the dates given for his death range from 1270 to 1415. In addition, he is frequently called Thomas Palmer, Palmerston or Palmeranus. The difficulty arises from a confusion of the author with two other medieval writers, the one also called Thomas Hibernicus, the other being a Thomas from Palmerstown in County Kildare. The conflation of these three Thomases was first noted and rectified some two and a half centuries ago; but the ghost stubbornly persists, making it advisable once again to distinguish our author's identity from those of his two namesakes.[2]

The earlier of the namesakes is the Thomas Hibernicus mentioned by Bartholomew of Pisa in his *De conformitate vitae beati Francisci*.[3] This Thomas was a Franciscan at the convent in Aquila, in Abruzzi, where he studied under Petrus de Hibernia. He is cited as an example of devotion to his vows, for when urged to become a priest he cut off his finger, deliberately rendering himself unwhole and thus unfit for the priesthood. He died ca. 1270. His conflation with the author of the *Manipulus florum* is first seen in the chronicle of the Franciscan Marianus of Florence, compiled in the second half of the fifteenth century.[4] Marianus includes the information about the Franciscan Thomas, which he has taken from Bartholomew. Elsewhere, however, he notes that the *Manipulus florum* was completed by "... Thomas de Hibernia, ordinis Minorum."[5] Those who read

[1] The best available discussion of Thomas' life and works is that of B. Hauréau in *Histoire littéraire de la France* 30 (1888) 398-408.

[2] The perpetuation of the confusion owes much to the first edition of the *Dictionary of National Biography*, where Thomas is described once under the name Palmer or Palmarius, and again under Thomas Hibernicus, in two articles by Mary Bateson, vols. 43 (London 1895) 160 and 56 (1898) 174-175.

[3] Bartholomew of Pisa, *Liber conformitatum* (Milan 1510) fols. LXXII, CXXIIII^v.

[4] Theophilus Domenichelli *et al.*, eds., "Compendium chronicarum fratrum minorum scriptum a patre Mariano de Florentia," *Archivum Franciscanum Historicum* 2 (1909) 458.

[5] Ibid. 463.

this naturally assumed—and probably rightly so—that Marianus was referring to the Thomas at Aquila. The merging of the two authors into one was completed and embellished by the early modern bio-bibliographers. James Ware, *De scriptoribus Hiberniae...* (1639) was the first to make this conflation. It was thereupon widely popularized in Lucius Wadding's *Scriptores ordinis minorum* (1650).[6]

The second namesake is the late-fourteenth-century Anglo-Irish Dominican, Thomas Palmer, who probably came from Palmerstown in County Kildare.[7] He was a friar at Winchester in 1371, prior provincial of his order in England in 1393-96, and prior of the London convent 1397-1407; the last known reference to him is in 1415. He is thought to have written the *Determinatio in materia schismatica*, formerly in the library of Westminster Abbey. Again, it was Ware in the *De scriptoribus Hibernicis* who first merged Thomas Palmer with the two continental Thomases and, again, Wadding who picked this up and gave it wide currency in the *Scriptores ordinis minorum*, from whence it was adopted by the early modern bibliographers. Although, as early as 1719, Quétif and Échard had painstakingly disentangled the three authors,[8] the three-part ghost frequently reappears; and, doubtless, our attempt at exorcism will be no more effective than our predecessors'.

When extricated from the embellishments of later centuries, the author of the *Manipulus florum* can be reasonably well identified. Thomas de Hibernia in all probability came from Ireland, as his name indicates. The insular features of his handwriting suggest that he received his initial formation in Ireland or England.[9] After receiving his basic education, Thomas went to Paris, where he was a fellow of the Sorbonne. He had become a fellow by 9 June 1295, on which date he witnessed a judgment concerning Sorbonne affairs.[10] The document also refers to him as a master (i.e., of arts), indicating that he must have been at least twenty years old, the usual age for a mastership in the Faculty of Arts. This would suggest that he was born no later than 1275, perhaps as early as 1265.

---

[6] James Ware, *De scriptoribus Hiberniae...* (1639) cites Waddings' *Annales* (1628) 2: AD 1269, 1270, for this information; but Wadding has not made the conflation. Wadding first joins the Thomases, presumably on the basis of Ware, in his *Scriptores ordinis minorum* (Rome 1650) 326-327.

[7] A. B. Emden, *A Biographical Register of the University of Oxford to A.D. 1500* (Oxford 1959) 3: 1421-1422.

[8] J. Quétif and J. Échard, *Scriptores ordinis praedicatorum* (Paris 1719) 1: 744-746. The matter was also properly dealt with by Hauréau, *Histoire littéraire* 30: 398-408.

[9] Concerning Thomas' hand, see below pp. 97-98.

[10] The Sorbonne cartulary is edited by P. Glorieux, *Aux origines de la Sorbonne* 2. *Le cartulaire*, Études de philosophie médiévale 54 (Paris 1965) 484-485 no. 393.

Apparently Thomas remained at the Sorbonne long enough to become a bachelor in theology, a minimum of seven years, but did not attain the rank of master of theology. This is implied by the fact that he is called "bac- calarius in theologia" in the explicit of the *De tribus punctis religionis christiane* in B.N. MS lat. 15966 f. 6, a manuscript written after Thomas' student days were over, if not after his death; the writer would not have given him the lesser title if he had right to the greater.[11]

It is probable that Thomas' years as a student and fellow of the Sorbonne ended before 1306, the date of the publication of the *Manipulus florum*. The earliest manuscrits of the work call him "... quondam socius." There is no clear indication of his career after his baccalaureate. However, such evidence as can be pieced together from various sources suggests that he was awarded a cure somewhere in Paris and that he remained closely associated with the Sorbonne. His three later works, especially the *De tribus punctis*, indicate a concern for and knowledge of the work of the parish priest, and the *Manipulus florum* itself is primarily a manual for sermon preparation. One might wonder if Thomas did not receive a benefice from Nicholas of Bar-le-Duc, bishop of Mâcon, for whom he made a copy of the *Manipulus*, now B.N. MS lat. 15985.[12] While his holding a benefice is mere conjecture, we can at least be certain that he was a secular and not a regular cleric. His fellowship in the Sorbonne, his authorship of a "rule for seculars," the *De tribus punctis*, and the absence of any mention of a religious order in the early manuscripts of his works leave no room for doubt on this point. That he remained in Paris is indicated by the fact that the earliest surviving manuscripts of his works are Parisian and by his con- tinuing connection with the Sorbonne. We know that Thomas compiled the *Manipulus florum* from Sorbonne books and that shortly after completing the work he presented the college with a copy, now B.N. MS lat. 15986. He also gave the college a manuscript, now B.N. MS lat. 16397 ff. 1-18, of his three small tracts soon after he had completed them in 1316. At some time in this period Thomas secured two small volumes of sermons from the Sor- bonne's *parva libraria* for Master Christian de Rubeo Monte, not a member of the house. Christian's pledge, a mid-thirteenth-century manuscript of Peter Lombard's *Sentences*, was apparently not redeemed. It became part of the *parva libraria*, and was entered in the catalog after the bequest of Peter Crespin and before the bequest of Bernard of Pailly (d. 1324)—hence, be-

[11] See Hauréau, *Histoire littéraire* 30: 400.
[12] Concerning Nicholas see P. Glorieux, *Aux origines de la Sorbonne* 1. *Robert de Sor- bon*, Études de philosophie médiévale 53 (Paris 1966) 165, 320, 322, 331; and vol. 2: 412. For the manuscript, see below, pp. 164-165.

tween 1310 and 1324.[13] Finally, at his death Thomas left the college his books and the substantial sum of sixteen pounds Parisian to cover his debts.[14] Such a life-long association with the college was common among the early Sorbonnists and was in part responsible for the continuity and vitality of the college, and, certainly, for the growth of its library.[15]

The date of Thomas' death is unknown. We can be certain that he died before 1338, because the books from his bequest are described in the 1338 catalog of the *parva libraria*. The last positive date in his life is 1316, the year in which he completed the *De tribus punctis*. In all probability, however, he died after 1329; Bruges MS 362, a glossed manuscript of the sixth book of the Decretals copied in that year, was evidently made for him—"scriptus magistro Thome de Ybernico, in civitate Parisiensi."[16] It cannot be proved that this is the same Thomas who wrote the *Manipulus florum*, but the identity of place and the plausibility of date add weight to the evidence of the name itself. In sum, we can say that Thomas died after 1316, probably after 1329, and before 1338.

At his death, as we have seen, he left the Sorbonne money and at least seven books. These included Thomas Aquinas on the second book of the *Sentences* (Cat. 1338, XXIII, 107; Delisle, 3: 29);[17] a collection of *quaestiones* of Thomas on the *Sentences*, followed by a tract *De predestinatione et paradiso* (Cat. 1338, XXIII, 108; Delisle, 3: 29); Thomas' *Summa theologiae*, book two part two, now B.N. MS lat. 15797, s. xiii ex. (Cat. 1338, XXIII, 105; Delisle, 3: 29); Peter of Tarentaise on the four books of the *Sentences* (Cat. 1338, XXIII, 106; Delisle, 3: 29); the quodlibets (1286-1291) of Giles of Rome, now B.N. MS lat. 15862, s. xiii ex. (Cat. 1338, XXIV, 107; Delisle, 3: 32); the letters of Peter of Blois in a

[13] See L. Delisle, *Le cabinet des manuscrits de la Bibliothèque nationale* (Paris 1874) 2: 176; Glorieux 1: 298, 331 (incorrectly treats Christian as a fellow of the Sorbonne); and R. H. Rouse, "The Early Library of the Sorbonne," *Scriptorium* 21 (1967) 243-244.

[14] The bequest is entered in the Sorbonne obituary, ed. Glorieux 1: 170: "Obiit magister Thomas Hybernicus quondam socius domus, qui compilavit manipulum florum et tres parvos tractatus, scilicet de tribus punctis religionis christiane, de tribus ordinibus angelice hierarchie et ecclesiastice, de tribus sensibus sacre scripture, quos et misit nobis et multos alios libros; legavit eciam xvi. lib. pro emendis redditibus. pictancia x. sol. par."

[15] See Rouse, "Early Library" 42-71, 227-251.

[16] A. de Poorter, *Catalogue des manuscrits de la Bibliothèque publique de la ville de Bruges: Catalogue général des manuscrits des bibliothèques de Belgique* (Gembloux 1934) 2: 399-400. The manuscript, written in Paris, bears *peciae* notes enclosed in pink boxes, as does the *Summa confessorum* of John of Fribourg in B.N. MS lat. 15924, written in 1318 in Paris "per Droconem Loquet clericum." See C. Samaran and R. Marichal, *Catalogue des manuscrits en écriture latine...* (Paris 1974) vol. 3 Texte 463, Planches XCI.

[17] The references indicate the description of each manuscript in the Sorbonne's library catalog of 1338, ed. Delisle, *Cabinet des manuscrits* vol. 3.

mid-thirteenth-century manuscript to which Thomas added a subject index, now B.N. MS lat. 16714 (Cat. 1338, XLII, 74; Delisle, 3: 46); and Alan of Lille's *De planctu naturae*, now Vatican MS Reg. lat. 1006, s. xiii (Cat. 1338, LII, 21; Delisle, 3: 62). Both this manuscript and the collection of letters of Peter of Blois may have been used and cited in the *Manipulus florum*. If Thomas left other books, as he may well have done, they remain hidden by the anonymity of the catalog of the Sorbonne's chained library.[18]

If we take this as Thomas' library and add to it the book of decretals in Bruges MS 362 and the works which he wrote, we find what we might expect among the books of a late thirteenth to early fourteenth-century Parisian theology student, namely the standard apparatus on the *Sentences*, the *Summa theologiae* of Saint Thomas, the public debates of a significant master, and a collection of decretals. More interesting, however, is the inclusion, along with the scholastic material, of the works of two twelfth-century writers, Peter of Blois (with an index) and Alan of Lille. One would hope for as much from the author of the *Manipulus florum*, who draws little from the scholastics in his works and much from the patristic, ancient and twelfth-century moralists. Of the four surviving manuscripts, two—15797, the *Summa*, and 15862, the quodlibets—were written during Thomas of Ireland's lifetime. 15797 bears decorated initials, tendrilled capitals and alternating red and blue paragraph marks; it is written in that black uneven hand often found in late thirteenth- or early fourteenth-century Parisian manuscripts. MS 15862, the quodlibets, is unevenly written in a drab brownish ink and is undecorated save for occasional red slashed capitals. Neither manuscript is annotated save for occasional marginal corrections. The manuscripts of Peter of Blois' letters, MS 16714, and Alanus in Vatican MS Reg. lat. 1006, Thomas must have acquired second hand, because they were written somewhere in north France in the mid-thirteenth century.

Manuscript 16714 (see plate 6) furnishes numerous examples of Thomas' notarial hand: ff. 2-3, subject index; and numerous marginal index notes in pencil, many of which are rewritten in ink, throughout the text. The only other known examples of Thomas' notarial script can be found in B.N. MS lat. 15982 (s. xiii; Sorbonne), *Flores paradysi*, f. 3ᵛ, marginal note lower left (see plate 5); and f. 179ʳ⁻ᵛ, list of authors and works quoted. Thomas'

[18] B.N. MS lat. 15470, a thirteenth-century Bible, is erroneously listed as belonging to Thomas by Delisle, 2: 176, because bound in it is the flyleaf of B.N. MS lat. 15797, Thomas Aquinas' *Summa* II, ii, which of course bears the *ex legato* note of Thomas of Ireland. It was an inadvertent slip, for Delisle elsewhere (3: 29 n. 1) noted the misplaced flyleaf himself.

hand reflects the following English features: a round abbreviation mark for *-er* attached to the line $\int$ or $\mathfrak{I}$; an *O* with the internal tail ϑ; the letter *r* which descends below the line—though not excessively; looped ascenders for the letters *b*, *h*, *l* and *v*; carrot-topped *l*'s occasionally; and two forms of the letter *a*, the small tear drop *a*, and the large double-looped $\mathfrak{a}$ extending far above the midline. It reflects the influence of notarial scribal practice in its uneven, horizontally looped, and slightly cursive appearance. Two specific features stand out and may serve to distinguish it from other hands of the same time and place: first, the lower loop of the minuscule *g* is oblong, is heavy on its upper edge, and extends two or three letters to the left; secondly, the round *r*, the *r* being made in two forms, bears a long tail made with a separate stroke which often reaches far to the left.

It is also possible that we have as well Thomas' formal or book hand in the two most authoritative manuscripts of the *Manipulus florum*, B and C (see plates 2 and 3). There is little doubt in our minds that B and C were written by the same hand. While there are slight individual variations in appearance, these are wholly natural for two manuscripts written at different times. A change in quill would explain them. The feature tying the two is the appearance of the abbreviation for *er* $\mathfrak{I}$, which appears, although rarely, in each manuscript. It is not coincidental, since the abbreviation is not common in French manuscripts of the period.

The possibility that Thomas was the writer arises from the colophon of C and the verses in the margins, f. 111ᵛ. These are written in a cursive rather than a book hand, distinguished by three features common to Thomas' cursive: *r*'s that drop below the line, flat looped *d*'s, and the looped abbreviation $\mathfrak{I}$. At first sight one might suppose that they were added by another writer, who logically could only be Thomas himself. However, closer inspection reveals that (1) the ink is the color of that in the text, (2) the colophon is rubricated in the same manner as the end of the text, and (3) as noted above, the same looped abbreviation $\mathfrak{I}$ appears in the text of both manuscripts. That is as far as it goes, however; we would venture that there is not a single looped *d* or descending *r* in the text of either manuscript. Nevertheless, it is not at all unlikely that Thomas could write a book hand as well as a cursive, and that the cursive would retain strong English features while the book hand (in which the differences between Oxford and Paris are much less pronounced) would conform to local practice. If Thomas himself were the writer, that fact could explain the very plain appearance of B and C which distinguishes them from all other manuscripts of the *Manipulus*. On the basis of present evidence, however, this must remain a supposition.

Thomas' achievements and his bequest to the college were sufficiently noteworthy to earn him a memorial day, 28 July, on the Sorbonne's calendar of obituaries. At the end of the fifteenth century (ca. 1481) when a new library was built, Thomas was among the thirty-eight illustrious members of the college commemorated in the stained glass windows.[19] His window apparently rested between that of Godfrey of Fontaines and that of Henry of Hassia.

So far as is known, Thomas' writings consist solely of the *Manipulus florum* and the three brief tracts enumerated in his obituary: "... compilavit Manipulum florum et tres parvos tractatus, scilicet De tribus punctis religionis christiane, De tribus ordinibus angelice hierarchie et ecclesiastice, De tribus sensibus sacre scripture...." The minor works were probably all three written within the span of a year or two, probably in the order in which the obituary names them. *De tribus punctis*, the only one which bears a date, was written in 1316. It unquestionably antedates the *De tribus ordinibus* (usually called *De tribus hierarchiis*), in which the *De tribus punctis* is heavily quoted and is twice cited by name. The *De tribus hierarchiis* and *De tribus sensibus* seem to have been written much at the same time, with little indication of which preceded the other. There is a brief passage at the end of *De tribus sensibus* which refers to the three hierarchies, but in such general terms that one cannot be certain whether the *De tribus hierarchiis* had already been completed, or was merely projected, at the time the passage was written. Since there is no cross-reference in the other direction, from the tract on hierarchies to the tract on scriptural meaning, we must accept the obituary notice as being as near to chronological order as one can, or needs to, come. The *terminus ad quem* for the two undated works is ca. 1321, because all of Thomas' works appear in the analytical catalog of the Sorbonne's *magna libraria*, compiled in or just after 1321.[20]

Among the manuscripts of the minor works two stand out with regard to the history of the text. Each is a collection of Thomas' works. The first, B.N. MS lat. 16397 ff. 1-18, was in all likelihood commissioned by Thomas for the College. The manuscript bears a long *ex libris* without an *ex legato* note, and each text begs the prayers of the reader for the author, in closing. The manuscript contains, ff. 1-9ᵛ; *De tribus punctis christiane religione*;

---

[19] A first-hand description of the windows in this building (torn down to make room for the present building in the seventeenth century) is given by Claude Héméré in his *Sorbonae origines, disciplina, viri illustres* (B.N. MS lat. 5493 f. 98), from which it is printed by Delisle, 2: 200-201; Hauréau, *Histoire littéraire* 30: 399-400; and A. Franklin, *La Sorbonne: ses origines, sa bibliothèque...* ed. 2 (Paris 1875) 98.

[20] Regarding the date of the analytical catalog see Rouse, "Early Library" 232-241.

f. 10^{r-v}, blank; ff. 11-17^v [*De tribus sensibus sacre scripture*]; f. 18^r, blank; f. 18^v, *ex libris.* According to the *ex libris* note, the manuscript also contained the *De tribus hierarchiis.* Each work was written on a separate quire with the quire containing the *De tribus hierarchiis* first. This quire was lost sometime after the volume was given to the library and chained, since it is described in the catalog of ca. 1321 as containing all three works. The manuscript is small, its written space measuring qu. 1: 125 × 172 mm, qu. 2: 135 × 197 mm. It now consists of two quires, the first made up of five leaves, the second of four. The inside leaf of the first, written in a contemporary but different hand, is a replacement. Otherwise, the two gatherings are written by one person, probably a scribe, writing a careful upright text hand. The flourishes and hair lines are well made and the corrections are few. The text is written in two columns of thirty-six lines (qu. 1) and forty lines (qu. 2). The two quires are undecorated, though space is left for a decorated capital at the beginning of each text. The pages are ruled in ink. There are few marginal annotations; those on ff. 11 and 15 may be in Thomas' hand. The parchment of the first quire is of noticeably inferior quality, with blemishes, holes and stitches. Both gatherings show signs of wear and were in a soft cover when they were given to the Sorbonne, since the librarian treated them as a separate unit, entering the *ex libris,* shelf mark and value on the last leaf, f. 18^v: "Iste liber est pauperum magistrorum de Sorbona Parisius. In quo continentur tres tractatus quos compilavit magister Thomas Hybernicus, compilator Manipuli florum, quondam socius huius domus. Primus tractatus est de tribus ierarchiis tam angelicis quam ecclesiasticis. Secundus tractatus est de tribus punctis religionis christiane qui valde utilis est sacerdoti curato. Tertius est de tribus expositionibus sacre scripture ubi et plurima bona invenies. Precium xv solidarum Parisius. Inter summas morales lxxxiii. [Different hand:] Cathenatus." (1321 cat. S.c., not listed in shelf list *scamnum* S; 1338 cat., XLII, 83; Delisle, 3: 46, 108.) At some time after 1338 the works were bound in their present binding with a manuscript given by Gerard of Abbeville, now ff. 19-58, and with another given by Peter of Limoges, now ff. 59-194.

The second manuscript is the collection of the three works in B.N. ᴍꜱ 15966 ff. 1-14. This manuscript was assembled and left to the Sorbonne by a younger contemporary of Thomas, Gerard of Utrecht, and has a table of contents, f. ii^v, in Gerard's hand.[21] It contains (I) ff. 1-6, *Liber de regulis omnium christianorum seu christianitatis sive de tribus punctis*

---

[21] Gerard, who died between 1326 and 1338, left seventeen manuscripts to the Sorbonne; many contain notes in his hand. See M. Mabille, "Les manuscrits de Gérard d'Utrecht," *Bibliothèque de l'École des chartes* 129 (1971) 5-25; cf. plate IV.

christiane religionis; ff. 6-10 [*De tribus sensibus sacre scripture*, called *Commendatio theologie* in the table]; ff. 10-14 [*De tribus ierarchiis*]; ff. 14ᵛ-15ᵛ, blank; (II) ff. 1-118ᵛ, Bernard Gui, *Sermones dominicales*; ff. 119-121ᵛ, table; ff. 121A-216ᵛ, Bernard Gui, *Sermones in adventu*, beginning with a table, ff. 121A-121Bᵛ; ff. 217-234, James of Lausanne, *Moralitates super Mattheum*; f. 234ᵛ, blank; (III) ff. 1-2, table and notes; (IV) ff. 1-43, collection of extracts from a *De regimine principum*, beg. "Omnes principatus ait philosophus non esse equaliter... (text): Generalis procedendi modus in regimine principis et..." (*Larcastus de regimine principum quem compilavit quidam studens in domo de Sorbona*, in the table f. iiᵛ);²² f. 43ᵛ, notes; ff. 44-47, a table to the *De regimine principum*; f. 47ᵛ, notes.

The four parts are written by one hand. Two texts are dated; the text of Bernard's *Sermones dominicales* was finished 20 July 1319 (f. 118), and the *Sermones in adventu* were completed 21 October 1319 (f. 216ᵛ). The text of Thomas' three works was probably written in the same year. The manuscript is large, the written space measuring 183 × 257 mm. Thomas' works are written on quires 1¹⁰⁺¹, 2², 3², in two columns of fifty-four lines to the column. The quires are ruled in lead point, bear catchwords and contemporary foliation. The initial letters are decorated, the capitals bear tendrils, and the paragraph marks alternate in blue and red. There are copious marginalia in several hands, prominent among them that of the donor. The manuscript is in medieval boards covered by calf, with chain marks front top center, back bottom center. With respect to the works of Thomas Hibernicus both manuscripts, B.N. mss lat. 16397 and 15966, are very early, and both are close to the original. Short of a careful collation, one can only say that ms 16397 should, by all rights, contain the more authoritative text; but we are dependent upon 15966 to supply the *De tribus ierarchiis*, missing from 16397. Our discussion of the minor works is hence based upon these two manuscripts.

The most popular of the three treatises was the *De tribus punctis religionis christiane* (also *De regulis omnium christianorum*, *Expositio articulorum fidei christiane*, *Regula christiane religionis*, etc.), beg. "Religio munda et immaculata apud Deum... (James 1:27). Volens religionem aliquam intrare...," ends "... Ideo huius collectionis auctor volens quasi inter Sillam et Caribdim navigare, opusculum non nimis obscurum nec nimis

---

²² See Hauréau, *Histoire littéraire* 596-597. The collection was composed by a G. Larcastus who was a *socius* of the Sorbonne in the early years of the thirteenth century. The collection also exists in B.N. ms lat. 15107 ff. i-129ᵛ (s. xv; Saint-Victor MM14).

prolixum compilare decrevit." In the prologue, Thomas describes the work as a summary of the obligations of a Christian, phrased in terms of a "rule" for seculars. He takes the opportunity to present an artful distinction between regulars and Christians. Using the word *religio* ambiguously to mean both "an order" and "a religion," he says, "Every *religio* has its patron or founder—as the *religio* of the monks has the blessed Benedict, the *religio* of the Preaching Friars has the blessed Dominic, the Friars Minor the blessed Francis, and so on. Now the Christian *religio* has as its founder, Christ..."[23]—an invidious comparison, with the implication that the *religio* of Christ and the *religio* of any other founder are mutually exclusive. The three points of the faith, each discussed with examples and commentary, are these: (1) a firm belief in the articles of faith, which are expressed most succinctly in the Apostles' Creed; (2) a strict adherence to the Ten Commandments; and (3) a careful avoidance of the seven mortal sins. The work concludes with an epilogue on the powers and duties of the priesthood, at different levels of the hierarchy, in matters of absolution of sins. This leads, in turn, to a lengthy aside on the hierarchical nature of the Church, in which Thomas reveals himself to be a convinced ultramontane; the pope encompasses in himself, says Thomas, all the powers of the lesser members of the ecclesiastical hierarchy—archbishops, bishops, parish priests. In short, "... sic voluit Deus et decuit, ut in tota ecclesiastica ierarchia esset unus principans, infundens omnibus inferioribus virtutem et potestatem."[24] While heavily scriptural in content, the tract also cites Augustine, Jerome, Hilary, Haymo, Dionysius, Maimonides, Pliny the Elder and Aristotle. The *De tribus punctis* survives in over 120 manuscripts,[25] and was first printed ca. 1476 by Conrad Fyner in Esslingen (Hain 13854).[26]

This rather ordinary little tract achieved a considerable local circulation in Eastern Europe after 1349 when it was incorporated into the first provincial statutes for the newly-created archdiocese of Prague.[27] In 1344,

---

[23] "Quelibet autem religio habet suum patronum sive fundatorem. Sicut religio monachorum habet beatum Benedictum, religio fratrum predicatorum habet beatum Dominicum, fratrum minorum beatum Franciscum et sic de aliis. Religio autem Christiana habet fundatorem Christum, unde Christianus sive Christianitas a Christo dicitur." In the passage preceding this, Thomas has said, "Quelibet religio est bona. Sed religio Christiana est optima...." Cited from B.N. MS lat. 16397 f. 1.

[24] B.N. MS lat. 16397 f. 8ᵛ.

[25] See below, Appendix 5.

[26] It appears on the basis of his surviving books that Fyner printed between 1472 and 1477. See *Catalogue of Books Printed in the XV. Century now in the British Museum* pt. 2 (London 1912) 515-516, IB. 8989. A second incunable edition was printed in 1496 by Stephan Arnd at Lubeck (Hain 8544).

[27] The statutes and the *De tribus punctis* were published by B. Dudik, *Statuten des ersten*

Emperor Charles IV secured from his friend and former teacher Pope Clement VI the elevation of Prague (formerly in the archdiocese of Mainz) to an archbishopric.[28] The first metropolitan was Arnost von Pardubitz (Ernest of Pardubice), the recently elected bishop of Prague. In his first provincial synod, November 1349, he embarked on a vigorous program of reform centering on a rejuvenation of the priesthood. Arnost promulgated the statutes, or "constitutions" as he called them, for the archdiocese, to serve as a guide for his clerics. Furthermore, to insure that his clergy understood the spirit as well as the letter of the statutes, he appended to them Thomas Hibernicus' *De tribus punctis religionis christiane.* Each cathedral and collegiate church in the archdiocese was to possess two copies of the statutes and the *De tribus punctis*, one copy to be kept in the sacristy and one to be chained to a reading desk in an accessible spot; and every parish priest in the archdiocese was to have a copy as well.[29]

That Arnost should pick this obscure tract is not so unusual as it might appear. He was himself the product of fourteen years' university training in Bologna and Padua; the roads between the Sorbonne and Bologna, Padua, and Prague were well traveled. If he had not encountered Thomas' work in Italy, Arnost very likely could have found it in Prague itself. Considering also the affection of his emperor for the University of Paris, and the association of his spiritual lord, Clement VI, with the Sorbonne (he had been provisor of the college, 1326-1338), it is not surprising to see Arnost choose Thomas Hibernicus' tract to prescribe the Christian life for the clerics of the archdiocese of Prague.[30] Arnost's choice doubtless enhanced the circulation of Thomas' works in Bohemia where, as a result, this Parisian scholar's books are at least as numerous as in Paris. Over forty manuscripts of the *De tribus punctis*, with or without the provincial statutes, are found in the archdiocese today, as well as seventeen manuscripts of the *Manipulus florum* (the largest concentration outside of Paris), and the only

---

Prager Provincial-Concils vom 11. und 12. November 1349 (Brünn 1872). *De tribus punctis* was first published with the statutes by A. Fasseau, *Collectio synodorum et statutorum almae dioecesis Olomucenae* pt. 2 (Retz 1766) 30-45.

[28] Concerning Charles IV, Arnost and the establishment of the archdiocese see S. H. Thomson, "Learning at the Court of Charles IV," *Speculum* 25 (1950) 1-20.

[29] Dudik, *Statuten* 11.

[30] Peter Roger, Pope Clement VI, studied in Paris while at Chaise-Dieu. It is possible that he may have known Thomas, and he clearly knew of him. He copied, for example, the list of authors and works appended to the *Manipulus florum* into one of his notebooks, ca. 1315 (see p. 217 below); and he began his provisorship of the Sorbonne probably before Thomas' death.

surviving copy of Thomas' *De tribus sensibus sacre scripture* outside of the Sorbonne's manuscripts.

The second work, called in the obituary *De tribus ordinibus hierarchie angelice et ecclesiastice* is more commonly known as the *De tribus hierarchiis*, beg. "Nunquid nosti ordinem celi et pones rationes eius in terra. Job xxxviii. Secundum beatum Dyonisium, ecclesiastica ierarchia ordinata est ad instar...," ending "... Nam illi de ecclesiastica ierarchia solum illa peccata committunt, et ipsi soli ab illis sacramentaliter absolvere possunt."[31] It is an expansion and an elaboration of the discussion of hierarchies included at the end of the *De tribus punctis*. The first two hierarchies, the supercelestial which is the Trinity and the celestial which is the angelical hierarchy, are dealt with rather briefly (in MS 15966, roughly two columns each); the bulk of the tract (fourteen and a half columns in 15966) is devoted to the subcelestial hierarchy, the Church Militant. The three, supercelestial, celestial, subcelestial, are ranged from highest to lowest; each is divided internally into three, likewise ranged in rank; for the celestial and subcelestial hierarchies, the three internal divisions are each themselves further divided into three. Thomas' purpose is to demonstrate that monarchical organization is the natural order of things in all three hierarchies, and that in the third hierarchy this order is epitomized in the ecclesiastical monarchy with the pope at its head. The tract concludes with a paragraph explaining the correspondence between the three hierarchies and the three points of the Christian religion described in the *De tribus punctis*. Thomas in this tract supports his argument with citations from a much wider range of authorities than he uses for the other two tracts, including the bestiary *Leo fortissimus bestiarum* which he places with Hugh of Saint-Victor's writings in the bibliography at the end of the *Manipulus florum*.[32] Neither the ideas nor the execution of *De tribus hierarchiis* is particularly original, nor is the tract of much interest in the history of Dionysian thought.[33] This in part explains why the *De tribus hierarchiis* survives in only eight manuscripts. The work has not been printed.[34]

The third tract, the *De tribus sensibus sacre scripture* (also called *De tribus expositionibus sacre scripture*, or *Commendatio theologie*), beg. "Sapientia edificavit sibi domum et excidit in ea columpnas septem. Proverbia ix. Sicut dicit beatus Augustinus libro primo super Genesim ad litteram

---

[31] B.N. MS lat. 15966 ff. 10-14.

[32] See below, Appendix 6, no. XIV: 38.

[33] G. Théry, "Catalogue des manuscrits dionysiens des bibliothèques d'Autriche," *Archives d'histoire doctrinale et littéraire du Moyen Age* 10 (1936) 205-209.

[34] The edition announced by Théry was not forthcoming.

c. 1: In omnibus sanctis libris...," ending "... Nam illi de ecclesiastica ierarchia solum indigent morali instructione," is an explanation of the four senses of the Scripture, literal, moral, allegorical and anagogic. Thomas explains briefly what the four senses are, placing the literal sense in contradistinction with what he calls the mystical senses: the literal sense tells what
things the words describe, the other three tell what these things signify, in
terms either of human behavior (the moral sense), or of the Church
Militant (the allegorical sense), or of the Church Triumphant (the anagogic
sense). The four reveal, respectively, what has been done, what one should
do, what one should believe, and what one may expect. The major portion
of the tract is given to an illustration of the four in practice, by means of in-
terpreting the text from Proverbs with which the tract begins. The literal
sense is quickly disposed of: Solomon, in his wisdom, built the Temple; it
had, to be sure, a multitude of columns, but they were constructed of seven
different materials (gold, cedar, silver, etc.). Most of his interpretation,
naturally, is devoted to the other three senses. For the "mystical" senses,
Sapientia is explained as the wisdom of God the Father, while the remainder of the passage is subject to numerous interpretations according to each
of the senses. Morally, for example, the *domus* is the cloister with its
columns being the seven observances; or, what better house for God's
wisdom than the University of Paris, with trivium and quadrivium as the
seven pillars, Law and Medicine as the two principal walls, and Theology,
of course, crowning the edifice. Allegorically, for example, the *domus* may
refer to the Church Militant, with its seven sacraments. Anagogically,
wisdom's house may refer, for example, to Christ's statement about His
Father's house with many mansions, whose pillars may be the seven orders
of spirits—angels, patriarchs, prophets, apostles, martyrs, confessors and
virgins. The tract concludes, abruptly and unexpectedly, with the explanation that the anagogic sense of the scriptures corresponds to the supercelestial hierarchy, the allegorical sense to the celestial hierarchy, the moral
sense to the subcelestial hierarchy. It must have been partly the result of
Thomas' emphasis on the three "mystical" senses, and partly the result of
the influence of the titles of the earlier tracts, that this work has always
been known as *De tribus* and not *De quattuor sensibus*. Like *De tribus punctis*, this tract relies heavily on biblical quotations; but the list of authors
cited is a bit more extensive, including Augustine, Damascenus, Isidore,
Prosper, Hugh of Saint-Victor, Chrysostom, Bernard, Dionysius, Bede,
Jerome, Basil, Strabo, Avicenna, Ptolemy, Alfraganus, and Maimonides.
The *De tribus sensibus sacre scripture* evidently had a very limited circulation, since, of the three extant copies, one is in the manuscript which
Thomas himself gave to the Sorbonne, and the second, likewise a Sorbonne

manuscript, is probably a copy of the first; in both instances, it is accompanied by Thomas' other two tracts. The third copy of this work is in a fifteenth-century Prague manuscript, where it appears without the other tracts; and two others are referred to, at Marienborn or Mariendaal near Arnhem (CRSA) and at Vallis Sancti Martini in Louvain (CRSA), in the sixteenth-century location list of books compiled at Rookloster.[35] This suggests that the *De tribus sensibus* may have circulated more widely than the number of surviving manuscripts would indicate. It has not been printed.

As we observed, the notice in the Sorbonne obituary constitutes, to the best of our knowledge, the complete and authentic list of Thomas' writings. The minor works we have discussed briefly here, and the one major work will be the concern of the remaining chapters of this book. However, in the intervening centuries the original list has, figuratively speaking, been subjected to numerous "Addenda et corrigenda," to the point that Thomas' authorship of the *Manipulus florum* has frequently been denied while, as if in recompense, a number of spurious works have been attributed to him. Before we begin a discussion of the *Manipulus florum* and its world, we must clear away this bibliographic tangle in order to justify, first, a discussion of the *Manipulus* under Thomas' name and, second, the exclusion of other works from consideration.

There is a strong tradition to the effect that the Franciscan doctor John of Wales began the *Manipulus florum*, leaving it unfinished at his death, and that Thomas Hibernicus merely completed the work.[36] This attribution can be traced back directly to the colophon of the text in one family, designated β, of the manuscripts of the *Manipulus florum*.[37] This colophon begins with a standard formula, "Explicit Manipulus florum compilatus a magistro Thoma de Hybernia quondam socio de Serbona...." This is comparable to the colophon in the manuscript which Thomas gave to the Sorbonne: "Explicit Manipulus florum collectus a magistro Thoma de Ybernia," and to the colophon common to the university stationers' text: "Hoc opus est compilatum a magistro Thoma de Ybernia quondam socio de Sorbona. Explicit Manipulus florum." However, the β colophon contains a further passage: "... et incepit frater Johannes Galensis ordinis fratrum

---

[35] Unfortunately the union catalogue of Rookloster is still unedited; it is cited from Vienna, Österreich. Nationalbibl. MS ser. nov. 12694 f. 351ᵛ. We are grateful to Prof. Albert Gruijs of the University of Nimegue for this reference.

[36] This tradition has most recently been accepted and used by R. A. Pratt, "Jankyn's Book of Wikked Wyves," *Annuale mediaevale* 3 (1962) 5-27, esp. 16-20.

[37] See below, Ch. 6, History of the Text.

minorum doctor in theologia istam tabulam et magister Thomas finivit."
From a strictly textual standpoint, the attribution to John of Wales appears
to be a later addition to the colophon; however, the earliest surviving example of this colophon, that in Université MS 215, can be dated 1315 or
before, that is, nine years at most after the *Manipulus florum* was written,
and during the lifetime of Thomas Hibernicus.

It is difficult to explain the addition of this note, at such an early stage in
the history of the text. On the surface, the simplest explanation would be to
say that its claim is true—that the note was added to the colophon because
it was common knowledge at Paris that it was John of Wales who conceived
the idea and began the work on the *Manipulus florum*. However, scarcely
beneath the surface, one finds considerable evidence both internal and external which indicates that the *Manipulus florum* was written wholly by
Thomas.

First, the earliest manuscripts and records point to Thomas and not to
John. B.N. MSS lat. 15985 and 15986 (both ca. 1306) are not merely
earlier, but preserve a text superior to β. The attribution to Thomas alone
is preserved in his presentation copy to the Sorbonne; in the two known
editions (1306 and undated) of the university stationers, from which the
great majority of surviving texts stem; and in the obituary of Thomas, in
the Sorbonne's records. Conversely, the earliest bibliographies of John of
Wales do not mention the *Manipulus florum*;[38] it is not until the fifteenth
century that Marianus of Florence adds this work to the list of John's
writings.[39] Marianus' source, at this late date, can only have been the
colophon of a manuscript of the β tradition (such as, for example, the San
Marco manuscript, now Florence, Biblioteca nazionale MS conv. sopp. J
6.12). Marianus' chronicle was in turn used by the early modern bibliographers, who gave life to the attribution. It was Marianus as well who first
explained John of Wales' failure to finish the *Manipulus florum*: "Sed heu
morte preventus imperfectum reliquit, quem perfecit Magister Thomas de
Hibernia, Ordinis Minorum." This explanation is simply another of
Marianus' assumptions, based on the information provided by the colophon.
It is no more reliable than his conflation of Thomas the Sorbonnist with
Thomas the Italian friar.

Secondly, it is difficult to conceive of the circumstances under which a
work begun by John of Wales would come to be completed by Thomas

---

[38] See, for example, Henry of Kirkestede (Boston of Bury) printed in Tanner, *Bibliotheca Britannico-Hibernica...* (London 1748) p. xxxiii.

[39] Ed. Domenichelli, "Compendium chronicarum" 463, where the work is called *Manipulus morum*.

Hibernicus. John was a Franciscan; Thomas was a secular cleric who reveals, in the *De tribus punctis*, distinct anti-Mendicant bias. A more important obstacle is the chronology of the two men's lives. Having already served as regent master at the Franciscan house at Oxford, John of Wales came to Paris ca. 1270, and died there probably in 1285.[40] Thomas must have been born between 1265 and 1275, and is not known to be connected with the Faculty of Theology before 1295. Probably Thomas had not even begun his studies in the Faculty of Arts before John's death. Thus, Thomas can scarcely have been a disciple of John's, and certainly not a colleague nor a confrère, whom one might expect to take over John's unfinished text and complete it as an act of piety or friendship for the deceased.

The internal evidence connecting the *Manipulus florum* with John of Wales is slim indeed. In sum, it consists of the fact that the works of John of Wales and the *Manipulus florum* cite two authors not commonly quoted in the thirteenth century. The first of these is Walter Map's *Valerius ad Rufinum*, which makes its first recorded appearance at the University of Paris in John's *Communiloquium*,[41] written between 1270 and 1285.[42] That a second author, writing at the Sorbonne, should use this same work twenty or thirty years later is in no way unusual, particularly since there were two manuscripts of it in the Sorbonne's library.[43] The second work is John of Salisbury's *Policraticus*, which John of Wales helped to reintroduce into scholarly literature.[44] The *Policraticus* is quoted six times in the *Manipulus florum*, but all six extracts are taken from the *Flores paradysi*, one of the two major sources from which Thomas compiled the *Manipulus florum* rather than from the *Policraticus* itself; all six extracts attribute the *Policraticus* to Chrysostom, a wonderful bit of misinformation deriving ultimately from a rubricator's error in the main manuscript of the *Flores paradysi*, Brussels Bibl. Royale MS 20030-32 (s. xiii). In comparing John's works with the *Manipulus florum*, thus, the closer one scrutinizes their common sources the less one sees to connect them.

As to a more general comparison, the *Manipulus florum* is markedly different in character from John of Wales' writings. While his works are certainly compendia of quotations from famous authors, both Christian and

---

[40] Regarding John's life see Emden, *BRUO* 1960-1961; and W. A. Pantin, "John of Wales and Medieval Humanism", in *Medieval Studies presented to Aubrey Gwynn S.J.*, ed. J. A. Watt *et al.* (Dublin 1961) 297-319.

[41] Pratt, "Jankyn's Book" 16.

[42] Pantin, "John of Wales" 298.

[43] At least one of these had been at the Sorbonne since ca. 1275, when the earliest catalog was made; see Rouse, "Early Library" 251.

[44] Pantin, "John of Wales" 304.

ancient, John wove the extracts into his own frequently elaborate framework, and consistently used them to point a moral. His borrowings consisted not only of *sententiae* but also, quite heavily, of anecdotes, an
element totally absent from the *Manipulus florum*.[45] In no sense do his
works resemble a dictionary of quotations such as the *Manipulus florum*.

If the internal evidence tends to reject John of Wales, it tends on the
contrary to support Thomas as the compiler of the *Manipulus florum*. The
prologue contains a pun on the name Robert; having referred to Ruth,
whose poverty forced her to glean after the reapers in the field of Boaz, the
prologue continues, "Sic ego pauperculus non habens copiam scriptorum
nec originalium acervum, agrum intravi Booz, quod interpretatur robur vel
virtus, scilicet Roberti utique robusti in quo virtutis robur vigere consuevit,
et ibidem originalium spicas, id est, diversas sanctorum auctoritates de
diversis libris, non sine labore collegi."[46] This flattering reference to the
founder of the College, Robert of Sorbon, and to his "field," the Sorbonne
and its collection of books, points to Thomas Hibernicus, former fellow of
the Sorbonne, rather than to the Mendicant John of Wales, who had no
such connection with the institution.[47] Also, in drawing up the list of
authors and works at the end of the *Manipulus florum*, the compiler has in
one instance used a manuscript, B.N. lat. 15730, bequeathed to the Sorbonne by Simon Widelin (d. 1285). If John of Wales died in 1285, then the
list, like the prologue, also points to Thomas rather than John. Finally, as
we shall see in more detail below, the arrangement of the authors in the list,
the arrangement of the quotations under each heading in the body of the
Manipulus, and the very extracts themselves, which come in large part from
two Sorbonne *florilegia*, indicate that the work could only have been compiled by someone with continued or repeated access to the Sorbonne books.
This fact points unmistakably to Thomas, for only fellows or former fellows
would have been granted such privileges at this date.[48]

In light of the counter evidence, both external and internal, it would appear that the attribution to John of Wales in the β colophon is the result of

---

[45] Concerning the character of John of Wales' writings see Pantin, esp. 299-302.

[46] For a fuller discussion of this passage see below, Ch. 5.

[47] The same conclusion was reached at the beginning of this century by Valentin Rose,
Die Handschriftenverzeichnisse der königlichen Bibliothek zu Berlin (Berlin 1901) 2: 304.

[48] See Delisle, *Cabinet des manuscrits* 2: 185, 196; Rouse, "Early Library" 228-230.
While there is some evidence to suggest that, despite the regulations, outsiders were occasionally given access to Sorbonne books in the thirteenth century, there is no indication
that an outsider, at this date, could have worked in the Sorbonne library on anything ap-
proaching the scale involved in the compilation of the *Manipulus florum*.

one person's mistake or misunderstanding;[49] that this person attempted to "correct" the colophon on his copy of the *Manipulus florum*; and that the family of manuscripts descended from this one codex perpetuated and disseminated the mistaken attribution. Thomas Hibernicus was the compiler of the *Manipulus florum*.

A number of other works are attributed to Thomas. Each of these, however, can be identified and shown to be spurious.

The most important of these is the *Flores Bibliae* or *Bibliorum*. This is a biblical *florilegium* in which the extracts from the scriptures are listed under ca. 270 alphabetically arranged topics: "Abstinencia, Abusio, Acceptio personarum, Accedia, Acquisitio iniusta, Adolescentia ... Vindicta, Unctiofacta, Voluntas dei, Votum." It has no author's prologue and begins "*Abstinentia*. Vir sive mulier, cum fecerint votum ... potest, abstinebunt. Num. 6. Tobias filium suum ab infantia ... ab omni peccato. Tob. 1...." It ends with "*Votum* ... Si quid vovisti Deo, ... et stulta promissio. Eccl. 5." The work was first printed by Guillaume Rouillé, Lyon, 1554.[50] It is quite probable that Rouillé commissioned the work. There is no evidence that it existed before this date; the work is not mentioned in the Middle Ages, and there are no manuscripts of it. Rouillé probably conceived the *Flores Bibliae* as a parallel and companion text for the *Manipulus florum*, which he had published with considerable success in the previous year; we know that Rouillé was interested in, and published a number of, collections of extracts or moral readings. Rouillé's editions of the *Flores Bibliae* were, however, anonymous. The Rouillé edition was reprinted in Antwerp in 1555, 1557 and 1567 by John Steele, who also published the *Manipulus florum* (again, from Rouillé's text). In the 1567 edition produced by Steele's widow and heirs, the *Flores Bibliae* is for the first time attributed to Thomas of Ireland. The *Flores Bibliae* continued to be published by the printers of the *Manipulus florum*. In all, it went through seventeen editions and was attributed to Thomas in at least ten of them.[51] By the nineteenth century the *Flores*

---

[49] P. G. C. Campbell, *L'Epitre d'Othéa: Étude sur les sources* (Paris 1924) 162, says, "Il serait difficile d'expliquer pourquoi le nom de [Jean de Galles] s'est glissé dans l'*explicit* de si bonne heure; il est beaucoup plus facile d'expliquer comment dans la plupart de nos manuscrits la dernière partie de l'*explicit* a été omise." Naturally, Campbell was unaware that there are five independent witnesses to the original, and that only one of these, not the most authoritative, contains the lengthier explicit (see below, Ch. 6, History of the Text). It is more reasonable to assume one addition than four independent omissions.

[50] Regarding Rouillé see N. Davis, "Publisher Guillaume Rouillé, Businessman and Humanist," in *Editing Sixteenth-Century Texts*, ed. R. J. Schoeck (Toronto 1966) 72-112.

[51] Also entitled *Flores sacrorum Bibliorum sive Loci communes ... ordine alphabeto Digesti per F. Thomam Hibernicum, ordinis praedicatorum* (Lyon, I. Certe 1579); or *Flores Bibliae sive Loci communes omnum fere materiarum ex veteri ac novo testimento excerpti. Et*

Bibliae had become firmly entrenched as a work of Thomas Hibernicus.[52]

The *Promptuarium morale* is a manual of sermons and addresses arranged by Sundays and feastdays, with extensive reference to scriptural and liturgical texts.[53] It was tentatively attributed to Thomas by Lucius Wadding in his edition of the work, and from there the attribution found its way into the notices of the early modern biographers and the later editors of the *Promptuarium*. Wadding's deductions, however, were based upon a string of mistaken premises: that Thomas was a Franciscan, that he died about 1269/70, and that he wrote the *Flores Bibliorum*. Kleinhans has shown that the work was probably written by an Irish ecclesiastic between 1254 and 1274.[54] There is, in addition, no medieval evidence associating it with the compiler of the *Manipulus florum*.

B.N. MS lat. 15853, *Questiones super primum et secundum sententiarum* (s. xiv in., Sorbonne, ex leg. Johannis Gorre), bears the following notes: "Thomas Hibernicus," on the flyleaf, f. 192, in a late fifteenth or early sixteenth-century hand; "Thomas Hibernicus super sententias," at the head of the text, f. 1, in a seventeenth- or eighteenth-century hand; and Guedier de Saint-Aubin's description of the manuscript, repeating this ascription, on flyleaf i[v]. The attribution was repeated, curiously enough, by Delisle, and also appears in the D.N.B., for example. Hauréau considered the ascription doubtful, and this has since been shown to be the work of Richard of Fitzralph.[55] It is possible that Thomas left his name on this manuscript, and that it was reproduced in the sixteenth century. The manuscript has lost its medieval binding and has been cropped, losing its title on f. 1 in the process, though it apparently retains its flyleaves. It came to the Sorbonne library with the books of John Gorre, who probably died in 1362. There is, frankly, no indication in the manuscript that it had any association with Thomas whatsoever, and the reason for the appearance of his name in the volume is a mystery.

De illusionibus daemonum, *De tentatione diaboli*, *De remediis vitiorum*—these three titles without incipits are first attributed to Thomas by John

---

alphabetico ordine digesti, à F. Thoma Hibernico, nuncque demum castigati (Antwerp, Plantin 1568).

[52] Cf. Hauréau, *Histoire littéraire* 30: 408.

[53] First printed by Lucius Wadding, *Concordantiae morales S. Antonii de Padua* (Rome 1624).

[54] A. Kleinhans, "De concordantiis biblicis S. Antonio Patavino...," *Antonianum* 6 (1931) 273-326, esp. 306-308.

[55] See the article by P. Glorieux in the *Dictionnaire de théologie catholique* (Paris 1943) 15: col. 778.

Bale in the *Scriptores*, 1557/59. They are not mentioned in the first edition, the *Summarium*, 1548; nor, unfortunately, do they appear in Bale's notebook, the *Index*, in which he frequently noted the source of his information.[56] Bale does not give an incipit for any of the three items, which suggests that he did not see manuscripts of them. From Bale, nevertheless, the attribution spread through the later English and continental bio-bibliographers. Quétif and Échard in the eighteenth century and Hauréau in the late nineteenth century declared themselves unable to identify any of the works which might have given rise to these attributions; and we can add nothing on this question.

In addition to the six works discussed above, there are various other titles ascribed to Thomas by individual bibliographers; these, however, are simply variant titles for Thomas' genuine works.

---

[56] John Bale, *Scriptorum illustrium maioris Brytannie...* (Basel 1557-59) 2: 242.

5

The *Manipulus florum*

Thomas of Ireland called his collection the *Manipulus florum*. The term *flores* or flowers, evoking the image of blossoms culled from a field, is the most common medieval name for a collection of extracts; the analogy between the fertile page and the fertile field was strongly felt. *Flores* is the Latin equivalent for anthology. Combined with the verb *legere* it becomes *florilegium*; and the two give birth to a variety of derivatives: *deflorare*, *deflorationes*, *flosculi*, *floretum*. The generic term *flores* is often combined with a second more colorful noun in the titles given to medieval *florilegia*. Thomas chose *manipulus*—sheaf, bouquet or handful of flowers. The usage is apparently original with him. Thomas' predecessors gave their collections such names as *Liber scintillarum*, *Liber florum*, *Flores paradysi*, *Liber exceptionum* and *Liber Pharetrae*; individual extracts are likened to sparks, flowers, or arrows in a quiver. In slight contrast to "quiver" or the non-committal *liber*, "handful" stresses the fact that it is a selection, a culling of a few from the many. While *manipulus* is a fairly common word, its only prior appearance in association with a collection of extracts is in the dedicatory epistle of the *Florilegium Angelicum*: "Defloravi tamen flosculos digniores et candidiores manipulos tuis oculis presentavi."[1] Although Thomas knew a manuscript of this *florilegium*, the chances that he saw the prefatory letter are negligible, since only the dedication copy, Rome Biblioteca Angelica MS 1895, contains the letter. With the popular reception of the *Manipulus florum* in the fourteenth century, its title and variations upon it become firmly associated with collections of extracts.[2]

Thomas explains the *Manipulus florum*, his reasons for compiling it, its purpose and its technical apparatus in detail in a prologue to the book. This prologue, unfortunately, was printed only in the two incunable editions,[3] being replaced in subsequent editions by dedicatory epistles of doubtful quality composed by later printers, editors and patrons. His was a good introduction to the *Manipulus*, growing out of, yet going beyond, the con-

[1] Concerning the *Florilegium Angelicum* see n. 27 below.
[2] See below, chap. 7, pt. VI.
[3] The prologue is edited below, Appendix 2.

ceptual framework of earlier ascetic and ethical *florilegia*. Thomas uses two metaphors, the one scriptural, the other classical, to illustrate his reasons for compiling the book and the purpose which it was to serve. Both metaphors are common in monastic literature.

As a scriptural basis for his prologue, Thomas chose a quotation from the second chapter of the Book of Ruth: "Abiit in agrum et collegit spicas post terga metentium." This text was often employed by medievals to describe their relationship to the Fathers. It is used in this sense, for example, by Stephen Langton, Philip the Chancellor, Jacques de Vitry, Engelbert of Admont and Philip of Moncalieri,[4] as well as by those who comment on the Old Testament such as Jerome, Bede, Rabanus and the *Gloss*. Far more people, it seems, preferred to see themselves as gleaners rather than as dwarves, even though the latter metaphor is the one usually singled out by modern scholars.

A century and a half before Thomas, Saint Bernard had employed this text as the basis for a sermon explaining the relationship of medieval writers and thinkers to the patristic authors.[5] The difference in the treatment of this same theme by a mid-twelfth-century monk and a fourteenth-century university master charts in miniature the distance between two intellectual worlds. Saint Bernard was dealing specifically with the matter of biblical commentary: how can one, at so late a date as the twelfth century, venture to comment upon the Bible when the patristic giants, the great "reapers," have long since worked over the field? One can only, with the humility of Ruth, glean after the reapers, picking up any stray wisps that have by hazard escaped them. Nor should he who has once devoted himself to the "disciplina christiana" glean the alien field of secular studies. One must truly follow after the reapers, so as not to stray from orthodoxy. In Ber-

---

[4] G. Lacombe and B. Smalley, "Studies on the Commentaries of Cardinal Stephen Langton," *Archives d'histoire doctrinale et littéraire du Moyen Age* 5 (1931) 100; Philip the Chancellor, *Summa de bono*, prologue, as found e.g. in Paris, B.N. mss lat. 3146, 15749, 16387; Jacques de Vitry, *Prologus in sermonibus cotidianis et communibus*, ed. G. Frenken in *Die exempla des Jacob von Vitry*, Quellen und Untersuchungen zur lateinischen Philologie des Mittelalters 5.1 (Munich 1914) 93-94; Engelbert, *Expositio super Ps. 118 "Beati immaculati,"* printed in B. Pez, *Thesaurus anecdotorum novissimus* (Augsburg 1729) 6.3: 6-8, discussed in G. B. Fowler, *The Intellectual Interests of Engelbert of Admont* (New York 1947) and idem, "Additional Notes on Manuscripts of Engelbert of Admont," *Recherches de théologie ancienne et médiévale* 28 (1961) 275-276; Philip of Moncalieri in the prologue to his *Postilla super evangelia* as found e.g. in Brussels Bibl. roy. ms 18016 (Van den Gheyn 1870) fol. 1, London, British Library ms Royal 4 D.ix fol. 1, Vatican ms Vat. lat. 1066 fol. 1, printed at Lyon in 1510.

[5] See J. Leclercq, "Inédits bernardins dans un manuscrit d'Orval," *Analecta monastica* 1 (1948) 157-158.

nard's approach to Christian tradition, one should humbly consider oneself "inter minimos qui sunt in ecclesia."

With Thomas of Ireland much of the humility is gone. To be sure, Thomas avows that he is, like Ruth, a pauper, with respect to writings. But in actuality he seems rather well satisfied with his efforts. He calls up the quotation from Ruth as an apologia for writing a book which consists of nothing but extracts from other writers: since he has no writings of his own, he is justified in gleaning ("non sine labore," he observes pointedly) various *auctoritates* from the books of the saints, doctors and philosophers. For Thomas, Bernard's restriction against "secular studies" is invalid, for he gleans after the ancients as well as the Fathers; if his favorite source is Augustine, Seneca easily takes second place. Again like Ruth, Thomas says that he did his gleaning in the field of *Boaz* (meaning *robur*), or in other words, the field of *Robertus utique robustus*—a rhetorical way of saying that he did his bibliographic gleaning in the library of the Sorbonne. (One is tempted to suspect that he first thought of the *robur-Robertus-robustus* pun on Robert of Sorbon's name, and erected the Ruth-analogy upon it.) This bibliographical allusion is typical of the fact that Thomas' attitude toward past authority is one more of interest than of awe. The writings to be found in Robert's "field" are not to be meditated upon, nor emulated; they are to be utilized. Thus the distinction between twelfth-century monastic saint and fourteenth-century scholastic is one of primary emphasis. Certainly, no more than Bernard, would Thomas consider himself on a plane with the writers of the patristic era. But in describing the import of their writings it would never have occurred to Bernard to apply to them, first and foremost, the adjective *useful*.[6] It was precisely their utility, in a technical sense, for preachers and students, which was Thomas' principal consideration. And this being the case, in Thomas' estimate the gleaner was no mean figure. Hence he says, "Let other reapers come rejoicing bearing their sheaves (Ps. 126:6); for my part, this sheaf collected after the doctors I shall offer, with the widow (Mark 12:41-44) to the Lord's treasury."

The classical metaphor is drawn from Seneca's letter to Lucilius[7] on gathering ideas, encouraging one to imitate the bees who collect honey from the flowers and distribute what they collect in combs. Seneca's letter has as its subject the creative process, namely, how something new is produced out

---

[6] Philip the Chancellor does intend to use the *auctoritates sanctorum patrum*, and the *rationes philosophorum*, as well as the *dicta modernorum* in support of his arguments. Engelbert would have one apply distinctions and tools as an aid to understanding what the "great reapers" missed, admitting that there is still work to be done; but he sees meditation as the primary route to understanding.

[7] Seneca, *Epistulae ad Lucilium*, ep. 88; ed. L. Reynolds (Oxford 1965).

of an assimilation of what is already known. He continues, "One's life must be made up of an equal balance of reading and writing, as the bees both cull the flowers and arrange in the cells what they have collected." The reference to honey permits Seneca a long digression, questioning whether honey already exists in certain plants known to bees, or whether instead— as he believes—the bees actually transform diverse elements into a new substance. Returning to his subject, he stresses the value of separating or classifying, as bees do, the different subjects covered in reading, and blending these ideas or flavors into one compound that, while its sources are apparent, is nevertheless distinct from its component parts—as the body does with food. All that our mind absorbs is to be hidden away; only that which is made of these materials should come to light. Like a chorus, the individual voices blend into one harmony, in which the identity of the individual sources of an idea are transformed into new thought. Seneca closes the letter with a resounding plea for variety, focus and devotion: one's mind should ideally be made up of many parts, precepts and patterns of conduct. This is to be accomplished by abandoning all distractions—riches, bodily pleasures, quest for office, and envy. Constant effort and guidance by reason are the route. The road to the heights of greatness is rough; but if you desire to scale the peak which lies above fortune, you will look down on what men regard as lofty.

To imitate the bees who fly about the flowers collecting nectar, transform it into honey and store it in their cells, becomes a commonplace in the Middle Ages. It was used by both Seneca and later by Macrobius (*Saturnalia*, praef. 5-10), as well as by Virgil in the Aeneid (1.432-3), and it is used in turn by the Fathers. It became with ease the basic image of the medieval florilegist: the produce of his searching the fields was honey, and his words were mellifluous. Already in the seventh century Defensor of Ligugé says in the prologue of the *Liber scintillarum*, "Melliflua grate suscipias verba." The emphasis, however, is normally on the aspect of gathering the best or the honey from the flowers. In contrast with this, and with Seneca's emphasis on the creation of new thought from old, Thomas focuses on the importance of classification and arrangement of ideas. Since the extracts which he had culled were without order, he gathered them into a bouquet and arranged them according to the letters of the alphabet in the manner of a concordance, so that simple folk might find them more easily. Since the sea of whole texts was so vast, it seemed better to have a few sayings of the doctors at one's fingertips than to be lost in the flood: as Seneca said, when you skim through many things, single out one which you actually digest that day. If one wishes to absorb something it is necessary to linger over it a while since memory is fragile and cannot cope with the whirling storm of things.[8] Thus we should imitate the bees, who wander about suckling the flowers to make honey and then distribute and arrange whatever they carry off in the honey comb. Then, skipping Seneca's digression on the nature of honey, Thomas passes to classification: hence, whatever we amass from diverse reading, we ought to separate out so that the individual items might be more useful; then we ought to arrange these varying tastes according to their proper function. Selection of the most useful and arrangement so that it can easily be found, these are the goals toward which Thomas strives.

Thomas' purpose in compiling the *Manipulus* emerges reasonably clearly from his use of these two metaphors, the judicious gleaner and the orderly bee. He wants to provide a selection of significant authorities, arranged in a manner which will permit everyone to get at those best suited to his own purpose. The function of this book is not to lead people back to the faith or to inspire new ideas. It is to be useful, to serve the reader well. No wonder the *Manipulus florum* was popular. Let us examine how, in practice, Thomas went about the business of selection and arrangement.

I. STRUCTURE

The body of the *Manipulus florum* consists of some 6000 extracts from the writings of the Fathers and doctors of the Church, along with acceptable ancients; these quotations are classified according to 266 alphabetically-arranged topics. In addition, there is a prologue and, at the end, a bibliography of 366 works complete with incipit and explicit. In all, the *Manipulus florum* would correspond to approximately 365 pages of modern printed text, at 300 words per page.

The number of topics was a felicitous choice. Earlier *florilegia*, with a negligible break-down into perhaps as few as twenty or twenty-five topics, were obviously not so amenable to searching as was the *Manipulus*. At the same time, Thomas' number was still small enough to permit one to become familiar rather quickly with all the topics the *Manipulus* contained. With planning, a preacher could supply himself with *auctoritates* for a year's worth of sermons without ever treating the same subject twice. As for the nature of the topics, the *Manipulus florum* from a preacher's standpoint was a clear improvement upon earlier *florilegia*, which centered upon theological and doctrinal subjects. It is true that Thomas claims, in his prologue, to have included the most notable topics which frequently occur in sermons or in "reading" (*que sepius in sermonibus vel lectionibus possent occurrere*)— which latter in this context most likely means "university lectures"; but in

---

[8] Source unidentified. This same quotation appears in the text of the *Manipulus florum*, *Doctrina ax*, attributed to Peter of Blois.

practice, well over 200 of the 266 topics were of a moral and ethical nature, which probably related more to the pulpit than to the schoolroom. It is likely that Thomas' principal source for his topics was the index of the *Liber exceptionum*. Virtually all of the *Manipulus'* topic headings appear there, though in view of the fact that the *Liber exceptionum*'s index contains approximately 2350 subjects, a major overlap is almost inevitable. Still, there is probably more than coincidence, or common purpose, in the fact that topics heavily documented in the early thirteenth-century Cistercian *florilegium* (e.g., *Mors, Oratio, Peccatum*) are likewise emphasized in the early fourteenth-century university *florilegium*. Thomas may well have selected the topics with the largest number of references in the index of the *Liber exceptionum* to form the basis of his own list.[9]

The arrangement of the *Manipulus florum*'s topics was probably the major factor in the work's popularity. First-letter alphabetization was the norm through the Middle Ages, on those occasions when alphabetical order was employed.[10] But Thomas alphabetized through the word, that is, he used complete or absolute alphabetization. In the prologue, Thomas describes such alphabetization as being in the manner of the concordances (*secundum ordinem alphabeti more concordantiarum*), not so much because the concordance was the immediate inspiration for this facet of the *Manipulus*, but because the concordance was the most commonly known work in alphabetical order. Thomas goes on to give a clear and simple explanation of the process of alphabetization, an indication perhaps that he assumed that a certain proportion of his readers would be less than familiar with the process. In practice, he deviates from strict alphabetical order himself on only some seventeen occasions (including cross-reference entries)— an above-average performance.[11] An addition to his alphabetical arrangement of topics is the inclusion, in their proper places in the alphabetical schema, of cross-reference or "dummy" entries, e.g., *Scientia: vide Sapientia*. There are some forty-four of these, in addition to the 266 real entries, which help to render the *Manipulus* completely searchable.

Under each heading Thomas listed all the extracts which he had collected

---

[9] Thomas' manuscript of the *Flores paradysi*, B.N. ms 15982, was lacking an index and thus, obviously, was not a potential source of topic-headings. The *Flores paradysi* is discussed later in this chapter.

[10] See the discussion of alphabetization in chap. 1 above, at n. 78ff.

[11] Occasionally, these aberrations result, not from carelessness, but from Thomas' permitting logical considerations to outweigh the alphabetic principle: thus we find *Gloria bona*, *Gloria mala* (*vana*: edd.), *Gloria eterna*—because the first two are opposite sides of the same coin, which the alphabet is not permitted to sunder. Likewise, *Vita humana*, *Vita eterna*—a logical progression not to be reversed by the alphabet.

that pertained to that subject. Obviously, as he notes in the prologue, a quotation often could fit almost as well under one heading as under another related one, requiring him to make a choice. The number of extracts naturally differs from one topic to another; a very few topics have only three or four entries, while the longest, *Amicitia* and *Mors*, have ninety-five and ninety-nine, respectively. The length of the extracts or quotations themselves varies too; none is longer than a half-column in manuscript, and very rarely are extracts less than three column-lines in length. If these are the extremes, the typical is something else. A representative subject has some twenty-five or thirty quotations; a typical quotation or extract is five to eight column-lines in length. By comparison, there are thus many fewer extracts per topic in the *Manipulus* than in the *Liber florum*; and the individual extracts are much shorter than those in the *Liber exceptionum* or the *Flores paradysi*. Thomas groups the extracts under each heading according to author—e.g., all quotations from the works of St. Augustine on the subject of abstinence follow one after another, with all those on the same topic taken from works of St. Ambrose coming next in a body, and so on. The author's name appears in the margin beside the first extract from his writings, under each topic for which he is cited. In addition, both author and work, along with book, chapter, epistle or sermon number, are cited in the text at the end of each extract. Customarily Thomas is more precise in his citations than the *Liber florum*, a fact which probably depends more on the precise citations available in his major sources than upon any inherent precision on his own part. At any rate, Thomas mentions in his prologue that it was occasionally difficult to determine the number of book or chapter for a given extract because of the fact that different copies of the same work sometimes have differing book and chapter divisions. We can see, thus, that despite lapses in practice, he was conscious of the problem.

Thomas identified each of the extracts in the margin, with a letter of the alphabet, recommencing with *a* for the first extract under each topic, *b* for the next, and so on, resorting to double alphabet (*ab, ac, ad..., ba, bc,* etc.) if the number of extracts on a given topic warranted it. Thomas used a twenty-two- or twenty-three-letter alphabet, omitting *j, v* and *w* of course, and with or without *z*, as he chose. His double alphabets were only twenty-one (or twenty-two) letters in length, because he eliminated the duplicatives—i.e., there is no *aa* before *ab*, no *bb* between *ba* and *bc*, no *cc* between *cb* and *cd*. The use of letters as identification or reference symbols we have examined in chapter 1. Thomas added two technical improvements of his own, however. First, in contrast to virtually all previous reference symbols, Thomas' were as specific as possible, with each extract having a precise reference of its own. Only one of the indexed *florilegia* known to us referred to each single extract by a symbol of its own, and other indexes and concordances referred to larger segments of text—chapter, book, column, etc. Secondly, in contrast to the earlier reference symbols that we have examined, Thomas' symbols were not designed for use with an alphabetical index. The *Manipulus florum*, because of its alphabetical arrangement, is its own index. Thomas' reference letters are, instead, intended strictly for the purpose of internal cross-references from one topic to another. By this means he circumvented the problem posed by those quotations which could fit under either one of two or three topics—so he explains in the prologue. He placed such extracts in the best location, according to his judgment, and then referred the reader to them at the conclusion of other topical groups to which they pertained. To give an example: at the end of the entries for *Ab- stinentia*, which run from *a* through *ao*, one finds the passage, "Ubi *Caro* e.r., *Coniugium* c., *Consuetudo* c., *Discretio* m.n., *Elemosina* l., *Gula*, *Ieiunium*, *Infirmitas* b., *Servitium* c., *Sobrietas*, *Temperantia*." This per- mitted a preacher to know that, when he was preaching on the subject of abstinence, he might find additional material by resorting to any or all of the extracts under the headings *Gula*, *Ieiunium*, *Sobrietas* and *Temperantia*, or to the one or two specific extracts mentioned under the other seven topics. In theory, then, a reader of the *Manipulus* will find collected in one place all the extracts relating primarily to a given topic, and cross- references to all others that are relevant. In practice, Thomas was more con- scientious at some times than at others. Also in practice, the cross-reference symbols proved susceptible to scribal error. For example, as we have said, the last letter in Thomas' alphabet was often *y*, followed by an entry marked *ab* if he needed to continue into the double alphabet. But in numerous manuscripts the scribes used an *a-z* alphabet invariably, thus changing and hence invalidating as cross-references all the succeeding references under that topic. The printed editions stray even farther from the original. The *editio princeps*, from which all later editions descend, added both *z* and *&* to Thomas' alphabet, and used duplicatives in the double alphabets as well. Thus, the final extract under *Abstinentia* is designated *al* in the printed editions, while it is marked *ao* in Thomas' manuscript and in any cross- references. In addition to such conscious alterations, there are ordinary mistakes, letters repeated, letters omitted, which again invalidate subsequent cross-references. On the whole, however, the reference letters proved less susceptible to error than numbers usually are, particularly roman numer- als.[12]

---

[12] The cross-references in the distinction collection of Peter of Capua consist of roman numerals only; they are replete with errors. See above, chap. 1, at nn. 12-13.

Thomas was among the first compilers of reference works to incorporate cross-reference as an integral part of the structure of his work. The only earlier example known to us is found in Peter of Capua's collection of distinctions; and the ultimate source, for both Thomas and Peter, was the heavily cross-indexed glossed scriptures of the late twelfth century. The cross-reference system must have contributed materially to the *Manipulus'* usefulness, and usability, for preachers.

The extracts, grouped by author, Thomas arranged in his own order of precedence under each topic-heading. While Thomas' arrangement of the topics in alphabetical order is immediately evident, the internal order of precedence under each heading is less obvious. Indeed, the existence of such an order might pass unperceived, although Thomas states in the prologue, "Sub qualibet autem dictione ponuntur diverse auctoritates sanctorum et aliorum doctorum per ordinem...." He does not elaborate. To verify that an order does exist, it was necessary to establish a composite of the arrangement under numerous headings, because of course no single topic-entry contains more than a fraction of the possible combinations. This procedure reveals that there is no definite order for the works cited—in fact, that citations from a single work are not even grouped together at times—but, on the contrary, that there is a consistent order of precedence for the authors cited. In part, this order is readily apparent, as soon as one consciously looks for it. A casual glance through the text reveals that the four major patristic authors, the four Doctors of the Church, when they are cited, invariably come first, invariably in this order—Augustine, Ambrose, Jerome, Gregory—and that Seneca, when he is cited, almost invariably comes last, as Thomas had promised in the prologue: "... Seneca, cuius dicta in fine cuiuslibet dictionis ponuntur." It requires but little further effort to discern that the three categories of authors, patristic, ecclesiastic, ancient, are arranged in that order, which is the descending order of their authority for Christians. However, the consistent order of precedence extends even to individual authors within these categories, to a point at which judgment of relative authority can scarcely have been the determining factor. Rather, the principle of arrangement is what we may call, for lack of a better name, Sorbonne order (see Table, pp. 122-123). The catalogs of the Sorbonne's books, both the catalog of 1338 and the 1290 catalog contained within the later document,[13] list the codices of *originalia* of individual authors in the same order that Thomas of Ireland has employed. It is easier to

---

[13] See R. H. Rouse, "The Early Library of the Sorbonne," *Scriptorium* 21 (1967) 42-71, 227-251, esp. 61-66.

TABLE

Sorbonne catalog[a]	List in the prologue[b]	Bibliography appended to the *Manipulus florum*	Order in which extracts are cited[c]
		Dionysius[d]	
Augustine	Augustine	Augustine	Augustine
Ambrose	Ambrose	Ambrose	Ambrose
Jerome	Jerome	Jerome	Jerome
Gregory	Gregory	Gregory	Gregory
Bernard	Bernard	Bernard	Bernard
Dionysius[d]			
Hilary	*Hilary*	Hilary	
Chrysostom	Chrysostom	Isidore	{ Chrysostom
Isidore	Isidore	Chrysostom	{ Isidore
	Damascenus[e]		
	Origen		
	Cyprian		
	Fulgentius		
	Basil		
	Maximus		
	Rabanus	Rabanus	Rabanus
	Caesarius		
	Leo		Leo
Bede and Anselm	Bede		Bede
	Prosper	Prosper	
		Damascenus[e]	
	Anselm	Anselm	Anselm

[a] Taken from the 1338 catalog of the *parva libraria*, sections XXV-XXXVI, L-LII (Delisle 3: 32-37, 60-62).

[b] The names in italics are authors whom Thomas of Ireland probably or certainly quotes through intermediate sources only, in the text of the *Manipulus florum*.

[c] This is a composite order, based primarily upon the articles *Adulatio, Amicitia, Apostoli, Ascensio, Avaricia, Ira, Sciencia, Scriptoria,* with recourse to others ad hoc for determining the placement of certain authors. We have included only those authors pertinent to the other three lists, eliminating as well those whose place in the sequence is unclear. Brackets indicate that the order of the names enclosed is variable.

[d] Dionysius' works are listed first in the bibliography, as compared with sixth position in the catalog (Dionysius does not appear in the two remaining categories).

[e] Damascenus precedes Rabanus and Prosper in the prologue, while his work follows theirs in the bibliography (he does not appear in the other two categories). Damascenus was belatedly tacked on to the

Hugh of
  St. Victor
	Richard	Richard	Hugh of
			  St. Victor

Richard of
  St. Victor
	Hugh	Hugh	Richard of
			  St. Victor

	Cassian		
	Cassiodorus[f]		Cassiodorus[f]
		Alcuin	
	Alanus[f]	Alanus[f]	Alanus[f]

	Petrus
	  Ravennas
			Petrus
			  Ravennas

	Pliny[f]	Pliny[f]	
	Solinus[f]		
	Maimonides	Maimonides	Maimonides
	Valerius Maximus[f]	Valerius[f]	Valerius[f]
	Vegetius		
	Agellius		
	Sidonius		
		Macrobius	
Seneca	Tully	Tully	Tully
Tully and Boethius	Boethius	Boethius	Boethius
	Seneca	Seneca	Seneca
"Libri Socratis, Plato- nis, Ciceronis, Valerii, Solini, Cassiodori, Pli- ni et aliorum acto- rum."			

---

list of Prosper's works in the bibliography, when Thomas came upon his work in the codex that supplied the list of Anselm's works, the following entry in the bibliography; see Appendix 6 below.

  [f] In the Sorbonne catalog of 1338 these authors' works should have been listed in section LII, "Libri Socratis, Platonis...." In actuality, however, most of them do not have their works described in this or any other section of the 1338 catalog, including those authors whose names appear in the rubric of section LII!

recognize the similarity, than it is to explain the relationship, between Thomas' order and the Sorbonne order. It is difficult to imagine that he utilized a sequence represented only in a catalog, a catalog which was essentially just an inventory of property. The explanation may lie instead in the arrangement of the codices in the Sorbonne library. Given the size of the Sorbonne's collection, 1,017 codices in 1290 and more by Thomas' time, we assume that a rough subject arrangement of the codices themselves, presumably in the order in which the authors were listed in the catalog, was necessary to facilitate both daily use and annual inventory-taking. It seems more likely that the physical arrangement of the codices, rather than the organization of a catalog, would have influenced the order of entry in the *Manipulus florum*. To anyone who works over a long period of time in a given library, the order of the books becomes second nature.

II. SOURCES

Thomas' source, in the widest sense, was the library of the Sorbonne College; one assumes so, he himself declares so, and surviving manuscripts verify the fact. We know that Thomas was a Sorbonnist, and he would be most likely to use the books of his house. Thomas refers to his use of the Sorbonne's library, in the play on words which opens the prologue: he, like Ruth, had done his gleaning in the field of "Boaz," which means in Latin *robur vel virtus*—hence, the field of *Robertus*. As we noted above, the "Robert" in question is Robert of Sorbon, and the "field" of his "virtue" was the Sorbonne and its books.

Thomas lists in the prologue the names of thirty-six authors whose works he claims to have quoted the most often. This list, one might assume, would aid in the process of identifying Thomas' specific sources; but in point of fact the list is not so straightforward as it looks. Eleven of the thirty-six are cited only ten or fewer times: Caesarius, Hilary and Richard of Saint-Victor ten times; Aulus Gellius, nine; Maximus and Pliny, eight; Anselm, Fulgentius and Solinus, five; Damascenus, four; Maimonides, two. Among those authors quoted in the text but not included in the list—and thus, by implication, quoted but rarely—are Gregory of Nazianzus, quoted ten times; Peter of Blois, thirty-three; and Pope Innocent III, thirty-eight. In other words, as is the case with the bibliography of 366 works and their authors at the end of the *Manipulus*,[14] there is no direct correlation between the

[14] See below, pt. III of this chapter.

authors listed and the texts cited in the body of the *Manipulus florum*. Therefore, the list in the prologue is not a reliable guide to identifying Thomas' manuscript sources; it is simply a list of notable authors made for the sake of advertisement.

Turning to the body of the *Manipulus*, it is first of all worthwhile to remind ourselves that the sources cited in medieval *florilegia* often bear little relationship to the actual identity of the source or text that has been used. *Florilegia* such as the *Manipulus florum* are a literary world apart. Their customary sources are earlier *florilegia*, and their most frequent literary heirs, subsequent *florilegia*. One also has to consider the possibility of fraud. We have previously examined a large family of *florilegia*, the *Lumen anime* texts, which treated citations of source rather like items of decoration, names to be inserted where they appear to best effect, without regard for reality.[15] Thus, an extract in a *florilegium* which is ascribed to the *City of God* may, in fact, have been taken from a manuscript of that work; it may, instead, have been taken from another *florilegium* which, correctly or not, ascribes the extract to the *City of God*; it may even have been made up out of whole cloth by the "compiler," who then chose to embellish it with Augustinian respectability. In effect, this means that no citations of source may ever be accepted at face value, without verification and, especially, without a search for an intermediate source.

We must also take into consideration the fact that individual quotations often had, as they have today, independent lives of their own. A concise, apt definition of a term, or a profound or well-phrased observation, often became a commonplace to be quoted in every *florilegium* and even in every sermon which dealt with the subject involved. To take an example from the *Manipulus florum*: Thomas' quotation from Gregory's *Moralia* on the subject of angels (*Angeli h*) can be found in the *Pharetra* and in the *Alphabetum auctoritatum* of Arnold of Liège. If one wonders which of these was his direct source, the answer is, neither; his actual source in this case was a manuscript of the *Moralia*. The fact that one, two or a dozen of these extracts in the *Manipulus* appear as well in an earlier *florilegium* does not prove Thomas' dependence upon it. Further proof is required—a similarity in sequence of the extracts, a peculiarity in the attribution or other common errors, mistakes which are explained by the physical appearance of the source, marks in the text or margin of the specific manuscript employed, or a frank avowal by Thomas that he has used a given secondary source.

---

[15] See M. A. and R. H. Rouse, "The Texts Called *Lumen anime*," *Archivum Fratrum Praedicatorum* 41 (1971) 5-113.

Finally, there is the problem that when we have identified a *florilegium* used by Thomas—or, again, in a later chapter, a *florilegium* which in turn used the *Manipulus*—it has often been necessary to sort out the history of this text as well, simply in order to be able to identify clearly what work we are dealing with. This proved true of the *Florilegium Angelicum*, the *Liber exceptionum*, the *Flores paradysi*, the *Alphabetum auctoritatum*, the *Lumen anime* and the *Liber Pharetrae*, none of which had been adequately described in print.

With this as background, one can make some progress toward identifying the sources of the extracts which Thomas of Ireland cites in the *Manipulus florum*. They are a mixture of *originalia*, of *florilegia*, and of secondary sources which are not *florilegia* in the strict sense (the *Decretum* and the *Gloss*).

A. *Major sources: the* Flores paradysi, *the* Liber exceptionum

Although Thomas cited many of his predecessors by name, he never names the two *florilegia* which were his major sources, the *Flores paradysi* and the *Liber exceptionum ex libris viginti trium auctorum*. Since Thomas does not name these two books among his sources, their identification was largely due to their survival among the Sorbonne books. It would seem natural, in hunting for the sources used by an author, to examine the books surviving from his library; how seldom this is done is rather surprising. In this instance, a review of *florilegia* known to have been at the Sorbonne in Thomas' time produced among others these two, which had a marked degree of overlap with the contents of the *Manipulus*. A search of the surviving Sorbonne books produced, as we shall see, the very manuscripts of these two which Thomas used. The *Flores paradysi* and the *Liber exceptionum* have not hitherto been examined in print.[16] Yet, beyond their specific significance as sources of extracts for the *Manipulus*, they are significant in their own right as the earliest indexed *florilegia* and, indeed, among the earliest examples of subject indexing of any sort. Hence, these two early thirteenth-century Cistercian preaching tools will be discussed here in detail.

The *Flores paradysi* is a large collection of short sentences from patristic and ancient authorities, which has been provided with an elaborate subject

[16] A brief description of the *Flores paradysi* appears in R. H. Rouse, "The *A* Text of Seneca's Tragedies in the Thirteenth Century," *Revue d'histoire des textes* 1 (1971) 93-121. Both *florilegia* are summarily discussed in R. H. Rouse, "Cistercian Aids to Study in the Thirteenth Century," *Studies in Medieval Cistercian History* 2 (1976) 123-134, and in chap. 1 above.

index and reference system. The work survives in three distinct states which
we shall designate *a*, *b* and *c*. Each state is represented by a single manuscript.[17] The text developed during the first half of the thirteenth century at
the Cistercian house of Villers-en-Brabant founded from Clairvaux in
1146.

The earliest version of the *Flores paradysi*, *a*, is contained in Brussels,
Bibliothèque royale MS 4785-93 (Van den Gheyn no. 970) ff. 1-133ᵛ,
s. xiii, beg. (f. 5), "Ambrosius super Lucam. Qui labore sibi victum
requirit...," and ending, "[Crisostomus:] ... Rectas enim mentes diligit et
sine fuco propositum." It includes sentences from the works of Ambrose,
Augustine, Jerome and Chrysostom, in that order. The sentences are entered in the order of the books from which they were taken: the order of the
sentences thus does not represent an artificial arrangement by subject, but
rather reflects directly the contents of a number of codices probably in the
library of Villers itself.[18] A subject approach to the sentences is afforded by
an elaborate alphabetical index on ff. 1-4. The index is written in three
columns and contains approximately 450 topics. The following are those
beginning with the letter A: *Abicere, Abire, Abscondere, Abstinere, Absens,
Abundare, Accedere, Accusare, Adherere, Adiuvare, Adversitas, Adulari,
Adulterium, Affectus, Amaritudo, Ambitio, Amicus, Amor, Angelus,
Angustia, Anima, Animus, Ascendere, Aperire, Appetere, Aqua, Artes,
Arguere, Arrogantia, Avaricia, Audacia, Audire, Aurum.* Ten additional
topics are added at the end of the list as afterthoughts, and two columns of
f. 4ʳ and all of f. 4ᵛ are left blank.

A greater variety of subjects is represented than one normally finds in the
narrower preaching *florilegia* of the fourteenth century. One is struck by the
appearance of such topics as *Artes, Aurum, Bestia, Clavis, Civitas, Color,
Corona, Dextra, Felicitas, Fortuna, Fructus, Lapis, Lingua, Lumen, Mar-
garita, Pinguis, Sensus, Via* and *Vir*, none of which appears, for example, in
the *Manipulus florum*. Those topics most heavily used are such as one
might expect in a monastic *florilegium: Abscondere, Amicus, Amor, Cupiditas, Humilitas, Inebriare, Iusticia, Laudare, Legere, Loqui, Mors, Oratio,
Patiencia, Peccatum, Prelatus, Servire, Timor, Videre, Virgo.*

[17] In addition, there is one quire from a second *b* text, bound at the end (fols. 134-145ᵛ)
of *Flores paradysi a*, Brussels Bibl. roy. MS 4785-93.
[18] Regarding the abbey library see H. Schuermans, "Bibliothèque de l'abbaye de Villers," *Société archéologique de l'arrondissement de Nivelles* 6 (1898) 193-236; he prints the
catalog of 1309. In 1796 the books passed to the Benedictine abbey of Afflighem and in
1837 to Termonde. Today some sixty-nine Villers manuscripts are in the Bibliothèque royale at Brussels, and another half-dozen are scattered among other libraries in Europe and
America.

Each subject-heading is supplied with from one to thirty-six (*Mors*) references. In order to produce a system of reference from index to text, the *florilegium* has been subdivided by means of three concentric sequences of the alphabet, resulting in reference notations such as *Aaa* or *Pcn* in the index. Each opening of the manuscript bears a designation composed of a large majuscule letter of the alphabet in the upper left corner and a medium-sized letter in the upper right corner. These proceed in sequence as one turns the leaves: *Ab, Ac, Ad, Ae ... Az, Ba, Bb, Bc...*. Within each verso-recto opening the sentences themselves are designated in the margin by the third and smallest alphabet. For the majority of pages the lettering of the sentences begins afresh at the head of each page. In these cases the appearance of a small dot to the upper right of the reference in the index— e.g., *Aba·*—indicates that the desired sentence appears on the right-hand page of opening *Ab*, whereas an index reference without the dot, *Aba*, would refer to the left-hand page of opening *Ab*. For a number of openings, however, the compiler follows the more practical method of lettering the extracts consecutively through both sides of the opening, thus avoiding confusion (see ff. 7^v-8, 9^v-10, 13^v-14, 14^v-15, 15^v-16, 16^v-17, 21^v-22, 39^v-40). The format of the references changes with the end of the quire 5. From this point on, both letters that designate the opening appear together, one red, the other black, in the upper left corner or in the center of the upper margin of the left-hand page. Far fewer sentences have their own reference letter; that is, the letters of the small alphabet become less specific and refer to larger portions of text. In some cases they dwindle to two per opening. This reference system is a primitive device still in a state of flux. The index is good only for this manuscript. If the text were to be copied and the amount of text on each page altered, the index would no longer function, since the two large alphabets in the reference system refer to physical parts of the codex rather than to portions of the text.

Brussels MS 4785-93 is lacking quires 6, 7, 10, 11, 17 and 18. That they were once part of the manuscript is confirmed by the signatures and by the gaps in the letter-sequence for the openings. For example, quires 6-7 contained openings *Bz* to *Cp*; quires 10-11, *Dk* to *Ed*; and 17-18, *Gf* to *Gv*.[19] Quire 21 is mislabeled 22. The manuscript was written by three people in the early thirteenth century. The first, who wrote the index only, also wrote the index in *Flores paradysi b*, and is probably the compiler or maker of the index rather than just a copyist. A second person wrote the majority of the

---

[19] More precisely, one is lacking p. 2 of opening *By* through p. 1 of *Cp*; p. 2 of *Dj* - p. 1 of *Ed*; and p. 2 of *Gd* - p. 1 of *Gv*.

text. His hand bears a number of conservative characteristics, particularly the cedillaed *e*. A third person, whose hand displays distinct charter features, wrote quire 8 and half of quire 9 (ff. 49-62ᵛ), and may also have written quires 6 and 7, now lost. The writers of the text are contemporary with the writer of the index, obviously, since they had to have completed their portions before he could carry out his work. The decoration of the manuscript is plain, with frequent use of green and silver for the initials.

The last quire in Brussels MS 4785-93 (ff. 134-145ᵛ) is an addition, and not a part of *Flores paradysi a*. This quire originally belonged to a manuscript of *Flores paradysi b*. It is a fragment, beginning with the last word of a sentence from the sermons of Peter of Ravenna and breaking in the middle of a sentence from Cicero's *Tusculan Disputations*. Its writer clearly skipped about in the sections of *Flores b* which contain *sententiae* from the works of Cicero and Seneca. The readings are similar, but occasionally superior, to the text of Brussels 20030-32, the only known text of *b*. The text of this quire has not been subdivided by letters of the alphabet, and it is of course not represented in the index of MS 4785-93. It was probably a part of that manuscript already in the thirteenth century.

Not long after the completion of *Flores paradysi a*, at least within the lifetime of the writer of the index, a second, much enlarged version of the work was produced, *Flores paradysi b*, Brussels 20030-32 (Van den Gheyn no. 1508); it begins, "[prologue:] Flores paradisi pro titulo.... [text:] Excerpta sententiarum de libris beati August[in]i episcopi. Ex libro de catezizandis rudibus: Nulla est maior ad amorem...," ends, "... suavitas ammirabilis respondens tactui. Ibi erit rex veritas, lex caritas." The new book, the text of which fills over 200 folios, was equipped with a vast index (ff. 2-18)[20] and a prologue (f. 1ʳ⁻ᵛ). The prologue is divided into two parts, the first explaining the nature and purpose of the work, the second dealing with the index.[21] The author states that his book, filled with the choicest sentences, offers grace to its readers, as if it were filled with the finest flowers of Paradise. Through them a knowledge of truth is attained, knowledge permitting one to recognize the good and pursue it and to shun evil—to fear the Lord, and to turn from the mortality of this world. Wishing to leave something to posterity, the author has collected the brief, useful and necessary sentences from the Fathers and men of renown, sentences which, like the flowers of Paradise, never alter, but rather alter their admirers for the better. Here one finds easily at hand all that one might find in the great

---

[20] Fol. 10ʳ⁻ᵛ is misplaced; it should follow fol. 16ᵛ.
[21] The prologue is printed below, Appendix 1.

books of many libraries, assembled by the author. There is more, in similar vein, but these are the salient points of the author's statement: his book provides grace and the knowledge of truth, coupled with the homely virtues of brevity, utility and compactness, salutary both for the reader and, as a pious and charitable deed, for the author as well. This first part of the prologue is not so much an introduction to the *Flores paradysi* in particular, as a general statement of the philosophy of the *florilegium* as a genre.

The second part of the prologue describes the purpose and the mechanics of the index and the reference system. The principal topics among the *sententiae*, which are also the most important for sermon-making, are listed alphabetically with references to their location, the purpose being to provide access to these materials. The author continues with a detailed and intricate description of the reference system upon which the index depends, complete with examples and with exhortations to the faint-hearted to persevere. The instructions are both practical and efficient, and display a sympathetic understanding of man's horror of the complicated.

The new index occupies seventeen folios—many times the size of that in *Flores paradysi a*. The index of *b* contains approximately 900 topics, incorporating virtually all those in *Flores a*. Those for the first letter of the alphabet are *Abicere vel repellere, Abire vel recedere, Abscondere vel occultum, Abstinere, Absorbere, Absentia, Abuti, Abundare, Accedere, Accipere, Accusare, Acquirere, Adherere, Adiuvare, Adorare vel orare, Adolescens, Adversitas, Adversarius, Adulari, Adulter, Affectus, Afflictio, Agere vel actio, Ager, Ala, Alienum, Altare, Altum, Amare vel diligere, Amaritudo, Ambitio, Ambulare, Amicus, Amplexus, Angelus, Angustia, Anima, Animus, Aperire, Apparere, Appetere, Apis, Aqua, Arbitrium, Arbor, Ardor, Arescere, Arguere vel corripere, Arma, Aromata, Ars, Arrogantia, Ascendere, Asperitas, Athleta, Avaricia, Audacia, Audire, Auferre, Auris, Aurum, Auctoritas.* Of the some 900 topics, those with the largest number of references are *Amare, Contempnere, Dare, Docere, Dolor, Mors mori vel mortuus, Pauper, Peccare vel peccatum, Prelatus, Superbia, Timere, Vincere, Vindicta, Virtus*—nothing unexpected for a monastic *florilegium*. The index is not a fair copy, but rather a rough version resulting from someone's going through the text and noting down references as he came to them. This must have been a staggering task. Some entries are squeezed, in order to fit in all the references; others were allotted more white space than they needed in the event. Omissions are handled in a supplementary index (ff. 17-18) of at least 160 repeated topic-headings, with from one to twenty additional references for each. Also inscribed here is the whole entry for the topic *Malicia malum vel malus*, which had been omitted from the initial alphabetical sequence in the index.

The text of *Flores paradysi b* is divided for purposes of reference in a fashion similar to that of *Flores a*, namely, into three concentric alphabets. There are, however, two distinct improvements in technique. First, the reference becomes more precise: in the third alphabet, i.e., the one with the narrowest reference point, an individual letter is assigned to a single *sententia*, whereas in *Flores paradysi a* the smallest referent was often attached to an entire excerpt, a passage which might be as much as a page in length. Secondly, the reference system as a whole in *Flores b* is divorced from the codex and attached, rather, to the text: whereas in *Flores a* the two larger alphabets designated the opening, and the smallest alphabet recommenced with the letter *A* for every opening or even on every page, in *Flores b* the smallest alphabet simply runs its full course (*A* to *V* or *A* to *T*—rarely, *A* to *X* or *Y*) through however many pages are required by the material, and when this smallest alphabet returns again to the letter *A* the intermediate alphabet moves forward by one letter, irrespective of the physical location in the codex; similarly, the largest alphabet advances by one letter whenever and wherever the intermediate alphabet returns again to the letter *A*. This change would make it possible to copy the *Flores paradysi* without risk of changing the relationship of the reference letters to the text, thus preserving the validity of the index references. It was of course a serious disadvantage in indexes which referred one to folios, columns or pages, that the amount of text in a given folio column or page was altered each time a manuscript was copied, thereby invalidating the original index references for all subsequent copies.[22] Indexes such as those made by Kilwardby to the Fathers referred one to book and chapter. But for a collection of extracts like the *Flores paradysi*, the artificial division via arbitrarily assigned reference-letters seems the ideal solution to the problem of indexing.

The index is followed (f. 18^{r-v}) by a table of contents, i.e., a list by

---

[22] A nice example is quoted by B. Smalley, *English Friars and Antiquity* (Oxford 1960) 35, from an early copy of Holcot on Wisdom, now Oxford, Bodleian Library MS Laud Misc. 562 fol. 194 (10 July 1347, Paris; belonged to Saint-Mary's of Eberbach): "Expliciunt tituli questionum huius libri qui completi fuerunt in die Septem Fratrum anno Domini MCC-CXLVII Parisius per fratrem Henricum de Stetthin de Alamania. Exemplar tabule parvum valuit presertim in cifris. Credo quod post 100 pauce sint vere, sed sub centenario numero major pars est vera, ut patet per se. Crede si vis." The references are to the numbered *lectiones* into which the text is divided—e.g., "228 B" meaning the second quarter of lectio 228. The manuscript, it might be added, was copied in Paris from a university edition— since it has *pecia* notes (87 or 88 *peciae*)—and is dated 1347. Holcot equipped his work with an index (probably that in Laud Misc. 562); but other indexes have been made. For example, the five copies of the work in Oxford today bear four different indexes. The colophons in Laud Misc. 562 are printed in H. O. Coxe, *Bodleian Library Quarto Catalogues* 2: *Laudian Manuscripts*, rev. R. W. Hunt (Oxford 1973) 403-404.

author of the works extracted, with references to the location of the extracts in the *Flores*. As one would expect, the works are listed in the order of their appearance in the *Flores paradysi*—save for a peculiar exception. The works of Saint Augustine are listed in quite different order in the table of *Flores b* from the order in the text of *Flores b*, although occasionally the sequence corresponds for from two to four works; likewise, the table and the text of *b* each present occasional correspondence with, but normally divergence from, the order of the Augustine works in the text of *Flores a* (*a* has no table). For the present, we can offer no explanation for this discrepancy.

The *florilegium* itself consists of extracts from the standard patristic and medieval authorities, followed by an equally large body of extracts from the ancients—a significant change from *Flores a*, which has extracts from only four authors. Saint Augustine dominates the field: he is the first author in the *florilegium*, and extracts from his works occupy at least forty folios. Among the lesser authors it is interesting to see relatively extensive extracts from Chrysostom (ff. 134-138, 150-158) and scarcely any from Isidore (*De summo bono* only). Along with the standard Christian authorities who appear in most twelfth- and thirteenth-century *florilegia* are several *rarae aves*, such as the sermons of Valerianus, fifth-century bishop of Cimiez (now in Nice), and the letter collection of Transmundus of Clairvaux. Others not quite so rare but far from usual are the *Policraticus* of John of Salisbury, the letters of Peter of Blois, the letter collection of Arnulf of Lisieux and the *De fide orthodoxa* of John of Damascus. The school authors and texts are totally lacking.

Among these authors two merit discussion in some detail. The homilies of Valerianus of Cimiez are very rare, surviving in one tenth-century manuscript from Corbie (now B.N. MS lat. 13387 ff. 1-51), with extracts from the homilies in Cues MS 29. Extracts appear in *Flores b* (ff. 143-144ᵛ), and in the quire of a *b*-text added to *Flores paradysi a* (Brussels MS 4785-4793 ff. 135-136). They are drawn from homilies 5, 7, 2, 3, 14, 12, 8, 13, 11, 9 and 20. They apparently derive from the text of Valerianus also represented by Cues MS 29, for in the following instances the *Flores* extracts preserve readings superior to those in the Corbie manuscript: Homily VIII, 2.717 *praeteriret* (Flores): *praeveniret* (Corbie); XIII 5.733 *nec*: *et*; XIII 6.734 *non invidet*: om. Corbie; XI 2.725 *abscesserit* (so also Cues 29): *discesserit*.[23] When Thomas of Ireland incorporated these extracts, many of them emerged in the *Manipulus florum* attributed to Valerius Maximus. The

---

[23] We are grateful to J. P. Weiss, who is preparing an edition of the homilies for *Corpus Christianorum*, for placing these extracts in the stemma of the text.

extracts from the letter collection of Transmundus (ff. 190ᵛ-191) are the only extracts known to have been made from this work.[24] They are detailed enough to permit one to say that they derive from the second collection assembled by Transmundus, that of sixty letters. This collection was represented at Clairvaux in what is now Troyes MS 1531, of which only a list of letters and the final quire survive; and it was also at Saint-Victor (B.N. MS lat. 11382). Both manuscripts date from the first half of the thirteenth century. The second collection was assembled between 1206 and ca. 1216. It is the latest work to be included in *Flores paradysi b*, and provides the only fixed *terminus a quo*.

Perhaps the most interesting feature of *Flores b* is the fact that over a fourth of the work (ff. 158ᵛ-210ᵛ) is devoted to ancient authors, both philosophers and poets. The extent of this is in large part explained by copious borrowings from two popular classical *florilegia*. Nevertheless it makes of *Flores paradysi b* an impressive mixture of Christian and profane authors, more common to mid-twelfth-century *florilegia* like that found in Troyes MS 215 and Douai MS 533 than to those of the thirteenth century like the *Liber exceptionum* or the *Liber Pharetrae*, whose classical authors are basically limited to Christianized ancients such as Seneca.

The major source for extracts from classical authors was the *Florilegium Gallicum.*[25] The borrowings in *Flores paradysi b* are extensive, and do not descend from any of the five known complete manuscripts of the *Florilegium Gallicum*. The *Florilegium* was compiled in the mid-twelfth century, the earliest evidence for its existence being its use by the author of the *Moralium dogma philosophorum*;[26] the oldest surviving manuscripts date

---

[24] Concerning Transmundus see S. J. Heathcote, "The Letter Collections attributed to Master Transmundus," *Analecta Cisterciensia* 21 (1965) 35-109, 167-238. We are grateful to Ann Dalzell, University of Toronto, who is currently engaged in a study of Transmundus, for identifying the "edition" of the collection from which the excerpts were taken.

[25] Concerning the *Florilegium Gallicum* see the series of articles by B. L. Ullman on classical authors in medieval *florilegia*, in *Classical Philology* 23 (1928) 128-174, 24 (1929) 109-132, 25 (1930) 11-21 and 128-154, 26 (1931) 21-30, 27 (1932) 1-42; A. Gagnér, *Florilegium Gallicum*, Skrifter utgivna av Vetenskaps-societeten i Lund 18 (Lund 1936); G. Ranstrand, *Querolusstudien* (Stockholm 1951); J. Hamacher, *Florilegium Gallicum: Prolegomena und Edition der Exzerpte von Petron bis Cicero De oratore*, Lateinische Sprache und Literatur des Mittelalters 5 (Frankfurt-am-Main 1975); R. H. Rouse, "*Florilegia* and Latin Classical Authors in Twelfth- and Thirteenth-Century Orléans," *Viator* 10 (1979, forthcoming); and Rouse, "The *A* Text" 106-108, for a full list of manuscripts and their provenance so far as has been determined.

[26] S. Jeffris, who is writing a doctoral dissertation for the University of California, Los Angeles on the medieval circulation of Suetonius' *Lives*, has recently discovered another early use: William of Saint-Denis borrowed from the *Florilegium Gallicum* the quotations

from the end of the twelfth or beginning of the thirteenth century. Portions of the *Florilegium Gallicum* have been edited. Using these as a basis for collation, we conjecture that the compiler of *Flores paradysi b* employed a manuscript of the eb tradition, though he used neither e (Escorial MS Q I.14 ff. 1-216ᵛ, s. xiii in.) nor b (Berlin MS Diez. B Sant. 60, s. xiii ex./xiv in.) itself. Both are north French, of unknown provenance. The borrowings in *Flores paradysi b* constitute one of the major instances of use of the *Florilegium Gallicum*, and provide an early thirteenth-century witness to its circulation.

A second source for classical extracts was the *Florilegium Angelicum*, compiled in the second half of the twelfth century, probably at Orleans.[27] The compiler of *Flores paradysi b* took extracts from the *Florilegium Angelicum*; but, in contrast with his treatment of material from the *Florilegium Gallicum*, he failed in this case to insert the names of the authors to whom the extracts were attributed. Instead, material from the *Florilegium Angelicum* bears such rubrics as *Sententie diversorum philosophorum* (ff. 186ᵛ-190ᵛ, with an admixture from other sources). The lack of attribution makes it difficult to single out the borrowings from this source. *Flores b*'s borrowings from the *Florilegium Angelicum* include the *Proverbia philosophorum* ("Cum quidam stolidus..."; see pp. 149-150 below) and extracts from Pliny's letters, Cicero's Verrine orations and the letters of Solinus, among other things. Using the rather lengthy extracts from Pliny as a basis for collation, we could unfortunately do no more than rule out all the known surviving manuscripts, whole or partial, of the *Florilegium Angelicum* as the source used by *Flores b*'s compiler.

Mingled with the texts taken from the *Florilegium Gallicum* and the *Florilegium Angelicum* are classical extracts from other sources. The compiler of *Flores b* used the *Distichs of Cato*, which are not found in either *florilegium*. In addition to the Pliny borrowed from the *Florilegium Angelicum*, there are several extracts from another source, probably from a text of the letters themselves.[28] Furthermore, a large number of the Seneca

from Suetonius used in his *Life of Louis VII*. Concerning William's work, see A. Wilmart, "Le dialogue apologétique du moine Guillaume, biographe de Suger," *Revue Mabillon* 32 (1942) 80-118.

[27] See R. H. and M. A. Rouse, "The *Florilegium Angelicum*: Its Origin, Content, and Influence," in *Medieval Learning and Literature: Essays presented to R. W. Hunt*, ed. J. J. G. Alexander and M. Gibson (Oxford 1976) 66-114.

[28] The compiler of *Flores paradysi b* included four extracts (from 1.8.14-15, 2.3.9, 1.3.4 and 2.8.3) drawn from a manuscript of the ten-book (β) or French family of the letters, which is known in at least five manuscripts and two medieval mentions before 1300; see R.

extracts in *Flores paradysi b* do not appear in the two classical *florilegia*. Among them are the extracts from one of the collections of Senecan epigrams which circulated under the title *Proverbia Senece*; those from the letters to Lucilius, for which a manuscript of the first eighty-two letters was used; extracts from the *Copia verborum*, from the *Natural Questions*, and from the tragedies. The body of extracts from this last, known to Seneca scholars (from the addition to *Flores paradysi a*) as the *Eclogae Burgundiae*, derive from a *florilegium* made from the tragedies. This *florilegium* is no longer extant, but it was also used in the first half of the thirteenth century by both Vincent of Beauvais and the writer of Exeter Cathedral MS 3549B.[29] Other portions of *Flores paradysi b* also appear to derive from earlier *florilegia*, but these have yet to be identified.

Flores paradysi b was probably compiled in large part at Villers itself. Despite the destruction of the cream of the Villers library when the abbot's residence burned in the late seventeenth century,[30] one can identify several codices which the compiler used. The extracts from the corpus of Bernard's works are taken from Brussels Bibl. roy. MS 20006-20017 (Van den Gheyn no. 1445) s. xiii. The extracts from Gilbert of Hoyland on the Canticles are supplied from Brussels MS II.938 (Van den Gheyn no. 1433) s. xiii. The second half of the extracts from Jerome's letters come from Brussels MS II.924 (Van den Gheyn no. 986) s. xiii.[31] The first half of the extracts from Jerome's letters corresponds with a manuscript at the nearby Cistercian house of Saint Mary of Aulne (now Brussels MS II.1071, Van den Gheyn no. 985, s. xiii).[32] However, it is more likely that the compiler's source was an identical collection, no longer surviving, at Villers itself. The Villers catalog of 1309 lists both a "prima pars" and a "secunda pars" of Jerome's letters, though only the second survives.[33] Since Villers, like Aulne, was a

---

A. B. Mynors, ed., *C. Plini Caecili Secundi Epistularum Libri Decem* (Oxford 1963) preface. Significant readings occur in the extract from 1.3.4: excude γ, exclude α, ex cute β FP; sortientur $\alpha\beta$ FP, sortiuntur γ; tuum *post* si semel ceperit *hab.* $\beta\gamma$ FP.

[29] Rouse, "The *A* Text" 98-101.

[30] Schuermans, "Bibliothèque de l'abbaye de Villers" 225.

[31] The rubric of the first extract (MS 20030-32 fol. 51ᵛ) reads "Ad Paulinum in secundo volumine." There are extracts from epp. 58, 52, 14, 60, 69, 66, 84, 78, 16, 21, 73, 17, 140, 71, *Ad Tyrasium* (PL 30.278), *Adversus Helvidium* (PL 23.183), *Contra Vigilantium* (PL 23.339), *Contra Ioannem Hierosolymitanum* (PL 23.355), ep. 68, *De honorandis parentibus* (PL 30.145), epp. 147, 6, 125, 7, 107, 64, 48. Brussels MS II.924, lacking its last folios, contains in this order all but the last (ep. 48).

[32] There are extracts from the following: *Ad Damasum papam* (PL 45.1716), epp. 53, 118, 133, 130, 117, 54, 79, *Ad Susannam lapsam* (PL 30.210), epp. 37, 148, 120, 22, 46, 31. Brussels MS II.1071 (Saint Mary of Aulne) contains all of these in this order.

[33] Schuermans, "Bibliothèque de l'abbaye de Villers" 202.

filial of Clairvaux, and since the mother house customarily provided a core collection of patristic works when it founded a new house, such duplication at Aulne and Villers would not be unusual. One would hope, but in vain, to find some trace of the long series of Augustiniana or Ambrosiana, if not among the surviving manuscripts, at least in the Villers library catalog of 1309. The library is very likely to have had a large set of collected works of the Fathers similar to that in Troyes MSS 30-40,[34] which is found at other daughter houses of Clairvaux. However, the existence of rare works in *Flores paradysi b* suggests the possibility that the compiler may have drawn on materials in other libraries to supplement those at Villers. The letter collections of Transmundus and of Valerianus of Cimiez, Pliny's letters, the *Florilegium Gallicum*, the *Florilegium Angelicum*, the *florilegium* of Seneca's tragedies, the *Policraticus*—any or all of these may represent libraries other than Villers itself.

The extracts are apparently in the state in which the compiler copied them from their sources. No effort was made to rearrange or group them in any fashion. They are thus in a state of disorder. A handful of extracts from an author often appears long after the main body of extracts from that author. Medieval texts crop up amid classical texts. This pristine state, while confusing for the reader, does preserve for us a view of the compiler's sources and of his method of work. The compiler clearly made an effort to group his codices by main author before he began. Then he worked through them codex by codex. If a codex containing principally Gregoriana, for example, should also contain one work of Augustine's, this fact would be reflected in the *Flores paradysi* as well, by the occurrence of extracts from Augustine in the midst of the section containing largely extracts from Gregory. If the compiler came across something new and interesting, he would interrupt what he was working on and enter the new material at once. Hence, for example, four folios of extraneous matter (ff. 190^v-194^v), including the letters of Transmundus and of Arnulf of Lisieux, appear in the midst of extracts from the *Florilegium Gallicum*. He sometimes went through a source a second time, as he did, e.g., with the extracts from Seneca's tragedies, from Arnulf of Lisieux's letters, and from the section of extracts from Pliny's letters found in the *Florilegium Angelicum*. In some cases he may have reshuffled his notes; there seems no other way to explain the rearrangement of large portions of the material taken from the *Florilegium Gallicum*.

Virtually all of *Flores paradysi a* was incorporated into *Flores paradysi b*.

---

[34] See n. 47 below.

For example, extracts from nineteen works of Ambrose appear in *b*; for sixteen of these, the extracts are identical with those in *a*, and the extracts from the other three may well have appeared in the portion of *a* now missing. Most of the Augustine extracts in *a* likewise appear in *b* and, again, if we had the large section of *a* now missing (two quires, constituting the end of the Ambrose extracts and the beginning of Augustine's), the correspondence would probably be exact.

The manuscript of *Flores paradysi b*, Brussels MS 20030-32, is written by four hands. The prologue (f. 1) and the table of contents (f. 18^{r-v}) may well be in the compiler's own hand, as the index (ff. 2-18) is clearly in the hand of the indexer, rather than being a fair copy of his work. The text is a fair copy written by two scribes (scribe 1, ff. 19^v-43; scribe 2, ff. 43-234^v). The decoration of the manuscript would place their work between 1230 and 1250. Evidently the scribes simply made a direct copy of the compiler's original notes, to judge from the second thoughts and the disruptions we have mentioned above. Improvement in the ordering of the extracts was left to the compiler of B.N. MS lat. 15982, *Flores paradysi c*.

Sometime in the middle of the thirteenth century someone thoroughly revised the *Flores paradysi*. The extracts were grouped strictly by author, a large number of extracts from Augustine were added, and the majority of the extracts from the *Florilegium Gallicum* were dropped. The prologue and marginal indexing symbols were retained, but a new index was not made. The revision, *Flores paradysi c*, survives in a single manuscript, B.N. lat. 15982, beg. "[prologue:] Flores paradysi pro titulo.... [text: Augustinus in libro confessionum:] Magnus es domine et laudabilis valde...," ends, f. 178, "... nec perficit laudem sed initiatur dignitatem." This manuscript made its way to the Sorbonne, to be used there by Thomas of Ireland in the compilation of the *Manipulus florum*.

Revision has rendered *Flores c* quite unrecognizable as a descendant of *Flores b*, save for the reappearance of the prologue; and it is only with some effort that one can determine what the relationship between Brussels 20030-32 and B.N. 15982 actually is. Clearly, the most significant change was the compiler's attempt to lend order to the haphazard first-draft state of *b*. The compiler of *c* gathered into one place the extracts of a given author that in *b* might be dispersed throughout the volume according to the order in which *b*'s compiler had come upon them. Hence, for each author in *Flores c* one will first meet the main body of extracts from that author's works in *Flores b*, followed by the extracts collected from various scattered locations in *b*. The extracts in this composite have been grouped by work. The result is a distinct improvement over the notebook quality of *Flores b*.

The other major revision was a focusing on patristic authority by means, first of all, of an increase in the already large body of Augustiniana. The compiler of *Flores c* added numerous extracts from Augustine's works, including additional extracts for works already cited in *Flores b*. There is a textual muddle in the Augustine entry (ff. 3^v-75^v), difficult to understand and equally difficult to describe. Two scribes are involved, which may be the source of the difficulty. Hand 1, the hand of the prologue (f. 3^{r-v}), wrote quires 6 and 7 (ff. 52-75^v), which contain the Augustiniana assembled from various parts of *Flores b*. On the last page of quire 7, f. 75vb mid-column, hand 2 begins writing the added Augustiniana peculiar to *Flores c*, starting with extracts from the Confessions, "Magnus es domine...." Folio 75vb ends with "... et usuras exigis. Su-", and obviously continues with what are now quires 2-5 (ff. 4-51^v), beginning "-pererogatur tibi..." and continuing with all the rest of the added Augustiniana, likewise written by hand 2 (with a brief appearance of hand 1, ff. 50va-51rb). Evidently, for reasons of his own, the compiler had intended that his own additions precede the borrowings from *Flores b*, a point he failed to make clear to the scribes. Therefore, he placed quires 2-5 in their present position. To correct their mutilated beginning, he had the initial "Magnus es ... usuras exigis. Su-" from f. 75vb recopied (by hand 1, writing large to fill the space) in the blank column at the end of the prologue, that is, on f. 3vb (see plate 5); and he neglected to cancel the now-meaningless half-column on f. 75^v. In summary, hand 1 has written f. 3^{r-v}, ff. 50va-51rb, ff. 52-75vb, ff. 76-178; hand 2, ff. 4-50va, f. 51^{rb-vb}, f. 75vb.[35]

The focus on patristic authority was further emphasized by the deletion of the majority of extracts from ancient authors other than Cicero and Seneca. With them went the large body of classical texts which the compiler of *Flores b* had taken from the *Florilegium Gallicum*. Of the extracts from this work in *Flores b*, only part of the entries for only a few of the works passed into *Flores paradysi c*, and thence into the *Manipulus florum*. Interestingly enough, the bulk of the classical borrowings from the *Florilegium Angelicum* were retained; perhaps the lack of attributions in *Flores b* disguised their true nature from the compiler of *c*.

The compiler of *Flores paradysi c* evidently intended to compile a new index. The index of *b*, which would have worked for a direct copy, was useless for a sweeping revision. *C*'s compiler retained the description of the index

[35] An alternative possibility is that the transplanting of quires 2-5 is a binder's error. That, however, would entail the assumption that fol. 3vb was written, and the marginal indexing symbols (in correct sequence as the MS now stands) were added, after binding. In particular, the writing of a full column of text in a bound volume seems unlikely.

and of its use, in the prologue copied from *b*; and he entered marginal reference letters in the text, employing the same sort of three-fold alphabet. However, the index was never added and presumably never composed.

B.N. MS lat. 15982 appears to be a finished copy. In contrast to Brussels MS 20030-32, there are virtually no author's slips, afterthoughts or changes of mind (saving the Augustine entry which, for all its complexity, is but one mistake). Where the work was written is not known. Since the only known copy of its source, *Flores b*, was at Villers, probably *Flores c* was written there. The text is written by two precise scribes of the mid-thirteenth century who, strikingly enough, seem to have been Parisian, on the basis of both script and decoration. Somehow, early in its existence, *Flores c* was conveyed (from Villers?) to Paris. It became the Sorbonne's property, evidently early in the history of the college since it was described in the first catalog of the Sorbonne library, ca. 1270.[36] Its donor is not known.

* *

The other major source from which Thomas of Ireland drew extracts for the *Manipulus florum* is the *Liber exceptionum ex libris viginti trium auctorum*. Like the *Flores paradysi*, it is an indexed Cistercian *florilegium*—a collection of some 5800-6000 extracts from twenty-three authorities (all patristic save Seneca), arranged in the order of the books from which the extracts are taken, provided with reference symbols, and followed by an alphabetical index of some 2350 topics.

The *Liber exceptionum* was compiled at Clairvaux, from Clairvaux books, during the first half of the thirteenth century, probably by William of Montague. Troyes MS 186 (s. xiii[1], Clairvaux L.50) is evidently the source for all later copies of the *Liber exceptionum*;[37] it is likely a fair copy of the compiler's own work. At the end (f. 229) is a note in a near-contemporary hand, "Liber Sancte Marie Clarevallis quem compilavit frater Guillermus de Monte Acuto monachus Clarevallis. Ora pro eo, lector." The same note, in the same hand, appears in another somewhat abridged thirteenth-century manuscript of the work, Troyes MS 705 f. 194[v].[38] A conflicting attribution appears in B.N. MS lat. 2115 (s. xiii/xiv; Nicholaus de S. Marcello,[39] s. xiv/xv), in a hand contemporary with the manuscript (f. 155): "Istam

[36] The surviving fragments of the 1270 catalog are edited by Rouse, "Early Library" 245-251.

[37] MS 186 is described without reproduction in C. Samaran and R. Marichal, *Catalogue des manuscrits en écriture latine portant des indications de date, de lieu ou de copiste* 5 (Paris 1965) 615.

[38] Ibid. 618.

[39] Frater Nicholaus gave B.N. MS lat. 17343 (s. xv) to the Carmelites in Paris.

tabulam composuit dominus frater Walterus episcopus Pictavensis de ordine fratrum minorum," and on f. 1, "Incipit tabula de ordine fratrum minorum." This can only refer to Walter of Bruges, o.f.m., bishop of Poitiers (d. 1306); Walter, however, is of the wrong time and place to have been the compiler of an early thirteenth-century work written at Clairvaux. The attribution to William of Montague seems secure, since it represents contemporary local knowledge of a work locally compiled.[40]

William of Montague was prior of Clairvaux, then abbot of La Ferté, and finally in 1227 abbot of Cîteaux.[41] At some time late in life (probably after 1239) he resigned the abbacy and retired to spend his final years as a monk at Clairvaux, where he died on 19 May 1246 (or 1245). Besides the *Liber exceptionum*, William compiled a second work and possibly composed a third. The second work is an indexed collection of extracts taken from the works of Saint Bernard. It survives in two Clairvaux manuscripts, now Troyes mss 497 (s. xiii, Clairvaux H.49)[42] and 911 (s. xv; commissioned by Master Richard de Plumbo; Clairvaux H.50).[43] The work apparently did not circulate outside the walls of Clairvaux. Troyes ms 497, a handsome fair copy, was written and decorated by the same hands that completed the *Liber exceptionum* in ms 186. The Bernard *florilegium* is constructed in the same fashion as the *Liber exceptionum*—that is, it is a large body of extracts (ms 497, ff. 1-179ᵛ) arranged according to the *originalia* from which they were drawn, provided with the same sort of reference symbols as those found in the *Liber exceptionum*, and followed by an alphabetical subject index (35 folios, in ms 497). William may also have written a third work, a *Summa de virtutibus*, known only in Dijon ms 179 (s. xiii; Cîteaux), 40

---

[40] The attribution of this work to John of Limoges is groundless; see Glorieux, *Répertoire des maitres* 2: 254 no. 316p, "Exceptiones e libris xxiii auctorum (ou Resina scripturarum)," among the *dubia*, with manuscript references including Troyes mss 1534 and 1916. The misapprehension arises from the combining of two pieces of information: 1) Troyes ms 1534, from Clairvaux, contains a number of works of John of Limoges, followed by William of Montague's *Liber exceptionum*. 2) Troyes ms 1916 (s. xii/xiii; Clairvaux L.79) contains a *florilegium* called "Resina scripturarum Johannis Clarevallis monachi." The *Resina* is on no account to be equated with the *Liber exceptionum*; and nowhere is there a manuscript of the *Liber exceptionum* with a manuscript attribution, early or late, to John of Limoges.

[41] William is as yet unstudied. There is a short biographical notice by Petit-Radel, "Guillaume iii de Montaigu...," in *Histoire littéraire de la France* 18 (Paris 1835) 338-346. "Guillaume, abbé de Cîteaux," the subject of a notice by Daunou in the same volume (149-152), is of course the same William of Montague.

[42] Samaran and Marichal 5: 618. An eighteenth-century hand notes on fol. 1 that the work was completed in 1220.

[43] Ibid. 664. Richard de Plumbo commissioned this ms, according to Pierre de Virey. Richard also commissioned Laon ms 34 (AD 1469).

folios. A seventeenth-century hand, frequently seen in Cîteaux manuscripts, has noted on the bottom of f. 2, "Fratris Guillelmi monachi summa de virtutibus. Claruit frater Guillelmus de Monte Acuto, monachus Clarae vallis auctor hujus libri, anno 1240." Finally, William compiled or directed the compilation of a series of *notule* primarily from canon-law texts, which follow the shortened *Liber exceptionum* in Troyes MS 705;[44] among them are works of Raymond of Pennafort that date from 1234, and Geoffrey of Trani's *summa* on decretal rubrics which dates from 1241-1243. The inclusion of these—an example of the rapid movement of school books to Clairvaux—demonstrates that William of Montague was still active in the years just prior to his death in 1246.

We know that both of the indexed *florilegia* were compiled at Clairvaux, since both the *Liber exceptionum* and the Bernard *florilegium* are based upon *originalia* from the Clairvaux library. One wonders whether William compiled them in his early years as a monk at Clairvaux, or after he retired to the abbey at the end of his life. The hands of Troyes MSS 186 and 497 suggest the later rather than the earlier period in William's life; however, paleographic evidence is not sufficiently precise to settle a question of dates that range over twenty-five years at most. The nature of the works is perhaps more suggestive of an old man in reflective retirement than of a young monk just beginning a climb to the highest position of his order. In sum, we feel the date of composition of the indexed *florilegia* lies in the years between 1239 and William's death in 1246, but we recognize this as largely a subjective judgment.

The *Liber exceptionum* (beg. "Augustinus de achademicis. Licentius: Non parvum in philosophia...," ends "... Meliorem facies ingratum ferendo, peiorem exprobando.") contains extracts from the works of the following authors: Augustine, Gregory, Jerome, Ambrose, Hilary, Isidore, Origen, Cassiodorus, John Chrysostom, Basil, Gregory of Nazianzus, Cyprian, Leo, Ephraem, Caesarius of Arles, Fulgentius, Maximus, Bede, Prosper, Peter of Ravenna, John Cassian, Boethius and Seneca.[45] Extracts from the works of the first four authors comprise over four-fifths of the text; Augustine's alone account for half of the entire work. According to the compiler's statement

---

[44] *Catalogue général des manuscrits des bibliothèques publiques des départements*, 4° ser. (Paris 1855) 2: 297: "Notule ex summa magistri Raymundi ... de casibus; ... ex summa ejusdem de matrimonio; ... ex summa magistri Goffredi de Trano super titulis decretalium; ... ex apparatu decretorum; ... ex summa magistri Guillermi Autissiodorensis de mundo creato; ... ex summa magistri Herberti decani Autissiodorensis de sacramentis; ... ex libro magistri Petri cantoris Parisiensis de consiliis; ... ex apparatu decretalium."

[45] The contents are analyzed in some detail by B. Bertomeu, *Los códices medievales de la catedral de Tortosa* (Barcelona 1962) 296-302.

(Troyes MS 186 f. 228ᵛ), he has not tampered with the wording of his extracts; and each passage as it stands, from the paragraph mark at its beginning to the paragraph mark which indicates the next excerpt, has been neither added to nor subtracted from.[46]

We are fortunate in the case of the *Liber exceptionum* to be able to identify among the large number of surviving Clairvaux books the actual manuscripts from which William compiled his work. Frequently, particularly among the works of Augustine and Ambrose, the order of the works extracted reproduces the sequence found in surviving codices. For Saint Augustine, William has used the great folio "edition" of the works of Augustine and others in ten volumes prepared at Cîteaux in the mid-twelfth century, which for a certain time apparently formed the original nucleus of the library of each succeeding daughterhouse.[47] Augustine works 1-17 in the *Liber exceptionum* come from Troyes MS 40.I (Clairvaux F.78), works 18-29 from MS 40.II (F.79), 30-38 from MS 40.III (F.80), and so on. Ambrose works 1-5 William drew from Troyes MS 874 (s. xii, F.47), 6-10 from MS 284 (s. xii, F.45), 11-20 from MS 39 (s. xii, F.44), and so on. The works of Cyprian are taken from Troyes MS 37 (s. xii, I.19). On occasion, a single codex supplied the extracts from more than one author's works. Thus, Troyes MS 38 (s. xii, F.29) supplied extracts from one work each of Ambrose and Chrysostom; MS 234 (s. xii, F.20), one work of Basil and one of Chrysostom; and MS 5 (s. xii, G.61) supplied all the extracts from works of Gregory of Nazianzus, all of Prosper, and one work of Chrysostom.

In some of these manuscripts—the folio volumes of Augustine, for example—we find notations which are probably physical vestiges of William's

---

[46] "Notandum quod auctoritates que hic continentur sunt omnino sicut sumpte sunt a libris originalibus. Ita quod a paragrapho usque ad paragraphum sequentem vel unum capitulorum vel librorum vel rubricam aliam, continuantur verba auctorum. Et ideo videat siquis transcripserit, quod nichil minuat vel addat vel mutet de paragraphis vel rubricis."

[47] Regarding the twelfth-century library of Clairvaux and this edition of the Fathers see T. Humpfner, "Archivum et bibliotheca Cistercii et quatuor primarum filiarum ejus," *Analecta sacri ordinis Cisterciensis* 2 (1946) 140-144; A. Wilmart, "L'ancienne bibliothèque de Clairvaux," *Collectanea ordinis Cisterciensium reformatorum* 11 (1949) 101-127, 301-319, repr. from *Mémoires de la Société académique de l'Aube*, ser. 3, 54 (1917) 125-190; J. de Ghellinck, "Une édition ou une collection médiévale des *opera omnia* de Saint Augustin," in *Liber Floridus: Mittellateinischen Studien P. Lehmann...* (St. Ottilien 1950) 63-82; J. Leclercq, "Les manuscrits de l'abbaye de Liessies," *Scriptorium* 6 (1952) 51-52; W. M. Green, "Mediaeval Recensions of Augustine," *Speculum* 29 (1954) 531-536. Plates and a detailed description of MS 40.I-III, VI and IX are given by Samaran and Marichal 5: 449-451 and pl. CXCIV. Regarding the later history of the library and the catalog of 1472 compiled by Pierre de Virey see A. Vernet, "Un abbé de Clairvaux bibliophile," *Scriptorium* 6 (1952) 80-83. Professor Vernet has in progress an edition of this catalog with descriptive notices of the Clairvaux manuscripts.

work in compiling the *Liber exceptionum*. Passages which reappear in the *Liber exceptionum*, and some others as well, are marked with a vertical *nota* in the margins of the text. We suppose that William read or skimmed through the *originalia*, designating with this symbol passages for inclusion in the *florilegium*. These passages were later copied out, by William himself or a scribe.

For purposes of reference William imposed artificial divisions upon his collection of extracts. In contrast with the triple alphabet of the *Flores paradysi*, the *Liber exceptionum* uses a combination of roman numerals and letters of the alphabet. The entire text is divided into forty-four numbered *distinctiones*, of roughly equivalent size (nearly five folios each). The number of a given *distinctio* appears in the upper left-hand margin of each opening, repeated on each of the openings required to complete that *distinctio*, thus: "iiii^a distinctio." Each *distinctio* is subdivided by marginal letters of the alphabet, customarily only two or three to the page, so that one can consider as a crude gauge that each letter represents something like three-quarters of a column of text. These subdividing alphabets usually run from *A* through *T*, though they are occasionally shortened by a few letters to enable the beginning of a new *distinctio* to coincide with a change in author. As William explains in his concluding statement following the index, the reference symbols of numbers and letters should be regarded as if they were *libri* and *capitula*, respectively.

The reference system is put to work in making the *Liber exceptionum* searchable, by means of an elaborate index similar to that in *Flores paradysi b*. The index consists of approximately 2200 subjects, beginning with *Abducere, Abesse, Abicere, Abiectio, Abiectus, Abyssus, Abluere, Abscidere, Abscondere, Absolvere, Absolutio, Abstinere, Abstinencia, Abuti, Accendere, Accidens, Accidia, Accipere, Accusare, Accusatio, Accusator*.... The subjects are arranged in erratic alphabetical order; while the alphabetization is often absolute, frequently it does not extend beyond the first two or three letters of the word. The index proper is followed by a further list of some 100 complex theological concepts, e.g., "Quod nichil potest digne dici de deo," or "De cognitione dei et quod non potest plene cognosci in presenti vita." The arrangement of these seems haphazard, though perhaps there is an underlying logic which we have not discerned. William offers as many as 101 references for an individual topic (*Peccatum*). Other heavily-cited topics are *Corpus, Deus, Dolor, Facere, Finis, Homo, Humilitas, Misericordia, Mors, Natura, Oratio, Penitentia, Voluntas, Virtus* and *Vita*. Each individual reference consists of a number, a letter, and a one- or two-word *lemma*; for example, "*Dissimulare*: ... xliiii B Manet." This indicates that an extract pertaining to the topic *dissimulare* is to be found in *distinctio* xliiii, section

B, somewhere in the paragraph that begins with the word *Manet*. This system of reference is less confusing and more readable, involving numbers, letters, and words, than that of the *Flores paradysi* which presents one with a string of letters sometimes hard to distinguish. It has the disadvantage, in comparison with the index of *Flores b*, of being less precise: the narrowest point of reference in the *Liber exceptionum* shares with *Flores paradysi b* the advantage of a reference system which is attached to portions of the text rather than to portions of one codex, which would permit the index to serve without alteration in any subsequent copies. Unlike *Flores b*, however, the permanent validity of the *Liber exceptionum*'s index was repeatedly demonstrated in fact.

Because it originated in a more cosmopolitan abbey than did the *Flores paradysi*, the *Liber exceptionum* had a greater opportunity for dissemination. It moved to both Paris and Oxford. Besides three manuscripts at Clairvaux itself, Troyes MSS 186 (s. xiii, Clairvaux L.50), 705 (s. xiii, L.71) and 1534 (s. xiii/xiv, D.89), the *Liber exceptionum* survives in seven other manuscripts: B.N. MSS lat. 2115 (s. xiii/xiv, Nicholaus de Sancto Marcello) and 15983 (s. xiii, Sorbonne, ex leg. Gerard of Abbeville; the manuscript used by Thomas of Ireland); Tortosa, Biblioteca de la catedral MS 139 (s. xiii, N. France); London, British Library MS Royal 7 B.xiii (s. xiii ex., Rochester); Oxford, Trinity College MS 41 (s. xiii, Trinity Coll., "ex dono fundatori," i.e., Thomas Pope); Worcester Cathedral MS F.51 (s. xiv); and Klosterneuburg, Stiftsbibliothek MS 331 (s. xv, Klosterneuburg).

The text of the *Liber exceptionum* was stable; we find no indication of the sort of revising and reworking evident in the *Flores paradysi*. Troyes MSS 705 and 1534 are independent abridgements of Troyes MS 186, retaining the same sequence and the same rubrics found in MS 186. The result of these changes is merely abbreviation, not revision. The manuscript of the *Liber exceptionum* used by Thomas of Ireland (now B.N. MS lat. 15983) presents a minor change in the index. The writer of this text has attempted to improve the index by incorporating the concluding list of 100 concepts into the alphabetical structure of the subject index. Strict alphabetization dependent on the first word would be meaningless, since all one hundred of the concepts begin with either *De* or *Quod*. The writer used, instead, the first major word as the denominator. Thus, following all of the subjects which begin with the letter *A*, the writer has added "De abrenunciatione proprietatis et proprie voluntatis et potestatis, Quod non amittitur sine dolore quod habetur cum amore, De tempore antichristi"; and similar additions to the index occur under each succeeding letter of the alphabet. Ironically, he was unable or unwilling to dispose of all hundred of them alphabetically, so that the intended improvement is incomplete; a list of twenty-eight concepts, arranged haphazardly, remains at the end of the alphabetical sequence. This change is not revision, but merely tinkering. It is significant only because it illustrates the ubiquity of the impulse to alphabetize and to increase "searchability," epitomized in the *Flores paradysi* and in the *Liber exceptionum* itself.

* * *

Not only do we know that Thomas of Ireland used these two Cistercian *florilegia* in compiling the *Manipulus florum*, but we can identify among the surviving Sorbonne books the very manuscripts that he used: B.N. MSS lat. 15982 (*Flores paradysi c*) and 15983 (*Liber exceptionum*). Both are well written, and both provide clear citations to their own sources—points which no doubt recommended them to Thomas. Moreover, each bears physical evidence of Thomas' use. For example, in the *Liber exceptionum* (MS 15983) there are numerous instances in which a marginal mark—the word "Nota" or a simple line—singles out a passage which has been selected for use in the *Manipulus florum*. A noteworthy example is the marginal mark in MS 15983 f. 114^v, beside the first three sentences ascribed to Seneca *De quattuor virtutibus*; in the *Manipulus* the same three sentences appear, in the same sequence, with the same ascription.[48] Signs of Thomas' use of MS 15982 are even more telling. There is, for example, the note in Thomas' own hand on f. 3^v recording the fact that the index mentioned in the prologue of the *Flores paradysi* is not to be found in MS 15982 (see plate 5): "Nota quod hic deficit tabula ad inveniendum diversas auctoritates concordantes in unam sentenciam que debet esse secundum ordinem alphabeti de diversis vocabulis ita quod post quodlibet vocabulum diverse littere combinate que ponuntur in margine subscribantur sicut docet iste prologus procedens. Sed in fine istius libri invenies tabulam ad inveniendum diversos auctores ac libros partiales ipsorum quorum dicta et auctoritates in hoc libro colliguntur." There are also examples of passages marked in MS 15982 which reappear in the *Manipulus*. Most revealing of all, however, is the fact that Thomas in the *Manipulus florum* consistently ascribes quotations from the *Policraticus* to John Chrysostom; this is directly traceable to an error in MS 15982. The extracts from the *Policraticus* in MS 15982 begin on the bottom of f. 132^v, immediately following the several pages of excerpts from the works of Chrysostom. However, the running headline across the top of the two-page opening continues to say, "Johannes [f. 132^v] Crisostomus [f. 133]," and again on f. 133^v, the final page of

---

[48] Such instances are, of course, rare because the *Manipulus florum* is arranged topically.

the *Policraticus* extracts, "Crisostomus." Added to the mistake in the running headline is the fact that the rubric in the text itself is ambiguous, at best: "Item ex libro qui dicitur Policratico Johannis de curialium nugis et vestigiis philosophorum" (f. 132ᵛ). It is true that both Thomas of Ireland in the *Manipulus florum* and the anonymous compiler in the *Flores paradysi* consistently refer to John Chrysostom simply as Chrysostom, without Christian name. But—given the facts that the running headlines (as opposed to the rubrics) do say "Johannes Crisostomus," that the running headline repeats Chrysostom's name on two pages which are pure John of Salisbury, and that, obviously, Thomas had no independent acquaintance with the *Policraticus*—Thomas quite naturally assumed that "John's *Policraticus*" was to be interpreted as "John Chrysostom's...." There is, of course, not the slightest tradition of such a misattribution; and if MS 15982 did not survive to provide the key, the ascription of the *Policraticus* to Chrysostom would remain one of the more baffling puzzles posed by the *Manipulus florum*.

The two, *Flores paradysi c* and the *Liber exceptionum ex libris viginti trium auctorum*, provided Thomas of Ireland with well over half of the titles which he cites. In the *Manipulus florum* Thomas includes roughly 6000 extracts, and cites as sources for them some 560 titles; it is better to call them *titles* than *works* since, as we shall see, a number of them are not actually works. Of these 560, the *Liber exceptionum* probably served as the sole source for all the extracts ascribed to some 175 titles; *Flores paradysi c* was probably the sole source for the excerpts ascribed to some 70 other titles. Moreover, there is considerable overlap in the contents of the *Flores paradysi* and the *Liber exceptionum*, despite the fact that neither of these works seems to have drawn upon the other. Thus, the two of them must be considered joint source (i.e., the source was either or both) for the extracts ascribed to some 75 more titles. In sum, all of the extracts purportedly derived from some 320 titles are in fact taken from these two major sources. In addition, the two *florilegia* are partial sources for the extracts ascribed to some thirty other titles.

These two *florilegia* provide a link, without intermediaries or transmitters, between the university world of the early fourteenth century and the milieu of Cistercian monasticism of the early thirteenth century. Via the *Liber exceptionum*, the *Manipulus florum* in effect is presenting extracts compiled from the twelfth-century collection of patristic manuscripts at Clairvaux. Via the *Flores paradysi* the *Manipulus* is perpetuating the literary interests of the Cistercian house of Villers-en-Brabant, and of the external sources used by the *Flores'* compiler. The *Manipulus* even reproduces a small amount of the mid-twelfth-century *Florilegium Gallicum*, transmitted

through the *Flores paradysi.* In turn, Thomas of Ireland served as the intermediate link in the chain which reached back from later fourteenth-, fif-
teenth- and sixteenth-century writers to the two Cistercian *florilegia.* For
example, one can trace back the genealogy of individual quotations in Geoffrey Chaucer's *Tale of Melibee* via the *Livre de Mellibée et Prudence*
through the *Manipulus florum* to the *Liber exceptionum* and the *Flores
paradysi*; or of quotations in Christine de Pisan's *Epitre d'Othea* via the
Chapelet des vertus through the *Manipulus florum* to the *Liber exceptionum* and the *Flores paradysi*—unexpected twelfth- or thirteenth-century
monastic roots feeding the literary renaissance of Northern Europe.

B. *Minor sources*

In addition to his use of the Cistercian *florilegia,* Thomas of Ireland
borrowed extracts from three other intermediate sources, and made extracts
of his own from a fair number of *originalia.*

The most interesting of the intermediate sources is the *Florilegium
Angelicum,* so called because the dedication copy is a manuscript of the
Biblioteca Angelica in Rome.[49] Although less well known today, it actually
enjoyed a wider circulation than did the similar, near-contemporary, *Florilegium Gallicum.* The *Florilegium Angelicum,* compiled in the second half
of the twelfth century probably at Orleans, was a collection of extracts
chosen for their eloquence, designed for use in letter-writing. Among them
were extracts from such rare texts as Pliny's letters, some of Cicero's rarer
orations (i.e., those in Paris B.N. MS lat. 7794), the *Querolus,* Ennodius
and Censorinus.

The *Florilegium Angelicum* survives basically complete in eleven manuscripts: Cambridge, Saint John's College MS 97 ff. 214-229[v] (s. xiv, Saint
Augustine's Canterbury); Evreux, Bibliothèque municipale MS 1 ff. 64-
114[v] (s. xiii med., France; Lyre); Florence, Laurenziana MS Strozzi 75
(s. xii[2], France); London, British Library MS Add. 25104 (s. xv, Italy);
Paris, Arsenal MS 1116E (s. xiii[1], France); Rome, Bibl. Angelica MS 1895
(s. xii[2], France); Sydney, University Library MS Nicholson 2 (s. xiii[1],
France); and Vatican MSS Vat. lat. 3087 (s. xiii, France) and 5994 (s.
xiii/xiv, France), Reg. lat. 1575 (s. xiii, France), and Palat. lat. 957 (s.
xii[2], France). Of these, Angelica 1895 is the dedication copy and Palat. lat.
957 is the exemplar from which it was copied. It survives in part or in
revision in nine other codices.[50] The manuscript which Thomas of Ireland

---

[49] See Rouse and Rouse, "*Florilegium Angelicum.*"
[50] Auxerre, Bibl. mun. MS 234 (s. xiv[2]; France); Brussels, Bibl. roy. MS 10098-10105,

used was one of that splendid collection of codices brought together by Richard de Fournival in the first half of the thirteenth century, which passed to the Sorbonne with the bequest of Gerard of Abbeville in 1272.[51] Fournival's manuscript of the *Florilegium Angelicum* has left no trace in the Sorbonne library catalogs, which is unfortunate but not unusual: books which were in use or not in the library at the time the 1338 catalog was made are represented in that catalog by a number only, without a description; and books which had been placed in the chained collection disappear almost as thoroughly, unless one can piece together a description from the incomplete analytical catalog (ca. 1320). However, Fournival himself left a lengthy description of the codex in his catalog, the *Biblionomia*, no. 84: "Censorini exceptiones florum ex operibus sanctorum et phylosophorum moralium: primo quidem de libro Machrobii Saturnariorum vel Saturnarium. Secundo proverbia quorumdam philosophorum. Tercio de epystolis beati Jheronimi. Quarto de libro Epuleii Madaurensis de Deo Socratis. Quinto de epystolis Plinii secundi. Sexto de harenga Tulii pridie quam in exilium iret. Septimo cum senatui gratias egit. Octavo de epystolis Sidonii. Nono de libro Senece de beneficiis. Decimo de epystolis eiusdem ad Lucilium. Undecimo sententie quorumdam philosophorum. Duodecimo de libro Tulii Tusculanarum. Tercio decimo de libro Agellii noctium Atticarum. Quarto decimo de comedia Plauti que dicitur Allularia."[52]

The surviving manuscript which most closely approximates the description of Fournival's manuscript in contents and sequence is Vatican Palat. lat. 957 ff. 97-184[v]. It was written in north France in the second half of the twelfth century and contains marginal notes in an early fourteenth-century French hand. MS 957 includes the following: excerpts from Macrobius, the *Proverbia philosophorum*, excerpts from Jerome's letters, from Apuleius, from Pliny's letters, from Cicero's orations, from Sidonius' letters, from Seneca's *De beneficiis* and *Ad Lucilium*, the *Sententie philosophorum*, excerpts from the *Tusculan Disputations*, from Aulus Gellius, from Cicero's *Verrines* and from Ennodius. At the end of f. 176[v] (quire 10) the text breaks in mid-sentence, indicating that a portion of the manuscript is

---

Van den Gheyn 1334 (s. xiii[1]; France); Leiden, Bibl. Rijksuniversiteit B.P.L. MS 191B (s. xiii[2]); London, British Library MS Royal 11 A.v (s. xii-xiii; Merton Priory, Surrey); Oxford, Trinity Coll. MS 18 (s. xiv[2]; England); Paris, B.N. MSS lat. 1860 (s. xiii; S. France); and 15172 (s. xiii[1]; France; Saint-Victor); Rome, Bibl. Angelica MS 720 (s. xiii; France); and Vatican, Reg. lat. MS 358 (s. xv; France; Tours).

[51] See R. H. Rouse, "Manuscripts belonging to Richard de Fournival," *Revue d'histoire des textes* 3 (1973) 253-269.

[52] Quoted from L. Delisle, *Le cabinet des manuscrits de la Bibliothèque nationale* 2 (Paris 1874) 529.

missing; the missing quire doubtless contained the *Querolus* ("Aulularia") and the brief extract from Censorinus, which normally conclude the *Florilegium Angelicum*. Palat. lat. 957 continues (ff. 177-184ᵛ) with a quire containing extracts from Gregory's letters and from Julius Paris' *Epitome* of Valerius Maximus, again with a break at the end indicating another missing portion. This last gathering is written by a hand contemporary with that which wrote the first ten quires; it bears, unexpectedly, the signature "l." Discounting this added gathering, Fournival's description is identical with Palat. lat. 957 to and including the extracts from Gellius; the differences consist, first, of the fact that Fournival does not name the *Verrines* and Ennodius as part of his codex, and secondly, that his manuscript concluded with extracts from Pseudo-Plautus that are no longer found in MS 957. While the *Querolus* extracts probably appeared in the gathering now missing in MS 957, the absence from Fournival's enumeration of the extracts from the *Verrines* and from Ennodius makes it very unlikely that MS 957 is the missing Fournival codex. In any event, however, it is evident that Palat. lat. 957 is a reliable witness to the text which Thomas of Ireland saw.

Thomas used the former Fournival manuscript as a source for quotations from the Greek philosophers. He cites the source as "Proverbia philosophorum," but examination reveals that he made use of both proverb collections, the one called *Proverbia philosophorum* and the one called *Sententie philosophorum* as well. *Flores paradysi b* and *c*, among their borrowings from the *Florilegium Angelicum*, likewise included portions of the *Proverbia philosophorum*; but they are without rubric, and the extracts are different from those which Thomas chose. These two collections, the *Proverbia* and the *Sententie*, have similarities which serve both to link them to one another and to distinguish them from many of the other Latin collections of Greek aphorisms which circulated in the Middle Ages. For one thing, they both preserve the names of the authors, or purported authors, of the proverbs, which is not the case with Publilius Syrus, for example, or with the Pseudo-Senecan collections. Secondly, they both are arranged in roughly topical fashion, whereas Publilius Syrus' aphorisms and the Proverbs of Seneca are alphabetized according to the first word of each proverb. Both of these aspects must have appealed to Thomas; the topical organization facilitated his use of the collections, and the presence of proper names fit in with his practice of normally citing the original source even when he was employing an intermediate source. A third similarity between the *Proverbia* and the *Sententie* is the existence of an appreciable amount of duplication. There are roughly 200 proverbs in the *Proverbia*, and 85 in the

Sententie; 25 proverbs are duplicates, which for the *Sententie* especially constitute a significant proportion.

Both of these collections of proverbs were edited by Eduard Wölfflin in his *Caecilii Balbi De nugis philosophorum* (Basel 1855),[53] in which he treats the two as different recensions of a lost archetype. However, the name Caecilius Balbus stems from a passing reference in the *Policraticus*, and the title derives, through a series of misunderstandings, from the title of the *Policraticus, sive de nugis curialium et de vestigiis philosophorum*. Furthermore, for as far back in time as one can trace them, the two collections have separate existences. The *Proverbia philosophorum*, beg. "Cum quidam stolidus audienti Pitagora diceret: Malle secum...," survives in numerous manuscripts, among the oldest of which is Clm 6292 ff. 84-91 (s. x/xi, Freising).[54] The compiler and the date of compilation are unknown. Meyer concluded, a century ago, that the *Proverbia philosophorum* was a Roman translation of a Greek *florilegium*, with a few interpolations from Publilius Syrus' proverb collection.[55] The *Sententie philosophorum*, beg. "Nulle sunt occultiores insidie quam hec...," also survives in numerous manuscripts, among the oldest of which is B.N. MS lat. 2772 (s. ix; Lyon?). The collection was known to Heiric of Auxerre.[56] Concerning its date and origin we can add nothing. The two proverb collections seem first to appear together, i.e., in a single codex, in the *Florilegium Angelicum*. Thus, although there were other manuscripts of each collection in circulation (none, that we know of, at the Sorbonne), Thomas' conflation of the two of them betrays the *Florilegium Angelicum* as his source.

From these two collections of Greek aphorisms Thomas of Ireland took twenty-two extracts; he ascribes them on six occasions simply to the collection itself, "In proverbia philosophorum," and on all other occasions to the supposed author, either with or without mention of the source, e.g., "Diogenes in proverbia philosophorum" or simply "Diogenes." To further

---

[53] E. Wölfflin, *Caecilii Balbi De nugis philosophorum* (Basel 1855) 18-35, the *Proverbia*, from Clm 6292; and 37-43, the *Sententie*, from B.N. MSS lat. 2772, 4718 and 4887.

[54] The manuscript represents a collection of texts that was, at an earlier stage, at the Court Library of Charlemagne. See F. Newton, "Tibullus in Two Grammatical *Florilegia* of the Middle Ages," *Transactions of the American Philological Association* 93 (1962) 253-286.

[55] W. Meyer, *Die Sammlungen der Spruchverse des Publilius Syrus* (Leipzig 1877) 44. See A. F. Pauly and G. Wissowa, eds., *Paulys Real-Encyclopädie der classischen Altertumswissenschaft* 3 (Stuttgart 1899) 1196-1198 and the works cited there; F. Giancotti, *Ricerche sulla tradizione manoscritta delle sentenze di Publilio Siro* (Messina 1963); and R. Quadri, ed., *I collectanea di Eirico di Auxerre*, Spicilegium Friburgense 11 (Fribourg 1966).

[56] Edited by Quadri 134-138. Items 1-37 are the same as the text published by Wölfflin; thereafter the collections, though similar, tend to vary.

complicate matters, Thomas also used on occasion a manuscript of the alphabetically arranged collection of proverbs that circulated under Seneca's name, which at times he cites as "Seneca" and at times simply as "In proverbiis." Thomas may have used other portions of the *Florilegium Angelicum*, but thus far we have not noticed any such use.

The two remaining intermediate sources, the *Decretum* and the *Gloss*, are not *florilegia* in any true sense; but Thomas of Ireland mined them for quotations as if they were. For entries taken from the *Decretum*, Thomas cites the secondary source quite consistently, thus: "Augustinus de unico baptismo libro v°, et ponitur de conse. di. 4 ca. Nunc autem" (*Baptismus a*). Obviously, there is no way to insure that the *Manipulus florum* does not contain extracts masquerading as citations taken directly from *originalia* which were actually taken from the *Decretum*. However, attempts to uncover unacknowledged borrowings from the *Decretum* proved fruitless. Therefore it is likely that, even if there were an occasional omission, there was no large body of them; Thomas' borrowings from the *Decretum*, in other words, can be limited essentially to those extracts which he labels as such. The *Decretum* was Thomas' sole source for roughly 60 of the 560 titles cited in the *Manipulus florum*.

The last intermediate source of which we are aware is the *Glossa ordinaria*. Thomas of Ireland cites the *Gloss* by name for some fifty-five entries, usually including the name of the author as well: "Augustinus, et est in glossa Jacobi 2 super illud: Fratres mei, nolite in personarum acceptione etc." (*Acceptio personarum a*); occasionally the name of both author and work are cited via the *Gloss*: "Augustinus super Johannem, et in glosa I Timothei i" (*Adventus domini a*). At times Thomas is content to cite the *Gloss* itself as his authority: "Glosa super illud proverbiorum xxv: Vetus aquilo dissipat pluvias et facies tristis linguas detrahentem" (*Detractio d*). In addition to the entries ascribed to the *Gloss*, there are some forty other titles, comprising about seventy-five entries, which probably came from the *Gloss*, even though Thomas neglected to cite it. These unattributed borrowings are easy to discern because of the manner in which Thomas phrases his citation. For example, citations to Augustine's *Tractatus in evangelium Ioannis*, which read simply "Augustinus super Johannem," are derived in part from the *Liber exceptionum*, in part from a manuscript of the work itself. In contrast, the citation "Augustinus super illud Johannis: Hec est vita eterna ut cognoscant" (*Beatitudo a*), by its reference to a specific verse and by its variation from the wording of the other citations, indicates that it probably comes from the *Gloss*.

Thomas of Ireland made extensive use of previous compendia to compile his own *florilegium*, a common practice. A more interesting aspect of his work is the extent to which he relied, as well, upon manuscripts of *originalia* or whole works to supply extracts for the *Manipulus florum*. The precise degree of his use of *originalia* cannot be known, and certainly cannot be demonstrated, save in an edition of the *Manipulus* itself. However, one can determine enough to form some notion of the scope involved.

The most promising place to begin an investigation of Thomas' use of *originalia* is with those works cited in the *Manipulus* (1) which do not normally appear in the homiletic *florilegia*, (2) which were represented by only one manuscript at the Sorbonne, or (3) for which Thomas' own copy survives. Within such restrictions it becomes relatively easy to verify whether Thomas did or did not use the *originale*. An important case in point— Thomas' use of Pliny's *Natural History*—actually provides a confirmation in reverse. The Sorbonne lost its Pliny sometime after 1338. In the mid-sixteenth century G. Pelicier collated manuscripts of the *Natural History* in and around Paris, entering the variants for books 1-4 in his copy of the 1545 Froben edition of Pliny.[57] The variant readings which are designated *Sor.* correspond to the text in B.N. MS lat. 6803;[58] and Thomas of Ireland's use of Pliny confirms the identification of this manuscript as the Sorbonne Pliny. Thomas cites the *Natural History* only eight times in the *Manipulus florum*. He has marked in the margin of MS lat. 6803 (f. 63), with strokes in hard point and a *nota*, the passages which constitute two of his borrowings, *Homo m* and *n*.

Thomas cites Maimonides ("Raby Moyses") only twice, *Discere l* and *Scriptura sacra bq*. The Latin *Guide of the Perplexed*, translated only in the 1240s, was a rare work which exists today in twelve manuscripts, only three of them from the thirteenth century.[59] Certainly material from this work was not available to Thomas through *florilegia*. B.N. MS lat. 15973 (s. xiii) is the copy left to the Sorbonne by Gerard of Abbeville; it bears a dry-point

---

[57] The volume is now Paris, B.N. Rés. S.118. For this information we are grateful to Dr. Herman Walter of Duisberg who is preparing a study of the manuscripts of the *Natural History*.

[58] The early history of this codex is unknown. At the Sorbonne Pliny's *Natural History* was chained, and thus there is no entry in the 1338 catalog to record the donor or the beginning of the second folio. MS 6803 dates from the second half of the thirteenth century; certain pages (fols. 202-204, 213, 218, 219) had been remade before the end of the century. It passed to the Royal Library via Colbert (no. 2417), who also owned other Sorbonne volumes.

[59] Concerning the Latin Maimonides see W. Kluxen, "Literargeschichtliches zum lateinischen Moses Maimonides," *Revue de théologie au Moyen Age* 21 (1954) 22-35; idem, "Maimonides und die Hochscholastik," *Philosophisches Jahrbuch* 63 (1955) 151-165; and idem, "Die Geschichte des Maimonides im lateinischen Abendland als Beispiel einer Christlich-judischen Begegnung," *Miscellanea medievalia* 4: *Judentum im Mittelalter* (Berlin 1966) 146-166.

nota in the margin (ff. 3ᵛ, 17ᵛ) beside each of the passages excerpted by Thomas. The volume bears only a few other *nota* marks throughout, perhaps marking passages of interest which Thomas did not use after all.

Walter Map's *Valerius ad Rufinum*, like the Latin Maimonides, appeared on the university scene too recently for Thomas to have found portions of it in preachers' *florilegia*. The use of Map by John of Wales constitutes the only appearance of this work in university circles prior to Thomas' use of it.[60] *Valerius ad Rufinum* is cited in the *Manipulus florum* three times under the heading *Mulier*, and eight times (extracts *r-ab*) under *Coniugium*. In the Sorbonne *Valerius*, now B.N. MS lat. 16359 ff. 221-225, there is a marginal *nota* beside the passage (f. 221ᵛ) which heads this latter series in the *Manipulus*.

When Thomas owned a manuscript of a work cited in the *Manipulus florum*, it is reasonable to suppose that he would have used it. The two which fit the description are Peter of Blois' letters and Alan of Lille's *Planctus naturae*. In fact, their inclusion in the *Manipulus*, particularly in the case of Peter's letters, was probably motivated by his having had them at hand.

There are seventeen quotations from the letters of Peter of Blois in the *Manipulus florum*, one of which (*Doctrina ax*) is also used in the prologue. Abundant evidence indicates that Thomas took these from his personal copy, now B.N. MS lat. 16714, a mid-thirteenth-century manuscript. To help him use this text, Thomas supplied it with a subject index of 108 topics, *Abstinencia-Ypocrisis* (ff. 2-3; see plate 6); the index refers one to the system of letters entered for this purpose in the margins of the text itself, indicating opening and column. Seventy-seven of the 108 topics are used in the *Manipulus* as well. Perhaps he referred to the index of MS 16714 in making selections from Peter's letters for inclusion in the *Manipulus*. Under the topic-heading *Medicina* in the *Manipulus florum* are two quotations (*m* and *n*) from Peter's letters; the sole reference s.v. *Medicina* in the index of MS 16714 indicates f. 33, where extract *m* appears, and the second, *n*, comes from the verso of the same folio where it is marked with a marginal *nota*. *Notas* again stud the margins of f. 80 where one finds en bloc the series of thirteen quotations that appear in the *Manipulus* under the heading *Militia* (*p-ae*).

Alan's *Planctus naturae* is cited nineteen times in the *Manipulus florum*.

---

[60] R. Pratt, "Jankyn's Book of Wikked Wyves: Medieval Antimatrimonial Propaganda in the Universities," *Annuale mediaevale* 3 (1962) 16-20; though see above, chap. 4 at n. 36, regarding Pratt's comments on the authorship of the *Manipulus florum* and the Lambeth Commentary.

The manuscript of Alan which Thomas left to the Sorbonne is now Vatican Reg. lat. MS 1006. There is unfortunately no indication in the *marginalia* of this manuscript whether or how Thomas used it in compiling the *Manipulus*. It is possible that he acquired it after having completed the *Manipulus florum.*

With respect to the foregoing works, it was an easy enough matter to search for evidence of Thomas' use. It is impossible to go farther with certainty, without editing the *Manipulus florum.* For example, when we come to works which survive in multiple copies from the Sorbonne, we can establish the identity of Thomas' source only through collation of texts—which, in turn, would require the establishment of a critical text of the *Manipulus.* Or, when we deal with works for which no Sorbonne manuscript survives, we would have to resort to the textual history of each work involved. However, the positive results obtained through a search of these five manuscripts prove that Thomas did use primary sources, *originalia,* and indicate by implication that he must have used manuscripts of *originalia* as his source for other works as well. In fact, in many instances the citations in the *Manipulus* are couched in terms which suggest that they have been taken from *originalia* rather than from *florilegia.* On the one hand, there are citations which refer to physical location in a text, e.g., "Hilarius in principio libri 10 de trinitate [*Detractio x*]," "Augustinus in libro contra mendacium circa medium [*Fabula a*]," "Bernardus super *Missus est* circa finem [*Superbia al*]." On the other hand are the citations which plainly state that they come from *originalia.* A good example, not only of the form but also of the reason for such citations, appears under the heading *Divitie.* Item *h* is ascribed to "Augustinus in originali super psalmum 51"; items *i* and *k* are ascribed to "Glosa Augustini" and "Glosa Augustini super illud ps. 68," respectively. Thomas inserted the phrase "in originali" here, as on other occasions, when he felt it necessary to contrast a primary source with a secondary source with which it might otherwise be confused. In all, there are twenty-four citations in the *Manipulus* which by their wording suggest *originalia* as sources.

Lastly, the bibliography at the end of the *Manipulus florum* is another rough indicator, though a treacherous one, of the works which Thomas supplied from *originalia.* In strictest fact, the bibliography does no more than establish possibilities: since, as we shall see below, the works in the bibliography represent Sorbonne codices, the appearance of a title there establishes the possibility that citations to that work in the *Manipulus* may have been taken from a manuscript of the whole work, because a manuscript of it was demonstrably available. We feel justified in speculating that he did indeed make use of many of these manuscripts which we know passed, literally, through his hands. In particular, when these circumstances combine: that a work which is cited in the *Manipulus florum* appears in the bibliography, but does not appear in the *Liber exceptionum*, the *Flores paradysi*, nor any of the less-frequently-used secondary sources—it is natural to assume that Thomas' sources were *originalia*.

With considerably larger margin of error than was true of other sources, we speculate that primary manuscript sources provided all of the extracts attributed to some seventy of the 560 titles cited in the *Manipulus*, and that they provided some of the extracts (in conjunction with others taken from *florilegia*) attributed to fifteen or twenty more titles.

* * *

As we have seen, Thomas' sources included two patristic *florilegia*, a classical *florilegium*, the *Decretum*, the *Gloss*, and an unknown but respectably large number of manuscripts of *originalia*. There may be another source or sources still undiscovered, but any such source would have, by process of elimination, to be of minor magnitude. From these several sources Thomas created a work that was his own in structure and arrangement, with the result, as he says of his extracts in the prologue (quoting Seneca), "ut etiam si apparuerit unde sumpta sint, aliter tamen esse quam unde sumpta sint appareat." Thomas integrated the material from his disparate sources into his own structure of topic-headings, and into his own order of precedence under each heading.

There is of course little evidence as to how this was done. Some florilegists used wax tablets on which they transcribed *sententiae* drawn from *originalia*. It is more likely that Thomas used the method common to compilers of concordances and indices in the thirteenth and fourteenth centuries, namely to take a blank quire and assign each page a subject heading—1 *Abstinencia*, 1ᵛ *Abusio*, 2 *Acceptio*, 2ᵛ *Accidia*, etc.—and then to proceed through a given body of material, entering the extracts on their proper pages. Given a minimum of second thoughts, this would account for the uniform sequence of authors under all headings.[61] Perhaps Thomas went first through the *originalia*, the Fathers, then the modern doctors, and finally the ancients. Into this sequence he must have added the basic contents of the *Flores paradysi* and the *Liber exceptionum*, and the other collections that he used. For each sentence that he selected, Thomas had first to determine to which topic in the *Manipulus florum* it pertained and what if

---

[61] In the entry for *Accidia* he apparently added an extract out of order, and his instructions for correcting the error were interpreted in several different ways. See below, chap. 6, pp. 166-167.

any cross-references should provide access to it; then he had to enter it in the position under its heading which was proper to the author of the extract. In an age that did not know index cards, it was an impressive accomplishment.

III. THE BIBLIOGRAPHY OF THE *MANIPULUS FLORUM*

At the conclusion of the *Manipulus florum* Thomas added a bibliography or booklist.[62] It differs in many ways from the body of the *Manipulus*—in purpose, in source, in method of compilation—even, as we shall see, in its circulation. Thomas states in the prologue of the *Manipulus*, and repeats in virtually the same words in a paragraph prefatory to the bibliography, his purpose for including this list of works: "Libros quantum ad principia et fines et nomina et partialium librorum numerum in fine huius operis signavi, ut facilius possent cognosci et securius allegari." The words indicate that, at least in Thomas' own (possibly wishful) thinking, the *Manipulus* was to be used in conjunction with, not in avoidance of, the *originalia*.[63] To this end he has even included virtually the whole of the *Retractationes* in the list of Augustine's *originalia*. The body of the *Manipulus florum* was a key to some of the more quotable words of the orthodox authors; the bibliography was a key to identification of some of their best-known works. Thomas added the list to encourage readers not to be satisfied with extracts alone, but to seek out the whole works. At the end of the prologue, Thomas admonishes, "May you not on account of these modest gleanings disdain the fertile field of the originals. He is indeed improvident who, ignoring the fire, strives to warm himself with little sparks;[64] and who, despising the fountain, tries to quench his thirst with drops of dew." While it is rather clear that the *Manipulus florum* in practice substituted for rather than encouraged wider reading, the intent nevertheless distinguishes Thomas' work from preceding *florilegia*, particularly twelfth-century works like the *Liber florum*. The inclusion of the bibliography indicates that, in

---

[62] The bibliography is printed for the first time in Appendix 6 below.

[63] See M. D. Chenu, *Introduction à l'étude de Saint Thomas d'Aquin*, Publications de l'Institut d'études médiévales 11 (Montreal 1950) 38-43; and J. de Ghellinck, "Patristique et argument de tradition au bas Moyen Age," in *Aus der Geisteswelt des Mittelalters*, Beiträge zur Geschichte der Philosophie und Theologie des Mittelalters supp. 3 (Münster 1935) 423-425 and n. 75.

[64] This is probably an allusion—rather snide, under the circumstances—to the most venerable of medieval *florilegia*, the seventh-century *Liber scintillarum* of Defensor of Ligugé, ed. H. M. Rochais, *Corpus Christianorum* 117 (Turnhout 1959); see Rochais, "Contribution à l'histoire des florilèges ascétiques du haut Moyen Age latin: Le 'Liber scintillarum'," *Revue bénédictine* 63 (1953) 246-291.

1306, the thirteenth-century mystique of the *originale* was still strong enough to require more than a token gesture.

The bibliography, which appears after the table of topics and the colophon of the *Manipulus florum*, lists 366 works of twenty-four authors. This is somewhat different from Thomas' intention, announced in the prologue, to list the works of the thirty-six authors whose names he gives in the prologue. In the bibliography, fifteen of the thirty-six are missing; and to the twenty-one who remain Thomas adds three names, Dionysius, Alcuin and Macrobius. The discrepancy was noted by the scribe of Cologne MS G.B. fo. 168 f. 177: "Not all the books of these [thirty-six] doctors are found here, but rather, so it seems, whatever he could find in the Paris library" (see Appendix 7 below). So far as we can discern, this change in "personnel" from the prologue list to the bibliography has no particular significance. Thomas omitted the fifteen authors from his bibliography simply because he did not make the effort to include them; more than half[65] of these fifteen were cited at second hand only, so that Thomas had no particular manuscripts of these authors' *originalia* ready to cite. Probably it did not seem to him that he was in any way obligated to tailor the bibliography to the specific size and shape of the list in the prologue. As for the three additions: Dionysius had become a favorite of Thomas' by the time he wrote his three minor works; perhaps an incipient interest in Dionysius' writings led Thomas to add them, as an afterthought, to the bibliography, even though Dionysius is quoted only twice in the body of the *Manipulus*.[66] Alcuin, who is mentioned only once (*Compassio q*) in the body of the *Manipulus*, is probably included in the bibliography on impulse, simply because Thomas had in his hand a codex (B.N. lat. 16362, of interest to him because of a work of Jerome's it contained) which happened to contain six works of Alcuin's. The explanation for the single work of Macrobius likely follows the same lines, but no manuscript survives to confirm this conjecture.

After a brief introductory paragraph, Thomas lists the works of two dozen authors, again following the "Sorbonne order"—the order of the Sorbonne library catalogs, the order of the authors' precedence under topic-headings in the *Manipulus florum*, the order of the names in the prologue list, and, possibly, the order of the Sorbonne books themselves in the

---

[65] Of the fifteen names in the prologue list which are absent from the bibliography, nine come entirely from secondary sources: Origin, *Liber exceptionum* and *Flores paradysi*; Cyprian, *L.E.*; Fulgentius, *L.E.* and *Gloss*; Basil, *L.E.* and *Gloss*; Maximus, *L.E.*; Caesarius, *L.E.*; Leo, *L.E.*, *F.P.* and *Decretum*; Bede, *L.E.* and *Gloss*; Cassian, *L.E.*

[66] See the discussion of Thomas' minor works above, chap. 4.

presses. The notable exception is the insertion of Dionysius at the head of the list, doubtless as an afterthought. Thomas distinguishes as *beatus* the first seven names: Dionysius, Augustine, Ambrose, Jerome, Gregory, Bernard and Hilary. Under each author's name is a list of his works, ranging in length from 148 for Augustine to one each for Damascenus, Pliny, Maimonides and Macrobius. For each work Thomas normally supplies the *incipit* and *explicit*. The principal exception is the group of titles, with their *incipits*, which he has taken from Augustine's *Retractationes*; he acknowledges this borrowing, in the preface to his bibliography, and notes that for some of these works "fines non vidi."[67]

Thomas' method of compilation for the list of works can be discerned from the bibliography itself. Aside from the *Retractationes* he simply took major codices from the presses of the Sorbonne and listed their contents, or so many of their contents as were attributed to his authors. Far from haphazard, his selection of manuscripts reveals that he consistently chose what he thought to be the most important codex or codices of an author's works available at the Sorbonne, to form the main part if not the whole of the list for any given author. A good example of his method is his list of works by St. Ambrose: there are thirty-four works, listed exactly in the order in which they appear in B.N. MS lat. 15641 (s. xiii; Sorbonne, ex leg. G. of Abbeville). Another example is found in Thomas' list of works attributed to Hugh of Saint-Victor. The first twenty-nine on the list are taken, in order, from two substantial collections of Hugh's works—the first nine from B.N. MS lat. 15693 (s. xiii, ex leg. G. of Abbeville), and the next twenty from MS lat. 15315 (s. xiii, ex leg. G. of Abbeville). The Dionysius list of five works, each in two translations, comes entirely from B.N. MS lat. 15629 (s. xiii, ex leg. Joseph of Bruges). Thomas has, in a sense, compiled a descriptive catalog of collections of *originalia*.

Of course, some of the manuscripts which Thomas used contain the works of more than one author. An example of his way of handling such a codex is his treatment of B.N. MS lat. 15310. Thomas' primary interest in this manuscript lay in a group of nine works of Richard of Saint-Victor, which he duly recorded in the bibliography as the major collection of Richard's works at the Sorbonne. However, the same codex also contains two works of Saint Augustine, two of Saint Jerome, and Saint Gregory's *Pastorale*, all five of which are entered under the appropriate names in the

---

[67] The order of St. Augustine's works in the *Retractationes* was not infrequently used as the guiding principle for arranging codices of Augustiniana. The *Retractationes* were also used, probably from the *Manipulus florum*, in the *Catalogus scriptorum ecclesiae* of Henry of Kirkestede, monk of Bury Saint-Edmunds; see chap. 7 n. 72ff. below.

bibliography. Whereas the major manuscript source or sources determined pretty strictly the basic structure or "order" for the list of an author's works, the incidental works taken from mixed codices were treated more casually. They could be added on at the end of a list (the commonest treatment); they could be squeezed in at odd spots, presumably because there was white space there (as at the beginning of an entry, for example, in the case of Richard of Saint-Victor); or they could be inserted in places that seemed logical to Thomas. The most readily apparent examples of this last process occur in the very lengthy Augustine entry. For instance, in listing the contents of a large codex of Augustiniana (B.N. ms lat. 15302, s. xiii, G. of Abbeville) Thomas recorded the *Regula tertia*, which appears on fols. 243-244 (ii. AUGUSTINE 46), and the *De penitentia* from fols. 245-249 (ii. AUGUSTINE 48); but between them is *Item alia regula* (ii. AUGUSTINE 47), from another manuscript (B.N. lat. 15988), which Thomas has obviously squeezed into the most appropriate place in the Augustine list.[68]

It is possible to identify with certainty, or a good degree of probability, the surviving manuscripts which provided Thomas with all but thirty-three of the 366 works listed.[69] The identifiable works were taken from approximately forty-six manuscripts. It is startling to realize that only five of these manuscripts are known to have reached the Sorbonne through a bequest other than that of Gerard of Abbeville. Thomas' reliance on them underlines the continuing importance of the codices of the Abbeville bequest, thirty years earlier, to the Sorbonne library at the beginning of the fourteenth century.[70] Here, in the case of the *originalia*, just as with the Cistercian *florilegia*, the books that Thomas drew on are a bridge between, on the one hand, the spirit of late twelfth-century humanism and early thirteenth-century return to the *originalia* reflected in the books brought together by Richard de Fournival (i.e., Abbeville's bequest), and, on the other, the preachers and writers of the fourteenth and fifteenth centuries. Abbeville's books formed the solid core of the Sorbonne's chained library or *magna libraria*, to judge from the catalog of that collection made sometime in the 1320s. However, it is doubtful that many of the manuscripts which Thomas used were chained at the time he was compiling the *Manipulus*

---

[68] On this basis, ii. AUG. 51 and 52, inserts, should follow ii. AUG. 48; he may simply have lacked space at that spot.

[69] Twenty-four of the missing thirty-three are works of Cicero, Boethius and Seneca; if we add the works of Rabanus, we account for twenty-nine of the thirty-three. For identification of the manuscripts, see the edition below in Appendix 6.

[70] Concerning Abbeville's bequest see Rouse, "Early Library" 47-51, and "Richard de Fournival" passim.

florum, since he used the manuscripts in the order of the unchained collection (the chained books were not grouped by topic or author) and since he used together manuscripts which, by the 1320s, were separated into the two collections. It is not surprising, however, that the majority of the manuscripts which Thomas used did eventually come to be included in the *magna libraria*; for the criterion used to select books for chaining, as expressed in the college statutes of 1321, was essentially that which guided Thomas: to select the best codex of each work. The statute reads, "De omni sciencia et de libris omnibus in domo existentibus saltem unum volumen quod melius est ponatur ad cathenas...."

Thomas' list of authors and works, including *incipit* and *explicit* for each, is one of the lengthiest and most elaborate of its type produced in the thirteenth and early fourteenth centuries. For that reason it came to have a life of its own; there are at least thirteen surviving manuscripts of the bibliography alone, without the body of the *Manipulus florum*. Conversely, many manuscripts of the *Manipulus* omit the bibliography, perhaps because it appears after the colophon to the table of contents and text, and thus has the semblance of being a separate work. Even in the present century, so able a scholar as Ghellinck failed to recognize that there was a relationship between the list of works and the text which precedes it. Manuscripts of the bibliography alone have given rise to varied scholarly speculation—that it represents the book collection from his student days of Peter Roger (later Clement VI), or a local or private library of some sort in fifteenth-century Trier.[71] Before this present edition, the bibliography has never appeared in print, although the body of the *Manipulus florum* has been printed some 59 times. As a result of the frequent sundering of the bibliography and the text, we shall occasionally have to treat the list of works as a separate entity in subsequent discussions of the use, influence and textual tradition of Thomas' work.

IV. CONCLUSION

The *Manipulus florum* grew out of the concording and indexing tradition of the thirteenth century. The purpose of the *Manipulus*—identical with the original impetus toward indexing—was to provide preachers with readily accessible materials for sermons. The materials, in this case, are the *auctoritates*, authoritative pronouncements made by the Fathers and doctors of the Church, and by those pagans who had been accorded posthumous or-

---

[71] See below, chap. 7, n. 62.

thodoxy. The use of such *auctoritates* in sermons, as a means of buttressing a preacher's expressed opinion, was not novel; but their employment was modest, in the nonstructured homilies common through the twelfth century. However, in the ever more highly structured sermons of the thirteenth century, particularly in sermons preached to or preached by schoolmen, the increasing citation of authorities had become an addiction by the end of the century. Obviously, preachers needed access to a source of supply. There existed *florilegia* in plenty, with the *flores* grouped by subject. However, in practice, the number of topics in such *florilegia* were too few and too broad to provide any meaningful categorization of the quotations; and, in addition, the topics of the earlier *florilegia* were heavily doctrinal, whereas a parish preacher, in particular, needed more materials which were divided into moral categories, to help him deal with his parishioners' problems in Christian behavior. Some seventy or more years before the *Manipulus florum*, the Cistercians devised a solution to the problem of accessibility, by doing away with subject arrangement and by placing reliance on an alphabetized subject index, instead, to provide access to individual excerpts. The disadvantage of this system, however, is readily apparent: working from index to text is clumsy, time-consuming, and prone to error.

The *Manipulus florum* adopted an organization which combined the advantages of alphabetized index and of topical arrangement, with the added element of cross-references or cross-indexing. This, while not the whole, is probably the greater part of Thomas of Ireland's achievement. An organization of this sort, in retrospect, may seem to be the logical, almost inevitable, next step beyond the organization of the *Flores paradysi* and the *Liber exceptionum*. Demonstrably, however, it was neither inevitable nor obvious at the time, since the step was not taken until some seventy years had passed. Thomas' innovation was no dazzling display of intellect, but it was at the least an honest artisan's eminently practical invention. In view of the number of surviving manuscripts, the number of printed editions, the number and variety of instances in which the *Manipulus* was used and referred to by other writers, we may be certain that Thomas' work received both instant recognition and long-term appreciation.

6

The History of the Text
in Manuscript and in Print

Upon completing his work, Thomas published it through the Parisian stationers. Its availability in *peciae* accounts in large part for the sizable and uniform body of manuscripts surviving from the early fourteenth century. Fortunately for the history of the text, Thomas also made or permitted to be made at least three private copies. Thus the text of this work is interesting for what it can tell us of publication in the early fourteenth century.

Our knowledge of the history of the text is based partly on external and partly on internal evidence. In gathering the latter, we have, for the major families of manuscripts, (1) compared the glosses on the text; (2) compared the number and the order of the extracts under each heading; and (3) collated the prologue, the chapters from *Abstinentia* through *Adventus*, and the concluding list of authors and works. We will discuss first the manuscripts of the private tradition, which are more important textually. Then we shall consider the university tradition, which is of course important in a quantitative sense because it comprises four-fifths of the surviving manuscripts; and we shall consider as well the information which this particular university text affords concerning the mechanics of university book production. We are interested not in preparing a critical edition of the *Manipulus florum*, but rather in determining on sound evidence how this text was disseminated.

Thomas' original, which we shall call manuscript ω, is not known to have survived. There are, however, two manuscripts which were almost certainly copied from it, and descendants of a third copy; they constitute three distinct witnesses from which one can reconstruct Thomas' text, and against which one can compare the two university "editions."

One of the closest manuscripts to ω is Paris B.N. lat. 15986 which we shall call B (see plates 1 and 2).

MS 15986 (former nos. 923, 834, 1002). I. Contains, f. 1ᵛ, original flyleaf, "Manipulus florum quem fecit magister Thomas Hybernicus / socius huius domus. Orate pro anima eius. / Precium 8to librarum," and "xix inter flores," along with the notice by

Guédier de Saint-Aubin; ff. 2-3, prologue, beg. "Abiit in agrum [glossed "scilicet Booz"] et collegit spi/caṣ...," ends "... gut/tas sitim conatur extinguere"; ff. 3-224ᵛ, text, beg. "*Abstinentia* / a. Bonum est in cibo cum gratiarum actio/ne...," ends "... *fabula b. humilitas b. / parentes o. / Explicit Manipulus / florum collectus a / magistro Thoma de Y/bernia.* / Iste liber est datus collegio ma/gistrorum de Serbona"; f. 225ʳ⁻ᵛ, table of subjects, beg. "Abstinentia / Abusio / Acceptio personarum...," ends "Uxor / Xp̄ianus / Xp̄c / *Finit.*" followed by an illegible note in leadpoint: "In hoc libro... / Manipulus... / ... in toto circa... / xi dictiones"; ff. 226-231, list of authors and works (this and ff. 232-33 constitute the last gathering), beg. "Notandum quod libros originalium sanctorum ac / doctorum...," ends "... nec / enim ulli flumini dulcior gustus." ff. 231ᵛ-233ᵛ, blank, save for faded pen and pencil notes on 233ᵛ.

Written by a single hand, probably before 1 July 1306, on twenty-nine quires of eight folios each, measuring 288 × 200 mm (text 227 × 142 mm); catchwords in red boxes, corrector's note "corr" to the right of the catchword; parchment ruled in ink; text in two columns of forty-four lines each, written in brown ink; running headlines; subject headings in large letters with red shadow and alternating red and blue paragraph marks; cross-references underlined in red; line ends filled out in red, frequently in this pattern: —ooo—. Binding late medieval, s. xv?, rebacked, calf over boards; marks of two fore-edge clasps, remains of a paper label in the center of the back cover; chain marks front flyleaf top and bottom center, front cover top center, back cover top and bottom center. Given to the Sorbonne by Thomas de Hibernia, probably in 1306; valued at eight pounds; entered among the *florilegia* in the *parva libraria*, and later chained in the *magna libraria* (1338 catalog, XXXIX, 19, *cathenatus*; shelf list Scamnum K? 1321 catalog, S.d.? Delisle, 3: 43, 74, 105).

II. Bound with a smaller manuscript of the mid-thirteenth century containing three works of Nicholas of Lisieux: ff. 234-238, "Liber de ordine preceptorum"; ff. 238-255, "Responsio ad questionem fratris Johannis de Peschant de ordine fratrum minorum"; ff. 255-259ᵛ, "Responsio ad questionem fratris Thomas de Alquino de ordine fratrum predicatorum." Written in a careful hand very similar to that which wrote the Sorbonne catalog of 1270; left to the college by Robert de Sorbon in 1270; valued at ten solidi and entered "inter summas morales 33"; apparently missing at the time the 1338 catalog was made, for there is no description of it (1338 catalog, XLII, 33; Delisle, 3: 45).

The designation of Thomas as "socius" rather than "quondam socius" in the early fourteenth-century *ex libris*, the use of the word "datus" rather than "legatus" in the colophon, and the position of the entry for this book in the 1338 catalog, all three indicate that this copy was made specifically for the college and that it probably entered the library in 1306.[1] It is a plain and quite accurate copy. Thomas took care to see that the text was accurate; for the manuscript was read by a corrector, whose mark can still be seen on the last page of a number of gatherings. His corrections are few in number.

The second probable copy of ω, equal in authority with B, is Paris B.N. MS lat. 15985, which we have called C (see plate 3).

MS 15985 (former nos. 922, 1007). Contains, pastedown, fly-leaf, (f. 1ᵛ), "Iste liber est magistri Nicolai de Barroducis," s. xiv in.; "Manipulus florum," s. xiv ex.; "Manipulus florum quem composuit magister Thomas Ibernicus quondam socius huius domus Sorbone," s. xiv ex.; and a note by Guedier de Saint-Aubin; f. 2ʳ⁻ᵛ, prologue, beg. "Abiit in agrum [glossed "scilicet Booz"] et col/legit...," ends "... per / roris guttas sitim conatur extinguere." ff. 2ᵛ-206, text, beg. "*Abstinentia* / a. Bonum est in cibo cum gratiarum actione / percipere...," ends "... *decima / a. fabula b. humilitas / b. parentes o. / Explicit Manipulus florum.* / Hoc opus est compilatum a magistro Thoma / de Ybernia quondam socio de Sorbona"; ff. 206ᵛ-207, table of subjects, beg. "Abstinentia / Abusio / Acceptio personarum...," ends "... Uxor / Xp̄ianus / Xp̄c̄ / Finit"; f. 207ᵛ, blank; ff. 208-213ᵛ, list of authors and works, beg. "Notandum quod libros originalium sanctorum / ac...," ends "... finis: / nec enim ulli flumini dulcior gustus. / Finit"; f. 214, pastedown, blank, save for ex-libris on upper verso: "Iste liber est pauperum magistrorum de Sorbona ex legato magistri Nicho. de barro ducis. Precium vi librarum. Inter flores originalium" (faded).

Written by a single hand, probably before 1 July 1306, on eighteen quires of twelve folios and one of five, measuring 290 × 205 mm (text 230 × 150); catchwords in red boxes; parchment ruled in ink; text in two columns of forty-four lines each, written in brown ink; initial *A* with red tendrils, alternating red

[1] See above, chapter 4 p. 98.

PLATE 1

Paris, Bibliothèque nationale MS lat. 15986 f. 1ᵛ,
Manipulus florum (B) (⅔ actual size)

PLATE 2

Paris, Bibliothèque nationale MS lat. 15986 f. 2,
Manipulus florum (B) (⅔ actual size)

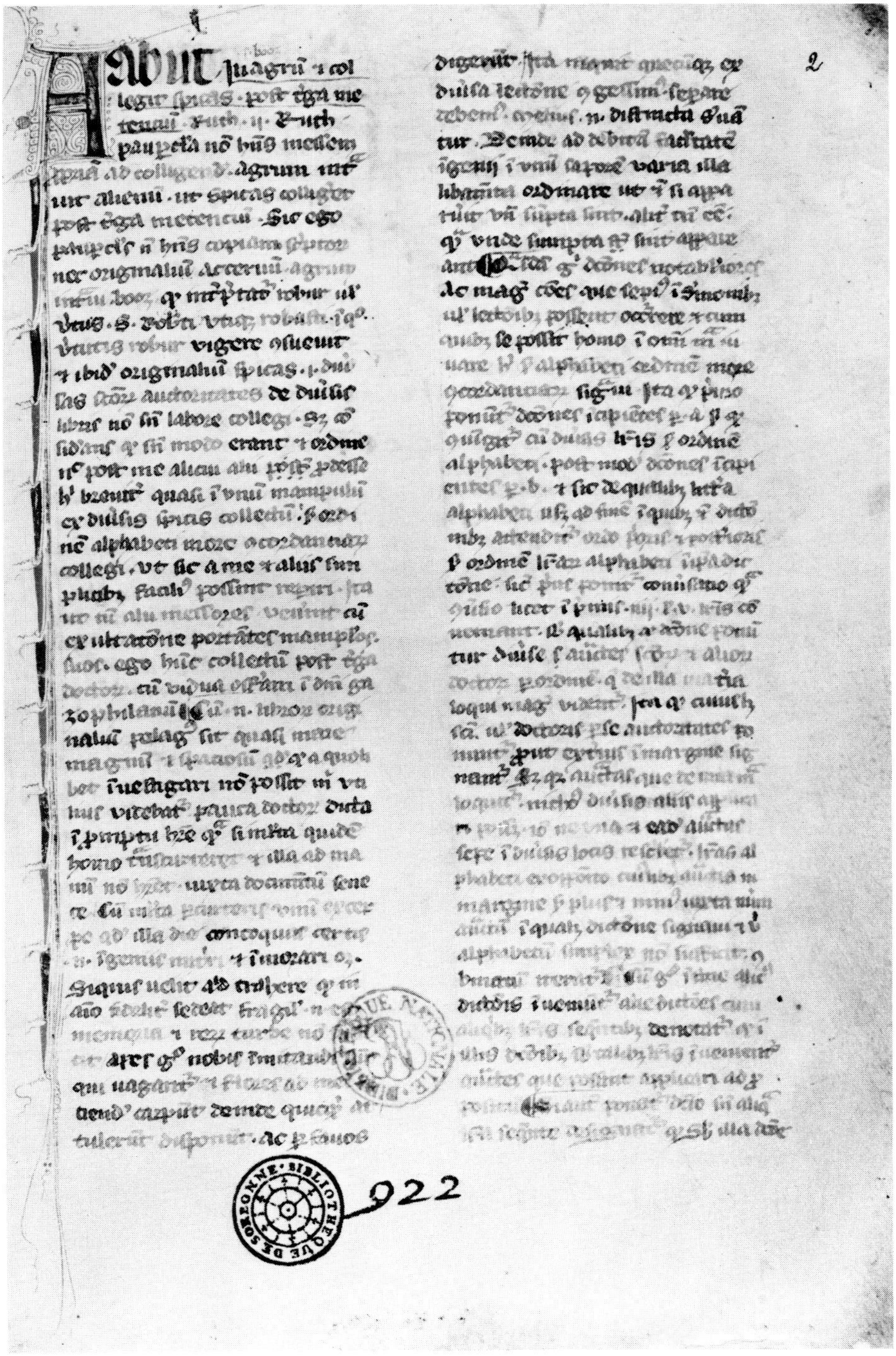

PLATE 3

Paris, Bibliothèque nationale MS lat. 15985 f. 2,
Manipulus florum (C) (⅔ actual size)

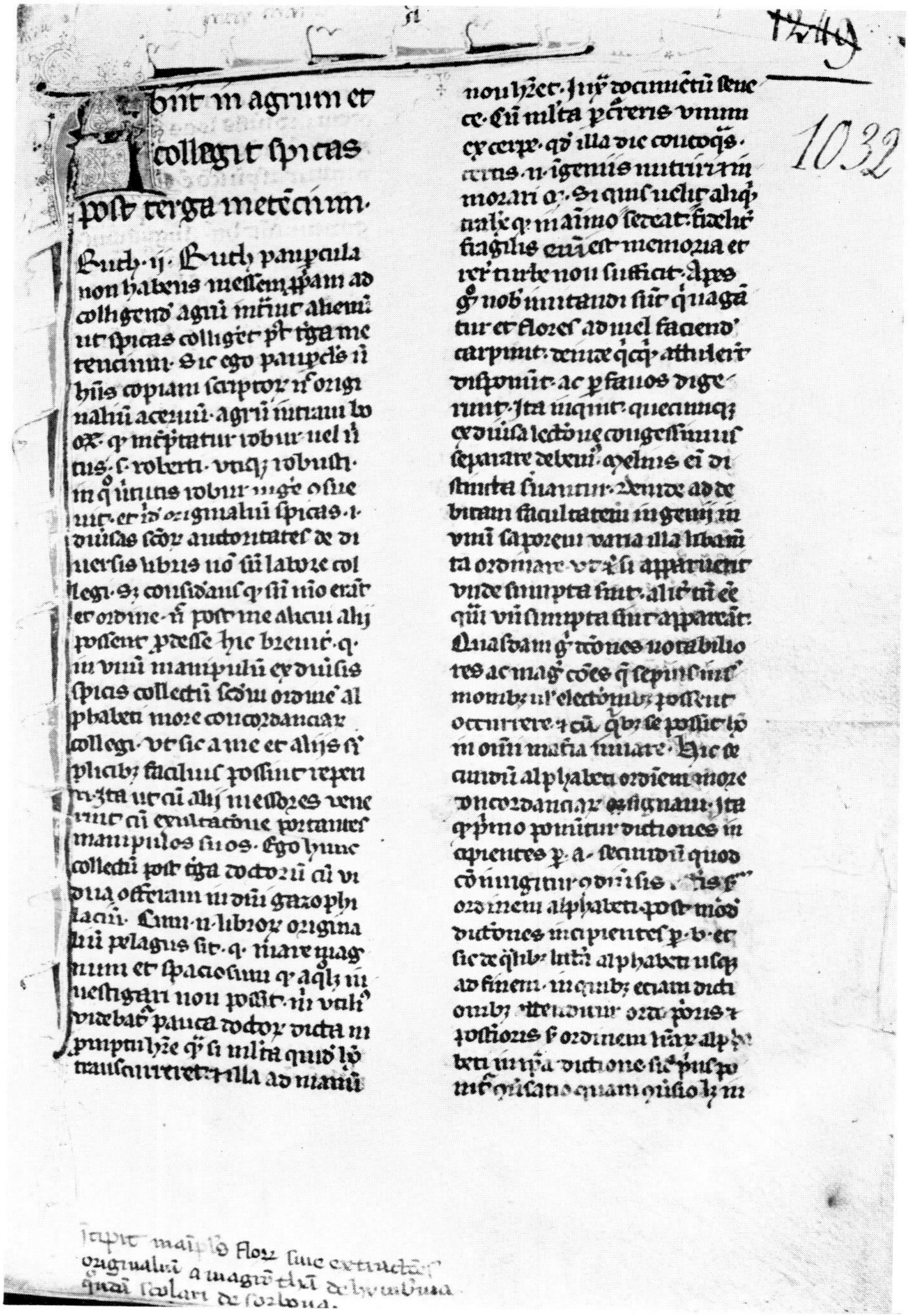

PLATE 4

Paris, Bibliothèque Mazarine MS 1032, f. 1,
Manipulus florum (M) (¾ actual size)

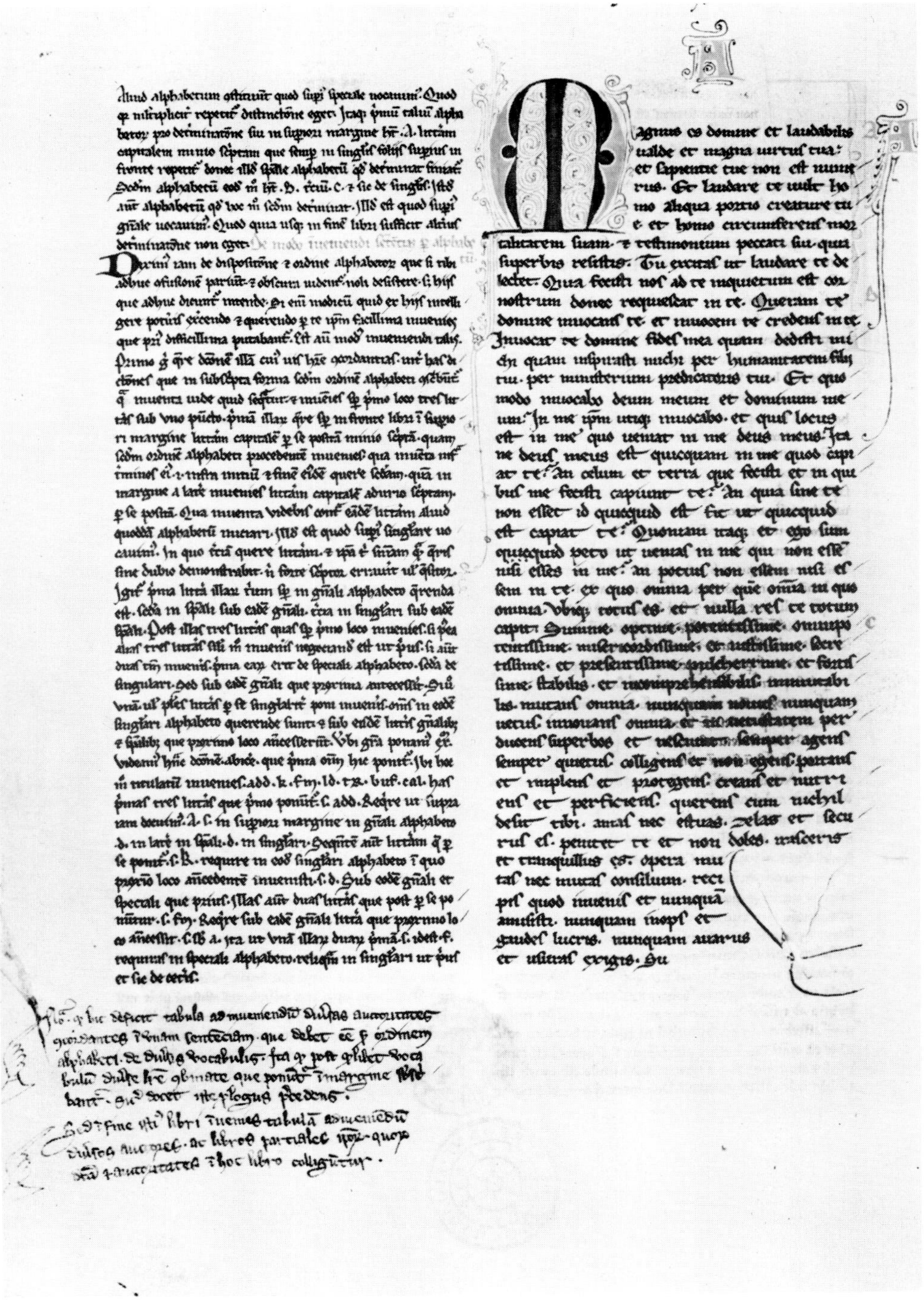

PLATE 5

Paris, Bibliothèque nationale MS lat. 15982 f. 3v,
Flores paradysi (c) (⅔ actual size)

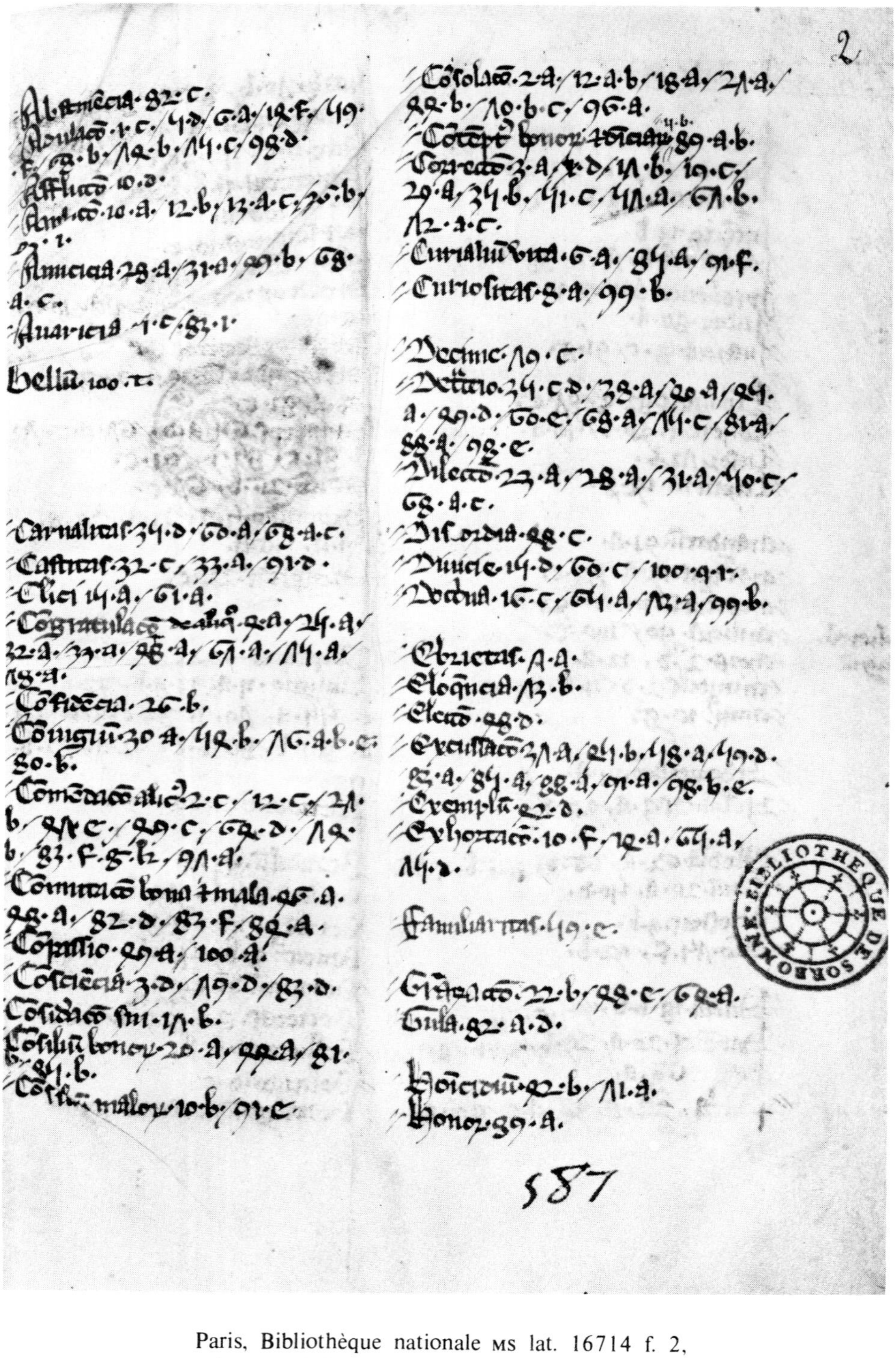

PLATE 6

2

587

Paris, Bibliothèque nationale MS lat. 16714 f. 2,
letters of Peter of Blois, index (actual size)

and blue descenders to foot of page; running headlines; subject
headings in large letters shadowed in red; alternating red and blue
paragraph marks; cross-references underlined in red; line ends
filled out in red, frequently in this pattern: —ooo—. Binding late
medieval, s. xiv-xv?, boards in calf; marks of two fore-edge
clasps; on back cover, the number 49, a paper label bearing the
number 49, and remains of a large paper label; chain marks front
top center, back bottom center, of flyleaves and covers. Left to
the college by Nicholas of Bar-le-Duc (d. 1310); valued at six
pounds; entered among the *florilegia* in the *parva libraria*; not
described in the 1338 catalog, probably because it was chained by
that time.

The manuscripts B and C are striking for their similarity in appearance.
Both are written in columns of forty-four lines each and are ruled in the
same dimensions—lines 5 mm apart, columns 18 mm apart. The shadowing
of the titles in red, the filled-out line endings, the underlining of the cross-
references, the running headlines, the notation of authors' names in the
margins, the placement of the catchwords in red boxes—these reflect a
manner of presentation common to both manuscripts and differing only in
the smallest details. The one noticeable difference is that C is slightly better
decorated; it bears a filigreed initial which descends on the left to the lower
margin, and each *auctoritas* is noted with a red or blue paragraph mark.
Even the glosses are remarkably similar, not only in content but in their
configuration and their placement on the page. The readings in the text of C
are of equal value with those in B, and any mistake or omission in one of
these manuscripts can be corrected or supplied from the other. The
closeness in content and appearance strongly suggests that B and C were
copied at virtually the same time, and by Thomas or at his instigation. One
wonders if Thomas wrote or commissioned the writing of C and gave it to
Nicholas of Bar-le-Duc as a form of recommending himself to Nicholas'
patronage.[2] Nicholas of Bar-le-Duc, bishop of Mâcon (from 1286) and a
former fellow of the Sorbonne, could conceivably have given help to
Thomas in securing a benefice; but the suggestion that he did so, or that
Thomas bid for his aid, is merely speculative. The combined BC text,
notably superior to those in the other surviving manuscripts, has served as
the basis for the edition of the list of authors and works and the prologue

---

[2] Concerning Bar-le-Duc see P. Glorieux, *Aux origines de la Sorbonne*, Etudes de
philosophie médiévale 53 (Paris 1966) 1: 165, 320, 322, 331; and vol. 2, Etudes phil. méd.
54 (1965) no. 412.

(Appendixes 2, 7), and as the source of our quotations from the *Manipulus florum*.

In addition to manuscripts B and C, which to our knowledge are without issue, there was a third private copy now unknown, β, progenitor of a family of manuscripts of which there are at least fourteen survivors. The β family rubric, "Incipit tabula originalium sive Manipulus florum secundum ordinem alphabeti extracta a libris xxxvi auctorum edita a magistro Thoma Ybernico quondam socio domus scolarium de Serbona Parisiensis civitatis," is very stable—that is, few of the β manuscripts lack this rubric and, conversely, only rarely has it been appropriated by manuscripts belonging to another tradition. In the text itself there are three significant features which serve to distinguish the β family from B and C and/or from the university editions. The first of these is the appearance of Petrus Blesensis in the list of authors contained in the prologue. This addition probably was made in the missing β itself, inserted by someone who noticed that the *Manipulus florum* contained a number of quotations from Peter of Blois. The writer did not bother to change the rubric, noted above, to read "extracta a libris xxxvii auctorum," and the discrepancy between the number stated in the rubric and the number of names contained in the list is present throughout the β tradition.

A major textual variation between BC and β (β's reading is shared by M) occurs under the topic-heading *Accidia*. In β the text begins with an extract from Gregory, labeled *a*.; item *b*., an extract from Bernard; and so on, to item *l*., an extract from Augustine's *De conflictu vitiorum et virtutum*, beg. "Torpor et ignavia..."; item *m*., etc.[3] BC begins with Augustine, *De conflictu vitiorum et virtutum*, beg. "Torpor et ignavia...," labeled *a*.; next, an item without a reference letter, the extract from Gregory; then item *b*., the Bernard extract; and so on, to item *k*., followed by item *m*., etc.—the letter *l*. being omitted. The reason for this variation is apparent when we take into account two factors: first, that the BC reading is in fact a rearrangement, as the discrepancy in reference-letters reveals; and second, that Thomas consistently lists first, under any heading, extracts from the works of Augustine.[4] In the extracts on the subject *Accidia* Thomas listed the Augustine extract out of order, perhaps as the result of a belated discovery of the quotation. He knew, as he wrote it down, that the extract was not in its proper place. (While there is no proof that it was Thomas himself who

---

[3] This is the order found in all printed editions—derived from M, however, and not from β.

[4] See the description of the order of entry in chapter 5 above, p. 121ff.

noted the error, it is a safe assumption to make, since no one else is likely to have considered that the order of entry was important, nor even to have been aware that a strict order of entry existed.) Therefore, he marked the autograph manuscript to indicate the passage which was out of place and to designate the spot to which it should be moved. BC and β (and M) reflect different interpretations of Thomas' autograph. The writer of B and C, probably Thomas himself, following the indication in ω, rearranged the *Accidia* entry, taking the Augustine extract out of the *l.* position and making it *a.* instead; but he left the lettering of all the other extracts in its original form (with the exception of *Gregorius in omelia*, left bare with its *a.* having been confiscated) in order to preserve the validity of whatever cross-references to this entry might be scattered through the text. The scribe of β, on the contrary (and the scribe of M, as we shall see below), either ignored or overlooked Thomas' directions, and copied the original version, mistake and all.

Far and away the most interesting distinctive mark of the β manuscripts is their colophon, which attributes the initial labor on the *Manipulus* to John of Wales, saying that Thomas then finished it: "Explicit Manipulus florum compilatus a magistro Thoma de Hybernia quondam socio de Serbona; et incepit frater Johannes Galensis ordinis fratrum minorum doctor in theologia istam tabulam et magister Thomas finivit." This colophon is unique to the β tradition (the only exception being Berlin lat. theol. quarto 17, where the colophon is no doubt a borrowing). Conversely, the John of Wales attribution is lacking only in those β manuscripts which have no colophon at all. We have discussed earlier the import of this colophon,[5] and at this point we shall merely repeat our conclusions: the attribution is not correct, and we are quite at a loss to explain its presence in a copy presumably made from Thomas' own autograph, at, presumably, a very early date.

So far as is known, the earliest surviving manuscript of this tradition is Paris, Bibliothèque de l'Université MS 215, which we have called D.

> MS 215 (former nos. 188.1.9, 256, 155). Contains, f. 1, "De domo Choletorum Parisius," s. xv; "ex bibliotheca Choletaeae (!) domus," s. xviii; "Ex Bibliotheca Domus Choletae," s. xviii; f. 2^{r-v}, prologue, beg. "Abiit in agrum [glossed "scilicet Booz"] et collegit / bat spicas....," ends "... si/tim conatur extinguere"; ff. 2^v-241, text, beg. "*Abstinentia* / a. Bonum est in cibo cum gratiarum acti/one....," ends "... *a.* / *fabula b. humilitas b. paren-*

---

[5] See above, chapter 4 p. 106 ff.

tes o. / Explicit Manipulus florum com/pilatus a magistro Thoma de Hyşber/nia quondam socio de Serbona. et / incepit frater Johannes Gallensis ordinis / fratrum minorum doctor in theologia / istam tabulam et magister Thomas finivit"; ff. 241-242ᵛ, table of subjects, beg. "Abstinentia / Abusio / Acceptio personarum...," ends "... Uxor / Xp̄ianus / Xp̄c̄ / Finit tabula"; ff. 243-248ᵛ, list of authors and works, beg. "Notandum quod libros originalium sancto/rum..."; the final gathering is lost, MS ends incomplete among the books of Cicero, "... De senectute. Principium: O Ty Tyte siquid...."

Written by a single scribe, before 1315, on twenty quires of twelve folios and one of eight (last cahier, probably a single folio, lost), measuring 290 × 210 mm (text 215 × 145 mm); catchwords in brown boxes; gatherings signed by corrector, ".-;- corr. per Mᵗ [Mattheum]," on lower left corner of last page; sheets lettered *a-f* or slashed *i-vi* in pencil; parchment ruled in lead point; text in two columns of thirty-six lines each, well written in dark brown ink; large decorated initial *A* in red and blue with filigree interior and a tendrilled descender in red and blue extending to bottom margin; initials of subject headings tendriled with small filigree interior, alternating red and blue; alternate red and blue paragraph marks. Modern binding.

D was made with considerable care; the manuscript is well written and more heavily decorated than B and C. It was read by a corrector, Matthew, who has left his mark at the end of each gathering. The manuscript was written in Paris before 1315; it belonged to the College des Cholets in the fifteenth century, and may have been there in the fourteenth, since the college was founded in 1295.

We know of one, and possibly three, descendants of D. The first is Vatican MS Borghese 247, ff. 20-21ᵛ (E), into which only the list of authors and works has been copied. The manuscript is a collection of notes made about 1315 by Peter Roger (later to become provisor of the Sorbonne, and later still, Pope Clement VI), who was then a student at Paris.[6] Salzburg MS a.IX.4 (s. xiv med.) and Clm 5345 (s. xv) may also be descendants of D (the latter possibly by way of the former); however, they occasionally sup-

---

[6] The manuscript is fully described and discussed by A. Maier, "Der literarische Nachlass des Petrus Rogerii (Clemens VI) in der Borghesiana," *Recherches de théologie ancienne et médiévale* 15 (1948) 332-356, 16 (1949) 72-98, esp. 92-96. Maier did not identify the list as part of the *Manipulus florum*, and instead thought it was the catalog of a library, perhaps a list of books at Peter's house, Chaise-Dieu (p. 93 n. 91).

ply readings which are missing in D, including the β rubric, despite perpetuating a number of mistakes unique, among surviving manuscripts, to D. It may be necessary to postulate another missing manuscript, which stood between β and D, as common progenitor of D and the two German manuscripts. A second β family, larger and close-knit, is the group of six English manuscripts which have the John of Wales colophon. These manuscripts (Cambridge, Peterhouse College 163; Lincoln Cathedral 48; London, British Library Add. 24,129; Oxford, Lincoln College 98 and Merton College 129; Worcester Cathedral F 153) are all descendants of the same rather corrupt text. Perhaps one of the six themselves is the parent from which the other five stem—the London or the Worcester manuscript, possibly. We know that the text from which this little cluster derives was in England before 1347, because Merton College MS 129 (not the parent manuscript) contains a borrower's note from that year.[7] A seventh English β manuscript, British Library MS Royal 7 C.iii, which has no colophon, does not belong to the same "branch" of the β family as these six; perhaps its text is related to Braunschweig MS 65 and Paris, B.N. MS nouv. acq. lat. 708, the only other manuscripts of this family which lack the John of Wales colophon. Three other β manuscripts are known to us: Berlin MS lat. theol. fol. 239, Florence, Bibl. naz. MS conv. sopp. I 6.12, and Hamburg MS s. Jacobi 15; in the colophons of all three, John of Wales is called simply "Galensis" ("... et incepit Galensis ordinis minorum istam tabulam..."). Possibly these three constitute another branch of β.

Aside from B and C and the manuscripts stemming from β, the remaining manuscripts represent the university stationers' editions; that is, either these are manuscripts produced by the copying of *peciae* rented from a university stationer, or they are descended from manuscripts so produced. The stationer's text is considerably more corrupt than the private traditions, although it is not devoid of value in establishing the text of the *Manipulus florum*. So far as we can tell, it is not descendent from B, C, or β, which would mean that the stationer's text represents, however poorly, a fourth witness to the autograph. Textual considerations aside, however, it is worth examining the university stationer's tradition as an end in itself, in order to add whatever possible to our still limited knowledge of this means of manuscript production. It is only on the basis of the bits and pieces provided in-

---

[7] The earliest evidence for the presence of the *Manipulus florum* in England occurs in a list of books from the estate of Ralph de Baldock, bishop of London, who died in 1313 (see Emden, BRUO 3: 2148; we thank Leonard Boyle for this reference). De Baldock's manuscript has not been identified, however, and there is no telling which recension of the *Manipulus* it may have contained.

cidentally by the editing of university texts such as the present one that we can hope eventually to amass enough specific data to permit a precise understanding of book production in the medieval university.

The method of reproducing manuscripts by means of *peciae* was first clearly described and convincingly documented by Jean Destrez; and later studies, especially the work of Saffrey, Battaillon and Dondaine on the manuscripts of Saint Thomas, have added to and modified Destrez's findings.[8] A Parisian university stationer produced an exemplar of a work in demand. The exemplar in theory, but evidently not often in practice, was an authoritative text, representing a carefully written and scrupulously corrected copy of the author's autograph or his fair copy. This exemplar was written in quires of four or eight folios, called *peciae*, which were numbered in sequence and were left separated, instead of being bound as a codex. Any scholar who wanted a copy of the work, rented, or had a scribe rent, the exemplar from the stationer, one or more *peciae* at a time—a practice which permitted several copies at varying stages of completion to be made concurrently. The scribe who made the scholar's copy was paid by the *pecia*, and so he noted in the margin the number of each *pecia* as he came to it, to serve as a record of his due and a witness of his completeness, or perhaps as a reminder to himself of where he was. The marks were not meant to be preserved. They were normally erased; those written in the outer or inner margins have been lost to the binder. Thus, of the many manuscripts of the *Manipulus florum* copied from Parisian exemplars, only a few still contain *pecia* notes or other evidence of having come from a university exemplar.

Two editions of the *Manipulus florum* were published by the Parisian

---

[8] The basic study of manuscripts in *peciae* is J. Destrez, *La pecia dans les manuscrits universitaires du XIIIe siècle* (Paris 1935); but one can also consult P. Delalain, *Etude sur la librairie parisienne du XIIIe au XVe siècle* (Paris 1891) with profit. Considerable progress on the work of the stationers has been made by the following studies and editions: A. Dondaine, *Secrétaires de saint Thomas* (Rome 1956) 168-184; idem, "Apparat critique de l'édition d'un texte universitaire," *L'homme et son destin*, Actes du premier congrès international de philosophie médiévale (Louvain 1960) 211-220; H. D. Saffrey, ed., *S. Thomae de Aquino super librum de causis expositio* (Fribourg 1954) xl-lxxiii. Introductions to volumes of the Leonine edition of the works of St. Thomas published since 1949 frequently contain valuable information concerning publication in pieces. See in particular vol. 26, *Expositio super Iob ad litteram*, ed. A. Dondaine (Rome 1965); vol. 41 pts. B, C, *De perfectione spiritualis vitae* and *Contra doctrinam detrahentium a religione*, ed. H. F. Dondaine (Rome 1969); vol. 47 pts. 1-2, *Sententia libri ethicorum*, ed. R. A. Gautier (Rome 1969); vol. 22 pts. 1-2, *Quaestiones disputatae de veritate*, ed. A. Dondaine (Rome 1970-1972). There are also interesting suggestions, which must be treated with considerable caution, in G. Fink-Errera, "Une institution du monde médiéval: la 'pecia'," *Revue philosophique de Louvain* 60 (1962) 184-243, and idem, "De l'édition universitaire," *L'homme et son destin* 221-228.

stationers. The one contained twenty-four *peciae*, the other seventy-five. Our knowledge of the twenty-four *pecia* text, γ, is limited; however, the existing evidence suggests that it was the earlier edition, and that the edition in seventy-five *peciae*, M, was copied from it. The two clearest indications are these: (1) Both γ and M contain an additional passage near the end of the prologue, beginning "Nomen autem collectoris..." (described below). This conventional modest disclaimer, absent from the private tradition of the *Manipulus*, must have been added by Thomas to the copy which he handed to the stationer. The fact that it appears in the same form in γ and M suggests that one of these must be copied from the other. (2) In the section headed *Accidia*, we know that the γ exemplar preserved the ambiguity of Thomas' original (ω), permitting different interpretations (see below); M presents a clear reading, equivalent to one of the interpretations permitted by the text of γ. While the reading of M could easily derive from γ, the state of γ could not possibly be derived from M but, on the contrary, must derive, at a very slight remove indeed, from ω itself. Consequently, we shall discuss γ, the first university edition, and M, the second university edition, in that order.

The aspect of the first university edition which strikes one immediately is its rarity; we have distinguished only four manuscripts which contain this text: El Escorial, MS Q III 11; Oxford, Magdalen College MS 87; Paris, B.N. MS lat. 3336; and Soissons, Bibl. mun. MS 112. Fortunately, at least one of the four, Paris MS 3336 (P), was copied from the exemplar and bears *pecia* notes.

MS 3336 (former nos. Colbert 4171, Regius 4106$^{5.5.}$). Contains, f. 2, rubric, "Incipit tabula librorum ori/ginalium, scilicet Augustini, Ambro/sii, et sic de aliis, qui sunt numero / xxxvi auctores, secundum ordinem alphabeti, qui vocatur Manipulus florum / edita a magistro Thoma de Ybernia / quondam sociu͂s de Sarbona. Prologus." f. 2^{r-v}, prologue, beg. "Abiit in agrum / scilicet Booz et collegit / spicas...," ends "... roris / guttas sitim cognatur (*sic*) extinguere"; ff. 2^{v}-223^{v}, text, beg. "*Abstinentia /* a. Bonum est in cibo cum gratiarum / actione...," ends "... *fabula / b. humilitas b. parentes o.* / Explicit Manipulus / florum compilatum (*sic*) a ma/gistro Thoma de Ybernia / quondam socius (*sic*) de Sarbo/na. Deo gratias"; f. 224^{r-v}, table of subjects, beg. "Abstinentia / Abusio / Acceptio...," ends "... Uxor / Xp̄ianus / Xp̄c̄ / Finit Amen." Lacks list of authors and works.

Written by a single scribe, before 1 July 1306, on eighteen quires of twelve folios and one of seven, measuring 248 × 175 mm (text 170 × 102 mm); catchwords; quires signed; sheets lettered *a-f* and/or slashed *i-vi*; parchment ruled in ink; text written in two columns of forty-four lines each; on f. 2, a decorated initial A with L-frame, bearing bird singing and greyhound chasing a hare; arms (unidentified) in center of capital A: bendy or and azure; initials of subject headings alternating red and blue, tendrilled and filigreed in red and blue; alternating red and blue paragraph marks. Provenance notes: f. 2, erased, "Iste liber est ... et post mortem eius ..."; f. 223^v, effaced and darkened with oak galls, "... et est conventu Arelatis ... de monte Majori [abbey of Montmajour near Arles]," s. xiv. Rebound, red morocco, Colbert arms; lacks medieval flyleaves.

Since P is the source of our knowledge of the *pecia* divisions of the first university edition, we shall also give a full list of P's *pecia* notes. These were written in the margins, many in pink boxes, and then carefully erased; we have found all but three of them, but the *pecia* number was legible only in those notes which are quoted here. Because some of them are very faint, we have noted, along with the folio, the portion of the text beside which each note is located.

First note missing; f. 22, "Finitur quaternus ii" (*Avaritia x.*); next note missing; f. 43 (*Contemplatio ad.*); f. 52^v (*Correctio cl.*); f. 61^v (*Dilectio a.*); f. 70, "Finit pecia vii" (*Dolor*, cross-references); f. 79, "... viii ..." (*Exemplum o.*); f. 88 (*Gratia q.*); f. 97 (*Ieiunium al.*); f. 106, "... xi quaternus" (*Ira t.*); f. 115, "Finit xii quaternus" (*Libido b.*); f. 124^v (*Meritum ac.*); f. 133^v (*Mors cn.*); f. 145^v (*Patientia a.*); f. 155^v (*Penitentia k.*); f. 165^v (*Prelatio s.*); f. 175, "Finit xix pecia" (*Regimen t.*); next note missing; f. 196, "Finit xxi quaternus" (*Sobrietas c.*); f. 206, "Finit xxii pecia" (*Taciturnitas n.*); f. 216^v, "Finit xx ..." (*Vitium m.*); none at the end, f. 224^v.

One can see from the above list that at some point between the twelfth and the eighteenth *peciae* an error in numbering has occurred (in P and, presumably, in γ); so that the *peciae* numbered xix, xxi and xxii are actually the eighteenth, twentieth and twenty-first, respectively. P, thus, is a copy of only twenty-three *peciae*. However, it is almost certain that γ included a twenty-fourth *pecia*, containing the list of authors and works, which the maker or commissioner of P did not choose to include. If we are correct in thinking that the second university edition, which contains the list, derives from the first, then the existence of a twenty-fourth *pecia* is a necessity. Furthermore, Escorial MS Q III 11 contains the list of authors and works, and the Oxford manuscript may once have contained it. Its absence from P follows a pattern common among manuscripts of the second university edition, many of which have omitted the list either by choice or from negligence.

Destrez's study showed the usual length of an exemplar *pecia* at Paris to be four folios, although editions in eights were not uncommon.[9] The *pecia* notes in P reveal that the first university edition of the *Manipulus florum* consisted, instead, of twelve-folio *peciae*. To call this a rarity would understate the case. Destrez's extensive search seems to have uncovered only two previous examples at Paris of *peciae* in twelves—the *Secunda secundae* of Saint Thomas, in a 15 February - 2 April 1290 edition; and St. Thomas' commentary on book four of the *Sentences*, which must date from the second half of the century.[10] Twelve-folio *peciae* were too long to be practical, because too large a portion of the text would be monopolized by an individual borrower. The two earlier attempts at *peciae* in twelves were evidently unsuccessful, according to Destrez, and the exemplars were withdrawn from circulation very soon, to be replaced by editions of shorter and more numerous *peciae*. Thus the exemplar of the commentary on the *Sentences*, Bk. 4, published in eighteen *peciae* of twelve folios, was replaced by three successive editions in fours, of ninety-one, ninety-three, and ninety-eight *peciae*, respectively.[11] Likewise, the first edition of the *Manipulus* was evidently not successful, and was quickly withdrawn and replaced by an edition of seventy-five *peciae* of four folios (2 sheets) each. (One wonders why, in the light of previous, presumably expensive, failures, the *Manipulus* was published in twelve-folio *peciae* at all.)

The text of γ is distinguished by the following features. (1) It has a standard rubric, "Incipit tabula originalium scilicet Augustini, Ambrosii, et sic de aliis qui sunt numero xxxvi auctores secundum ordinem alphabeti que vocatur Manipulus florum, edita a magistro Thoma de Ybernia quondam socio de Sarbona." (2) Almost at the end of the prologue, there is an additional sentence not found in BC or β; following the sentence which begins "Tu ergo lector ora pro collectore...," γ adds, "Nomen autem collectoris volui subticere, ne collectio vilesceret, cognito collectore." Evidently, on presenting his work to the general reading public of the university, Thomas added this conventional request for anonymity. The fact that his name did, indeed, appear in the standard rubrics on the first page of both university editions is an irony to be attributed to scribal conventions. (3) In the section *Accidia*, it is obvious from the surviving manuscripts that the γ exem-

[9] Destrez 27.

[10] Paris, Bibl. Mazarine MS 824 is an exemplar in 12s of the IIa IIae (Destrez 30); copies of an exemplar in 12s of St. Thomas on bk. 4 of the *Sentences* are noted in Destrez 92-94.

[11] See the notes to plates 8 and 12 in Destrez, representing the 91 and the 98 *pecia* texts. See also pp. 73-79 for examples of successive exemplars of the same text, for example, Jacques de Voragine's *Legenda aurea* which went through five editions, of 71 *peciae*, 80, 85 or 86, 90 and 95 *peciae* respectively.

plar presented a confusing picture. Magdalen 87 has the Augustine extract "Torpor et ignavia..." as entry *a* under this heading, the Gregory extract second, without a letter, and no extract lettered *l*.; in other words, this section agrees with the reading of BC. P has the Augustine extract entered by mistake before the *Accidia* heading, so that the text reads, "a. Torpor et ignavia ... ACCIDIA. b. Accidia est de ... [Gregory]; c. Accidia est anime ... [Bernard]," and so on, with the extracts re-lettered through *l* (= *k* in BC, β, *M*, and the rest of γ). The Escorial and Soissons manuscripts have the Augustine extract in the *l* position, like the reading of β. The source of this confusion probably lay in the fact that the scribe of γ reproduced here the state of Thomas' manuscript, which we have suggested must have contained the indications of the change in order desired by Thomas. The stationer's scribe in this instance seems to have copied into the exemplar the indications of the change, rather than making the change himself. In the manuscripts copied or descended from this exemplar, the text of Magdalen 87 displays the correct interpretation of the directions; the text of P reveals an unsuccessful attempt to follow the directions; and the texts in Escorial Q III 11 and Soissons 112 ignore the directions altogether. (4) The explicit of P is probably a variant of the exemplar's "Explicit Manipulus florum. Hoc opus est compilatum a magistro Thoma de Ybernia quondam socio de Sarbona."

The first university edition must have had a brief life span. This fact is evident, when one compares the four surviving manuscripts of the γ tradition with the some 160 manuscripts of the *M* tradition. Making all allowances for the caprice of chance in the disappearance of certain manuscripts and the preservation of others, it is nonetheless obvious that γ as an edition did not begin to approach the longevity of *M*. As we have suggested, it must have been the unwieldy length of the *peciae* in the first edition which led to its replacement by the second. Perhaps the stationer had not initially foreseen that the demand for copies of the *Manipulus florum* would be heavy; the lengthy *peciae* were not practical in such a situation. Perhaps also economics entered into the change. In theory, the number of lines per page and the number of letters per line were regulated by the university, as well as the price of the *pecia*. But in practice, this edition of twenty-four *peciae* in twelves was converted, not to seventy-two, but to seventy-five *peciae* in fours, which doubtless made the second edition more profitable as well as more practical.[12] The more rapid turnover permitted by the smaller

---

[12] See Destrez 73-79; it should be noted, however, that a change from pieces in 12s to pieces in 4s is not the same as a gradual increase in the number of pieces—e.g., 91, 93, 98—and each sort of change must be separately explained.

peciae was, of course, financially advantageous in itself. The first edition is undated; it is reasonable, however, to assume that it preceded the second edition of 1 July 1306 by a very short time.

The second university edition, in seventy-five *peciae*, is the source from which most surviving manuscripts stem. Our knowledge of this edition rests upon a collection of exemplar *peciae*, M (Paris, Bibliothèque Mazarine MS 1032; see plate 4) and manuscripts copied from exemplar *peciae* of this edition.[13] The *Manipulus florum* is one of the relatively small number of works for which exemplar *peciae* survive. Of the hundreds of texts which were circulated by stationers in Paris, Oxford and Bologna, only eighty-two "exemplars" were known to Destrez.[14] No doubt when the *Manipulus florum* ceased to be in demand, this set of *peciae* was bound into a codex and sold; the last *pecia* is now missing and possibly was never included in the made-up volume.

MS 1032 (former no. 1249). Contains, ff. 1-2, prologue, beg. "Abiit in agrum et / collegit..." [rubric at foot of f. 1, "Incipit Manipulus florum sive extractiones originalium a magistro Thoma de Hymbernia (*sic*) quondam scolari de Sorbona." At top of page in same ink as at bottom—indication of placement?— "Incipit Manipulus florum."], ends "... gutas / sitim conatur extinguere"; ff. 2-289, text, beg. "*Abstinentia* / a. Bonum est in cibo cum gratiarum actio/ ne...," ends [beg. of *pecia* seventy-three] "... *humilitas b. pa/ rentes o.* / Hoc opus est compilatum /a magistro Thoma de Ybernia / quondam socio de Sorbona. / *Explicit Manipulus florum*"; ff. 289-291, table of subjects, beg. "Abstinentia / Abusio / Acceptio personarum...," ends "Uxor / X͞pianus / X͞pistus / Finitus anno domini Mᵒ CCCᵒ / VIᵒ die veneris post pas/ sionem Petri et Pauli"; f. 291ᵛ, blank; f. 292, top, "Incipit pecia lxxiiii" [in error]; ff. 292-296ᵛ, list of authors and works, beg. "Notandum est quod libros origi/ nalium..." [note on f. 293 (correctly), top, "lxxiiii pecia"], breaks at end of *pecia* 74 among the *Libri beati Bernardi* ("De laude nove militie templi"), "... finis: et di/ gitos nostros ad bellum," catchword, "De diligendo deo."

---

[13] To summarize our *sigla* for the second university edition: M = Maz. 1032, a collection of exemplar *peciae* of this edition; m = another collection of exemplar *peciae*, twin of M, now missing; *M* = no single MS, but the second university tradition as a whole, and the consensus of its readings.

[14] J. Destrez and M. D. Chenu, "Exemplaria universitaires des XIIIᵉ et XIVᵉ siècles," *Scriptorium* 7 (1953) 68-80.

Probably written by a single scribe, completed 1 July 1306, on
seventy-four *peciae* or quires of four folios each (*pecia* seventy-
five missing), measuring 227×155 mm (text 165×108 mm);
pecia number at head (left) of each gathering in Roman numerals:
"xxv pᵃ" or number alone; catchwords; gatherings signed twice in
lower left corner of last page: "corr. corr."; parchment ruled in
ink; text in two columns of thirty-nine lines each; red and blue
initial A (red filigree interior) descending to the foot of the page
and extending across the upper margin in bands; alternating red
and blue paragraph marks; headline letters A, B, C, etc. Extensive
correction of omissions by corrector; MS is badly worn, esp.
peciae 8, 22; lower outside corner of *pecia* 25 (ff. 97-100)
remade by second hand, perhaps that of marginal corrector; f.
183, new lower outside corner added before writing; outer margin
of ff. 260-296 deteriorating. Modern binding; f. 61, "Gui[liel-
mus]."

This collection of seventy-five exemplar *peciae* represents the second university edition. As additional witnesses to it, there are at least eight manuscripts which bear evidence that they were copied from exemplar *peciae* of
this edition:[15] Paris, B.N. MSS lat. 14990, 16532; Melun, Bibliothèque
municipale MS 16; Arras MS 1001; Lyon MS 711; Assisi MS 244; Vatican MS
Barberini 458; and Bruges, Bibliothèque municipale MS 171. Bruges 171
has a large number of marginal *pecia* notes—e.g., on folios 3, 7, 11ᵛ, 13,
16, 19. B.N. 16532 has *pecia* notes in the margins of folios 45ᵛ, 52, 55ᵛ,
58ᵛ, 81, 84ᵛ, 104ᵛ. We have found no *pecia* notes in Melun 16; but there
are changes in the ink, indicative of an interruption, at places in the text
where one *pecia* ends and another begins.

While Destrez thought that there could be only one exemplar for any one
edition, later studies have shown that a stationer might be renting simultaneously two or more "identical" sets of *peciae*—identical, in that each
pecia in a given set contained precisely the same portion of the text as the
corresponding *pecia* in the other set or sets, although inevitable errors of
transcription made each of the "identical" *peciae* unique.[16] A stationer

---

[15] We are grateful to Father Louis Bataillon O.P., Le Saulchoir-Etiolles, who searched for
us Destrez's notebooks at Le Saulchoir. Among the *pecia*-MSS of the *Manipulus* Destrez
records Tours MS 37, because it contains on fol. 6ʳᵃ a marginal note which Destrez reads as
"pᵉ iiᵃ," *pecia secunda*; rather, it is "pᵉ rᵃ," Petrus Ravennas, author of the adjoining
quotation. Tours 37 does not contain an *M* text, but rather a *β* text.
[16] See Dondaine, "Apparat critique."

would invest the sum necessary to make and correct a second or even a third set of exemplar *peciae* for a given text when the demand for the text warranted the investment. The second set of *peciae* would probably be made from the first—or perhaps from the master copy which the stationer supposedly retained, if such was ever actually the practice. The stationer thereafter would not bother to guard the homogeneity of a set of *peciae* by keeping each set together and distinct; instead, he kept the *peciae* by text and number. Thus, in the bin for *pecia* 1 of a given text, there might be exemplar *peciae* from two, three, perhaps even four different sets of *peciae*. Furthermore, any *pecia* which was lost, destroyed or partially mutilated would be wholly or partially remade, a process which gave birth to *peciae* which did not "belong" to any set.[17] As a result, any manuscript made from an edition which was published in multiple parallel exemplars would be copied from a totally haphazard series of exemplar *peciae*. The chances of any other manuscript being copied from precisely the same sequence of exemplar *peciae* would be very small. The unit one must deal with, in establishing the text of a university book, is the *pecia*, rather than the codex.

In the case of the second edition of the *Manipulus florum*, we have found on the basis of a collation of *peciae* 1-2 and 73-74 either that two parallel sets of exemplar *peciae* were being rented, or that many of the *peciae*, including these four, were remade; and one must assume that M represents, not one "set"—a concept which the stationer would lack, himself—but a mixture of *peciae* from both sets, or a mixture of original and remade *peciae*. For the four *peciae* collated, Bruges 171 and B.N. lat. 16532 depended upon M's missing counterpart, m. Melun 16 was copied from m 1, M 2, m 73, m 74. Three other *pecia*-manuscripts (B.N. lat. 14990, Arras 1001, Assisi 244) have copied M 1 and M 2; we have not collated *peciae* 73-74 in these cases, nor have we collated the remaining *pecia*-manuscripts Lyon 711 and Vatican Barberini 458, since the evidence is sufficient for our purposes as it stands. In order to establish the text of the second university edition (*M*), an editor would have to establish a separate stemma for each of the seventy-five *peciae*. Fortunately, it would not be necessary to do this for an edition of the *Manipulus florum*, since we have the private tradition of B, C and β. And certainly for present purposes we have not undertaken anything so elaborate; we have, merely, been aware that M cannot stand alone as the representative of *M*, and that our conclusions concerning this

---

[17] The lower half of the outer column of M fols. 97-100 has been remade and glued in. Perhaps written in the hand of the second corrector.

seventy-five *pecia* edition must rely upon the composite readings of M and other M-manuscripts.

The following features distinguish the second university edition:

(1) The standard rubric of M reads "Incipit Manipulus florum sive extractiones originalium a (*or* editus a) magistro Thoma de Ybernia quondam scolari (*or* socio) de Sorbona." A sizable proportion of the manuscripts derived from this edition have no rubric at all preceding the opening words of the prologue, "Abiit in agrum..."; M itself has no rubric nor space left for one, but the words have been added by another, contemporary, hand in the bottom margin of the first page (see plate 4). The omission is worth noting because it may explain why, in a few instances, one finds an M text with a rubric which has been borrowed from elsewhere.

(2) In the prologue, this edition contains an error which may serve as a ready means of identification. Thomas lists in the prologue the names of thirty-six authors whose works will be cited, ending with the name of "Seneca, cuius dicta in fine cuiuslibet dictionis ponuntur...," a promise which he adheres to with fair regularity throughout the text. The prologue of M, only, reads "... Tullius, Boetius, Seneca, *quorum* dicta...." Because this reading is obvious nonsense—that all thirty-six will be cited last—and because the correct reading could be surmised with a minimum of thought, the absence of this error does not automatically exclude a manuscript from the M tradition; but the presence of this mistake is a thoroughly dependable sign that a given manuscript stems from the second university edition.

(3) The second university edition follows the first, and differs from the private traditions, in inserting near the end of the prologue the sentence "Nomen autem collectoris volui subticere...."

(4) As we have observed, the exemplar of the first university edition (γ) presented an ambiguous reading in the section *Accidia*; the second edition (M) adopted the reading found in two γ manuscripts, Soissons 112 and Escorial Q III 11—that is, it retains the extract from Augustine, beg. "Torpor et ignavia...," in the eleventh position, bearing the letter *l*.

(5) At the end of the text, prior to the table of subjects, is the standard M colophon, borrowed from the first edition: "Hoc opus est compilatum a magistro Thoma de Ybernia quondam socio de Sorbona. Explicit Manipulus florum."

(6) At the end of the table, prior to the list of authors and works, there is another feature unique to M, the date-colophon: "Finit anno domini M CCC VI die veneris post passionem Petri et Pauli [1 July 1306]." This we presume to be the date on which the exemplar *peciae* (the first set of them) were completed. The date colophon has been discarded by most M manuscripts; occasionally, it is replaced by a similar colophon which, *mutatis*

mutandis, notes the date at which a given manuscript was itself completed.[18] However, a few M manuscripts have retained the original date-colophon unchanged. This has naturally caused considerable confusion in dating such manuscripts.[19]

(7) At the beginning of the list of authors and works, where BC and the β tradition read "Notandum quod libros doctorum...," M reads "Notandum est quod...." This reading is probably derived from the first university edition, since it agrees with Escorial Q III 11, the only known descendant of the γ list.

We can scarcely label this a feature of the second university edition, but we should, in conclusion, note the tendency of manuscripts of this tradition to omit the list of authors and works. Some thirty-five M manuscripts lack the list. This fact should be coupled with another, the misplacement of *pecia* number 74 in M. *Pecia* 74 begins on f. 293; but the hand of the text has written "Incipit pecia lxxiiii" at the head of the list of authors and works on f. 292—that is, at the head of the last folio of *pecia* 73. Doubtless there are other possible reasons, but the one probable reason for such an error is that the exemplar from which M was copied likewise read "Incipit pecia lxxiiii" at the head of the list. To carry conjecture one step farther, it is plausible, at the very least, to assume that in one of the sets of exemplar *peciae* the beginning of the list actually did coincide with the beginning of a new *pecia*, *pecia* 74. This conjecture presents problems of its own, certainly; it would require *pecia* 73 to conclude with two blank pages, and—a more serious objection—it would mean that *peciae* 73-75 of the two parallel sets would not, in fact, be parallel. On the other hand, the conjecture has several advantages. It would conform with the natural tendency to begin something new on a new quire. It would parallel, in the second edition, the structure of the first edition, in which the list comprised a separate *pecia*. And it would help to explain the absence of the list from so many manuscripts. Since the

---

[18] Toulouse MS 222 bears a colophon which seems at first glance to antedate the stationer's exemplar by several months: "Iste liber finitur A.D. millesimo trecentesimo sexto die mercurii in festo sancti Albini [1 March]." This is, however, to be read as Wednesday, 1 March 1307 (N.S.).

[19] MSS containing this date-colophon are often themselves assumed to date from 1306. Attention is called to the problem in C. Samaran and R. Marichal, *Catalogue des manuscrits en écriture latine...* 1 (Paris 1959) x, and J. Destrez and G. Fink-Errera, "Des manuscrits apparemment datés," *Scriptorium* 12 (1958) 56-93, esp. 59-60. For an example of the confusion which may result, see F. Unterkircher, *Die datierten Handschriften der Oesterreichischen Nationalbibliothek bis zum Jahre 1400* 1 (Vienna 1969) 38 (MS 1334), 41 (MS 1555), 42 (MS 1611) and plates 75-77; Unterkircher recognizes that the date 1306 is that of the exemplar, yet he gives plates of three mid- or late fourteenth-century manuscripts under the date 1306—though see his introduction, p. 11 n. 12.

presence of the list is not necessary to the utility of the text which precedes it, a man with little interest in a booklist would not pay to rent the separate *peciae*. Furthermore, the position of the date-colophon at the end of the table of contents would tend to convey the impression that the "work proper" was ended, particularly if it were followed, not by the beginning of the list (as in M), but by two blank pages filling out the *pecia*.

There is no way to determine whether or not different stationers were involved in the publication of the *Manipulus florum*. Common sense suggests that only one stationer handled the text. Two editions, the latter perhaps in two sets of *peciae*, is not sufficient variety to suggest the presence of a second publisher. In addition, the two editions are tied by their decoration. MS 3336 (P) of the γ edition, and MSS B.N. 16532, Melun 16 and Vat. Ross. 217 of the M edition, share a common decoration on the first page: the left shaft of the initial A (for 'Abiit in agrum...") is elongated and extended across the foot of the page to form a frame on which a greyhound chases a hare. The greyhound-hare motif apparently was a standard decoration that one could request and have applied, for a fee, to the first page of any text. It is also interesting to see that the copyist of a manuscript of the *Manipulus*, P, also copied a manuscript purchased by Thomas (Bruges MS 362); both bear *pecia* notes in identical pink boxes. Scribes were probably associated with specific stationers; and it would seem natural for Thomas to publish through, and to purchase from, the same stationer.

Publication by the stationers had a significant effect upon the *Manipulus florum*—upon its circulation and, therefore, its influence, and even upon its textual integrity. Obviously, publication in pieces allowed the *Manipulus*, a useful book with a substantial buying public, to be multiplied rapidly after it was deposited with a stationer in 1306. The book was clearly in demand: not only was a shift in the number of *peciae* from 24 to 75 needed, to allow more pieces to be "out" simultaneously, but also a stationer found it necessary to invest in a second set of *peciae*. There is no indication of how long the *Manipulus florum* remained available in *peciae*. It was doubtless a short time, compared with the longevity of the set texts necessary to the training of masters, some of which were available in *peciae* for half a century or longer. Only eight surviving manuscripts are known to bear *pecia* marks or other evidence of having been copied directly from exemplar *peciae*. Yet at least forty manuscripts date, on paleographic grounds, from the Paris of the first third of the fourteenth century. If these are not all direct copies of exemplar *peciae*, they are at least descendants of such copies. The simultaneous availability of multiple copies at a cosmopolitan center like Paris meant that the *Manipulus florum* would spread quickly across Europe, carried by students returning to Clairvaux, Tours, and Bec, as well as to Oxford, Cologne, Prague, and Bologna, there to be copied again. Publication by the stationers, thus, has an effect on a given text that extends quantitatively beyond the number of stationer-produced copies, extends culturally to literary history outside the university, and extends chronologically to the vanishing point. In the period of time during which the *Manipulus florum* was available in pieces, enough copies were produced to father at least three-quarters of the some 200 surviving manuscripts. The foundation for the some 80 copies of the *Manipulus* produced in the fifteenth century was laid within Thomas' lifetime.

To speak of the stationers' effect on textual integrity may seem contradictory, in light of our insistence on the corruption of the university text. Perhaps the phrase we need, rather, is integrity of content. The contents of *florilegia* are characteristically unstable. The nature of the genre invites alteration—enlargement, abridgement, rearrangement, or all three at once. We have discussed in the preceding chapter the *Flores paradysi*, which survives in three manuscripts, each in turn a thorough revision of its predecessor. In chapter 7 we describe a mare's nest of *florilegia* called the *Lumen anime*, which was steadily altered and adapted by owner-writers to the point that perhaps two-thirds of the 200 surviving manuscripts can be classified into three distinct versions, with the other third being hybrids or *unica*. In contrast, the contents of the *Manipulus florum* remained basically stable during nearly two centuries of reproduction in manuscript. By enabling a substantial number of copies to be made, within a short period, from a common exemplar, publication by the stationers probably contributed to this relative uniformity.

For the text of the *Manipulus florum*, the university tradition is the most, not the best. Any edition of the *Manipulus florum* should be produced from a collation of B and C and occasional reference to β, with resort to γ and M only for help in resolving a three-way conflict among the private traditions. But inevitably, if unfortunately, it was the ubiquitous M-text which fell into the hands of the first printer of the *Manipulus*; and, through four centuries, no subsequent printer ever looked at a manuscript.

The *Manipulus florum* was first printed at Piacenza on 5 September 1483 by Jacobus de Tyela (Hain no. 8542). After he had already begun the printing, it seems that he revised his notion of the work's potential popularity and increased the size of his run.[20] Tyela's exemplar contained the second

[20] This is apparently the only book printed by Tyela. See C. F. Bühler, "The Two Issues of the First Edition of the *Manipulus florum*," *Gutenberg Jahrbuch* 28 (1953) 69-72. The copy we have used in this study is described in the *Catalogue of Books Printed in the xvth Century Now in the British Museum* pt. 7 (London 1935) 1072.

university stationers' text. The 1483 printing includes the prologue, beg. "Abiit in agrum...," the text from *Abstinentia* to $\overline{Xpus}$, and the table of topics at the end; but it does not contain the list of authors and works. Furthermore, the edition contains additional extracts not found in the original text. Rather than being additions of the printer they probably appeared in his manuscript exemplar.[21] All subsequent editions of the *Manipulus florum* include these additions, thus confirming that the whole of the printed tradition derives from the *editio princeps*. An edition (Hain no. 8543) containing the same matter—Thomas' prologue, text from *Abstinentia* to $\overline{Xpus}$, and table—was printed by Joannes Rubeus Vercellensis in Venice, 20 December [1493/5?].[22] A half-century later, there began a new interest in the *Manipulus florum*, which saw at least twenty-four editions in a span of thirty years. The first of these, from which all later editions derive, is the edition published in 1550 at Venice "Ad signum spei."[23] Four changes in this edition are significant for the subsequent printed tradition: (1) It abandons the title *Manipulus florum*, substituting instead *Flores omnium fere doctorum...*; henceforth the work is published under some form of the name *Flores doctorum* (*Flores omnium pene doctorum...*, *Flores doctorum pene omnium...*, *Flores doctorum insignium...*). (2) The 1550 edition eliminates Thomas' prologue, substituting an editor's prologue which paraphrases, and occasionally quotes from, Thomas; as a result, the prologue beginning "Abiit in agrum..." does not appear in print after the incunables. (3) The editor has compiled a list of authors whose works are quoted in the text, and has classified them into five groups—Hebrews and Egyptians, Arabs, Greek Christians, Latin Christians, and Latin pagans; this list appears in virtually all later editions. (4) The topic headings $\overline{Xp\imath anus}$ and $\overline{Xpus}$ are altered to *Christianus* and *Christus*, and these two chapters are moved from the end of the work to the appropriate place under the letter *C*, where they remain through all subsequent editions.

Although the text was transmitted via Venice, Lyon was the point from which the *Manipulus florum* was distributed in print, specifically through

---

[21] The following extracts in the Piacenza edition do not appear in the manuscripts (в, с, β, γ, м): *Incarnatio* u; *Ingenium* m; *Iuventus* k-n; *Lacrima* o; *Luxuria* ae; *Maria* aq-bs; *Monachus* ai; *Mors* a, dl; *Mulier* y; *Passio* au; *Perfectio* a; *Providentia* ab; *Relinquere* ap; *Scriptura* e, f, aq; *Tentatio* ae, af; *Tribulatio* k. These, of course, persist through all printed editions. The extracts *Maria* aq-bh (only) appear in this same order in the *Pharetra*; cf. *Sancti Bonaventurae Opera omnia*, 6 (Rome 1596) chapter 5, 108-110.

[22] Concerning John of Vercelli see F. J. Norton, *Italian Printers 1501-1520* (London 1958) 157-160; and *Catalogue of Books Printed in the xvth Century* pt. 5 p. 420. Concerning the source of this edition see Bühler 72.

[23] The printer has not been identified. Examples of this printing are quite rare; the only easily available copy known to us is at the Bayerische Staatsbibliothek, Munich.

the agency of the publisher Guillaume Rouillé.[24] From 1553 to 1580, fifteen editions appeared in Lyon alone, nine of them with Rouillé's name on the imprint and the others bearing the imprint of publishers associated with him, such as Cloquemin & Michel or, most notably, Thibaud Payen.[25] Rouillé, though a Frenchmen, had spent his apprenticeship in publishing at the Venetian establishment of the Giolito family, and he retained his connections in Venice after coming to Lyon around 1543;[26] from this aspect, it is not surprising that the text of the *Manipulus florum* should come from Venice to Lyon by way of Rouillé. From another aspect, however, it is puzzling that Rouillé, with his humanist interests, should have wished to publish this text. It seems an alien among his other publications. Perhaps he produced the *Manipulus florum* as a money-maker, to help finance some of his expensive illustrated editions.[27] Or perhaps he was more favorably impressed by the amount of classical quotation in the *Manipulus florum* than one would have expected. Certainly it is this latter aspect which Rouillé emphasizes in the one-page letter to the reader, which he substitutes for the prologue of the 1550 Venice edition: the *Manipulus florum*, he says, constitutes a treasure, not only of theology but also of all philosophy, from which the reader may freely pick and choose what he likes, concerning elegance of mores and the dignity and integrity of life. Rouillé's edition of 1553 is the immediate source of the Lyonnais editions; of the three Paris editions of 1556-57, which are set up in type line by line from Rouillé ; and of the Antwerp editions, which begin to appear in 1558. Moreover, this 1553 edition is the ultimate source of all later editions, the majority of which, through the eighteenth century, still faithfully reproduce as if it were their own, Rouillé's address to the reader beginning "Anthologiam habes a nobis, candide lector...."

We must note in passing that the Antwerp edition of Joannes Bellerus, 1558, substitutes numbers for letters of the alphabet, as the reference symbols for each of the extracts in the text of the *Manipulus florum.*[28] This

[24] The editions of the *Manipulus* with the locations of known copies are listed in H. L. Baudrier, *Bibliographie lyonnaise* (Lyon 1895-1921).

[25] Concerning printing and the intellectual life of Lyon see René Fédou et al., *Cinq études lyonnaises*, Histoire et civilisation du livre 1 (Paris 1966); and Roger Chartier et al., *Nouvelles études lyonnaises*, Histoire et civilisation du livre 2 (Paris 1969).

[26] The publishing house of Rouillé has been carefully examined by Natalie Davis, "Publisher Guillaume Rouillé, Businessman and Humanist," in *Editing Sixteenth-Century Texts*, ed. R. J. Schoeck (Toronto 1966) 72-112.

[27] We thank Natalie Davis for this assessment of Rouillé's relationship with the *Manipulus florum.*

[28] Regarding Joannes Bellerus see A. Rouzet, *Dictionnaire des imprimeurs, libraires et éditeurs des xve et xvie siècles dans les limites géographiques de la Belgique actuelle* (Nieuwkoop 1975) 8-10.

change, repeated in the subsequent Antwerp editions, was not adopted elsewhere, save in the French editions 1664-1887. Of more consequence was Bellerus' addition to his 1563 Antwerp edition of a selection of extracts from the scriptures and the Fathers under the title *Exceptiones sanctorum patrum*; this, he says, was brought to him by Jacob Place, citizen and bibliophile of Bruges, from a very old exemplar in which they were attributed to Bede and entitled *Scintillae sacrae scripturae*.[29] Finding it useful and a complement to the *Manipulus*, he has included a selection of the extracts at the end of the work for the use of the reader. This added element became firmly attached to the text, and was reproduced as an addendum in at least a dozen subsequent editions extending through the eighteenth century.

It was evidently the Lyon 1567 edition of Thibaud Payen which was the first of the "enlarged" editions. Payen, a publisher-printer, is known to have produced other works on short-term partnership with Rouillé,[30] and this was almost certainly the case for the *Manipulus florum* as well, during the 1550s; evidently Payen did the printing, and he and Rouillé appeared alternately in the title-page imprint. However, Payen sold his press and became strictly a merchant-publisher during the 1560s.[31] It is probable, then, that the edition of 1567 was Payen's own venture. The enlargement comprises many added quotations in the text, including a new chapter entitled *Animal brutum*; the additions are marked with asterisks. Moreover, five new names are included in the list of authors which precedes the text.[32] Payen's additions were widely adopted in later editions, including Rouillé's own subsequent editions.[33] Perhaps more important in the long run was the idea, itself, that the text could be added to and otherwise altered.

This idea was seized with enthusiasm by the Calvinist printer Jacob Stoer in Geneva, who energetically proceeded to transform the *Manipulus florum*

---

[29] "Absoluta prope modum huius operis editione, commodum ad me tulit Jacobus Placius, civis et bibliopola Brugensis, vetustissima quoddam exempla scintillarum sacrae scripturae venerabilis Bedae, a scrutario fortuito casu comparata, in quo praeter caetera habebantur Exceptiones sanctorum patrum ad aedificationem morum...," beginning "Dei omnipotentis filius, verae sacrae suae ... Isidorus: Primum scientiae studium est...," and ending, "... non impletur nisi voluntas Dei." It consists of ca. 160 extracts from the Fathers, the scriptures and Seneca.

[30] Davis 76 n. 13.

[31] Davis 77 n. 15.

[32] The five were Tertullian, Lactantius, Demosthenes, Plutarch and Stobaeus. There was obvious intent to inflate the importance of the classical content, not only by the addition of the last three names but also by a change in the designation of the last group, "Auctores humanitatis *Graeci et* Latini," with the insertion of the words italicized here.

[33] The exceptions are the Antwerp editions, which reproduce Antwerp 1563; the "royal" editions of 1664, 1669, 1678; and the two nineteenth-century editions.

into a Protestant polemic.[34] In his foreword to the reader, which is dated January 1593 (N.S. 1594) and which reappears in his subsequent printings, Stoer observes that he secured the aid of a learned Christian to correct the text, and that this latter emended the corruptions, restored the omissions, and, Stoer notes casually, "added whatever seemed necessary." These additions included three new chapters—*Adulterium, Clementia, Zelus*—and a large number of extracts added to existing chapters; he marked his additions with daggers, to distinguish them from the Payen additions, marked with asterisks, which are likewise included. Furthermore, Stoer made numerous excisions from the text, which are not indicated in any way. The total effect of additions and omissions was to give the *Manipulus florum* a thoroughly Calvinist bias. Stoer's text was placed on the Index in 1642[35] and remained there in every revision of the Index including the last, in 1948. One final remark concerning Stoer's editions: he frequently printed a title page *sine loco*, and very often supplied a location—either Geneva or Cologne—with a hand stamp. Thus, for example, the editions of 1593/4, 1596, 1601 were printed without designation of place, and it appears that the 1614 edition was also. (Although Stoer died on 30 October 1610, works continued to be printed under his name until 1639.) We have seen at the Bibliothèque Nationale in Paris a 1614 edition with Cologne added by hand stamp, and another at the University Library in Cambridge in which the designation Cologne (possibly hand-stamped) has been canceled by stamp and Geneva substituted. Aside from the reissues and new editions in Stoer's name, his version of the text was never adopted by any other publisher. However, in 1606 Stoer's Calvinist version evoked a Catholic edition. This consisted of the 1567 Thibaud Payen text and the added *Exceptiones SS. Patrum* of the Antwerp 1563 edition, with a new introduction denouncing the Stoer editions. Bernhard Wolter, publisher at Cologne, wrote this attack on Stoer (not mentioned by name) in the form of a dedicatory epistle addressed to Bernhard Xylander.[36] Wolter singled out those of Stoer's changes which were particularly irksome to orthodox Catholics, in the chapters *Anti-*

---

[34] Regarding Stoer see Paul Chaix, *Recherches sur l'imprimerie à Genève de 1550 à 1564* (Geneva 1954) 223-224; and H. J. Bremme, *Buchdrucker und Buchhandler zur Zeit der Glaubenskämpfe* (Geneva 1969) 231-233. Ties between Protestant printers in Geneva and Lyon were obviously close. Stoer, for example, printed two titles for Louis Cloquemin, who in 1567 had moved from an association with Rouillé in Lyon to set up shop in Geneva.

[35] See *Catalogue des ouvrages mis à l'Index*, ed. 2 (Paris 1826) 153, s.n. *Hibernicus; Index librorum prohibitorum* (Rome 1900) 293, s.n. *Thomas* ; J. Hilgers, *Der Index der verbotenen Bücher* (Freiburg/Breisgau 1904) 423, s.a. *1642, 7 apr.*

[36] Regarding Wolter see the brief note in Josef Benzing, *Die Buchdrucker des 16. und 17. Jahrhunderts im deutschen Sprachgebiet* (Wiesbaden 1963) 234 no. 92. We have not managed to identify Xylander any further.

christus, Confessio, Ecclesia, Eucharistia, and *Maria.* By excision and addition, he notes, Stoer had altered the first of these, for example, in such a way as to make the description of Antichrist point unmistakably toward the papacy; the quotations on confession had been altered so that their cumulative effect was to support confession directly to God and to denigrate confession to the priest, as if the two were mutually exclusive; and so on. And if one should say in Stoer's defense that he has, nonetheless, employed authentic *sententiae* of the Fathers in his collection, Wolter counters by noting that just as the devil can quote scripture, so a Calvinist can quote the Fathers, and for similar purposes. Wolter published this edition at least once more, a decade later, and it was also reproduced by Martin Endter at Nuremberg in 1699, by which time the issue was surely dead.[37]

The period from 1550 through 1622, which saw the *Manipulus florum* published at least thirty-two times, obviously marked the high point of interest in the work. However, it continued to be printed on occasion, sometimes in isolated editions, sometimes in a brief series of printings which reflected renewed interest in the *Manipulus florum* at a given time and place. P. Variquet at Paris acquired royal permission to print the *Manipulus florum,* giving him exclusive rights for a ten-year period 1663-1673. Variquet's two editions are interesting in that his text combines elements from several previous editions. The basis of his text was the original, pre-asterisk, Rouillé text, following Rouillé in the wording of his title and reproducing Rouillé's letter to the reader, "Anthologiam habes a nobis...." However, Variquet substituted numbers for letters as reference symbols for each extract in the text; he may have done this independently, but it is more likely that he borrowed this element from one of the various editions of Joannes Bellerus, Antwerp, 1558-1576. Finally, although they are not included in his table of chapters, Variquet added three chapters at the end out of alphabetical sequence, *Adulterium, Clementia* and *Zelus,* which come from the Jacob Stoer editions.[38] After Variquet's royal permission had lapsed, Johannes Certe of Lyon acquired permission for a three-year period, 1678-1681. His edition, 1678, was simply a reprinting of Variquet's, with the novelty that it was published in two volumes. The edition of Endter at Nuremberg, 1699, has already been mentioned. The eighteenth-century editions, of Lehmann and Krauss or of Krauss only at Vienna, and of the Jesuits at Turin, reproduce the Endter text, save that they omit the older

[37] Regarding Martin Endter see Benzing 343 no. 70.

[38] Neither Stoer's nor Bellerus' editions could have provided Variquet with the Rouillé preface nor with the wording of Rouillé's title. Therefore, at least three earlier editions went into the making of Variquet's edition.

Wolter dedicatory epistle dated 1606. In other words, these editions contain the Lyon 1567 text of Payen, followed by the *Exceptiones SS. Patrum* from the Antwerp 1563 edition of Bellerus.

In the nineteenth century the *Manipulus florum* was printed twice, in 1858 at Monteregali (= Mondoví), and in 1887 at Paris. The former edition we have not seen. The latter, the editors say, derives from the Variquet edition of 1654 (i.e., 1664),[39] save that they have corrected typographical errors and have added a chapter on St. Joseph. Among their corrections was the placing of Variquet's three final chapters, *Adulterium*, *Clementia* and *Zelus* (taken from Jacob Stoer), into their proper positions in the alphabetical structure; it is ironic to find this condemned Calvinist material incorporated into an edition with the official blessing of the French hierarchy. The editors have undoubtedly made other additions to the text which are not indicated in any way; thus, for example, the last extract under the topic *Maria* comes from the bull *Ineffabilis* of 1854. Prefaced to the text is a letter from Jean-Marie Bécel, bishop of Vannes, commending the new edition of this work as a signal service for preachers, who should quote from "the living sources of our Tradition" in order to give more authority to their teaching. It is a fitting denouement to find at the end of its printed tradition that the *Manipulus florum* was regarded, not as a curious relic for antiquarians nor as an object for scrutiny by historians, but, rather, that it was considered to be a useful tool for preachers, precisely as Thomas of Ireland had intended it at the beginning of its life in manuscript some 580 years earlier.

---

[39] There is no other evidence of a 1654 Variquet edition ; and Variquet's license to print the *Manipulus florum* covered only the years 1663-1673.

7

The Use and Influence
of the *Manipulus florum*

The *Manipulus florum* was a tool, a reference book, carefully compiled for practical purposes. There can be no doubt that it was useful, and that it was used: this is implicit in the very quantity of copies of the work, both in surviving manuscripts and in printed editions. There is no need, then, for any elaborate proof that the *Manipulus florum* was used. Rather, we wish here to deal with specific aspects of its use and influence—such matters as how it was used, and why, and by whom, and to what effect. Thomas of Ireland intended the *Manipulus* primarily as a device to assist preachers in the preparation of sermons. We shall consider first, therefore, how it was employed by preachers, examining especially the "instructions for use" in various *Artes praedicandi*. But with any effective tool, whether *florilegium* or claw-hammer, the scope of its utility is determined by the needs of its users rather than by the intent of its creator. Besides the preachers, the *Manipulus florum* was seized upon by a host of others—florilegists, theologians, mystics, lawyers, vernacular poets—who mined it for authorities with which to shore up the arguments or enliven the language of their various works; this chapter will provide examples to demonstrate the myriad uses to which the *Manipulus* was put. We shall even see the bibliography at the end of the *Manipulus* being employed in ways which Thomas likely did not anticipate. Finally, we shall consider evidence of a less tangible nature, which helps to complete our picture of the influence of the *Manipulus florum*.

1. SERMON COMPOSITION

First and foremost, the *Manipulus florum* was a tool for sermon-writing. It was as such a device that it was published by the university stationers and that it received its widest use. Its value to the compilation of sermons was recognized and advertised by three fourteenth-century manuals on preaching, written by Thomas Waleys, John of Chalons, and an anonymous writer.

The Oxford Dominican, Thomas Waleys, wrote his *De modo componendi sermones*[1] soon after his release in 1342 from house arrest earned by his opposition to John XXII in the "Beatific Vision" controversy. His lengthy and detailed treatise, surviving in six manuscripts, has been edited and thoroughly described by Th.-M. Charland, so that we may confine our discussion to the pertinent part of his work. It is in the last chapter, "Quomodo praedicator dilatare se possit in sermone...," that the *Manipulus florum* is mentioned. Waleys names three methods of expanding the parts or "members" of a sermon—by a logical discussion, by use of *exempla*, and, in the first position, by citation of authorities. The citation of authorities is not to be a haphazard recitation of any and all *sententiae* relevant to the theme; rather, the authorities must be linked together, or connected, in a meaningful way. Waleys' description of the various types of *connexio auctoritatum* is, of course, neatly divided and subdivided in best scholastic fashion. The *connexiones* fall into two large classes, according to the nature of the relationship established between the authorities, namely the intrinsic and the extrinsic. Intrinsic connections themselves may be either direct or indirect. Of direct connections Waleys names eleven types: similitude—that is, when the second authority expresses an idea similar to the first; mediation—when an authority serves as a bridge between the one preceding it and the one following it, by its mutual connection with both; definition—when the second authority defines an important word or idea in the first authority; exposition—when the second authority explains or expounds the sense of the first; and so on, through the connections of description, of causality, of specification, of modification, of confirmation, the relationship of whole to part or part to whole, and the complementary relationship. Indirect connections, though they may travel under three or four different designations, are all essentially connections by opposition—the second authority refers to the contrary of the idea alleged in the first; or the second authority states an exception to a general rule posed by the first, etc. The extrinsic relations between authorities are those imposed from without, that is, the relationships which the preacher himself imposes with his divisions, distinctions, and *acceptiones pluralitatis*.[2] The reason why Waleys presents

[1] Edited by T. M. Charland, *Artes praedicandi: Contribution à l'histoire de la rhétorique au moyen âge*, Publ. of the Institut d'études médiévales d'Ottawa 7 (Paris 1936) 325-403. Concerning Waleys see also T. Kaeppeli, *Le procès contre Thomas Waleys, O.P.*, Institutum hist. FF. praedicatorum Romae ad S. Sabinae, Dissertationes historicae 6 (Rome 1936); B. Smalley, "Thomas Waleys O.P.," *Archivum Fratrum Praedicatorum* 24 (1954) 50-107; idem, *The English Friars and Antiquity in the Early Fourteenth Century* (Oxford 1960); and Kaeppeli, "Le *Campus floretum* de Thomas Waleys," *AFP* 35 (1965) 85-92.
[2] Charland, *Artes praedicandi* 151-152.

this minute analysis of the *connexio auctoritatum* lies in the fact that many sermons, particularly those of the less enterprising preachers, used no other method of expansion; the entire sermon was composed of biblical and saintly authorities carefully chained together. As Waleys observes, "This method of preaching—by linking together of authorities—is quite easy, because it is easy to get hold of the authorities, since alphabetical concordances have been made, of the Bible and of the works of the saints, so that the authorities may easily be found. And similarly, several works have been compiled, such as the one called *Manipulus florum* and other larger ones, in which authorities extracted from the works of the saints are compiled in alphabetical order; so that there is no great difficulty for anyone to get hold of authorities *ad libitum.*"[3]

The *Manipulus florum* is recommended again in an *ars praedicandi* published at Deventer and at Cologne in 1479, *Informatio notabilis et preclara de arte predicandi in thematibus de tempore et de sanctis artificialiter deducta incipit*, beg. "Quattuor sunt genera predicationis. Primum genus est...," ending "*Probat* ... felicitas, excellentia, rosa."[4] The work was also printed with the *De faciebus mundi* of William of Auvergne in two editions, Cologne 1482 and a printing probably at Paris, date and printer unknown. The author of this treatise, and the place and date of its composition, are unknown. Charland identified the text in this book with the second *ars praedicandi* attributed to John of Wales;[5] however, the printed text bears no relationship to the text found in B.N. ms lat. 15005 ff. 79-86 s. xiii and Mazarine MS 569 ff. 80ᵛ-86ᵛ s. xiv (i.e., the text to which Charland refers); and furthermore, several of the sources noted in the printed text are posterior to John of Wales (d. ca. 1285). While this *ars praedicandi*, thus, is difficult to date, its reference to the *Manipulus florum* is straightforward enough. At the close of the text, the author merely observes, "Ad predicandi artem sunt necessarii hii libri—scilicet, Biblia, concordantia, Manipulus florum, Milleloquium August[in]i, dictionarius Bertholdi, Catholicon."[6]

In contrast with the single mention of the *Manipulus florum*, in both the anonymous tract and in Waleys' lengthy treatise, John of Chalons gives us a more concrete picture of the ways in which the *Manipulus florum* could prove useful in the construction of a sermon. The *ars praedicandi* written by

---

[3] Charland, *Artes praedicandi* 390-391. Charland (390 n. 2) mistakenly thought Thomas of Ireland to have been a Dominican.

[4] Charland, *Artes praedicandi* 58 nn. 1, 2; Hain 1861; Copinger 2 no. 3265; Pellechet 1374; *Gesamtkatalog* 2669-2670.

[5] Charland, *Artes praedicandi* 56-58.

[6] We have used the Cologne 1479 edition at the Bibliothèque Nationale, Paris.

John of Chalons, abbot of Pontigny ca. 1372, survives in eight manuscripts.[7] Because it has not been described in print, we shall give a brief
overview here.[8]

The treatise, beg. "Hec est ars brevis et clara faciendi sermones secundum formam sillogisticam...," is divided into fourteen parts which are
grouped into six chapters: 1. *Debiti thematis inventio*; 2. *Divini adiutorii
postulatio, assumpti thematis applicatio, maioris ad propositum formatio*;
3. *Maioris formate probatio, minoris correspondentis subscriptio, minoris
subscripte deductio*; 4. *Materie dilatatio seu prolongatio*; 5. *Conveniens ad
mores disgressio, de proposito in propositum pertinens transitio, auctoritatum
scripture circumlocutio et concordatio*; 6. *Thematis conclusio, divisio et
divisionis prosecutio, totius negotii decens et grata* (?) *titulatio.* John has
called his treatise "The Art of Making Sermons according to the Syllogistic
Form"; and, as the chapter headings indicate, he employs the terminology
of logic rather than of rhetoric. This practice is more than a little discon-
certing. Beneath the surface, one can usually discern a similarity with the
parts of the normal sermon; so that, upon inspection, "Divini adiutorii
postulatio," for example, is seen to be nothing more than the protheme and
prayer. Nevertheless, one gets the impression that a sermon constructed
along these lines—with major premise (stated, confirmed and subdivided),
minor premise (stated, confirmed and subdivided) and conclusion—would
be somewhat at variance with the presumably standard sermon structure
described by Charland.

The most evident utility of the *Manipulus florum* was as an abundant
source of the authorities used to develop or expand the divisions and subdivisions of the theme. It is in this regard that Waleys recommends the
Manipulus florum to his readers, and John of Chalons follows suit. In chapter four, *Materie dilatatio seu prolongatio*, John outstrips Waleys by listing
no less than fourteen modes of expanding one's material. For the eleventh
of these, *Potest materia prolongari per auctoritatum applicatam intermixtio-
nem*, he says, "When anything in any member of the minor premise makes
mention of any virtue, or of any operation of a virtue, one should take note
of that virtue and of the *dictio* which expresses it; and then one should look
for that *dictio* in the Concordance, or in the *Manipulus florum*, or [the
Distinctiones of] Mauritius or the Dictionary [of William Brito]. Then one

[7] Concerning John of Chalons see Charland, *Artes praedicandi* 53, and P. Glorieux,
Répertoire des maîtres en théologie de Paris au xiiie *siècle* 2, Etudes de philosophie
médiévale 18 (Paris 1933) no. 367 *i*.

[8] Our texts are based on B.N. MSS lat. 14580 fols. 152-160 and 15173 fols. 12-24[v],
with 14909 fols. 126-138.

should or could mix together the pertinent authorities."[9] He adds, that not only virtues but other qualities may be "looked up" in the same fashion.

Happily, John of Chalons has not confined his recommendation of the *Manipulus florum* to the obvious, but has mentioned three other ways in which it might prove useful. Two of these mentions appear in his explanation of how one constructs the major premise. John describes the formation of five types of major premise—the illative, the integrative, the divisive, the remotive, and the comparative. It is worthwhile to quote at length John's descriptions of the types of major premise for whose service he adduces the *Manipulus*, that is, the divisive and the remotive.

> The divisive major is that which through many members of division proceeds to elicit that which has been taken as the theme.... An example of the divisive major: suppose that one takes this theme, referring to the Blessed Virgin: 'Ego sum mater pulchre dilectionis.' I shall consider, for the sake of example, that the principal term which occurs in this theme is the term *dilectio*; from this principal term, one constructs the divisive major, saying, from the Scriptures, *dilectio* is revealed as three-fold...,

and he gives them, as is traditional, in parallel rhyming phrases, the effect of which would in this case disappear in translation:

> Una qua Deus super omnia proficitur,
> Alia qua proximus tamquam ipsemet diligitur,
> Tertia qua ad seipsum plus aliis afficitur.

Following the example comes practical advice.

> Concerning the method of constructing this sort of divisive major, the preacher should well and diligently note the *dictio* on the basis of which the division is to be made; he should at once look up that principal *dictio* in the Concordance, and, according to the diversity of authorities written therein, he should note in how many different ways this *dictio* is treated. And if the *dictio* appears in the *Manipulus florum*—as it might be, *Humilitas, Patientia*, and so on—the preacher should look up that *dictio* in the *Manipulus florum*, and should form his division on the basis of the multitude of authorities written therein.... I give as a general rule, that in as many ways as any *dictio* may be taken—or however many ways it may be predicated—just so many members may the divisive major have.[10]

---

[9] "Unde aliquis in aliquo membro minoris fecit aliquam mentionem de aliqua virtute vel aliqua operatione virtutis, debet bene notare illam virtutem, et dictionem per quam signatur, et tunc illam dictionem querere in concordantiis vel in Manipulo florum vel Mauritio vel dictionario; et tunc debet vel potest auctoritates pertinentes intermiscere."

[10] "Maior divisiva est que per multa membra divisionis procedit ad inferendum illud quod sumptum fuerat pro themate.... Exemplum de maiore divisiva: Sumatur istud thema de

The second for which the *Manipulus florum* is useful is the remotive major,

> which infers or elicits through its opposite the chosen theme.... An example
> of the fourth type of major: if the following theme is selected, "Ero humilis in
> oculis meis," a remotive major can be formed. According to that which is
> drawn from Holy Scripture, there are four principal characteristics which op-
> pose humility and proclaim pride, namely,
>> Pomposity in conversation,
>> Singularity in opinion,
>> One's own reputation
>> And one's neighbors' denigration.
> Here you can plainly see that one proceeds to the remotive major by op-
> posites; and note that you can and should take *dictiones* of this sort, in con-
> sidering carefully the *dictio* of the theme and the *dictio* opposed to it. And
> then you should seek out the opposite *dictio* in the Concordance and see its
> conditions and properties—how, and in what manner, and in how many ways,
> the opposite of the theme is taken. For example, in the theme given above, the
> principal *dictio* is *humilitas*, and the *dictio* opposed to it is *superbia*.
> Therefore, in the Concordance under the *dictio Superbia*, or in the *Manipulus
> florum* under the same *dictio*, or in Mauritius or in the Dictionary, look up the
> conditions and properties of *superbia*, and select several of them, and form a
> polymembered proposition which asserts that something-or-other is *superbia*.
> This is the direct opposite of the chosen theme.[11]

---

beata virgine, 'Ego sum mater pulchre dilectionis,' et considerabo principalem terminum qui
ponitur in istud thema. Sit igitur, gratia exempli, iste terminus *dilectio*. Et penes istum terminum principalem sumat divisivam maiorem, dicendo ex scripturis triplex dilectio reperitur,
nam Una qua Deus super omnia proficitur, / Alia qua proximus tanquam ipsemet diligitur, /
Tertia qua ad seipsum plus aliis afficitur. / Ecce maiorem divisivam. Et est notandum quod
circa modum inveniendi huiusmodi maiorem divisivam, predicator debet bene et diligenter
notare illam dictionem penes quam sumitur divisio; statim debet videre in concordantiis
illam principalem dictionem, et secundum diversitatem auctoritatum ibi scriptarum, notare
quot modis accipitur; quod si talis dictio reperiatur in Manipulo florum—sicut esset humilitas, patientia, et sic de aliis—predicator debet illam dictionem in Manipulo florum querere,
et secundum multitudinem auctoritatum ibidem scriptarum, divisionem formare.... Unde do
pro regula generali, quod quot modis aliqua dictio sumitur, de quot etiam aliqua dictio
predicatur, tot membra potest habere maior divisiva."

[11] "Maior remotiva est que per locum ad oppositum infert vel elicit thema sumptum....
Exemplum quarte maioris: Si sumatur istud thema, 'Ero humilis in oculis meis,' potest sic
formari maior remotiva. Secundum quod ex sacris scripturis elicitur, quattuor principales ad-
versantur humilitati et protestantur superbiam, videlicet, Pompositas in conversatione, /
Singularitas in opinione, / Sui ipsius reputatio, / Et proximorum vilipensio. / Hic plane vides
quod proceditur ad remotivam maiorem per oppositum; et notes quod huiusmodi dictiones
potes et debes accipere considerando bene dictionem thematis et dictionem sibi oppositam.
Et tunc debes in concordantiis querere dictionem oppositam, et videre ipsius conditiones et
proprietates, quomodo et que et quot modis inferat oppositum thematis. Verbi gratia, in

The third example appears toward the end of chapter three in a section titled "Ad minoris probationem." Both the major premise and the minor premise are subject to *probatio* (analogous with Charland's "confirmation des parties"); that is to say, according to the elaborately formalized sermon structure of the time, before the preacher could proceed to expand upon the various members of the major or the minor premise, the premise itself must be "proved" or "confirmed." In this discussion of the *probatio* of the minor premise, John observes that, whatever it may be, "oportet quod deducatur per scripturam pertinentem ad propositum, et per glosas coniunctas et sermones et expositiones sanctorum doctorum ... revolventes." Customarily the "proof"—an authoritative statement which verified the preacher's own phrasing of the proposition—was drawn from Scripture, but John of Chalons admits *auctoritates sanctorum* on an equal footing. Hence, the utility of the *Manipulus florum* for this procedure. John gives a hypothetical case of a minor premise in commendation of Holy Scripture; for this, one may find verification or "proof" either through a scriptural concordance, under such headings as *Sapientia, Scientia, Doctrina, Lex dei*; or in the *Manipulus florum* under the headings *Sapientia, Scientia, Scriptura* or *Doctrina*—"unless one is so well provided with authorities that he has no need to resort to volumes of this kind."[12] Again, if one's statement of the minor premise treats directly of any virtue or similar quality, John advises a search under the name of that virtue, and under its opposite, in the Concordance, the *Manipulus florum*, and Mauritius.

Without assuming that John of Chalons' "school" of the syllogistic sermon found any large number of disciples, one may safely suppose that the ideas which occurred to him, for use of the *Manipulus florum*, occurred to others as well; that the *Manipulus florum* served, then, not only as a source of the quotations which were linked together to develop a point, but that it was also a source of ideas for the construction of the sermon divisions, as well as a source of the authoritative confirmation for such divisions. And in all three of the *Artes praedicandi* discussed above, the tacit assumption that every preacher would have knowledge of and access to the text of the *Manipulus florum*, gives a fair indication of the book's importance to fourteenth-

---

proposito thematis, principalis dictio est *humilitas*, et dictio que sibi opponitur est ista dictio *superbia*. Vide igitur in concordantiis in dictione *superbia*, vel in Manipulo florum in eadem dictione, vel in Mauritio vel in dictionario, conditiones et proprietates superbie, et sumas plures ex ipsis, et formes unam propositionem polimembrem que inferat aliquod esse superbiam. Et hoc est directe oppositum thematis assumpti."

[12] "... nisi tamen [tantum: *add.* 15173] sit aliquis auctoritatibus copiosus que non indigeat huiusmodi volumina visitare."

century sermon writing. For how long preachers continued to draw upon the *Manipulus florum* with any regularity we cannot say. The uninterrupted production of new manuscripts through the fifteenth century, discussed below, suggests continued use by preachers. Blench's study of English preachers has noted, in passing, the use of the *Manipulus* by the sixteenth-century Franciscan preacher Stephen Baron.[13] It is likely that future monographic studies of early modern preachers will uncover many more such examples.

When we note the works with which the *Manipulus florum* circulated, we find confirmation of its usefulness for sermons. Although the *Manipulus florum* usually constitutes a codex in itself, it occasionally travels with collections of sermons, with other *florilegia*, or with alphabetical *tabulae*—sourcebooks, in short, for the composition of sermons of one's own. Oxford, Oriel College MS 10 (s. xv) is a large collection of preaching materials which include John Bromyard's *Distinctiones* (called *Summa predicantium* in this manuscript), John Felton's *Sermones dominicales*, with a table to their contents, and the *Manipulus*. In a fifteenth-century manuscript probably from Bohemia (now Winston-Salem, Wake Forest University lat. 1410a), a body of excerpts from the *Manipulus* forms part of a preaching manual. The collection of extracts ("alique auctoritates sanctorum doctorum in materia predicabili necessarie extracte a manipulo florum") is preceded by an anonymous *Ars praedicandi*, and followed by a Bible that is equipped with a calendar, a lectionary, and prayers for before and after sermons. In several codices one finds the *Manipulus florum* in company with other collections of *flores* or *auctoritates*—with extracts from the *Florilegium Gallicum* (Arras MS 305); with extracts from the *Pharetra* (Tours MS 35); with a *flores philosophie* and an *auctoritates Porphirii* (Linz MS 379, El Escorial MS Q III.11, respectively); and, in Braunschweig MS 65, with two collections, an *auctoritates biblie* and an *auctoritates decretorum*. In addition, the *Manipulus florum* travels with *tabulae*, that is, alphabetically-arranged subject indexes to standard works—with John de Fayt's *Tabula moralium Aristotilis* in Graz Univ. MS 445; and with two *tabulae* in Oxford, Merton College MS 129, Kilwardby's on Peter Lombard's *Sentences* and an anonymous table to the Acts of the Apostles and the Pauline and canonical epistles. Finally, one manuscript, Cambridge U.L. MS Ff VI.35, represents an interesting cross-fertilization between the *Manipulus florum* and a

---

[13] J. W. Blench, *Preaching in England* (Oxford 1964) 210-211 and nn. 11-12. We should add that Baron's quotation from Saint Bernard (p. 119) also comes from the *Manipulus florum* (*Tempus g*).

biblical concordance.[14] Following the text of the *Manipulus*, slightly abridged, an anonymous compiler has taken Thomas' topic-headings one by one and has assembled under each a few selected entries found under the same *dictio* in a concordance; it begins, "Abstinentia: Ecclesiasticus [xxv]iii *Abstine te a lite.* i. the.[i]iii *Absti. vos a fornicatione....*" And the compiler reminds us that, just as with the preceding collections, the purpose of his compilation is to facilitate preaching: "Explicit tractatus breviter exceptus de libro concordantiarum secundum titulos contentos in libro qui dicitur Manipulus florum. Qui quidem liber cum dicto tractatu non modicum utilis erit collationem volenti facere vel sermonem."

Two Graz manuscripts of the *Manipulus florum* (Univ. 1254 and a copy of it, Univ. 888) contain an elaborate new *tabula* to the *Manipulus* itself. The compiler of this *tabula*—perhaps the scribe of MS 1254, Andreas Kurzmann, a Cistercian of Neuberg—introduced his work with thirteen lines of verse, beginning "Nunc pagina verte ibique videbis aperte / Tabulam...."[15] After having written the first page of his *tabula* (f. 137), he evidently decided that the verse, after all, would not suffice as an introduction; therefore, he canceled that page and wrote (f. 137[v]) a less fanciful, more practical explanation of the *tabula* and its use.[16] The *tabula* consists of ex-

---

[14] A brief description is given in *A Catalogue of the Manuscripts Preserved in the Library of the University of Cambridge* 2 (Cambridge 1857) 537.

[15] Graz Univ. MS 1254 f. 136[v]:
"(rub.) *Versus super tabulam huius opusculi*
Nunc pagina [*sic*] verte ibique videbis aperte
Tabulam que docet querere quod minime nocet.
Nam facile discit anima quod avide gliscit.
Mox oculis patet liquido quod rusticos latet.
Repperies bona, cupiens celestia dona
Que dominus pie matris prestabit Marie
Fidelibus cunctis crismate cum sacra perunctis.
¶ O genitrix Dei, miserere supplico mei
Ut tibi devotus merear existere totus
Et audiam rite, Benedicti Patris Venite,
Percipite digne regnum, liberati ab igne
Qui Sathane datus angelis eiusque paratus.
Respondeas amen, quia desinit ecce dictamen."

[16] Graz Univ. MS 1254 f. 137[v]: "Ad habendam noticiam tabule subnotate scire debes o lector quod unaqueque auctoritas opusculi suprascripti designata est per litteram alphabeti. Ad inveniendam igitur cuiuslibet auctoritatis concordancia [*sic*] recursum habeas ad tabulam per quam tua caritas docetur quicquid invenire desideras et in diversis locis habetur. Verum si per negligencia [*sic*] littera alphabeti non ponitur, invenies in eodem loco paragrafum qui tripliciter est depictus. Primus enim a parte anteriori, secundus a parte superiori rotundus habetur, tertius vero triangularis describitur. Nec te moveat si due littere consimiles sub uno tytulo describuntur quia propter prolongacione [*sic*] materie interdum eciam ipsum alphabetum duplicatum esse conspicitur. Verbi gratia: Sub titulo qui dicitur *Prelacio* invenies

tensive lists of cross-references, collected under the tituli of the *Manipulus florum*. The compiler has included s.v. *Abstinentia*, for example, not only Thomas' cross-references, taken from the end of that section in the *Manipulus*, but also additional cross-references of his own. The result is a forty-page index "for finding the concordance of any topic" in the *Manipulus florum*; it begins, "*Abstinentia*. ubi Caro f, Coniugium q, Consuetudo b c, Decima y, Discretio f...." A similar, less elaborate table of cross-references appears in Fulda MS Fritzlar 10; in effect, this manuscript has even made a *tabula* of the list of authors and works, by arranging the authors in alphabetical order.

II. *FLORILEGIA*

However, if the preachers were the first and most numerous users of the *Manipulus florum*, others soon recognized its value as a handy book of authorities or quotations. The most extensive and, surely, the most unremarkable borrowing from the *Manipulus* occurs in the propagation of its own species: Thomas of Ireland's collection of extracts was used, repeatedly, in the compilation of other collections of extracts. Some of these *florilegia* were private or personal collections, informal in structure, intended solely for the use of the compiler. Others were public works, that is, works of a formal nature, complete within their own terms of reference, intended to be used by, and designed so as to be usable for, persons other than the compiler. The *Manipulus florum* was mined for both types of collection, the notebook and the finished work.

An example of the former is an anonymous fourteenth-century collection, B.N. MS lat. 3711, written in several hands.[17] The manuscript contains various collections of extracts, largely for contemplation or meditation: a *florilegium* on virtues and vices (fols. 1-114^v); a series of short treatises, on the virtues and vices *inter alia* (fols. 115-154); and extracts from Pseudo-Dionysius (fols. 154-157^v), Jerome (fols. 157^v-158), and Pseudo-Augustine (fols. 159-216). On fols. 217-244^v, in a meridional hand, is yet another *florilegium* on virtues and vices, beg. "Ista sunt originalia quedam acta pluribus materiis...," some ninety-four extracts from works of Augustine, Gregory, Jerome, Leo, Chrysostom, Basil, Cyprian, Valerianus

---

litteram alphabeti videlicet F bis positam, et sub titulo qui dicitur *Predicatio* litteram I. Ergo in tabula si prima littera non concordat cum compendio tunc secunda, et econverso. Hiis ita premissis, precor ut legas, hortor ut repetas et pro collectore preces ad dominum fundas, ne tamen collectori, verum eciam quod pluris est, conditori tuo, ingratus existas."

[17] We are grateful to M. Pierre Gasnault for calling this manuscript to our attention.

of Cimiez, Isidore, Peter of Ravenna, Hugh of Saint-Victor, Bernard, Anselm, and Innocent III. Among the extracts are at least ten from the *Manipulus florum*. The source can be identified not merely because these ten extracts appear in the *Manipulus*, but principally because of the anonymous compiler's attributions: he refers, not to a specific work of each author, but to the *Manipulus*'s topic-heading under which he found the extract. For example, extracts designated "Bernardus de loquacitate" and "Hugo de eadem" (fol. 231) come from Thomas of Ireland's *Loquacitas* (*q* and *u* respectively); "Valerius episcopus in quodam sermone de laude humilitatis" (fol. 228) comes from the section on *Humilitas* in the *Manipulus*; and so on.

A second example falls midway between our two types of *florilegia*: it is a finished work, Arnold of Liège's *Alphabetum auctoritatum*, which has been revised, abridged and added to, to form a private notebook.[18] This work, B.N. MS lat. 3752, is the only version of the *Alphabetum auctoritatum* to contain borrowings from the *Manipulus florum*. Since the history of the *Alphabetum* is as yet unstudied and, as a result, rather muddled, we will take a moment to add what information we have.

The *Alphabetum* survives in four manuscripts, none of which bears Arnold's name; only one, a fifteenth-century manuscript (Maria Saal MS 24 ff. 1-153ᵛ, "Incipit alphabetum auctoritatum....") bears the title *Alphabetum auctoritatum*. The source of the attribution to Arnold lies in the prologue of his better-known work, the *Alphabetum narrationum* (1297-1308), in which Arnold mentions having previously compiled an *Alphabetum auctoritatum*, a collection of authorities arranged alphabetically by topic. The text found in the following manuscripts fits this description, and no other surviving work does: Milan, Ambrosiana MS D 61 sup.; Naples, MS VII G 20; and Troyes MS 1922 fols. 1-86 (Clairvaux L.73). Two of these manuscripts contain a prologue indicating that the work was completed in 1276. The prologue begins, "Tempore quodam cum devotionis..."; text beg. "*De abusionibus seculi*. Cyprianus in libro de duodecim abusionibus seculi; XII sunt...." The manuscript formerly at Münster, Universitätsbibliothek 656, was destroyed in World War II. Troyes 1922 is described in the catalog as extracts from the *Alphabetum*; but a cursory examination indicates that it contains the full text. Munich Clm 8954, mistakenly called *Alphabetum auctoritatum*, is in fact a collection of extracts from the *Manipulus florum*, of which only this manuscript is known. The manuscript formerly Venice SS. Giovanni e Paolo 374 has not been traced.

---

[18] Concerning Arnold of Liège see T. Kaeppeli, *Scriptores ordinis praedicatorum medii aevi* 1 (Rome 1971) 130-133.

Manuscript B.N. lat. 3752 evidently represents a complete revision of the standard text. MS 3752 begins, without prologue, "*De amore hominis ad deum.* Augustinus in libro confessionum xiii: Ponderibus suis...." The order of chapters has been rearranged—for what purpose it is hard to imagine, since the standard text follows two-letter alphabetical order which has been often disrupted in the change, and since the changed order reveals no attempt at logical, as opposed to alphabetical, arrangement. The sequence of the extracts under a given heading is usually altered and the number of extracts drastically reduced, but occasionally new extracts are included as well. In addition, at the end of each chapter is a lengthy section of commentary or exegesis upon a text or texts of the Bible pertinent to the topic at hand. Despite rearrangement, excisions, and additions, enough of the base text of the *Alphabetum auctoritatum* is preserved in MS 3752 to permit one to consider it a version of the *Alphabetum*, rather than a distinct and separate work. One of the changes may be a clue to this version's origin: where the standard text has a chapter *De monachis bonis*, MS 3752 has substituted the heading *De monachis albis*; and the standard text's body of extracts from the works of a variety of Fathers has been reduced to comprise only the quotations from Saint Bernard, plus one brief *auctoritas* attributed to Anselm which was presumably inoffensive to the compiler. From this we may speculate that the compiler was Cistercian; and, from the hand, we judge the manuscript to be southern French, beginning of the fourteenth century. Further than that we cannot go at present.

It would normally be very difficult to spot an instance of borrowing involving an individual extract, but there are fortunately several instances in which the compiler of MS 3752 has preserved the sequence of the extracts as they are found in the *Manipulus*; and this order is, of course, unique. For example, under the heading *Avaricia* (MS 3752 fol. 31^v) are four extracts attributed respectively to "Augustinus in quodam sermone," "Augustinus ibidem," "Augustinus in epistola ad comitem," and "Augustinus de verbis domini." These extracts comprise the first four entries in the *Manipulus* s.v. *Avaricia.*

Specifically, the compiler of MS 3752 borrowed extracts from the *Manipulus florum* for use in the following chapters of his version of the *Alphabetum*: *De amore hominis ad deum* and *De amore dei ad nos* (both s.v. *Amor* in the *Manipulus*), *De anima, De adventu, De avaritia, De angelis, De apostolis*; it is probable that he also borrowed for the chapters *De ambitione* and *De accidia* (only two extracts, both of which reappear in the *Manipulus*), but the evidence is insufficient. And that, evidently, is the sum of it. There seems to be no point in inquiring why the compiler went no further than the letter A, because the possibilities are several and the evidence nil.

In total, this revision of the *Alphabetum auctoritatum* derived some forty-five or fifty extracts from the *Manipulus florum*.

Florilegia intended for public consumption are not necessarily better gauges of the extent of the *Manipulus florum*'s use and influence, but they were at any rate more efficient vehicles of dissemination for Thomas of Ireland's work and (often, but not always) his name. Not surprisingly, examples of such *florilegia* are also easier to find, since they tend to survive in more than one manuscript.

The *Manipulus florum* was used extensively in the version of the *Lumen anime* compiled by Godfrey of Vorau in 1332.[19] The *Lumen* is a manual which provides preachers with *exempla* from the world of natural history with which to illustrate homiletic points. The work exists in three basic versions, the oldest of which, *Lumen* A, was compiled between 1317 and 1330 by Berengar of Landorra, archbishop of Compostella. *Lumen* A was rewritten and enlarged in 1332 by Godfrey, canon of Vorau, producing *Lumen* B. *Lumen* C, considerably smaller than B, was made sometime before 1357, date of the earliest surviving manuscript. In addition to these three basic versions of the *Lumen*, there are numerous variations and combinations of them. The latter account for at least one-third of the approximately 200 surviving manuscripts. This brief review should serve at least to warn the unsuspecting of the morass of problems surrounding the textual tradition of the *Lumen anime*.

Lumen anime B, the version compiled by Godfrey of Vorau which used the *Manipulus florum*, exists in its entirety in only two manuscripts, Vorau 130 (AD 1332) and Klosterneuburg 384; but B was published four times between 1477 and 1482, and it is, thus, the best-known version of the *Lumen*. *Lumen* B consists of three parts: (1) a collection of *exempla* drawn from works of natural history, supplied with "proofs" from the authorities and moralizations from the author, and listed under seventy-six alphabetically arranged topics; (2) a brief illustrated tract on the combat of the virtues and vices; and (3) a collection of extracts from the Fathers, doctors, and philosophers, classified under 267 alphabetically arranged topics. In part 3, the first twelve headings (*De abiectione-De acceleratione*) and the extracts ranged under them appear to be the work of Godfrey. The remaining 255 topic headings (*De abusione, De acceptione personarum, De accidia*, etc.) and the extracts under them are taken from the *Manipulus florum*. Usually only a small portion of the extracts available in the *Mani-*

<hr />

[19] Concerning the *Lumen anime* see M. A. and R. H. Rouse, "The Texts Called *Lumen anime*," *AFP* 41 (1971) 5-113, esp. 38-39; and Kaeppeli 191-194.

pulus are employed in the *Lumen anime*; on the other hand, virtually every one of Thomas of Ireland's 265 topic headings is used in the *Lumen anime*.[20]

This classified list of "sayings" of the authorities bears little relationship to the moralized natural history and the disquisition on virtues and vices which constitute the rest of this work; in addition, this section does not appear in most manuscripts of *Lumen* B. Therefore, when explaining the presence of the alphabetical *florilegium* in the fifteenth-century printings of the *Lumen*, scholars have implied or asserted that it represents an addition made by the fifteenth-century editor, Matthias Farinator. Quite to the contrary, however, we know that this collection of extracts from the *Manipulus florum* was compiled and included by Godfrey of Vorau in 1332. The same authorities are cited in the twelve "original" chapters of part 3 as Godfrey cites in part 1, and the explicit of part 3 reads: "Explicit registrum precedentis libri qui dicitur Lumen anime, excerptum de Manipulo florum." Rather amusingly, this *florilegium* which Godfrey drew, for the most part, from the *Manipulus* to constitute the third part of his *Lumen anime*, assumed a life of its own, and survives apart in three fifteenth-century manuscripts.

Another instance of borrowing from the *Manipulus florum* occurs in the collection called, from its incipit, *Omne bonum*, compiled in England ca. 1350-1360 by an English ecclesiastic named Jacobus. The *Omne bonum* exists, so far as we know, in only one two-volume copy, British Library MS Royal 6 E.vi and 6 E.vii.[21] It is a voluminous encyclopedia of extracts concerning canon law, theology and general information, arranged according to 242 topics which are listed in rough alphabetical order: *absolutio, abbas, abbatissa, abusiones*, etc. In his prohemium the compiler lists approximately 115 sources for his material, including the *Manipulus florum.* Instead of reproducing large portions of the *Manipulus florum* in a separate section, as Godfrey did in the *Lumen anime*, Jacobus has incorporated his borrowings from Thomas of Ireland with his borrowings from other sources, to produce a work that, in its organization and emphasis, is his own. The procedure followed in the *Omne bonum*, rather than that in the *Lumen anime*, is typical of the subsequent use of the *Manipulus florum* by compilers of extract collections.

---

[20] Besides the 255 topics in sequence, 10 of the initial 12 are duplicates of topics in the *Manipulus florum*.

[21] The *Omne bonum* is described by G. F. Warner and J. P. Gilson, *Catalogue of Western Manuscripts in the Old Royal and King's Collections* 1 (London 1921) 157-159; and by Aubrey Gwynn, "The Sermon-Diary of Richard Fitzralph, Archbishop of Armagh," *Proceedings of the Royal Irish Academy* 44 (1937-1938) sect. C, 1-57, esp. 15-16.

The *Tabula originalium* of Andreas de Curtili (Cortile, near Modena?) borrows regularly from the *Manipulus*. Andreas' *Tabula* is known in only one manuscript, Padua, Biblioteca Antoniana 113 (s. xiv[1]; OFM Padua, ex leg. Bp. Hildebrand of Padua, 1352); the author, papal penitentiary under John XXII, identifies himself in the rubric and again in the explicit of MS 113: "Frater Andreas de Curtili ordinis minorum, domini pape penitenciarius."[22] The *Tabula* consists of extracts largely from patristic and medieval authors, entered under several hundred topic-headings arranged alphabetically; those for the letter A begin "Aaron, abba, abbas, abbatissa, Abel, abesse, abicere, abissus, abnegare, abominari, abortivus, Abraham, abreviare, abscendere, abscondere, absintium, absolvere, absorbere, abstinere, abstraere, abuti...." Andreas says in the prologue that he has taken his extracts from a number of works that he lists; and that "the remaining *auctoritates* in this work that are not cited from the preceding books were taken from another work called the *Manipulus florum*."[23] His borrowings from the *Manipulus* are selective rather than inclusive; they are customarily added on, after his extracts from originalia—e.g., the last two extracts s.v. *Abstinere* (s. and t.), the last two s.v. *Advocare* (e. and f.)[24]—but occasionally the *Manipulus* provides all the extracts for a given topic—e.g., *Abuti*, *Accidiari*. The *Tabula* derives techniques as well as extracts from the *Manipulus*. Andreas has given each individual extract a reference-letter, or *siglum*, as he calls it; and his extensive use of cross-references takes both its inspiration and its style from Thomas of Ireland—e.g., "*Accedere*: require *Ordinare* h., *Sacrificare* t." There are, in sum, at least four *florilegia*—from France, Austria, England and Italy—that drew upon the *Manipulus florum* before the middle of the fourteenth century.

More significant in terms of extending its influence was the use made of the *Manipulus florum* by the compiler or compilers of the Lollard compilation known as the *Floretum*.[25] It consists of several thousand extracts from basically patristic authors, grouped by approximately 509 subjects

---

[22] The manuscript is described by Giuseppe Abate and Giovanni Luisetto, *Codici e manoscritti della Biblioteca Antoniana*, Fonte e studi per la storia del santo a Padua 1, 2 vols. (Vicenza 1975) 147-148 and plate 21. Andreas de Curtile appears in a list of papal penitentiaries for October 1316; see K. H. Schäfer, *Die Ausgaben der apostolischen Kammer unter Johann XXII* (Paderborn 1911) 548.

[23] MS 113 fol. 2rb: "Relique autem auctoritates que sunt in isto opere et non notantur in libris predictis fuerunt recepte de quodam alio opere vocato manipulus (!) florum...."

[24] Taken from the *Manipulus florum*, *Abstinentia ab.*, *af.*, and *Advocati b.*, *c*.

[25] We are indebted to Christina von Nolken, Somerville College, Oxford, for having discovered this use of the *Manipulus* and for much of what follows regarding the *Floretum* and *Rosarium*. See C. von Nolken, "An Edition of Selected Parts of the Middle English Translation of the *Rosarium theologie*," D.Phil. diss. (Oxford 1976).

alphabetically arranged from *Absolutio* to *Zizania*. The entries in the *Floretum* are divided into numbered sections, and its index makes clear that further division by letter, probably on the model of the *Manipulus*, was intended; but no surviving manuscript bears letters. The *Floretum* was compiled sometime between 1384 and 1396. It is anonymous and neither its prologue nor its text reveals anything regarding its author. Because it quotes Wycliffe and reveals the pertinent preoccupations in its entries, one can see that it was developed in a Wycliffite context.[26] Its use can be traced in Lollard tracts and sermons, and its compiler is described by Thomas Netter as a disciple of Wycliffe.[27] It was apparently quite popular.

Moreover, the *Manipulus* was transmitted not only through the *Floretum* but also through the abbreviations and translation made of it. Shortly after its compilation the *Floretum* was abridged, producing a text resembling Cambridge, Trinity College MS 1358; and from that state it was reworked into the text known to us as the *Rosarium theologie*. This involved both excisions and the introduction of fresh material. On the basis of its text, it seems likely that the *Rosarium* was produced and copied at a center, and that it is not far removed in date from the *Floretum*. A Middle English translation of the *Rosarium* was made shortly thereafter.

The use of the *Manipulus* in the *Floretum* is relatively easy to discern, for the compiler of the latter borrowed large chunks. Under the letters A-E, taken as a sample, the *Manipulus* has 82 subject headings and the *Floretum* 135; 63 headings coincide. The subjects omitted in the *Floretum* are of unlikely interest to Wycliffites, while those introduced often seem to have a particular interest—for example, *Absolutio*, *Additio*, *Adoratio*. The compiler of the *Floretum* used material from at least forty-one of the sixty-three common subject headings in the *Manipulus*, and sometimes quite extensively. The length of borrowed extracts corresponds, save in a very few cases where the compiler of the *Floretum* has abbreviated a citation—for example, (*Floretum*) *Divitie* 3, where texts from (*Manipulus*) *Divitie c* and *d* are shortened, although *Divitie o, p, x* and *y* are borrowed in full. The attributions also correspond exactly, including those for which Thomas of Ireland was vague, such as "Aug. in quodam sermone" or "Jer. in quadam epistola." Since the compiler of the *Floretum* was selective, he occasionally had to replace Thomas's *ibidem* with the original reference found further up the column in the *Manipulus*, and at times he looked too far up the column.

---

[26] Regarding the *Floretum* and the *Rosarium* see A. Hudson, "A Lollard Compilation and the Dissemination of Wycliffite Thought," *Journal of Theological Studies* 23 (1972) 65-81, and "A Lollard Compilation in England and Bohemia," ibid. 25 (1974) 129-140.

[27] Thomas Netter, *Doctrinale* 2.135, 145.

This explains several curious attributions in the *Floretum*. Another clear indication that the *Floretum* used the *Manipulus* is the fact that the order or sequence of the citations in the latter is preserved, in spite of the fact that the compiler of the *Floretum* drew on the *Manipulus* selectively. For example, (*Floretum*) *Adiutorium* 3 quotes (*Manipulus*) *Adiutorium* b, c, d, f, h and ab in that order; (*Floretum*) *Excusatio* reproduces in order (*Manipulus*) *Excusatio* a, b, c, h, i, k, l, n, q and r. Very occasionally the order is changed, and then only slightly. Thomas of Ireland's order can be seen even in the *Rosarium*, despite the substantial rearrangement of that text—for example, under the heading *Monachus*, where the order (*Manipulus*) i, l, n, ae has survived. The selection of extracts from the *Manipulus* for the *Floretum* appears to be random, though there is a tendency to prefer shorter examples. The entire entry in the *Manipulus* for *Excommunicatio* reappears, with additional material, under that heading in the *Floretum*. Occasional entries in the *Floretum* (e.g., *Conversatio*, *Excusatio*) derive wholly from the *Manipulus*. More often at least one of the numbered sections under a heading comes from the *Manipulus* (e.g., *Confessio* 2, *Conscientia* 6 and 7, *Consuetudo* 2); and frequently the *Manipulus* provides part of a section (e.g., *Bona* 2, *Castitas* 2). At times more intelligent use has been made of the *Manipulus*, as in the dispersal of its material under *Amicitia*, *Amor* and *Adventus*. Thomas's cross-references were heeded, material from his entry *Lacrima* appearing under the heading *Fletus* as he suggests. The *Manipulus* accounts for the *Floretum*'s entire knowledge of certain authors, among them Chrysostom (apart from the *Opus imperfectum in Matheum*, for which a separate classified source must have been used), Cassian, Cassiodorus, and probably Boethius and Seneca. It is not that these authors were unavailable, or less available than others; they were just more readily available in the *Manipulus* than in the *armaria*.

The *Floretum* and the texts deriving from it are known in at least 47 manuscripts. It circulated in Bohemia as well as in England, carrying within it sizable portions of the *Manipulus florum* for the use of Wycliffite and Hussite preachers.

The *Pharetra doctorum et philosophorum* printed by Mentelin at Strasbourg in 1472, also has borrowed from the *Manipulus*.[28] This *Pharetra* is a revision and considerable enlargement of the well-known mid-thirteenth-century *Liber Pharetrae*. The latter, organized by subjects arranged in four books, was written by an anonymous Franciscan sometime before 1261, the

[28] *Catalogue of Books Printed in the xvth Century now in the British Museum* 1 (London 1908) 56; Hain-Copinger 12908.

date of the earliest dated manuscript.[29] The revised and enlarged *Pharetra* is
not known before 1472; the only surviving manuscript is one copied from
the Mentelin edition.[30] It is possible that the enlargement was produced for
this publication. The enlarged version begins, "In conversionis mee primor-
dio cum pro mentis recreatione [this, and at least half of the prologue, are
taken verbatim from the smaller *Pharetra*].... *Incipit nomina doctorum*. Ambrosius, Anastius [*sic*], Augustinus.... *Tabula materiarum in generali*. De
abbate, De abbatissa, De abysso.... *De abbate*. Gregorius in registro...,"
and ends, "... recte dicitur in libro Job: Qui affert stellas pluvie et effundit
ymbres ad instar gurgitum." Although his model, the early *Pharetra*, is
arranged topically in scholastic order beginning, inevitably, with *De deo*,
the compiler of the revision has classified his material according to some
930 topics alphabetically arranged, and his list of *nomina doctorum* contains
approximately 180 names. There is no acknowledgement that he has
gleaned some of his material from the *Manipulus florum* (just as there is no
mention of the earlier *Pharetra*, which he has plundered thoroughly), but
the agreement in length of quotation and manner of citation betrays his
source. For example, under the heading *De acceptione personarum* the
Pharetra lists four extracts from book 3 of Isidore's *De summo bono* (i.e.,
Sententiae), the first two with chapter references, the last two without; these
last two are identical with the only extracts ascribed to Isidore under the
same topic in the *Manipulus florum*, where they are cited as coming from
De summo bono book 3, without chapter numbers.[31] As a general observation, one may say that the compiler of the enlarged *Pharetra* used the
Manipulus florum from beginning to end of his work, but used it sparingly.

Finally, the *Manipulus florum* provided material used in the compilation
of a series of classified, alphabetically arranged anthologies in the early

---

[29] Salzburg, St. Peter's MS IV.34. This older *Pharetra* is printed among the works of
Saint Bonaventure, *Opera* 6 (Rome 1596) 102-208; see *Opera omnia* 8 (Quaracchi 1898)
cxv. This text, still anonymous, is variously ascribed, on the basis of manuscript at-
tributions, to William of Fourmenterie (British Library, Royal MS 8 C.xvi; Glorieux, *Réper-
toire* 2.45), Albert of Cologne (Toulouse MS 175), and Gilbert of Tournai (E. Longpré,
Tractatus de pace auctore fr. Gilberto de Tornaco [Quaracchi 1925] xxiv-xxviii). This
Pharetra survives in over two hundred manuscripts and is to be distinguished from the
Pharetra fidei catholici.

[30] Paris, B.N. MS lat. 3275, copied for Jean Budé shortly before 5 December 1487 by
Jean de Bailleul. See M. C. Garand, "Les copistes de Jean Budé (1430-1502)," *Bulletin*, Institut de recherche et d'histoire des textes, 15 (1969) 298-299.

[31] Other examples: *De accidia*, the last entry under *Gregorius* equals the only entry attributed to Gregory under this heading by Thomas; *De abstinentia*, of the twelve quotations
from Gregory's works six are taken from the *Manipulus florum*, of the more than thirty attributed to Jerome three come from the *Manipulus*; *De ambitiosis*, the first of the three extracts attributed to Gregory comes from the *Manipulus florum*.

modern period. At least three of these drew upon the *Manipulus florum* directly (as opposed to indirect use through borrowing from another collection which had mined the *Manipulus florum*). The *Manipulus florum* was used, without acknowledgement, in the compilation of perhaps the earliest significant printed anthology of extracts, the *Polyanthea* of Dominicus Nannus Mirabellius, 1503.[32] The *Manipulus florum* was only one of Nani's sources for patristic quotations; and although he sometimes borrows heavily—of the thirty-five extracts which Thomas of Ireland lists under *Abstinentia*, eighteen reappear in the *Polyanthea*[33]—Nani does not reproduce Thomas' order. Almost a century later, in 1598, Joseph Lang used and acknowledged the *Manipulus florum* as his major source for patristic *sententiae* in the *Loci communes...* or *Anthologia...*.[34] Since he acknowledged this source in his prologue, Lang was under no compulsion to disguise his borrowings but rather reproduced long strings of extracts in the same order in which they appeared in the *Manipulus florum*. As Ullman notes, Lang could not have derived these indirectly through Nani because, using *Abstinentia* as a test, Ullman found that "only eight (i.e., eleven in the 1517 edition available to us) of Lang's seventeen from Thomas are identical with Nani's."[35] In addition, Lang's reproduction of *Manipulus florum* order is proof in itself of direct borrowing. When Lang in 1604 produced a revision and enlargement of Nani's *Polyanthea*, the *Polyanthea nova* (Lyon 1604) he not only combined with Nani's material much of his own *Anthologia*, but incorporated additional material, including a fresh infusion from the *Manipulus florum*. On both occasions Lang's use of the *Manipulus florum* was uncritical, to the extent that he even perpetuates Thomas' attribution of the *Policraticus* to John Chrysostom.[36] As far as we can tell on the basis of a rapid survey, Lang did not draw upon the *Manipulus florum* for his *sententiae philosophorum*; but he included, in the *Polyanthea nova*, virtually all

[32] We have used the edition of Strasbourg, 1517. Our awareness of this use of the *Manipulus florum* stems from a discussion of early anthologies and their sources by B. L. Ullman, "Joseph Lang and his Anthologies," in *Festschrift for John G. Kunstmann*, University of North Carolina Studies in Germanic Languages and Literatures 26 (Chapel Hill 1959) 186-200.

[33] Our count is slightly at variance with Ullman's, p. 195.

[34] *Anthologia...* is on the first page of the 1598 edition, to be replaced by *Loci communes...* on the title page in the 1605 edition. Ullman, p. 187, suggests that Lang may have borrowed from Thomas "the very arrangement of material, beginning with *Abstinentia....*" This perhaps overstates the case, since by the end of the sixteenth century alphabetically arranged *florilegia* were not rare; and one could name others among them which began with *Abstinentia*, including the *Flores bibliorum*, another of Lang's sources.

[35] Ullman, "Joseph Lang" p. 195.

[36] See, for example, *Adulatio* in both works. The misattribution stems originally from a rubricator's error in Thomas of Ireland's source, the *Flores paradysi*; see above, ch. 5, p. 145f.

of the *Manipulus florum*'s patristic quotations, reproduced in Thomas of Ireland's order. Thus, from 1604 on, it becomes next to impossible to judge whether any borrowings from the *Manipulus florum* come directly from that work or whether, instead, they are taken from Lang. Certainly the various enlargements of Lang's work, the *Novissima Polyanthea* (first printed 1613), the *Polyanthea novissimarum* (probably first printed 1615), and the posthumous *Florilegium magnum* (first ed. 1620),[37] do not represent direct use of the *Manipulus florum*.

III. LATIN AUTHORS

Extracts from the *Manipulus florum* doubtless found their way into numerous other homiletic aids, such as the logically and alphabetically arranged *florilegia*, the moralized biblical dictionaries, and the collections of model sermons which abound in fourteenth- and fifteenth-century libraries. However, its usefulness was not limited to these. Anyone, from theologian to secular poet, who needed ready access to quotations from the authorities might resort to the *Manipulus florum*. But the use of the *Manipulus* by such writers of original compositions is much harder to trace. Authors would see no need to cite the *Manipulus*, and modern textual scholars until recently have not paid particularly close attention to the intermediate sources upon which medieval authors relied. The following examples, not intended to be exhaustive, will illustrate the variety of services which the *Manipulus*, often unnoticed, might perform.

William of Pagula, an early fourteenth-century doctor of law and vicar of Winkfield near Windsor, drew on the *Manipulus florum* for his *Summa summarum* written sometime between 1319 and 1322.[38] The *Summa* is a collection of questions and answers on canon law, arranged according to the Decretal-rubrics with a number of Pagula's own topics inserted, and supplied with fairly precise citation of sources; according to Boyle, it is the only

---

[37] These are discussed in Ullmann, "Joseph Lang" 196. We have seen only the 1620 version.

[38] William of Pagula is discussed by Leonard E. Boyle, O.P., "A Study of the Works Attributed to William of Pagula with Special Reference to the *Oculus sacerdotis* and *Summa summarum*," 2 vols., D.Phil. diss. (Oxford 1956); summarized in "The *Oculus sacerdotis* and Some Other Works of William of Pagula," *Transactions of the Royal Historical Society* ser. 5, 5 (1955) 81-100. See now Boyle, "The *Summa summarum* and Some Other English Works of Canon Law," in *Proceedings of the Second International Congress of Medieval Canon Law*, ed. Stephan Kuttner and J. J. Ryan, Monumenta iuris canonici, ser. C, 1 (Vatican City 1965) 415-456; for the date, see 419 n. 21.

summa of canon law produced in the fourteenth and fifteenth centuries in England.[39] Naturally, this summa of canon law contains none of the *sententiae* of fathers, doctors and ancients which compose the body of the *Manipulus florum*; but William's prologue contains borrowings from Thomas' prologue. This borrowing, admittedly a bit surprising, is by no means an illogical occurrence. The *Manipulus florum* and the *Summa summarum*, despite their obvious differences, are both collections of materials drawn from other sources; and each required a prologue explaining the purpose of the work, the method of its compilation, and the manner in which it should be used. When William came to write his prologue, he found an existing one, Thomas's, which contained several passages suitable, *mutatis mutandis*, to his own needs. We give below the parallel passages.

Summa summarum[40]	*Manipulus florum*
Incipit speculum ... per quod quilibet litteratus quascumque materias et questiones iuris canonici cuiuscumque ponderis *faciliter poterit invenire, et breviter eisdem materiis et questionibus respondere...* (p. 440, lines 8-11).	Istorum autem auctorum libros ... signaui *ut facilius possent cognosci et securius allegari* (infra, p. 238, lines 3-5).
Quidquid igitur in prato spinoso iuris tanquam lato et diffuso sparsim seritur *quasi in unum manipulum ex diversis spicis collectum breviter hic collegi ... ut sic a me et aliis simplicibus possint* dubia lata et obscura et diffusa alibi hic sub compendio *faciliter reperiri* (p. 440, lines 19-27; *reperiri: inveniri*, Boyle).	*... hic breuiter quasi in unum manipulum ex diuersis spicis collectum ... collegi ut sic a me et aliis simplicibus facilius possint reperiri* (p. 236, lines 9-11).
Tu ergo lector ora pro collectore et diligenter suscipe quesita cum alieno labore et gaude de inventis sine labore. Nomen autem collectoris exprimere nolo ne collectio vilescerit cognito collectore (p. 443, lines 127-129).	*Tu ergo lector ora pro collectore et utere quesitis cum labore alieno et gaude de inuentis sine labore proprio.*[41] (University editions add:) *Nomen autem collectoris uolui subticere ne collectio uilesceret cognito collectore* (p. 238, lines 5-7).

In explanation of their respective systems of designating items with letters of the alphabet to facilitate reference to them:

---

[39] Boyle, diss. 1: 418-423.

[40] Edited by Boyle, "The *Summa summarum*" 440-443.

[41] The phrase "utere ... proprio" that Pagula borrows from the prologue of the *Manipulus florum*, Thomas of Ireland had in turn borrowed from the prologue of *Flores paradysi* c; see below, Appendix 2 n. 10.

*... et ubi una litera alphabeti non suffi-
cit tunc litere combinantur. Et hec patent plenius intuenti* (p. 443, lines 135-
136).

*... et ubi alphabetum simplex non suf-
ficit combinatum iteratur ... et hec planius* (univ. edd.: *plenius*) *patent intuenti*
(p. 237, lines 18-26).

The first of the above parallels is an echo rather than a quotation, but the
two passages express the same thought with the same rhetorical device,
"faciliter poterit inuenire et breuiter respondere" versus "facilius possent
cognosci et securius allegari." Given the other unmistakable instances of
borrowing, we are probably justified in assuming that in this instance as
well William of Pagula's choice of expression was influenced by Thomas of
Ireland.

There were doubtless many writers whose borrowings from the *Manipulus
florum* were so scant, and so thoroughly merged with other materials, that
their reliance on Thomas of Ireland would be hard to discover. Such cases
come to light only upon the occasion of a thorough study of an individual
work. An example is the use of the *Manipulus florum* by Johannes of Dambach (1288-1372), an Alsatian Dominican, in writing his *Consolatio theologiae*. The detailed study of the *Consolatio* by P. Albert Auer[42] ferreted out
numerous instances in which Johannes borrowed from the *Manipulus*, instances which would otherwise have passed unnoticed. Johannes of Dambach used the *Manipulus florum* as a source particularly for classical
quotations, and he used it as well for material from Valerius Maximus and
from the *Proverbia philosophorum*. Auer concludes that the *Manipulus* did
not provide any of Johannes' quotations from Cicero; however, if the *sententiae* which Auer cites *in extenso*[43] are a fair indication, it seems likely to
us that some of the Cicero material also was provided by Thomas of
Ireland. Johannes of Dambach composed the *Consolatio theologiae*, his
most important work, over a lengthy time period—the prologue was written
as early as 1338/41, and the finished product appeared in 1366. During
this time Johannes lived briefly in Prague, where he served in 1347 as the
first lecturer at the Dominican *studium generale*; as we have seen,[44] Thomas

---

[42] Albert Auer, o.s.b., *Johannes von Dambach und die Trostbücher vom 11. bis zum 16.
Jahrhundert*, Beiträge zur Geschichte der Philosophie und Theologie des Mittelalters 27
(Münster i.W. 1928); F. Stegmüller, "Die *Consolatio theologiae* des Papstes Pedro de Luna
(Benedikt xiii)," in *Gesammelte Aufsatze zur Kulturgeschichte Spaniens* 21 (Münster i.W.
1903) 209-215; and Kaeppeli, *Scriptores* 2: 400-405.

[43] Auer, *Johannes von Dambach* 97-98.

[44] See above, ch. 4, pp. 102-103.

of Ireland was "in vogue" at Prague for a time. The major part of this
period of composition, from around 1350 on, was spent in Strasbourg; it
may, instead, have been there that Johannes made use of the *Manipulus
florum*.

Quite the opposite in magnitude is the next example, in which materials
from the *Manipulus florum* abound. This work is the long anonymous commentary on *Valerius ad Rufinum ne ducat uxorem*, found in Lambeth Palace
Library MS 330. As Robert Pratt describes the commentary, "Here the fifteen pages of *Valerius ad Ruffinum* are treated in some two hundred pages
of smothering discourse, almost wholly moralistic in tone."[45] The work
begins with a four-part prologue on the true meaning of friendship (ff. 1-
11ᵛ), followed by the commentary proper; both prologue and commentary
consist of innumerable quotations from authorities, Christian and pagan,
strung together with the author's own moralizations. Of these quotations, a
very high percentage—nearly half, according to Pratt—are found in the
Manipulus florum. We have examined carefully the first few pages of the
prologue, where the incidence of borrowings from the *Manipulus florum* is
considerably higher. For example, the prologue contains the following extracts: fol. 1ʳ, *Discordia i, Amicitia az, ay, bf, by, bs*; fol. 1ᵛ, *Amicitia ai,
Fortitudo u, Dilectio y, Amor ao, Amicitia i*; fol. 2ʳ, *Amicitia k, m, u, at, ca*;
fol. 2ᵛ, *Amicitia x, ch, e, ca, cr, ce, al, cd, bo, l*. For these four pages every
quotation, save those from the Bible, comes from the *Manipulus florum*.
Pratt, in his study of the commentary, argued that it was written by the
author of the *Manipulus florum*, having assumed that author to be John of
Wales. However, that cannot be the case because, first, as was shown above,
John did not compile the *Manipulus florum*; and second, the relationship is
not that of two works having a common author but, quite simply, of two
works one of which, the commentary, has borrowed profusely from the
other, the *Manipulus florum*. While the commentary must thus return to
anonymity, one can at least provide a piece of factual evidence regarding its
date, namely, that the commentary was written after 1306.

One often assumes, and with some justification, that works such as the
Manipulus florum were responsible for a deterioration in vitality and originality, since they were used as substitutes for the whole works, and since
they were usually applied mechanically. It is on these grounds that Petrarch
castigated an opponent for making use of the *Manipulus*: John of Hesdin,
who lectured on the scriptures at Paris ca. 1340-1378, championed the
French cause in the war of words with Petrarch, who was attempting to woo

---

[45] R. A. Pratt, "Jankyn's Book of Wikked Wyves," *Annuale mediaevale* 3 (1962) 16-18.

the papacy away from Avignon and back to Rome in the 1360s.[46] Hesdin wrote ca. 1368-1370 an invective against Petrarch's position, defending Avignon and vilifying Rome and the Romans, in a letter liberally sprinkled with classical quotations used as *auctoritates* in support of his position. The letter of course provoked a scathing response. Among other things, Petrarch sneers at Hesdin (whom he identifies only as "a certain nameless Frenchman") for daring to do polemical battle with him, dragging along "all the books he could find, or rather, a *Manipulus florum*—a truly French work—which the frivolous French regard as the equivalent of all books."[47]

We know—but it is questionable whether Petrarch did so—that John of Hesdin elsewhere used the *Manipulus florum*. In his *lectura* on Titus (written 1362-1367), Hesdin not only employed the *Manipulus* but even cited it as his source on at least one occasion: commenting on Titus 3.5, Hesdin quoted Saint Bernard with the reference, "in Manipulo florum ponuntur."[48] In his invective, however, there are no borrowings from the *Manipulus*. Petrarch's shot was, thus, wide of the mark; but doubtless the specifics were unimportant to him. He meant unmistakably to convey the insult that his opponent was a man who read, not books, but extracts only. The point to notice here is that Petrarch did not say merely, "a *florilegium*," but singled out the name of the most famous collection of extracts of his day. Evidently, the defender of all things Italian and classical had, himself, a ready acquaintance with that "truly French work," the *Manipulus florum*.

Besides the discouraging instances represented by Hesdin and the Valerius commentator, we have seen the enthusiastic acceptance of the *Manipulus florum* by the codifiers of the scholastic sermon, whose work demonstrates, according to Charland, that "one had to know a prodigious amount in order to preach so badly."[49] But we must remember that the

---

[46] Concerning John of Hesdin see Beryl Smalley, "Jean de Hesdin O.Hosp.S. Ioh.," *Recherches de théologie ancienne et médiévale* 28 (1961) 283-330, and E. Cocchia, "Magistri Iohannis de Hysdinio Invectiva contra Fr. Petrarcham et Fr. Petrarchae contra cuiusdam Galli calumnias Apologia," *Atti della Reale accademia di archeologia, lettere e belle arti di Napoli* n.s. 7.1 (1920) 91-202. On the exchange with Petrarch, see P. de Nolhac, *Pétrarque et l'humanisme* 2 (Paris 1907) 303-312.

[47] "Donec emendicatis ostiatim stipendiariis, ut sic dixerim, auxiliis, omnesque quos invenire potuit libros, sive unum manipulum florum—opus vere Gallicum—et quod Gallica levitas pro omnibus libris habet in proelium secum trahens, auderet in aciem venire...." Cocchia 141-142. Neither Cocchia, who translates "*manipulum florum*, 'mazzo di fiori', bouquet," (141 n.), nor B. L. Ullman, who in "Some Aspects of the Origins of Italian Humanism," *Studies in the Italian Renaissance* (Rome 1955) 34, translates it as "only a handful of extracts," recognized Petrarch's reference to Thomas of Ireland.

[48] Smalley, "Jean de Hesdin" 303.

[49] Charland, *Artes praedicandi* 224.

Manipulus florum was a tool, whose use, good or ill, depended upon the workman. Therefore, we should not be surprised to find that Thomas of Ireland's work could render service to a new and vital movement, that of the late fourteenth- and early fifteenth-century Dutch mystics. While the sources drawn upon by the Windesheim Congregation are still in the process of being studied, we know that one of the brothers, John of Schoonhoven, drew upon the *Manipulus florum* for his *De contemptu mundi*; and there is reason to suppose that further investigation will show this source being used by other writers of the community as well.

John was born in 1356 at Schoonhoven, some ten miles south of Gouda.[50] He studied at the arts faculty in Paris, was licensed in 1374, and went to the Augustinian house of Groenendael in 1377. There he knew John Ruysbroeck (d. 1381) and John of Leeuwen (d. ca. 1378). He became prior of Groenendael, probably in 1386, and retained the position until his death in 1432. His *De contemptu mundi* was completed between 1384 and 1419 and survives in thirty-one manuscripts.[51]

De contemptu huius mundi is a brief treatise on the text, "Do not love the world nor those things which are in the world," 1 John 2:5. The life of this world is not life but death, and those who love the world constitute themselves enemies of God. Fortunately, there are seven signal disadvantages of the worldly life itself which, when well considered, make it easy for a man to rise above his attachments to the world. Schoonhoven discusses the seven points in turn, couching much of his argument in quotations adapted from the fathers—principally from Gregory, with much also from Bernard, as well as from Augustine, Jerome, Anselm and others. Much of this material was taken according to Gruijs from intermediate sources, *florilegia* and collections of proverbs and verses, such as the *Florilegium Gottingense* and the *Pharetra*.[52] With the exception of the biblical concordance, the *Manipulus florum* was the single most heavily used intermediate source. On perhaps as many as eleven occasions, the quotations have been derived by

[50] Much of our discussion of John of Schoonhoven is based upon the doctoral dissertation (Thèse de doctorat du 3ᵉ cycle [Philosophie médiévale] soutenue le 10 juin 1967 à la Faculté des Lettres et Sciences humaines de l'Université de Paris) of Albert Gruijs, *Jean de Schoonhoven (1356-1432) ... De contemptu huius mundi: Textes et études*, 3 vols. (Nijmegen 1967). Concerning his life see 3: xvi-xvii, app. 2; and A. Gruijs, "Jean de Schoonhoven, *De contemptu huius mundi*," *Bulletin Du Cange: Archivum latinitatis medii aevi* 32 (1962) 135-187, 33 (1963) 35-97. The comments on Thomas of Ireland and the *Manipulus florum* should be used with caution.

[51] Manuscripts are listed by Gruijs, diss. 1: 23.

[52] Ibid. 3: 9-24, "Les sources: S. Augustin, S. Grégoire, S. Bernard, S. Jérôme à travers les florilèges..."; for Thomas of Ireland see p. 9 n. 11.

way of the *Manipulus florum*; the extracts listed under the heading *Mundus* have provided most of these.[53]

The use of the *Manipulus florum* by a Dutch mystic of the *Devotio moderna* finds a curious echo across the Channel, in two manuscripts in which the *Manipulus* text has been adapted to make it suitable for devotional reading. In one of these (Cambridge, Univ. Library Ii VI.39 ff. 67-71), the process of adaptation was simply one of selection. On these folios one finds a few selected passages, from each of the first twelve topics in the *Manipulus florum*, from *Abstinentia* through *Amor*. In the same codex are a variety of devotional tracts, on chastity ("A Tretis of Maydenhod," possibly by Richard Rolle), on the Passion, on prayer and contemplation, including the *Cloud of Unknowing*. The other manuscript (Cambridge, Peterhouse 268) consists of an altered *Manipulus florum* text. The small format of the codex ($4\frac{1}{2}$" × $3\frac{3}{4}$") emphasizes that this was a book for private devotional reading, a handbook rather than one intended for a lectern. In this version, again, the *Manipulus florum* is heavily abridged, with only selected topics and, under each heading, only selected extracts, beginning with "*Amor*. Augustinus: Nichil tam durum...." For each letter of the alphabet, following the topics which begin with that letter the adapter has added a section called *Narratio*, which is an extract from the writings, or about the life, of a saint whose name begins with the given letter.

IV. VERNACULAR AUTHORS

Our last examples find the *Manipulus florum* far removed from its scholastic origins, serving as a sourcebook for secular literature in the vernacular.

Christine de Pisan (1364-1430), in vernacular works which were written for the French court circle, borrowed freely from the *Manipulus florum* and other compendia. This fact, and the extent of her borrowing for one major work, were established by P. G. C. Campbell.[54] *L'épitre d'Othéa*, the work which is Campbell's central concern, is a treatise on the character and deportment of a true *chevalier*. It is divided into one hundred parts, each dealing with a particular virtue to be emulated, a particular vice to be

[53] Citing Gruijs's edition (diss. vol. 1) and the *Manipulus* references: 3, lines 9-11, *Mundus d.*; lines 82-85, *Mundus c.*; lines 88-89, *Mundus z.*; 4, lines 78-80, *Consolatio i.*; 5, lines 4-8, *Mundus u.*; line 23, *Mundus q.*; lines 24-27, *Mundus s.*; lines 102-104, *Mundus t.*; 6, lines 44-47, *Mundus c.*; lines 54-63, *Mundus o*. We have not located 1, lines 3-7, for which Gruijs gives the reference "Hib. 'mors'."

[54] P. G. C. Campbell, *L'épitre d'Othéa: Etude sur les sources de Christine de Pisan* (Paris 1924), esp. 163-168.

avoided, or an admonition to be obeyed (e.g., the Decalogue); each part begins with a "text" in verse, setting forth the theme, followed in prose by a "gloss'—a story or anecdote illustrative of the topic—and an "allegory," a brief explanation of the Christian moral of the tale, including usually one biblical and one patristic quotation. For the latter, one can see how the *Manipulus florum* would readily have lent itself to use. Christine had merely to find in Thomas' work the topic most closely related to her own theme, and to translate an appropriate quotation. By Campbell's count, eighty-seven of the hundred sections in the *Epistre* contain patristic quotations, and sixty-nine of these are found in the *Manipulus florum*. Commencing with *L'epistre d'Othéa* (ca. 1400), her first work to be written primarily in prose, Christine evidently used the *Manipulus florum* as the principal source for patristic quotations in all her later works; Campbell found evidence of such borrowings in her *Livre de Prudence, Vision, Chemin de Long Estude, Livre des Trois Vertus, Mutacion de Fortune*—to which list Solente has added the *Livre des Fais et bonnes meurs du sage Roy Charles v.*[55]

Christine's use of the *Manipulus* is thus well-documented. However, Curt Bühler, in his recent edition of Scrope's *Pistell of Othea* and earlier publications,[56] has demonstrated that some thirteen of the quotations in the *Epistre d'Othéa* which can be found in the *Manipulus florum* were really taken from another source, the late fourteenth-century *Chapelet des Vertus*.[57] This anonymous work is derived, evidently at one remove, from a fourteenth-century Italian work, the *Fiore di virtù*. First the *Fiore* was literally translated into the French *Fleurs de toutes vertus*; the *Fleurs* was then altered, rearranged, and augmented to create the *Chapelet des Vertus*. Among the added portions—those passages in the *Chapelet* not found in the *Fiore*—are patristic quotations, evidently including all of the thirteen borrowed by Christine. Neither work has been edited, to permit a comparison of texts; but in four instances, Bühler explicitly states that the given patristic quotation in the *Chapelet* does not appear in the *Fiore*, and for the other nine his wording leads one to assume that such was the case. In addition to the thirteen borrowed by Christine, three other patristic quotations in the *Chapelet* can be found in the *Manipulus florum*.[58] It seems to us

[55] *Livre des Fais...*, ed. S. Solente, 2 vols. (Paris 1936-1940); see 1: lxvii.
[56] C. F. Bühler, ed., *The Epistle of Othea*, trans. Stephen Scrope, Early English Text Society 264 (London 1970).
[57] Regarding the *Chapelet* see C. F. Bühler, "The *Fleurs de toutes vertus* and Christine de Pisan's *L'épitre d'Othéa*," PMLA 62 (1947) 32-44; idem, "The *Fleurs de toutes vertus*," PMLA 64 (1949) 600-601; and the notes to his edition of Scrope.
[58] Specifically, in the *Chapelet*'s chapter *Glotonnie* is the *Manipulus*' *Gula k.*; in *Misericorde, Misericordia n.*; in *Humilité, Humilitas q.*

evident that the anonymous author of the *Chapelet* has taken most of his added patristic quotations from Thomas of Ireland. If we consider the sixteen quotations common to the *Chapelet* and the *Manipulus*, we find that the *Chapelet* in most cases preserves the quotation under the same subject heading as in the *Manipulus florum*. Thus, the extract designated *Temperantia a.* in the *Manipulus* appears in the *Chapelet*'s chapter on *Atrempance*; *Iusticia s.* appears under *Justice*; *Superbia aq.* is in the chapter on *Orgueil*—none of these, according to Bühler, is found in the *Chapelet*'s Italian source; *Ira b.* is under *Ire*, *Invidia d.* under *Envie*, *Gula k.* under *Glotonnie*, and so on. In sum, the *Chapelet des Vertus* represents a second example of use of the *Manipulus florum* in French vernacular. And, in thirteen instances, Christine de Pisan has borrowed from the *Manipulus florum* indirectly via the *Chapelet*, in addition to her scores of direct borrowings from Thomas of Ireland's work.

A probable third use of the *Manipulus florum* in French vernacular literature would link the *Manipulus* at one remove with Geoffrey Chaucer. *The Tale of Melibeus*, one of the most derivative of the Canterbury Tales, is little more than a translation of the French *Livre de Mellibée et Prudence* which derived in turn from the Latin *Liber consolationis et consilii*.[59] Albertano of Brescia composed the *Liber consolationis* in 1246. The work survives in at least four French versions, of which the *Livre de Mellibée et Prudence* was the most popular. This version, "an adaptation rather than a translation," was written after 1336 by Renaud de Louens, Dominican of Poligny. Renaud heavily abridged the Latin original, and added a small proportion of new material. Allusions in this work are heavily classical; patristic quotations in Renaud's Latin source are few, and those in the *Livre de Mellibée* itself can literally be counted on the fingers of one's hands. Six of the quotations (five ascribed to Cassiodorus and one to Innocent) are taken from the *Liber consolationis*, leaving only four which are additions made by Renaud: two ascribed to Augustine, one to Gregory (neither of these authors is cited even once in the *Liber consolationis*), and one to Innocent. All four of these quotations are found in the *Manipulus florum*. In terms of raw numbers, this is slender evidence to justify a claim that Renaud used the *Manipulus florum*; however, in terms of percentage, it would be impossible to improve upon. Given the virtual ubiquity of Thomas of Ireland's work in fourteenth-century France, it requires no effort to suppose that Renaud both knew of, and had access to, the *Manipulus florum*.

[59] See J. B. Severs in *Sources and Analogues of Chaucer's Canterbury Tales*, ed. W. F. Bryan and G. Dempster (Chicago 1941) 560-614.

Whether Renaud actually used the work, and, hence, whether Chaucer was indirectly dependent upon it, must remain problematical.

Finally, the *Manipulus florum* served the minor Elizabethan poet and pamphleteer, Thomas Lodge, for his *Wits Miserie, and the Worlds Madnesse* (1596). In this pamphlet, "the mediaeval classification of the seven deadly sins serves as a framework for satiric pictures of London types in the last decade of the sixteenth century."[60] Lodge was notorious among contemporaries for his plagiarism, even in an age where a certain amount of plagiarism was acceptable and even expected. Alice Walker has studied Lodge's borrowings for his prose works. In *Wits Miserie* she found about twenty patristic and Senecan quotations derived from the *Manipulus florum*. "Generally the 'flores' appear in batches of three or four and in the order in which [Thomas of Ireland] arranged them."

* *

To summarize, the *Manipulus florum* was principally used for sermon writing. It also served in the compilation of other *florilegia* or commonplace books, some of them as late as the seventeenth century. As examples of its use by authors we have noted borrowings from its prologue by a canonist; of its classical quotations by Johannes von Dambach and the Valerius commentator; and of its patristic quotations by a Dutch mystic and by French and English vernacular authors. In quantity and quality, surely, this is a better than average record.

v. Bibliographies

The list of authors and works which Thomas of Ireland appended to the *Manipulus florum* has its own history of use and influence. Not many years after the *Manipulus florum* was written, the list began to circulate by itself.[61]

---

[60] Alice Walker, "The Reading of an Elizabethan," *Review of English Studies* 8 (1932) 264-281, esp. 265-266, 272-273.

[61] The surviving manuscripts in which the list appears without the body of the *Manipulus florum* are Vat. Borgh. MS 247 ff. 20-21ᵛ (ca. 1315, written by Peter Roger); Munich, Universitätsbibliothek, 2° Cod. MS 22 ff. 581-585 (s. xiv²; Northern Italy, Bologna?); Cambridge, Corpus Christi College MS 518 ff. 166ᵛ-169 (ca. 1376); Prague, Narodni Museum MS XII G.5 ff. 105ᵛ-114ᵛ (1384); Budapest, National Museum MS 74 ff. 145-146ᵛ (s. xiv); Paris, B.N. MS lat. 16533 ff. 3-11 (s. xiv ex. - xv in.); two Cologne Hist. Archiv. MSS, G.B. 4° 215 ff. 40-45ᵛ (1424-1436), and G.B. 4° 152 ff. 46-53ᵛ (1439); Vat. Pal. lat. MS 226 ff. 50-58 (1447); Trier, Stadtbibliothek MS 91/1075 ff. 272-277ᵛ (post 1453); and four manuscripts dated only s. xv: Berlin, Deutsche Staatsbibliothek MS lat. theol. fol. 131 ff. 1-7; Brussels, Bibliothèque Royale MS 3672-90 (V. de G. 1503) ff. 180ᵛ-186; Budapest, Natl. Museum MS 196 ff. 3-6ᵛ; and Würzburg, Universitätsbibliothek MS M.p.th. 9.72 ff. 191-206. Another manuscript, no longer extant, is mentioned in the late fifteenth-century

There are at least fifteen instances in which the list was copied alone. This has been the source of some confusion; the list alone is not easily recognizable as part of the *Manipulus florum*, and it was never included in the printed editions. It has the appearance of a library catalog, since the incipit and explicit of each work is given. Ghellinck thought the list in Merton College MS 129 reflected an effort to assemble a canon of Hugh of Saint-Victor's works. Paul Bissels felt that the list in Trier MS 91/1075 was a fifteenth-century private library, and Anneliese Maier suggested that the copy of the list made by Peter Roger might be a list of the books at Chaise-Dieu.[62]

As far as one can tell, the earliest example of the list alone is this last, the copy made by Peter Roger (later Clement VI), which survives in his hand in Vat. Borgh. 247, a notebook of some seventy miscellaneous extracts which Peter made as a student.[63] Since he notes at the end of one piece, on f. 117, "Anno domini M.ccc.quinto-decimo," we know that he must have copied the list (ff. 20-21^v) by 1315 at the latest. By good fortune, the manuscript from which his copy was made still survives, Paris, Bibl. de l'Univ. 215, which contains prologue, text and table, as well as the list; thus we may be certain that Peter Roger deliberately chose to reproduce the list only. This would seem also to be the case for the two Cologne manuscripts, G.B. 4° 215, which contains the list (ff. 40-45^v), and G.B. 4° 152, which contains the *Manipulus florum*'s prologue (f. 45^{r-v}), the table (ff. 45^v-46) and the list (ff. 46-53^v); presumably both were copied from manuscripts containing the whole work. The same is evidently true of Budapest Natl. Museum MS 74, which contains only the last part of the list, the philosophers (ff. 145-146^v), followed by Thomas' prologue (ff. 146^v-147). Paris B.N. MS lat. 16533 contains not only the list (ff. 3-11) but

---

catalog of the Dominikanerkloster of Vienna, "H.52, Principia et fines librorum originalium doctorum Dyonisii, Augustini, Ambrosii, Jeronimi, Gregorii, Bernardi, Hylarii, Ysidori, Crysostomi, Rabani, Damasceni, Anselmi, Richardi de S. Victor, Hugonis de S. Victor, Alchuini id est Albini, Alani, Plinii, Rabby Moyses, Valerii Maximi, Marcialis, Tullii, Boecii, Senece; Augustinus ad fratres de contemptu mundi..." etc.; T. Gottlieb, *Mittelalterliche Bibliothekskataloge Oesterreichs* 1 (Vienna 1915) 352-353, item H 52. It is possible that Henry of Kirkestede (English, d. ca. 1379) used a copy of the list alone, which no longer survives; see below.

[62] J. de Ghellinck, "Un catalogue des œuvres de Hugues de Saint-Victor," *Revue néo-scolastique de philosophie* 20 (1913) 226-232; idem, "A propos d'un catalogue des œuvres de Hugues de Saint-Victor," *Revue néo-scolastique de philosophie* 21 (1914) 86-88; P. Bissels, "Wissenschaft und Bibliographie im spätmittelalterlichen Trier," *Kurtrierisches Jahrbuch* 6 (1965) 54-60; A. Maier, "Der literarische Nachlass des Petrus Rogerii," *Recherches de théologie ancienne et médiévale* 16 (1949) 92-96.

[63] For an analysis of the manuscript see Maier, "Der literarische Nachlass."

almost forty folios of other extracts from the body of the *Manipulus florum* (ff. 104-143)—indicating, once more, that the reproduction and preservation of the list as a separate entity was done in this case by choice rather than necessity. It is evident that the reason for people's interest in the list *per se* was as a reference work, a useful bibliographic tool. This much is indicated by the company with which the list travels. In Vatican Pal. lat. MS 226, there are several other works of a reference nature, including a Latin-German lexicon and a *consensus evangelistarum* in tabular form; in Budapest Natl. Mus. MS 196 Thomas' list is followed by a list of the books of the Bible with their first and last words. In Cologne Hist. Arch. MS G.B. 4° 215 the list is accompanied by numerous works of a bibliographic nature or reference works of a more general nature. The manuscript contains the *Philobiblon* of Richard de Bury, *De laude scriptorum*, a table of contents for the *Catholicon*, and *Mystice acceptiones terminorum secundum alphabeti*, in addition to the list from the *Manipulus florum*. And in Munich Univ. MS 2° cod. 22, a manuscript of early fourteenth-century northern Italian origin, Thomas of Ireland's list forms part of the apparatus to a Bible; the text of the Bible is preceded by a table of contents (with folio and chapter references), and followed by (1) interpretations of Hebrew names, (2) a selection of liturgical readings, (3) the list of authors and works from the *Manipulus*, and (4) a list of commentators on the individual books of the Bible.

One need not rely on inference alone to conclude that the list was used as a bibliographic authority; it is cited as such by two authors nearly contemporary with Thomas of Ireland. Nicholas Trevet in his commentary on *Valerius ad Rufinum* cites Thomas' testimony on the problem of Valerius' identity: "Sciendum quod tres fuerunt Valerii et omnes erant romani. Unus erat Valerius Martialus Cocus qui fecit epigramata ludica. Alius fuit Valerius Maximus qui scripsit de dictis et factis memorabilibus ad Tiberium Cesarem. Tertius fuit iste Valerius et non fuit idem alicui primorum, licet auctor manipulus (*sic*) florum dicat eum esse secundum predictorum."[64] This must be a reference to the list at the end of the *Manipulus florum*; for while Thomas nowhere states explicitly that the two Valerii are one, in the list he couples their names in such a fashion as to make it fairly evident that he regarded them as one and the same. Jordanus of Saxony (Jordanus of Quedlinburg) also cites the list, in his *Liber vitasfratrum*, as supporting evidence for the fact that there are two separate rules attributable to Augustine. Having stated the case, on the basis of other evidence, he adds,

[64] Unpublished; cited from Oxford, Lincoln Coll. MS lat. 81 fol. 94. See also Pratt, "Jankyn's Book" 19.

"Ad huius confirmationem facit magister Thomas Hibernicus, olim socius in Sorbona Parisius, qui in compilatione sua, quam Manipulum florum appellat, inter alios libros Augustini duas Regulas distinctas computat et designat...."[65] Unquestionably, Jordanus found this information in the list at the end, not in the body, of the *Manipulus florum*.

In several manuscripts Thomas' list has been added to, showing that the list was regarded as a useful record of bibliographic information, hence a logical place to record further bibliographic information. Lincoln Cathedral MS 191 (s. xv), a manuscript of the whole *Manipulus florum*, contains at the end of the list (following the works of Seneca) a list of the works of Bede, taken from Bede's bibliography in his *Historia ecclesiastica* (5.24). And immediately following the list (ff. 191ᵛ-196ᵛ) there appears on f. 197ʳ⁻ᵛ the Pseudo-Gelasian *Decretum ... de scripturis recipiendis....* In Klosterneuburg Stiftsbibliothek MS 391 (1422), also a manuscript of the whole work, the list again is enlarged. Following the works of Seneca, a different hand has added a list of six works of Bede, six works of Honorius of Autun, and eleven works of Rupert of Deutz. All twenty-three of the works are supplied with incipits and explicits, a fact which makes it easy to confirm that the information was taken from Klosterneuburg manuscripts.[66] The list in B.N. MS lat. 16533 has two additions, inserted by another hand, in the section *Libri diversorum auctorum*: Josephus *De bello judaico* and Solinus *De mirabilibus mundi*. The titles (without incipits) and the names of their respective authors were very likely found in the extracts from the body of the *Manipulus florum* which appear toward the end of this manuscript. In the previously mentioned Vat. Borgh. MS 247, Peter Roger has added, on f. 20ᵛ at the end of the list of Augustine's works, a note summarizing the number of Augustine's writings, for which his sources were the *Retractationes* and Vincent of Beauvais' *Speculum historiale*: "Unde Augustinus in libro retractationum (*altered to* speculum) loquens de suis operibus enumeratis aliquibus libris ait sic: Hec opera lxxxxiii in libris cclxxxii (*sic*) me dictasse recolui, utrum aliquos essem dictaturus ignorans. Ultimo librum quem uocauit speculum ad ... < illeg. > etiam omnium librorum suorum

[65] *Liber vitasfratrum* 2.14; ed. R. Arbesmann and W. Hümpfner (New York 1943) 171.
[66] Bede: *Super Lucam*, MS 242; *Super Marcum*, MS 247; *Super canonicas epistolas*, MS 246; *De planetis*, unident.; *De tabernaculo*, MS 245; *Scintille*, MS 244; Honorius: *De con...tione uite*, unident.; *De imago mundi*, unident.; *Super cantica*, MS 158; *In primam quinquagesimam*, MS 160; *In secundam quinquagesimam*, MS 161; *In tertiam quinquagesimam*, MS 162; Rupert: *Super Genesim*, MS 260; *Super Exodum, Leviticum*, MS 255; *Super Numerum., Deut., Iud., Ruth*, MS 253; *Super cantica*, unident.; *Super prophetas* and *Super prophetas minores*, MS 258; *Super Johannem* pt. 1, MS 256, pt. 2, MS 257; *Super Apocalipsim*, MS 254; *De victor ... vi diei*, unident.; *De officiis*, MS 252.

composuit.[67] Unde quidam loquens de ipso sic ait: Mille uoluminibus pater (ms patet) Augustine refulges. Mentitur qui te totum legisse fatetur (ms faretur)."[68] The case of Peter Roger's addition is a unique one; since the extra material is not added in a later hand (the case with Klosterneuburg and B.N. lat. 16533), and since we possess the manuscript from which Peter made his copy, we know in this instance that the addition originated with the writer.

Thomas' bibliography was not infrequently used in the compilation of other bibliographies. In Paris B.N. ms lat. 14237 (Saint-Victor, s. xiii) there appears on f. 181ᵛ (end of the manuscript) a tribute to Richard of Saint-Victor, written in a fourteenth-fifteenth century hand. Following a eulogy in verse, the same hand has inscribed a list of twenty-two works attributed to Richard, the first thirteen works with their incipits, followed by nine other works, titles alone. Ludwig Ott, who has printed the list, thought it must have come from a codex which contained the works inscribed here.[69] But in actuality the list can only come from Thomas's—since the first thirteen in lat. 14237 correspond to the *Manipulus florum* list, not only in contents but in order; and secondly, because the last nine have no incipits, indicating that the last part of the list came from a source different from that of the beginning.[70] Likewise, the *Manipulus florum* has provided the list of twenty works of Seneca added to the flyleaf of a manuscript collection of Seneca's works (Paris, B.N. ms lat. 11376 f. 1).[71] Again, the list corresponds in both content and sequence with Thomas' bibliography.

The most elaborate use of the list was its employment by Henry of Kirkestede, a monk of Bury St. Edmunds, in the compilation of his

---

[67] *Retractationes*, ed. P. Knöll, *C.S.E.L.* 36 (Vienna 1902) 204, followed by a paraphrase of the passage "Libri qui post istorum editionem..." that appears at the end of some mss. including a Parisian one; cf. p. 205.

[68] A paraphrase and a quotation from *Speculum historiale* lib. 19 (20) c. 28.

[69] L. Ott, *Untersuchungen zur theologischen Briefsliteratur der Frühscholastik*, Beiträge zur Geschichte der Philosophie und Theologie des Mittelalters 34 (Münster 1937) 563-564. Ott also prints and discusses the list of Richard's works in the *Manipulus florum* (562-563) from three Munich mss. but does not recognize the connection between these and the list in the Saint-Victor ms.

[70] Nos. 1-13 of the list in B.N. lat. 14237 are identical with Thomas of Ireland's list of Richard of Saint-Victor's works, with these exceptions: (1) 14237 has no explicits; (2) 14237 omits *De verbis apostoli*, no. 5 in the *Manipulus* bibliography; (3) 14237 divides *De contemplatione sive de xii patriarchis*, *Manipulus* no. 11, into two titles and provides a separate incipit, no doubt taken from a manuscript of the work, for the *De contemplatione*.

[71] The manuscript is a composite: part I, s. xii; and part II, s. xv; the Seneca bibliography has been added in a fifteenth-century hand. This list was brought to our notice by Jeannine Fohlen, Institut de recherche et d'histoire des textes, Paris.

Catalogus scriptorum ecclesiae (c. 1360-1378).[72] Kirkestede not only
borrowed bibliographic information from every available source, but he also
appropriated ideas on structure, scope, etc. Thus, for example, stripped to
its most basic element, the *Catalogus* may be described as a location list of
books; that is, for most of the works which he lists, Kirkestede supplies
one or more arabic numerals corresponding to one or more monastic or
cathedral libraries where this book might be found. This idea (and his key
list of numbered libraries, and most of his references to them) Kirkestede
borrowed from the earlier *Registrum*, the location list of books produced by
the English Franciscans. To this original notion, Kirkestede added the idea
of a biobibliography—that is, that for every author mentioned he should
give a biographical notice, and that he should attempt to list all of a man's
writings, including those for which no location could be indicated. This idea
of biobibliography, as well as vast amounts of data, Kirkestede took equally
and impartially from Jerome, Gennadius, Isidore and Vincent of Beauvais.
On the model of the *Manipulus florum*'s bibliography, Kirkestede decided
that thorough identification of a work required that one provide not only its
first words, the practice followed by the *Registrum*, but its last words also.
In addition to this aspect of his format, Kirkestede borrowed from the
Manipulus florum virtually every work of every author that Thomas had included.[73] It is essential that any user of the *Catalogus* take cognizance of
this fact, lest he assume that every title followed by an incipit and an explicit represents an actual English manuscript seen by Kirkestede—whereas,
in reality, if such titles are borrowed from the *Manipulus florum*, the
presence of incipit and explicit usually indicates a manuscript seen in Paris
by Thomas of Ireland.[74] In addition to borrowing Thomas' bibliographic
information and Thomas' method of identifying a work, Kirkestede
paraphrased or quoted portions of Thomas' brief prefatory explanation of
his list (the passage, "Notandum quod libros..."), in the preface to the
Catalogus. Since Kirkestede's preface has not been edited, it is worth

[72] Concerning Henry of Kirkestede and the *Catalogus* see R. H. Rouse, "Bostonus
Buriensis and the Author of the *Catalogus scriptorum ecclesiae*," *Speculum* 41 (1966) 471-
499.

[73] The major exception is Jerome, since Kirkestede's other sources for Jerome, the
Registrum and the Bury manuscripts, dwarf completely the meager list provided by the
Manipulus florum.

[74] For example, in compiling his entries for Cicero and Seneca Kirkestede borrowed virtually the whole of Thomas of Ireland's bibliography for these two authors—reflecting Sorbonne, not Bury, books. See R. A. B. Mynors, "The Latin Classics Known to Boston of
Bury," in *Fritz Saxl 1890-1948: A Volume of Memorial Essays from his Friends in England*,
ed. D. J. Gordon (London 1957) 199-217.

reproducing in full the significant paragraph. The italicized portions are borrowed from Thomas of Ireland:

> Utilitati et expeditioni studentium et praedicatorum quidam S. Edmundi monachus ex informatione aliorum et eorum exemplaribus pro modulo suo volens proficere, *nomina actorum, doctorum et librorum eorum originalium* secundum ordinem alphabeti *ac partialium librorum numerum* in uno colligere, *principia pariter et fines,* locaque quibus huiusmodi libri poterint inveniri per numerum algorismi locorum nominibus correspondentem *hic scribere et intitulare curavit, ut quum alicui occurrerint facilius possint ea cognoscere et securius allegare. Quandoquidem tamen* ... (illeg.) ... *multorum librorum* principia non novit, *vidit neque fines* nec ubi potuerunt inveniri, *ideo si alicui occurrant poterit eos in spatio vacuo ad hoc reservato intitulare.* Primo enim ponuntur nomina doctorum seu auctorum et anni quibus ipsi doctores floruerunt, secundo tituli et nomina librorum.[75]

One may conjecture that Kirkestede employed a manuscript which contained only Thomas' list. This is suggested by three facts, all admittedly arguments from silence: (1) Kirkestede includes nothing which cannot be found in the list alone; (2) we know, from a discrepancy in the Pseudo-Dionysian epistles, that Kirkestede did not use Peterhouse MS 163, a surviving Bury manuscript of the whole *Manipulus florum*; (3) Kirkestede did not list Thomas of Ireland among the authors in the *Catalogus*, an omission which tallies neatly with the fact that, whereas the text was nearly always plainly attributed to Thomas of Ireland, the list alone seldom if ever bore any attribution of authorship.

The value of Thomas' bibliography assumes a larger dimension when one notes that it was used in the compilation of a fifteenth-century Rhenish location list of books, the beginning of which survives in Basel Universitätsbibliothek MS F VI 53.[76] The location list was compiled in the second

---

[75] The text is quoted from the eighteenth-century copy of the *Catalogus* made by Thomas Tanner, now Cambridge Univ. Lib. MS Add. 3470. The rest of Kirkestede's preface is a borrowed disquisition on the "authenticity"—a term that encompasses "orthodoxy" as well—of books, both biblical and patristic, and a numbered list of 195 libraries. The final paragraph, quoted here, is the only part of Kirkestede's prologue which attempts to explain the *Catalogus* itself. It is printed in T. Tanner, *Bibliotheca Britannico-Hibernica...* (London 1748) xvii-xxiv.

[76] We are grateful to Richard Marks who first noted the similarity and brought it to our attention. The Basel catalog is described by P. Lehmann, "Alte Vorläufer des Gesamtkatalogs," *Erforschung des Mittelalters* 4 (Stuttgart 1961) 172-183, esp. 173-176; and H. Knaus, "Ein rheinischer Gesamtkatalog des 15. Jahrhunderts," *Gutenberg Jahrbuch* (1976) 509-518.

half of the century, probably at some religious house in Cologne, since two
Cologne university masters and a number of Cologne religious houses are
represented in the location *sigla*. The catalog consists of lists of works of
patristic and medieval authors. Each author is introduced by a biographical
notice—as in the case of the *Catalogus*, or the Erfurt catalog. *Sigla*
representing institutional and private owners of individual works were added
in the margins of the catalog, in the years following its compilation. The
compiler has drawn on a variety of sources. For Ambrose, Anselm, Alan of
Lille and Alcuin, he clearly used the bibliography of the *Manipulus florum*
as the basis for his lists of works, fleshing them out from other sources,
particularly from manuscripts of the works themselves; occasional references
to printed books were included. Since the titles under each author's name
appear in alphabetical order, they do not reproduce the order of the *Manipulus florum*. Nonetheless, one can be quite certain that the *Manipulus'*
bibliography was used, on the basis of other evidence. For example, thirty-
three of the thirty-four Ambrose works in Thomas' bibliography recur in
identical words (title, number of books, incipit, explicit) in the Basel
fragment. The incipits and explicits given for the same works are normally
identical; the only exception is the list of Anselm's works, where the compiler of the Basel list usually shortened both incipits and explicits.
Moreover, certain errors in the Basel fragment are explicable only in terms
of the *Manipulus florum*. For example, Anselm's *De veritate* (fragment p. 9)
has the explicit of the *Cur deus homo* (fragment p. 8); the error has been
corrected, doubtless from a text of *De veritate*, by a second hand. Although
these works occur on two different pages in the Basel list, in the *Manipulus'*
bibliography the *Cur deus homo* immediately precedes the *De veritate*.
Neither the Augustine nor the Jerome entries in the *Manipulus* bibliography
suited the compiler; he preferred an extensive analysis of the sermons and
letters. (The Jerome entry had not suited Kirkestede either.) We cannot tell
to what extent the compiler may have drawn upon the *Manipulus* bibliography for such authors as Bernard, Cicero, or Seneca, because the Basel
fragment ends at the letter I, and has lost the leaves containing B-F.

Identification of the source of some of the lists of works in the Basel list
is important, lest the unwary editor be misled, because of the presence of
the opening and closing words, into thinking that he is dealing with the
books of some fifteenth-century Rhenish library—whereas in actuality it is
the library of the Sorbonne in 1306. While the history of late fifteenth-
century Rhenish location lists of books, encompassing the catalogs of
Gerard Roelants at St. Martin's, Louvain, and that at Rookloster, has not
yet been sorted out, certain facts are clear: they are interrelated, and

Thomas of Ireland's descriptions of Sorbonne codices are incorporated in the earliest of them.[77]

VI. INFLUENCE AND CIRCULATION

To document that a work was widely used is, surely, to demonstrate its influence. Yet there is other evidence, less tangible than specific borrowings, which likewise attests to the influence of the *Manipulus florum*.

A prime example is the effect of this work on nomenclature, as witnessed by the number of fourteenth-century and later works that use *Manipulus* in their titles. While, as we have seen, *manipulus* was not an uncommon word in the thirteenth century, Thomas was the first to make it the title of a work. At least four later fourteenth-century authors followed his example. The Spanish priest Guido de Monte Rocheri entitled his manual for parish priests the *Manipulus curatorum*, which was completed ca. 1330-1333 and dedicated to Raymond, bishop of Valencia.[78] Galvaneus de Flamma compiled a history or chronicle of Milan, completed 1336, which he called simply *Manipulus florum*: "Ex his viginti quatuor chronicis hanc chronicam adnotavi, quam Manipulus florum appellari placuit."[79] John of Fayt (d. 1395), abbot of St. Bavon in Ghent and compiler of numerous aids to study and preaching, employed the term for his *Manipulus exemplorum*; it should not be confused with the anonymous collection of *exempla* also entitled *Manipulus exemplorum* which exists in a single manuscript, Liège, Bibliothèque de l'Université MS 391 ff. 124-321 (s. xv; Convent of the Holy Cross, Huy).[80] Compiled in the second half of the century, Fayt's *Manipulus exemplorum* is an alphabetically arranged collection of some 2000 *exempla* ranged under 576 titles from *Absolutio, Abstinentia* to *Xp̄istus*. The term appears again in the colophon of John's *Tabula moralis philosophie* (before 1358)—e.g., Bruges MS 508: "Explicit milliloquium philosophi, sive manipulus moralis philosophie." For John of Fayt, we might add, the *Manipulus florum* was the source not only of his titles but also of his structure; as he says in the prologue of his *Tabula* to Robert of Bardi's *Collec-*

---

[77] The relationship is studied by P. J. F. Obbema, "The Rookloster Register Evaluated," *Quaerendo* 7 (1977) 325-353.

[78] See J. F. von Schulte, *Die Geschichte der Quellen und Literatur des Canonischen Rechts* 1 (Stuttgart 1875) 429-430.

[79] Regarding G. de Flamma see A. Potthast, *Bibliotheca historica medii aevi* 1 (Berlin 1895) 489; the chronicle is printed, L. A. Muratori, *Rerum italicarum scriptores* 11 (Milan 1727) 537-740, esp. col. 539.

[80] See J. Th. Welter, *L'exemplum dans la littérature religieuse et didactique du moyen âge* (Paris 1927) 402-405.

torium, "In this table I have included cross-references from one subject-heading to another on the example of the *Manipulus florum*, just as I did in another table that I made on Aristotle's *Libri morales*"[81]—i.e., the *Tabula moralis philosophie*. Yet another fourteenth-century *Manipulus florum* (also called *Manipulus florum minor*) survives in at least four manuscripts, beginning "*Abstinentia*: Ecclesiastici 37[:34], Qui abstinens est...." This is an anonymous alphabetically arranged collection of biblical extracts compiled in the archdiocese of Prague late in the century.[82] Earlier than any of these uses of *Manipulus* as a title are the references to *manipuli* in the sense of "things collected" by Johannes Hautfuney, perhaps a member of the *familia* of Cardinal Simon de Ariacho (1320-1323) and later (from 1330) bishop of Avranches. Hautfuney, between 1320 and 1323, compiled a massive alphabetical name-place-subject index to Vincent of Beauvais' *Speculum historiale*. His familiarity with the *Manipulus florum* is revealed in the dedicatory preface; there he uses the word *manipulus* more than a half-dozen times, and even employs the same biblical imagery found in Thomas of Ireland's prologue, likening the condition of a compiler to that of Ruth gleaning after the reapers.[83]

So thorough and widespread was the adoption of this generic title that it is even applied, after the fact, to older works. Thus, among the later manuscripts of the *Liber de exemplis sacre scripture* of Nicholas of Hanapis (d. 1291) is Arras MS 806 ff. 1-121ᵛ (s. xiv) with the title *Manipulus sacre scripture*. And an anonymous thirteenth-century collection of sermons and extracts in Erlangen MS 319 is given the title *Manipulus rosarum* on its fifteenth-century binding. Of course, the practice continued with new works as

[81] "In presenti tabula posui remissionem de uno vocabulo ad aliud instar Manipulo florum, sicut etiam feci in alia tabula quam edidi super libros morales Aristotilis"; cited from G. Pozzi, "La 'Tabula' di Jean de Fayt al 'Collectorium' di Roberto de' Bardi," *Miscellanea G. G. Meersseman*, Italia sacra 15-16 (Padua 1970) 264.

[82] See for example Prague, Bibl. Met. Kap. MSS C.xxxix.1 ff. 4-106ᵛ (s. xv), C.xxxiv.3 ff. 1-153ᵛ (s. xv), C.xxxvii.3 ff. 2-164 (AD 1442) and N.xxxii ff. 121-232ᵛ (s. xiv-xv). Two other alphabetical texts bearing the title *Manipulus florum* are found in the same library, MSS C.xxxv ff. 1-93 (AD 1437), beginning "*Aron*. Quod Aron sacerdotium approbatur d xxii..."; and O.xl ff. 144ᵛ-262ᵛ (s. xv), beginning "Abutens privilegio sibi concesso..."; see F. Schulte, *Die canonistischen Handschriften...* (Prague 1868) 114 n. 289.

[83] Oxford, Lincoln College MS lat. 99 f. 2 (s. xiv): "Velud alia Ruth in eundem agrum abii, spicas post terga metencium collecturus; quas collectas et secundum species suas in distinctos redactas manipulos.... Prefatorum manipulorum contexui nomina.... Sub certis distinctis ad ordinatis redigerentur manipulis....," and so on. Concerning Hautfuney and his index, see A. D. von den Brincken, "Tabula alphabetica von den Anfängen alphabetischer Registerarbeiten zu Geschichtswerken," in *Festschrift für Hermann Heimpel* 2 (Göttingen 1972) 900-923, esp. 907-912 and works cited there; and R. H. Rouse, *The Development of Aids to Study in the Thirteenth Century*, Rosenbach Lectures in Bibliography, University of Pennsylvania (forthcoming).

well in the fifteenth century, including the above-mentioned *Manipulus exemplorum*; the *Manipulus diversarum materiarum*, a collection of moral anecdotes and tales in Brussels MS II.2294 (Van den Gheyn 2246); the *Manipulus chronicorum* in Cambridge, Gonville-Caius College MS 26; and yet another *Manipulus florum*, a collection of patristic extracts logically arranged by topic, in Brussels MS 10001-02 (Van den Gheyn 1509). The latest example known to us is Elizabethan: in 1570 Peter Levins compiled an English rhyming dictionary, alphabetized by last syllable, with the Latin title *Manipulus vocabulorum*.[84]

For Thomas of Ireland, the use of the word *manipulus* was a biblical allusion. His prologue says, in effect, Let other authors "come rejoicing, bringing in their sheaves" (*manipuli*; Ps. 126:6); I am content with my sheaf of extracts (*Manipulus florum*). But thenceforward the title *Manipulus* is an allusion to Thomas's work, referring either to the matter or to the arrangement of the *Manipulus florum*. After 1306, a *manipulus* will be either a collection of extracts, of whatever sort (from the Fathers, from sermons, from chronicles), however arranged; or an alphabetically arranged compilation, whatever the matter (extracts, *exempla*, even the last syllables of English words).

The fourteenth- and fifteenth-century circulation of manuscripts of the *Manipulus florum* outline in an almost graphic fashion the spreading influence of Thomas's work, chronologically, geographically, and—for want of a better term—sociologically. Many manuscripts of the *Manipulus florum* must, in the nature of things, have disappeared without trace. However, we assume that the lost manuscripts, if recoverable, would not alter by much the picture presented by the large number of surviving manuscripts and of medieval records of manuscripts no longer extant.

Of the 181 surviving manuscripts of the *Manipulus florum*, 100 date from the fourteenth century. The majority of these—perhaps as many as two-thirds—date from the first half of the century,[85] beginning with an initial dissemination from the stationers. The manuscripts B, C, D, and those that bear *pecia* marks all date from 1306 or shortly thereafter. Toulouse MS 222 was completed on 1 March 1307, and was taken to the Dominican convent at Toulouse. On 22 March 1312, Robert de Marcelliaco finished copying Troyes MS 1785 (Clairvaux A.56) in Paris for Peter de Ceffons,

---

[84] P. Levins, *Manipulus vocabulorum*, ed. H. B. Wheatley, Camden Society 95 (1867).

[85] Since the majority of manuscripts are not dated, this is an estimate, based on the following evidence: of those fourteenth-century MSS that bear a date, or that can be assigned with some assurance to either the first or the second half of the century, 27 belong to the first half, 14 to the second.

scholar and monk of Clairvaux.[86] Bishop Ralph de Baldock owned a text of the *Manipulus florum* in London by 1313.[87] Graz MS 746 was finished on 18 October 1318, and eventually went to the Cistercians at Neuburg. Peter Roger (later Clement VI) copied the list of authors from D at Paris before 1315. From the inventories of prelates' estates in the registers of papal spoils we see that the *Manipulus florum* was also owned by Peter's uncle, another Peter Roger, bishop of Carcassonne, who died 25 December 1329, and by John Grand Furstat, archbishop of Bremen, who died on 30 May 1327; it appears as well among the books of Frederick archbishop of Riga in an inventory dated 31 May 1325. Two copies appear in an inventory of books dated 1328 which belonged to Walter Stapeldon, bishop of Exeter. For these last, obviously, the manuscripts themselves may antedate the inventories by many years.[88] The Basel Carthusians possessed a copy finished in 1324 (now Basel MS B.IV.9). The *Manipulus florum* was used in England by William of Pagula in 1319-1322, and in Austria by Godfrey of Vorau before 1332. As one might expect, however, the majority of fourteenth-century manuscripts were French.

Reproduction of the *Manipulus florum* continued, at a slower pace, throughout the fourteenth century, and the first half of the fifteenth century brought a new flurry of manuscript production. Of the eighty-one fifteenth-century manuscripts, perhaps as many as three-quarters were written before mid-century.[89] The bulk of the new manuscripts were German or Central European. The importance of fifteenth-century Germany as a source for new manuscripts of older works is a phenomenon that has been observed in relationship to many texts.[90] For the *Manipulus florum* the figures clearly substantiate the point: of 100 fourteenth-century manuscripts, 23 are of probable German provenance; of 81 fifteenth-century manuscripts, 52 probably were written in Germany and farther east.

Who were the owners of the *Manipulus florum*? One expects, and quite rightly, to find this work, composed at the university and intended for

[86] See Samaran and Marichal, *Catalogue des manuscrits en écriture latine* 5: *Texte* p. 517, *Planches* 42. Regarding Peter see D. Trapp, "Peter Ceffons of Clairvaux," *Recherches de théologie ancienne et médiévale* 24 (1957) 101-154.

[87] See chap. 6 n. 7 above.

[88] Concerning papal spoils, see n. 91 below. Concerning Stapeldon, see *The Register of Walter de Stapeldon Bishop of Exeter*, ed. F. C. Hingeston-Randolph (London 1892) 564: "Item, Manipulus Florum, sine asseribus, precii xiij s. iiij d. Item, Manipulus Florum, cum asseribus, precii xl s." We are grateful to Susan Cavenaugh for this reference.

[89] Of the dated or datable fifteenth-century MSS (including 5 dated s. xiv ex./xv in.), 33 belong to the first half of the century, 10 to the second half.

[90] Cf. Rouse and Rouse, "*Lumen anime*" 64-72; and E. C. Higonnet, "Spiritual Ideas in the Letters of Peter of Blois," *Speculum* 50 (1975) 218 and n. 4.

preachers, in the hands of university-trained preachers—parish priests, houses of mendicant orders, newly revitalized houses of canons regular. But we also find the *Manipulus florum* in older or more conservative institutions: Clairvaux, Saint-Martin of Tours, Bec, Jumièges—all have copies of the *Manipulus* before the end of the fourteenth century. In most cases this reflects not so much the interests of the house as those of its donors.

The fact that prelates both preached and wrote, in the conduct of their duties, readily accounts for the number of manuscripts of the *Manipulus florum* found in the registers of papal spoils. There are between seventeen and thirty-two copies (fifteen of the entries are possible duplications) in the estates of cardinals, archbishops, bishops and officials who died at Avignon between 1327 and 1409.[91] Among these is an expensive book, evidently a *Manipulus florum*, that Clement VI commissioned in 1352: "Pro tabula super Manipulo sanctorum in quo sunt sexterni 25: 66 fl., 15 s., 6 d."[92] Another instance, not of ownership but of specific interest, is that of Robert de Baubigny, abbot of Saint-Paul of Besançon; the *Manipulus florum* is among the books, principally canon law and pastoral theology, that he borrowed in 1409 from his former abbey, Saint-Etienne of Dijon.[93]

[91] These book records are to be edited for the C.N.R.S., Paris, by Daniel Williman and Jacques Monfrin. Williman has collected the following notices of owners of the *Manipulus florum* in his doctoral dissertation, "The Books of the Avignonese Popes and Clergy: A Repertory and Edition of the Book-Notices in the Vatican Archives, 1287-1420" (University of Toronto 1973); numbers refer to his repertory: 327.5 (20), Johannes Grand Furstat, abp. of Bremen; 329.9 (2), Petrus Rogerii, bp. of Carcassonne; 341.6 (8), Fredericus de Pernstein, OFM, abp. of Riga; 347.8 (85), Guillelmus de Veyraco, canon of Salisbury, papal chaplain; 348.64 (26), Arnaldus de Roseto, bp. of Asti; 352.1 (9), Bertrandus de Pogeto, cardinal; 352.9 (8), purchased by Clement VI; 364.7 (5), Deodatus de Canillaco, OSB, bp. of Maguelonne; 368.7 (37), Joannes Peissoni, abp. of Aix; 369.4 (408, 590, 786, 1311, 1552, 1720), six copies in the papal inventory of before 4 May 1369—some or all of these are probably duplicates of the preceding; 373.7 (17), Gaucelmus de Deux, bp. of Maguelonne; 375.9 (1092, 1114, 1115, 1116, 1117), five copies in the catalog of Oct. 1375, probably duplicates of 369.4 above; 377.3 (42), Goffridus de Veyrols, abp. of Toulouse; 378.4 (17), Jacobus, abp. of Taranto; 380.3 (34), Guillelmus de Vesencay, abbot of Saint-Maxence, Poitiers; 394.2 (12), Joannes Stephani, bp. of Toulon; 394.7 (1592), Pedro de Luna (Benedict XIII); 407.5 (5), three copies in the catalog of 28 Sept. 1407, probably duplicates of preceding notices; 409.3 (c 20), Franciscus Eximensis, OFM, patriarch of Jerusalem; 420.5 (206), one copy in the papal library at Peniscola, arranged and cataloged as it had been at Avignon—probably a duplicate of a preceding notice.
[92] Evidence that this refers to a *Manipulus florum* consists of the mention of the word "Manipulus," the fact that 25 sexterns (300 folios) is an appropriate length for a manuscript of the *Manipulus florum*, and the use of the word "tabula," which indicates the work in question to be an alphabetical compilation. However, the cost is startling, compared with the evaluation of copies of the *Manipulus florum* in the spoils registers: 10 fl. is the highest figure given.
[93] Pierre Cockshaw, "Une source d'information codicologique: les protocoles de notaires conservés aux Archives de la Côte-d'Or," *Scriptorium* 25 (1971) 67-70, esp. 70.

The *Manipulus* was also among the books removed from Queen's College Oxford in the late 1370s by John of Trevisa, the translator of Higden, and others.[94] And finally, Françoise Autrand has found the *Manipulus florum* in the estates of two turn-of-the-century members of the *parlement* of Paris, Nicolas de l'Espoisse (will dated 1 August 1419) and Guillaume d'Estouteville (will dated 21 December 1414).[95]

* * *

The *Manipulus florum* was intended by Thomas of Ireland for the use of preachers; and evidence indicates that preachers did make extensive use of it for the writing of sermons. But in practice the utility of a reference tool is defined not by the intent of its creator but by the demands of its users. Thus the *Manipulus* was of service to anyone whose profession involved composition—theological, literary, legal or other. Its influence extended from 1306 to the end of the Middle Ages and beyond; from new order to old, from priest, canon and friar to prelate and pope. It served theologians, anthologists, literary figures and pamphleteers, male and female. For virtually anyone whose career put a premium on a choice of phrase, the *Manipulus florum* was of ready use.

[94] The list of books is printed by D. C. Fowler, to whom we owe this reference, in his "John of Trevisa and the English Bible," *Modern Philology* 58 (1960) 94, "*Manipulus florum* [2ndo folio] *quisque.*"

[95] Françoise Autrand, "Les libraries des gens du Parlement au temps de Charles vi," *Annales: Economies, Sociétés, Civilisations* 28 (1973) 1233.

When the present work was already in the press, we were kindly informed by Peter S. Lewis that Jean Juvénal des Ursins ii, archbishop of Rheims 1449-1473, used the *Manipulus florum* extensively in his political writings. The *Manipulus*, though never mentioned by name, is the source of over one hundred extracts in Juvénal's eleven political treatises written between 1432 and 1468. The treatises are being edited by Lewis: Jean Juvénal des Ursins, *Ecrits politiques*, Société de l'histoire de France (Paris, forthcoming). Regarding Juvénal, see P. L. Péchenard, *Jean Juvénal des Ursins: Etudes sur sa vie et ses œuvres* (Paris 1876); and P. S. Lewis, *Later Medieval France: The Polity* (London 1968), esp. 177-178.

Appendix 1

Prologue to the *Flores paradysi*

Prologue to the *Flores paradysi*, taken from Paris, Bibliothèque nationale MS lat. 15982 fol. 1^{r-va} (*c*; see plate 5); and Brussels, Bibliothèque royale MS 20030-32 fol. 14^{r-v} (*b*).

Flores paradysi pro titulo nomen non immerito sortitus est liber iste. Qui sanctorum catholicorum patrum, philosophorum et poetarum electissimis plenus sententiis tanquam paradysi prestantissimis refertus floribus gratiam sui cunctis prebet legentibus. Paradysi etenim nomine non incongrue sacra scriptura signatur, in cuius medio lignum uite apprehenditur,[1] id est, in cuius intimo intellectu ueritatis cognitio attingitur, sicut testatur Salomon in parab[olis], dicens, Lignum uite est hiis qui apprehenderint illam;[2] et item, Vita sunt inuenientibus ea,[3] scilicet archana sacre scripture intelligentibus. Veritatis autem cognitio atque fruitio uita est cunctorum beate uiuentium qui in sacra scriptura a studiosis mentibus et deuotis utcumque apprehenditur et gustatur, dum per illam et cognoscuntur mala ad detestationem et cautelam, et agnoscuntur bona ad amorem et sequelam. Hec autem est tota sapiencia hominis et uera anime uita, in huius uite mortalitate declinare scilicet a malo et facere bonum. Sicut dicit Salomon, Quia omnis sapiencia timor domini,[4] et item, Deum time et mandata eius observa: hoc est omnis homo,[5] ergo absque hoc nichil homo. Per timorem itaque domini declinatur a malo, sicut dicitur in Ecclesiastico, Timor domini expellit peccatum.[6] Item per timorem domini fiunt bona, sicut dicit idem Salomon, Qui timet Deum nichil negligit,[7] et item in Ecclesiastico, Qui timet Deum faciet bona.[8] Ad hanc ueram hominis sapienciam et ueram anime uitam ipsa scriptura quam superius paradysi nomine signari diximus nos uocat dicens, Venite filii, audite me. Timorem domini docebo uos,[9] et quod ipse timor Dei[a] sit

---

[a] domini *b*.

[1] Cf. Gen. 2:9.
[2] Prov. 3:18.
[3] Prov. 4:22.
[4] Ecclus. 19:18.
[5] Eccles. 12:13.
[6] Ecclus. 1:27.
[7] Eccles. 7:19.
[8] Ecclus. 15:1.
[9] Ps. 33:12 (AV Ps. 34:11).

hominis uita, consequenter exponit et dicit, Quis est homo qui uult uitam etc.[10] Quid sit etiam timere Deum in consequentibus ostendit, dicens, Declina a malo et fac bonum.[11] Ecce, uita hominis timor domini. Timor autem domini nichil aliud est quam declinare a malo et facere bonum, quod dum per assiduam sacre scripture lectionem facere docemur et ad hoc faciendum eiusdem sacre scripture et terremur minis et monemur exemplis et informamur consiliis et accendimur promissis, proculdubio tanquam lignum uite in medio paradysi pascimur et nutrimur. Merito igitur sacra scriptura paradysus uocatur que cognitione ueritatis tanquam ligno uite suos pascit amatores que quot utiles habet libros, tot habet fructuosas arbores et salutares; quot sententias, tot flores. Per huius igitur paradysi medium dum quasi transitum facerem plurima sacre scripture uolumina percurrendo, uolensque posteris aliquem laboris mei fructum relinquere. De dictis sanctorum catholicorum patrum magnorumque et nominatorum uirorum breues et utiles ac necessarias eligere ac colligere curaui sententiae tanquam paradysi amenissimos flores, specie, odore et sapore prestantissimos. Qui et in hoc ipso ceteris materialibus prestant floribus quod nunquam marcescunt, immo semper in ipsa ueritate tanquam sua uita radicate uiuunt, et quod semel sunt semper esse noscuntur, nec deficiunt unquam aut mutantur in peius, sed pocius suum fidelem possessorem et amatorem in melius mutare consueuerunt. In hiis et studiosus eruditionem et deuotus gratiam et quilibet pius lector et fidelis edificationem inueniet. In hiis et docentur bona et dedocentur mala, ut et auidius appetantur bona et prudentius mala caueantur. In hiis ad timorem Dei eruditur animus et ad amorem Dei inflammatur affectus, quibus duobus nichil est hominibus in hac uita utilius. Et hec est omnis sapiencia nostra et uita nostra, ut supra ostensum est, timere Deum, scilicet, et amare, quod qui ignorat pro nichilo est et nichil est, quamlibet multa scire uideatur. Disputent igitur doctores, litigent sophiste, studeant studentes, nouerint scientes, si huius artis fuerint expertes in uacuum currunt, et pro totius sui laboris fructu nisi huic arti prius manus dederunt, nichil aliud in fine nisi mortem eternam inuenient. Quisquis igitur es qui utilem et salutarem scientiam apprehendere niteris, qui salutis fructum ex scientia queris, qui non ad ostentationem sed ad tuam et aliorum edificationem erudiri desideras, in hoc opere te exercere curato. Hic enim breuiter et summatim ad manum inuenies quicquid in multorum armariorum multis et magnis uoluminibus ad honeste uite informationem, ad uitiorum detestationem et morum edificationem utiliter et eleganter dictum inuenire

---

[10] Ps. 33:13 (av Ps. 34:12).
[11] Ps. 33:15 (av Ps. 34:14).

potuisses, etiam si omnia illa perscrutari licuisset. Utere igitur quesitis cum labore meo et gaude inuentis sine labore tuo.

Ut autem in hoc opere studiosis exercendi ingenii materia preberetur simul que utilitas multo amplior proueniret, uniuersum hoc opus pro diuersa alphabeta distinximus per que singule sententie concordate inueniri breui compendio et facillimo possent. Plurimas siquidem dictiones quas in ipsis sententiis magis celebres ac principales inuenimus et quas ad materiam sermonis magis necessarias credidimus, hic secundum ordinem alphabeti subscriptas inuenies, simulque attitulatas eisdem dictionibus litteras alphabeti punctis distinctas, per quas sententie ex diuersis locis in quibus eedem dictiones uel similes eis uel equales inueniuntur, ad easdem concordationis gratia reducuntur, ita etiam ut una sententia secundum diuersas dictiones quas in se habet quasi principales ad diuersa loca per earumdem[b] dictionum concordantiam referatur. *De dispositione alphabetorum*: Est autem dispositio alphabetorum talis. In hoc opere tria genera alphabetorum suo modo currentium inuenies, que exempli gratia suis sunt appellanda uocabulis. Primum ergo uocemus generale, secundum speciale, tertium singulare. Sicut enim genus continet species, species autem indiuidua continent; sic[c] primum continet secundum, sicut genus species, secundum continet tertium, sicut species indiuidua. Tertium autem non continet sed continetur, et idcirco dicitur illud singulare, quia ulterius non diuiditur tanquam indiuiduum. Secundum autem idcirco speciale uocamus quia et continetur et continet, tanquam species. Primum autem idcirco generale dicimus quia non continetur ab aliquo, tanquam genus, sed continet sub se secundum, et sub illo tertium. Continet enim sub se tot alphabeta que specialia diximus quot sunt littere in ipso alphabeto, ita ut singule littere alphabeti generalis aliquod speciale sub se contineant alphabetum. Unumquidque autem speciale alphabetum tot sub se continet singularia alphabeta quot sunt littere in ipso alphabeto, ita ut singule singula. Singulare autem alphabetum nullum aliud sub se continet alphabetum, sed singule illius littere singulas demonstrant sententias. Habent enim singule sententie singulas litteras appropriatas sibi, quas contra initia sententiarum in margine poteris inuenire. Que quia per ordinem alphabeti currunt, alphabeta plurima faciunt que singularia uocamus, ita ut uno finito aliud continuo inchoetur, donec singule sententie singulas habeant litteras, usque in finem. Et quam talium alphabetorum multiplicitas confusionem pareret nisi ab inuicem distinguerentur, habent et singula alphabeta huiusmodi[d] singulas litteras attitulatas sibi, quas circa initium uniuscuiusque alphabeti in margine poteris inuenire, ita ut primum alphabetum in principio sui iuxta se in margine habeat .A., secundum eo

[b] eandem *b*.   [c] sicut *b*.   [d] huius *c*.

modo .B., tertium .C., quartum .D. et sic de singulis—que littere, quia per ordinem alphabeti currunt, aliud alphabetum constituunt, quod superius speciale uocauimus. Quod quia multipliciter repetitur, distinctione eget. Itaque primum talium alphabetorum pro determinatione sui in superiori margine habet .A. litteram capitalem minio scriptam, que semper in singulis foliis superius in fronte repetitur donec illud speciale alphabetum quod determinat finiatur. Secundum alphabetum eodem modo habet .B., tertium .C. et sic de singulis. Istud[e] autem alphabetum quod hoc modo secundum determinat, illud est quod superius generale uocauimus. Quod quia usque in finem libri sufficit, alterius determinatione non eget. *De modo inueniendi sententias per alphabetum*: Diximus iam de dispositione et ordine alphabetorum, que si tibi adhuc confusionem pariunt et obscura uidentur, noli desistere, sed his que adhuc dicuntur intende. Si enim modicum quid ex hiis intelligere potueris exercendo et querendo per te ipsum facillima inuenies que prius difficillima putabantur. Est autem modus inueniendi talis: Primo igitur quere dictionem illam cuius uis habere concordantias, inter has dictiones que in subscripta forma secundum ordinem alphabeti conscribuntur. Qua inuenta, uide quid sequitur et inuenies semper primo loco tres litteras sub uno puncto; primam illarum quere semper in fronte libri in superiori margine litteram capitalem per se positam minio scriptam, quam secundum ordinem alphabeti procedentem inuenies. Qua inuenta, infra terminos eius, id est, infra initium et finem eiusdem, quere secundam, quam in margine a latere inuenies litteram capitalem incausto[f] scriptam per se positam. Qua inuenta, uidebis contra eandem litteram aliud quoddam alphabetum iniciari. Illud est quod superius singulare uocauimus, in quo tertiam quere litteram et ipsa tibi sententiam quam queris sine dubio demonstrabitur, nisi forte scriptor errauerit vel quesitor. Igitur prima littera illarum trium semper in generali alphabeto querenda est, secunda in speciali sub eadem generali, tertia in singulari[g] sub eadem speciali. Post illas tres litteras quas semper primo loco inuenies, si postea alias tres litteras simili modo inueneris, negociandum est ut prius. Si autem duas tamen inueneris, prima illarum[h] erit de speciali alphabeto, secunda de singulari, sed sub eadem generali que proxima antecesserit. Si uero unam uel plures litteras per se singulariter poni inueneris, omnes in eodem singulari alphabeti querende sunt et sub eisdem litteris generalibus et specialibus que proximo loco antecesserunt. Verbi gratia ponamus exemplum: Videamus hanc dictionem, *Abicere*, qui prima omnium hic ponitur. Ibi hoc modo titulatum inuenies: Add.k.fm.ld.tr. Bvf.Cal. Has primas tres litteras que primo ponuntur, scilicet, Add., require ut supra iam docuimus: .A., scilicet, in superiori margine in generali

---

[e] Illud *b.*　　[f] adurio *c.*　　[g] singulari sed sub *b.*　　[h] earum *c.*

alphabeto, .d. in latere in speciali, .d. in singulari. Sequentem autem litteram que per se ponitur, scilicet, .k., require in eadem singulari alphabeto
in quo proximo loco antecedentem inuenisti, scilicet, .d., sub eodem generali
et speciali que prius. Illas autem duas litteras que post per se ponuntur,
scilicet .fm., require sub eadem generali littera que proximo loco antecessit,
scilicet, sub .A., ita ut unam illarum duarum, primam scilicet, id est .f.,
requiras in speciali alphabeto, reliquam in singulari, ubi prius, et sic de
ceteris.

Appendix 2

Prologue to the *Manipulus florum*

Abiit in agrum[a] et collegit spicas post terga metencium. Ruth ii.[1] Ruth paupercula non habens messem propriam ad colligendum, agrum intrauit alienum, ut spicas colligeret post terga metencium. Sic ego pauperculus non habens copiam scriptorum nec originalium aceruum, agrum intraui Booz, quod interpretatur robur[2] uel uirtus, scilicet Roberti utique robusti in quo uirtutis robur uigere consueuit, et ibidem originalium spicas id est diuersas sanctorum auctoritates de diuersis libris non sine labore collegi. Sed considerans quod sine modo erant et ordine nec post me alicui alii possent prodesse, hic breuiter quasi in unum manipulum ex diuersis spicis collectum secundum ordinem alphabeti more concordanciarum collegi, ut sic a me et aliis simplicibus facilius possint reperiri. Ita ut cum alii messores uenerint cum exultatione portantes manipulos suos,[3] ego hunc collectum post terga doctorum cum uidua offeram in Domini gazophilacium.[4] Cum enim librorum originalium pelagus sit quasi mare magnum et spaciosum[5] quod a quolibet inuestigari non possit, michi utilius uidebatur pauca doctorum dicta in promptu habere quam si multa quidem homo transcurreret et illa ad manum non haberet, iuxta documentum Senece: Cum multa[6] percurreris unum excerpe quod illa die concoquas; certis enim ingeniis nutriri et immorari oportet. Siquis uelit aliquid trahere quod in animo fideliter sedeat, fragilis enim est memoria et rerum turbe non sufficit.[7] Apes ergo nobis imitandi sunt qui uagantur et flores ad mel faciendum carpunt deinde quicquid attulerunt disponunt ac per fauos digerunt. Ita inquit quecumque ex diuersa lectione congessimus separare debemus. Melius enim distincta seruantur. Deinde ad debitam facultatem ingenii in unum saporem uaria illa libamenta ordinare ut etiam si apparuerit unde sumpta sint, aliter tamen

---

[a] scilicet Booz *suprascript in* BCD *and most* MSS *of private tradition*

[1] Ruth 2:3.

[2] This is a commonplace found in any number of lists of Hebrew names which accompanied the text of the Scripture: "Booz: in quo robur, vel in quo virtus, vel in ipso fortitudo, vel ipse in fortitudine."

[3] Ps. 125:6 (AV Ps. 126:6).

[4] Cf. e.g., Mk. 12:41-44.

[5] Ps. 103:25 (AV Ps. 104:25).

[6] Seneca, *Ad Lucilium ep.* 84. Quoted in the body of the *Manipulus florum, Studium ab.*

[7] Unidentified. Quoted in the body of the *Manipulus florum, Doctrina siue doctor ax,* attributed to Petrus Blesensis (without title of work).

esse quam unde sumpta sint appareant.[8] Quasdam igitur dictiones nota-
biliores ac magis communes que sepius in sermonibus uel lectionibus
possent occurrere et cum quibus se possit homo in omni materia iuuare, hic
secundum alphabeti ordinem more concordanciarum signaui. Ita quod primo
ponuntur dictiones incipientes per *a* secundum quod coniungitur cum
diuersis litteris secundum ordinem alphabeti, post modum dictiones incipientes per *b*, et sic de qualibet littera alphabeti usque ad finem, in quibus
etiam dictionibus attenditur ordo prioris et posterioris secundum ordinem
litterarum alphabeti in ipsa dictione, sicut prius ponitur *conuersatio* quam
conuersio licet in primis quattuor uel quinque litteris conueniant. Sub
qualibet autem dictione ponuntur diuerse auctoritates sanctorum et aliorum
doctorum per ordinem que de illa materia loqui magis uidentur. Ita quod
cuiuslibet sancti uel doctoris per se auctoritates ponuntur prout exterius in
margine signantur. Sed quia auctoritas que de una materia loquitur nichilo-
minus diuersis aliis applicari posset, ideo ne una et eadem auctoritas sepe in
diuersis locis rescriberetur, litteras alphabeti ex opposito cuiuslibet auctoritatis in margine secundum plus et minus iuxta numerum auctoritatum in
qualibet dictione signaui et ubi alphabetum simplex non sufficit, combinatum iteratur. Cum ergo in fine alicuius dictionis inueniuntur alie dictiones cum aliquibus litteris sequentibus denotatur quod in illis dictionibus
sub talibus litteris inuenientur auctoritates que possint applicari ad
propositum. Si autem ponatur dictio sine aliqua littera sequente designatur
quod sub illa dictione quasi per totum de illa materia potest inueniri. Ita
quod si aliqua auctoritas in loco proprio non situatur quelibet tamen ad
proprium locum remittitur uel in proprio collocatur, et hec planius patent
intuenti. Auctoritates autem quantum ad librorum capitula non potui deter-
minate signare cum in diuersis libris diuersimode signentur, et sepe eadem
auctoritas a diuersis doctoribus scribitur, quin immo una et eadem ab eodem
in diuersis locis frequenter inuenitur. Sed omne uerum a quocumque dicatur
a Spiritu Sancto est. Auctores autem quorum dicta hic sepius allegantur
sunt hii: Augustinus, Ambrosius, Ieronimus, Gregorius, Bernardus,
Hylarius, Crisostomus, Ysidorus, Damascenus, Origines, Cyprianus, Ful-
gencius, Basilius, Maximus, Rabanus, Cesarius, Leo, Beda, Prosper, Anselmus, Ricardus, Hugo, Iohannes Cassianus, Cassiodorus, Alanus, Petrus
Rauennas, Plinius, Solinus, Rabymoyses, Valerius Maximus, Vegecius,
Agellius, Sydonius, Tullius, Boecius,[b] Seneca, cuius[c] dicta in fine cuiuslibet
dictionis ponuntur, quia secundum ipsum eundem illa pars in finem

[b] Boecius, Petrus Blesensis, Seneca *β*   [c] cuius: quorum *M*

[8] See note 6.

reseruari debet quam quilibet etiam satiatus appetere potest. Deditum enim uino pocio extrema delectat et quod in se iocundissimum hominis uoluntas habet in finem suum differt.[9] Istorum autem auctorum libros quantum ad principia et fines et nomina et parcialium librorum numerum in fine huius operis signaui ut facilius possent cognosci et securius allegari. Tu ergo lector ora pro collectore et utere quesitis cum labore alieno[10] et gaude de inuentis sine labore proprio.[d] Propter has autem modicas spicas agrum fertilem originalium non despicias; improuidus enim est qui neglecto igne se per scintillas nititur calefacere, et qui contempto fonte per roris guttas sitim conatur extinguere.

[d] Nomen autem collectoris uolui subticere, ne collectio uilesceret cognito collectore γ *and* M *add here*.

[9] Seneca, ep. 12, ¶ 4-5; ed. L. D. Reynolds (Oxford 1965) 1.27 lines 5-7: "Deditos vino potio extrema delectat...; quod in se iocundissimum omnis voluptas habet in finem sui differt."

[10] Prologue of the *Flores paradysi c* (B.N. lat. MS 15982 fol. 1ᵛ): "Utere igitur quesitis cum labore meo et gaude inuentis sine labore tuo."

Appendix 3

Pecia Divisions in Bibliothèque Mazarine MS 1032

We give below the *loci* in the text of the *Manipulus florum* at which new *peciae* commence in Maz. MS 1032, the surviving collection of exemplar *peciae* of the second and more important university stationers' edition. This should aid in determining whether or not a given manuscript was copied from *peciae*. The list includes the number of the *pecia*; the topic-heading under which the new *pecia* begins; the reference-letter of the passage in which the change in *peciae* occurs, taken from the *editio princeps* (Jacobus Tyela, Piacenza 1483); and an excerpt from the passage, with a slash marking the spot where the new *pecia* begins. While the reference-letters vary slightly from one edition to another, the references from the 1483 edition taken in combination with the context passages should enable one to locate the *pecia* divisions easily.

1. Prologue: *Abiit in agrum, et collegit spicas post terga mententium.* Ruth II. Ruth paupercula non

2. [*Accidia i./k.*] sed resistendo superandam. In eodem libro. / Accidia est solitariis magis

3. [*Aduocati c./d.*] oppressisti de falsitate uicisti. Ambrosius in sermone. / Iustus aduocatus nullo modo

4. [*Amicitia ai.*] exhibite subuentionis elucidat. / Cassiodorus in quadam epistola

5. [*Amor m.*] labores amantium sed ipsi delectant / sicut uenantium aucupantium

6. [*Anima ac.*] altitudinem et profunditatem maris / animi tui abyssum intra et mirare

7. [*Ascensio e.*] agnosce milite celestis obsequium / non auxilium seruitium non subsidium

8. [*Auaritia bx.*] Modus pecunie querendus / est, qui nec maior necessitate presenti

9. [*Bellum as.*] non laborat ut carus militibus / sit armare (*sic*) militis nescit

10. [*Caritas ac.*] tua dicere possum quam ut deum / de celo traheres et hominem de terra

11. [*Clericus n./o.*] Bernardus super Canticum sermone XXXIII. / Peccata populi mei comedunt. Sed

12. [*Confidentia i.*] sed deum rogare qui aduersarium pos/sit opprimere. Cassiodorus super illud psalmum

13. [*Consideratio x.*] quid intra se, quid extra, quid infra, quid supra, / quid contra, quid ante, quid post sit

14. [*Consuetudo p.*] quia ubi sponte diu perstitit, ibi / et cum noluerit coacta cadit. Gregorius

15. [*Conuersatio e.*] Falsus rumor cito opprimitur / et uita posterior indicat de priori

16. [*Conuersio ad.*] acutior, auditus promptior, incessus rectior, / uultus iocundior qui in hac etate

17. [*Correctio ak.*] non dominando preueniat; sed / simulando subsequatur, et notum

18. [*Crudelitas h.*] Plerique homines in suis domibus / seuissimi tyranni, in alienis humillimi

19. [*Curiositas af.*] ac deinde dissoluimus. Quid mihi uocum / similitudines distinguis quibus

20. [*Detractio p./q.*] ueritatis uideant. Gregorius ibidem. / Linguas detrahentium sicut

21. [*Dilectio e.*] Non habet callidus hostis / machinamentum efficacius

22. [*Discretio d.*] iusto discutimus de ipso discre/tionis studio indiscretius erramus

23. [*Doctrina siue doctor a./b.*] Augustinus de doctrina christiana. / Doctor et ductor id agere debet

24. [*Ebrietas k./l.*] uultus. Augustinus ibidem. / Sobrietas cum summa trepidatione

25. [*Elemosina c.*] nihil est maius quam cum ex / corde dimittimus peccata. Augustinus in Enchiridion

26. [*Error c.*] reuocare uellet, sed quod reuocare / deberet emisit. Non mihi igitur

27. [*Exemplum b.*] eorum quibus prepositus est / quantum in ipso est occidit et forte

28. [*Fides siue fidelitas z.*] credit nec in se sperat factus / sibi tanquam uas perditum

29. [*Gloria mala siue uana b.*] uel maxime cauendum esse perfectis / quo primo enim uitio lapsa

30. [*Gratia d./e.*] ducta causa creationis. Augustinus in Enchiridion. / Dei gratia cur ad istum ueniat

31. [*Heresis h.*] de scriptura est; sensus et non / sermo sit crimen. Hylarius de Trinitate

32. [*Humilitas e.*] qui querit patriam quid / recusat uiam. Augustinus super Iohannem

33. [*Ignorantia h.*] de ignorantia tui superbia, ac de / Dei ignorantia uenit desperatio

34. [*Ingratitudo m.*] Quidam quo plus debent / magis oderunt, leue es alienum

35. [*Inuidia ab.*] Africano iustitia uirtutem / uirtus gloriam, gloriosa emulatione comparauit

36. [*Ira q./r.*] cupiditas esse consueuit. Ambrosius de paradyso. / Est ira que iustitiam Dei non operatur

37. [*Iusticia et iustus k./l.*] in estimatione fulget operantis. Gregorius lib. 5 moralium / Humana iusticia diuine iusticie comparata

38. [*Laus am.*] diues est, non credo fortune; / ualidus est, egritudine fatigabitur

39. [*Loquacitas u.*] subdola; lata et parata ad exhauri/enda bona et miscenda mala

40. [*Mandatum c.*] iocundamque gustabis, si eius qui eam / promisit precepta dilexeris. Augustinus

41. [post *Martirium*] Matrimonium, ubi coniugi/um. Maturitas, ubi modestia

42. [*Militia o.*] nisi ex occasione aut nimia necessi/tate confligunt. Magna dispositio

43. [*Misericordia p.*] subiicitur; sed ipsas pias mentes ad compassion/nem dolentium necessario cogit affectu

44. [*Mors b.*] Mortis diem omnes affuturum / sciunt, et cum tamen omnes aut pene

45. [*Mors da./db.*] semper ibas nullum sine exitu iter est. Seneca lxxviii epistola. / Mors non est gloriosa sed fortiter

46. [*Murmur e.*] Anime que sane sunt portari non / indigent, ac per hoc nec onus sunt

47. [*Obedientia x.*] adimplere, locus uero aliquando placet, / aliquando displacet, placet quibusdam

48. [*Oratio bd.*] humilitatem dominus filios uocat iude/os, et illa dominos nec doluit in

49. [*Paciencia ag.*] te digne que pateris et cum te humili/aueris atque dixeris iustum de te factum iudicium

50. [*Patria a.*] tribulatio, quando in patria non / est delectatio. Augustinus super illud psalmum In die tribulationis

51. [*Peccatum m.*] mens oblectatur illicitis, non quidem / decernens esse facienda

52. [*Penitentia o.*] uxor et mundus ad se / uocent multos enim solet serotina

53. [*Petitio g.*] reprehenditur, ubi de dantis miseri/cordia non dubitatur

54. [*Predestinatio n.*] uictoribus munera parantur. Non solum ergo / bonis utitur Deus ad opus bonum

55. [*Prelatio x.*] Domino parcente prosterneret; utrobique / legatus fortis, utrobique mediator

56. [*Presumptio n.*] preesse festinant, nunquam senior/ibus ipsi subiiciantur et a superbia inchoantes

57. [*Prouidentia p.*] non dicit; non putaui hoc fieri / quia non dubitat sed expectat

58. [*Religio b.*] unicuique, sicut cuique opus fuerit / sicut legitur in actibus apostolorum, quia

59. [*Relinquere g.*] ostendat, licet in limine pater iaceat, / percalcatum perge patrem

60. [*Resurrectio r.*] resurrectionis et soluta est obser/uantia omnis pietatis. Chrisostomus super illud Matt. xxii

61. [*Sacramentum /a.*] Sacramentum / Ab ipsa Dei sapientia homine assumpto

62. [*Sapientia uel sciencia al.*] amare didicerit et ei sepius / uacare uoluerit, iocundam ualde

63. [*Scriptura sacra bo.*] Schola celestis, / eruditio uitalis, auditorium ueritatis

64. [*Simplicitas c.*] explicando enim te a mundo, simplex / implicando duplex eris. Augustinus

65. [*Solitudo et tumultus d./e.*] uirtutum est. Ieronimus in epistola ad Rusticum. / Si carni, quod licet, abscindimus

66. [*Studium f.*] Omnino iniquum est, nobiliora in/genia studiis dehonestari minoribus

67. [*Superbia al.*] non mentium et dignos se estimare / dignitate, ad quam ambiando peruenerunt

68. [*Tentatio aq.*] Quatuor sunt cause temptationum. / Prima est loci amenitas

69. [*Tribulatio ad.*] Afflicti terrena perdimus / si afflictione humiliter sustinentes

70. [*Verecundia r.*] magistra innocentie, cara proxi/mis, accepta alienis, omni loco

71. [*Virtus n.*] Mensuretur perfectorum fidelium / uita per quadrum et tantum habeat

72. [*Voluntas ae.*] uoluntas rebus istis esset contenta / ne ipsum horribile dictu deseuiret

73. [*Xp̄us al.*] probabilem fieri scelere abstinere / bonum uelle, amare omnes, odisse malum

74. [bibliography ii: 26] Contra epistolam fundamenti. Principium: / Unum uerum Deum

75. [bibliography vi: 9] et digitos nostros ad bellum. / De diligendo Deo

Appendix 4

Printed Editions of the *Manipulus florum*

The following have been seen by us, unless another source is cited.[1] This list does not distinguish among editions, issues, reprintings and the like, but (save for the incunables) refers to the information on the title pages.

1483, Piacenza; Jacobus de Tyela (Hain 8542)
[1493/5], Venice; Joannes Rubeus Vercellensis (Hain 8543)
1550, Venice; "Ad signum spei"
1553, Lyon; Guillaume Rouillé
1554, Lyon; G. Rouillé
1554, Lyon; Thibaud Payen
1555, Lyon; G. Rouillé
1555, Lyon; T. Payen
1556, Paris; J. Macé
1556, Paris; Joannes Baillerius[2]
1557, Paris; Jerome de Marnef (in the Bibliothèque municipale, Lyon)
1557, Lyon; Jacques Brossart (H. L. Baudrier, *Bibliographie lyonnaise*, 12 vols. [Lyon 1895-1921] 1:68)
1558, Lyon; G. Rouillé
1558, Lyon; T. Payen
1558, Antwerp; Joannes Bellerus
1563, Antwerp; J. Bellerus
1566, Lyon; G. Rouillé
1567, Lyon; T. Payen
1572, Lyon; G. Rouillé (Baudrier 9:341)
1575, Lyon; G. Rouillé
1575, Lyon; Louis Cloquemin & Etienne Michel

---

[1] The following libraries were searched for printed editions: Antwerp, Stadsbibliotheek; Brussels, Bibliothèque royale; Cambridge University Library; Florence, Biblioteca nazionale centrale; London, British Library; Lyon, Bibliothèque municipale; Munich, Bayerische Staatsbibliothek; Oxford, Bodleian Library; Paris, Bibliothèque de l'Arsenal, Bibliothèque Mazarine, Bibliothèque nationale; Vienna, Oesterreichische Nationalbibliothek; Vatican, Bibliotheca apostolica.

[2] The publisher is evidently not to be identified with his contemporary and near namesake at Antwerp, Joannes Bellerus; see A. Rouzet, *Dictionnaire des imprimeurs, libraires et éditeurs...* (Nieuwkoop 1975) 8-10.

1576, Venice; M. Leuum
1576, Antwerp; J. Bellerus
1577, Cologne; Ludovicus Alectorius
1579, Lyon; G. Rouillé
1580, Lyon; G. Rouillé
1593, s.l.; Jacob Stoer
1596, s.l.; J. Stoer
1601, s.l.; J. Stoer
1606, Cologne; Bernhard Wolter
1614, Cologne; J. Stoer
1614, Geneva (altered, from Cologne); J. Stoer
1616, Cologne; B. Wolter
1622, s.l.; J. Stoer
1622, Cologne (added to t.p. ?); J. Stoer
1664, Paris; Pierre Variquet
1669, Paris; P. Variquet
1678, Lyon; J. Certe (in 2 vols.)
1699, [Nuremberg]; Martin Endter
1735, Vienna; G. Lehmann & J. P. Krauss
1736, Vienna; G. Lehmann & J. P. Krauss
1746, Turin; Society of Jesus
1751, Vienna; J. P. Krauss
1752, Vienna; J. P. Krauss
1758, Vienna; J. P. Krauss
1770, Turin; Society of Jesus
1858, Monteregali; P. Rossi; ed. I. T. Gelardi (in the Vatican Library)
1887, Paris; Bloud et Barral

We have been unable to verify the following editions. While many of the references are doubtless mistakes, there may well be genuine reports among them. Normally we cite only a single source, in which further bibliography may be found.

1555, Paris (L. Ott, *Untersuchungen zur theologischen Briefliteratur der Frühscholastik*, Beiträge zur Geschichte der Philosophie und Theologie des Mittelalters: Texte und Untersuchungen 34 [Münster i.W. 1937] 562 n. 36)

1568, Antwerp (P. Glorieux, *Répertoire des maitres en théologie de Paris* 2, Etudes de philosophie médiévale 18 [Paris 1934] 118 no. 322 x)

1570, Antwerp (P. Feret, *La faculté de théologie de Paris* 3 [Paris 1896] 240 n. 1)

1572, Antwerp (F. Stegmüller, *Repertorium biblicum medii aevi* 5 [Madrid 1955] 365 no. 8128.1)

1575, Antwerp (Stegmüller)

1579, Cologne (Glorieux; B. Hauréau, "Thomas d'Irlande," *Histoire littéraire de la France* 30 [Paris 1888] 401)

1580, Antwerp (Glorieux; Hauréau)

1611, Cologne (Stegmüller)

1622, Paris (Stegmüller)

1622, Geneva (Stegmüller; Hauréau)

1624, Rome (Stegmüller)

(1654, Paris; Pierre Variquet. This, mentioned in the preface of the 1887 edition, is a mistake for the genuine 1664, Paris; P. Variquet.)

Appendix 5

Manuscripts of the Minor Works of Thomas of Ireland

The following is a summary list of the surviving manuscripts, compiled from the catalogs of extant collections, from the *Manuscript Sources for the History of Irish Civilization* (ed. R. J. Hayes, 11 vols. [Boston 1965]), from the list printed by B. Dudik (*Statuten des ersten Prager Provincial-Concils vom 11. und 12. November 1349* [Brünn 1872] 18-32), and from notes collected and kindly shared by Ludwig Bieler. Since the inflated circulation of the *De tribus punctis* is the result of its inclusion in the 1349 statutes of the archdiocese of Prague (see chapter 4 above), we have noted each time that the statutes are found in the same codex with Thomas' work.

1. *De tribus punctis religionis christiane, Expositio articulorum fidei christiane, Regula christianorum, Regula fidei christiane,* etc.

   Berlin, Deutsche Staatsbibliothek MS Lat. theol. fol. 241 (Rose 800) ff. 26^v-33^v (s. xv)
   — Lat. theol. fol. 503 (now in Berlin [West], Staatsbibliothek Preussischer Kulturbesitz) ff. 309^v-319 (s. xiv^2); with statutes
   Brno, Archiv Města MS 106/120 ff. 13-25^v (AD 1351)
   Brno, Statni Archiv MS 360 pp. 37-46 (AD 1378); with statutes
   Brno, Universitní Knihovna MS 21 (II.98) ff. 75^v-84^v (AD 1403-04); with statutes
   — MS 33 (II.203) ff. 20^v-32^v (AD 1420-28); with statutes
   — MS 43 (II.48) ff. 85^v-94^v (s. xiv^2); with statutes
   — MS 70 (II.112) ff. 185-200 (s. xv); with statutes
   — MS 79 (I.57) ff. 389^v-392 (AD 1419)
   — MS 86 (II.39) ff. 38-56 (AD 1410-16); with statutes
   — MS Rajhrad R. 365 ff. 1-12^v (s. xv)
   Budapest, Országos Széchényi Könyvtár MS 89 ff. 95-103 (s. xiv ex.)
   Český Krumlov, Bibliotheca capellanorum MS I-6 allig. ff. 17^v-31^v (s. xv)
   Edinburgh, University Library MS 78 ff. 62-81^v (AD 1464)
   Escorial, MS F. II 18 ff. 185-189 (s. xiv); with *Manipulus florum*
   Evreux, Bibliothèque municipale MS 13 ff. 3-43 (s. xiv)
   Göttingen, Niedersächsische Staats- und Universitätsbibliothek MS Theol. 119 ff. 259-266 (AD 1455)

Graz, Universitätsbibliothek MS 611 ff. 103-111 (s. xv); with colophon of statutes

Innsbruck, Universitätsbibliothek MS 381 ff. 73-91 (s. xiv ex.)

Kiel, Universitätsbibliothek MS Bordesholm 49 quarto ff. 134-147 (AD 1455)

Klosterneuburg, Stiftsbibliothek MS 731 B ff. 222-232^v (s. xv)

— MS 797 ff. 48^v-65^v (s. xiv)

København, Kongelige Bibliotek MS GKS 63 fol. ff. 180-189^v (s. xv)

Kraków, Biblioteka Jagiellońska MS 1426 (AA III 11) pp. 599-617 (s. xv)

— MS 1685 (AA IV 5) pp. 502-513 (AD 1418-19)

— MS 2068 (BB XI 18) ff. 326-349 (s. xv^2)

Kremsmünster, Stiftsbibliothek MS 9 ff. 157^v-167 (s. xv)

— MS 22 ff. 225^v-240 (AD 1470)

— MS 82 ff. 69-79^v (s. xiv, after 1353)

Lambach, Stiftsbibliothek MS chart. 437 ff. 77-102^v (s. xv)

Leipzig, Universitätsbibliothek MS 613 ff. 175-186^v (AD 1419)

— MS 1244 ff. 102^v-110^v; with statutes

Lüneberg, Ratsbücherei MS theol. fol. 77 ff. 94^v-103 (s. xv med.); with *Manipulus florum*

Marburg, Universitätsbibliothek MS 75 (D 38) ff. 295-305^v (AD 1465-75)

Melk, Stiftsbibliothek MS 1059 (175; D 12) pp. 161-184 (s. xv^1)

München, Bayerische Staatsbibliothek Clm 915 ff. 1-37 (s. xvi)

— Clm 12389 ff. 115-133^v (s. xv); with statutes

Olomouc, Statni Archiv MS CO 54 ff. 187^v-195 (AD 1410); with statutes

— MS CO 68 ff. 133^v-143 (s. xv)

— MS CO 162 ff. 195^v-201^v (AD 1394); with statutes

— MS CO 215 ff. 111-122^v (s. xv)

— MS CO 232 ff. 57^v-71^v (s. xv)

— MS CO 286 ff. 20^v-25^v (AD 1407); with statutes

— MS CO 362 ff. 22-36 (s. xiv-xv); with statutes

Olomouc, Universitní Knihovna MS II 188 ff. 161-168 (s. xv); with statutes

— MS II 220 ff. 290-295 (s. xiv^2); with statutes

Opava, Institute of Silesian Studies MS 14 ff. 237^v-249 (AD 1386); with statutes

Osek, Stiftsbibliothek MS 15 ff. 75^v-86 (AD 1396); with statutes

— MS 31 ff. 17-26 (s. xiv?)

Padova, Biblioteca Universitaria MS 1575 ff. 1-24 (s. xv)

Paris, Bibliothèque Nationale MS lat. 15966 ff. 1-6 (ca. 1319); with *De tribus hierarchiis* and *De tribus sensibus*

— MS lat. 16397 ff. 1-9^v (ca. 1316); with *De tribus sensibus* and formerly with *De tribus hierarchiis* (now lost)

Philadelphia, University of Pennsylvania MS lat. 92 ff. 146-159^v (AD 1421)

Praha, Knihovna Metropolitní Kapituli MS A lix. 3 (Podlaha 91) ff. 180-192^v (AD 1422-1435)

— MS C lv.1 (Podlaha 483) ff. 16^v-26^v (AD 1388); with statutes

— MS C lv.2 (Podlaha 484) ff. 13-21 (AD 1403); with statutes

— MS C cxix (Podlaha 551) ff. 25^v-33 (s. xiv^2); with statutes

— MS E lvi (Podlaha 816) ff. 82-87 (s. xv^1)

— MS E lxxviii.2 (Podlaha 840), with statutes, inclusive ff. 20^v-42 (s. xiv ex.)

— MS I lx.2 (Podlaha 1173) ff. 19-30 (ca. 1385); with statutes

— MS I lxxvi (Podlaha 1189) ff. 10^v-17 (s. xiv^2); with statutes

— MS K xx (Podlaha 1214) ff. 39^v-62 (s. xiv^2); with statutes

— MS N ix (Podlaha 1533) ff. 15^v-24 (s. xv); with statutes

— MS N xvi (Podlaha 1540) ff. 287^v-296 (s. xiv-xv); with statutes

— MS N xxxvii (Podlaha 1561) ff. 18^v-29 (AD 1408); with statutes

— MS N xli (Podlaha 1565) ff. 157-161 (s. xv in.); with statutes

— MS N liii (Podlaha 1577) ff. 370^v-386 (s. xv^1)

— MS O xxiii (Podlaha 1607) ff. 200-213^v, 261^{r-v} (s. xv^1)

— MS O xxxiii (Podlaha 1617) ff. 21-29 (s. xiv-xv)

— MS O xli (Podlaha 1625) ff. 15-17^v (s. xv^1); with statutes

— MS O xlii (Podlaha 1626) ff. 28-46^v (s. xv^1); with statutes

— MS O lxvi (Podlaha 1650) ff. 46^v-59^v (s. xiv^2);

— MS O lxix (Podlaha 1653) ff. 1-15 (s. xiv^2); with statutes

Praha, Narodni Museum MS XIII F 4 ff. 28^v-38^v (s. xv); with statutes

— MS XVI A 11 ff. 121-128 (s. xiv^2); with statutes

— MS XVI E 21 ff. 170-184^v (AD 1453); with statutes

Praha, Universitní Knihovna MS I G 19 (Truhlář 295) ff. 22^v-35^v (s. xiv^2) with statutes

— MS I H 3 (Truhlář 328) ff. 374-406^v (s. xv)

— MS III D 13 (Truhlář 465) ff. 12^v-18^v (s. xiv^2); with statutes

— MS IV A 11 (Truhlář 587), with statutes, inclusive ff. 92^v-130^v (s. xiv-xv)

— MS IV G 7 (Truhlář 739), with statutes, inclusive ff. 1-42 (s. xiv^2)

— MS V B 3 (Truhlář 820) ff. 57-65 (s. xv); with statutes

— MS V B 5 (Truhlář 822) ff. 132-137^v (s. xiv-xv); with statutes

— MS V G 8 (Truhlář 960), with statutes, inclusive ff. 85-116^v (s. xiv ex.)

— MS V G 13 (Truhlář 965), with statutes, inclusive ff. 13-51^v (AD 1457-67)

— MS VI B 21 (Truhlář 1055) ff. 15-25^v (s. xv); with statutes

— MS VIII D 29 (Truhlář 1524), with statutes, inclusive ff. 73^v-95^v (s. xiv, after 1384)

— MS X A 26 (Truhlář 1829) ff. 50-58 (AD 1403-16); with statutes

— MS X C 1 (Truhlář 1854), with statutes, inclusive ff. 96-117 (s. xiv²)

— MS X E 20 (Truhlář 1921), with statutes, inclusive ff. 39^v-53 (s. xiv²)

— MS X G 15 (Truhlář 1969) ff. 101^v-113 (s. xiv²); with statutes

— MS XIII G 7 (Truhlář 2374) ff. 213^v-226^v (s. xiv-xv)

— MS XIV E 26 (Truhlář 2560), with statutes, inclusive ff. 125-148^v (AD 1453-55)

— MS XIV F 5 (Truhlář 2576), with statutes, inclusive ff. 1-26 (s. xiv ex.)

— MS XIV H 5 (Truhlář 2650) ff. 1-17^v (s. xiv)

— MS XX A 1 (olim Admont, Stiftsbibliothek MS 133) ff. 17^v ff. (s. xv)

Regensburg, Kollegiatstift U.L. Frau zur Alten Kapelle MS 1890 ff. 256-265 (s. xv)

Rein, Stiftsbibliothek MS 5 ff. 57-76 (s. xv)

— MS 60 ff. 92-99 (AD 1410)

Salzburg, Bibliothek der Erzabtei St. Peter MS B viii.20 ff. 1-14 (s. xv)

Schlägl, Stiftsbibliothek MS 46 (454a.61) frag., f. 348^v (s. xiv-xv); with statutes

— MS 204 (817.146) ff. 160v-173 (s. xv); with statutes

Seitenstetten, Stiftsbibliothek MS 193 ff. 120^v-128^v (s. xv)

— MS 205 ff. 102-110^v (s. xv); with statutes

Třeboň, Statni Archiv MS 5 (A 3) ff. 21^v-34^v (s. xv); with statutes

— MS 8 (A 6) ff. 2-18^v (AD 1454-56); with colophon of statutes

— MS 19 (A 18) ff. 447-454^v (s. xv)

Uppsala, Universitetsbiblioteket MS C 27 ff. 220^v-232^v (s. xv)

— MS C 212 ff. 98^v-111^v (s. xiv-xv)

— MS C 218 ff. 91-95 (s. xiv-xv)

— MS C 449 ff. 70-90^v (s. xiv-xv)

Vyšší Brod, Stiftsbibliothek MS 16 ff. 17-27 (s. xiv²); with statutes

— MS 59 ff. 19-30 (s. xiv²); with statutes

Wien, Österreichische Nationalbibliothek MS 537, with statutes, inclusive ff. 38-62 (AD 1386)
— MS 616 ff. 19^v-32^v (s. xiv^2); with statutes
— MS ser. nov. 3618 ff. 44-58 (s. xiv-xv)
Wien, Schottenkloster MS 76 (50.h.10) ff. 81-94^v (s. xv)
— MS 314 (54.e.8) ff. 190-207^v (s. xv)
Wilhering, Stiftsbibliothek MS IX.25 ff. 168-178 (AD 1383); with statutes

2. *De tribus ordinibus hierarchie angelice et ecclesiastice, De tribus hierarchiis*

Bruxelles, Bibliothèque Royale MS 9608-19 (Van den Gheyn 1498) ff. 232-237 (s. xv)
Klosterneuburg, Stiftsbibliothek MS 361 ff. 131-139^v (s. xiv)
Marseilles, Bibliothèque Municipale MS 210 ff. 123^v-125^v (s. xiv)
Oxford, Bodleian Library MS Digby 33 ff. 1-16 (s. xiv)
Oxford, Merton College MS 68 ff. 224-232^v (s. xv)
Praha, Knihovna Metropolitní Kapituli MS F ii (Podlaha 848) ff. 98^v-103^v (s. xiv)
Paris, Bibliothèque Nationale MS lat. 15966 ff. 10-14 (ca. 1319); with *De tribus punctis* and *De tribus sensibus*
— [MS lat. 16397]: title in contents list; with *De tribus punctis* and *De tribus sensibus*
— MS lat. 16536 ff. 63-67^v (s. xiv^1)

3. *De tribus sensibus sacre scripture, Commendatio theologie, De tribus expositionibus sacre scripture*

Paris, Bibliothèque Nationale MS lat. 15966 ff. 6-10 (ca. 1319); with *De tribus punctis* and *De tribus hierarchiis*
— MS lat. 16397 ff. 11-17^v (ca. 1316); with *De tribus punctis* and formerly with *De tribus hierarchiis* (now lost)
Praha, Knihovna Metropolitní Kapituli MS N x (Podlaha 1534) ff. 5-9 (s. xv)

Appendix 6

List of Authors and Works
or
Bibliography Appended to the *Manipulus florum*

The following text is based on Paris, Bibliothèque nationale MSS lat. 15986 (B) and 15985 (C), both probably in Thomas of Ireland's hand; there are no significant variants between them. The bibliography was compiled from manuscripts available at the Sorbonne ca. 1306; in practice, nearly all of those which Thomas used stem from the bequest of Gerard of Abbeville (see R. H. Rouse, "The List of Authorities Appended to the *Manipulus florum*," *Archives d'histoire doctrinale et littéraire du moyen âge* 32, 1965 [1966] 243-250). For each item we have tried to identify the surviving Sorbonne manuscript source, and the mentions in the Sorbonne catalogs: Cat. 1275, edited by R. H. Rouse, "The Early Library of the Sorbonne," *Scriptorium* 21 (1967) 245-251 and pl. 5; Cat. 1321, the analytical catalog of the chained library, edited by Delisle, 3: 72-114; and Cat. 1338, the catalog of the unchained collection, ibid. 9-72. The following abbreviations have been used:

CC = *Corpus christianorum*

CSEL = *Corpus scriptorum ecclesiasticorum latinorum*

Clavis Patrum = *Clavis patrum latinorum*, rev. ed. E. Dekkers, *Sacris erudiri* 3 (1961)

Delisle = L. Delisle, *Le cabinet des manuscrits*, 3 vols. (Paris 1868-1881)

JTS = *Journal of Theological Studies*

Mittelalterliche Bibliothekskataloge = *Mittelalterliche Bibliothekskataloge Deutschlands und der Schweiz* 2, ed. P. Lehmann (Munich 1928)

RB = *Revue bénédictine*

RTAM = *Recherches de théologie ancienne et médiévale*

Stegmüller = F. Stegmüller, *Repertorium biblicum medii aevi*, 7 vols. (Madrid 1940-1961)

Wilmart, *Auteurs spirituels* = A. Wilmart, *Auteurs spirituels et textes dévots du moyen âge latin* (Paris 1932)

Notandum quod libros originalium sanctorum ac doctorum, quantum ad principia et fines ac parcialium librorum numerum, hic signare curaui ut, si alicui occurrerent, facilius possit eos cognoscere et securius allegare. Quorundam autem librorum Augustini, precipue quos ipse in suo libro retractationum enumerat, fines non uidi; ideo si alicui occurrant, eos hic poterit signare.

1. Libri Beati Dyonisii

> The works in this entry comprise B.N. ms lat. 15629 (s. xiii; Joseph of Bruges; Cat. 1321, ms Y.a.; Cat. 1338, XXX, 1, *cathenatus*; Delisle, 3: 35, 99-100). See H. F. Dondaine, *Le Corpus dionysien de l'Université de Paris au xiiie siècle* (Rome 1953) p. 81 n. 39. The incipit and explicit for works 1, 2, 4 and 5.xi are those of the Scotus translation; for works 3 and 5.i-x, those of the Sarracenus translation.

1. Ecclesiastica ierarchia secundum duas translationes. Principium: *Quia quidem secundum nos ierarchia etc.* Finis: *diuini ignis ascendens usque uapores* uel *scintillas.* Continens capitula vii.

    > B.N. ms lat. 15629 ff. 43ᵛ-67ᵛ; the alternate explicit is that of the Sarracenus translation, ff. 112-135. P. Chevallier, *Dionysiaca: Recueil donnant l'ensemble des traductions latines des ouvrages attribués au Denys de l'Aréopage* (Bruges 1937) 2: 1071-1476.

2. Celestis ierarchia secundum duas translationes. Principium: *Omne datum optimum etc.* Finis: *secretum* uel *occultum silentio honorificantes.* Capitula xv. Commentatores iiii: Iohannes Scotus, Iohannes Sarracenus, Maximus, Hugo.

    > ff. 6-23, exp. ... *secretum silentio honorificantes*; the alternate explicit is that of the Sarracenus translation, ff. 23-42ᵛ, ... *occultum silentio uenerantes.* Ibid., 2: 727-1039. This manuscript contains only the initial portion of the *Compellit me*, inc. *Breuis et valde necessaria declaratio...*, rather than the commentaries themselves.

3. De diuinis nominibus secundum duas translationes. Principium: *Nunc o beate post theologicas* Finis: *ad simbolicam theologiam duce Deo transibilis.* Capitula xiii.

    > ff. 136-170, inc. *Nunc autem o beate...*, exp. ... *transibimus.* Ibid., 1: 5-561, exp. ... *Deo duce, transibo.*

4. De mistica theologia secundum duas translationes. Principium: *Trinitas super essencialis* Finis: *simpliciter perfectione et summitas omnium* uel *simpliciter absoluti et supra tota.* Capitula v.

    > ff. 99ᵛ-101ᵛ; the alternate explicit is that of the Sarracenus translation, ff. 170ᵛ-172ᵛ. Ibid., 1: 565-602, exp. ... *super tota.*

5. Epistole eiusdem x.

    > ff. 172ᵛ-182ᵛ. Ibid., 1: 605-669; 2: 1479-1578.

    Prima Gaio que incipit *Tenebre*

    Secunda eidem. *Quomodo quidem*

    > Ibid., 1: 608, inc. *Quomodo qui est...*

    Tercia eidem. *Subito est*

    Quarta eidem. *Quomodo dicis*

    Quinta Dorotheo. *Diuina caligo*

Sexta Sosipatro. *De opineris*

    Ibid., 2: 1479, inc. *Ne opineris...*.

Septima Policarpo. *Ego quidem non sciui*

    Ibid., 2: 1482, inc. ... *non sum...*.

Octaua Demophilo. *Hebreorum hystorie*

Nona Tito. *Sanctus quidem Thimotheus*

Decima Iohanni ewangeliste. *Salutate sanctam animam*

    f. 182, inc. *Saluto te...*.

Undecima Apoliphano de eclipsi solis in passione Christi. *Nunc mihi ad te sermo etc.*

    ff. 110ᵛ-111ᵛ. Chapter 15 of the *Areopagitica* of Hilduin. PL 106: 33A-34C.

Et omnis secundum duas translationes.

II. LIBRI BEATI AUGUSTINI

This entry has been compiled primarily from the following manuscripts: works 2-3, 5-11, B.N. MS lat. 15659 (s. xiii; Gerard of Abbeville; Cat. 1275, no. 5; Cat. 1321, MS T.b.; Cat. 1338, XXV, 20, *cathenatus*; Delisle, 3: 33, 93-94); works 4, 12-24, B.N. MS lat. 15658 (s. xiii; Gerard of Abbeville; Cat. 1321, MS Y.k.; Cat. 1338, XXV, 19, *cathenatus*; Delisle, 3: 33); works 26-46, 48-50, 53-67, B.N. MS lat. 15302 (s. xiii; Gerard of Abbeville; Cat. 1275, no. 4; Cat. 1321, MS Y.l.; Delisle, 3: 94); works 68-73, 75-78, 146, B.N. MS lat. 15655 (s. xiii; Gerard of Abbeville; Cat. 1275, no. 9; Cat. 1321, MS Y.e.; Delisle, 3: 94); works 51, 79-84, B.N. MS lat. 15687 (s. xiii; Gerard of Abbeville; Cat. 1321, MS Q.q.; Cat. 1338, XXXVII, 14, *cathenatus*; Delisle, 3: 38), also used for IV. HIERONYMUS 14, XI. DAMASCENUS 3, XII. ANSELMUS 1-18; works 74, 87-88, 92-94, 99, B.N. MS lat. 15289 (s. xiii; Gerard of Abbeville; Cat. 1275, no. 1; Cat. 1321, MS Y.m.; Cat. 1338, XXV, 1, *cathenatus*; Delisle, 3: 32, 94); works 86, 89-100, 109-132, supplied from the text of Augustine's *Retractationes* in B.N. MS lat. 15737 ff. 143-163 (s. xiii; Gerard of Rheims; Cat. 1338, XXXVII, 25; Delisle, 3: 39); works 85, 134-145, 147, B.N. MS lat. 15662 (s. xiii; probably Gerard of Abbeville, companion volume to B.N. MS lat. 15655 cited above; Cat. 1321, MS Y.g.).

1. De ciuitate dei libri xxii. Principium: *Gloriosissimam ciuitatem dei etc.* Finis: *nisi peruenire ad regnum cuius nullus est finis.*

    Perhaps B.N. MS lat. 15648 ff. 2ᵛ-214ᵛ; preceded by table and *Retractationes* 2: 69 (s. xiii; Gerard of Abbeville; Cat. 1338, XXV, 3; Delisle, 3: 33). Thomas omits the final paragraph ending ... *deo in excelsis in secula seculorum. Amen.* PL 41: 13-803; ed. Dombart and Kalb, CC, 47, 48 (1955); the explicit is that of bk. 22 c. 30 ¶ 5.

2. De trinitate libri xv. Principium: *Lecturus hec que de trinitate* Finis:
precatione melius quam dispositione concludam.

> B.N. MS lat. 15659 ff. 2ᵛ-68ᵛ, exp. ... *quam disputatione...*; preceded by
> *Retractationes* 2: 41, the prologue and table, f. 2. PL 42: 819-1097; the
> explicit is that of bk. 15 c. 27, because c. 28 in this manuscript bears the
> explicit *Retractatio Aurelii Augustini episcopi de trinitate...*.

3. Super Genesim ad litteram libri xii. Principium: *Omnis diuina scriptura*
bipartita est Finis: *isto tandem fine concludamus.*

> ff. 70ᵛ-123, exp. ... *concludimus*; preceded by table, ff. 69ᵛ-70. PL 34:
> 245-486; ed. Zycha, CSEL, 28, 1 (1894) 3-435.

4. De confessionibus libri xiii. Principium: *Magnus es domine et laudabilis*
ualde Finis: *ex quo omnia per quem omnia in quo omnia ipsi gloria in*
secula seculorum. Amen.

> B.N. MS lat. 15658 ff. 51-97; preceded by *Retractationes* 2: 32. Thomas
> has inadvertently given the explicit of the *De uera religione*, no. 17 below,
> which follows the *Confessiones* in this manuscript. PL 32: 659-868; ed.
> M. Skutella (Leipzig 1934).

5. De libero arbitrio libri iii. Principium: *Dic michi queso te utrum deus*
non sit auctor mali Finis <re> *quiescere aliquando compellit.*

> B.N. MS lat. 15659 ff. 131-150ᵛ. PL 32: 1221-1310; ed. Green, CSEL,
> 74 (1956).

6. De predestinatione diuina liber unus. Principium: *Dum sacrarum uolu-*
minibus litterarum Finis: *in una contumacie uoragine damus.*

> ff. 123ᵛ-126ᵛ. Ps. Augustine; see *Clavis Patrum* 382. PL 45: 1665-1678,
> inc. *Cum in sacrarum...*.

7. De natura boni liber unus. Principium: *Summum bonum quo nichil*
superius est Finis: *uitam eternam preponant.*

> ff. 126ᵛ-131, inc. ... *quo superius nichil est...*, exp. ... *eternamque...*;
> preceded by *Retractationes* 2: 35. PL 42: 551-572; ed. Zycha, CSEL, 25,
> 2 (1892) 855-889.

8. De questionibus Orosii liber unus. Principium: *Licet multi ac*
probatissimi Finis: *qui preesse desiderat non prodesse.*

> ff. 150ᵛ-155ᵛ. Pseudo-Augustine; see *Clavis Patrum* 373 n. PL 40: 733-
> 752. Same as 101 below.

9. De mirabilibus sacre scripture libri iii. Principium: *Cum omnipotentis dei*
auxilio Finis: *et ceteri exemplo castigarentur.*

> ff. 156ᵛ-171ᵛ; preceded by the prologue and table. "Augustinus Hiber-
> nicus"; see *Clavis Patrum* 1123. PL 35: 2151-2200. (ff. 171ᵛ-174, the
> letters of Prosper and Hilary to Augustine, *De querela gallorum*, PL 44:
> 947-960.)

10. De predestinatione et perseuerancia sanctorum libri duo. Principium:

Dixisse quidem apostolum scimus Finis: *dignanturque nosse quod scribo.*

    ff. 174-189. PL 44: 959-45: 1034.

11. De unico baptismo liber unus. Principium: *Respondere diuersa sentientibus* Finis: *qua detinetur baptismi sacramentum.*

    ff. 189-193; preceded by *Retractationes* 2: 60. PL 43: 595-614; ed. Petschenig, CSEL, 53 (1910) 3-34.

12. De doctrina christiana libri iiii. Principium: *Due sunt res quibus innititur* Finis: *adiuuante domino qui uiuit et regnat.*

    B.N. ms lat. 15658 ff. 2ᵛ-26ᵛ, exp. ... *regnat in secula seculorum. Amen*; preceded by *Retractationes* 2: 30, and the prologue. PL 34: 19-122; ed. Martin, CC, 32 (1962).

13. Contra v hereses liber unus. Principium: *Debitor sum fratres* Finis: *qui credentes in se custodit in secula seculorum. Amen.*

    ff. 26ᵛ-31. Quodvultdeus; see *Clavis Patrum* 410. PL 42: 1101-1116.

14. De fide rerum inuisibilium liber unus. Principium: *Sunt qui putant christianam* Finis: *cum ceperint in littore separari.*

    ff. 31-33. PL 40: 171-180; ed. M. F. McDonald (Washington 1950).

15. De ecclesiasticis dogmatibus liber unus. Principium: *Credimus unum esse deum et patrem* Finis: *similitudinem in moribus inueniri.*

    ff. 33ᵛ-35ᵛ, exp. ... *inuenire*; preceded by table. Gennadius; see *Clavis Patrum* 958. PL 42: 1213-1222; ed. C. Turner, JTS 7 (1906) 78-99, 8 (1907) 103-114. Same as xv. ALCUINUS 5.

16. Encheridon liber unus. Principium: *Dici non potest dilectissimi fili Laurenti* Finis: *de fide spe et caritate conscripseram.*

    ff. 37-50ᵛ, inc. ... *dilectissime...*, exp. ... *Amen*; preceded by table, ff. 35ᵛ-37. PL 40: 231-290; ed. O. Scheel (Tübingen 1930).

    (ff. 51-97, *Confessiones*, used for no. 4 above.)

17. De uera religione. Principium: *Cum omnis uite bone* Finis: *ex quo omnia per quem omnia etc.*

    ff. 97-109ᵛ. PL 34: 121-172; ed. Daur, CC, xxxi (1961).

    (ff. 109ᵛ-110ᵛ, *Expositio de uerbo apostoli*; Caesarius of Arles; ed. Morin, CC, 104 [1953] 724-729, serm. 179.)

18. De deitate et incarnatione uerbi liber unus. Principium: *Species uero uerorum que per* Finis: *illa pocius quam hec recipiantur.*

    ff. 110ᵛ-116. Extracts from Rufinus' translation of Origen's *Periarchon*. PL 42: 1175-1194.

19. De opere monachorum liber unus. Principium: *Iussioni tue sancte frater,* <uel> *Ut de opere monachorum* Finis: *rescriptis tue beatitudinis nouerim.*

    ff. 116-124ᵛ; the first incipit is that of the text and the second is that of the prologue, perhaps added as an afterthought since both bear the rubric *Incipit liber de opere....* PL 40: 549-582; ed. Zycha, CSEL, 41 (1900) 531-595.

20. De immortalitate anime liber unus. Principium: *Si alicubi est disciplina* Finis: *de quo dictum est probatur.*

   ff. 124ᵛ-128. PL 32: 1021-1034.

21. De magistro liber unus. Principium: *In eadem urbe scripsi,* uel *Quid tibi uidemur* Finis: *ut tuis uerbis asserebatur.*

   ff. 128-136ᵛ; the first incipit is that of *Retractationes* 1: 7, *De animae quantitate,* which is incorrectly prefixed to the *De magistro* in this manuscript, and the second incipit is that of the work itself. PL 32: 1193-1220; ed. G. Weigel, CSEL, 77 (1961) 3-56.

22. De lxxxiii questionibus. Principium: *Omne quod est aliud est quo constat,* uel *Utrum anima sit a se ipsa* Finis: *si fideles ambo essent.*

   ff. 138ᵛ-167; preceded by *Retractationes* 1: 25, and table, ff. 136ᵛ-138ᵛ. The first incipit is that of the text in this manuscript, which begins with *Quaestio* 18. The second is that found in *Retractationes* 1: 25, and is that of *Quaestio* 1. The text in this manuscript contains *Quaestiones* 1-81, 83, in a different order from that in Migne, e.g., *Quaestiones* 18, 23, 63, 16, 37, 42, etc.; and its adds seventeen short passages, probably extracted from other works of Augustine, on ff. 148-150, 166. PL 40: 11-97, 100. (ff. 167ᵛ-168, blank.)

23. De corpore Christi liber unus. Principium: *Sicut ante nos* Finis: *ne fueris curiosus.*

   ff. 168ᵛ-171ᵛ. Hériger of Lobbes; see J. Lebon, "Sur la doctrine eucharistique de Hériger de Lobbes," in *Studia medievalia in honorem ... Raymundi Josephi Martin* (Bruges 1948) 61-84. To the text printed under the name of Gerbert in PL 139: 179-188, that in this manuscript adds a passage of 13 lines inc. *Quoniam modo panis efficiatur caro...,* exp. *... semper et in pluribus eius ne fueris curiosus.* This work, with the added passage, follows the *De magistro* in the catalog of Salvatorberg in Erfurt; *Mittelalterliche Bibliothekskataloge,* 2: 538, lines 27-28. (f. 172ʳ⁻ᵛ, blank.)

24. De baptismo contra Donatistas libri vii. Principium: *In eis libris quos scripsimus* Finis: *edificamur in petra.*

   ff. 173-214, inc. *... quos aduersus epistolam Parmeniani quam dedit ad Tychonium scripsimus....* PL 43: 107-244; ed. Petschenig, CSEL, 51 (1908) 145-375.

25. Super Iohannem omelie cxxii. Principium: *Intuentes quod modo audiuimus* Finis: *meum terminare sermonem.*

   Probably B.N. ms lat. 15295 (s. xiii; probably Gerard of Abbeville; Cat. 1321, ms T.g.; Delisle, 3: 94). Homilies 21 and 22 are omitted in this manuscript. PL 35: 1379-1976; ed. Willems, CC, 36 (1954).

26. Contra epistolam fundamenti. Principium: *Unum uerum deum om-nipotentem* Finis: *deo permittente atque adiuuante arguantur.*
    B.N. MS lat. 15302 ff. 2-10; preceded by *Retractationes* 2: 28. PL 42: 173-206; ed. Zycha, CSEL, 25, 1 (1891) 193-248.
27. Contra Adamancium Manichei discipulum liber unus. Principium: *Eodem tempore uenerunt* Finis: *ab errore uincuntur.*
    ff. 10-22; incipit is that of *Retractationes* 1: 21, which precedes the text. PL 42: 129-172; ed. Zycha, CSEL, 25, 1 (1891) 115-190.
28. Soliloquia liber unus. Principium: *Solenti,* uel *Voluenti michi multa ac uaria* Finis: *fiat ut speramus.*
    ff. 22ᵛ-32, second incipit *Volenti....* The first incipit is that of the text, in which the rubricator has drawn an *S* for a *V*; Thomas supplies the alternate, correct incipit from *Retractationes* 1: 4, which precedes the text. PL 32: 869-904.
29. De disciplina Christiana. Principium: *Locutus est ad nos sermo dei* Finis: *conuersi ad deum et est amen.*
    ff. 32-34ᵛ. PL 40: 669-678, ending with the first line of paragraph 16.
30. De uita Christiana liber unus. Principium: *Ut ego peccator* Finis: *absentes conferamus.*
    ff. 34ᵛ-39. Attributed to Pelagius; see *Clavis Patrum* 730 and R. F. Evans, "Pelagius, Fastidius and the Ps. Augustinian *De Vita Christiana*," JTS 13 (1962) 72-98. PL 40: 1031-1046.
31. De natura et origine anime ad Vincencium libri iiii. Principium: *Quod michi ad te scribendum* Finis: *remotis plausibus alienis.*
    ff. 39-49; preceded by *Retractationes* 2: 82. Bks. 3-4 of the *De natura et origine anime.* PL 44: 509-548; ed. Vrba and Zycha, CSEL, 60 (1913) 359-419. See nos. 62-63 below.
32. De baptismo paruulorum libri iii. Principium: *Quamuis in mediis et magnis curarum estibus* Finis: *tandem aliquando finitus.*
    ff. 49ᵛ-74; preceded by *Retractationes* 2: 59. PL 44: 109-200; ed. Vrba and Zycha, CSEL, 60 (1913) 3-151.
33. Questiones ueteris lvi et noui testamenti cxxi. Principium: *Deus hoc est quod nulla attingit opinio.* Finis: *facile eos uinci posse quam persuaderi.*
    ff. 76ᵛ-135; preceded by table, ff. 74-76ᵛ. Ambrosiaster; see *Clavis Patrum* 185. The text in this manuscript contains the first recension (Migne: *secundum genus*), consisting of 150 *quaestiones* numbered in two series: 56 Q. ex V.T. and 94 Q. ex N.T. (ed. Souter, CSEL, 50 [1908] 418-480, with concordance to those *quaestiones* which are printed in the second recension, 3-416). As a result of some error made in the process of copying this manuscript, the final paragraph of Q. 94 was omitted here (f. 103ᵛ) and appears below on f. 132; it has, however, been added in the lower margin of f. 103ᵛ. Then follow twenty-six additional *quaestiones*

(numbered 95-117, 119-121), namely Q. ex N.T. (*primum genus*) 78 (Souter: 74) and 94, and Q. ex utroque mixtim 100-122, 127 (PL 35: 2271-2272, 2288-2290, 2300-2369, 2378-2386). The text concludes with the final paragraph of Q. 94 (see above), and Jerome's *Altercatio inter orthodoxum et luciferianum* (PL 23: 155-182), which bears the headline and the colophon of the *quaestiones*.

34. De correctione et moribus Donatistarum. Principium: *Dilectissimo fratri Vincencio* Finis: *acceptione curauerint.*

    ff. 135-142ᵛ. PL 33: 321-347; ed. Goldbacher, CSEL, 34 (1898) 445-496, ep. 93.

35. De correctione eorum ad Bonifacium liber unus. Principium: *Laudo et gratulor* Finis: *saluandosque commendat.*

    ff. 142ᵛ-149ᵛ, exp. ... *sanandosque...*; preceded by *Retractationes* 2: 74. PL 33: 792-815; ed. Goldbacher, CSEL, 57 (1911) 1-44, ep. 185.

36. De x cordis. Principium: *Dominus et deus noster misericors* Finis: *ut quod ibi desideramus ibi inueniamus.*

    ff. 150-154v, exp. ... *Amen.* PL 38: 75-91, serm. 9.

37. De uita beata liber unus. Principium: *Si philosophie portum* Finis: *facto disputationis fine discessimus.*

    ff. 155-160, inc. *Si ad philosophie...*; preceded by *Retractationes* 1: 2. PL 32: 959-976; ed. W. Green, *Stromata* 2 (Utrecht 1955) 73-95.

38. Acta contra Fortunatum Manicheum liber unus. Principium: *Ego iam errorem* Finis: *te polliceris deo gracias.*

    ff. 160ᵛ-165, exp. ... *te polliceris. Augustinus dixit, deo gracias*; preceded by *Retractationes* 1: 15. PL 42: 111-130; ed. Zycha, CSEL, 25, 1 (1891) 83-112; the incipit is that of Augustine's first speech.

39. De duabus animabus liber unus. Principium: *Opitulante dei misericordia* Finis: *parci sibi postulat longitudo.*

    ff. 165ᵛ-169ᵛ. PL 42: 93-112; ed. Zycha, CSEL, 25, 1 (1891) 51-80.

40. De achademicis libri iii. Principium: *Utinam romaniane hominem sibi* Finis: *quam sperabam fecimus.*

    ff. 170-185ᵛ, exp. ... *speraueram....* PL 32: 905-958; ed. Green, *Stromata* 2: 13-72.

41. De ordine libri duo. Principium: *Ordinem rerum Zenobi cum* Finis: *cum nocturnum lumen fuisset illatum.*

    ff. 186-198ᵛ, exp. ... *cum iam nocturnum....* PL 32: 977-1020; ed. Green, *Stromata* 2: 97-148.

42. De Genesi contra Manicheos libri duo. Principium: *Primum ergo librum ueteris testamenti* Finis: *que michi uidebantur exposui.*

    ff. 199-211, exp. ... *que nichil uidebantur...*; preceded by the prologue. PL 34: 173-220; the incipit is that of c. 2. (f. 211ᵛ, blank.)

43. De moribus ecclesie catholice et Manicheorum libri duo. Principium: *In aliis libris satis* Finis: *multitudine non uelitis.*
    ff. 212-230ᵛ. PL 32: 1309-1378.

44. Contra mendacium liber unus. Principium: *Multa michi legenda* Finis: *terminum quem loco fiximus ueniremus.*
    ff. 230ᵛ-238ᵛ. PL 40: 517-548; ed. Zycha, CSEL, 41 (1900) 469-528.

45. De cura pro mortuis agenda liber unus. Principium: *Diu sanctitati tue* Finis: *profecto interrogationi tue mea responsio defuisset.*
    ff. 238ᵛ-243, rubric ... *mortuis gerenda.* PL 40: 591-610; ed. Zycha, CSEL, 41 (1900) 621-660.

46. De regula Augustini ad clericos liber unus. Principium: *Hec sunt que ut* Finis: *ne inducatur.*
    ff. 243-244. *Regula tertia*; see *Clavis Patrum* 1839b. Ed. D. de Bruyne, RB 42 (1930) 320-326; and T. van Bavel, *Augustiniana* 9 (1959) 16-73. (f. 244ᵛ, *Sermo b. Augustini episc. ad penitentes*; Geoffrey Babion, cf. *Clavis Patrum* 285; PL 39: 1713-1715 spur. serm. 393.)

47. Item alia regula eiusdem incipiens *Ante omnia fratres.*
    Inserted, probably from B.N. ᴍs lat. 15988 pp. 308-311; used also for xiv. Hugo 30-32, and probably for no. 102 below and vi. Bernardus 14. *Regula tertia*, same as no. 46 above; but in this manuscript it begins with the first sentence of the *Regula secunda*: *Ante omnia fratres karissimi diligatur ... principaliter nobis data. Hec igitur sunt que ut....*

48. De penitencia liber unus. Principium: *Quam sit utilis* Finis: *mors eterna uitatur.*
    B.N. ᴍs lat. 15302 ff. 245-249. Dubious authorship; see *Clavis Patrum* 284. PL 39: 1535-1549 serm. 351.

49. De pastoribus liber unus. Principium: *Spes tota nostra* Finis: *ad unitatem.*
    ff. 249-255ᵛ. PL 38: 270-295 serm. 46; ed. Lambot, RB 63 (1953) 165-210.

50. De ouibus liber unus. Principium: *Verba que cantauimus* Finis: *dominus deus noster.*
    ff. 255ᵛ-261. PL 38: 295-316 serm. 47.

51. De penitencia alius liber. Principium: *Vox penitentis* Finis: *correctus.*
    Inserted, from B.N. ᴍs lat. 15687 ff. 166ᵛ-170, exp. .... *correctus accepit*, used for nos. 79-84 below. PL 39: 1549-1560 serm. 352. To the text in Migne, ending ... *datus est dies mortis incertus*, this manuscript adds three and a half columns, ff. 169-170, inc. *Quid enim est infelicius quid peruersius quam de illo uulnere...*, exp. ... *penitencie consilium ab ipso Petro correctus accepit.*

52. Item alius incipiens *Excepto baptismatis* Finis: *bonos constituisse.*
    Inserted, probably from B.N. MS lat. 15310 ff. 34-36, rubric *De utilitate penitencie...*; also used for IV. HIERONYMUS 15-16, XIII. RICARDUS 2-10, and probably for no. 101 below and V. GREGORIUS 2. The preface of the *Collectio canonum Dacheriana.* Ed. d'Achery, *Spicilegium* 1 (Paris 1723) 510-512.

53. De mendacio liber unus. Principium: *Magna questio est de mendacio* Finis: *etiam exitum ut possis sustinere.*
    B.N. MS lat. 15302 ff. 261-268ᵛ, exp. *... possitis...*; preceded by *Retractationes* 1: 26. PL 40: 487-518; ed. Zycha, CSEL, 41 (1900) 413-466. (ff. 268ᵛ-269, *Sermo de corpore Christi,* inc. *Veritas ait caro mea uere est...*, exp. *... et in hoc uerbo creatur illud corpus*; an anonymous late twelfth-century collection of extracts from the fathers and the early masters concerning the Eucharist.)

54. De xii gradibus abusionis liber unus. Principium: *Primo sine operibus* Finis: *incipiat esse Christus in futuro.*
    ff. 269-271ᵛ, inc. *Primo si sine....* Pseudo-Augustine; see *Clavis Patrum* 1106. PL 40: 1079-1088; ed. S. Hellmann, Texte und Untersuchungen 34.1 (Leipzig 1909) 32-60.

55. De conflictu uitiorum et uirtutum. Principium: *Apostolica uox clamat* Finis: *narrantem fidem prebeto.*
    ff. 271ᵛ-275, inc. *Apostolia....* Ambrosius Autpertus. PL 40: 1091-1103; the explicit is that of c. 26.

56. De paciencia liber unus. Principium: *Virtus animi que paciencia dicitur* Finis: *donatum est caritati.*
    ff. 275-278. PL 40: 611-626; ed. Zycha, CSEL, 41 (1900) 663-691.

57. De utilitate credendi. Principium: *Si michi Honorate* Finis: *in ceteris promptior.*
    ff. 279-286; preceded by *Retractationes* 1: 13, ff. 278-279. PL 42: 65-92; ed. Zycha, CSEL, 25, 1 (1891) 3-48.

58. De gracia noui testamenti. Principium: *Quinque michi proposuisti* Finis: *magistrum nos habere testamur.*
    ff. 286-297; preceded by *Retractationes* 2: 62. PL 33: 538-577; ed. Goldbacher, CSEL, 44 (1904) 155-234, ep. 140.

59. De cathezizandis rudibus liber unus. Principium: *Petisti a me frater Deogracias* Finis: *plus quam possunt sustinere.*
    ff. 297-306ᵛ, inc. *Petis...*; preceded by *Retractationes* 2: 40. PL 40: 309-348.

60. De quantitate anime liber unus. Principium: *Quoniam uideo te habundare* Finis: *oportuniorem obseruabo.*
    ff. 307ᵛ-320, exp. *... oportunionem...*; preceded by table and *Retractationes* 1: 7, f. 307ʳ⁻ᵛ. PL 32: 1035-1080.

61. De adulterinis coniugiis libri duo. Principium: *Prima questio est frater dilectissime* Finis: *occasio castitatis.*

    ff. 320-328ᵛ; preceded by *Retractationes* 2: 83. PL 40: 451-486; ed. Zycha, CSEL, 41 (1900) 347-410.

62. De natura et origine anime ad Renatum liber unus. Principium: *Sinceritatem tuam erga nos* Finis: *aliqua dilectione conscripsi.*

    ff. 328ᵛ-333ᵛ. Bk 1. PL 44: 475-496; ed. Vrba and Zycha, CSEL, 60 (1913) 303-335. See also nos. 31 above and 63 below.

63. De eadem re ad Petrum presbyterum liber unus. Principium: *Omnino dilectissimo fratri* Finis: *epistola ista uel fecerit.*

    ff. 333ᵛ-337ᵛ. Bk 2. PL 44: 495-510; ed. Vrba and Zycha, CSEL, 60 (1913) 336-359, inc. *Domino...*. See also nos. 31, 62 above.

    (ff. 337ᵛ-341, *Epistola Augustini de orando deo*, PL 33: 494-507, ep. 130).

64. De uidendo deo ad Paulinam liber unus. Principium: *Memor debiti quod ex tua* Finis: *quid disputare ualeamus.*

    ff. 341-346ᵛ; preceded by *Retractationes* 2: 67. PL 33: 596-622; ed. Goldbacher, CSEL, 44 (1904) 274-331, ep. 147.

65. De fide et operibus liber unus. Principium: *Quibusdam uidetur indiscrete* Finis: *facillime redargui posset.*

    ff. 347-355, exp. *... regardui...*; preceded by *Retractationes* 2: 64. PL 40: 197-230; ed. Zycha, CSEL, 41 (1900) 35-97.

66. Commonitorium sub qua cautela Manichei recipi debent liber unus. Principium: *Cum Manichei qui* Finis: *commendati deserant.*

    ff. 355ʳ⁻ᵛ. Pseudo-Augustine; see *Clavis Patrum* 533. PL 42: 1153-1156; ed. Zycha, CSEL, 25, 2 (1892) 979-982.

67. De perfectione iusticie liber unus. Principium: *Sanctis fratribus et episcopis* Finis: *anathematizandam non dubito.*

    ff. 355ᵛ-361ᵛ, exp. *... anathematizandum...*. PL 44: 291-318; ed. Vrba and Zycha, CSEL, 42 (1902) 3-48.

68. Contra Faustum libri <x> xxiii. Principium: *Faustus quidam fuit gente Afer* Finis: *ut aliquando et catholici esse possitis.*

    B.N. ᴍꜱ lat. 15655 pp. 211-376; preceded by *Retractationes* 2: 33. PL 42: 207-518; ed. Zycha, CSEL, 25, 1 (1891) 251-797.

69. De natura et gracia liber unus. Principium: *Librum quem misistis karissimi filii* Finis: *eterna bonitas in secula seculorum.*

    pp. 377-397, exp. *... eternitas ... Amen.* PL 44: 247-290; ed. Vrba and Zycha, CSEL, 60 (1913) 233-299.

70. De gracia et libero arbitrio. Principium: *Propter eos qui hominis liberum arbitrium* Finis: *cum patre et spiritu sancto in secula seculorum.*

    pp. 398-413, exp. *... Amen.* PL 44: 881-912.

(pp. 413-428, *Liber secundus s. Augustini de correctione et gracia*, PL 44: 915-946.)

71. De heresibus que sunt xci liber unus. Principium: *Quod petis sepissime frater* Finis: *ne orationibus adiuuetis.*

   pp. 429-440, inc. ... *petis sepissime atque instantissime sancti fili...*, exp. ... *me orationibus....* PL 42: 21-50, inc. ... *sepissime fili....*

72. Yponosticon ubi responsiones v liber unus. Principium: *Aduersarii catholice fidei* Finis: *qui super omnes et per omnia et in omnibus nobis.*

   pp. 440-465. Pseudo-Augustine; see *Clavis Patrum* 381. PL 45: 1611-1658, bks. 1-4.

   (p. 466, *Sermo Augustini de oratione et ieiunio*; Peter Chrysologus; PL 52: 678-679, spur. serm. 6.)

73. Contra Maximum hereticum libri duo. Principium: *Disputationem Maximini* Finis: *de tua fraternitate gaudeamus.*

   pp. 466-501. PL 42: 743-814.

   (pp. 501-502, *Sermo b. Augustini quomodo factus est homo ad ymaginem et similitudinem dei*; Pseudo-Alcuin, *Dicta de imagine Dei*, PL 100: 565-568; equivalent to the beginning and end of the Pseudo-Ambrosian *De dignitate conditionis humanae* [PL 17: 1015-1016 to ... *non habeat memoria*, 1018 from *et haec de imagine habeto...*]; see M. Schmaus, "Das Fortwirken der Augustinischen Trinitätspsychologie...," *Vitae et Veritati: Festgabe für Karl Adam* [Düsseldorf 1956] 51 n. 2.)

74. Alius contra eundem. Principium: *Cum Augustinus* Finis: *ero culpabilis.*

   Inserted from B.N. ms lat. 15289 ff. 120-129. PL 42: 709-742.

75. De origine anime ad Ieronimum et sententia Iacobi libri duo. Principium: *Deum nostrum qui nos* Finis: *in suis sacramentis commendauit posse liberari.*

   B.N. ms lat. 15655 pp. 502-508; the *Sententia Iacobi* (PL 33: 733-742 ep. 167) is not included in the rubric or the text. PL 33: 720-733; ed. Goldbacher, CSEL, 44 (1904) 545-585, ep. 166.

   (p. 509, *Rescriptio Ieronimi ad Augustinum*, PL 22: 1161-1162, ep. 134.)

76. De diuinatione demonum liber unus. Principium: *Quodam die in diebus sanctis* Finis: *quantum dominus adiuuat respondebimus.*

   pp. 509-513; preceded by *Retractationes* 2: 56. PL 40: 581-592; ed. Zycha, CSEL, 41 (1900) 599-618.

77. De sancta uirginitate. Principium: *Librum de bono coniugali nuper* Finis: *et superexaltate eum in secula.*

   pp. 514-528, exp. ... *Amen.* PL 40: 397-438; ed. Zycha, CSEL, 41 (1900) 235-302.

78. De professione sancte uiduitatis. Principium: *Augustinus episcopus seruus seruorum* Finis: *perseueres in gracia dei.*

pp. 529-538, exp. ... *Amen.* PL 40: 431-450; ed. Zycha, CSEL, 41 (1900) 305-343.

(pp. 538-544, *Liber s. Augustini de paciencia,* same as no. 56 above. pp. 544-549, *Liber eiusdem de elemosina;* Cyprian; same as no. 133 below.)

79. De bono coniugali liber unus. Principium: *Quoniam unusquisque homo* Finis: *propter Christum patres fuerunt.*

> B.N. MS lat. 15687 ff. 161-166ᵛ. PL 40: 373-396; ed. Zycha, CSEL, 41 (1900) 187-231.

80. De nuptiis et concupiscentiis libri duo. Principium: *Heretici noui dilectissime fili* Finis: *lectioni uigilanter impendas.*

> ff. 155ᵛ-161; preceded by the prologue. PL 44: 413-436; ed. Vrba and Zycha, CSEL, 42 (1902) 211-252.

81. Contra Felicianum Arrianum liber unus. Principium: *Exorsisti michi dilectissime* Finis: *cum iustis ceperit retribuere mercedem.*

> ff. 151-155ᵛ, inc. *Extorsisti....* Vigilius of Thapsus; see *Clavis Patrum* 808. PL 42: 1157-1172. (ff. 149-150ᵛ, blank.)

82. Retractationum libri duo. Principium: *Iam diu istud facere cogito* Finis: *retractare cepissem.*

> ff. 130ᵛ-148ᵛ; preceded by table, f. 130ʳ⁻ᵛ. PL 32: 583-656; ed. Knöll, CSEL, 36 (1902).

83. De agone Christiano liber unus. Principium: *Corona uictorie non promittitur* Finis: *coronam uictorie mereamur.*

> ff. 125ᵛ-129ᵛ; preceded by *Retractationes* 2: 29. PL 40: 289-310; ed. Zycha, CSEL, 41 (1900) 101-138.

84. De fide ad Petrum libri duo. Principium: *Epistolam fili Petre* Finis: *hoc quoque reuelabit illi deus.*

> ff. 118-125ᵛ. Fulgentius of Ruspe: see *Clavis Patrum* 826. PL 40: 753-778; ed. Fraipont, CC, 91ᴀ (1968) 709-760; the explicit is that of c. 44.

85. Ad inquisitiones Ianuarii libri duo. Principium: *Ad ea que me interrogasti* Finis: *multis daturam atque lecturam.*

> Probably B.N. MS lat. 15662 ff. 188-196, inc. *... que interrogasti malem...;* used for nos. 134-145, 147 below. PL 33: 199-223; ed. Goldbacher, CSEL, 34 (1898) 158-213, epp. 54, 55.

86. De Genesi ad litteram liber unus imperfectus. Principium: *De obscuris naturalium rerum*

> B.N. MS lat. 15737 ff. 151ᵛ-152; *Retractationes* 1: 17.

87. De sermone domini in monte libri duo. Principium: *Sermonem quem locutus est dominus* Finis: *faciam quod hortaris.*

> Probably B.N. MS lat. 15289 ff. 33-55ᵛ; preceded by table. This manuscript contains the text as in PL 34: 1229-1307 to bk. 2 ¶ 85 ... *illa*

miracula facere. The text in this manuscript adds another column, inc. *Venite ad me omnes qui laboratis.... Huius non esse audiens sancta Cecilia...,* exp. *... dei angelus sit faciam quod hortaris.* The work also appears with the addition in the catalog of Salvatorberg, Erfurt; *Mittelalterliche Bibliothekskataloge,* 2: 536, lines 27-28.

88. Questiones ewangeliorum libri duo. Principium: *Hoc opus non ita scriptum est* Finis: *patrem deum esse arbi<trantur>.*

    Probably B.N. MS lat. 15289 ff. 266-283; preceded by *Retractationes* 2: 38. This manuscript contains the text as in PL 35: 1321-1364, followed, as is often the case, by the *Quaestiones 17 in Evangelium Matthaei,* PL 35: 1365-1374.

89. De consensu ewangelistarum libri iiii. Principium: *Inter omnes diuinas auctoritates*

    B.N. MS lat. 15737 f. 158; *Retractationes* 2: 42.

90. Contra epistolam Parmeniani libri iii. Principium: *Multa quidem alias aduersus Donatistas*

    f. 158; *Retractationes* 2: 43.

91. Contra litteras Petriliani libri iii. Principium: *Nostis nos sepe uoluisse*

    f. 159; *Retractationes* 2: 51, title *Petiliani.*

92. Ad Cresconium gramaticum partis Donati libri iiii. Principium: *Quando ad te Cresconi mea* Finis: *reuocare dampnatos.*

    f. 159, *Retractationes* 2: 52; and the text of this work in B.N. MS lat. 15289 ff. 129ᵛ-168ᵛ, preceded by *Retractationes* 2: 52. PL 43: 445-594; ed. Petschenig, CSEL, 52 (1909) 325-582.

93. Contra sermonem Arrianorum liber unus. Principium: *Eorum precedenti disputtationi* Finis: *et tandem in fine isto conclusimus.*

    f. 161ᵛ, *Retractationes* 2: 78; and the text of this work in B.N. MS lat. 15289 ff. 202ᵛ-210, exp. *... quo tandem isto fine conclusimus.* PL 42: 683-708.

94. Locutionum libri vii. Principium: *Locutiones scripturarum* Finis: *domus confirmata est super eas.*

    ff. 161ᵛ-162, *Retractationes* 2: 80; and the text of this work in B.N. MS lat. 15289 ff. 1-16, preceded by *Retractationes* 2: 80. PL 34: 485-546; ed. Fraipont, CC, 33 (1958) 381-465.

95. Questionum libri vii. Principium: *Cum scripturas sanctas*

    f. 162, *Retractationes* 2: 81.

96. Contra aduersarium legis et prophetarum libri duo. Principium: *Libro quem misistis fratres*

    f. 162ᵛ, *Retractationes* 2: 84.

97. Contra Gaudencium episcopum libri duo. Principium: *Gaudencius Donatistarum*

f. 162ᵛ, *Retractationes* 2: 85.

98. Contra duas epistolas Pelagianorum libri iiii. Principium: *Noueram te quidem fama*

f. 162ᵛ, *Retractationes* 2: 87.

99. Contra Iulianum libri vi. Principium: *Contumelias tuas et uerba.* Finis: *ueritatem poteris qua uinceris.*

f. 162ᵛ, *Retractationes* 2: 88; and the text of this work in B.N. MS lat. 15289 ff. 56-120. PL 44: 641-874.

100. De octo Dulcitii questionibus. Principium: *Quantum michi uidetur dilectissime*

f. 163, *Retractationes* 2: 91.

101. Ad Orosium dyalogice traditus liber unus. Principium: *Licet multi ac probatissimi* Finis: *qui preesse desiderat non prodesse.*

Probably B.N. MS lat. 15310 ff. 157-163, also used for IV. HIERONYMUS 15-16, XIII. RICARDUS 2-10, and probably for no. 52 above and V. GREGORIUS 2. Same as no. 8 above.

102. De contemplatione domini nostri Ihesu Christi liber unus. Principium: *Quoniam in medio loquere* Finis: *michi dicere ut amem deum meum.*

Probably B.N. MS lat 15988 pp. 302-307, inc. ... *laqueorum...*, also used for XIV. HUGO 30-32, and probably for no. 47 above and VI. BERNARDUS 14. Identified by Wilmart as an anonymous early thirteenth-century collection of extracts taken in part from John of Fécamp's *Meditatio theorica*; see *Auteurs spirituels*, 195. More recently suggested to be the work of Peter Comestor by G. Raciti in *Rivista di filosofia neo-scolastica* 53 (1961) 385-401. PL 40: 951-962; ed., with two Dutch translations, by J. J. Lub, 1 (Assen 1962) 84-212; the explicit is that of c. 25 (c. 24 in Migne). Approximately the same as XIV. HUGO 10, bk. 4, cc. 1-11.

103. De spiritu et anima secundum quosdam liber unus. Principium: *Quoniam dictum est michi* Finis: *aliud non sit quam ratio.*

Probably B.N. MS lat. 15660 ff. 24ᵛ-27 (s. xiii; Cat. 1338, XXXVII, 22; Delisle, 3: 39). Anonymous; the common attribution to Alcher of Clairvaux is discounted by Wilmart, *Auteurs spirituels*, 174-178, 194. More recently suggested to be the work of Peter Comestor by Raciti, *Revista di filosofia neo-scolastica* 53 (1961) 385-401. PL 40: 779-803; the explicit is that of c. 33. Same as XIV. HUGO 10, bk. 2.

104. De collatione x preceptorum ad x plagas. Principium: *Non est sine causa fratres* Finis: *auxiliante domino nostro Ihesu Christo in secula seculorum.*

Probably supplied from the text in the missing portion of B.N. MS lat. 15660 which is described in the 1338 catalog; the only other text of this sermon at the Sorbonne, B.N. MS lat. 15309 ff. 34-35 (s. xiii; Godfrey of Fontaines; Cat. 1321, MS Y.h.), lacks the final sentence. Caesarius of

Arles. PL 39: 1783-1786, spur. serm. 21; ed Morin, CC, 103 (1953) 406-413, serm. 100.

105. Speculum siue manuale liber unus. Principium: *Adesto michi uerum lumen* Finis: *sempiternaliter uiuis et regnas per omnia secula seculorum. Amen.*

Probably B.N. MS lat. 16359 ff. 85-94, also used for XVI. DIVERSI AUCTORES 4. Part I of the *Confessio fidei*, attributed by Wilmart to John of Fécamp; *Auteurs spirituels*, 195 n. 7. PL 40: 967-984.

106. Super epistolam Iohannis omelie siue sermones X. Principium: *Quod erat ab initio* Finis: *tu Christo predicanti.*

B.N. MS lat. 15296 ff. 1-24ᵛ, preceded by table and prologue (s. xiii; Cat. 1321, MS T.s.; Cat. 1338, XXV, 13, *cathenatus*; Delisle, 3: 33). PL 35: 1977-2062.

107. De musica libri VI. Principium: *Modus qui pes est Pirrichius*, uel *Satis diu pene* Finis: *hereticorum necessitate fecisse uideremus.*

ff. 98ᵛ-134. Thomas supplied the alternate incipit, which is that of bk. 6, from *Retractationes* 1: 10, which is prefixed to this work. PL 32: 1081-1194.

108. De uera innocencia liber unus. Principium: *Innocencia uera est* Finis: *si te ipsum respexeris.*

Probably B.N. MS lat. 15653 ff. 2-8 (s. xiii; Gerard of Abbeville; Cat. 1321, MS Y.j.). Prosper of Aquitaine. *Sententiae ex operibus S. Augustini.* Same as XI. PROSPER 2.

109. De fide et symbolo liber unus. Principium: *Quoniam scriptum est*

B.N. MS lat. 15737 f. 151ᵛ, rubric *De fide uel symbolo, Retractationes* 1: 16.

110. Psalmus contra partem Donati liber unus. Principium: *Omnes qui gaudetis de pace*

ff. 152ᵛ-153; *Retractationes* 1: 19.

111. Contra epistolam Donati heretici. Principium: *Abs te ipso presente audiemus*

f. 153, inc. ... *audieram...*; *Retractationes* 1: 20.

112. Ad Simplicianum libri duo. Principium: *Gratissimam sane atque suauissimam*

f. 156ʳ⁻ᵛ; *Retractationes* 2: 27.

113. Contra partem Donati libri duo. Principium: *Quoniam Donatiste nobis*

ff. 156ᵛ-157; *Retractationes* 2: 31.

114. Contra Felicem Manicheum libri duo. Principium: *Honorio*

f. 157; *Retractationes* 2: 34.

115. Contra Secundinum Manicheum. Principium: *Beniuolenciam in me que apparet*

f. 157ᵛ; *Retractationes* 2: 36, inc. *Beneuolentia....*

116. Contra Hylarium liber unus. Principium: *Qui dicunt mentionem ueteris testamenti*

  f. 157ᵛ, rubric ... *Hilarum*; *Retractationes* 2: 37.

117. Annotationes in Iob. Principium: *Et opera magna erant ei*

  f. 157ᵛ; *Retractationes* 2: 39.

118. Contra quod attulit centurius a Donatistis. Principium: *Dicis eo quod scriptum est*

  f. 158ᵛ; *Retractationes* 2: 45.

119. Probationum et testimoniorum contra Donatistas liber unus. Principium: *Qui timetis consentire ecclesie*

  f. 159ʳ⁻ᵛ; *Retractationes* 2: 53.

120. Contra nescio quem Donatistam liber unus. Principium: *Probationes rerum necessariarum*

  f. 159ᵛ; *Retractationes* 2: 54.

121. Ammonitio Donatistarum de Maxianistis. Principium: *Quicumque calumpniis hominum*

  f. 159ᵛ; *Retractationes* 2: 55, title ... *Maximianistis.*

122. Expositio epistole Iacobi ad duodecim tribus liber unus. Principium: *Duodecim tribus que sunt in dispersione*

  f. 160, inc. ... *tribubus...*; *Retractationes* 2: 58.

123. De Maxianistis contra Donatistas liber unus. Principium: *Multa iam diximus*

  f. 160; *Retractationes* 2: 61, title ... *Maximianistis....*

124. De spiritu et litera ad Marcellinum. Principium: *Lectis opusculis*

  f. 160ᵛ; *Retractationes* 2: 63.

125. Breuilocus collationis cum Donatistis libri iii. Principium: *Cum catholici episcopi*

  f. 160ᵛ, rubric *Breuiculus...*; *Retractationes* 2: 65.

126. Post collationem contra Donatistas liber unus. Principium: *Siluanus senex*

  f. 160ᵛ, ... *Sic quippe incipit Siluanus senex ... concilio tercensi ad Donatistas [Hic liber sic incipit: Quid ad] huc Donatiste seducemini*; the omission in this manuscript of the *Retractationes* explains why Thomas gives the incipit of the *Acta Concilia Zertensis* rather than that of the work itself; *Retractationes* 2: 66.

127. Contra Priscillianistas ad Orosium presbyterum liber unus. Principium: *Responderi tibi querenti*

  f. 161, rubric *Ad Horosium presbyterum contra Priscillianistas*; *Retractationes* 2: 70, inc. *Respondere....*

128. Ad Emeritum episcopum Donatistarum. Principium: *Si uel nunc frater Emerite*

> f. 161; *Retractationes* 2: 72.

129. De gestis Pelagii liber unus. Principium: *Postquam in manus uestras*

> f. 161^{r-v}, inc. *Posteaquam...*; *Retractationes* 2: 73, inc. *... manus nostras...*.

130. De presencia dei ad Dardanum liber unus. Principium: *Frater dilectissime Dardane*

> f. 161^v; *Retractationes* 2: 75, inc. *Fateor, frater...*.

131. De gracia Christi et peccato originali contra Pelagium et Albinum libri duo. Principium: *Quantum de uestra corporali*

> f. 161^v, rubric *Contra Pelagium et Celestium de gracia Christi et de peccato originali ad Albinum, Pinianum et Melauiam*; *Retractationes* 2: 76.

132. Gesta cum Emerito Donatista liber unus. Principium: *Gloriosissimo Honorio*

> f. 161^v; *Retractationes* 2: 77.

133. De elemosina liber unus. Principium: *Multa et magna sunt fratres* Finis: *purpuream geminabit.*

> Probably B.N. ms lat. 15655 pp. 544-549, also used for nos. 68-78 above and 146 below. Cyprian; see *Clavis Patrum* 47. PL 4: 601-622; ed. Hartel, CSEL, 3, 1 (1868) 371-394.

134. Ad Ieronimum de eo quod scriptum est qui totam legem seruauerit liber unus. Principium: *Quod ad te scripsi honorande* Finis: *nobiscum communicare digneris.*

> B.N. ms lat. 15662 ff. 3^v-7. PL 33: 733-742; ed. Goldbacher, CSEL, 44 (1904) 586-609, ep. 167.
>
> (ff. 3-115^v, eighty epistles, used for no. 147 below.)

135. De vi questionibus contra paganos liber unus. Principium: *Mouet quosdam et requirunt* Finis: *sine salutis dispendio tolerandum.*

> ff. 116^v-123^v; preceded by *Retractationes* 2: 57, prefatory letter, and table, f. 116^{r-v}. PL 33: 371-386; ed. Goldbacher, CSEL, 34 (1898) 545-578, ep. 102.

136. De quatuor uirtutibus caritatis. Principium: *Desiderium caritatis uestre* Finis: *fructum inueniat operis non folia laudis.*

> ff. 124-127, exp. *... fructum in uos inueniat...*. Attributed to Quodvultdeus; see *Clavis Patrum* 368. PL 39: 1952-1957, spur. serm. 106.

137. De cantico nouo liber unus. Principium: *Omnis qui baptismum Christi desiderat* Finis: *in orationibus uestris.*

> ff. 127-130^v, exp. *... nos orationibus uestris.* Quodvultdeus; see *Clavis Patrum* 405. PL 40: 677-686.

138. De quarta feria liber unus. Principium: *Celesti gracie et spirituali pluuie* Finis: *cum sancto spiritu in secula seculorum. Amen.*

    ff. 130^v-134^v. Quodvultdeus; see *Clavis Patrum* 406. PL 40: 685-694.

139. De catheclismo liber unus. Principium: *Quoniam in proximo est dies redemptionis* Finis: *salutem uestris orationibus parciar.*

    ff. 134^v-138. Quodvultdeus; see *Clavis Patrum* 407. PL 40: 693-700.
    (f. 138, *De contempnenda morte*, treated as ep. lxxxi, part of no. 147 below, in the table of contents; anonymous; ed. Fraipont, CC, 90 [1961] 260.)

140. De tempore barbarico liber unus. Principium: *Admonet dominus deus noster* Finis: *recipiant uos in eterna tabernacula.*

    ff. 138-142^v, exp. ... *Amen.* Quodvultdeus; see *Clavis Patrum* 411. PL 40: 699-708.

141. De trinitate tractatus quidam. Principium: *Catholice fidei* Finis: *nisi credideritis non intelligetis.*

    ff. 142^v-147^v. Spurious; see *Clavis Patrum* 843. PL 65: 707-720; ed. Fraipont, CC, 90 (1961) 235-259.
    (ff. 147^v-148, *S. Augustini de fide catholica*, treated as ep. lxxxii, part of no. 147 below, in the table of contents; Pseudo-Augustine, see *Clavis Patrum* 368; PL 39: 2180-2181, spur. serm. 235.)

142. Expositio symboli contra Iudeos et paganos liber unus. Principium: *Inter pressuras atque angustias* Finis: *inmortalem. Amen,* uel *optinet caritas.*

    ff. 148-150. Quodvultdeus; see *Clavis Patrum* 404. The text follows that in Migne to the beginning of c. 5, ... *mutantes patrem mutate hereditatem,* PL 42: 1117-1119. Here it adds two and a quarter columns, inc. *Renuntiate diabolo et angelis eius...,* exp. ... *suscepisse mortalem ut faceret inmortalem. Amen.* The text with this addition also appears in B.N. MS lat. 15294 f. 223^{r-v} (s. xiii; Godfrey of Fontaines). The alternate explicit is that of the whole text, PL 32: 1117-1130, lacking the closing benediction; it may be supplied from B.N. MS lat. 15737 ff. 89-94, exp. ... *obtinet caritas. Ipse est enim qui uiuit et regnat ... seculorum. Amen,* which contains the text of the *Retractationes* used for nos. 86, 89-100, 109-132 above.

143. Expositio super prouerbia de muliere forti. Principium: *Prestabit nobis dominus* Finis: *beati qui habitant in domo tua in secula seculorum.*

    ff. 150-156, exp. ... *seculorum laudabunt te.* PL 38: 221-235, serm. 37.
    (ff. 156-160^v, seven sermons attributed to Augustine: *De oratione et ieiunio,* PL 39: 1886-1887, spur. serm. 73. *De diuite,* PL 40: 1358, *Ad fratres in eremo serm.* 75; see J. Bonnes in RB 56 [1945-46] 178 n. 1. *De penitencia,* Caesarius of Arles, serm. 63; ed. Morin, CC, 103 [1953] 272-274. *De fornicatione,* inc. *Fratres ut aliquid sub argumento dicamus quero*

iustis iudex..., exp. *... ecclesiam cotidie de minucis purgat*; this anonymous
piece is also included in the *Collectorium* of Robert of Bardi, chancellor of
the Sorbonne 1336-49, and in the list of sermons which follows John of
Fayt's analytical table to the *Collectorium* in B.N. MS lat. 2032 f. 157; see
G. Pozzi in *Italia medioevale e umanistica* 1 [1958] 141-153. *Quomodo
factus est homo ad ymaginem et similitudinem dei*, same as no. 73
[pp. 501-502] above. *In laudibus dei*, Caesarius of Arles, serm. 206;
ed. Morin, CC, 104 [1954] 824-828.)

144. Expositio super epistolam ad Romanos. Principium: *Sensus hii sunt*
Finis: *quorum deus uenter est.*

    ff. 161-170^v. PL 35: 2063-2088.

145. Expositio in epistola ad Galathas. Principium: *Causam propter quam
scribit apostolus* Finis: *Ihesu Christi cum spiritu sancto fratres. Amen.*

    ff. 170^v-187, exp. *... spiritu uestro fratres...*; preceded by *Retractationes*
1: 23. PL 35: 2105-2148.

    (f. 187^{r-v}, *Epistola Origenis apologetica*, PG 17: 624-626. ff. 188-196,
Liber Augustini ad inquisitiones Ianuarii, same as no. 85 above. ff. 196-
198, *Omelia s. Augustini ep. de igne purgatorio*, treated as ep. lxxxiii, part
of no. 147 below, in the table of contents; same as no. 17 [ff. 109^v-110^v]
above.)

146. Epistole eius ad diuersas personas et econuerso cxii.

    B.N. MS lat. 15655 pp. 1-210 contains 112 letters to and from
Augustine, and is used for nos. 68-78, 133 above. The corpus of letters in
no. 147 below is referred to in the contemporary table of contents, *In alio
uolumine continentur epistole lxxxiii cum aliis libris Augustini.*

147. Epistole eius ad Ieronimum et quosdam alios lxxviii.

    B.N. MS lat. 15662 ff. 3-115^v, 138, 147^v-148, 196-198; table of con-
tents, *lxxxiii.*

148. Sermones eius multi que omnia longum esset signare.

    This entry does not represent any specific codex of Augustine's sermons.

III. LIBRI BEATI AMBROSII

    The works in this entry comprise B.N. MS lat. 15641 (s. xiii; Gerard of
Abbeville; Cat. 1321, MS Y.p.; Cat. 1338, XXVI, 1, *cathenatus*; Delisle,
3: 34, 95-96).

1. De officiis libri tres. Principium: *Non arrogans uideri* Finis: *plurimum
instructionis conferat.*

    B.N. MS lat. 15641 ff. 4-35^v. PL 16: 23-183; ed. J. B. Krabinger
(Tübingen 1857).

2. Exameron id est de opere vi dierum libri vii. Principium: *Tantum
opinionis assumpsere* Finis: *perpetuitas a seculis nunc et semper et in
omnia secula seculorum. Amen.*

ff. 35ᵛ-74; table of contents reads *libri vii.* The manuscript treats cc. 7-10 of bk. 6 as a separate book with the rubric *De homine ad imaginem dei creato*, inc. *Quis hoc dicit nonne deus qui te fecit....* PL 14: 123-274; ed. Schenkl, CSEL, 32, 1 (1897) 3-261.

3. De excessu fratris liber unus. Principium: *Deduximus fratres* Finis: *cogar exsoluere.*

    ff. 74-79ᵛ. PL 16: 1289-1316; ed. Faller, CSEL, 73 (1955) 207-251.

4. De fide resurrectionis liber unus. Principium: *Superiori libro* Finis: *timere nequeamus.*

    ff. 79ᵛ-88ᵛ, with separate rubric, bk. 2 of 3 above. PL 16: 1315-1354; ed. Faller, CSEL, 73 (1955) 251-325.

5. De bono mortis liber unus. Principium: *Quoniam de anima* Finis: *perpetuitas a seculis et nunc et semper in secula seculorum. Amen.*

    ff. 89-95ᵛ, exp. *... semper et in....* PL 14: 539-568; ed. Schenkl, CSEL, 32, 1 (1897) 703-753.

6. De uirginitate libri iiii. Principium: *Si iuxta celestis sententiam* Finis: *in isto quia mundum ignorauit.*

    ff. 95ᵛ-112ᵛ. *De uirginibus libri tres* (PL 16: 187-232; ed. E. Cazzaniga [Torino 1948]), followed by *De uirginitate* as bk. 4 (PL 16: 265-302; ed. Cazzaniga [Torino 1954]).

7. De uiduis libri iii. Principium: *Bene accidit fratres* Finis: *fili cui seruare digneris.*

    ff. 112ᵛ-130ᵛ, exp. *... filii tui....* *De uiduis* (PL 16: 234-262), followed by *De uirginitate* (PL 16: 265-302) and *Exhortatio uirginitatis* (PL 16: 335-364) as bks. 2 and 3.

8. De lapsu uirginis liber unus. Principium: *Audite qui longe estis* Finis: *ab ipso querere remedium.* Et ibidem epistola et lamentatio eiusdem.

    ff. 130ᵛ-132ᵛ, exp. *... quere....* Uncertain authorship, discussed among the dubious works of Nicetas of Remesiana in *Clavis Patrum* 651. PL 16: 367-379, cc. 1-8; ed. Cazzaniga, *Incerti auctoris "de lapsu Suzannae"* (Torino 1948) 1-23.

    (ff. 132ᵛ-133, the *Epistola eiusdem ad uiolatorem* and the *Lamentatio eiusdem*, which appear with separate rubrics, comprise cc. 9-10 of the *De lapsu uirginis.* PL 16: 379-384; ed. Cazzaniga, 23-31.)

9. De misteriis iniciandis liber unus. Principium: *De moralibus cotidianis* Finis: *ueritatem regenerationis consequuntur.*

    ff. 133ᵛ-136, exp. *... consequuntur ueritatem regenerationis operetur.* PL 16: 389-410; ed. Faller, CSEL, 73 (1955) 1-12.

10. De sacramentis libri vi. Principium: *De sacramentis que accepistis* Finis: *et in omnia secula seculorum. Amen.*

    ff. 136-143. Attributed to Ambrose; *Clavis Patrum* 154. PL 16: 417-462; ed. Faller, CSEL, 73 (1955) 13-85.

11. De Naboth paupere liber unus. Principium: *Naboth hystoria tempore* Finis: *mereamur paupere.*

> ff. 143-148^v. PL 14: 731-756; ed. Schenkl, CSEL, 32, 2 (1897) 469-516.

12. De Helya et ieiunio liber unus. Principium: *Diuinum ad patres* Finis: *meruit insigne pietatis.*

> ff. 148^v-155. PL 14: 697-728; ed. Schenkl, CSEL, 32, 2 (1897) 411-465.

13. De Thobia liber unus. Principium: *Lecto prophetico libro* Finis: *et usura perpetua.*

> ff. 155-162^v. PL 14: 759-794; ed. Schenkl, CSEL 32, 2 (1897) 519-573.

14. De interpellatione Iob liber i. Principium: *Multas nobis perturbationes* Finis: *abstinere autem a malis disciplina est.*

> ff. 162^v-165^v. *De interpellatione lib. i.* PL 14: 797-812; ed. Schenkl, CSEL, 32, 2 (1897) 211-232.

15. De interpellatione Dauid et psalmis lxxii liber i. Principium: *Multi quidem deplorauerunt* Finis: *et in omnia secula seculorum. Amen.*

> ff. 165^v-169. *De int. lib. ii.* PL 14: 811-828; ed. Schenkl, CSEL, 32, 2 (1897) 267-296.

16. De interpellatione Iob alius liber. Principium: *Superiori nobis* Finis: *et pax que super omnem intellectum est.*

> ff. 169-171. *De int. lib. iii.* PL 14: 827-838; ed. Schenkl, CSEL, 32, 2 (1897) 233-247.

17. De interpellatione Dauid alius liber. Principium: *Decursa est interpellatio* Finis: *et in omnia secula seculorum. Amen.*

> ff. 171-174. *De int. lib. iv.* PL 14: 837-850; ed. Schenkl, CSEL, 32, 2 (1897) 248-267.

18. De apologia Dauid ad Theodosium Augustum libri duo. Principium: *Apologiam prophete Dauid* Finis: *quia futura prescripsit.*

> ff. 174-187^v. Includes the *Apologia altera* as bk 2. PL 14: 851-884, 887-916; ed. Schenkl, CSEL, 32, 2 (1897) 299-355, 357-408.

19. Pastorale eiusdem qui intitulatur de dignitate sacerdotali. Principium: *Si quis fratres* Finis: *dare promisisti perpetua. Amen.*

> ff. 187^v-189^v. Gregory of Elvira; see *Clavis Patrum* 551. PL 17: 567-580; ed. A. C. Vega, *España sagrada* (Madrid 1957) 55: 83-127; 56, 67-77.

20. De Gedeon liber unus. Principium: *Ieroboal cum sub arbore* Finis: *honor et gloria in secula seculorum. Amen.*

> ff. 189^v-190^v. A brief extract from the prologue of *De spiritu sancto.* PL 16: 703-708 line 5.

21. Epistola eiusdem de misterio pasche. Principium: *Pasche misterium* Finis: *nunc et semper et in secula seculorum. Amen.*

> ff. 190ᵛ-191. Pseudo-Ambrose; see *Clavis Patrum* 180. PL 17: 673-675, spur. serm. 35.
> (f. 191ʳ⁻ᵛ, B. *Cyprianus de ecclesie catholice unitate,* exp. ... *noctem pro die interitum pro salute.* PL 4: 495-498; ed. Hartel, CSEL, 3, 1 [1868] 207-211 line 27.)

22. De penitencia libri iii. Principium: *Penitencia officia* Finis: *mundi istius nexu debemus absoluere.*

> ff. 191ᵛ-211ᵛ, inc. *Penitentie....* Victor of Cartenna, *De paenitentia* (see *Clavis Patrum* 854; PL 17: 971-1004), followed without rubric by Ambrose, *De paenitentia* (PL 16: 465-524; ed. Faller, CSEL, 73 [1955] 117-206).

23. De patriarchis libri ii. Principium: *Sanctorum uita ceteris norma* Finis: *Apollo rigauit.*

> ff. 211ᵛ-223. Contains the *De Ioseph* (PL 14: 642-672; ed. Schenkl, CSEL, 32, 2 [1897] 73-122) as bk. 1 and the *De patriarchis* (PL 14: 673-694; ed. Schenkl, CSEL, 32, 2 [1897] 125-160) as bk. 2.

24. De penitencia epistole iiii.
Prima: *Audisti frater*

> ff. 223-224. PL 16: 1254-1257 ep. 74.

Secunda: *Etsi sciencia*

> f. 224ʳ. PL 16: 1257-1259 ep. 75.

Tercia: *Si Abraham credidit*

> f. 224ʳ⁻ᵛ. PL 16: 1267-1269 ep. 78.

Quarta: *Audisti frater lectionem*

> ff. 224ᵛ-226. PL 16: 1271-1278 ep. 80.

25. De incarnatione domini liber unus. Principium: *Debitum fratres* Finis: *intelligibilium.*

> ff. 226-230ᵛ. PL 16: 818-846.

26. De fuga seculi. Principium: *Frequens nobis* Finis: *et omnia secula seculorum. Amen.*

> ff. 230ᵛ-236ᵛ. PL 14: 569-596; ed. Schenkl, CSEL, 32, 2 (1897) 163-207.

27. De Iacob et uita beata liber i. Principium: *Necessarius ad disciplinam* Finis: *attroci peremptus est morte.*

> ff. 236ᵛ-245ᵛ. PL 14: 597-638; ed. Schenkl, CSEL, 32, 2 (1897) 3-70, in two books.

28. De Ysaac et anima liber unus. Principium: *In patre nobis sancto Ysaac* Finis: *seruare se debet et custodire.*

> ff. 245ᵛ-253. PL 14: 501-534; ed. Schenkl, pt. 1, 641-700.

29. De paradyso. Principium: *De paradyso adoriendus est sermo* Finis: *metemus ea que sunt spiritualia.*
> ff. 253-263. PL 14: 275-314; ed. Schenkl, CSEL, 32, 2 (1897) 265-336.
> (f. 263^{r-v}, *Epistola Graciani ... ad S. Ambrosium.* PL 16: 875-876.)

30. De trinitate libri iiii. Principium: *Regina Austri uenit* Finis: *nam qui se imparem nescit fecit equalem.*
> ff. 263^v-287^v, exp. ... *equaleo.* Comprises lib. i-ii to c. 7 ¶ 57 of the *De fide* (PL 16: 527-571), followed by lib. i-ii of the *De spiritu sancto* as bks. 3-4 (PL 16: 703-776).
> (f. 288^{r-v}, blank.)

31. Epistole v.
> Prima incipit: *Clementissimo imperatori*
> f. 289^{r-v}. PL 16: 1002-1007 ep. 21.
> Secunda: *Video uos*
> ff. 289^v-292. *Sermo contra Auxentium.* PL 16: 1007-1018 ep. 21.
> Tercia: *Quoniam omnibus epistolis*
> ff. 292-293^v. PL 16: 994-1002 ep. 20.
> Quarta: *Exercitus semper*
> ff. 293^v-295^v. PL 16: 1101-1113 ep. 50.
> Quinta: *Hoc nobis motus terrarum*
> ff. 295^v-299^v. *De obitu Theodosii.* PL 16: 1385-1406; ed. Faller, CSEL, 73 (1955) 369-401.

32. De consolacione Valentiniani liber i. Principium: *Etsi incrementum doloris sit* Finis: *matura re compenses.*
> ff. 299^v-304^v, exp. ... *matura resuscitatione compenses. De obitu Valentiniani.* PL 16: 1357-1384; ed. Faller, CSEL, 73 (1955) 229-367.

33. Epistola ad Vercellensem ecclesiam. Principium: *Ambrosius seruus.*
> ff. 304^v-311^v. PL 16: 1188-1220 ep. 63.

34. De sancto Abraham libri iii. Principium: *Abraham libri huius titulus est* Finis: *sed in confusione uiciorum est.*
> ff. 312-340. *De Abraham lib. ii* (PL 14: 419-500; ed. Schenkl, CSEL, 32, 2 [1897] 501-638), followed by the *De Noe* as bk. 3 (PL 14: 361-416; ed. Schenkl, CSEL, 32, 2 [1897] 413-497).

IV. LIBRI BEATI IERONIMI
> Works 1-7, 9-13, 18 appear in B.N. MS lat. 15287 (s. xiii; Gerard of Abbeville; Cat. 1321, MS T.e.; Cat. 1338, XXVII, 1, *cathenatus*; Delisle, 3: 34, 103), also used for IX. CHRYSOSTOMUS 3. Thomas has singled out nos. 1-7 from the corpus of letters which comprises the first part of this codex, and then has itemized the rest of the codex, as nos. 9-13.

1. De xlii mansionibus populi Israelitici liber unus. Principium: *Mouerunt autem castra* Finis: *preuaricatores autem corruerunt in eis.*

    B.N. ms lat. 15287 ff. 28-33ᵛ, exp. ... *corruent....* PL 22: 700-724; ed. Hilberg, CSEL, 55 (1912) 49-87, ep. 78.

2. De perpetua uirginitate Marie contra Helindium hereticum liber i. Principium: *Nuper rogatus a fratribus* Finis: *Tulli Philippi scribere.*

    ff. 64-69, rubric ... *Heluidium....* PL 23: 183-206. Thomas has given the explicit of the following letter *Ad Pammachium*, ff. 69-72, exp. ... *Philipicas scribere* (PL 22: 568-579; ed. Hilberg, CSEL, 54 [1909] 503-526, ep. 57).

3. De questionibus scripturarum ad Hedibiam. Principium: *Quomodo perfectus esse quis possit* Finis: *extinguntur in nobis bonis.*

    ff. 76ᵛ-83ᵛ. PL 22: 981-1006; ed. Hilberg, CSEL, 55: 470-515, ep. 120.

4. Liber questionum Syminicon ad Algasiam. Principium: *De hac questione* Finis: *antichristum suscepturi sunt.*

    ff. 84ᵛ-92ᵛ, exp. ... *sint.* PL 22: 1006-1038; ed. Hilberg, CSEL, 56 (1918) 1-55, ep. 121; the incipit is that of c. 1.

5. De seraphin et calcalo et forcipe in Ysaia. Principium: *Septuaginta* Finis: *studeamus et lingua.*

    ff. 96ᵛ-100ᵛ, rubric ... *calculo....* PL 22: 361-376; ed. Hilberg, CSEL, 54: 73-103; the incipit is that of ep. 18ʙ, the explicit is that of ep. 18ᴀ.

6. Symbolum de fide Nicheni consilii. Principium: *Credimus in unum deum* Finis: *non ambigua sunt sortiti.*

    ff. 106ᵛ-108ᵛ. Pseudo-Jerome; see *Clavis Patrum* 633 and 1746. PL 30: 176-181, spur. ep. 17; ed. C. Turner, *Ecclesiae occidentalis monumenta iuris antiquissima* (Oxford 1913) 1: 355-363.

7. Sermo de uirtutibus. Principium: *Tres quodammodo uirtutes* Finis: *et imperium in secula seculorum. Amen.*

    ff. 111-112ᵛ. Pseudo-Jerome; see *Clavis Patrum* 633. PL 30: 116-122, spur. ep. 8.

8. De habitatione clericorum et mulierum. Principium: *Promiseram quid uobis* Finis: *et dilectionis erit uobiscum.*

    This work does not appear in B.N. ms lat. 15287 and has been added from another manuscript. The only text of this work identified among the Sorbonne manuscripts appears without rubric in B.N. ms lat. 15294 ff. 420ᵛ-427, inc. ... *quidem...,* exp. ... *Amen* (s. xiii; Godfrey of Fontaines), which was probably not used. Pseudo-Cyprian; see *Clavis Patrum* 62. PL 4: 835-870; ed. Hartel, CSEL, 3, 3 (1871) 173-220; inc. *Promiseram quidem....*

9. Liber eiusdem aduersus Rufinum. Principium: *Lectis litteris prudencie* Finis: *a te laudatus uideatur.*

    B.N. ms lat. 15287 ff. 154-158ᵛ. *Liber tertius aduersus libros Rufini;* see

Clavis Patrum 614. PL 23: 457-474 ¶ 23 med. Thomas omits the final
portion of the *Liber tertius* on ff. 158ᵛ-162ᵛ, which is treated as a separate
work with the rubric *De epistolis epiphanii*, inc. *Te autem frater liberet
deus et sanctum...*, exp. *... ab locuti sunt falsa.* PL 23: 474ʙ-490ᴅ.

10. Rufini ad Ieronimum libri duo. Principium: *Relegi scripta* Finis: *siue
aduersus tuos datam.*
    ff. 162ᵛ-181. PL 21: 541-624; ed. Simonetti, CC, 20 (1961) 29-123.
    (f. 181, *Epistola Ieronimi ad Rufinum.* PL 22: 735-736, ep. 81.)

11. Ad Pammachium et Marcellam libri duo. Principium: *Et uestris et
multorum litteris* Finis: *nomine sustinere.*
    ff. 181-195. *Apologia aduersus libros Rufini.* PL 23: 397-456.
    (ff. 195-198ᵛ, *Epistola Ieronimi ad Thesifontem*, PL 22: 1147-1161,
    ep. 133; and *Epistola b. Ieronimi contra hereticos predictos*, PL 23: 495-
    498.)

12. Expositio fidei catholice. Principium: *Credimus in deum patrem* Finis:
non me hereticum comprobabit.
    ff. 198ᵛ-199. Pelagius, *Libellus fidei ad Innocentiam papam*; see *Clavis
    Patrum* 731. PL 45: 1716-1718.

13. Aduersus Iouinianum libri duo. Principium: *Pauci admodum* Finis:
Epicuri luxuriam susceperunt.
    ff. 199ᵛ-226ᵛ. PL 23: 211-338.
    (ff. 227-249ᵛ, *De dignitate sacerdotali*, used for ɪx. Cʜʀʏsᴏsᴛᴏᴍᴜs 3.)

14. De essentia diuinitatis et de dictis de deo translatiue. Principium: *Om-
nipotens deus pater et filius* Finis: *se manifestum demonstrare.*
    B.N. ᴍs lat. 15687 ff. 114-116ᵛ; also used for ɪɪ. Aᴜɢᴜsᴛɪɴᴜs 51, 79-
    85, xɪɪ. Aɴsᴇʟᴍᴜs 1-18, and probably for xɪ. Dᴀᴍᴀsᴄᴇɴᴜs 3. The short
    version of an anonymous collection of extracts taken primarily from the
    Formulae spiritalis intelligentiae of Eucherius of Lyons; it comprises part
    1 of the *Formulae.* PL 42: 1199-1206; ed. Wotke, CSEL, 31 (1894) 3-
    62.

15. De litterarum hebraicarum interpretatione. Principium: *Nudius tercius*
Finis: *pedibus nostris uelociter.*
    B.N. ᴍs lat. 15310 ff. 130ᵛ-131; also used for xɪɪɪ. Rɪᴄᴀʀᴅᴜs 2-10, and
    probably for ɪɪ. Aᴜɢᴜsᴛɪɴᴜs 52, 101, and v. Gʀᴇɢᴏʀɪᴜs 2. PL 22: 441-
    445; ed. Hilberg, CSEL, 54: 243-249, ep. 30.

16. De osanna liber i. Principium: *Multi super hoc.* Finis: *sentenciam finit.*
    ff. 131-132. PL 22: 375-379; ed. Hilberg, CSEL, 54: 104-110, ep. 20;
    exp. *... fictam ferre sententiam.*

17. De tribus naturis anime. Principium: *Anima tres habet in se naturas*
Finis: *habete pacem cum deo.*
    B.N. ᴍs lat. 16362 f. 55ʳ⁻ᵛ; also used for xv. Aʟᴄᴜɪɴᴜs 1-6. An
    unidentified text, inc. *Anima tres habet in se naturas uidelicet rationem,*

uoluntatem, appetitum..., exp. ... *de qua dicit apostolus habete pacem cum deo.* Probably identical with the text noted in the 1321 catalog (Delisle, 3: 84) without pressmark, inc. *Anima in se habet tres naturas....* This text also appears among the works of Jerome in the catalog of Salvatorberg, Erfurt, *Mittelalterliche Bibliothekskataloge*, 2: 531, line 22, inc. *Anima in se tres habet naturas....*

18. Epistole eius de diuersas personas cv.

> B.N. ms lat. 15287 ff. 3-150ᵛ.

v. Libri Beati Gregorii

1. Super Iob libri xxxv. Prologus: *Reuerentissimo et sanctissimo fratri Leandro* Principium libri: *Inter multos sepe queritur* Finis: *pro me lacrimas reddit.*

> B.N. ms lat. 15674 ff. 2-333 (s. xiii; Gerard of Abbeville; Cat. 1321, ms N.k.; Cat. 1338, XXVIII, 6, *cathenatus*; Delisle, 3: 35, 100). PL 75: 510-76: 782; the incipits are those of the dedicatory epistle and the preface.

2. Pastorale eiusdem libri iiii. Principium: *Pastoralis cure me pondera* Finis: *meriti manus leuet.*

> Probably B.N. ms lat. 15310 ff. 3ᵛ-34, also used for iv. Hieronymus 15-16, xiii. Ricardus 2-10, and probably for ii. Augustinus 52, 101; the text in B.N. ms lat. 15309 ff. 1-15 is incomplete. PL 77: 13-128.

3. Dyalogorum eiusdem libri iiii. Principium: *Quadam die nimis quorundam* Finis: *deo hostia ipsi fuerimus.*

> Probably B.N. ms lat. 15309 ff. 35-70ᵛ, inc. *Quadam die dum nimis...* (s. xiii; Godfrey of Fontaines; Cat. 1321, ms Y.h.; Cat. 1338, XXXVII, 36, *cathenatus*; Delisle, 3: 40, 100). PL 77: 149-429.

4. Super Ezechielem partes due. Principium prime: *Deus prophecie locutionis* Finis: *roborare Ihesus Christus qui uiuit et regnat etc.* Continens omelias x. Principium secunde partis: *Quia multis curis* Finis: *sit itaque gloria omnipotenti domino nostro Ihesu Christo qui uiuit et regnat etc.* Omelie x.

> Probably B.N. ms lat. 15309 ff. 73-139ᵛ, exp. pt. i ... *Christus dominus noster qui...*; pt. i contains 12 homilies. Thomas accidentally omits homily 1; the incipit of pt. i is a misreading of the beginning of homily 2, *Usus prophetice locutionis...*, caused in part by the florid rubrication of this manuscript. Positive identification with this manuscript is difficult because of the variations in incipit and explicit and because of the late date of Godfrey's bequest, ca. 1306. However, the misreading of *Deus...*, and the fact that the only other manuscript of this work at the Sorbonne by 1306 (B.N. ms lat. 15308; s. xii in., John Clarambout) is a very doubtful candidate, strengthens the identification. PL 76: 785-1072.

VI. LIBRI BEATI BERNARDI

> Works 1-13 comprise B.N. MS lat. 16371 ff. 2-186^v, 288-434^v (s. xiii; Cat. 1321, MS Y.b.; Cat. 1338, XXIX, probably no. 2, *cathenatus*; Delisle, 3: 35, 97).

1. De consideratione ad Eugenium libri v. Principium: *Subit animum dictare* Finis: *sed non finis querendi.*

   > B.N. MS lat. 16371 ff. 2-29^v. PL 182: 727-808; eds. Leclercq and Rochais, *S. Bernardi Opera* 3 (1963) 393-493.

2. Super Cantica omelie siue sermones lxxxiii. Principium: *Vobis fratres alia quam aliis* Finis: *quid est super omnia deus benedictus in secula seculorum. Amen.*

   > ff. 288-434^v, exp. ... *qui est ... in secula. Amen.* PL 183: 785-1181; eds. Leclercq, Talbot and Rochais, *S. Bernardi Opera*, 1 (1957); 2 (1958), 1-302.

3. De precepto et dispensatione liber unus. Principium: *Qua mente iam tacebo* Finis: *quod et studui satisfacere uoluntati.*

   > ff. 30-42^v; preceded by the prologue. PL 182: 861-894; Leclercq and Rochais, 254-294.

4. Super Missus est qui dicitur de laudibus uirginis omelie iiii. Principium: *Missus est angelus Gabriel* Finis: *deuotissime destinaui.*

   > ff. 42^v-56; preceded by the prologue. PL 183: 55-88.

5. De gratia et libero arbitrio liber unus. Principium: *Loquente me coram fratribus* Finis: *hos magnificauit.*

   > ff. 56-67^v, exp. ... *hos et magnificauit*; preceded by the prologue. PL 182: 1001-1030; Leclercq and Rochais, 165-203.

6. De xii gradibus humilitatis. Principium: *Rogasti me frater* Finis: *inquirendo uiam humilitatis.*

   > ff. 68-74^v, exp. ... *in querendo...*; preceded by table. PL 182: 941-958; Leclercq and Rochais, 16-37.

7. De xii gradibus superbie. Principium: *Primus itaque superbie* Finis: *generatio cum caritate procedit.*

   > ff. 75-80^v; PL 182: 957-972; Leclercq and Rochais, 38-59. The explicit is that of a brief unidentified passage which is added without rubric to the end of the text, inc. *Quicunque fecerit uoluntatem patris* (Matth. 12, 50). *Notandum ordo prius...*, exp. ... *pulchra generatio cum caritate procedit.* A longer form of this passage also follows this work in Paris, Bibl. Mazarine MS 775 ff. 139-141^v, s. xiii.

8. De laude noue milicie templi. Principium: *Nouum milicie genus ortum* Finis: *et digitos nostros ad bellum.*

   > ff. 81-88; preceded by table and prologue. PL 182: 921-940; Leclercq and Rochais, 214-239; exp. ... *digitos uestros....*

9. De diligendo deo liber i. Principium: *Viro illustri domino Hamerico*
Finis: *qualem littere uestre predicant.*

> ff. 88-98. *De diligendo deo* (PL 182: 973-1000; Leclercq and Rochais,
> 119-154) in this manuscript includes the final paragraph of the letter to
> Guigo, PL 182: 115, ep. 11.

10. De amore dei liber unus. Principium: *Ascendamus ad montem domini*
Finis: *et nouissimi primi.*

> ff. 98-115, inc. *Venite ascendamus....* William of Saint-Thierry, *De con-
> templando deo* (PL 184: 367-380; incipit is that of c. 1), followed without
> rubric by his *De natura et dignitate amoris*, PL 184: 379-408.
> (f. 115ᵛ, blank.)

11. De colloquio Symonis ad Ihesum. Principium: *Dixit Symon Petrus*
Finis: *Ihesus Christus filius tuus dominus noster.*

> ff. 116-131ᵛ. Geoffrey of Auxerre. PL 184: 437-476; incipit is that of
> c. 1.

12. Super Qui habitat omelie xvi. Principium: *Considero laborem uestrum*
Finis: *benedictus in secula.*

> ff. 131ᵛ-159ᵛ; this manuscript contains the usual seventeen homilies, but
> the rubricator has misnumbered them as sixteen. PL 183: 185-254.

13. De professione monachorum siue expositione regule beati Benedicti.
Principium: *Tractatus iste qui est* Finis: *animaduertunt omnia.*

> ff. 160-186ᵛ. William Peyraut; see A. Dondaine, "Guillaume Peyraut, vie
> et œuvres," *Archivum fratrum praedicatorum* 18 (1948) 162-236. Ed. B.
> Pez (Vienna-Graz 1721) cols. 567-650. Same as xiv. Hugo 30.
> (ff. 186ᵛ-187ᵛ, *Sermo b. Bernardi de trinitate*; PL 183: 667-669,
> serm. 45. ff. 188-284ᵛ, Boethius, *Opuscula sacra*, with commentary of
> Gilbert of Poitiers; used for xviii. Boethius 1. ff. 285-287ᵛ, blank.
> ff. 288-434ᵛ, *Super Cantica*, no. 2 above.)

14. Meditationes Bernardi. Principium: *Multi multa sciunt* Finis: *uiuit et
regnat per omnia secula seculorum. Amen.*

> Probably B.N. ms lat. 15988 pp. 581-595; also used for xiv. Hugo 30-
> 32, and probably for ii. Augustinus 47, 102. Pseudo-Bernard. *Meditatio
> de humana condicione.* Recently suggested to be the work of Peter
> Comestor by G. Raciti in *Rivista di filosofia neo-scolastica* 53 (1961)
> 385-401. PL 184: 485-508. Same as xiv. Hugo 10, bk. 1.

vii. Libri Beati Hylarii

> The works in this entry comprise B.N. ms lat. 15637 ff. 3-92 (s. xiii;
> Gerard of Abbeville; Cat. 1321, ms Q.h.; Cat. 1338, XV, 9, *cathenatus*;
> Delisle, 3: 20, 100).

1. De trinitate libri xii. Principium: *Circumspicienti michi proprium* Finis:

dominus meus Ihesus Christus manens in te et ex te et apud te semper deus qui est benedictus in secula seculorum. Amen.

B.N. MS lat. 15637 ff. 3-68ᵛ. PL 10: 25-472.

2. De synodis liber unus. Principium: *Constitutum habebam mecum* Finis: *per omousion oportet intelligi.*

ff. 68ᵛ-78, inc. ... *mecum habebam....* PL 10: 479-546.

3. Tractatus eiusdem tres ad Constancium imperatorem. Principium: *Tempus est loquendi* Finis: *iuxta ista non dissonans.*

ff. 78-83ᵛ. Includes the *Liber contra Constantium imperatorem* (PL 10: 577-603), the *Epistola Synodi Sardicensis* (PL 10: 558-564; ed. Feder, CSEL, 65 [1916] 181-184), and the *Liber [ii] ad Constantium imperatorem* (PL 10: 563-572; Feder, 197-205).

4. Exemplum blasphemie Auxencii. Principium: *Beatissimis et gloriosissimis* Finis: *hec retractari non oportere.*

f. 83ᵛ. PL 10: 617-618 ¶ 13-15.

5. Tractatus eiusdem aduersus Auxentinum Arrianum Mediolanensem episcopum. Principium: *Dilectissimis fratribus* Finis: *uerum deum predicabunt.*

ff. 83ᵛ-85, exp. ... *deum uerum predicabunt.* PL 10: 609-617 ¶ 1-12.

6. Tractatus describens hystoriam a principio mundi usque ad Christum.

ff. 85-92, unattributed, without title, inc. *Considerans hystorie sacre prolixitatem nunc non et difficultatem scolarium...*, exp. ... *ipse fuit electus cum Ioseph inter dies ascensionis et pentecostes.* Petrus Pictauensis, *Compendium historie in genealogia Christi.* This text is seldom found with the works of Hilarius Pictauensis; its inclusion in this manuscript no doubt rests upon a confusion of the surnames. For a discussion of this work, see Philip S. Moore, *The Works of Peter of Poitiers*, Publications in Medieval Studies 1 (Notre Dame 1936) 97-117.

VIII. LIBRI YSIDORI

1. Ysidorus de summo bono libri iii. Principium: *Summum bonum deus est* Finis: *letificandos includit.*

Probably B.N. MS lat. 15734 ff. 215ᵛ-242ᵛ, preceded by the prologue (s. xiii; Gerard of Abbeville; Cat. 1338, XXXVII, 6; Delisle, 3: 37-38); also used for XIII. RICARDUS 1, and XVIII. BOETHIUS 1. *Sententiarum libri iii.* PL 83: 537-738.

2. Ysidorus ethimologiarum libri xx. Prologus: *Domino meo* Principium libri: *Disciplina a discendo* Finis: *ut uis morbi ignis ardore siccetur.*

Perhaps B.N. MS lat. 16216 ff. 2-241ᵛ (Cat. 1321, MS S.o.; Cat. 1338, XXXIII, 4, *cathenatus*; Delisle, 3: 36, 103); but see 3 below. PL 82: 73-728; ed. W. Lindsay (Oxford 1911).

3. Ysidorus de officiis ecclesiasticis. Prologus: *Domino meo* Principium libri: *Primum a beato Petro* Finis: *paternis sentenciis firmaretur*.

This work and 2 above were probably taken from the manuscript represented by Cat. 1321, MS S.p.; Delisle, 3: 103. No surviving Sorbonne manuscript of this work has been identified. PL 83: 737-826.

IX. LIBRI IOHANNIS CRISOSTOMI

1. Super Matheum incomplete et sunt due partes. Prima incipit: *Oportuerat quidem* Secunda: *Liber generationis Ihesu Christi* Fines non uidi.

B.N. MS lat. 15642 ff. 1ᵛ-187ᵛ (s. xiii; Gerard of Abbeville; Cat. 1321, MS Q.s.; Cat. 1338, XXXII, 3, *cathenatus*; Delisle, 3: 35, 98); Thomas omits prologues of parts i and ii. Pt. i, ff. 1-83ᵛ, is Chrysostom, *Homeliae in Matthaeum* 1-25 (trans. Anianus of Celeda; Stegmüller 4348), printed in *Opera* 4 (Venice 1503); homilies 1-8 are printed in PG 58: 975-1058. Pt. ii, ff. 84-187ᵛ, is Pseudo-Chrysostom, *Opus imperfectum in Matthaeum*, hom. 1-22, 32-46 (on Matth. 1-8, 19-23), Stegmüller 4350. PG 56: 611-897 med.

2. Super Iohannem omelie lxxxviii. Prologus primus: *Omnibus in Christo* Secundus qui est Crisostomi: *Hunc igitur librum* Liber sic incipit: *Qui agonum que foris sunt* Finis: *cum sancto spiritu nunc et semper etc.*

B.N. MS lat. 15284 ff. 1-159 (s. xiii; Gerard of Abbeville; Cat. 1321, MS Q.r.; Cat. 1338, XXXII, 1 or 4, *cathenatus*; Delisle, 3: 35, 98). Trans. of Burgundio of Pisa. Stegmüller 4355. Unpublished. The first prologue is that of Burgundio, extracts of which are printed in E. Martène and U. Durand, *Veterum scriptorum et monumentorum ... collectio* 1 (1724) 819, 828, and C. H. Haskins, *Studies in Medieval Science*, rev. ed. (Cambridge 1927) 151, 185.

3. Dyalogorum eius libri vi qui intitulatur de dignitate sacerdotali. Principium: *Michi quidem multi fuerunt* Finis: *tabernaculum*.

B.N. MS lat. 15287 ff. 227-249ᵛ; also used for IV. HIERONYMUS 1-7, 9-13, 18. Printed, Ulrich Zell, Cologne, ca. 1472 (Hain 5048, Proctor 857); ed. Fronton du Duc, *Opera* (Paris 1614) 4: 1-111.

4. De eo quod nemo leditur ab alio nisi a semetipso fuerit lesusa iniiiium: *Scio quod crassioribus quibusque* Finis: *a semetipso non leditur*.

B.N. MS lat. 16382 ff. 74ᵛ-82 (s. xiii; Gerard of Abbeville; Cat. 1321, MS Q.m.; Cat. 1338, XXXVII, 7, *cathenatus*; Delisle, 3: 38, 98-99); also used for XI. PROSPER 1-2. Sermon 39, in A. Wilmart, "La collection des 38 homélies latines de S. Jean Chrysostome," JTS 19 (1918) 305-327. Printed, n.p., n.d. (Hain 5044, Proctor 4748) ff. 42-52ᵛ; ed. Fronton du Duc, *Opera* 4: 569-595.

5. De laudibus Pauli omelie vi. Principium: *Nichil prorsus errauerit* Finis: *cum sancto spiritu in secula seculorum. Amen.*

ff. 82-93^v; the manuscript contains seven homilies incorrectly numbered as six. Trans. of Anianus of Celeda. PG 50: 473-514.

x. Libri Rabani

Works 1-4 may represent a manuscript similar to Troyes Bibliothèque Municipale MS 31 (s. xii, Clairvaux D.49), which contains Strabo's *Abbreviatio* of Rabanus on the Pentateuch, followed by the complete text of Rabanus on Deuteronomy; analyzed in Stegmüller, 7027, 8316-21. No Sorbonne manuscripts of works 1-5 have been identified.

1. Super Genesim. Principium: *In principio fecit deus celum et terram* Finis: *in dextera tua usque in finem.*

   Probably Walafrid Strabo, *Abbreviatio Rabani Mauri in Genesim libri i-iv.* Stegmüller 8316. Unpublished.

2. Super Exodum. Principium textus: *Exodus exitus dici debet* Finis: *a sensibus obsecatis.*

   Strabo, *Abbreviatio in Exodum*, lacking the final lines of the text. Stegmüller 8318. Unpublished.

3. Super Leuiticum. Principium: *Sequentis libri id est Leuitici* Finis: *de filiabus Saphat iam diximus.*

   Strabo, *Abbreviatio in Leviticum* (Stegmüller 8319, PL 114: 795-850), followed by the *Abbreviatio in Numeros*, which lacks the final lines of the text (Stegmüller 8320, unpublished).

4. Super Deuteronomium. Principium: *Hec sunt uerba que locutus est* Finis: *idem per omnia permanet secula. Amen.*

   The incipit and explicit given here may include Strabo's *Abbreviatio in Deuteronomium* (Stegmüller 8321, unpublished), followed by the whole of Rabanus on Deuteronomy (Stegmüller 7027; PL 108: 837-998), as in Troyes MS 31 ff. 144-213^v discussed above. The text of the Rabanus commentary as printed in Migne and noted by Stegmüller is incomplete; the explicit given here is that of the full text. See J. de Blic, "Walafrid Strabon et la *Glossa ordinaria*," RTAM 16 (1949) 19 n. 38.

5. Super Mattheum. Principium prologi: *Memor illius sibi precepti* Principium textus: *Expositionem itaque* Finis: *deinde in Galilea.*

   Rabanus Maurus, *Expositio in Matthaeum*, lacking the final lines of the text. Stegmüller 7060. PL 107: 727-1156A.

xi. Libri Prosperi et Damasceni

1. Prosper de uita contemplatiua libri iii. Principium: *Contemplatiua uita* Finis: *uerba sunt instituta.*

   B.N. MS lat. 16382 ff. 51^v-74^v; preceded by the prologue. Julian Pomerius. PL 59: 418-520.

(ff. 74ᵛ-93ᵛ contain IX. CHRYSOSTOMUS 4-5).

2. Sentencie eiusdem uel propositiones ccclxxx<x>. Principium: *Sentencia uera est que nec sibi nocet nec alteri* Finis: *si te ipsum re-spexeris.*

> ff. 94-105, inc. *Innocentia uera ... sibi nec alteri nocet.... Sententiae ex operibus S. Augustini.* PL 51: 427-496. Same as II. AUGUSTINUS 108.

3. Damasceni libri iiii. Principium: *Deum nemo uidit unquam* Finis: *quod ab ipso est gaudium fructificantes.*

> Probably B.N. MS lat. 15687 ff. 175-201ᵛ (Delisle, 3: 100); used also for XII. ANSELMUS 1-18, II. AUGUSTINUS 51, 79-84, and IV. HIERONYMUS 14. *De fide orthodoxa,* trans. of Burgundio of Pisa. Ed. E. M. Buytaert, Franciscan Institute Publications, Text Series 8 (New York 1955).

XII. LIBRI ANSELMI

> Works 1-18 comprise B.N. MS lat. 15687 ff. 1-113ᵛ; also used for II. AUGUSTINUS 51, 79-84, IV. HIERONYMUS 14, and probably for XI. DAMASCENUS 3.

1. Cur Deus homo libri duo. Principium: *Sepe et studiosissime a multis* Finis: *attribuere debemus qui est benedictus in secula.*

> B.N. MS lat. 15687 ff. 2ᵛ-16ᵛ, exp. ... *Amen;* preceded by the prologue and table. PL 158: 361-432; ed. F. S. Schmitt (Edinburgh 1946) 2: 47-133.

2. De ueritate liber unus. Principium: *Quoniam deum ueritatem esse credimus* Finis: *ueritas uel rectitudo.*

> ff. 16ᵛ-20ᵛ; preceded by the prologue and table. PL 158: 468-486; ed. Schmitt, 1: 176-199.

3. De libertate arbitrii. Principium: *Quoniam liberum arbitrium* Finis: *quod necesse habeam de illis interrogare.*

> ff. 20ᵛ-24. PL 158: 489-506; ed. Schmitt, 1: 207-226.

4. De casu dyaboli. Principium: *Illud apostoli quid* Finis: *et uti potestate loquendi.*

> ff. 24-31ᵛ. PL 158: 325-360; ed. Schmitt, 1: 233-276.

5. De incarnatione uerbi liber unus. Principium: *Domino et patri uniuerse* Finis: *libro aperte inueniet.*

> ff. 31ᵛ-36ᵛ. PL 158: 261-284; ed. Schmitt, 2: 3-35.

6. De conceptu uirginali et peccato originali. Principium: *Cum in omnibus religiose tue uoluntati* Finis: *si uera probari poterit.*

> ff. 37-43. PL 158: 431-464; ed. Schmitt, 2: 139-173.

7. De processione spiritus sancti contra Grecos. Principium: *Negatur a Grecis quod spiritus sanctus* Finis: *non sensui latinitatis.*

> ff. 43ᵛ-51. PL 158: 285-326; ed. Schmitt, 2: 177-219.

8. Epistola eius de azimo et fermentato. Principium: *Anselmus seruus ecclesie* Finis: *rationabiliter repudiandum iudicatur.*

> ff. 51-52, exp. ... *repudiandum rationabiliter....* PL 158: 541-548; ed. Schmitt, 2: 223-232.

9. Monologion. Principium: *Si quis unam naturam* Finis: *solus deus ineffabiliter trinus et unus.*

> ff. 53-66; preceded by the prologue and table. PL 158: 144-224; ed. Schmitt, 1: 13-87.

10. Proslogion. Principium: *Eya nunc homuncio* Finis: *et unus deus benedictus in secula. Amen.*

> ff. 66ᵛ-70; preceded by the prologue and table. PL 158: 225-242; ed. Schmitt, 1: 97-122.

11. Disputatio pro insipiente. Principium: *Dubitanti utrum sit* Finis: *et laude suscipienda.*

> ff. 70-71. Gaunilo, *Liber pro insipiente aduersus S. Anselmum.* PL 158: 241-248; ed. Schmitt, 1: 125-129.

12. Contra respondentem pro insipiente. Principium: *Quoniam non me reprehendis* Finis: *non maliuolencia reprehendisti.*

> ff. 71-73, inc. ... *reprehendit....* PL 158: 247-260; ed. Schmitt 1: 130-139.

13. Meditaciones eiusdem. Principium: *Terret nos uita* Finis: *gloriaris per interminata secula. Amen.*

> ff. 73-74, inc. *Terret me uita....* PL 158: 722-725 (*Meditatio* 2); ed. Schmitt, 3: 76-79 (*Meditatio* 1).

14. De concordia presciencie predestinationis et gracie cum libero arbitrio. Principium: *De tribus illis questionibus* Finis: *petentibus impendere,* uel *quod non sit dissolubile.*

> ff. 74-82ᵛ. First explicit is that of the complete work; second explicit is that of *Quaestio* 1, f. 77 (PL 158: 519). PL 158: 507-542; ed. Schmitt, 2: 245-288. See also nos. 17, 18 below.

15. Disputatio Iudei cum Christiano de fide catholica. Principium: *Reuerendo patri et domino*

> ff. 82ᵛ-86ᵛ. Gilbert Crispin. PL 159: 1005-1036; ed. B. Blumenkranz, *Stromata* 3 (Utrecht 1956).
> (ff. 87-89ᵛ, six letters of Anselm: Schmitt epp. 37, 2, 183, 161, 160, and *Ad Waleramnum de Sacramentis ecclesiae*, ed. Schmitt, 2: 239-242.)

16. De similitudinibus in quo continetur liber de beatitudine celestis patrie. Principium: *Tripliciter intelligitur uoluntas* Finis: *in quantum uolunt.*

> ff. 90-113ᵛ. Alexander of Canterbury; see Wilmart, *Auteurs spirituels* 300. PL 159: 605-702; explicit is that of c. 192.
> (ff. 113ᵛ-114, a second text of the *Epistola ad Waleramnum*, which concludes the Anselm portion of this manuscript.)

Nos. 17-18 below appear as individual works in this manuscript with these rubrics, and were probably added by Thomas as an afterthought.

17. De predestinatione et libero arbitrio. Principium: *Nunc ergo in eo* Finis: *quod fecit fecisset.*

> f. 77^{r-v}. *Quaestio* 2 of 14 above. PL 158: 519-521; ed. Schmitt, 2: 260-262.

18. De gracia et libero arbitrio. Principium: *Restat nunc ut de gracia* Finis: *gratis uolui petentibus impendere.*

> ff. 77^v-82^v. *Quaestio* 3 of 14 above. PL 158: 521-542; ed. Schmitt, 2: 263-288.

19. Epistole plures et sermones multi.

> This entry does not represent any specific manuscript of Anselm's letters or sermons.

XIII. LIBRI RICARDI DE SANCTO VICTORE

> Works 2-10 comprise B.N. MS lat. 15310 ff. 134^v-191^v (Cat. 1321, MS N.l.; Delisle, 3: 104-105); also used for IV. HIERONYMUS 15-16, and probably for II. AUGUSTINUS 52, 101, and V. GREGORIUS 2. The list of this author's works has been edited from Munich, Bayerische Staats-bibliothek MSS 5404 f. 323^{r-v}, s. xv; 5345 f. 287^{r-v}, s. xv; and 12310 f. 286^v, s. xv, by Ludwig Ott, *Untersuchungen zur theologischen Brief-literatur der Frühscholastik*, Texte und Untersuchungen 34 (Munster 1937) 562-565.

1. De trinitate libri vi. Prologus: *Iustus meus* Principium libri: *Si ad sublimium scientiam* Finis: *cum personarum pluralitate*, uel *in altero doctrinam discens.*

> Probably B.N. MS lat. 15730 ff. 2-33^v, also used for XIX. SENECA 1-7. The alternate explicit is that of an incomplete text of this work ending with bk. 6 c. 24 (PL 196: 989C), which appears in B.N. MS lat. 15734 ff. 64-88^v, ... *est doctrina docens, in altero doctrina discens* (s. xiii; Gerard of Abbeville; Cat. 1338, XXXVII, 6; Delisle, 3: 37-38); also used for XVIII. BOETHIUS 1, and probably for VIII. ISIDORUS 1, XIV. HUGO 33, and no. 11 below. PL 196: 887-992; ed. J. Ribaillier, Textes philosophiques du moyen âge 6 (Paris 1958); cf. p. 37.

2. De potestate ligandi et soluendi. Principium: *Quodcumque ligaueris super terram* Finis: *non imputauit dominus peccatum.*

> B.N. MS lat. 15310 ff. 134^v-140. PL 196: 1159-1178.

3. De spiritu blasphemie. Principium: *Que in ewangelio leguntur* Finis: *tu me coegisti.*

> ff. 140-141^v. PL 196: 1185-1192.

4. De tribus appropriatis. Principium: *Queris a me mi Bernarde* Finis: *iudicantur munda et bona.*

ff. 142-143. *De tribus appropriatis* (PL 196: 991-994), followed by the first paragraph of the *Declarationes nonnullarum difficultatum scripturae* (PL 196: 255-256).

5. De uerbis apostoli. Principium: *Queris quomodo ab apostolo azimi* Finis: *reficiamus intellectum nostrum.*

   ff. 143-146. Pt. ii of the *Declarationes nonnullarum difficultatum scripturae.* PL 196: 256-266.

6. Super Ysaiam exponens illud: Ad me clamat ex Seyr. Principium: *Ad me clamat ex Seyr* Finis: *tu me co<e> gisti.*

   ff. 146-150ᵛ. *Liber de verbo incarnato.* The text in PL 196: 995-1010 is incomplete; the complete text is printed in the edition of John of Toulouse (Rouen 1650) 272-280. See Ott, *Briefliteratur* 599-600.

7. De differencia peccati mortalis et uenialis. Principium: *Quoniam questioni tue*

   ff. 150ᵛ-151. PL 196: 1191-1194.

8. De uerbis apostoli. Principium: *Si ea que de lege ab apostolo* Finis: *nil nisi amor retribuitur.*

   ff. 151-157. *Explicatio aliquorum passuum difficilium apostoli.* PL 196: 665-684.

   (ff. 157-163, *Dialogus quaestionum lxv*, probably used for II. AUGUSTINUS 101.)

9. Super Danielem libri iii. Principium: *Quid illud Nabugodonosor* Finis: *regnum peccati destruitur.*

   ff. 164-   ; preceded by table, ff. 163-164. The manuscript is incomplete, ending on f. 191ᵛ, ... *cuinam queso dubium esse queat* (PL 196: 1330c, bk. 2 c. 32). *De eruditione hominis interioris.* PL 196: 1229-1366.

10. De potestate iudiciaria. Principium: *In regeneratione cum se<derit>* Finis: *uix poterit credi.*

    This title appears as the last work in the contents list of B.N. MS lat. 15310 f. 1, but has since disappeared from the codex. PL 196: 1177-1186.

11. De contemplatione siue de xii patriarchis. Principium: *Beniamin adolescentulus in mentis ex<cessu>* Finis: *humana ratio applaudit.*

    Probably B.N. MS lat. 15734 ff. 3ᵛ-16, rubric *De contemplatione*, used for no. 1 above; also to be considered, however, is B.N. MS lat. 15692 ff. 45ᵛ-77ᵛ (s. xii), rubric *De patriarchis*, in which the incipit reads ... *ex-/cessu...*. In either case, the alternate title is not uncommon and is in all probability taken from another manuscript of this work. *Beniamin minor.* PL 196: 1-64.

12. De exterminio mali. Principium: *Quid est tibi mare quod fugisti* Finis: *promereri non meretur.*

    Perhaps B.N. MS lat. 16381 ff. 59-78 (s. xiii; Gerard of Abbeville; Cat.

1321, MS Q.ac.; Cat. 1338, XXXVI, 2, [*cathenatus*]; Delisle, 3: 36, 105), which is the only text of this work found in the catalogs or surviving manuscripts of the Sorbonne; rubric, *De exterminatione mali et promotione boni*; inc. ... *mare quo...*, exp. ... *promoueri....* Attributed to Richard of Saint-Laurence by J. Châtillon, *Revue du moyen âge latin* 2 (1946) 163-164. PL 196: 1073-1116.

13. De statu interioris hominis. Principium: *Omne capud languidum* Finis: *neque fota oleo.*

Perhaps B.N. MS lat. 16351 ff. 27-28 (s. xiii; Gerard of Abbeville; Cat. 1338, XXXVII, 3; Delisle, 3: 37). This work may, however, have been supplied from Cat. 1321, MS S.p. (Delisle, 3: 105), probably used for VIII. ISIDORUS 2-3. PL 196: 1117-1160.

XIV. LIBRI HUGONIS DE SANCTO VICTORE

Works 1-9 comprise B.N. MS lat. 15693 (s. xiii; Gerard of Abbeville; Cat. 1321, MS Q.p.; Delisle, 3: 101f.). Works 10-29 comprise B.N. MS lat. 15315 (s. xiii; Gerard of Abbeville; Cat. 1321, MS Q.o.; Cat. 1338, XXXV, 7, *cathenatus*; Delisle, 3: 36, 101f). This list of Hugh of Saint-Victor's works has been edited from Merton College, Oxford, MS 129 ff. 135A^v-136^r (s. xv, Merton College), by J. de Ghellinck, "Un catalogue des œuvres de Hugues de Saint-Victor," *Revue néo-scolastique* 20 (1913) 226-232.

1. De sacramentis libri duo, primi libri partes xii, secundi libri partes xviii. Prologus: *Quisquis ad diuinarum* Principium libri: *Arduum profecto et labo<riosum>* Finis: *ecce quid erit in fine sine fine.*

B.N. MS lat. 15693 ff. 12^v-111^v; preceded by the preface and table. PL 176: 173-618.

(ff. 2-10, *Liber de dogmatibus philosophorum*, ed. J. Holmberg [Uppsala 1929] 5-76; for a review of the discussion concerning the authorship, see M. Th. d'Alverny, *Alain de Lille: Textes inédits*, Etudes de philosophie médiévale 52 (Paris 1965) 65; the text in this manuscript adds in the margin the brief extract from Boethius' *De consolatione philosophiae* 5.6.47-48, and continues for four columns beyond the normal explicit with sentences from the fathers, inc. *Primum querite regnum dei. Ysidorus: Primum sciencie studium est...*, exp. ... *recipiunt gradum si sordes.* ff. 111^v-136, *M. Richardus de S. Victore de summa trinitate*, same as XII. RICARDUS 1.)

2. De medicina anime. Principium: *Homo microcosmus id est minor* Finis: *uerecundie fronti superponat.*

ff. 136^v-139^v; preceded by the prologue. Spurious; see R. Baron, "Hugues de Saint-Victor: Contribution à un nouvel examen de son œuvre," *Traditio* 15 (1959) 243. PL 176: 1183-1202.

3. De meditatione. Principium: *Meditatio est frequens cogitatio* Finis: *suo tempore apprehendat.*

> ff. 139ᵛ-140ᵛ. PL 176: 993-998.

4. De incarnatione uerbi. Principium: *Quidam fuerunt heretici* Finis: *forma glorificationis.*

> ff. 140ᵛ-141ᵛ. This text comprises bk. 2 pt. 1 c. 6 of the *De sacramentis*, no. 1 above. PL 176: 383-387D.

5. De tribus uoluntatibus in Christo. Principium: *Queris de uoluntate dei* Finis: *quod enim uiuit uiuit deo.*

> ff. 141ᵛ-142ᵛ. *De quatuor uoluntatibus...*; the title *De tribus...* is not unusual. PL 176: 841-846.

6. De potestate et uoluntate dei. Principium: *Queritur de potestate dei* Finis: *non predestinauit sed presciuit.*

> ff. 142ᵛ-143. *Si pares Dei uoluntas et potentia.* PL 176: 839-842.

7. De sapiencia Christi. Principium: *Queritis de anima Christi id est de illo* Finis: *non arroganter presumere.*

> ff. 143-145; preceded by the prologue. PL 176: 847-856.

8. De substancia dilectionis. Principium: *Cotidianum de dilectione* Finis: *sed inordinata cupiditas.*

> f. 145ʳ⁻ᵛ. Attributed to Hugh by Baron, 243, 279-280. Printed as c. 4 of the *Institutiones in Decalogum*, PL 176: 15-18.

9. De operibus trium dierum. Principium: *Verbum bonum et uita* Finis: *octauus pertinet ad resurrectionem.*

> ff. 145ᵛ-151. Printed as the seventh book of the *Didascalicon*, PL 176: 811-838.

10. De anima libri iiii. Principium: *Multi multa sciunt* Finis: *quantum dei potestas ualet dimittere.*

> B.N. MS lat. 15315 ff. 2-33ᵛ. An anonymous thirteenth-century collection which consists of part or all of the following works, and additional material: Bk. 1, Pseudo-Bernard, *Meditatio de humana conditione* (same as VI. BERNARDUS 14), PL 184: 485-506, to the end of c. 14; bk. 2, Pseudo-Augustine, *De spiritu et anima* (same as II. AUGUSTINUS 103), PL 40: 779-816, to the end of c. 50; bk. 3, Pseudo-Bernard, *De interiori domo*, PL 184: 507-552, followed by PL 177: 165-170; bk. 4, Pseudo-Augustine, *De contemplatione domini*, or *Manuale* (same as II. AUGUSTINUS 102), PL 40: 951-962, followed by PL 177: 183B-190 (also printed as *De anima*, bk. 4, in PL 177: 171-190). The collection is described by E. Bertola, "Di alcuni trattati psicologici attribuiti ad Ugo da S. Vittore," *Rivista di filosofia neo-scolastica* 51 (1959) 436-455. The authorship of the individual treatises is discussed by Raciti, ibid. 53 (1961) 385-401.

11. De claustro anime libri iiii. Principium: *Rogasti nos frater a<matissime>* Finis: *immortalitatis benedictus deus. Amen.*

    ff. 33^v-75. Hugh of Folieto; see Baron, 288-89 and n. 272. PL 176: 1017-1182.

12. Libellus ad socium uolentem nubere. Principium: *Dum te karissime mundi* Finis: *et regnat per eterna secula. Amen.*

    ff. 75-79. Spurious, *De nuptiis*; see Baron, 289. PL 176: 1201-1218.

13. Expositio dominice orationis. Principium: *Inter omnia que humana* Finis: *feruor etiam interne dilectionis.*

    ff. 79^v-80^v. Printed as *Allegoriae in Novum Testamentum* bk. 2 c. 2, PL 175: 767-774.

14. De archa Noe libri v. Principium: *Primum in planicie* Finis: *in te edificatam esse lateris.*

    ff. 81-103. *De arca Noe mystica* (PL 176: 681-704), followed by the four books of *De arca Noe morali* (PL 176: 641-680, a truncated text; the final paragraph is printed in B. Hauréau, *Hugues de Saint-Victor...* [Paris 1859] 103). Sometime after the manuscript was described in the 1321 catalog two quires of three leaves each, containing the first part of this text, were inverted. The folios should proceed as follows: ff. 87-92^v, *De arca Noe mystica*; ff. 81-86^v, *...illu-/ 93 minat...*-103, *De arca Noe morali.* The accident is of long standing, since the interruption of the text is marked by a mid-fourteenth-century hand on f. 86^v, *Deficit hic multum de libro.*

15. Didascalicon de studio legendi libri vi. Principium: *Omnium expetendorum prima* Finis: *primum uenit.*

    ff. 103^v-121^v; preceded by the prologue. PL 176: 741-812; ed. C. H. Buttimer (Washington, D.C. 1939).

16. De uirtute orandi. Principium: *Quo studio et quo affectu* Finis: *sacrificium in ara cordis adolet<ur>.*

    ff. 121^v-124^v; preceded by the prologue. PL 176: 977-988.

    (ff. 124^v-130. *Liber de medicina anime*, same as no. 2 above.)

17. De institutione nouiter conuersorum ad religionem. Principium: *Quia fratres largiente domino* Finis: *quomodo obseruari debeat.*

    ff. 130-132^v. *De institutione novitiorum*, prologue—c. 10. PL 176: 925-935.

18. De disciplina monachorum. Principium: *Disciplina est conuersatio bona* Finis: *bonitatem orate ut uobis det deus. Amen.*

    ff. 132^v-137^v, exp. *... bonitatem uero orate.... De institutione novitiorum* cc. 10-21. PL 176: 935-952.

19. De arra anime libri duo. Principium: *Loquar in secreto anime* Finis: *de fabricatione arche sapiencie prosequimur.*

ff. 137ᵛ-148, inc. *Loquar secreto...*, exp. *... prosequamur*; preceded by the prologue. *De arrha animae* (PL 176: 951-970; ed. K. Müller [Bonn 1913] 3-25), followed by bk. 3 of the *De arca Noe morali* (PL 176: 647-664).

20. De uanitate mundi libri iiii. Principium: *O munde inmunde* Finis: *ad mutabilitatem non mutetur.*

    ff. 148-158ᵛ. PL 176: 703-740.

21. De laude caritatis. Principium: *Iam multos laudatores* Finis: *et regnat deus per omnia secula seculorum. Amen.*

    ff. 159-160ᵛ, inc. *Iam multos iam laudatores...*; preceded by the prologue. PL 176: 971-976; ed. F. G. Schöpf (Dresden 1857).

22. De cantico beate Marie. Principium: *Maximam hanc in scripturis* Finis: *Abraham et semini eius in secula.*

    ff. 160ᵛ-165ᵛ. PL 175: 413-432.

23. De dominica oratione. Principium: *Septem sunt uicia principalia* Finis: *et adiuua impotentes. Libera nos a malo.*

    ff. 165ᵛ-170. Attributed to Hugh by Baron, 261, 278. Printed as bk. 2 cc. 3-14 of the *Allegoriae in Novum Testamentum*, PL 175: 774-789.

24. De vii donis. Principium: *Scriptum est si enim uos* Finis: *illinc qui operatur ex quo operatur.*

    ff. 170-171. Printed as c. 5 of the *De quinque septenis*, PL 175: 410-414.

25. De amore sponsi ad sponsam. Principium: *Ibo michi ad montem Mirre* Finis: *in unum congregamur.*

    ff. 171-172ᵛ, exp. *... Amen.* PL 176: 987-994.
    (ff. 172ᵛ-173ᵛ, *De substantia dilectionis*, same as no. 8 above. ff. 173ᵛ-174, *Expositio super prologum in pentathecum*, PL 175: 29-32.)

26. De sacra scriptura et eius scriptoribus. Principium: *Lectorem diuinarum* Finis: *qui Iacobum interfecit.*

    ff. 174-179ᵛ. PL 175: 9-28.

27. Epitoma in philosophiam. Principium: *Sepe uobis Indaleti* Finis: *legentis animus ad reliqua libet euadet.*

    ff. 179ᵛ-182, inc. *Sepe nobis....* Ed. R. Baron, *Traditio* 11 (1955) 91-148.

28. Note de v libris Moysi et Iudicum et Regum. Principium: *Sciendum quod Moyses* Finis: *Assur capiet te.*

    ff. 182ᵛ-204, exp. *... Assur enim capiet....* In Genesim, In Exodum, In Leviticum, In librum Iudicum, In libros Regum, Note de libro Numerum (i.e., on Deuteronomy and Numbers both). PL 175: 32-86, incipit is that of c. 3.

29. Speculum eiusdem de mysteriis ecclesie. Principium: *De sacramentis ecclesiasticis* Finis: *uerius inuenit amans quam disputans.*

ff. 204ᵛ-217, exp. ... *uerius enim inuenit*.... Attribution to Hugh is doubtful; see Baron, 269. PL 177: 335-380.

30. De professione monachorum. Principium: *Tractatus iste* Finis: *animaduertunt omnia.*

    B.N. MS lat. 15988 pp. 356-389 (Stephen of Alvernia; Cat. 1321, MS C.o.; Cat. 1338, XXXVII, 28, *cathenatus*; Delisle, 3: 40, 101-102), probably also used for II. AUGUSTINUS 47, 102, and VI. BERNARDUS 14. William Peyraut. Same as VI. BERNARDUS 13.

31. De consciencia. Principium: *Domus hec in qua habitamus* Finis: *uel quomodo uel ubi nescire.*

    pp. 485-502. Spurious, but often attributed to Hugh or Saint Bernard; see Baron, 290. Sometimes called (as in Migne) *De interiori domo*, it forms bk. 3 cc. 1-28 of the *De anima*, no. 10 above. PL 184: 507-538.

32. Confessio eiusdem. Principium: *Solus solitudinem* Finis: *custodiatur.*
    pp. 502-512. Spurious. Bk. 3 cc. 29-41, 50 of *De anima*, no. 10 above. PL 184: 538-552, 177: 165-170.

33. De differencia diuine ac mundane theologie super celestem ierarchiam capitula xv. Principium: *Iudei signa querunt* Finis: *sanctitas condescendit.*

    Probably B.N. MS lat. 15734 ff. 245-279ᵛ; also used for XVIII. BOETHIUS 1, XIII. RICARDUS 1, and probably for RICARDUS 11 and VIII. ISIDORUS 1; however, the work also appears in B.N. MS lat. 15637 ff. 93-150, used for VII. HILARIUS 1-6. Both of these bear the title *De differencia mundane theologie atque diuine ex demonstrationibus earum*, which is that of the first chapter; the description of the former, however, in its fourteenth-century table of contents and in the 1338 catalog reads *De differencia diuine theologie atque mundane.* PL 175: 923-1154.

34. Beniamin eiusdem. Principium: *Spiritalis diiudicat omnia* Finis: *ibi lutum hic puluis.*

    B.N. MS lat. 16368 ff. 2-41ᵛ (s. xii; Gerard of Abbeville; Cat. 1321, MS Q.y.; Cat. 1338, XXXV, 12, *cathenatus*; Delisle, 3: 36, 101-102). A collection of *sententiae* which are printed among the *Miscellanea* 1, PL 177: 469ff. For the title Thomas apparently used the opening word of the following text in this manuscript, Richard of Saint-Victor's *Beniamin minor*, ff. 44-88 (without rubric).

35. Misterium ecclesie. Principium: *Oportet ut sacramentorum Christi* Finis: *in quo uiuit et regnat per cuncta secula.*

    ff. 135-165ᵛ, exp. ... *secula seculorum. Amen.* Without rubric; attributed to Hugh, with this title, in the early fourteenth-century table of contents and in the 1321 catalog. It is an anonymous collection of texts explaining the Mass for the use of novices and members of the lower orders. A somewhat similar collection appears in B.N. MS lat. 1207 ff. 10-113,

150^v-152 (s. xi, near Orléans). The collection in B.N. MS lat. 16368 contains a text on the sacraments, ff. 135-141^v, exp. ... *salutem custodire cuius imperium permanet in s. s. Amen*; an explanation of the Mass, ff. 141^v-160, inc. *Prima statio sacerdotis ad dextram altaris in initio misse...*, exp. ... *de ministro et omnis respondeant deo gracias*; and an instructional text for Holy Week, ff. 160-165^v, inc. *Isti dies qui modo sunt et qui modo ueniunt hi sunt dies quos obseruare debetis....*

36. Expositio litteralis uisionis Ezechiel. Principium: *Multis diuine scripture* Finis: *complendam necessaria adiectio.*

   Probably supplied from the manuscript described in Cat. 1321, MS R.t., Delisle, 3: 101, which has not been identified. Richard of Saint-Victor; see Stegmüller, 7337. PL 196: 527-600; explicit is that of c. 19.

37. Super Cantica. Principium: *In principio librorum tria requiruntur* Finis: *utriusque operis gracias agamus. Amen.*

   Probably B.N. MS lat. 16294 ff. 1-83^v (s. xiii; Gerard of Abbeville; Cat. 1338, XIIII, 1; Delisle, 3: 19); beginning of manuscript lacking, inc. ... *humana natura sponsa...* (PL 172: 360). Honorius of Autun; see Stegmüller, 3573. PL 172: 347-496.

38. Bestiarium eiusdem. Principium: *Leo fortissimus bestiarum* Finis: *ut ad passionem peruveniant.*

   Probably supplied from the manuscript represented by Cat. 1321, MS Z.o.; Delisle, 2: 113 (see also p. 83, MS Z). The incipit and explicit given here are those of a collection of natural history texts which circulated together in the thirteenth and fourteenth centuries and which can be seen in Oxford MS Ashmole 1511 ff. 11-104, exp. ... *inobediencie debachatur*, s. xiii; B.N. MS lat. 11207, s. xiii (f. 1, *Usibus fratrum praedicatorum re ... communitatis ... erasure ...*, later hand *Sanctae Mariae A...*, s. xvii-xviii); and Nîmes, Bibl. Mun. MS 82.I pp. 1-121, exp. ... *inobediencie debacchatur*, paper, s. xvi in. The collection, described from B.N. MS lat. 11207, consists of, ff. 1-39, *Incipiunt nature animalium et moralitates naturarum eorum*, inc. *Leo fortissimus bestiarum / ad nullius...* (a bestiary of the "second family" distinguished by F. McCulloch, *Medieval Latin and French Bestiaries* [Chapel Hill 1960] 30-38); ff. 39-42, [*De natura arborum*]; ff. 42-54, [*De natura hominis*] (extract from Isidore's *Etymologiarum lib. xi*); ff. 54-76, [*Glossarium*] (dependent upon the *De proprietatibus rerum* of Bartholomaeus Anglicus); ff. 76-78^v, [*De lapidibus*], exp. ... / *ut ad passionem peruveniant.* There is some evidence to suggest that this might be the manuscript which Thomas used. The collection is not a common one. The description in the 1321 catalog calls it a "libellus," which aptly describes this little codex. And the incipit and explicit are not only those of the first and last works in this manuscript, but they coincide exactly with the first and last lines of the codex; the length of the first and last lines, in many instances, determines the length of

Thomas' incipit and explicit. The manuscript was written in northern France in the thirteenth century.

XV. LIBRI ALQUINI ET ALANI

Works 1-6 comprise B.N. MS lat. 16362 ff. 3-52 (s. xii; Gerard of Abbeville; Cat. 1275, nos. 10, 16; Cat. 1321, MS T.r.; Delisle, 3: 97), also used for IV. HIERONYMUS 17.

1. Alquinus de trinitate libri iii. Principium: *Domino glorioso Karolo* Finis: *regnum cuius nullus est finis.*

    B.N. MS lat. 16362 ff. 3-20ᵛ. PL 101: 11-54; the explicit is that of bk. 3 c. 22.

2. Questiones eiusdem de sancta trinitate. Principium: *Desideratissimo filio* Finis: *emisit in cruce spiritum Christus.*

    ff. 20ᵛ-22ᵛ. *Ad Fredegisum.* PL 101: 57-64.

3. Idem de ratione anime. Principium: *Karissime in Christi caritate* Finis: *perfecta meritorum claritate.*

    ff. 22ᵛ-26. *Ad Eulalium.* PL 101: 639-647.

4. De proprietate nominum deo conueniencium. Principium: *Domino Dauid rectori optimo* Finis: *dignetur dulcedine.*

    ff. 26-27. Alcuin. MGH Epp. 4 (1895) 263-265, ep. 163.

5. De ecclesiasticis dogmatibus. Principium: *Credimus unum deum esse* Finis: *similitudinem in moribus inuenire.*

    This title appears, attributed to Gennadius, as the final work in the contents list of this manuscript, f. 1ᵛ, but has since disappeared from the codex. The work appears, followed by no. 6 below, among the works of Alcuin in the catalog of Salvatorberg, Erfurt; *Mittelalterliche Bibliotheks-kataloge*, 2: 569, lines 10-11. Gennadius. Same as II. AUGUSTINUS 15.

6. Speculum paruulorum. Principium: *In scriptura sacra* Finis: *per eundem Iohannem apte nunc dicitur.*

    ff. 45ᵛ-52. Ambrose Autpert, *Commentarius in Apocalypsin libri decem*; see J. Winandy, "L'œuvre littéraire d'Ambroise Autpert," RB 60 (1950) 96-97. *Maxima bibliotheca veterum patrum* 13 (Lyon 1677) 403-657. See no. 5 above.

7. Alanus de maximis theologie. Principium: *Communis animi conceptio* Finis: *sed ut plenius possideatur.* Principium commenti: *Omnis sciencia* Finis: *id etiam quo fit confirmatio sed crisma.*

    B.N. MS lat. 16084 ff. 178-192 (Cat. 1321, MS Q.9; Delisle, 3: 109). This text and no. 8 below may once have been a separate codex; sometime after 1321, the first folios of this manuscript were lost, and the text now begins in the middle of the commentary on Reg. V, ... *Dicitur autem aliquid...* (PL 210: 626A). PL 210: 622-680, ending with the commentary on Reg. CXI.

8. De fide catholica. Principium: *Quicquid est causa cause* Finis: *et spiritus sanctus cum filio iudicabunt.* Principium commenti: *Clemens papa cuius rem* Finis: *hominibus homo iudex.*

> ff. 192-198. Nicolaus Ambianensis. *Ars fidei catholicae* (PL 210: 595-618), with the addition *Potentia est uis facilius ... iudicandis hominibus homo iudex*, which in some manuscripts concludes the *Ars fidei cath.* and which is edited by P. C. Balić, "De auctore 'Ars fidei catholicae' inscribitur," in *Mélanges Joseph de Ghellinck S.J.* 2 (1951) 793-814 (text 802-814). The attribution to Nicholas is established by M.-Th. d'Alverny, *Alain de Lille...* 68-69, 319-322.

9. De complanctu siue conquestione nature. Principium: *In lacrimas risus* Finis: *aspirationis derelinquit aspectus.*

> Thomas' manuscript of the *De planctu naturae*, doubtless to be identified with this entry, is Vatican MS Reg. lat. 1006 (s. xiii; Cat. 1338, LII, 24). Alanus. PL 210: 431-482.

XVI. LIBRI DIVERSORUM AUCTORUM

1. Plinius de naturali hystoria mundi ad Vaspasianum continens libros xxxvii. Principium: *Plinius secundus nouem quo menses* Finis: *experimenta pluribus modis constant primum pondere*

> B.N. MS lat. 6803 (s. xiii, [Gerard of Abbeville]; the only reference to Pliny in the Sorbonne catalogs is in the section title, Cat. 1338, LII, "Libri Socratis, Platonis, Ciceronis, Valerii, Solini, Cassiodori, Plini et aliorum actorum"; Delisle, 3: 62), beginning with the *De vita Plini* from Suetonius' *De viris illustribus* (ed. Reifferscheid [Teubner, 1860] 92-93). Variant readings designated *Sor.* appear in a copy of the 1545 Froben edition (B.N. Rés. S 118) which correspond to the readings of this manuscript; and Thomas of Ireland marked passages in this manuscript (see p. 152 above). Ed. L. Jan and C. Mayhoff (Teubner, 1892-1909) I-V, 474; title, ... *Vespasianum...*, inc. ... *nouocomensis...* .

2. Raby Moyses qui intitulatur dux dubiorum uel neutrorum continens partes tres. Principium: *In nomine domini dei mundi notam fac mihi uiam* Finis: *sedentibus in regione umbre mortis lux oriatur eis.*

> B.N. MS lat. 15973 ff. 1-228ᵛ, followed by table ff. 229-236ᵛ (s. xiii; Gerard of Abbeville; shelf-list 1321, P; Cat. 1338, LII, 4, *cathenatus*; Delisle, 3: 62, 75). Moses Maimonides, trans. of Augustinus Iustinianus (Giustiniani). Printed Paris, 1520. See W. Kluxen, "Literargeschichtliches zum lateinischen Moses Maimonides," RTAM 21 (1954) 23-50.

3. Valerius Maximus de memorabilibus dictis et factis romanorum et exterarum gencium continens libros ix. Principium: *Urbis Rome exterarum gencium* Finis: *usque ad primum annum Iustini sub quo factus est episcopus fuerunt anni lxviii.*

This entry makes possible the identification of the Sorbonne Valerius as B.N. MS lat. 5839, s. xiii, which contains this work (inc. ... *exterarumque gencium...*), followed by three short biographical extracts concerning Simmachus, Fulgentius and Sidonius (f. 64^r−v) which bear this explicit. This manuscript is probably the one described in the only notice of this work in the Sorbonne catalogs, Cat. 1321, MS X.k. (Delisle, 3: 77, 87). Ed. C. Kempf (Teubner, 1888).

4. Dissuasio Valerii ad Rufinum ne ducat uxorem. Principium: *Loqui prohibeor et tacere non possum* Finis: *sed ne Horestem scripsisse uidear. Vale.*

   Probably B.N. MS lat. 16359 ff. 221-225 (s. xiii; Cat. 1275, no. 20; Cat. 1338, XXXVII, 11; Delisle, 3: 38), also probably used for II. AUGUSTINUS 105, and XI. DAMASCENUS 3; or perhaps the text of this work in Cat. 1338, LIII, 14, "epistola Valerii," Delisle, 3: 63. Attributed to Walter Map. PL 30: 254-261; ed. M. R. James, *Anecdota Oxoniensis* 4, Medieval and Modern Series 14 (Oxford 1914) 143-158.

5. Macrobius de sompnio Sipionis. Principium: *Cum in Affricam uenissem* Finis: *philosophie continetur integritas.*

   Probably B.N. MS lat. 6367 ff. 4-59^v (s. xii ex.; Cat. 1321, MS P.b.; Cat. 1338, LII, 6, *cathenatus*; Delisle, 3: 62, 87), or perhaps the text of this work in Cat. 1338, LVI, 6; Delisle, 3: 67. Ed. I. Willis (Teubner, 1963).

XVII. LIBRI TULLII

   This list does not comprise a single codex, as do a number of the other lists in this work. Instead, it can be seen from the descriptions of the works of Cicero in the catalogs of 1321 and 1338 that this list was compiled from a number of manuscripts containing one or two works each. The manuscripts themselves are no longer among the Sorbonne codices, and many have not been identified. When there is more than one notice for a given work in the Sorbonne catalogs it is usually impossible to determine which one represents the manuscript that Thomas used; and in such cases the notices up to 1306 are listed in the order of their appearance.

1. Rethorica uetus libri duo. Principium primi: *Sepe et multum hoc mecum* Finis: *in secundo libro dicemus.* Principium secundi: *Crotomate quondam cum flo<rerent>* Finis: *In reliquis dicemus.*

   Probably Leiden, Bibliotheek der Rijksuniversiteit MS Voss. lat. Q.104 ff. 1-46 (s. xii², [Gerard of Abbeville]; Cat. 1338, LI, 11; Delisle, 3: 61), probably also used for no. 2 below. There were, however, other copies of this text available at the Sorbonne, including two other bequests by Abbeville, Cat. 1338, LI, 19 and LIII, 9; Delisle, 3: 61, 63. *De inventione.* Ed. E. Stroebel (Teubner 1915) 1-156; bk. 2, inc. *Crotoniatae...*.

2. Rethorica noua eiusdem libri vi. Principium: *Etsi negociis familiaribus* Finis: *diligencia consequemur exercitationis.*

Probably Voss. lat. Q.104 ff. 52ᵛ-102, used for no. 1 above. Pseudo-
Cicero. *De ratione dicendi ad C. Herennium.* Ed. F. Marx (Teubner 1894)
187-377.

3. De accusatione Ciceronis libri iiii. Principium: *Antequam de re* Finis:
    libertatis exarsimus.

    B.N. ᴍs lat. 6602 ff. 48-49 (s. xiii, [Gerard of Abbeville]; Cat. 1338, LI,
    25; Delisle, 3: 61), also used for no. 12 below. *Orationes in M. Antonium
    Philippicae.* The text of the Philippics in this manuscript is a member of
    the c family which contains only bks. 1-4. Ed. A. Klotz and F. Schoell
    (Teubner 1918) 128-229.

4. De amicitia. Principium: *Quintus Mucius augur* Finis: *nihil prestabilius
    esse putetis.*

    Appears in Cat. 1338, LI, 3 (Gerard of Abbeville) and 19 (Gerard of
    Abbeville); LIII, 14; Cat. 1321, ᴍs Z.m.; Delisle, 3: 61, 63, 87. Ed. C. F.
    W. Mueller (Teubner 1898) 162-196; exp. ... *nihil amicitia praestabilius
    putetis.*

5. De officiis libri iii. Principium: *Quamquam te Marche* Finis: *precep-
    tisque letabere.*

    Appears in Cat. 1338, LI, 3 (Gerard of Abbeville); Cat. 1321, ᴍs Z.m.;
    and Vatican, ᴍs Reg. lat. 1623 (s. xiii; Gerard of Abbeville; Cat. 1338,
    LI, 24); B.N. ᴍs lat. 15449 ff. 271-291 (s. xiii; Cat. 1321, ᴍs X.b.), not
    used; Delisle: 3: 61, 87. Ed. C. Atzert (Teubner 1963) 1-123.

6. De senectute. Principium: *O Tite si quid ego* Finis: *experti probare
    possitis.*

    Appears in Cat. 1338, LI, 3 (Gerard of Abbeville); and B.N. ᴍs lat.
    16203 ff. 59-77ᵛ (s. xiii, John of Mitri; Cat. 1338, LI, 31); Delisle, 3: 61.
    Ed. C. F. W. Mueller (Teubner 1898) 131-162.

7. Dispositiones eiusdem libri v. Principium: *Non eram nescius Brute*
    Finis: *perreximus omnes.*

    Probably supplied from the text in Cat. 1321, ᴍs P.l.; Delisle, 3: 87,
    which is the only notice of this work at the Sorbonne. *De finibus bonorum
    et malorum libri quinque.* Ed. T. Schiche (Teubner 1915).

8. De natura deorum uel de deo Socratis libri iii. Principium: *Quam multe
    res philosophice* Finis: *similitudinem uideretur esse propensior.*

    Probably supplied from the text in Cat. 1321, ᴍs Z.n., Delisle, 3: 87,
    which is the only notice of this work at the Sorbonne. Ed. W. Ax (Teub-
    ner 1961), inc. *Cum multae res in philosophia....*

9. De uniuersalitate. Principium: *Multa sunt a nobis* Finis: *neque dabitur,*
    uel *non est finis.*

    Probably supplied from the text in Cat. 1321, ᴍs P.l., Delisle, 3: 87,
    which is the only notice of this work at the Sorbonne. The second explicit

may be that of another manuscript. *Timaeus*. Ed. W. Ax (Teubner 1938) 154-187.

10. De paradoxis liber unus. Principium: *Animaduerte o Brute* Finis: *pauperes estimandi sunt.*

   Appears in Cat. 1338, LI, 3 (Gerard of Abbeville); Cat. 1321, MS Z.b.; B.N. MS lat. 15449 ff. 268ᵛ-271, not used; Delisle, 3: 61, 87. Ed. O. Plasberg (Teubner 1908) 1-26; inc. *Animaduerti Brute...*, exp. *... existimandi....*

11. De diuinatione et fato. Principium: *Vetus opinio est* Finis: *si uolunt omnibus naturaliter.*

   Probably supplied from the text in Cat. 1338, LI, 26; Delisle, 3: 61, which is the only notice of these works at the Sorbonne. Ed. W. Ax (Teubner 1938) 1-129, 130-152.

12. Catelinarius qui dicitur philosophia eiusdem continens libros iiii. Principium: *Quo usque tandem abutere* Finis: *prestare possit.*

   B.N. MS lat. 6602 ff. 99-124, used for no. 3 above. Ed. P. Reis (Teubner 1933) 5-68.

13. Epistolarum eius liber unus. Principium: *M. Cicero salutem* Finis: *impediendi moram.*

   Probably supplied from the text in Cat. 1338, LI, 28 (Gerard of Abbeville); Delisle, 3: 61, which is the only notice of this work at the Sorbonne. The explicit indicates that it belongs to that family of manuscripts which contain bks. 1-8 only, which is represented in the stemma by B.N. MS lat. 17812 ff. 51-91ᵛ s. xii (M). *Epistolae ad familiares*, to lib. 8 ep. 8 ¶ 6. Ed. H. Sjögren (Teubner 1925) 5-247.

XVIII. LIBRI BOECII

1. Boecius de trinitate libri iii. Principium: *Inuestigatio nobis* Finis: *omnium bonorum causa perscribit.* Et super hoc commentum Porretani.

   B.N. MS lat. 15734 ff. 59-64, inc. *Inuestigatam nobis...*, easily misread in this manuscript for *Inuestigatio...* (also used for XIII. RICARDUS 1, and probably for RICARDUS 11, VIII. ISIDORUS 3, and XIV. HUGO 33). The reference to the commentary of Gilbert of Poitiers could have been supplied from any one of a number of manuscripts, e.g., B.N. MS lat. 16371 ff. 188-284ᵛ (also used for IV. HIERONYMUS 1-7, 9-13, 18), or B.N. MS lat. 16341 ff. 1-78 (s. xiii; Gerard of Abbeville). *Opuscula sacra*. Ed. H. F. Stewart and E. K. Rand (London 1918), inc. *Inuestigatam diutissime questionum, quantum nostrae...* The commentary is printed, PL 64: 1255-1300, 1301-1310, 1313-1334, 1353-1412.

2. Boecius de diffinitionibus liber unus. Principium: *Dicendi ac disponendi prima semper oratio* Finis: *et omnia et satis esse dixi.*

   The manuscript cannot be distinguished with certainty from among the following: Cat. 1321, MS AB.h.; Bern, Burgerbibliothek MS 300 ff. 43-48ᵛ, without title and incomplete (s. xi-xii; Laurence of Quesnes; Cat. 1338, XLVI, 8); the work also appeared in Cat. 1338, LI, 27 (Gerard of Abbeville), if this is the manuscript described in Richard de Fournival's *Biblionomia* no. 17; Delisle, 2: 525, 3: 57, 61, 87. Marius Victorinus; see *Clavis Patrum* 94. Ed. T. Stangl, *Tulliana et Mario-Victoriana* (Munich 1888) 17-48, inc. ... *ac disputandi...,* exp. ... *et omnia et singula satis esse duxi.*

3. Boecius de consolatione libri v. Principium: *Carmina que quondam* Finis: *iudicis cuncta cernentis.*

The manuscript used cannot be distinguished with certainty from among the following: Cat. 1338, XXXVIII, 7 (Gerard of Rheims); LI, 8 (perhaps Gerard of Abbeville), 12 (Robert de Sorbon), 13, 20, 21, 33 (Godfrey of Fontaines). B.N. MS lat. 16094 (s. xiii; probably Cat. 1321, MS C.b.), not used. Delisle, 3: 41, 61-62, 86. PL 63: 581-862; ed. Bieler, CC, 94 (1957).

4. Boecius de disciplina scolarium libri iii. Principium: *Vestra nouit intentio* Finis: *inquinamenta permanebunt.*

Probably supplied from the text in Cat. 1338, XXXVIII, 9 (Gerard of Abbeville). However, the work also appears in Cat. 1338, XXXVII, 30; LIII, 46 (Peter of Limoges); B.N. MS lat. 16082 ff. 353-363 (s. xiii; Adenulf of Anagni; Cat. 1338, XLVII, 18); B.N. MS lat. 16089 ff. 39-50, s. xiii. Delisle, 3: 40-42, 59, 64. Spurious; see J. Porcher, "Le 'De disciplina scholarium'...," *Ecole nationale des chartes: Positions des thèses* (Paris 1921); and A. Steiner, "The Authorship of *De disciplina scholarium,*" *Speculum* 12 (1937) 81-84. PL 64: 1223-1238; ed. Olga Weijers, *Pseudo-Boèce De disciplina scolarium* (Leiden 1976).

XIX. LIBRI SENECE

Works 1-7 comprise B.N. MS lat. 15730 ff. 33ᵛ-153ᵛ (s. xiii; Simon Widelin; Cat. 1321, MS X.n.; Cat. 1338, XXXVIII, 2, *cathenatus*; Delisle, 3: 41, 87), also probably used for XIII. RICARDUS 1.

1. Epistole eius ad Paulum apostolum et e conuerso xiiii. Principium: *Credo tibi Paule* Finis: *ad deum istinc properantem.*

B.N. MS lat. 15730 ff. 33ᵛ-34ᵛ. Pseudo-Seneca. Ed. F. Haase (Teubner, 1897) 476-481; and C. W. Barlow, American Academy in Rome 10 (1938) 123-138.

2. Epistole eius ad Lucilium et e conuerso lxxxviii. Principium: *Ita fac mi Lucili* Finis: *ubique horenda ad hunc peruenire mansueta sunt.*

ff. 34ᵛ-97, exp. ... *Vale.* Ed. O. Hense (Teubner 1914) 1-330, and L. Reynolds (Oxford 1965) 1: 1-297; the explicit is that of ep. 85.

3. De beneficiis libri vii. Principium primi: *Inter multos ac uarios* Secundi:

Inspiciamus Liberalis Tercius: *Non referre graciam* Quartus: *Ex omnibus que tracta< uimus>* Quintus: *In prioribus libris* Sextus: *Quedam Liberalis* Septimus: *Bonum mi Liberalis* Finis totius: *hoc est magni animi dare et perdere.*

> ff. 97-136ᵛ. Ed. C. Hosius (Teubner 1914) 1-209.

4. De clemencia ad Neronem libri duo. Principium: *Scribere de clemencia* Finis: *quomodo in rectum praua flectantur.*

> ff. 136ᵛ-144. Ed. C. Hosius (Teubner 1914) 210-251.

5. De copia uerborum siue quatuor uirtutibus. Principium: *Quatuor uirtutes* Finis: *que per negligentiam sit.*

> ff. 144-149. Martin of Braga, *Formula honestae uitae* (PL 72: 23-51; ed. Barlow [New Haven 1950]), followed by the first paragraph of Seneca's second letter to Lucilius (ed. O. Hense [Teubner 1914] 3).

6. Rethorica eiusdem libri x. Principium: *Exigitis rem magis* Finis: *proditor malo inuentus.*

> ff. 149-153ᵛ. The manuscript has lost its final quire; the text ends, ... *circa declamaret apte et...*. Seneca Rhetor. The prefaces of bks. 1-4 and 7 of the *Controuersiae*. Ed. A. Kiessling (Teubner 1872) 57-67, 150-152 line 11, 241-247, 257-260, 292-295 line 21.

7. Ludus Senece. Principium: *Quid actum sit in celo* Finis: *in qua aliquis nenus esset.*

> This title appears as the last work in the contents list of B.N. MS lat. 15730 f. 1ᵛ, but the work has disappeared from the codex. Ed. F. Haase (Teubner 1898) 264-275. The explicit is that of a short passage from Seneca Rhetor's *Controuersiae* 2: 2, 12, inc. *Naso rogatus aliquando ab amicis suis ut tolleret...*, which was appended to the text. It is also appended to this work in B.N. MS lat. 8542 f. 188ʳ⁻ᵛ (s. xiii), from which it is cited here. See C. F. Russo, "Studii sulla divi Claudii Apokolokintosis," *La parola del passato: Rivista di studi classici* 2 (1946) 241-259.

8. De sentenciis diuersorum oratorum. Principium: *Deliberat Cicero* Finis: *nolite a me omnia exigere que scio.*

> This is the only description we have of the Sorbonne *Suasoriae* and *Controuersiae*. It may be the manuscript described in Richard de Fournival's *Biblionomia* no. 33 (Delisle, 2: 526), which bears this title and forms a separate codex with no. 6 above. Seneca Rhetor. *Suasoriae*, beginning with bk. 6 or bk. 7, followed by the *Controuersiae* ending a few lines short in bk. 10 c. 35. Ed. A. Kiessling (Teubner 1872) 34 or 49-515 line 19.

9. De consolacione filii sui ad Marciam. Principium: *Nisi te Marcia scirem* Finis: *qui ista iam non nouit.*

> *Dialogorum lib.* 6. Ed. E. Hermes (Teubner 1905) 151-194, and L. Reynolds (Oxford 1977) 129-166; exp. *... iam nouit.* Nos. 9-13, 17-19 contain the only description we have of the *Dialogues* at the Sorbonne.

They probably represent one manuscript, which may have also included the three short works in nos. 14-16.

10. De uita beata ad Gallicionem. Principium: *Viuere Gallio* Finis: *qui laudat nauigatorem.*
    Dial. 7 and 8. Ed. Hermes, 195-241, and Reynolds, 167-206; exp. ... *quamquam laudet navigationem.*

11. De tranquillitate animi ad Serenum. Principium: *Inquirenti michi in me* Finis: *id animum labentem.*
    Dial. 9. Ed. Hermes, 242-278, and Reynolds, 207-238.

12. De breuitate uite ad Paulinum. Principium: *Maior pars mortalium* Finis: *fremitus circumsonat.*
    Dial. 10 and 11. Ed. Hermes, 279-339, and Reynolds, 239-290.

13. De consolatione filii ad Helbiam matrem suam. Principium: *Sepe iam mater optima* Finis: *omnibus seculis.*
    Dial. 12. Ed. Hermes, 340-370, and Reynolds, 291-317.

14. De moribus. Principium: *Omne peccatum actio uoluntaria* Finis: *quicquid libuit licuit.*
    Appears in Cat. 1321, MS X.o.; and Cat. 1338, LII, 5; Delisle, 3: 62, 87. Spurious; see *Clavis Patrum* 1090. Ed. E. Wölfflin (Leipzig 1869) 136ff. The explicit is that of the Pseudo-Aristotelian *Enigmata* which often follows the *De moribus*, and which is printed by B. Hauréau, *Notices et Extraits* 33.1 (1890) 227-228.

15. De remediis fortuitorum. Principium: *Licet cunctorum* Finis: *quam domi sit ista felicitas.*
    Appears in Cat. 1321, MS X.o., and B.N. MS lat. 16364 ff. 242-244 (s. xiii; Cat. 1338, XXXVIII, 15); Delisle, 3: 42, 87. Pseudo-Seneca. Ed. Haase, 446-457.

16. De paupertate. Principium: *Honesta inquit Epicurus res est paupertas leta* Finis: *dant diuicie insolenciam.*
    Appears in Cat. 1321, MS X.o., and Cat. 1338, LII, 5; Delisle, 3: 62, 87. Spurious; see *Clavis Patrum* 1089. Ed. Haase, 458-461.

17. Liber eiusdem ad Lucilium cum mundus prouidencia regatur quare multa mala bonis uiris accidunt. Principium: *Quesisti a me Lucili* Finis: *quod tam cito fit timetis diu.*
    Dial. 1. Ed. Hermes, 1-20, and Reynolds, 1-17.

18. Liber eiusdem ad Serenum quomodo in sapientem nec iniuria nec contumelia cadit. Principium: *Tantum inter Stoycos Serene* Finis: *generis humani est.*
    Dial. 2. Ed. Hermes, 21-45, and Reynolds, 18-38.

19. Liber eiusdem ad Nouatum de ira libri iii. Principium primi: *Exegisti a me Nouate* Finis eiusdem: *nisi quod simul placidum.* Principium

secundi: *Primus liber Nouate* Finis: *non ira dominetur.* Principium tercii: *Quod maxime desideras* Finis: *immortalitas aderit.*
>   *Dial.* 3-5. Ed. Hermes, 46-150, and Reynolds, 39-128.

20. De naturalibus questionibus libri viii. Principium: *Grandinem hoc modo
    fieri si tibi affirmauero* Finis: *nec enim ulli flumini dulcior gustus.*
>   This is the only description we have of the Sorbonne manuscript of the
>   *Natural Questions.* It may be the manuscript described in Richard de
>   Fournival's *Biblionomia* no. 93. Another text, or extracts from one, may
>   be contained in Cat. 1338, LII, 14, *Seneca de naturalibus*; Delisle, 2: 530,
>   3: 63. Ed. A. Gercke (Teubner 1907); inc. p. 160, exp. p. 157. The
>   manuscripts in family φ of this text contain bks. 4b-7, 1-4a, in that order.

Index of Incipits
in the List of Authors and Works

Appendix 7

Catalog of the Manuscripts
of the *Manipulus florum*

Since this study has been written largely from the manuscripts of the *Manipulus florum*, it seems sensible to include a detailed description of them. This catalog was compiled on the basis of lists of manuscripts given in standard sources—Glorieux's *Répertoire des maîtres*, Ott's *Briefliteratur*, Stegmüller's *Repertorium biblicum*—and in the files of the Institut de recherche et d'histoire des textes, Paris; the Hill Monastic Manuscript Library, St. John's University; and those of the Royal Irish Historical Society, Dublin, largely the work of Ludwig Bieler who kindly sent us references to additional manuscripts. These complemented an extensive search of the catalogs. We have examined firsthand as many as possible of these manuscripts, with the generous assistance of the Service des prêts of the Bibliothèque nationale, Paris. Where this was impossible we have in many cases relied upon microfilm; the Hill Monastic Manuscript Library, the Institut de recherche et d'histoire des textes, and the Knights of Columbus Vatican Film Library at St. Louis University rendered valuable service here. Richard Marks, Mirella Ferrari and Stephanie Jefferis kindly provided us with descriptions of a number of manuscripts which we were unable to see. Finally, for specific details we have relied on questionnaires which for the most part received the considerate attention of a large number of librarians, to whom we are indebted. The quality of the descriptions of those manuscripts not seen by us naturally varies; and, inevitably, there remain a few manuscripts for which we have no information beyond the shelf-number.

Insofar as possible we have given for each manuscript four types of information: (1) the contents, including the rubrics and colophon of the *Manipulus florum*; (2) a physical description, including decoration, dimensions of the ruled space (and of the page), and specific features of the layout; (3) information concerning the provenance, including the second folio reference, marks of ownership, and any references in medieval catalogs; and (4) a reference to a printed description or reproduction when one exists. As a whole, the catalog provides a body of precise statistics regarding the format of one early fourteenth-century handbook as it was marketed in Paris, and as it was reshaped by later generations in England, Italy and Germany.

The physical appearance of those manuscripts of the *Manipulus florum* that were produced at the University of Paris in the first half of the fourteenth century is fairly uniform in size, layout and decoration. The opening initial A may vary in height from two to eight or more lines, but its decoration is standard: parted red and blue, usually with a cascade. Other elements of decoration and layout that appear almost without exception in the early Paris manuscripts of the *Manipulus* are also found frequently in later French manuscripts, and fairly frequently in the fourteenth-century English and German ones: (1) alternating red and blue secondary initials, virtually all with tendrils and many with filigree as well; (2) alternating red and blue paragraph marks; (3) running headlines, consisting usually of the initial letter of the subject-heading on each page, but occasionally consisting of the tituli themselves; and (4) the names of the authors noted in the margin, each beside the first quotation from a given author under each subject-heading. Many, though by no means most, of these early university manuscripts of the *Manipulus* bear as frontispiece an L-frame supporting hound and hare, or hounds and hares, often accompanied by a bird and occasionally by another beast or two. This was obviously a "set piece" of decoration available, for a price, at Paris shops throughout the fourteenth century.

The dimensions of the written or ruled space in the some forty manuscripts of the *Manipulus florum* written in or around Paris in the first half of the century vary little. The text is invariably written in two columns, within a ruled frame roughly 180×110 mm; the dimensions of the ruled space in more than half of the early Parisian manuscripts fall within a centimetre of this norm. Among those that fall outside this near-standard size are the only manuscripts of the *Manipulus* (of this time and place) that do not contain the "university stationers' edition" of the text—namely, B.N. MSS lat. 15986 (B) and 15985 (C), and Université MS 215 (D). Their exception serves to emphasize the uniformity of layout for those manuscripts of the *Manipulus florum* that stemmed from exemplars in *peciae*.

The "secundo folio," the initial word or words of the second folio of a manuscript, was frequently used in medieval library catalogs after ca. 1300 as a method of identifying the specific manuscript of a given text. We have, therefore, recorded the secundo folio for the majority of manuscripts listed here, with the hope that this information may provide clues to their provenance. While this was our original motive, we found that the index to the second folio references also provided an opportunity to see just how reliable—which is to say, how distinctive—the secundo folio is, as a means of positive identification. We conclude that it is good, but not perfect.

Though this conclusion is unlikely to startle anyone, nonetheless it contains a caveat that should not be ignored. In at least nine cases, the secundo folio gives one a choice of two manuscripts of the *Manipulus*—and in one instance a choice of three—rather than giving positive identification of a single one. We are dealing here with dozens of near-contemporary manuscripts of the same text—many of them, moreover, having been written on near-standard-size ruling. Perhaps as many as three-quarters of the manuscripts begin their second folios at some point within a rather small segment of text, which extends from the closing portion of the prologue through the sixth extract s.v. *Abstinentia* (the first subject-heading). Although it is not inevitable (as witness the near misses), it is also not surprising that occasionally two different scribes began the second folio with precisely the same words. Since this is so for the *Manipulus florum*, it is likely to prove true for other works produced in the same circumstances, that is, for works written in great numbers during a restricted time-period at a given university center. For medievalists, this merely implies that one may be reasonably, rather than absolutely, certain of the identification of a manuscript—of St. Thomas, say—on the basis of the secundo folio alone.

Were there, in fact, set formats employed for different types of books at specific times and places, before the invention of printing? This question can be answered only through systematic collection and comparison of data for specific works.[1] The manuscripts of the *Manipulus florum*, for their part, suggest that the Paris book trade of the early fourteenth century had a fairly well-defined conception of the "appropriate" size, layout and decoration of handbooks of this sort. This relatively standard format doubtless resulted in large part from the standard sizes in which parchment was sold, and from the commercialization of both parchment and book production.

Admont, Stiftsbibliothek MS 81, s. xv[1], Austria

ff. 1-127   Thomas of Ireland, *Manipulus florum*. ff. 1-2v, table. f. 3r-v, prologue, beg. "Abiit in agrum...." ff. 3v-221v, text. ff. 222-227, list of authors and works.
Parchment; 2 cols., 44 lines. 235×160 mm (330×240 mm); one hand, littera textualis hybrida. Initial (5 line) decorated with flowers and gold balls. Primary initials decorated; secondary initials and paragraph marks in red. Running headlines (A, B, c). Label inside front cover, "Manipulus florum; diversae sanctorum auctoritates." Bound in leather over boards, s. xv.
2ndo folio, *Modestia* (of text, *qui sic*). Belonged to Admont, O.S.A. MS seen on film.

---

[1] N. R. Ker, "The English Manuscripts of the *Moralia* of Gregory the Great," in *Kunsthistorische Forschungen Otto Pächts zu seinem 70. Geburtstag* (Salzburg 1972) 77-89, provides a good example.

Admont, Stiftsbibliothek MS 580, s. xiv^1, Austria.

Pt. I

ff. 2-46v   Eutropius, *Compendium historiae romanae* (index, ff. 24-46v)

f. 47r-v   Extracts on the properties of iron

ff. 48-53v   Sybilla, *Erithrea*, beg. "Exquiritis me o illustrissima...."

Pt. II

ff. 54-65v   Thomas of Ireland, *Manipulus florum*. f. 54r-v, prologue, beg.
               (rub.) "Incipit manipulus florum sive extractiones originalium a
               magistro Thoma de Hybernia. [text] Abiit in agrum...." ff. 56-
               65v, text; remainder of manuscript missing, breaks s.v. Angelus,
               "... nescivit qui scientem omnia... [*catchword*: sciunt. Grego-
               rius].

Pt. III

ff. 66-75v   Milianus de Spoleto, *Extractiones de libro ethicorum* (one-line
               sententiae in alphabetical order).

ff. 76-78v   *Interpretatio somniorum* (in alphabetical order).

Pt. IV

ff. 79-114v   *Tractatus de quatuor virtutibus cardinalibus* (table, ff. 111-114v).

ff. 115-130v   *Tractatus de lapidibus pretiosis.*

               Pt. II: Parchment; 2 cols., 49 lines; one quire of 12 leaves. Catch-
               words. 185 × 125 mm (250 × 165 mm), ruled in lead; one
               hand, littera textualis. Opening initial left blank (6 lines). Red
               initials and paragraph marks.

               2ndo folio, *nota* (pt. I), *mater sanitatis* (pt. II). Belonged to Ad-
               mont, O.S.A.

               MS seen on film.

Alba-Iulia, Biblioteca Batthyaneum MS III-32, s. xv^1, Germany

ff. 1-254v   Thomas of Ireland, *Manipulus florum*. ff. 1-2, prologue, beg.
               (rub.) "Incipit liber qui intitulatur manipulus florum con-
               scriptus et collectus ab quodam theologo. [text] Abiit in
               agrum...." ff. 2-254v, text, ends "... parentes o. etc. et sic est
               finis manipuli florum. Merces scriptoris gaudium perhennis (?)
               decoris." Followed by eight lines of added extract, beg. "Augu-
               stinus super illud Ps. 93, 'Numquid adheret tibi sedes iniqui-
               tatis': Sicut stellas..."; rest of page blank.

               Parchment; 2 cols., 30 lines. Quires mostly of 10 leaves.
               175 × 110 mm (222 × 145 mm), ruled in ink; three hands (i,
               ff. 1-36v; ii, 37-193; iii, 193v-254v), littera textualis and lit-
               tera currens. Initial (5 line) in red. Red secondary initials.
               Foliation in roman numerals. Bound in leather over pasteboard
               (s. xviii).

               2ndo folio, *etiam satiatus*. Brought from Vienna by the founder of
               the library, Cardinal Cristofor Migazzi (s. xviii).

               Robertus Szentiványi, *Catalogus concinnus librorum manuscrip-
               torum Bibliothecae Batthyányanae* (Szeged 1958) 197-198.

Angers, Bibliothèque municipale MS 325, s. xv, France

ff. 1-88v	Thomas of Ireland, *Manipulus florum.* ff. 1-86v, text, beg. "Augustinus. *Abstinencia.* Bonum est in cibo...," ends "... Explicit manipulus florum." ff. 87-88, table (in 3 cols.).
ff. 89-95v	Blank
ff. 96-109v	Fragment of an *exempla* collection, beg. "De quodam homine dicebatur quod...."
ff. 110-111v	Blank
ff. 112-115v	"Valerius, libro 3, ponit septem enigmata Aristotelis...."
ff. 115v-124	Seneca, *Declamationes*

Paper; ca. 35 long lines (ff. 1-88); quires of 16 leaves. 182×117 mm (218×144 mm), ruled (frame only); three hands (ff. 1-88, 96-109, 112-124), littera cursiva. Running headlines (ff. 1-88: A, B, C). Bound in half calf (s. xix).

2ndo folio, *Seneca. Malum.* Belonged to St-Aubin, O.S.B., Angers: "Ex libris monasterii S. Albini Andegavensis congregationis S. Maur."

Catalogue général des manuscrits des bibliothèques publiques de France: Départements 31 (Paris 1898) 309.

MS seen.

Arras, Bibliothèque municipale MS 305, s. xiv[1], France (Paris?)

Pt. I

ff. 1-63v	*Florilegium Gallicum* (prose authors)

Pt. II

ff. 64-81v	Thomas of Ireland, *Manipulus florum* (abbreviated). ff. 64-80, text, beg. "*Abstinencia.* Augustinus in quarta dominica de Adventu: Qui sic a criminibus..., Jeronimus ad Celancium: Quid prodest..., *Acceptio personarum..., Amicitia...*," ends "*Xpistus.* Bernardus in epistolis ... solempne gaudium manducare vita beata. Expliciunt auctoritates extracta a manipulo florum"; followed ff. 80-81 by further extracts. f. 81v, table (added s. xv-xvi).

Two MSS brought together at an unknown date. Pt. II: Parchment; 2 cols., 48 lines; quires of 6 leaves, with added leaves. 217×161 mm (280×208 mm), ruled in lead; one hand, littera textualis currens. Alternating red and blue initials (with tendrils) and paragraph marks. Bound in soft parchment.

2ndo folio, (Pt. I) *nec penitus,* (Pt. II) *magna virtus.* Pt. I belonged to Hellerus de Dury, doctor of theology, master of the Sorbonne and priest of St. Sulpice de Fairers in the diocese of Paris, 1354. Pts. I-II belonged to the abbey of St. Vaast, O.S.B., Arras, in 1628 (no. C 24).

Catalogue général des manuscrits des bibliothèques publiques des départements, 4° ser., 4 (Paris 1872) 126-127.

MS seen.

316 APPENDIX 7

Arras, Bibliothèque municipale MS 580, s. xiv, S. France.

ff. 2-212v   Thomas of Ireland, *Manipulus florum*. ff. 2-3, prologue, beg.
"Abiit in agrum...." ff. 3-205v, text. ff. 205v-206v, table,
ends "Hoc opus est compilatum a magistro Thoma de Hybernia, quondam socio de Sorbona. Deo gracias explicit." ff. 207-
212v, list of authors and works, upper half of final leaves
lacking; incomplete, ends "[Boethius, *De disciplina scholarium*] ... finis: inquinamenta permanebunt." Manuscript has
been burned; much of opening folio illegible; lacks the final 66
folios.

Parchment; 37 long lines; quires of ca. 10 leaves, with many leaves
cut out. Catchwords in decorated boxes. 195×127 mm
$(298 \times 225$ mm), ruled in ink; one hand, littera textualis. Initial
(9 line), spiky vine leaves on gold rectangular frame; alternating
red and blue initials (with tendrils) and paragraph marks.
Authors noted in marg. Upper portions of MS severely damaged.
Bound in parchment over boards.

2ndo folio, *sub]ticere ne collectio*. Arms (s. xv) on frame f. 2, tree
flanked by two birds argent (unidentified). Belonged to the abbey of St. Vaast, O.S.B., Arras, in 1628 (no. B 33).

*Catalogue général des manuscrits des bibliothèques publiques des
départements*, 4° ser., 4 (Paris 1872) 232.

MS seen.

Arras, Bibliothèque municipale MS 771 (1001), s. xiv¹, France (Paris)

ff. 1-280v   Thomas of Ireland, *Manipulus florum*. ff. 1-2, prologue, beg.
(rub.) "Incipit manipulus florum sive extractiones originalium
editus a magistro Thoma de Hibernia quondam socio de Sorbona. [text] Abiit in agrum...." ff. 2-271v, text, ends '... Explicit manipulus florum. Hoc opus est compilatum a M. Thoma
de Hybernia, quondam socio de Sorbona." ff. 271v-272v, table
(in 4 cols.). ff. 273-280v, list of authors and works, ends "...
dulcior gustus. Explicit ipsa secunda tabula." The final 107
folios of the manuscript are missing.

Parchment; 2 cols., 40 lines; quires of 8 leaves. Catchwords.
170×97 mm $(212 \times 145$ mm), ruled in ink; one hand, littera
textualis. Initial (6 line) parted with cascade; alternating red and
blue initials with tendrils. Running headlines (A, B, C). Authors
noted in marg. Pecia notes, ff. 96, 107, 112, 150v, 205. Bound
in soft parchment.

2ndo folio, *cognosci et*. Given by Master Enguerran *de Sancto
Furciano*, provost of the cathedral (s. xiv ex.), to the Celestines
of St-Antoine of Amiens: f. 1, "Magister Inguerranus de Sancto
Furciano prepositus ecclesie Ambianensis dedit hunc librum
huic monasterio Sancti Anthonii Celestinorum de Ambianis.
Orate pro eo"; f. 281, "Liber Sancti Anthonii Celestinorum de
Ambianis. In quo continentur manipulus florum. Item, tabula
quedam in qua ponitur numerus librorum cum principiis et

finibus eorundem originalium sanctorum ac doctorum." Belonged to the abbey of St. Vaast, o.s.b., Arras, in 1628 (no. A 165). *Catalogue général des manuscrits des bibliothèques publiques des départements*, 4° ser., 4 (Paris 1872) 308.

MS seen.

Assisi, Biblioteca comunale MS 244, s. xiv (before 1381), Italy (?)

ff. 1-168   Thomas of Ireland, *Manipulus florum*. f. 1r-v, prologue, beg. (rub.) "Incipit manipulus florum sive extractiones originalium a magistro Thoma de Hibernia quondam socio de Sorbona. [text] Abiit in agrum...." ff. 1v-162, text, ends "Explicit manipulus florum. Hoc opus est compilatum a magistro Thoma de Ybernia quondam socio de Sorbona." ff. 162v-163, table. ff. 163-168, list of authors and works, ends "... dulcior gustus. Explicit fructus totius libri."

Parchment; 2 cols., 50 lines; quires of 12 leaves. Catchwords; leaves signed. 237 × 155/160 mm (313 × 225 mm), ruled in lead; one hand, littera textualis. Initial (8 line) parted red and blue, with filigree. Alternating red and blue initials, with filigree. Running headlines. Medieval foliation in arabic numerals. Modern binding.

2ndo folio, *a licitis caute*. Belonged to the Convent of St. Francis in Assisi, no. LXIX in the catalog of 1381; L. Alessandri, *Inventario dell'antica biblioteca del S. Convento di S. Francesco...* (Assisi 1906) 16.

G. Mazzatinti and A. Sorbelli, *Inventari dei manoscritti delle biblioteche d'Italia* 4 (Forlì 1894) 61-62.

Augsburg, Staats- und Stadtbibliothek MS fol. 348, s. xv (1447), Germany

ff. 1-274v   Thomas of Ireland, *Manipulus florum*. f. 1r-v, prologue, beg. "Abiit in agrum...." ff. 1v-266v, text. ff. 266v-268, table. ff. 268-274v, list of authors and works, ends "Finitus est liber iste. In nomine Ihesu Christi. Scriptum per manus (!) Eucharii Sinknecht sub anno Domini MCCCCXLVII, sabbato die post festum sancti Laurencii martyris, hora quasi decima."

Paper; 2 cols., ca. 36 lines; quires of 10 and 14 leaves. Ca. 220 × 150 mm (295 × 210 mm), ruled in ink; written by Eucharius Sinknecht, littera cursiva. Red initial (3 line)

2ndo folio, *gaudium est*. Belonged to Sigismund Meisterlin; f. 274v, "... est fratris Sigismundi. Et iste liber est hosp... Sancti Valentini in Rüffach ... 1473." f. 1, "Iste ... est d. Sigismundi presbiteri in Lauttenbach comparatus de sola... in Br...bach." Belonged later to the monastery of Sts. Ulrich and Afra, o.s.b., no. 9 f 3; ex-libris note, f. 1. Bound in pigskin over boards.

R. Ruf, *Mittelalterliche Bibliothekskataloge* 3 (1932) 48; P. Braun, *Notitia historico-literaria de codicibus manuscriptis in bibliotheca ... ad SS. Udalricum et Afram Augustae extantibus* 4 (Augsburg 1793).

Barcelona, Biblioteca de Catalunya MS 656, s. XV, Catalonia?

ff. 2-287v   Thomas of Ireland, *Manipulus florum.* ff. 2-277, text (first folios lacking), beg. "[*Apostoli* af.] ... speculum adhibere ut generosi...," ends "... parentes o. Explicit manipulus florum." ff. 277-279, table (in 3 cols.). ff. 279-287v, list of authors and works; ends incomplete (s.n. Alanus, XV.7), "... confirmacio sed crisma. [*catchword*: De fide catholica]".

Paper; 2 cols., ca. 42 lines; quires of 12 leaves, signed. Ca. 220 × 165 mm (276 × 200 mm), ruled in dry point; several hands, littera cursiva.

2ndo folio missing.

Cincuenta años de la antigua Biblioteca de Cataluña (Barcelona 1968) 143.

Basel, Oeffentliche Bibliothek der Universität MS B IV 9, s. XIV (AD 1324), Germany

ff. 1-214   Thomas of Ireland, *Manipulus florum.* f. 1, prologue, beg. "Incipit manipulus florum. Abiit in agrum...." ff. 1v-213, text, ends "... Explicit manipulus florum. Hoc opus compilatum est a magistro Thoma de Ybernia quondam socio de Sarbona." ff. 213-214, table (in 4 cols.), ends "... Laus tibi sit Christe quoniam liber explicit iste. Explicit manipulus florum. Hoc opus compilatum est a magistro Thoma de Ybernia quondam socio de Sarbona."

Parchment; 2 cols., 38 lines. Catchwords; signed in roman numerals. 215 × 145 mm (295 × 200 mm), ruled in ink; one hand, littera textualis. Red initials and paragraph marks. Authors noted in marg. Late medieval binding rebacked (diamond crosshatch); chain mark, back board bottom; index tabs on fore edge.

2ndo folio, *doleant se.* At head of prologue, f. 1, "Sancti Spiritus assit nobis gratia." Written by William Zuremont, AD 1324: f. 214, "Anno Domini MCCCXXIIII in vigilia Epyphanie finitus est liber iste. Wilhelmus Zuremont sit semper crimine liber. Iste liber est Vallis Sancte Margarethe in minori Basilea ordinis Carthusiensium" (Carthusians of .Basel, fd. 1406). This is probably the MS referred to in the chronicle of Prior Albert Buer (d. 1439): "Procuravit filiis meis ipse manipulum florum"; *Basler Chroniken* 1 (Leipzig 1872) 291.

G. Meyer, M. Burckhardt, *Die mittelalterlichen Handschriften der Universitätsbibliothek Basel* 1 (Basel 1960) 330-333.

Basel, Oeffentliche Bibliothek der Universität MS B IX 23, s. XIII-XIV, Germany

Pt. I, s. XIII-XIV

ff. 1-4   Hugh of St. Victor, *Soliloquium de arrha animae*

f. 4   *Carmen de exhortatione poenitentiae*
Biblical and patristic excerpts
Iubilus

f. 4v   Hymn *Veni creator*
ff. 5-13   St. Bernard, *De diligendo Deo*
ff. 13-16v   Excerpts, including ones from a Thomas of Cîteaux and from St.
             Bernard
Pt. II, s. xiv (f. 17, s. xv)
ff. 17-49v   Thomas of Ireland, *Manipulus florum* (abbreviated). f. 17r-v,
             table (in 3 cols., added s. xv), beg. "Tabula in summulam
             sequentem imperfectam. *De abstinencia*...," ends "... *De peni-*
             tencia." ff. 18-49v, text, beg. "*De abstinencia*. Augustinus.
             Bonum est in cibo...," ends "[*De penitencia*.] Augustinus in
             libro de x cordis. Melior est modica ... quam eternum tor-
             mentum in visceribus."
ff. 50-68   Ps.-Augustine, *De spiritu et anima*
f. 68   Ps.-Cyprian, *De xii abusionibus* (beginning only)
f. 68v   Astrological excerpts
             Pt. II: Parchment; 2 cols., 41-43 lines; quire structure varies.
             Catchwords cropped. 132/143 × 105/110 mm (177 × 127
             mm); one hand, littera cursiva. Fifteenth-century binding.
             2ndo folio, *misericorditer* (Pt. I); *negocium ut* (Pt. II). Belonged to
             the Basel Carthusians (fd. 1406): ff. 1, 16v, 50, "Liber Cartu-
             siensium Basilee."
             G. Meyer, M. Burckhardt, *Die mittelalterlichen Handschriften der*
             Universitätsbibliothek Basel 2 (Basel 1966) 329-336.

Berlin, Deutsche Staatsbibliothek (now in the Preussischer Kulturbesitz) MS
          lat. theol. fol. 131 (Rose 514), s. xv², Germany

ff. 1-7   Thomas of Ireland, *Manipulus florum*. List of authors and works.
ff. 9-290   Jordan of Quedlinburg, *Sermones de tempore*; ff. 269-272, table
             of contents to the sermons; ff. 273-290, three additional ser-
             mons of Jordan. The sermons continue in two additional
             volumes, Berlin lat. theol. fol. 132-133; see below.
             Paper; 2 cols, 40-48 lines; quires of 12 leaves, signed. Dimensions
             of written space vary (205/210 × 50/60 mm), not ruled; three
             hands, littera bastarda (i, ff. 1-7; ii, 9-129; iii, 130-290).
             Opening initial left blank. Red secondary initials. Bound in
             leather over old boards; marks of 2 fore-edge clasps; 5 bosses.
             2ndo folio, *esse nobiscum*. f. 268, "Scriptum per Ioannem Tanner
             de Lypczk notarium publicum." Front pastedown, "Clemens
             Tasser de Ebern, presbyter, recepi ad fraternitatem vestram pure
             propter Deum venditor quatuor voluminum doctoris Iordani de
             tempore et de sanctis [including MSS lat. theol. fol. 132 and 133
             noted above] cupiens esse particeps omnium bonorum pro vinis
             et de fructibus." See S. Krämer, "Neue Nachrichten über die
             ehemalige Pfarrbibliothek von Ebern," *Mainfränkisches Jahr-*
             buch für Geschichte und Kunst 28 (1976) 36ff.
             V. Rose, *Verzeichniss der lateinischen Handschriften* 2 (Berlin
             1901) 387-391.

Berlin, Deutsche Staatsbibliothek (now in the Preussischer Kulturbesitz) MS
        lat. theol. fol. 150 (Rose 451), s. xiv[1], France (Paris?)

ff. 3-29   Henry of Ghent, *De sacra virginitate*
ff. 30-261v   Thomas of Ireland, *Manipulus florum*. f. 30, prologue, beg.
                (rub.) "Incipit manipulus florum sive extracciones originalium
                librorum a magistro Thoma de Ybernia quondam socio de Sar-
                bona. [text] Abiit in agrum...." ff. 30v-254, text. ff. 254v-
                255v, table (in 4 cols.). ff. 256-261v, list of authors and
                works.
                Parchment; 2 cols., 44 lines; quires of 6 leaves. Catchwords.
                173 × 106 mm (252 × 168 mm), ruled in ink; one hand, littera
                textualis. Gold initial (6 line) with L-frame supporting grey-
                hound chasing a stag; two additional gold initials; alternating
                red and blue minor initials, parted with filigree. Running head-
                lines (A, B, C). Authors noted in marg. Bound in leather over
                boards.
                2ndo folio, *pauper de.*
                V. Rose, *Verzeichniss der lateinischen Handschriften* 2 (Berlin
                1901) 302-304.
                MS seen on film.

Berlin, Deutsche Staatsbibliothek (now in the Preussischer Kulturbesitz) MS
        lat. theol. fol. 239 (Rose 450), s. xiv (ca. 1384), Ger-
        many

ff. 1-231   Thomas of Ireland, *Manipulus florum*. f. 1, prologue, beg. (rub.)
                "Incipit tabula originalium sive manipulus florum secundum or-
                dinem alphabeti extracta a libris xxxvi actorum edita a magistro
                Thoma Ybernico quondam socio de Cerbona Parisiensis villa.
                [text] Abiit in agrum...." ff. 1-231v, text, ends "Explicit mani-
                pulus florum compilatus a magistro Thoma de Ybernia opido
                (!) socio de Cerbona et incepit Galensis istam tabulam et
                magister Thomas finivit."
                [Guido de Columna, *Historia de destructione Troie*, now missing,
                recorded in this position in the table of contents, s. xv]
ff. 232-286v   *Gesta Romanorum*
ff. 286v-289v   Robert Holcot, *Moralitates* cc. 1-6
ff. 290-320   Jacobus de Cessolis, *De ludo scaccorum*, with alphabetical subject
                index, ff. 315-320
ff. 321-343v   Vegetius, *De re militari*, epitome
                Paper; 2 cols., ca. 46 lines; quires of 12 leaves. Catchwords.
                220 × ca. 155 mm (286 × 212 mm), ruled (frame only); several
                hands, littera bastarda (i, ff. 1-24; ii, 25-56; iii, 57-195; iv,
                196-231; v, 232-289; vi, 290-320; vii, 321-343). Initial
                (5 line). Red secondary initials. Bound in leather over old
                boards, restored 1962.
                2ndo folio, *est proprius gradus.* The last work was written by
                Gerhard Borkenhagen in 1384, in Lübeck (Lebus: Rose);

f. 343v, "Scriptus per Gherardum Borkenhagen clericum Caminensis dyocesis, anno Domini MCCCLXXXIIII, in civitate Lubic'." The front pastedown is a leaf from a s. xii calendar (July and August), on which a later hand has entered at VIIII kal. Sept. "Bernardus confessus," suggesting that the leaf and thus the book may have belonged to a Franciscan house.

V. Rose, *Verzeichniss der lateinischen Handschriften* 2 (Berlin 1901) 300-302.

Berlin, Deutsche Staatsbibliothek (now in the Preussischer Kulturbesitz) MS lat. theol. qu. 17 (Rose 449), s. xiv¹, Germany

ff. 1-289   Thomas of Ireland, *Manipulus florum.* f. 1, prologue, beg. "Incipit manipulus florum. Abiit in agrum...." ff. 1v-287, text, ends "... Explicit manipulus florum compilatus a magistro Thoma de Hybernia quondam socio de Serbona et incepit frater Iohannes Galensis ordinis fratrum minorum doctor in theoloya istam tabulam et magister Thomas finivit." ff. 287-289, table.

Parchment; 2 cols., 34 lines; quires of 6 leaves. 130 × 80 mm (188 × 125 mm), ruled in ink; one hand, littera textualis formata. Initial (8 line) with filigree and L-frame; alternating red and blue initials (with cascade and tendrils) and paragraph marks. Running headlines (A, B, C). Authors noted in marg. Nineteenth-century binding.

2ndo folio, *subti]cere ne collectio.* On cover and f. 1 (s. xvii), "Sub custodia fratris Antonii Rhe Hammonensis," and on the last leaf (s. xvii), "Fratris Hantonii."

V. Rose, *Verzeichniss der lateinischen Handschriften* 2 (Berlin 1901) 300.

MS seen on film.

Braunschweig, Stadtbibliothek MS 65, s. xv¹, Germany

ff. 1-247   Thomas of Ireland, *Manipulus florum.* f. 1r-v, prologue, beg. (rub.) "Incipit tabula originalium sive manipulus florum secundum ordinem alphabeti extracta a libri triginta sex auctorum edita a magistro Thoma de Ybernia quondam de Serbona socio Parisiensis civitatis. [text] Abiit in agrum...." ff. 1v-2v, table (in 4 cols.). ff. 2v-237, text. ff. 237v-247, list of authors and works, ends "Et sic est finis huius opusculi...."

ff. 247v-299v   *Auctoritates Bibliae*

ff. 300-339   *Auctoritates decretorum*, beg. "Absconsa sapiencia...."

ff. 339v-342   Johannes Andreae, *Summula super quarto decretalium*

f. 342v   *Modus allegandi locos decretalium*, beg. "Notandum quod quelibet questio...."

f. 343r-v   Sermon *De regeneratione*, beg. "Expurgate vetus fermentum...."

Paper; 46-51 long lines; quires of 12 leaves. Catchwords. Ca. 231 × 161 mm (340 × 220 mm), ruled in ink (frame only); (ff. 1-247:) one hand, littera currens. Red initial (3 line). Red secondary initials. Medieval foliation in arabic numerals.

Leather over boards; boss mark; clasp marks; chain mark, back cover.

2ndo folio, *vomellis non.* Bought by Johann Gardeleghen in 1442 from Otto of Haghen; front pastedown, "Hunc librum emi Johannes Gardeleghen a domino Ottone de Haghen in festo Simonis et Jude apostolorum, anno MCCCCXLII, pro duabus marcis Stendal."

H. Nentwig, *Die mittelalterlichen Handschriften in der Stadtbibliothek zu Braunschweig* (Wolfenbüttel 1893) 45-46.

Bremen, Staatsbibliothek MS A 160, s. xv (1457), Germany

ff. 2-166   Thomas of Ireland, *Manipulus florum.* f. 2r-v, prologue, beg. (rub.) "Incipit manipulus florum sive extracciones originalium editus a magistro Thoma de Hybernia quondam socio de Sorbona. [text] Abiit in agrum...." ff. 2v-165v, text. ff. 165v-166, table.

ff. 167-200   Sermon *De conceptione B.V.*

ff. 201-231   A universal history, to the year 1450.

Paper; 2 cols, 47 lines. 241×148 mm (285×204 mm), ruled. 2ndo folio, *dives cito.* Ex-libris note, "Ex legato domini Egberti, vicarii in ...."

Brugge, Stadsbibliotheek MS 171, s. xiv[1], France (Paris)

ff. 1-244   Thomas of Ireland, *Manipulus florum.* ff. 1-235, text (first folio lacking), beg. "[*Abstinencia* c.] Quam suave michi subito...," ends "... Hoc opus compilatum a magistro Thoma de Ybernia quondam socio de Sorbona. Explicit manipulus florum." ff. 235-237v, table, ends "Finitum anno Domini MCCCVI, die veneris post Passionem apostolorum Petri et Pauli." ff. 237v-244, list of authors and works.

Parchment; 2 cols., 38 lines; quires of 12 leaves. Catchwords; leaves signed (a[1], a[2], a[3]). 193×127 mm (290×205 mm), ruled in ink; one hand, littera textualis. Initial with L-frame; alternating red and blue initials. Running headlines (A, B, C). Authors noted in marg. Pecia notes, ff. 3, 7, 11v, 13, 16, 19, 22v (75-pecia edition). Corrector's signature, f. 244: "Cor. per Robertum." Bound in calf over boards (like Brugge MS 59).

2ndo folio (present f. 1), *Quam suave.* Hymn or prayer to St. Anthony, f. 244. Belonged to the abbey of St. Mary of Ter Duinen, O.Cist.; f. 244, "Iste liber est ecclesie Beate Marie de Dunis...," and anathema.

A. de Poorter, *Catalogue des manuscrits de la bibliothèque publique de la ville de Bruges* (Gembloux 1934) 221-222.

MS seen.

Bruxelles, Bibliothèque royale MS 3672-3690 (Van den Gheyn no. 1503), s. xv (1410-1440), Low Countries

ff. 1-66v   Conrad of Soltau, Lectures *De fide catholica* completed at Heidelberg 19 April 1388 (see K. Krause, *Forschungen zur deutschen Geschichte* 19 [1879] 600-608); subject index, ff. 65-66v.

ff. 67-68v	blank
ff. 69-125v	Commentary on various biblical passages
ff. 126-127v	blank
ff. 128-132	*Epistola de fuga mundi*
f. 132r-v	Extracts
ff. 133-153	*Expositiones prologorum super libros biblie per literatum Britonem collecte*
ff. 153v-155	*Algorismus metrificatus*
ff. 155v-156	Poem on the year 1366
f. 156	Extracts from Bernard and Ambrose, and extracts in Flemish
ff. 157-160	*De horis canonicis*
f. 160	Extracts from *De erudicione religiosorum*
ff. 160v-166	Humbert of Romans, *Super regulam s. Augustini de laudibus caritatis* c. 13
ff. 167-168	Gerard Groot, two letters
ff. 168-170v	Extracts on spiritual and ascetic topics
ff. 171-172v	blank
ff. 173-178	Bulls of popes Eugenius, Martin v (dated 1433), Boniface ix
ff. 178-179	*Sermo in festo Visitationis*
ff. 179-180	*Questio cur natalicia sanctorum in leticia*
ff. 180v-186	Thomas of Ireland, *Manipulus florum*. List of authors and works.
ff. 186-187v	Bull of Pope Nicholas iv to the Order of Penitence
f. 188r-v	blank
ff. 189-194v	Henry of Hassia, *Speculum anime*

Paper (Briquet no. 6842, AD 1387-1402); 2 cols. Ca. 215×150 mm (295×202 mm); several hands, littera currens. Binding, s. xix.

2ndo folio, *articulus s[cil.] crede*. Belonged to the Augustinian canons of Bethlehem near Louvain; f. 1, "Liber monasterii de Bethleem prope Lovanium canonicorum regularium ordinis Sancti Augustini."

J. Van den Gheyn, *Catalogue des manuscrits de la Bibliothèque royale de Belgique* 2 (Brussels 1902) 396-398.

MS seen.

Budapest, Egyetemi Könyvtár MS 90, s. xv (before 1439), Poland

f. 1	flyleaf containing extracts from David of Augusta, *De regula honeste vite*
ff. 2-56	Conrad of Soltau, *Glossa in psalterium*
ff. 56v-60v	David of Augusta, *Instructio novitiorum*; cf. ff. 176v-178 below
ff. 61-173	Thomas of Ireland, *Manipulus florum*. f. 61r-v, prologue, beg. "Abiit in agrum...." ff. 61v-172, text; incomplete, ends "... tractans illud Mathei Jugum meum suave est. Ubi adventus animarum etc." ff. 172v-173, table.
ff. 173v-175	Extracts *De luxuria*
ff. 175v-176	blank

ff. 176v-178   Conclusion of David of Augusta, *Instructio novitiorum* (above)

ff. 179-190v   Thomas Aquinas, *De duobus preceptis caritatis et decem legis preceptis*

Paper; 2 cols; quires of 12 leaves. 235 × 165 mm (309 × 218 mm); one hand, littera currens. Red initials.

Bequeathed in 1439 by Nicholas Czipser of Cracow to the Carthusians of *Lechnicz*; front pastedown, "Dominus Nicolaus Czipser altarista ecclesie Beate Virginis in Cracovie legavit librum presentem venerabilibus patribus dominis Carthusiensibus in Lechnicz, qui obiit in vigilia Corporis Christi, alias in die sancti Erasmi tercie mensis juni, anno Domini MCCCCXXX nono."

L. Mezey, *Codices latini medii aevi* (Budapest 1961) 154-155.

Budapest, Egyetemi Könyvtár MS 92, s. xv¹, Poland

ff. 2-6   *Augustinus ad Probam*
ff. 6v-15   *Pelagius ad viduam*
ff. 15-17   Ps. Augustine, *De contemptu mundi*
ff. 17v-19   Ps. Augustine, *De speculo anime*
ff. 19-40   Ps. Augustine, *Soliloquium anime ad Deum*
ff. 40-41   Ps. Maximus Taurinensis, *Sermo de adventu Domini*
ff. 41-42   Ps. Augustine, *Sermo de adventu et nativitate Domini cum questionibus contra Iudeos*
ff. 42-44   Paul the Deacon, *Homilia XII*
ff. 44-51   *Adalgarius ad Hrodsuindam reclusam*
ff. 51-55v   William of St-Thierry, *De domo conscientie*
ff. 55v-57v   Anselm, *Meditatio I*
ff. 58-61v   blank
ff. 62-130v   William of Auvergne, *Rhetorica divinalis*
ff. 131-148   *Tractatus de novissimis* or *Cordiale*
f. 149r-v   Bonaventure, *Soliloquium*, extract
ff. 150-261v   Carthusian customal, 1259-1368
ff. 262-344v   Thomas of Ireland, *Manipulus florum*. Prologue, text; incomplete, ends s.v. *Gaudium*, "... interius cautiores reddunt. [*catchword*: Ibidem]"
ff. 345-356   Isidore, *De summo bono*

Paper; 2 cols; quires mostly of 12 leaves. Catchwords. 225 × 150 mm (308 × 210 mm); three hands, littera currens. Red and blue initials.

Bequeathed by Johannes de Pnyowo, archdeacon of Cracow, to a Carthusian house; f. 1, "Liber Iohannis Pnyowski decretorum doctoris archidiaconi Cracoviensis legatus per eum testamentaliter fratribus Carthusiensibus anno Domini millesimo quadringentesimo septuagesimo sexto."

L. Mezey, *Codices latini medii aevi* (Budapest 1961) 156-159.

Budapest, Országos Széchényi Könyvtár MS lat. 74, s. xiv, Germany

ff. 1-37   Peregrinus, *Sermones de sanctis*, and a *Sermo de BMV*, f. 37
ff. 37v-40v   Ps. Anselm, *Dialogus de Beate Marie et de passione Domini*

ff. 40v-58v   *Sermones de domo Dei, sermones de BMV et Christi passione*
ff. 59-78   James of Genoa, *Legenda aurea*
f. 78r-v   *Sermo de quattuor thronis*
ff. 79-81v   *Orationes Domini*, from various patristic and scholastic authorities
ff. 82r-v,142r-v *Exposicio dominice orationis secundum Catholicon*
ff. 83-141v   Peregrinus, *Sermones dominicales*
ff. 143-144v   blank
ff. 145-147   Thomas of Ireland, *Manipulus florum*. ff. 145-146v, partial list of
                       authors and works (Alcuin-Seneca), beg. "Libri Alquini et
                       Alani...," ends "... dulcior gustus. Amen." ff. 146v-147,
                       prologue, ends "... sitim conatur extinguere."
ff. 147-160v   Patristic extract
ff. 160v-162   *Nota casus de sacramentis ipsius Christi*
ff. 162-163v   *Octo species turpitudinis*
ff. 164-188   *Questiones super sententiarum libros*
               Paper; 2 cols. 217 × 159 mm (294 × 220 mm); eight hands.
               Binding, s. xv.
               2ndo folio, *qui amicitiam.* f. 188, "Expliciunt questiones libri
               quarti sententiarum disputate a magistro sollempni lectore
               secundario fratrum minorum ordinis sancti Francisci Erfordie,
               scripte et finite per manum Alexandri de nullius villa, complete
               anno Domini millesimo trecentesimo quinquagesimo, sexta
               nonas februarii etc." Belonged to Nicholaus de Jankovich,
               s. xix.
               E. Bartoniek, *Codices latini medii aevi* (Budapest 1940) 62-64.

Budapest, Országos Széchényi Könyvtár MS lat. 196, s. xv, Bohemia
ff. 1-2v   Notes
ff. 3-6v   Thomas of Ireland, *Manipulus florum*. List of authors and works.
ff. 7-19   Books of the Bible, with first and last lines of each
f. 19v   blank
ff. 20-31v   Nicholas of Lyra, on the Psalms
ff. 32-34v   Extracts on the Psalms, from Jerome, Remigius, Cassiodorus,
               Gregory, etc.
ff. 35-153v   Psalms, with gloss
ff. 153v-155   *Canticum trium puerorum*
ff. 155v-156   blank
ff. 156v-157v *Expositio verborum psalmorum*
ff. 158-229v   Hymns, with commentary
ff. 230-241v   Livy, *Ab urbe condita*, pref., cc. 1-28.1
               Paper and parchment; long lines; quires of 12 leaves. Catchwords;
               signatures. 226 × 135 mm (316 × 217 mm); two or more
               hands. Binding, s. xv.
               2ndo folio, *finis retractare.*
               E. Bartoniek, *Codices latini medii aevi* (Budapest 1940) 155-157

Cambrai, Bibliothèque municipale MS 242, s. xiv, France
ff. 1-425   Thomas of Ireland, *Manipulus florum*. ff. 1-2, prologue, beg.
               (rub.) "Incipit tabula originalium sive manipulus florum secun-

dum ordinem alphabeti extracta a libris xxxvi auctorum edita a magistro Thoma Hibernico quondam socio de Sorbona Parisiensis civitatis. [text] Abiit in agrum...." ff. 2-421v, text, ends "... Explicit liber qui vocatur manipulus florum compilatus a magistro Thoma de Hybernia socio de Narbona [sic]." ff. 422-425, table

ff. 425v-426v   blank

Parchment; 25 long lines; quires of 8 leaves. Catchwords; quires signed in roman numerals. 176×90 mm (260×177 mm), ruled in ink and lead; one hand, littera textualis. Initial (5 line) parted with tendrils, cascade and roundels containing the names of the authors listed in the prologue; alternating red and blue initials (with tendrils) and paragraph marks. Running headlines (*Abstinencia*, etc.). Authors noted in marg. Medieval foliation with letters of the alphabet (a-z, ba, bb, bc, etc.) and roman numerals. Bound in brown calf.

2ndo folio, *Fulgentius*. Belonged to the chapter library (no. 88) of the cathedral of Cambrai.

Catalogue général des bibliothèques publiques de France: Départements 17 (Paris 1891) 81.

MS seen.

Cambridge, Corpus Christi College MS 518, s. xiv (1376)-xv[1], Germany

ff. 1-43	*Questiones Sentenciarum*
ff. 43v-64	*Meditaciones Augustini, De occultacione viciorum sub specie virtutum, Hugo de arra anime*, intermingled through misbinding
ff. 64-72	*Tractatus de quatuor instinccionibus*
f. 72v	blank
ff. 73-77	Anselm, *De commensuracione crucis*
ff. 77v-80	*Sermo de Spiritu Sancto*, in verse
ff. 80v-94v	Extracts (ff. 85-90r, 93-94r blank)
ff. 95-109v	Innocent IV, *De miseria humane conditionis*
ff. 109v-118v	Bernard, *Meditationes*
ff. 118v-124	Anselm, *Proslogion*
ff. 124-137v	Augustine, *Soliloquium*
ff. 138-140	Bernard, *De odore Christi*
f. 140v	blank
ff. 141-155	Ps.-Bonaventure, *Stimulus amoris*; and anonymous extracts
ff. 155-166	*Paradisus anime*
ff. 166v-169	Thomas of Ireland, *Manipulus florum*. List of authors and works
ff. 169v-170	blank
ff. 170v-172	*De laude Dei*
ff. 172v-176v	blank
ff. 177-188v	Unidentified theological tract (incomplete)

Paper; 2 cols., varying number of lines (ca. 77 lines, ff. 166v-169); quires mostly of 12 leaves. 233×147 mm (280×210 mm), ruled in ink (frame only); several hands, littera cursiva. Red initials. Table of contents, f. i[v] (refers to list on 166v-169 as "Multorum librorum initia et fines"). Bound in leather over boards; chain mark, front bottom center; 4 metal bosses; fore-edge tabs in pink leather; metal tabs projecting on fore-edge. 2ndo folio, *ad quod.* Probably belonged to the Brigittine monastery at Elbing, near Danzig; see James, vol. 1, xxvii-xxviii. f. 1v bottom (s. xvii), "Mary Pernham."

M. R. James, *A Descriptive Catalogue of the Manuscripts in the Library of Corpus Christi College Cambridge* 2 (Cambridge 1911) 469-471.

MS seen.

Cambridge, Gonville and Caius College MS 402, s. xiv, England

ff. 1-181v	Thomas of Ireland, *Manipulus florum.* f. 1r-v, prologue, beg. "Abiit in agrum...." ff. 1v-176v, text, ends "... parentes o. Hoc opus est compilatum a magistro Thoma de Ybernia quondam socio de Sorbona. Explicit manipulus florum." ff. 176v-177, table (in 6 cols.), ends "Finit anno Domini MCCCVI, die veneris post Passionem apostolorum Petri et Pauli." ff. 177v-181v, list of authors and works.
ff. 182-183v	blank
ff. 184-201	Table of St. Augustine, *De civitate Dei*, incomplete (Abel-Salomon), beg. "Abel qui interpretatur...."
ff. 201-203	blank
ff. 204-213v	*De meteoris*
ff. 214-219	*De arithmetica*
ff. 219v-246v	*Epistola Aristotelis ad Alexandrum de regimine dominorum*
ff. 247-255	Bede, *De imagine mundi*
ff. 255v-264v	Dares Frigius, *De excidio Troiani*
ff. 265-347	*De vitiis et virtutibus*, beg. "Dicturi de septem viciis primo...."
ff. 347-349	*Historia de crucis*
ff. 349v-359	*Testamenta duodecim patriarchum*

Fols. 1-181v: Parchment; 2 cols., ca. 50 lines; quires usually of 12 leaves. Catchwords in boxes. 170×105 mm (210×140 mm), ruled in lead and ink; two hands (i, ff. 1-148; ii, 148-181v), littera textualis. Initials and paragraph marks in red. Running headlines (A, B, C; tituli added). Authors noted in marg. Fol. iv^v, table of contents. Ff. 204-347, folio and column numbers. Bound in white leather over boards, rebacked; chain mark, front top center; 2 fore-edge clasp marks, ff. 1-4.

2ndo folio, *quia si consuetudinem.* Inscription erased, f. iii. Note, verso of last flyleaf: "Anno ab Incarnatione Domini millesimo CCCC^{mo} XXII obiit Henricus quartus in festo Michaelis iuxta festum Egidii abbatis."

M. R. James, *A Descriptive Catalogue of the Manuscripts in the Library of Gonville and Caius College* 2 (Cambridge 1908) 466-468.

MS seen.

Cambridge, Peterhouse MS 163, s. xiv[1], England

ff. 1-141   Thomas of Ireland, *Manipulus florum*. f. 1r-v, prologue, beg.
                   (rub.) "Incipit tabulula (!) originalium sive manipulus florum
                   secundum ordinem alphabeti extractus libris scilicet XXXVI auc-
                   torum editus a magistro Thoma Hybernico quondam socio de
                   Serbona. [text] Abiit in agrum...." ff. 1-136v, text, ends "...
                   parentes o. Explicit manipulus florum compilatus a magistro
                   Thoma de Hybernia quondam socio de Sorbona et incepit super
                   (!) Iohannes Galensis ordinis fratrum minorum doctor in
                   theologia istam tabulam et magister Thomas finivit." ff. 136v-
                   137, table (in 3 cols.). ff. 137-141, list of authors and works.
                   Parchment; 2 cols., 61 lines; quires of 12 leaves. Catchwords.
                   229 × 116 mm (290 × 195 mm), ruled in lead; one hand, littera
                   textuali. Initial (6 line) with blue and purple frame. Blue initials
                   with red tendrils, alternating red and blue paragraph marks.
                   Authors noted in marg. Medieval foliation. Bound in parch-
                   ment.
                   2ndo folio, *extenditur.* Belonged to Bury St. Edmunds, O.S.B.
                   (Bury pressmark M 4). Given to Peterhouse by John Wark-
                   worth.
                   M. R. James, *A Descriptive Catalogue of the Manuscripts in the
                   Library of Peterhouse* (Cambridge 1899) 191-192.
                   MS seen.

Cambridge, Peterhouse MS 164, s. xiv[1], England

ff. 1-208v   Thomas of Ireland, *Manipulus florum*. f. 1r-v, prologue, beg.
                   (rub.) "Incipit manipulus florum sive extracciones originalium
                   editis (!) a magistro Thoma de Hybernia quondam socio de
                   Sorbona. [text] Abiit in agrum...." ff. 1v-207, text, ends "Hoc
                   opus est compilatum a magistro Thoma de Hybernia quondam
                   socio de Sorbona. Explicit manipulus florum." ff. 207v-208v,
                   table (in 3 cols.)
                   Parchment; 2 cols., 45 lines; quires of 8 leaves. Catchwords;
                   leaves signed (a, ã, ã̃, ã̅). 185 × 100 mm (242 × 155 mm), ruled
                   in lead; one hand, littera textualis. Blue initials with red tendrils,
                   alternating red and blue paragraph marks. Running headlines.
                   Authors noted in marg. Bound in parchment.
                   2ndo folio, *abstinencia.*
                   M. R. James, *A Descriptive Catalogue of the Manuscripts in the
                   Library of Peterhouse* (Cambridge 1899) 192.
                   MS seen.

Cambridge, Peterhouse MS 268, s. xv, England

ff. 1-73v   Thomas of Ireland, *Manipulus florum* (abbreviated and in-
                   terpolated). Text, beg. "*Amor.* Augustinus. Nichil tam durum
                   atque ferreum...," ends "... castus esto in omnibus et salvus
                   eris. Amen. Explicit manipulus florum. Omne quod est nichil
                   est preter amare Deum." Each alphabetical section is followed
                   by a paragraph or two labeled *Narratio*, an extract from a hagio-

graphy or some other text usually regarding a saint whose name begins with that letter of the alphabet.

Parchment; 27 long lines; quires of 8 leaves. Catchwords; leaves signed (ai, aii, aiii). 100 × 70 mm (145 × 103 mm), ruled in lead (frame only); one hand, littera currens. Alternating red and blue initials. Authors underscored in red. Bound in parchment.

2ndo folio, *devo]cio introducit.* Belonged to John Fulwell, monk, treasurer and cellarer of Westminster Abbey (fl. 1508-1535); f. 76 (pastedown), "Johannes ffulwell monachus West[monasteriensis]"; see E. H. Pearce, *The Monks of Westminster* (Cambridge 1916) 181. Also f. 76, "Robertus Aflyn (?)." Belonged to Westminster Abbey; see N. R. Ker, *Medieval Libraries of Great Britain*, ed. 2 (1964) 196. Given to Peterhouse by 18 February 1716, by Master Osbaldeston, who also gave MS 276.

M. R. James, *A Descriptive Catalogue of the Manuscripts in the Library of Peterhouse* (Cambridge 1899) 340.

MS seen.

Cambridge, University Library MS Ff VI 35, s. xv, England

ff. 1-171   Thomas of Ireland, *Manipulus florum* (abbreviated). ff. 1-170, text, beg. (rub.) "Incipit tractatus breviter exceptus de libello qui dicitur manipulus florum. [text] Bonum est in cibo...," ends "... parentes o. Explicit tractatus breviter exceptus de libello qui dicitur manipulus florum." ff. 170v-171, table (in 5 cols.)

f. 171v   blank

ff. 172-200v   Alphabetical index to Scripture according to *Manipulus florum* headings, beg. (rub.) "Tractatus breviter exceptus de libro concordanciarum secundum titulos contentos in libro qui dicitur manipulus florum. [text] Abstinencia: Ecc. iii. Abstine te a lite..., Abusio..., Acceptio personarum...," ends "... carnalis estis. Explicit. Explicit tractatus breviter exceptus de libro concordanciarum secundum titulos contentos in libro qui dicitur manipulus florum, qui quidem liber cum dicto tractatu non modicum utilis erit collationem volenti facere vel sermonem."

Parchment; ff. 1-171, 30 long lines; ff. 172-200v, 2 cols., 32 lines; quires mostly of 8 leaves. Catchwords in red boxes. 126 × 83 mm (159 × 120 mm), ruled in ink (frame only); one hand, littera currens. Red initials and paragraph marks. Running headlines added (*Abstinencia*, etc.). Authors noted in marg. Rebacked, 1961.

2ndo folio, *rem bonam sine.*

A Catalogue of the Manuscripts preserved in the Library of the University of Cambridge 2 (Cambridge 1857) 537.

MS seen.

Cambridge, University Library MS Ii.VI.39, s. xii-xv (Pt. II: s. xv), England

A composite manuscript: ff. 1-4, 241-248, notes in various hands. Pt. I (ff. 5-66v), s. xiii; Pt. III (ff. 190-214), s. xiv; Pt. IV (ff. 218-240v), s. xii.

Pt. II

ff. 67-71   Thomas of Ireland, *Manipulus florum*; selected extracts from the first twelve tituli. beg. "*Abstinencia.* Bonum est in cibo...," ends s.v. *Amor*, "... amor non est."

ff. 71v-74   Richard Rolle, *A tretis of mayndenhod*

ff. 75-120v   Walter Hilton, *Cloud of Unknowing*

ff. 120v-122v   *A Sermoun of Seynt Austin*

ff. 122v-133   Richard of St-Victor, *Benjamin minor* in Middle English

ff. 133-157   Hugh, *De consciencia*

ff. 158-162   Ailred of Rievaulx, *De amicitia* (extract)

ff. 162v-163v   Bernard, *De dignitate sacerdotum*

ff. 163v-165   *Oratio Thome de Alquin* in Middle English

ff. 166-177   Albertano of Brescia, *Liber de doctrina dicendi et tacendi*

ff. 177v-188v   A dialogue between Adversity and Reason, in Middle English; incomplete

     Pt. II: Parchment; 30 long lines; quires of 8 leaves. Catchwords in boxes. 106 × 70 mm (190 × 130 mm), ruled in ink (frame only); two hands (i, ff. 67-174v; ii, 175-188v). Bound in half-leather in 2 vols. by Grey, Cambridge (1935).

     2ndo folio, *In prima* (Pt. I); *maximum* (Pt. II). f. 66v, "Petri Durant." f. 67, "Per Thomam Col[man?]."

     A Catalogue of the Manuscripts preserved in the Library of the University of Cambridge 3 (Cambridge 1858) 535-538.

     MS seen.

Chambéry, Bibliothèque municipale MS 25, s. xiv, France

ff. 3-202   Thomas of Ireland, *Manipulus florum. f. 3r-v, prologue, beg. (rub.) "Incipit manipulus florum sive extracciones originalium a magistro Thoma de Hybernia quondam socio de Sarbona. [text] Abiit in agrum...." ff. 3v-196, text, ends "Hoc opus est compilatum a magistro Thoma de Hybernia quondam socio de Sorbona. Explicit manipulus florum." ff. 196-197, table (in 4 cols., folio nos. added), ends "Finit anno Domini* MCCCVI, *die veneris post Passionem apostolorum Petri et Pauli." ff. 197v-202,* list of authors and works, with attempts at numbering individual works.

     Parchment; 2 cols, 45 lines; quires of 12 leaves. Catchwords in boxes. 179 × 108 mm (235 × 140 mm), ruled in lead; one hand, littera textualis. Initial (5 line) parted with filigree and cascade. Alternating red and blue initials (with tendrils) and paragraph marks. Authors noted in marg. Medieval foliation (top center recto) in arabic numerals. Bound in parchment over pasteboard; chainmark, f. 202 top center.

     2ndo folio, *libero ad.*

     Catalogue général des manuscrits des bibliothèques publiques de France: Départements 21 (Paris 1893) 207-208.

     MS seen.

Charleville, Bibliothèque municipale MS 10, s. xiv[1], France

ff. 1-178v   Thomas of Ireland, *Manipulus florum.* f. 1r-v, prologue, beg. (rub.) "Incipit manipulus florum sive extractiones originalium a magistro Thoma de Hybernia quondam socio de Sorbona. [text] Abiit in agrum...." ff. 1v-171, text, ends "... parentes o. Hoc opus est compilatum a magistro Thoma de Hybernia quondam socio de Sorbona. Explicit manipulus florum." ff. 171-172v, table (in 3 cols.), with references to subject numbers in red roman numerals in hand of the scribe. ff. 172v-178v, list of authors and works.

Parchment; 2 cols., 33 lines; quires usually of 12 leaves. 155 × 112 mm (209 × 152 mm), ruled in lead; one hand, littera textualis currens. Initial (7 line) parted red and brown with filigree. Red initials (with brown tendrils) and paragraph marks. Tituli numbered as running headlines.

2ndo folio, *necessariis non est.* Belonged to the Premonstratensian house in Belleval (no. 465); f. 1 (s. xviii), "Canonicorum S. Augustini Bellaevallensium." Last flyleaf contains a fifteenth-century French poem (printed in catalogue); f. 178v (s. xv), effaced, "De ... Johannis scripsit...," referring to the verses rather than to the MS.

Catalogue général des manuscrits des bibliothèques publiques des départements, 4⁰ ser., 5 (Paris 1879) 548.

MS seen.

Charleville, Bibliothèque municipale MS 38, s. xiv[1], France

ff. 1-234v   Thomas of Ireland, *Manipulus florum.* f. 1r-v, prologue, beg. (rub.) "Incipit manipulus florum sive extracciones originalium a magistro Thoma de Hybernia quondam socio de Sorbona. [text] Abiit in agrum...." ff. 1v-226, text, ends "Hoc opus est compilatum a Thoma de Hybernia quondam socio de Sorbona. Explicit manipulus florum." f. 227r-v, table (in 4 cols.). ff. 228-234v, list of authors and works.

Parchment; 2 cols., 42 lines; quires of 12 leaves. Leaves signed (Ai, Aii, Aiii). 182 × 115 mm (230 × 170 mm), ruled in lead; one hand, littera textualis. Historiated initial (9 line), Virgin and Child confronted by a supplicant in white robe; L-frame containing two greyhounds chasing two hares. Alternating red and blue initials (with tendrils) and paragraph marks. Tituli washed in yellow. Authors noted in marg. Bound in parchment over pasteboard.

2ndo folio, *quare extolleris.* Belonged to the Premonstratensian house at Belleval (no. 459); f. 1 (s. xviii), "Canonicorum S. Augustini B[ellaevalen]sium."

Catalogue général des manuscrits des bibliothèques publiques des départements, 4⁰ ser., 5 (Paris 1879) 560.

MS seen.

Cordoba, Biblioteca del Cabildo MS 37, s. XV

> Thomas of Ireland, *Manipulus florum*. Beg. (rub.) "Manipulus
> florum a magistro Thoma de Ybernia quondam socio de Sar-
> bona...."
> Innocent III, *Super canonem missae*
> Parchment.
> R. Beer, *Handschriftenschätze Spaniens* (Vienna 1894) 140.

Douai, Bibliothèque municipale MS 458, s. XV, France

ff. 1-205v
> Thomas of Ireland, *Manipulus florum*. f. 1r-v, prologue, beg.
> (rub.) "Incipit tabula originalium sive manipulus florum secun-
> dum ordinem alphabeti extracta a libris 36 auctorum, edicta a
> magistro Thoma Ybernico quondam socio de Sorbona Pari-
> siensis civitatis. [text] Abiit in agrum...." ff. 1v-197, text, ends
> "... parentes o. Hoc opus est compilatum a magistro Thoma de
> Hibernia quondam socio de Sorbona. Explicit manipulus
> florum. Deo gratias." ff. 197v-199, table. ff. 199v-205v, list
> of authors and works.

ff. 205v-206
> *Praecepta Pithagore.*
> Parchment and paper; 2 cols., 47 lines; quires of 12 leaves. Catch-
> words. 202 × 141 mm (300 × 210 mm), ruled (frame only); one
> hand, littera currens. Initials left unfinished. Authors noted in
> marg. Bound in calf over boards.
> 2ndo folio, *sunt et.* Belonged to the abbey of Anchin, O.S.B.
> (nos. G 331, D 475).
> *Catalogue général des manuscrits des bibliothèques publiques des
> départements*, 4° ser., 6 (Paris 1878) 269.
> MS seen.

Dublin, Trinity College MS 312, s. xiv², England

> A collection primarily of devotional works, including *De modo
> confessionis, De virtutibus et vitiis*, Hugo de Scotia *De otiositate
> hominis*, St. Basil *De vita feliciter regenda*, the apocryphal
> Gospel of the Infancy, a poem in OF on Tindal's Visions, a life
> of St. Margaret, and the hours of the Virgin and other offices
> (184 folios).

ff. 101-127
> Thomas of Ireland, *Manipulus florum*. Extracts, with tituli not in
> alphabetical order, beg. (rub.) "Hic incipiunt auctoritates
> cuiusdam libri qui dicitur manipulus florum. [text] De morte.
> Boni vocantur ante tempus...," followed by *De muliere, De
> luxuria, De peccato, De inferno*, etc.; ends s.v. *De conversatione*,
> "... estimatione prosequi valent. Valerianus Maximus de mira-
> bilibus."
> Parchment; 31-35 long lines; quires of varying lengths (4-14
> leaves). Catchwords; signatures. 170/200 × 110/135 mm
> (233 × 162 mm), ruled in lead; three or four hands, littera
> currens (i, ff. 4-144v; ii, 145-175; iii, 175-176; iv [= i?], 176-
> 184v). Red initial (2 line) with purple tendrils. Alternating red
> and blue initials with purple and red tendrils. Medieval foliation

in arabic numerals. Bound in calf over boards (ca. 1830); chain marks, last two leaves, bottom.

2ndo folio, *ut si VIII*; f. 1 bottom (s. xvi), "Cundale" (= Cundall, Yorkshire N.R.?). Belonged to Henry Savile of Banke (Yorks.), MS 82. Belonged to Archbishop James Ussher. See A. G. Watson, *Manuscripts of Henry Savile of Banke* (London 1969) 34.

T. K. Abbott, *Catalogue of the Manuscripts in the Library of Trinity College, Dublin* (Dublin 1900) 48.

El Escorial, MS F.II.18, s. xiv¹, Low Countries-England?

ff. 1-176v	James of Genoa, *Legenda aurea*
ff. 177-184v	Bonaventure, *Viduarum consolatio*
ff. 185-189	Thomas of Ireland, *De tribus punctis christiane religionis quos edidit magister Thomas le Roys commorans in Sorbona, anno MCCLXXXIX*
ff. 189v-206	Thomas of Ireland, *Manipulus florum*. ff. 189v-190, prologue, beg. "Abiit in agrum...." ff. 190-206, a short portion of the text, ends "... pro patre stantem, sine patre morientem. Bernardus super Cantica. Explicit manipulus florum."
ff. 206-208	Thomas Aquinas, *De articulis fidei*
f. 208v	Alphabetical list of saints in the *Legenda aurea* (see above)

Parchment; 2 cols., 48 lines. Ca. 220 × ca. 150 mm (280 × 180 mm), ruled in lead. Alternating red and blue initials.

2ndo folio, *ex parte*. Purchased in the Netherlands by Arias Montano in 1569.

G. Antolín, *Catálogo de los códices latinos de la Real biblioteca del Escorial* 2 (Madrid 1911) 172-184.

El Escorial, MS Q.III.11, s. xiv, France

ff. 1-227v	Thomas of Ireland, *Manipulus florum*. f. 1r-v, prologue, beg. (rub.) "Incipit tabula librorum originalium scilicet Augustini et sic de aliis qui sunt numero xxxvi auctores secundum ordinem alphabeti qui vocatur manipulus florum, edita a magistro Thoma de Ybernia quondam socio de Sarbona. [text] Abiit in agrum...." ff. 1v-219v, text, ends "... parentes o. Hoc opus est compilatum a magistro Thoma de Ybernia quondam socio de Sorbona. Explicit manipulus florum." ff. 219v-220v, table (in 3 cols.). ff. 221-227v, list of authors and works.
ff. 228-230	Extracts from Porphyry

Parchment; 2 cols., 38 lines; quires of 12 leaves. Catchwords. 177 × 120 mm (243 × 160 mm); one hand, littera textualis. Initial (6 line) in gold, with frame. Alternating red and blue initials (with tendrils) and paragraph marks. Running headlines (A, B, C). Authors noted in marg.

2ndo folio, *d. utantur divites*. Belonged to the library of the Conde-Duque de Olivares.

G. Antolín, *Catálogo de los códices latinos de la Real biblioteca del Escorial* 3 (Madrid 1913) 428.

MS seen on film.

Fermo, Biblioteca comunale MS 97, s. XV, Italy

A miscellany of extracts from ancient, patristic and medieval authors (257 folios), including two groups of extracts from the *Manipulus florum.*

ff. 93-140   Thomas of Ireland, *Manipulus florum.* Extracts, rearranged; beg. (mutilated) "[*Consideratio*] ... cessatione quod fuit quatenus attendens...," including extracts s.vv. *Consilium, Consolacio, Consuetudo, Contemplatio, Contemptus, Contricio, Conversatio, Conversio, Cor sive mens, Discretio, Cogitatio, Ascensio Domini, Auditor, Baptismus, Beatitudo, Bellum*, and concluding (from ca. f. 132?) with one or more lengthy excerpts from another source.

ff. 181-257v   Further extracts, beg. "Quedam abstractio de manipulo florum per fratrem Ob'. [from the prologue:] Flagilis (!) est memoria ... unde sumpta sint appareant. *De abstinencia.* Quam suave mihi...," ends s.v. *Gratitudo*, "... habui quia tu dedisti... (illeg.). Augustinus super illud psalmum *Custodi animam.*"

Paper; ca. 20-30 long lines; ca. 130×100 mm (ca. 150×110 mm); one hand, littera currens. Bound in parchment (1958).

2ndo folio, *dominus.* f. 147 upper margin, "Maestro Michelozo da Pietra pola, pantaleo de serra sardo (?)."

S. Prete, *I codici della Biblioteca comunale di Fermo* (Florence 1960) 135-144.

MS seen on film.

Firenze, Biblioteca Medicea Laurenziana MS Plut. XXXIV Sin. 4, s. xiv[1], France

ff. 1-112   Thomas of Ireland, *Manipulus florum.* f. 1, prologue, beg. "Abiit in agrum...." ff. 1-108, text, ends "Explicit manipulus florum compilatus a magistro Thoma de Hybernia cuidam (!) socio de Serbona." ff. 108v-109, table (in 3 cols.). ff. 109-112, list of authors and works.

Parchment; 2 cols., 64 lines; alternating quires of 14 and 10 leaves. Catchwords. 252×203 mm (332×233 mm), ruled in ink; one hand, littera textualis. Initial (10 line) with cascade and filigree. Alternating red and blue initials (with filigree) and paragraph marks. Running headlines (A, B, C). Authors noted in marg.

2ndo folio, *al. Ipsis enim.* Belonged to the convent of San Croce in Florence; ff. 1, 112, "Iste liber est ad usum fratris Sebastiani Ioannis de Bucellis de Florentia ordinis minorum, quem emit a Ioanne domini Laurentii Redulfis ducatos tres cum dimidio, quem assignavit armario Florentini conventus anno Domini MCCCCXLIV, die XX ianuarii."

A. Bandini, *Catalogus codicum latinorum Bibliothecae Mediceae Laurentianae* 4 (Florence 1777) 303-304.

MS seen on film.

Firenze, Biblioteca nazionale centrale MS conv. sopp. F III 570, s. xiv[1], France (Paris)

ff. 1-255v   Thomas of Ireland, *Manipulus florum.* f. 1r-v, prologue, beg. (rub.) "Incipit manipulus florum sive extractiones originalium a magistro Thoma de Hybernia compositus. [text] Abiit in agrum...." ff. 1v-247v, text, ends "... parentes o. Hoc opus compilatum a magistro Thoma de Hybernia quondam socio de Sarbona. Explicit manipulus florum." ff. 247v-248, table (in 4 cols.). ff. 248v-255, list of authors and works.

              Parchment; 2 cols., 39 lines; quires usually of 8 leaves. Catchwords in red boxes; leaves signed (*/, //, ///*). 190 × 116 mm (246 × 167 mm), ruled in lead; one hand, littera textualis. Frontispiece: frame supporting two greyhounds chasing hares, and bird. Primary initials with cascades; secondary initials in alternating red and blue (filigree and tendrils), and alternating red and blue paragraph marks. Running headlines (A, B, C). Authors noted in marg. Pecia marks (ff. 16, 23), from 75-pecia edition. Rebound in half leather; chain mark, f. 257v bottom center.

              2ndo folio, *vel quantum quis.* Pastedown (s. xiv, Italian hand): "Iste liber fuit fratris Michaelis de Pilestris...." Belonged to the Dominican convent of S. Maria Novella (1489); f. 248, "Conventus Sancte Marie Novelle de Florentia ordinis predicatorum"; see S. Orlandi, *La biblioteca di S. Maria Novella in Firenze dal sec. XIV al sec. XIX* (Florence 1952) 58, no. 572 (catalog of 1489). Fol. 256, " In xxv BB. ponatus in xx3 armario ex parte ortus."

              MS seen.

Firenze, Biblioteca nazionale centrale MS conv. sopp. I VI 12, s. xiv, Italy

ff. 1v-116   Thomas of Ireland, *Manipulus florum.* ff. 1v-2, prologue, beg. (rub.) "Incipit manipulus florum sive extractiones originalium a magistro scil. Booz [*sic*] Thoma de Hybernia quondam scolari de Sorbona. [text] Abiit in agrum...." ff. 2-112v, text, ends "... Explicit manipulus florum compilatus a magistro Thoma de Hybernia totio [*sic*] de Serbona et incepit Galensis ordinis minorum tabulam istam et magister Thomas finivit." ff. 112v-113, table (in 3 cols.). ff. 113-116, list of authors and works, ends "... dulcior gustus. Explicit manipulus florum, Deo gracias. Explicit, expliceat. Scriptor semper cum Domino vivat," followed by a repetition of the final entry in the list.

              Parchment; 2 cols., 54 lines; quires of 12 leaves. Catchwords in boxes. 240 × 160 mm (332 × 252 mm), ruled in lead; one hand, littera textualis. Alternating red and blue initials (with tendrils and filigree) and paragraph marks. Authors noted in marg.

              2ndo folio, *proprio. Nomen.* Belonged to the convent of San Marco in Florence (no. 828); see B. Ullman and P. Stadter, *The Public*

Library of Renaissance Florence, Medioevo e umanesimo 10 (Padua 1972) 244 no. 1019.

MS seen.

Frankfurt a/M., Stadt- und Universitätsbibliothek MS Leonh. 4, s. XV (1470), Germany (Amorbach)

ff. 2-237v   Thomas of Ireland, *Manipulus florum*. ff. 2-3, prologue, beg. "Abiit in agrum...." ff. 3-236, text, beg. (rub.) "Incipit manipulus florum editus a magistro Thoma de Hybernia socio in Zurbona ville Parisiensis ubi est collegium scolarium theologye sacre. Et finita est prefacio. Sequntur consequenter auctoritates diccionum incipiencium a littera A. [text] *Abstinencia.* Bonum est...," ends '... Explicit manipulus florum scriptus per me dominum Johannem Gerhardi de Seligenstat socium divinorum Amorbach in opido. Anno etc. MCCCCLXX, altera die post festum Katherine virginis et martiris." ff. 236-237 v, table (in 2 cols.).

f. 238r-v   Medical notes

f. 238v   Table of biblical lessons for the summer and autumn months. Paper; 50-57 long lines; quires mostly of 10 leaves. 245 × 150 mm (285 × 210 mm); one hand, littera bastarda. Red initials, paragraph marks and underlining. Leonhardstift binding (s. xix).

2ndo folio, *fer]tilem originalium non.* Written at Amorbach in 1470 by Johannes Gerhardi of Seligenstadt, who matriculated at the University of Erfurt in 1463. Belonged to the collegiate church of St. Leonhard; f. 2, "Ecclesiae collegiatae S. Leonardi" (AD 1673).

G. Powitz, *Kataloge der Stadt- und Universitätsbibliothek Frankfurt am Main* 2.1 (Frankfurt 1968) 440-441.

Frankfurt a/M., Stadt- und Universitätsbibliothek MS Praed. 17, s. XV (1459), Germany (Leipzig)

f. 1r-v   blank

ff. 2-216v   Five collections of extracts, each arranged alphabetically by topic. ff. 2-8, tables of contents to the collections. ff. 8v-12v, blank. ff. 13-36v, extracts from the O.T., beg. "*Abscondere.* Absconsa sapiencia thesaurus...." ff. 36v-70, extracts from the O. and N.T., beg. "*Adventus.* Ecce virgo concipiet...." ff. 70v-109v, extracts from the *Decretum*, beg. "*Abstinencia.* Abstinencia sanat quos...." ff. 110-137v, extracts from the *artes*, beg. "Accidencia esse interdum mixtim...." ff. 137v-216v, extracts from the *Decretum*, the decretals and the poets, beg. "*Abutens.* Abutens privilegio sibi concesso...."

ff. 217-222   Thomas of Ireland, *Manipulus florum*. List of authors and works.

ff. 222v-332 *Rosarium theologiae*, with alphabetical table ff. 331-332.

ff. 332v-338v blank

ff. 339-432   Nicholas of Hanapis, *Liber exemplorum sacre scripture*

Paper; 2 cols., 43-50 lines; quires of 12 leaves. Catchwords; signatures. 230/235 × 140/150 mm (310 × 215 mm); four hands (i, ff. 2-8, 331-332; ii, 13-216; iii, 217-330; iv, 339-432), littera bastarda cursiva. Red initials, paragraph marks and underscoring. Bound in pigskin over boards (s. xv).

2ndo folio, *29 Claudicare.* f. 330v, "Expliciunt distinctiones Gwidonis finite anno Domini MCCCCLIX in studio Lipczenzi." The volume is one of a group of books written at the University of Leipzig in the 1450s which passed to the Dominican house in Frankfurt; f. 13 (s. xvi), "Conventus Franckfordensis ordinis predicatorum."

G. Powitz, *Kataloge der Stadt- und Universitätsbibliothek Frankfurt am Main* 2.1 (Frankfurt 1968) 36-38.

Frankfurt a/M., Stadt- und Universitätsbibliothek MS Praed. 143, s. xv (1443), Germany (Augsburg)

ff. 2-252   Thomas of Ireland, *Manipulus florum.* f. 2r-v, prologue, beg. (rub.) "Incipit manipulus florum sive extracciones originalium a magistro Thoma de Ybernia quondam socio de Sorbona. [text] Abiit in agrum...." ff. 2v-243v, text, ends "Explicit manipulus florum scriptus in Augusta, anno Domini 1443 in crastino Sancti Jacobi expletus [*corr. from* completus]." ff. 243v-245, table. ff. 245-252, list of authors and works, ends "... dulcior gustus. Et sic est finis, Deo gracias."

ff. 252-254   Nicholas V, bull *Immensa et innumerabilia* (19 Jan. 1449), added
ff. 255-264   St. Bonaventure, *Lignum vite,* added
f. 265   "Tabulam libri manipulus florum nuncupati generalem quere quasi in fine. Abstinencia.... Residua quere retro" (s. xv ex.).

Paper; 2 cols., 47-51 lines; quires of 12 leaves. Catchwords. 155 × 90 mm (200 × 135 mm); one hand, Italian minuscule. Alternating red and blue initials. Stamped leather binding (s. xv).

2ndo folio, *utantur divites.* Written by Siegfried Enemer who also wrote MSS Praed. 9, 36, 41, 48, 68, 72, 153; he matriculated at Erfurt in 1425, was in Pavia in 1434, in Augsburg between 1438 and 1447, and a physician in Frankfurt 1452-1453. MS Praed. 143 passed with many of his books to the Frankfurt magistrate Georg von Breidenbach, who gave them to the Frankfurt Dominicans in 1491; ff. 2, 95, 243, "K 11. Fratrum predicatorum est Franckfordie. 1491."

G. Powitz, *Kataloge der Stadt- und Universitätsbibliothek Frankfurt am Main* 2.1 (Frankfurt 1968) 327-328.

Fulda, Bibliothek der bischöflichen Priesterseminars MS Fritzlar 10, s. xv, Germany

ff. 1-231   Thomas of Ireland, *Manipulus florum.* ff. 1r-v, prologue, beg. (rub.) "Incipit manipulus florum sive extractiones originalium a magistro Thoma de Hybernia quondam socio de Sorbona. [text]

Abiit in agrum...." ff. 1v-209, text, ends "... parentes o. Explicit manipulus florum, Deo gracias." ff. 209v-211v, table. ff. 212-215, list of authors and works in alphabetical order (Alanus-Valerius), ends "Amen." ff. 215v-231, additional table, consisting of the collected cross-references taken from the end of each entry, beg. "*Abstinencia.* Caro e.r., Coniugium c., Consuetudo c," ends "[*Xpus*] ... parentes o. Explicit." (Cf. similar table in Graz MS 1254.)

ff. 232-239   blank

Paper: 2 cols., 36-73 lines; quires of 12 leaves. Catchwords. 220 × 150 mm (307 × 220 mm), ruled in dry point; two hands, littera bastarda (i, ff. 1-96; ii, 97-231). Red initial (10 line). Red secondary initials. Running headlines. Bound in grey leather (s. xv).

2ndo folio, *quia nimirum tanto.* On front cover, "Ad liberariam dominorum [i.e., parochial library in Fritzlar] pro memoria Iohannis Swartz [priest of St. Peter's in Fritzlar]."

Gdańsk, Gdańska Polskiej Akademii Nauk MS 1984, s. xv[1], Germany

ff. 1-256   Thomas of Ireland, *Manipulus florum.* f. 1r-v, prologue, beg. "Abiit in agrum...." ff. 1v-256, text, ends "... parentes o. Gloria tibi Domine qui natus es de Virgine ... in sempiterna secula, amen."

Paper; 2 cols., 35-39 lines; quires of 12 leaves. 211/214 × 155/163 mm (290 × 220 mm), ruled in ink; one hand, littera currens. Red initial (6 line) with filigree and tendrils. Initials in red. Running headlines (A, B, C).

2ndo folio, *vel necesse.* Belonged to the Franciscan house in Gdańsk; label "P" on cover.

O. Günther, *Katalog der Handschriften der Danziger Stadtbibliothek* 3 (Gdańsk 1909) 132.

MS seen on film.

Göttweig, Stiftsbibliothek MS 134, s. xiv-xv, Austria

ff. 1-267v   Thomas of Ireland, *Manipulus florum.* ff. 1v-2, prologue, beg. "Abiit in agrum...." ff. 2-259, text, ends "... patiencia c." ff. 259-261, table, folio references added. ff. 261-267v, list of authors and works.

Parchment; 2 cols., 37 lines; quires of 10 leaves. Quires signed in roman numerals. 225 × 154 mm (312 × 225 mm), ruled in lead; one hand, littera textualis. Red initials. Running headlines (at the beginning only). Medieval foliation: A[1], A[2], A[3], B[1], etc.

2ndo folio, *qui sic se.* Belonged to the abbey of Göttweig, O.S.B., no. H 64. f. i, "Manipulus florum domini Throni Beate M... Cemmiko. Manipulus florum sive extractiones originalium editus a magistro Thoma de Hybernia quondam socio de Serbona."

MS seen on film.

Graz, Universitätsbibliothek MS 445, s. xiv-xv, Austria

ff. 1-221v   Thomas of Ireland, *Manipulus florum*. ff. 1r-v, prologue, beg. "Abiit in agrum...." ff. 1v-220, text. ff. 220v-221v, table (in 3 cols.), ends "Et sic est finis registri etc."

ff. 222-229v   blank

ff. 230-348v   John of Fayt, *Tabula moralium Aristotelis*
Paper; 2 cols., 46 lines. 216 × 144 mm (300 × 210 mm), ruled in ink (frame only); one hand, littera cursiva. Red initial (7 line). Primary initials in red (later initials left blank); secondary initials slashed. Authors noted in marg. Medieval foliation in arabic numerals, upper right. Bound in white leather over boards.
2ndo folio, *ut alias*. Belonged to Ulrich von Albeck, bishop of Verden (1407-1417), who gave it to the Augustinian canons of Seckau; f. 1, "Iste liber est domini Ulrici episcopi Verdensis" (s. xv in.). Seckau no. Trop. 42.
A. Kern, *Die Handschriften der Universitätsbibliothek Graz* 1 (Leipzig 1939) 256-257; B. Roth, *Aus mittelalterlichen Bibliotheken der Seckauer Bischöfe* (n.p. 1960) 16; G. Möser-Mersky, *Mittelalterliche Bibliothekskataloge Oesterreichs* 3 (Vienna 1961) 89.
MS seen on film.

Graz, Universitätsbibliothek MS 574, s. xv[1], Germany/Austria

ff. 1-265   Thomas of Ireland, *Manipulus florum*. f. 1r-v, prologue, beg. (rub.) "Incipit liber qui dicitur manipulus florum collectus ab originalibus xxxvi doctorum secundum ordinem alphabeti. [text] Abiit in agrum...." ff. 1v-265, text, ends "... paciencia c. etc. Et sic est finis, sit laus et gloria trinis."
Paper; 2 cols., 44 lines. 216/223 × 146/160 mm (300 × 210 mm), ruled in ink (frame only); one hand, littera currens. Initial (7 line) parted red and blue. Red initials. Running headlines (tituli). Bound in leather over medieval boards; 2 fore-edge straps.
2ndo folio, *corruerunt*. Belonged to the Cistercians of Neuberg, no. 75.
A. Kern, *Die Handschriften der Universitätsbibliothek Graz* 1 (Leipzig 1939) 334-335.
MS seen on film.

Graz, Universitätsbibliothek MS 746, s. xiv (1318), Austria

ff. 1-319   Thomas of Ireland, *Manipulus florum*. ff. 1-2, prologue, beg. (rub.) "Incipit manipulus florum sive extractiones originalium a magistro Thoma de Hybernia quondam scolari de Sorbona Parisiensi. [text] Abiit in agrum...." ff. 2-309v, text. ff. 309v-310v, table (in 4 cols.), ends "Finit anno Domini 1318, xv die kal. novembris" (18 October 1318). ff. 311-319, list of authors and works, ends "Explicit manipulus florum. [later hand:] Cum magna (?) difficultate complevit."

Parchment; 2 cols., 32 lines; quires of 10 leaves. Quires signed in roman numerals. 200 × 145 mm (300 × 210 mm), ruled in ink; one hand, littera textualis. Historiated gold initial (2 haloed figures). Alternating red and blue initials with tendrils. Authors noted in marg. Contemporary red leather binding.

2ndo folio, *ap*]*petere potest*. Belonged to the Cistercians of Neuberg, no. 144.

A. Kern, *Die Handschriften der Universitätsbibliothek Graz* 2 (Vienna 1956) 23.

MS seen on film.

Graz, Universitätsbibliothek MS 888, s. XV, Austria

ff. 1-180v   Thomas of Ireland, *Manipulus florum*, abbreviated and interpolated (copy of Graz MS 1254). ff. 1-154, text, beg. "*Abstinencia. Bonum...*," ends s.v. *Zelus*, "... honorat. Beda." f. 154v, "Explicit libellus ... completus. Laus resonet.... *Versus*... Nunc pagina...." ff. 155-177v, table (in 2 cols.), beg. "*Abstinencia. ubi Caro f....*" See MS 1254 for full description.

ff. 181-253v   Siboto Viennensis, *Super Ave Maria*

ff. 254-263   *Sermones de visitatione et de Assumptione BMV*

Paper; 33 long lines. 154/160 × 90/95 mm (220 × 150 mm), ruled in ink (frame only); one hand, littera currens. Contemporary dark brown leather binding with rules.

2ndo folio, *duodecimi sunt*. Belonged to the Cistercians of Neuberg, no. 264.

A. Kern, *Die Handschriften der Universitätsbibliothek Graz* 2 (Vienna 1956) 108.

MS seen on film.

Graz, Universitätsbibliothek MS 1254, s. XIV (1396), Austria

ff. 1-157   Thomas of Ireland, *Manipulus florum*, abbreviated and interpolated. f. 1, table (in 3 cols.), *Resurrectio-Xp̄istus*. ff. 1v-136v, text, beg. "Abstinencia. Bonum est...," ends s.v. *Zelus* (an interpolated section), "... et hos sue presencia virtutis honorat. Beda. Explicit libellus qui dicitur manipulus florum, non sine grandi labore collectus, et tandem adiutorio Christi et beatissime genitricis eius completus," followed by a verse, "Laus resonet Christum, libellum terminans istum / Et genitrix pia laudetur Virgo Maria / Subsidiis quorum explicit manipulus florum / (rub.) *Versus super tabulam huius opusculi*: Nunc pagina [*sic*] verte ibique videbus aperte / Tabulam...," 13 lines. f. 137 (= same text as f. 138), canceled. f. 137v, an explanation of the subsequent table, beg. "Ad habendam noticiam tabule subnotate scire debes, o lector, quod unaqueque auctoritas opusculi suprascripti designata est per litteram alphabeti. Ad inveniendam igitur cuiuslibet auctoritatis concordancia [*sic*] recursum habeas ad tabulam...." ff. 138-157, table (in 2 cols.) consisting of the cross-references, taken from the end of each entry in the text, collected here under the tituli; beg. "*Absti-*

nencia. ubi Caro f, Coniugium q, Consuetudo b c, Decima y, Discretio f.... *Abusio.* ubi Compassio m...," ends "Explicit tabula super manipulum florum."

ff. 157-160   Chrysostom, *Opus imperfectum in Matheum* hom. xv

f. 160r-v   Ps.-Augustine, *Sermo de defunctis*

ff. 160v-169   Office of Corpus Christi

ff. 169-176   *Collectae sanctorum* and calendar

ff. 176-180   Legends

f. 180   *Summa indulgenciarum monasterii Novimontis,* ends "Anno Domini 1396, in die sancti Thome de Aquino completus est libellus iste a fratre Andrea [Kurzmann] quondam cantore monasterii Novimontis ibique professo sub venerabili patre ac domino Jacobo abbate, quarto regiminis sui anno."

Paper; 31 long lines; quires of 12 leaves, signed (A, B, C). 158 × 95 mm (210 × 150 mm), ruled in ink; one hand, littera currens and littera textualis. Initials in red. Contemporary grey leather binding.

2ndo folio, *enervatur.* Written by Andreas Kurzmann, monk of Neuberg (d. 1428), who also wrote Graz Universitätsbibliothek MS 1253 (Gregory, *Regula pastoralis*) in 1403. See *Verfasserlexicon* 2 (Berlin 1936) cols. 1000-1001. Belonged to the Cistercians of Neuberg.

A. Kern, *Die Handschriften der Universitätsbibliothek Graz* 2 (Vienna 1956) 142, 144.

MS seen on film.

Halle, Universitäts- und Landesbibliothek MS Quedlinburg 215, s. xiv-xv (*Manipulus florum* ca. 1390-1400), Germany

A composite manuscript containing a theological miscellany (339 folios) of some 16 items—sermons, tracts, excerpts.

ff. 153v-175v   Thomas of Ireland, *Manipulus florum.* ff. 153v-174, text (extracts), beg. "*Abstinentia.* Bonum est in cibo...," ends s.v. *Xp̄ianus.* ff. 174v-175v, list of authors and works (abbreviated), beg. "Libri beati Augustini. De civitate Dei...," ends "Expliciunt excerpta manipuli florum, Deo gracias."

ff. 153v-175v: paper; 2 cols., ca. 71 lines. 255 × 175 mm (285 × 200 mm), unruled; one hand, littera bastarda. Red initials. Binding, s. xv ex.

2ndo folio, *distin]ctio ut dicebat.* Belonged to St. Benedicti-Kirche in Quedlinburg, s. xv in. Belonged to the canon Johannes Goebing, s. xv ex., who gave it to the canons of St. Servatius of Quedlinburg; f. i, "Ex testamento domini Johannis Goebing."

Hamburg, Staats- und Universitätsbibliothek MS Jacobi 15, s. xv[1] (*Manipulus,* AD 1441), N. Germany

Part I

ff. 1-48v   Nicholas of Lyra, *Postilla super Proverbia,* written "per N[icholaum] Grabowe" (f. 48v).

Part II
ff. 49-60   *Postilla in Cantica Canticorum*
ff. 60v-61   blank
Part III
ff. 61v-103   Johannes Holt, *Lectura super canonem misse*, probably autograph
ff. 103v-105v   blank
Part IV
ff. 106-327   Thomas of Ireland, *Manipulus florum.* f. 106r-v, prologue, beg.
                (rub.) "Incipit tabula originalium sive manipulus florum secun-
                dum ordinem alphabeti extracta a libris xxxvi auctorum edita a
                magistro Thoma de Ybernia. [text] Abiit in agrum...." ff. 106v-
                318, text, ends "... parentes o. Explicit manipulus florum com-
                pilatus a magistro Thoma de Hybernia quondam socio de Ser-
                bona. Et incepit Galensis ordinis minorum istam tabulam et
                magister Thomas finivit." ff. 318-319v, table, ends "Finit
                fabula (!). Amen." ff. 319v-327, list of authors and works,
                ends "... dulcior gustus. Explicit. Anno a nativitate Domini
                MCCCCXLI, prima die septembris."
ff. 327v-334v   blank
                Four manuscripts, brought together in the mid or late fifteenth
                century. Paper; 2 cols. (save ff. 61-103), 32-52 lines; quires of
                12 leaves. A few catchwords. 215 × 145 mm (290 × 220 mm);
                five hands (i, ff. 1-48v; ii, 49-54v; iii, 54v-60; iv, 61-103; v,
                106-327). f. iᵛ, table of contents (s. xv). Contemporary bind-
                ing, restored 1964; label, front cover; title, back cover.
                2ndo folio, *hoc modo* (pt. I), *subli]mior sed non* (pt. IV). Belonged
                to the church of St. James, Hamburg. Former no. 27.
                T. Brandis and H. Maehler, *Katalog der Handschriften der Staats-
                und Universitätsbibliothek Hamburg* 4 (Hamburg 1967) 171-
                172.

Klosterneuburg, Stiftsbibliothek MS 391, s. xv (1422), Austria
ff. 1-220v   Thomas of Ireland, *Manipulus florum.* ff. 1-2, table (in 3 cols.).
                f. 3r-v, prologue, beg. "Abiit in agrum...." ff. 3v-213v, text.
                ff. 214-220v, list of authors and works, ends "Et sic est finis.
                Expliciunt principia necnon fines librorum diversorum doc-
                torum. Omnis creatura laudat Deum in secula seculorum.
                Amen. Anno Domini milesimo quadringentesimo xxii anno. In
                vigilia Goerii martiris."
ff. 220v-222   List of the works of Bede and of Rupert of Deutz, as additions to
                ff. 214-220 above
ff. 222v-228v   blank
ff. 229-242v   David of Augusta, *Tractatus de vii profectibus religiosorum*
ff. 243-246v   blank
ff. 247-294   Index to Gregory's *Moralia*, beg. "Abel de innocencia eius...."
ff. 294-317   Table to scriptural passages in Gregory's *Moralia*, beg. "Incipit
                prefacio super tabulam infrascriptam, docentem invenire illas
                auctoritates...."

ff. 317v-318v   blank

Paper; 2 cols., ca. 40 lines. 206 × 139 mm (298 × 212 mm), ruled (frame only); several hands, littera currens. Initials in red or left blank. Medieval foliation in arabic numerals.

2ndo folio, *f. Augustinus in.* Belonged to Klosterneuburg, C.S.A.; ex-libris, ff. 1, 143v, 317, "Liber Sancte Marie in Newburga claustrali."

B. Černík, *Catalogus codicum manuscriptorum qui in bibliotheca canonicorum regularum S. Augustini Claustroneoburgi asservantur* 2 (Klosterneuburg 1931) 162-163.

MS seen on film.

Koblenz, Landeshauptarchiv MS Best. 701 no. 759.15, s. xiv (AD 1320), N. France

Thomas of Ireland, *Manipulus florum*; list of authors and works (4 leaves unfoliated). Incomplete at beginning but appears to have been a copy of the list alone, beg. s.n. Augustinus, ends "... dulcior gustus. Expliciunt assignationes librorum origi nalium quoad eorum principia et fines sanctorum et doctorum sub scriptorum, videlicet Dyonisii, libri iiii, epistole xi; ... Senece, libri xx..., Macrobii liber i. [in a later cursive:] Rescripta sunt hec anno dominice Incarnationis millesimo trecentesimo xx°. Tibi laus et gloria qui est benedictus in secula."

Parchment; 2 cols., 43 lines. 210 × 130 mm (254 × 183 mm); one hand, littera textualis. Alternating red and blue initials and paragraph marks. Edges cropped. Has been used as binder's scrap; final leaf once served as a pastedown.

No known provenance.

MS seen on film.

Köln, Dombibliothek MS 182 (Darmst. 2159), s. xiv (6 Feb. 1347), Germany

ff. 2-160   Thomas of Ireland, *Manipulus florum.* f. 2r-v, prologue, beg. (rub.) "Incipit tabula originalium sive manipulus florum secundum ordinem alphabeti extracta a libris XXXVI auctorum edita a magistro Thoma de Ybernia quondam socio de Serbona Parisius civitatis. [text] Abiit in agrum...." ff. 2v-154, text, ends "... parentes o. Explicit manipulus florum, Deo gracias. Hoc opus est compilatum a magistro Thoma de Ybernia quondam socio domus magistrorum de Sarbona Parisius." ff. 154v-155, table. f. 155v, blank. ff. 156-160, list of authors and works, ends "Explicit consignatio librorum sanctorum ecclesie et aliorum quorundam auctorum, penes sua inicia seu principia et fines, manipulo florum annexa. Finita anno Domini 1347, mensis februarii die sexta, ad laudem Dei omnipotentis, gloriose Virginis Marie et omnium sanctorum, et utilitatem legentium in eo et proficientium. Deo gratiarum actio per infinita seculorum secula, amen."

Parchment; 2 cols., 50-51 lines; quires of 6 leaves. Catchwords; quires signed in arabic numerals. 200 × 145/150 mm (277 × 207 mm), ruled in drypoint (frame only); one hand, littera textualis. Decorated initial (5 line) with cascade. Alternating red and blue initials and paragraph marks. Authors noted in marg. Bound in parchment (s. xix).

2ndo folio, *tamen ymmo interdum.* Left to the cathedral library by William of Duren, rector of St. Margaret's of Cologne, according to a slip pasted into the binding (s. xv): "Dominus Wilhelmus de Duren, olim rector capelle Beate Margarete Coloniensis, legavit hunc librum ecclesie Coloniensis ut ad novam librariam ipsius ecclesie ponatur et ibidem cathenatus perpetuo remaneat. Orate pro eo."

P. Jaffé and G. Wattenbach, *Ecclesiae metropolitanae Coloniensis codices manuscripti* (Berlin 1874) 75-76.

MS seen on film.

Köln, Historisches Archiv MS G.B. fol. 168, s. xv (19 August 1450), Germany (Cologne)

ff. ii-177   Thomas of Ireland, *Manipulus florum.* f. ii^{r-v}, prologue, beg. (rub.) "Incipit prologus in librum sequentem. [text] Abiit in agrum...." ff. ii^v-176, text, beg. (rub.) "Incipit manipulus florum. [text] Abstinencia. Bonum est...," ends "... parentes o. Explicit manipulus florum per fratrem Danielem professum et conventualem domus Sancte Crucis in Colonia anno ab Incarnacione Domini millesimo quadringentesimo quinquagesimo, in crastino Sancte Helene regine." ff. 176-177, table. f. 177, "Notandum quod autor huius libri precedentis in fine post Explicit et tabulam ponit omnes libros originales sanctorum atque doctorum quos in magna copia allegat ut promisit in prohemio, videlicet Augustini, Ambrosii, Gregorii, Iheronimi, Bernardi, Hylarii, Crisostomi, Ysidori, Damasceni et ceterorum, ut patet ibidem. Sed hic causa brevitatis pretermissa sunt. Et habentur de verbo ad verbum quemadmodum prefatus magister Thomas doctor Parisiensis conscripserat. Et non habentur omnes libri eorundem doctorum; sed ut videtur quoscumque in libraria Parisiensi invenit, posuit. Nos eciam conscripsimus simili modo eadem opuscula in libro Philobiblon signato cum R.xviii.C [now MS G.B. 4° 215 ff. 40-45v]. Item in libro qui Opus pacis dicitur habentur omnia [now MS G.B. 4° 152 ff. 45-53v]."

ff. 177v-178   Table of contents to the quires now missing; f. 177v i.m., "Nota: Omnia que hic signata sunt habentur in alio libro signato cum numero A 14 [now MS G.B. fol. 130] in eisdem foliis in quibus hic signatur."

f. 178v   blank

[ff. 179-   ]   now MS G.B. fol. 130 ff. 81-197v

Paper; 2 cols., 38-41 lines; quires of 6 leaves. Catchwords; leaves signed in roman numerals. 203 × 142 mm (282 × 197 mm), ruled in brown ink (frame only); one hand, littera bastarda textualis. Initials in red, typical of Cologne Crosiers, with tendrils in bluish purple, and occasional white flowers in a blue background as the infilling. Bound in leather with rectangular and lozenge fillet decoration with blind stamps common to the Cologne Crosiers.

2ndo folio (present fol. 1), *Ante annos*. Fol. i, "т xvii" (erased); "m.xix. Liber fratrum Sancte Crucis canonicorum regularium domus Coloniensis, in quo habetur manipulus florum, liber multum notabilis habens 177 folia. Tabula secundum alphabetum habetur retro in fine huius folio clxxvi. Quem frater noster Daniel et plura alia scripsit circa annum mccccl"; exlibris written by the librarian Fr. Conrad Grunenberg, who copied the list from the *Manipulus florum* in mss G.B. 4° 152 and 215.

J. Vennebusch, *Die theologischen Handschriften des Stadtarchivs Köln* 1 (Cologne 1976) 146-147.

Köln, Historisches Archiv ms G.B. 4° 152, s. xv (1429-1430), Germany (Cologne)

ff. 1-44v   Oswald of the Grande Chartreuse, *Opus pacis* (written 1429).
ff. 45-53v   Thomas of Ireland, *Manipulus florum*. f. 45r-v, prologue, beg. (rub.) "Prologus libri qui manipulus florum dicitur secundum ordinem alphabeti dispositus etc. [text] Abiit in agrum...," ends "Explicit prologus magistri Thome de Ybernia quondam socii domus magistrorum de Sarbona Parisiensis in librum qui manipulus florum dicitur." f. 45v i.m., same hand as text, "Liber scilicet manipulus etc. iam scriptus est totus et signatus cum 174 [now ms G.B. fol. 168]." ff. 45v-46, table. ff. 46-53v, list of authors and works; same hand adds to the end of the introductory paragraph, "... signare. Verte folium et invenies plura. Et notandum quod non omnes libri doctorum hic habentur conscripti ac signati, sed tantum qui reperiuntur in libraria Parisiensis universitatis quia alios ab hiis nos habemus etc. [list begins,] Libri beati Dionysii...."

ff. 54-56v   blank
ff. 57-72   *De orthographia*
ff. 73-120v   *Tabula de Catholicon*
Paper; ca. 40 long lines; quires of 12 leaves. 165 × 105 mm (212 × 150 mm), ruled in dry point (frame only); one hand, cursiva textualis. Small red initials. Bound in leather, fillet decoration in rectangle and lozenges with stamp of the "Hilf Maria" master; very similar to ms G.B. 4° 215.

2ndo folio, *Maxi]miani pretulit*. Written by Conrad Grunenberg, mid-fifteenth-century librarian of the Cologne Crosiers. Belonged to the Crosiers; f. i, hand of Conrad, "... pertinetque conventui fratrum Sancte Crucis in Colonia...." Pressmarks erased.

Köln, Historisches Archiv MS G.B. 4° 215, s. XV, Germany (Cologne)

ff. 1-30	Richard de Bury, *Philobiblon*
ff. 30-39	J. Gerson, *De laude scriptorum* (written 1423)
f. 39v	blank
ff. 40-45r	Thomas of Ireland, *Manipulus florum*; list of authors and works (written by Conrad Grunenberg)
ff. 46-47	Bede, excerpt from *Historia ecclesiastica*, list of his own writings, and epitaph
ff. 47v-48v	blank
f. 49r-v	*Tabula libri Catholicon*
f. 50r-v	blank
ff. 51-124	*Mystice acceptiones terminorum secundum ordinem alphabeti*, beg. "Abissus est vetus et novum testamentum...," ends "... mysticario etc., per manum fratris Abbonis de Middelburch Zelandie. Anno Domini MCCCCXXVI...."
ff. 124v-134	blank

Paper; 35-38 long lines; quires of six leaves. 165 × 110 mm (214 × 148 mm), unruled; several hands, cursiva textualis. Small red initials. Bound in leather, fillet decoration in rectangular lozenges with stamp of the "Hilf Maria" master; very similar to MS G.B. 4° 152.

2ndo folio, *facilius est*. Belonged to the Canons Regular of the Cross, Cologne. Ex-libris, f. i: "R [erased: XVIII; R XVIII]. Iste liber pertinet conventui fratrum Sancte Crucis in Colonia."

Konstanz, Heinrich-Suso-Gymnasium, Jesuiten Bibliothek MS 42, s. XIV²

ff. 1-187v	Thomas of Ireland, *Manipulus florum*. ff. 1-182v, text; beg. mutilated, s.v. *Antichristus*, "... quippe ante adventum iudicis...," ends "... parentes o. Explicit manipulus florum. Hoc opus est compilatum a magistro Thoma de Ybernia quondam socio de Sorbona." ff. 182v-183v, table, ends "Finit." ff. 183v-187v, list of authors and works.

Parchment; 2 cols., 42 lines; quires of 12 leaves. Catchwords; quires signed. 145 × 110 mm (215 × 150 mm), ruled with dry point; two hands, littera textualis (i, ff. 1-168; ii, 169-187). Alternating red and blue initials. Pigskin binding, badly damaged.

2ndo folio, missing. f. 1v (s. XVII?), "Bibliothecae FF. min. conv. Constantiae," the Franciscan convent in Konstanz, no. M 1.

Kraków, Biblioteka Jagiellońska MS 401 (BB.III.27), s. XV (1417), Poland (Lwów)

ff. 1-204v	Thomas of Ireland, *Manipulus florum*. f. 1r-v, prologue, beg. "Abiit in agrum...." ff. 1v-202v, text, ends "... parentes o. etc. Non laus scriptori sed laus summo Genitori etc. Hoc opus compilatum est a magistro Thoma de Ybernia, finitus autem est iste liber in Lamborg post festum Laurencii, anno Domini MCCCC decimo septimo etc." ff. 202v-204v, table, ends "Explicit

registrum manipuli florum, pro quo sit benedictus Deus in secula seculorum. Amen etc."

Paper; 2 cols., 24-51 lines; quires of 12 leaves, signed. 262 × 180 mm (310 × 220 mm), ruled in ink; two hands, littera textualis currens (i, ff. 1-172v; ii, 173-204v). Opening initial (6 line) left blank. Red initials, sometimes left blank. Running headlines (ff. 163-202 only). Bound in leather over boards; label, front cover.

2ndo folio, *incentiva viciorum*. f. 1 (s. xv), "Memoriale magistri Sigismundi [de Pyzdry]; vobis reverendus magister, qui petivit propter Deum, ut eum memorie vestre, temporibus vite vestre imprimatis"; f. 204v, same hand, the same note ending "imprimatis, cum Christus per vos pertractatur," and with the words "reverendus magister" cancelled and written over with "Johannis Dambrowka questiones [?]." The name, and sometimes the hand, of Joannes de Dąbrówka appears on the front label, the inside front cover, ff. ii^{r-v}, and twice on iii^v, including "Det Jacobus redimendo librum quatuordecim grossis"; see W. Szelińska, "Dwa testamenty Jana Dąbrówki," *Studia i Materiały z Dziejów Nauki Polskiej* ser. A, 5 (Warsaw 1962) 3-40. Former no. (s. xviii) 720, f. ii.

W. Wisłocki, *Katalog rękopisów Biblioteki Uniwersytetu Jagiellońskiego* 1 (Cracow 1887) 130.

Kraków, Biblioteka Jagiellońska MS 402 (Aaa.I.14), s. xv (1404), Poland

ff. 2-188v   Thomas of Ireland, *Manipulus florum*. f. 2r-v, prologue, beg. "Abiit in agrum...." ff. 2v-187v, text, ends "... parentes o. Hoc opus est compilatum a magistro Thoma de Ibarnia quodam socio de Sorbona. Explicit manipulus florum." ff. 187v-188v, table (in 4 cols.), ends "Anno Domini MCCCCIV, in crastino octave Epiphanie Domini finitus."

Paper; 2 cols., 42-45 lines; quires mostly of 24 leaves. Catchwords. 215/225 × 155 mm (295 × 215 mm), ruled in ink; two hands, littera cursiva (i, ff. 2-166v; ii, 170-188v; i and ii alternating, 167-169v and 175). Opening initial (9 line) left blank. Red initials. Running headlines. Bound in leather over boards (s. xv); title, back cover (s. xv).

2ndo folio, *corpus non edomat*. Belonged to Michael *de Wartha*, priest of St. Anne's of Cracow, who sold it to Matthew *de Glowno*, B.A.; f. 187v (s. xv), "Magistri Michaelis de Wartha decretorum et arcium baccalarii liber"; f. 1, same hand, "Manipulus florum seu concordancie iurium Michaelis de Wartha decretorum et arcium baccalarii, predicatoris ad Sanctam Annam Cracovie" and "Pro quatuor mercis [!]"; in another hand (s. xv), "Et est Mathie de Glowno arcium liberalium baccalarii."

W. Wisłocki, *Katalog rękopisów Biblioteki Uniwersytetu Jagiellońskiego* 1 (Cracow 1877) 130-131.

348 APPENDIX 7

Kremsmünster, Stiftsbibliothek MS 222, s. xiv, Austria

ff. 1-205v   Thomas of Ireland, *Manipulus florum*. f. 1r-v, prologue, beg.
"Abiit in agrum...." ff. 2-205, text. f. 205r-v, table (in 4
cols.), ends "... Amen, Amen, Amen. Explicit expliceat. Liber
iste manipulus florum vocat. Tres digiti scribunt, tamen corpus
omne laborat etc."

Parchment; 2 cols., 45 lines; quires of 12 leaves. Catchwords
(cropped); quires signed in roman numerals; list of catchwords
and signatures, f. 205v. 205 × 135 mm (272 × 192 mm); one
hand, littera textualis. Decorated initial (9 line). Initials in red.
Running headlines. Formerly chained. Label, front cover.

2ndo folio, *ad prelium*. Given to St. Agapetus of Kremsmünster,
o.s.b., by Michael of Holabrunn; f. i (pastedown), label, "Iste
liber est S. Agapeti in Chremssmünster quem dedit dominus
Michahel de Holabrunn; idem est sepultus in ambitu."

MS seen on film.

Lambach, Stiftsbibliothek MS Ccl 128, s. xv, Germany/Austria

A miscellany (315 folios) of some 29 items—excerpts, tracts,
verses and sermons, including (ff. 73-201v) *Sermones fune-
rales*.

ff. 264-266v   Thomas of Ireland, *Manipulus florum*. f. 264r-v, prologue
(abbrev.), beg. "Abiit in agrum...." ff. 264v-266v, text;
manuscript breaks off, s.v. Adiutorium, "... si eum adiuvare
oportet quem non...."

Paper; 2 cols., 43 lines. 185 × 150 mm (290 × 210 mm), ruled in
ink (frame only); written by numerous hands, and possibly
made up of several separate books.

2ndo folio, *ā ām̄* (?). Given to the monastery of Lambach; f. i,
"Venerabilis dominus Oswaldus Cysentalem (?) vicarius in
Scherding dedit hunc librum monasterio Lambacens'."

E. Hainisch, ed., *Die Kunstdenkmäler des Gerichtsbezirkes Lambach*, Oesterreichischen Kunsttopographie 34 (Vienna 1959)
259.

MS seen on film.

Leipzig, Karl-Marx-Universitätsbibliothek MS 629, s. xv (1410), Germany
(Saxony?)

ff. 1-244v   Thomas of Ireland, *Manipulus florum*. f. 1r-v, prologue, beg.
"Abiit in agrum...." ff. 1v-237, text, ends "Explicit manipulus
florum compilatus a magistro Thoma de Ybernis (!) opido
cocio quondam socio de Serbona ville Parisiensis." ff. 237-
238, table (in 4 cols.). ff. 238-244v, list of authors and works,
ends "Scriptus est iste liber in conventu Hilden' pro reverendo
patre fratre Henrico Voernigherod (?) domus Lipzen' ordinis
predicatorum per contratam Misne tunc vicario a fratre Johanne
Rasoris domus Hilden' tunc subpriore ordinis antedicti et completus anno Domini MCCCCX, die XIIII, mensis novembris."

Parchment; 2 cols., 45-51 lines. Catchwords. 174 × 114 mm (252 × 180 mm), ruled in lead and ink; two hands, littera textualis. Initial (7 line) parted with tendrils. Alternating red and blue initials. Leather over boards; clasp marks; label.

2ndo folio, *da pauperibus*. Belonged to the Dominicans of Leipzig. f. 1 top, "Dexteram scribentis dirigat, regat, corrigat vis omnipotentis."

MS seen on film.

Lincoln, Cathedral Library MS 48 (C.3.1), s. xv, England

ff. 1-196   Thomas of Ireland, *Manipulus florum*. f. 1r-v, prologue, beg. (rub.) "Incipit tabula originalium sive manipulus florum secundum ordinem alphabeti extracta a libris xxxvi auctorum. [text] Abiit in agrum...." ff. 1v-187, text, ends "Explicit manipulus florum a magistro Thoma de Hybernia condam socio de Serbona et incepit super [*corr. to*: frater] Johannes Galensis ordinis fratrum minorum doctor in theologia istam tabulam et magister Thomas finivit." ff. 187v-189, table (in 3 cols.). ff. 189-196, list of authors and works.

Parchment; 2 cols., 40 lines; quires of 12 leaves. Catchwords. 241 × 138 mm (310 × 203 mm), ruled in lead; one hand, littera textualis. Initials left unfinished. Running headlines added (A, B, C, and tituli). Rebound in half leather.

2ndo folio, *o. hostem*. Fol. 1 bottom: "Tabula originalium sive manipulus florum per ff. W. de Stoke."

R. M. Wooley, *Catalogue of the Manuscripts of Lincoln Cathedral Chapter Library* (Oxford 1927) 24.

MS seen.

Lincoln, Cathedral Library MS 191 (B.4.4.), s. xv, England

ff. 2-196v   Thomas of Ireland, *Manipulus florum*. f. 2r-v, prologue, beg. "Abiit in agrum...." ff. 3-190v, text, ends "Explicit manipulus florum compilatus a magistro Thoma de Hybernia quondam socio de Sorbona et incepit Galieni (!) ordinis minorum istam tabulam et magister Thomas finivit." ff. 190v-191, table (in 4 cols.). ff. 191v-196v, list of authors and works, to which has been added (hand of the scribe) the list of Bede's works taken from the *Historia ecclesiastica*.

f. 197r-v   *Decretum Gelasii de scripturis recipiendis seu non recipiendis*

ff. 198-218v   St. Bernard, *De consideratione*

ff. 218v-228v   St. Bernard, *Sermo de evangelio Missus est...* (5 sermons)

ff. 228v-255v   Nigellus, *Speculum stultorum*

Parchment; 2 cols., 41 lines; quires of 12 leaves. Occasional catchwords. 229 × 137 mm (278 × 190 mm), ruled in lead; one hand, littera textualis. Opening initial parted red and blue, with white leaf relief and cascade. Blue initials (primary initials decorated), alternating red and blue paragraph marks. Running headlines (A, B, C). Authors noted in marg. Medieval boards rebacked; marks of two fore-edge clasps.

2ndo folio, *Gregorius. m. Abstinencia.* Belonged to Lincoln Cathe-
dral; f. 1 in faded red ink, "Liber ecclesie cathedralis Beate
Marie Lincolniensis" no. M.4, and an evaluation: "pret. VIII s.
IIII d."; table of contents.

R. M. Wooley, *Catalogue of the Manuscripts of Lincoln Cathedral
Chapter Library* (Oxford 1927) 138-139.

MS seen.

Linz, Studienbibliothek MS 117 (379), s. xiv[1], Germany/Austria

ff. 1-99v   Thomas of Ireland, *Manipulus florum.* f. 1r-v, prologue, beg.
(rub.) "Incipit manipulus florum sive extractiones originalium
editus a magistro Thoma de Ybernia quondam socio de Sorbona. [text] Abiit in agrum...." ff. 1v-99v, text, ends "Hoc
opus est compilatum a magistro Thoma de Ybernia quondam
socio de Sorbona. Explicit manipulus florum." ff. 96v-97,
table (in 4 cols.). ff. 97-99v, list of authors and works.

ff. 99v-113   Joannes de Fayt (?), *Auctoritates philosophorum,* beg. "Cum omnem nostrum appetitum...."

Parchment; 2 cols., 65 lines; quires of 12 leaves. Catchwords;
leaves signed (a, b, c). 234 × 161 mm (310 × 220 mm), ruled in
ink; one hand, littera textualis. Initial (13 line) parted and
decorated, extending into a frame. Alternating red and blue
initials, with tendrils. Pastedowns taken from another manuscript of the *Manipulus florum* (s. xiv[2], Germany).

2ndo folio, *accipiantur.* Belonged to the monastery of BMV, Gar-
sten. Former pressmark, Cc V 3.

MS seen on film.

Lisboa, Academia das Ciencias MS Convento de Nossa Senhora de Jezus de Lisboa 400, s. xiv

ff. 1-156v   Thomas of Ireland, *Manipulus florum.* Final quires missing, ends
s.v. *Mulier.*

London, British Library MS Add. 15340, s. xiv[1], France (?)

ff. 1-168v   Thomas of Ireland, *Manipulus florum.* f. 1, prologue, beg. (rub.)
"Incipit manipulus florum sive extractiones originalium a
magistro Thoma de Hybernia quondam scolari de Sarbona.
[text] Abiit in agrum...." ff. 1-164, text. f. 164, table (in long
lines). ff. 164-168v, list of authors and works.

Parchment; 2 cols., 55 lines; quires of 12 leaves. Catchwords in
boxes; leaves signed (a-f). 176 × 113 mm (270 × 185 mm),
ruled in lead; one hand, littera textualis currens. Decorated
opening initial (blue and gold diamond cross-hatch) and frame
supporting (i) a lion and an ox, (ii) a king instructing an archer,
(iii) an archer shooting a figure tied to a tree, (iv) birds on the
supports. Alternating red and blue initials (with tendrils) and
paragraph marks. Running headlines (A, B, C). Authors noted in
marg. Rebound in half leather, 1969; quires separately moun-
ted.

2ndo folio, *ad hoc in quantum.* F. 1, "flor. VI"; f. 168v, "Manipulus florum precio flor. VII"; flyleaf, "Purchased of Jos. Lilly 14 Nov. 1844 Sussex sale lot 494."
Catalogue of Additions to the Manuscripts in the British Museum in the Years MDCCCXLI-MDCCCXLV (London 1850) a. 1844 p. 129.
MS seen.

London, British Library MS Add. 17809, s. xiv[1], England

ff. 1-241   Thomas of Ireland, *Manipulus florum.* f. 1, prologue, beg. (rub.) "Incipit manipulus florum sive extractiones originalium edita a magistro Thoma de Ybernia quondam socio de Serbona. [text] Abiit in agrum...." ff. 1-232, text, ends "Explicit manipulus florum compilatus a magistro Thoma de Ybernia quondam socio de Serbona." ff. 232-234, table. ff. 234-241, list of authors and works, ends "Explicit Deo gracias. Filia pro pena scriptori detur amena, amen. Explicit iste liber, scriptor sit crimine liber, amen. Explicit manipulus florum sive extractiones originalium compilatus a magistro Thoma de Ybernia quondam socio de Serbona Deo gracias. Scriptor qui scripsit cum Christo vivere possit. Johannes de Syaco."
Parchment; 2 cols., 45 lines; quires of 8 leaves. Catchwords. 186 × 143 mm (273 × 188 mm), ruled in ink; one hand, littera textualis formata. Opening initial historiated: cleric kneeling before Virgin and Child; frame with spiky leaves. Primary initials gold with spiky leaf frames. Blue secondary initials with red tendrils; alternating red and blue paragraph marks. Authors noted in marg. Rebound in brown calf.
2ndo folio, *enim vino et vino.* f. i, "Purchased of Asher 30 June 1849."
Catalogue of Additions to the Manuscripts in the British Museum ... MDCCCXLVIII-MDCCCLIII (London 1868) 56; J. W. Bradley, *A Dictionary of Miniaturists, Illuminators, Calligraphers and Copyists* 3 (London 1889) 280.
MS seen.

London, British Library MS Add. 24129, s. xiv[1], England

ff. 1-4   blank
f. 4v   two extracts from the *Manipulus florum*
f. 5r-v   blank
ff. 6-169   Thomas of Ireland, *Manipulus florum.* f. 6, prologue, beg. (rub.) "Incipit tabula originalium sive manipulus florum secundum ordinem alphabeti extracta a libris xxxvi auctorum.... [text] Abiit in agrum...." ff. 6v-162v, text, ends "Explicit manipulus florum compilatus a magistro Thoma de Hybernia quondam socio de Serbona et incepit frater Iohannes Galensis ordinis fratrum minorum doctor in theologia istam tabulam et magister Thomas finivit." ff. 163-164, table, ends "Finit tabula, amen. Siquis amat Christum non mundum diligit istum, alleluya." ff. 164-169, list of authors and works.

Parchment; 2 cols., 56 lines; quires of 12 leaves. Catchwords in decorated boxes; leaves signed (a-, a=, aᵉ). 235 × 135 mm (308 × 190 mm); one hand, littera textualis. Opening initial (cut out) supported by frame. Primary initials decorated in frame. Secondary initials blue with red tendrils; occasional blue paragraph marks; majuscules slashed in red. Running headlines (A, B, C). Authors noted in marg. Tituli numbered in roman numerals, upper right. Occasional contemporary corrections and other notes in marg. Bound by Gough of Andrews Bristol, 1836; chainmarks bottom and top center, front and back flyleaves and pastedowns.

2ndo folio, *gaudiis*. f. 5, "[cut out] de Lund"; f. 168v, "Johe."; f. 3v, dealer's catalog notice; f. 1, "Purchased at Puttich's 4 May 1861, lot 10101."

Catalogue of Additions to the Manuscripts in the British Museum ... MDCCCLIV-MDCCCLXXV 2 (London 1877) 13

MS seen.

London, British Library MS Egerton 652, s. xiv¹, France

ff. 1-197v   Thomas of Ireland, *Manipulus florum*. f. 1r-v, prologue, beg. (rub.) "Incipit manipulus florum sive extracciones originalium a magistro Thoma de Hybernia quondam socio de Sorbona. [text] Abiit in agrum...." ff. 1v-191, text, ends "Hoc opus est compilatum a magistro Thoma de Hybernia quondam socio de Sorbona." ff. 191-192, table (folio references added), ends "Finit anno Domini MCCCVI, die veneris post Passionem Petri et Pauli." ff. 192-197v, list of authors and works, ends "... dulcior gustus. [line filling:] ambmcmdm. Explicit, expliceat, ludere scriptor eat."

Parchment; 2 cols., 46 lines; quires of 12 leaves. Catchwords outlined as fishes. 196 × 135 mm (283 × 200 mm), ruled in lead; one hand, littera textualis. Opening initial parted with tendrils and filigree. Alternating red and blue initials and paragraph marks. Running headlines (added). Authors noted in marg. Foliation in arabic numerals (s. xiv). Egerton vellum binding.

2ndo folio, *extin]guenda sunt*. No. 46 in the sale catalog of Baynes and Son, 1836. Purchased from Baynes by Dr. Adam Clark, 29 May 1838 (no. CI of Clark's collection).

Catalogue of Additions to the Manuscripts in the British Museum ... MDCCCXXXVI-MDCCCXL (London 1843) 25.

MS seen.

London, British Library MS Royal 7 C.III, s. xiv¹, England

ff. 1-4   flyleaves

ff. 5-202v   Thomas of Ireland, *Manipulus florum*. f. 5, prologue, beg. (rub.) "Incipit tabula originalium sive manipulus florum secundum ordinem alphabeti extracta a libris XXXVI auctorum edita a magistro Thoma Ybernico [*i.m.*: quondam socio de Sarbona

Parisiensis civitatis]. [text] Abiit in agrum...." ff. 5v-196v, text. ff. 196v-197, table. ff. 197v-202v, list of authors and works.

Parchment; 2 cols., 50 lines; quires of 12 leaves. Catchwords; leaves signed (i, ii, iii). 246 × 131 mm (310 × 198 mm), ruled in ink; two hands (i: ff. 5-6; ii, 6v-202v), littera textualis. Alternating red and blue initials (with tendrils) and paragraph marks. Authors noted in marg. Rebound, half leather (1970); quires detached.

2ndo folio, *necesse est.*

G. F. Warner and J. P. Gilson, *Catalogue of Western Manuscripts in the Old Royal and King's Collections* 1 (London 1921) 177.

MS seen.

Lüneburg, Ratsbücherei MS theol. fol. 77, s. xv med., Germany

ff. 1-35v	Giles of Rome, *De regimine principium*
ff. 35v-42v	*Speculum artis bene moriendi*
ff. 43-46	Ps.-Bernard of Clairvaux, *Magnificat*
ff. 46-61	Bernard, *Super Missus est*
ff. 61v-65	Rudolf of Biberach, *De septem donis Spiritus Sancti,* abbreviated
ff. 65v-66v	blank
ff. 67-94v	Gerhard of Vliederhoven (?), *De quatuor novissimis sive cordiale*
ff. 94v-103	Thomas of Ireland, *De tribus punctis christianae religionis*
f. 103	Gregory, *Moralia* bk. 12 c. 2 (extract)
f. 103v	Extracts (verse and *sententiae*)
ff. 104-174v	Thomas of Ireland, *Manipulus florum,* abbreviated and interpolated. Beg. (rub.) "Infrascripta sunt collecta de libro qui dicitur manipulus florum sive tabula originalium procedens secundum ordinem alphabeti extracta a libris xxxvi auctorum edita a magistro Ybernico quondam socio de Sarbona Parisiensis civitatis; et primo De adventu Domini.... [text] Augustinus super Iohannem...: Nulla causa veniendi...," ends s.v. *De Ihesu* (an interpolation), "... quid dulcius lacrimis caritatis." Includes lengthy extracts from *De interiori domo,* cc. 1, 6-7, 10-11, 14-22, on ff. 166v-173 (s.v. *De conscientia*).
ff. 174v-175v	*De visitatione infirmorum*
f. 175v	An absolution from the Council of Basel
ff. 178-233	Rudolf of Biberach, *De septem donis Spiritus Sancti*
ff. 233v-292v	Supposititious letters of Eusebius, Augustine and Cyril concerning St. Jerome
ff. 293-296v	*Tractatus Cassiani de octo viciis principalibus*

Paper; long lines (ff. 1-177v) and 2 cols. (178-296v), 33-48 lines; quires mostly of 12 leaves. Catchwords; leaves signed, in some quires. 200/230 × 130/140 mm (295 × 210 mm), ruled in ink (frame only); several hands, littera bastarda. Red initials, tituli and paragraph marks. Bound in old brownish red leather; clasp marks; chain mark, back cover, top.

2ndo folio, *capitulum sextum quod.* Binding scraps include fragments of a notarized document of Albertus of Rethem, cleric of the diocese of Minden, issued at Rome on 15 Nov. 1432 and incorporating a letter of Eugene IV, dated 27 April 1431, to the bishop *Adriensis*, the abbot of St. Michael's Lüneburg, and the prior of Heiligenthal, directing that a certain Henry be installed as priest of Hittbergen (in the Landkreis Lüneburg). Bequeathed to the Franciscan house of Lüneburg by Gerpert Everwin in 1501; f. 1, "Ex donatione testamenti domini Gerperti Euerwyn plebani Sancti Lamberti in Luneborch. Orate pro eo fratres. MDI."

I. Fischer, *Handschriften der Ratsbücherei Lüneburg* 2 (Wiesbaden 1972) 149-153.

Lyon, Bibliothèque municipale MS 711, s. xiv[1], France (Paris)

ff. 1-224 Thomas of Ireland, *Manipulus florum*. First folio lacking, save the parts of a few words of rubric and text; f. 1r-v formerly contained the prologue; ff. [lv] 2-216v, text, ends "Explicit manipulus florum. Hoc opus est compilatum a magistro Thoma de Ybernia quondam socio de Sorbona." ff. 216v-218v, table. ff. 218v-224, list of authors and works.

Parchment; 2 cols., 40 lines; quires of 8 leaves. Catchwords; signatures. 180×111 mm (234×161 mm), ruled in ink; one hand, littera textualis. Alternating red and blue initials and paragraph marks. Running headlines (A, B, C). Copied from a 75-pecia exemplar; pecia note, "p xviii," f. 56v. Rebound, s. xix.

2ndo folio, *infirmitatis sue.*

Catalogue général des manuscrits des bibliothèques publiques de France: Départements 30 (Paris 1900) 193-194.

MS seen on film.

Madrid, Biblioteca nacional MS 234 (A 120), s. xiv[1], Germany (?)

ff. 1-132v Thomas of Ireland, *Manipulus florum*. f. 1r-v, prologue, beg. (rub.) "Incipit tabula originalium Augustini et Ambrosii et sic de aliis qui sunt numero XXXVI auctores secundum ordinam alphabeti qui vocatur manipulus florum. [text] Abiit in agrum...." ff. 1v-132v, text; final quires missing, ends s.v. *Liberalitas*, "... et non labia sua denique perfecta...."

Parchment; 2 cols., 40 lines. $153/162 \times 106/112$ mm (232×165 mm); one hand, littera textualis. Opening initial (7 line), secondary initials and paragraph marks left incomplete. Pen grotesques in lower marg. Running headlines (tituli). Authors noted in marg.

2ndo folio, *luce clarior.* MS came to Madrid from Messina.

W. von Hartel, *Bibliotheca patrum latinorum Hispaniensis* 1 (Vienna 1887) 351-352; *Inventario general de manoscritos de la Biblioteca nacional* 1 (Madrid 1953) 181.

MS seen on film.

Magdeburg, Dom-Gymnasium MS 66, s. xv (1470)

ff. 1-233   Thomas of Ireland, *Manipulus florum.* We do not know where, or whether, this manuscript survives.

Magdeburg, Dom-Gymnasium MS 130

ff. 1-223   Thomas of Ireland, *Manipulus florum.* We do not know where, or whether, this manuscript survives.

Marseille, Bibliothèque municipale MS 331, s. xiv, France (?)

ff. 1-165   Thomas of Ireland, *Manipulus florum.* f. 1 cut out. ff. 2-159, text, beg. s.v. *Abstinencia*, "... Per Symonem qui significantur...," ends "Hoc opus est compilatum a magistro Thoma de Ybernia quondam socio de Sorbona. Explicit manipulus florum." ff. 159-160, table with folio references, ends "Explicit." ff. 160-165, list of authors and works, ends "... dulcior gustus. Explicit."

Parchment; 2 cols., 50 lines; quires of 12 leaves. Catchwords; leaves signed (A1, A2, A3). 208 × 145 mm (276 × 195 mm), ruled in lead; one hand, littera textualis. Alternating red and blue initials (with tendrils) and paragraph marks. Contemporary foliation in letters and arabic numerals (a1, a2-a20, b1-b20, etc.), on upper left verso. Early calf binding over boards; clasp marks; title on back cover.

2ndo folio, *Per Symonem.* Belonged to the Carthusian priory of Villeneuve-lès-Avignon (fd. 1356); ff. 2, 165, "Iste liber est domus Cartusiensis Ville nove prope Avinionem."

Catalogue général des manuscrits des bibliothèques publiques de France: Départements 15 (Paris 1892) 118-119.

MS seen.

Melun, Bibliothèque municipale MS 16, s. xiv[1], France (Paris)

ff. 1-265   Thomas of Ireland, *Manipulus florum.* f. 1r-v, prologue, beg. (rub.) "Incipit manipulus florum sive extractiones originalium a magistro Thoma de Hymbernia quondam socio de Sorbona. [text] Abiit in agrum...." ff. 1v-258, text. ff. 258-259, table (in 4 cols.). ff. 259-265, list of authors and works; final leaves missing, ends "[Boethius] ... satis esse dixi...."

Parchment; 2 cols., 37 lines; quires usually of 12 leaves. Catchwords in boxes. 150 × 97 mm (197 × 136 mm), ruled in lead; one hand, littera textualis. Initial (7 line) parted with filigree and cascade. Alternating red and blue initials (with tendrils) and paragraph marks. Running headlines added (A, B, C). Authors noted in marg. Copied from a 75-pecia exemplar (revealed by ink changes). Bound in whittawed leather, original boards; chain mark, front top center.

2ndo folio, *calefacere et.*

Catalogue général des manuscrits des bibliothèques publiques de France: Départements 3 (Paris 1885) 361.

MS seen.

Milano, Biblioteca Ambrosiana MS T 124 sup., s. xiv med., France

ff. 3-250v   Thomas of Ireland, *Manipulus florum*. f. 3r-v, prologue (rub. effaced), beg. "Abiit in agrum...." ff. 3v-245, text, ends "... parentes o. Hoc opus est compilatum a magistro Thoma de Ybernia quondam socio de Serbona." ff. 245-246, table (in 4 cols.); tituli numbered in arabic numerals (added s. xiv-xv). ff. 246-251v, list of authors and works; last leaves out of order: f. 249 (end of list) should follow present f. 251, which ends s.n. Anselmus, "... de similitudinibus...."

Parchment; 2 cols., 40 lines. Quires of 10 leaves; catchwords in red boxes. 164 × 115 mm (228 × 174 mm), ruled in lead; one hand, littera textualis. Opening initial (6 line) parted red and blue, with filigree and cascade. Alternating red and blue initials (with filigree and tendrils) and paragraph marks. Partly foliated, N1-N35, P1-P49 (s. xiv-xv) on verso. Authors noted in marg. Edges of the manuscript damaged. Ambrosiana binding, quarter leather over paper boards (s. xix[1]).

2ndo folio, *metus fuerat*. "Ex legato Bernardini Ferrarii Mediolanis machinatoris, MDCCCXXX."

A. L. Gabriel, *A Summary Catalogue of Microfilms of One Thousand Scientific Manuscripts in the Ambrosian Library, Milan* (Notre Dame 1968) 372 no. 926.

MS seen.

München, Bayerische Staatsbibliothek MS lat. 3212, s. xv, Germany

Pt. I

ff. 1-97v   Thomas of Ireland, *Manipulus florum*. ff. 1-2, table (in 4 cols.). f. 2r-v, prologue, beg. "Abiit in agrum...." ff. 3-97v, text, much abbreviated but with most tituli represented, ends "[Christus] ... Cassiodorus super illud psalmum: Dominus soluit compeditos."

Pt. II

ff. 98-140   *Flores bibliae* (from Proverbia, Ecclesiastes, Sapiencia, Ecclesiasticus), beg. "[prologue:] Flores librorum iiii[or] sapientialium paucis obmissis abbreviati reductique ad ordinem alphabeti licet.... [text:] Parabola Salamonis filii David regis Israel...," ends "... fuerit in maledictione erit pars vestra etc. Expliciunt flores iiii librorum sapientialium reducti ad ordinem alphabeti...."

Pt. I: Parchment; 34-38 long lines; quires of 10 leaves. Quires signed in roman numerals. 162 × 96 mm (216 × 155 mm), ruled in ink; two hands (i: ff. 1-97v, littera textualis currens; ii: ff. 98-140, littera currens). Red initial (3 line). Pt. I, red initials and paragraph marks; pt. II, alternating red and blue initials and paragraph marks. Authors noted in marg. Subject headings and cross references frequently added in marg. Medieval foliation in arabic numerals. Contemporary binding, leather stained pink over boards; label, front cover; 2 fore-edge clasps (missing).

2ndo folio, *Tribulatio.* Belonged to the monastery of Astach o.s.b. (no. 12).

K. Halm, W. Laubmann, *Catalogus codicum latinorum Bibliothecae regiae Monacensis* ed. 2, 1.2 (Munich 1894) 81.

MS seen.

München, Bayerische Staatsbibliothek MSS lat. 3724-3725, s. xv in., Germany

A two-volume set.

i, ff. 1-163v   Thomas of Ireland, *Manipulus florum.* Extensive extracts, beg. "*Abstinencia*: est in cibo cum gratiarum...," ends s.v. *Luxuria.*

ii, ff. 1-93   A continuation, beg. s.v. *Maria,* ends s.v. *Religio,* "... cognacionibus. Ieronimus in epistola ad Rusticum." The remaining quires of MS 3725 are left blank.

Paper; 24-26 long lines; quires of 12 leaves. Catchwords. 151 × 95 mm (212 × 147 mm), ruled in lead (frame only); one hand, littera currens (text) and littera textualis (tituli). Most tituli, initials, majuscule letters and paragraph marks in red. Binding: 3724, skin stained pink over medieval boards; fore-edge strap; label, front center, "Flores diversorum doctorum"; chain mark, bottom front center; pastedown and quire reinforcement from a Psalter (s. xii). 3725, whittawed skin over medieval boards; fore-edge strap mark; chain mark, bottom front center; label, top front center, "d"; pastedown and quire reinforcement from a liturgical book (s. xiv).

2ndo folio, *eisdem alimentis* (i), *quid vos* (ii). Belonged to the cathedral library of Augsburg (nos. 24, 25).

K. Halm, W. Laubmann, *Catalogus codicum latinorum Bibliothecae regiae Monacensis* ed. 2, 1.2 (Munich 1894) 127.

München, Bayerische Staatsbibliothek MS lat. 5345, s. xv¹, Germany

ff. 1-289v   Thomas of Ireland, *Manipulus florum.* ff. 1-2, prologue, beg. (rub.) "Incipit tabula originalium sive manipulus florum secundum ordinem alphabeti extracta a libris xxxvi auctorum edita a magistro Thoma Ybernico quondam socio de Sorbona Paris. civitatis. [text] Abiit in agrum...." ff. 2-280v, text, ends "Explicit manipulus florum compleatus (!) a magistro Thoma de Hybernia quondam socio de Sorbona et incepit frater Iohannes Galensis ordinis fratrum minorum doctor in theologia istam tabulam et magister Thomas finivit etc." ff. 280v-281v, table (in 4 cols., folio numbers added). ff. 282-289v, list of authors and works.

ff. 290-304   Prosper of Aquitaine, *De vera innocentia*; breaks off incomplete at end of quire, "ca. cccvi ... accipere deo pocius miserante..." (PL 51: 487).

Paper; 2 cols., 37 lines; quires of 12 leaves. Catchwords; quires signed in arabic numerals on first leaf; leaves signed (1-6). 197 × 140 mm (290 × 210 mm), ruled in ink (frame only); two hands (i: ff. 1-24v; ii: 25-304), littera cursiva. Squat initials, and paragraph marks, in red. Authors noted in marg. f. 1 top, added: "Tabulam super presente libro cum numero foliorum reperies in fine eiusdem folio 280." Medieval foliation in arabic numerals. Bound in original whittawed leather over boards; title written across top and bottom edge of leaves; two fore-edge clasps, missing.

2ndo folio, *originalium non.* Similar to Salzburg MS a.IX.4, which may be its exemplar. Given to the episcopal library of Chiemsee (no. 45) by Bernhard von Kraiburg, doctor of canon law at Vienna in 1442 and secretary to the archbishop of Salzburg (d. 1477); see Paul Ruf, "Eine altbayerische Gelehrtenbibliothek des 15. Jahrhunderts und ihr Stifter Bernhard von Kraiburg," in *Festschrift Eugen Strollreither* (Erlangen 1950) 219-239. Kraiburg arms, f. 1 bottom.

K. Halm et al., *Catalogus codicum latinorum Bibliothecae regiae Monacensis* 3.3 (Munich 1873) 8.

MS seen.

München, Bayerische Staatsbibliothek MS lat. 5404, s. xv (AD 1428), Germany

ff. 1-325v   Thomas of Ireland, *Manipulus florum.* f. 1r-v, prologue, beg. (rub.) "Incipit manipulus florum sive extractiones originalium a magistro Thoma de Hybernia quondam socio de Sorbona. [text] Abiit in agrum...." ff. 1v-315, text, ends "Explicit manipulus florum compilatus a magistro Thoma de Hybernia quondam socio de Sorbona et incepit frater Iohannes Galensis ordinis fratrum minorum doctor in theologia istam tabulam et magister Thomas finivit. Et est finitus liber iste quando scribebatur anno Domini millesimo quadringentesimo vigesimo octavo, in die conceptionis Virginis gloriosa. Qui me scribebat Echardius Perckhaymer nomen habebat." ff. 315v-317v, table (in 2 cols.). ff. 317v-325v, list of authors and works, ends "Finito libro, sit laus et gloria Christo. Kui scripsit scripta, manus eius sit benedicta. Est michi precium krankch cum nil datur nisi habdankch."

Paper; 2 cols., 38 lines; quires of 12 leaves. Catchwords; quires signed in roman numerals; leaves signed (a-f). 200 × 140 mm (298 × 211 mm), ruled in pencil (frame only); one hand, littera currens. Red initial (5 line) with filigree and tendrils. Red initials (with tendrils) and paragraph marks. Authors noted in marg. Bound in calf rebacked; 5 bosses, 2 fore-edge clasps, and title, formerly on front cover.

2ndo folio, *scilicet ad deitatem.* Written 8 Dec. 1428 by Erckhard Perckhaymer. Belonged to the episcopal library of Chiemsee (no. 104).

K. Halm et al., *Catalogus codicum latinorum Bibliothecae regiae Monacensis* 3.3 (Munich 1873) 13.

MS seen.

München, Bayerische Staatsbibliothek ms lat. 8954, s. xiv (1394-1395), Germany

ff. 1-28v   *De septem peccatis, de septem sacramentis et de septem donis Spiritus Sancti*
ff. 29-40v   *Evangelium Nicodemi*
ff. 41-49v   *De virtutibus*
ff. 50-109   Thomas of Ireland, *Manipulus florum*. Extracts from the text, beg. "Incipiunt auctoritates sanctorum et philosophorum secundum ordinem alphabeti. Abstinencia. Quid prodest actenuari corpus per abstinenciam...," ends "[Christianus] ... est divine consolationis impedimentum."
ff. 110-118v   St. Bernard, *De interiori homine*
ff. 119-206v   *Dialogus de passione Christi et de gaudio Paschali*
ff. 207-266v   *Sermones Germanici a dominica quadragesimali*
ff. 267-326v   *Sermones latini*
                 Paper; 29-33 long lines; quires of 12 leaves. Catchwords. 156 × 108 mm (208 × 150 mm), ruled in ink (frame only); one hand, littera currens. Initials left incomplete. Contemporary table of contents, front pastedown. Bound in whittawed skin over boards, rebacked; fore-edge clasp mark and chain mark (back top inner); labels on front cover, "Tractatus diversi. Vide in principio libri. N."
                 2ndo folio, *per mortali.* f. 167v, "finitus ... per me Johannem." Belonged to the Franciscans in Munich (no. 254).
                 K. Halm et al., *Catalogus codicum latinorum Bibliothecae regiae Monacensis* 4.1 (Munich 1874) 67.
                 ms seen.

München, Bayerische Staatsbibliothek ms lat. 12310, s. xv, Germany

ff. 1-288v   Thomas of Ireland, *Manipulus florum*. f. 1r-v, prologue, beg. (rub.) "Incipit manipulus florum sive extractiones originalium editus a magistro Thoma de Hybernia quondam socio de Sarbona scilicet Booz (!). [text] Abiit in agrum...." ff. 1v-280v, text, ends "Hoc opus compilatum est a magistro Thoma de Ybernia quondam socio de Sarbona. Libro completo, sursum salio pede leto. Deus sit benedictus in secula seculorum, amen." ff. 280v-281v, table (in 4 cols.). ff. 281v-288v, list of authors and works, ends "... dulcior gustus. Et sic est finis, de quo sit ille benedictus ex quo omnia, per quem omnia, in quo omnia ipsi gloria in secula seculorum, amen etc. Laus Christi."
                 Paper; 2 cols., 35-47 lines; quires usually of 12 leaves, some of 10. Catchwords. 226 × 144/145 mm (306 × 212 mm), ruled in ink (frame only); one or two hands (ff. 169-206 may be a second hand), littera currens. Initials not entered. Authors noted in marg. Bound in paper boards.
                 2ndo folio, *nonnulli vitam.* Belonged to the Augustinian canons of Rottenbuch (no. 110).

K. Halm et al., *Catalogus codicum latinorum Bibliothecae regiae Monacensis* 4.2 (Munich 1876) 68.

MS seen.

München, Bayerische Staatsbibliothek MS lat. 14367, s. xiv, Germany

ff. 1-226 Thomas of Ireland, *Manipulus florum*. f. 1r-v, prologue, beg. (rub.) "Incipit manipulus florum sive exacciones (!) originalium a magistro Thoma de Hybernia quondam socio de Serbona. [text] Abiit in agrum...." ff. 1v-218, text, ends "Hoc opus compilatum a magistro Thoma de Ybernia quondam socio in Sorbona. Explicit manipulus florum." ff. 218-220, table (in 2 cols.). ff. 220-226, list of authors and works, ends "... dulcior gustus. Bibales dico scriptori porrige cito."

f. 226v *De scriptura secreta*; fifteen lines (three of them erased) on secret writing

Parchment; 2 cols., 39 lines; quires of 12 leaves. Catchwords in boxes; quires signed; leaves signed (1-6). 198 × 127 mm (268 × 180 mm), ruled in lead; one hand, littera textualis. Initial (3 line) parted red and blue. Alternating red and blue initials and paragraph marks. Running headlines (A, B, C). Authors noted in marg. Modern binding.

2ndo folio, *Abstinencia tua*. Given to St. Emmeram's, O.S.B., Regensburg (no. Em. D 92) by Abbot Albertus: f. 226v, "Hunc librum dedit nobis dominus Albertus abbas."

K. Halm et al., *Catalogus codicum latinorum Bibliothecae regiae Monacensis* 4.2 (Munich 1876) 162.

MS seen.

München, Bayerische Staatsbibliothek MS lat. 14545, s. xv, Germany

ff. 1-191v Thomas of Ireland, *Manipulus florum*. ff. 1-2v, prologue, beg. (rub.) "Incipit manipulus florum sive exactiones (!) originalium a magistro Thoma de Hibernia quondam socio de Gerbona (!). [text] Abiit in agrum...." ff. 3-191v, text; incomplete, MS breaks at "*Fortitudo*. a. Qui vera virtute fortis...."

Paper; 26-28 long lines; quires of 16 leaves. Catchwords. 172 × 87 mm (219 × 150 mm), ruled in ink (frame only); one hand, littera currens. Initial (4 line) parted red. Secondary initials and majuscules slashed in red. Citations underlined in red. Authors occasionally noted in marg. Bound in soft parchment covers, once pages of a fourteenth-century book.

2ndo folio, *Quasdam igitur dictiones*. Belonged to St. Emmeram s, O.S.B., Regensburg (no. Em. F 46).

K. Halm et al., *Catalogus codicum latinorum Bibliothecae regiae Monacensis* 4.2 (Munich 1876) 190.

MS seen.

München, Bayerische Staatsbibliothek MS lat. 14591, s. xv (1465-1467), Germany

ff. 1-12v *Sermo de passione Domini* (incomplete)

ff. 13-21	Nicholas of Lyre, *Super epistolam ad Hebreos*
ff. 21v-24v	*Sermo de corpore Christi*
ff. 25-36	Gregory, *Moralia on Job*; extracts (cont. below, f. 52ff.)
ff. 37-41v	Thomas of Ireland, *Manipulus florum*. Abbreviation of the prologue, followed by extracts from the sections *Abstinentia-Conscientia*, beg. "Tu lector ora pro collectore.... Abstinencia. Utantur divites consuetudine...," ends "[Consciencia] ... fama consciencia numquam. Seneca" followed by several random excerpts from the Manipulus.
ff. 42-47	*Questiones theologice*
f. 48	blank, followed by 3 unnumbered folios, blank
ff. 52-59	Gregory, *Moralia on Job*; extracts
ff. 60-64	*Sermo de cena Domini factus Vienne ad predicatores*
f. 64r-v	Nicholas Starck (Vienna Augustinian), sermon to the clergy of St. John's
ff. 65-66v	*Sermo de annuntiatione BMV*
ff. 67-71	*Questiones theologice*
f. 71v	blank
ff. 72-83	Commentary on Canticles
f. 83v	*Epistola Soldani Babyloniorum ad papam cum huius responsione*

Paper; 2 cols., 36-42 lines; quires usually of 12 leaves. 161 × 115 mm (224 × 163 mm), ruled in ink (frame only); one hand, littera currens. Red initials; majuscules slashed in red. Bound in leaves from manuscripts over paper boards.

2ndo folio, *Dominica vero.* Belonged to St. Emmeram's O.S.B., Regensburg (no. Em. F 94).

K. Halm et al., *Catalogus codicum latinorum Bibliothecae regiae Monacensis* 4.2 (Munich 1876) 199.

MS seen.

München, Bayerische Staatsbibliothek MS lat. 16463, s. xv (1415), Germany

ff. 1-333	Thomas of Ireland, *Manipulus florum*. f. 1r-v, prologue, beg. (rub.) "Incipit liber qui dicitur manipulus florum secundum alfabetum. [text] Abiit in agrum...." ff. 1v-321v, text, ends "... Hoc opus compilatum est a magistro Thoma de Ybernia quondam socio de Sorbona. Quod opus nuncupatur manipulus florum." ff. 321v-323, table (in 3 cols.). ff. 323v-333, list of authors and works, ends "Finito libro sit laus et gloria Christo, et explicit opus magistri Thome de Ybernia quod florum manipulus nuncupatur."
f. 333v	Notes regarding an eclipse
ff. 334-351	Henry of Hassia, *Utrum rarius an saepius communicandum*
f. 351v	blank
ff. 351bis-360	Idem, *De symbolo apostolico* (dated AD 1414)
ff. 360v-361v	blank
ff. 362-367v	Thomas Aquinas, *De symbolo apostolico*
ff. 368-373v	Idem, *Orationes ad singulos psalmos*
f. 374r-v	blank

ff. 375-425   Idem, *In epistolas S. Pauli*
ff. 425v-426v   blank
ff. 427-462   Hugh of St-Victor, *De claustro materiali*
f. 462v   blank
ff. 463-474   *Versus et tractatus de vitiis*

              Paper; 2 cols., 32-38 lines; quires of 12 leaves. Catchwords. 214 × 140 mm (295 × 200 mm), ruled in ink (frame only); at least four hands, littera currens: i, ff. 1-333; ii, 334-367; iii, 368-462; iv, 463-474. Initial (4 line) red with tendrils. Initials and tituli in red; other majuscules slashed in red. Running headlines (A, B, C). Authors noted in marg. Foliated in arabic numerals. Bound in parchment over boards; 5 boss marks, 2 fore-edge clasps; label front center top, "Manipulus florum S.3"; label bearing arms now missing; pastedowns from psalter with notation (s. xi ex. - xii in.).

              2ndo folio, *edendum precepit*. Belonged to the Augustinian canons of St. Zeno, Reichenhall (S. Zen. 63).

              K. Halm et al., *Catalogus codicum latinorum Bibliothecae regiae Monacensis* 4.3 (Munich 1878) 68.

              MS seen.

München, Universitätsbibliothek MS 2º cod. 22, s. xiv[1], North Italy (Bologna)

ff. 1v-3   Table of contents to books of the Bible, with folio and chapter references (ff. 1 and 3v blank)
ff. 4-528   Bible (O. and N.T.); followed by a bibliographic apparatus consisting of the following:
ff. 529-576   *Interpretationes nominum Hebraicorum*
ff. 577-581   Pericopes
ff. 581-585   Thomas of Ireland, *Manipulus florum*; list of authors and works only, beg. (rub.) "Incipit tabula omnium inceptionum et finium originalium sive librorum doctorum in dicta tabula positorum. [text] Notandum quod libros...," ends "... dulcior gustus. Explicit tabula originalium sive librorum doctorum supradictorum, Deo gratias. Amen."
ff. 586v-587   List of commentators on the scriptures, to St. Bernard, beg. (rub.) "Isti sunt expositores veteris ac novi testamenti.... [text] Genesim: Augustinus, Beda, Jeronimus, Rabanus, Gregorius; Exodum: ...," ends "Apocalipsim: Jeronimus, Beda."

              Parchment; 2 cols., 44-49 lines; quires of 12 leaves. Catchwords. 182 × 132 mm (307 × 223 mm), ruled in ink; four or five north Italian hands (littera Bononensis: i, ff. 1v-3; ii, 4-528; iii, 529-576; iv, 577-585 [-587?]). Decorated initials at the beginnings of books; alternating red and blue secondary initials with elaborate tendrils terminating in birds, dragons and human forms; majuscules with yellow wash. Running headlines. Medieval foliation in roman numerals. Bound in stamped leather over boards (s. xix).

2ndo folio, *destruitur*. Pledge notes in Hebrew, f. 586 [Ricanti (Ricanati?) ... 20 June 1423] and f. 586v [Stephanus, servus protonotarius Rin...]. f. 586v, "Ista biblia est ordinis fratrum predicatorum cōē ... [erased]. Ad usum ... predictum.... Anno Domini MCCLXVI (= MCCCLXVI?) transmissione sancti Pauli apostoli et ... atque (?) fratris professionum...." Belonged to the University Library of Ingolstadt (s. xvi or later).

N. Daniel et al., *Die lateinischen mittelalterlichen Handschriften der Universitätsbibliothek München* 1 (Wiesbaden 1974) 36-37. MS seen.

München, Universitätsbibliothek MS 2° cod. 107, s. xv (1460-1463), south Germany

ff. 1-138   Thomas of Ireland, *Manipulus florum*; two sets of extracts. i: ff. 1-125; f. 1r-v, table (in 4 cols.), with folio numbers added in the first column; ff. 2-125, text, beg. (rub.) "Incipiunt extracta de manipulo florum magistri Thome de Hibernia. Et primo de abstinencia.... [text] Bonum est in cibo...," ends "[Xpistus] ... moriendo conquerit. Bernardus. Per infinita secula seculorum, amen." ii: ff. 125-138, beg. (rub.) "Collecta sunt hec de manipulo florum magistri Thome de Hybernia quondam socii de Sorbona Parysyus scilicet que secuntur. [text] Abstinencia: Gregorius. Intus est custodia modestiaque composita...," ends "[Excommunicacio] ... facis proprie vite eterne. Et sic est finis, Deo gracias. Sequitur ulterius." Despite the rubric, this second set of extracts does not come from the *Manipulus florum*; source unidentified.

ff. 138-143   Four tracts *De arte sermocinandi*; cf. Charland, *Artes praedicandi* pp. 102, 79, 99ff., and H. Caplan, "Artes praedicandi" nos. 98, 49.

ff. 143-150   Notes for sermon themes
[17 unnumbered blank leaves follow]

ff. 151-204v   Innocent III, *De sacro altaris mysterio*

ff. 205-209v   Honorius of Autun, *Inevitabile* (extracts)

Paper; 37-44 long lines; quires of 12 leaves. Catchwords. 197 × 142 mm (275 × 210 mm), ruled in drypoint; two hands, littera currens: i, ff. 1-150; ii, ff. 151-209v. Red initial with tendrils. Secondary initials and tituli in red. Contemporary foliation in arabic numerals. Bound in stamped leather over boards (s. xv), with two fore-edge clasps and label: "Extracta de manipulo florum magistri Thome de Hybernia. Liber de missarum mysteriis Innocencii tercii." On bottom edge: "62 Auctoritates sanctorum. Innocentius 39." Table of contents added (s. xv ex.; see below), f. 1v: "Manipulus florum, liber de missarum misteriis [...], Honorius de libero arbitrio."

2ndo folio, *Incipiunt*, or *Bonum*. Owned by Urban Klugkheimer (arms, f. 2), who added the table of contents and the rubrics to the *Manipulus florum*; a resident of Basel, he gave the book to

the University of Ingolstadt in 1502. See P. Ruf, "Ein Ingol-
städter Bücherschenkung vom Jahr 1502," *Sitzungsberichte der
Bayerischen Akademie zu München, phil.-hist. Klasse* (Munich
1933).

N. Daniel et al., *Die lateinischen mittelalterlichen Handschriften
der Universitätsbibliothek München* 1 (Wiesbaden 1974) 172-
173.

MS seen.

Namur, Musée archéologique, Fonds de la Ville MS 90, s. xv

ff. 1-161v   Thomas of Ireland, *Manipulus florum.* ff. 1-158v, text; extracts,
              beg. "*Abstinencia.* Bonum est in cibo...," ends '... B[ernardus]
              in sermone. Ubi amor." ff. 159-161v, table.

              Parchment; 32 lines. Some catchwords. (215 × 130 mm).
              Paginated in roman numerals. Binding from Floreffe, s. xviii.

              Belonged to the Premonstratensian abbey of Floreffe; f. 161v
              (s. xvi, xvii), "Benedictio utenti, abutenti maledictio. Liber B.
              Marie monasterii Floreffiensis."

              P. Faider, *Catalogue des manuscrits conservés à Namur* (Gem-
              bloux 1934) 177.

New Haven, Yale University Library MS 380, s. xv med., Italy

ff. 1-3   Ps.-Seneca, *De quattuor virtutibus* (excerpts)
ff. 3-10v   *Salomonis dicta*
ff. 11-12v   blank
ff. 13-198v   Thomas of Ireland, *Manipulus florum*; abridged, with some ad-
              ditions (including extracts from the Bible and from Petrarch).
              Beg. (rub.) "Sanctorum doctorum ac etiam aliorum quamvis
              paganorum rationi tamen congruentia dicta memoria et aucto-
              ritate digna ad instructionem fidelium ex locis plurimis ut flores
              collecta feliciter incipiunt: [text] Vix vidi continentem quem vidi
              abstinentem. [i.m.: Ambrosius.] Bonum est in cibo...," ends
              "[Superbia] ... pergitis meministis. F. Petrarca libro secundo
              capitulo De duro itinere."
ff. 199-202v blank
ff. 203-268v Petrarch, *De remediis utriusque fortunae* (excerpts)
ff. 269-274   Isidore, *De temporibus* (excerpts)
ff. 274-281v Miscellaneous definitions and etymologies
ff. 282-285   Table of contents (added, 3 Dec. 1495)

              Paper; 24-34 long lines; quires of 12 leaves. 130 × 80 mm
              (213 × 140 mm), ruled in ink; one hand, littera humanistica.
              5 illuminated initials. Authors noted in marg. (ff. 13-198v).
              Bound in half-leather and paper boards.

              2ndo folio, *duodecim sunt.* Belonged to the Visconti-Litta library.

              C. U. Faye and W. H. Bond, *Supplement to the Census of
              Medieval and Renaissance Manuscripts in the United States and
              Canada* (New York 1962) 92 (no. 244).

Nice, Bibliothèque municipale MS 29, s. xiv¹, France

ff. 1-195   Thomas of Ireland, *Manipulus florum.* ff. 1-190, text, lacks first
                   folio, beg. "[*Abstinencia d*] ... aliter non posse, melius enim
                   possent...," ends "... parentes o. Hoc opus est compilatum a
                   magistro Thoma de Ybernia quondam socio de Sorbona. Ex-
                   plicit manipulus florum." ff. 190-191, table, ends "Finit anno
                   Domini MCCCVI, die veneris post passionem apostolorum Petri
                   et Pauli." ff. 191-195v, list of authors and works.
                   Parchment; 2 cols., 42 lines; quires of 12 leaves. Catchwords;
                   leaves signed (a, b, c, d). 141 × 100 mm (188 × 130 mm), ruled
                   in lead; one hand, littera textualis. Alternating red and blue
                   initials (with tendrils) and paragraph marks. Running headlines
                   added (A, B, C). Authors noted in marg. MS suffering from
                   damp, lower and outer edges occasionally destroyed. Rebound,
                   parchment over pasteboard.
                   2ndo folio, *intervalla* (f. 1, original 2ndo folio, *aliter non posse*).
                   *Catalogue général des manuscrits des bibliothèques publiques de
                   France: Départements* 14 (Paris 1890) 445.
                   MS seen.

Nürnberg, Stadtbibliothek MS Cent. III 63, s. xiv-xv, Germany

f. 1r-v   Notes regarding events of ca. 1452-1454, cont. f. 115v.
ff. 2-114v   Thomas of Ireland, *Manipulus florum.* f. 2r-v, prologue, beg.
                   (rub.) "Incipit manipulus florum compilatus a magistro Thoma
                   de Ybernia. [text] Abiit in agrum...." ff. 2v-109, text, ends
                   "Explicit manipulus florum." ff. 109-110, table. ff. 110v-
                   114v, list of authors and works.
                   Parchment; 2 cols., 41-56 lines; quires of 8 leaves. Catchwords;
                   signatures. 260/275 × 165/180 mm (353 × 240 mm), ruled in
                   ink (sporadically); various hands, littera currens. Initial (6 line)
                   with tendrils in red and blue. Red initials with tendrils. Bound
                   in leather over boards; former no., "28 E."
                   2ndo folio, *ante annos robuste.* Belonged to the Carthusian house
                   in Nuremberg (fd. 1382); on cover, "Iste liber est Cartu-
                   siensium Nuremberge."
                   K. Schneider, *Die Handschriften der Stadtbibliothek Nürnberg* 2.1
                   (Wiesbaden 1967) 208-209.

Oxford, Lincoln College MS lat. 98, s. xiv¹, England

ff. 2-265   Thomas of Ireland, *Manipulus florum.* f. 2r-v, prologue, beg.
                   "Abiit in agrum...." ff. 2v-256v, text, ends "Explicit mani-
                   pulus florum compilatus a magistro Thoma de Hybernia quon-
                   dam socio de Serbona et incepit super (!) Johannes Galensis
                   ordinis fratrum minorum doctor in theologia istam tabulam et
                   magister Thomas finivit etc. Qui regnat cum Christo in secula
                   seculorum, amen." ff. 257-258, table. ff. 258-265, list of
                   authors and works.
                   Parchment; 37-41 long lines; quires usually of 12 leaves. Catch-
                   words in boxes; leaves signed (1, 11, 111, 1111). 153 × 102

mm (178 × 120 mm), ruled; one hand, littera anglicana. Alternating red and blue initials (with tendrils and filigree) and paragraph marks. Binding, s. xix.

2ndo folio, *Augustinus in.* f. iii^v (back flyleaf), "Liber collegii Lincolniensis Oxoniensis ex dono fundatoris... [Richard Flemming, d. 1431]." Corresponds to no. 30 in the 1474 catalog of Lincoln College Library, ed. R. Weiss, "The Earliest Catalogues of the Library of Lincoln College," *Bodleian Quarterly Record* 8 (1935-1937) 348: "Item Manipulus florum ex dono fundatoris. 2° fo. *Augustinus in sermone.*" Label f. 1, "Liber collegii Lincolniensis de methaphysica Boneti," from another manuscript.

H. Coxe, *Catalogus codicum MSS qui in collegiis aulisque Oxoniensibus hodie adservantur* 1.8 (Oxford 1852) 46-47.

MS seen.

Oxford, Magdalen College MS 87, s. xiv^1, England

ff. 1-218v   Thomas of Ireland, *Manipulus florum.* f. 1r-v, prologue, beg. (rub.) "Incipit tabula librorum originalium secundum ordinem alphabeti qui vocatur manipulus florum edita a magistro Thoma de Ybernia quondam socio de Serbona Parisius. [text] Abiit in agrum...." ff. 1v-218v, text, ends "Explicit manipulus florum. Hoc opus est compilatum a magistro Thoma de Ybernia quondam socio de Sarbona." f. 218v, table; last leaves missing, ends "*Dolor/ Ebrietas/....*"

Parchment; 2 cols., 41 lines; quires of 12 leaves. Catchwords in yellow boxes; leaves signed (a^i, a^ii, a^iii). 216 × 144 mm (290 × 204 mm), ruled; one hand, littera textualis. Alternating red and blue initials with filigree and tendrils. Running headlines. Authors noted in marg. Binding s. xix.

2ndo folio, *ho]nore sublimior.* Given to Magdalen College (fd. 1458) by Simon Alcock (MA 1420, d. 1459; see Emden, BRUO 1.20); f. 1, "Ex dono magistri Simonis Alcok."

H. Coxe, *Catalogus codicum MSS* 2.1 (Oxford 1852) 47.

MS seen.

Oxford, Merton College MS 129, s. xiv^1 (before 1347), England

Pt. I

ff. 2-25v   Robert Kilwardby, *Tabula super sententiarum libros*

Pt. II

ff. 26-136v   Thomas of Ireland, *Manipulus florum.* f. 26r-v, prologue, beg. (rub.) "Incipit tabula originalium sive manipulus florum secundum ordinem alphabeti extracta a libris scilicet XXXVI auctorum. [text] Abiit in agrum...." ff. 26v-134, text, ends "Explicit manipulus florum compilatus a magistro Thoma de Hybernia quondam socio de Serbona et incipit super (!) Johannes Galensis ordinis fratrum minorum doctor in theologia istam tabulam et magister Thomas finivit." ff. 133v-134, table, ends "Explicit tabula aurea." ff. 134v-136, list of authors and works, added in a slightly later hand.

Pt. III

ff. 137-148v Alphabetical table on the Pauline epistles, Acts and the Gospels, beg. "*Abba*, idem est quod pater et quare.... *Abraham*...." Incomplete, breaks f. 148v, "*Tribulatio* ... quanta erit in fine mundi. Math. 24a [*catchword*: consurget]"; complete text in Merton MS 197.

The table of contents (s. xiv) on f. ii indicates that the volume once contained additional tables: "In hoc volumine tot continentur: tabula super librum sententiarum; manipulus florum; tabula super epistolas Pauli; tabula super actus apostolorum; tabula super apocalipsim; tabula super epistolas canonicas; tabula super libros Salomonis."

Three manuscripts of approximately the same date, brought together by their first owner; pts. I and III may have been written by the same scribe, since the dimensions of the written space are identical (690 × 400 mm). Pt. II: parchment; 2 cols., 60 lines; quires of 12 leaves. Catchwords in red flourished boxes. 692 × 445 mm (862 × 560 mm), ruled; two hands: i, ff. 26-134 (littera anglicana); ii, 134v-136v (littera bastarda). Blue initials with red tendrils and filigree; alternating red and blue paragraph marks. Merton College binding.

2ndo folio, *Quod sicut*. Left to Merton by Robert of Gillingham, Merton fellow 1327-1333 and vicar of St. Peter's in the East 13 May 1338 until his death, January 1346: f. ii^v, "Liber quondam magistri Roberti de Gillynham in sacra pagina quondam professoris et vicarii Beati Petri in Oriente Oxoniensis, legatus domui aule de Mertone ad catenandum in librario eiusdem domus." See F. M. Powicke, *The Medieval Books of Merton College* (Oxford 1931) 128-129, and Emden, BRUO 770.

H. Coxe, *Catalogus codicum MSS* 1.3 (Oxford 1852) 57.

MS seen.

Oxford, Oriel College MS 10, s. xv (after 1431), England

ff. 1-272v John Bromyard, *Summa praedicantium*

ff. 273-337 John Felton, *Sermones dominicales* (completed in 1431; see Emden, BRUO 2.676)

ff. 337-340 Idem, alphabetical subject index to the sermons

ff. 340-446v Thomas of Ireland, *Manipulus florum*. f. 340r-v, prologue, beg. "Abiit in agrum...." ff. 340v-446v, text, ends "Hoc opus est compilatum a magistro Thoma de Hibernia."

Parchment; 2 cols., 62-64 lines; quires of 12 leaves. Catchwords in boxes; leaves signed (1-6). 267 × 175 mm (350 × 240 mm), ruled; one hand, littera cursiva. Blue initials with red herringbone tendrils; alternating red and blue paragraph marks. Occasional fore-edge tabs, ff. 1-272v. Modern Oriel College binding, original (?) whittawed leather covers bound in.

2ndo folio, *monachi etiam*.

H. Coxe, *Catalogus codicum MSS* 1.5 (Oxford 1852) 3-4

MS seen.

Padova, Biblioteca Antoniana MS 208, s. xiv[1], France (Paris?)
Pt. I
ff. 1-259   Thomas of Ireland, *Manipulus florum.* ff. 1-2, prologue, beg.
                 (rub.) "Incipit tabula librorum originalium scilicet Augustini,
                 Ambrosii, et sic de aliis qui sunt numero xxxvi auctores secun-
                 dum ordinem alphabeti qui vocatur manipulus florum, edita a
                 magistro Thoma de Hibernia quondam socius (!) de Sarbona.
                 [text] Abiit in agrum...." ff. 2-251v, text, ends "... parentes o.
                 Explicit manipulus florum compilatus a magistro Thoma de
                 Hybernia quondam socio de Sarbona. Corpus scriptoris servet
                 Deus omnibus horis." f. 252r-v, table (in 4 cols.). ff. 253-
                 259, list of authors and works, ends "... dulcior gustus. Corpus
                 scriptoris servet Deus omnibus horis."

Pt. II
ff. 261-351   Bertrand de Turre, *Sermones dominicales et de sanctis*
                 Two manuscripts brought together before 1449. Pt. I: parch-
                 ment; 2 cols., 39 lines. Quires mostly of 12 leaves; leaves
                 signed in arabic numerals. Catchwords in decorated boxes.
                 164/172 × 105 mm (230 × 160 mm), ruled in lead; one hand,
                 littera textualis. Opening initial (9 line) parted red and blue on
                 red and blue penwork, with cascade. Alternating red and blue
                 initials and paragraph marks. Bound in wooden boards covered
                 with whittawed white leather (s. xv, Italian); remains of a label,
                 back cover; remains of two ties.
                 2ndo folio, *despicias improvidus enim.* f. 259, "Iste liber est
                 assignatus ad usum ffratris Leonis" (s. xiv; French hand?);
                 "de plebe saccii" (s. xiv-xv; Italian hand; "Plebs Saccii"
                 probably = Piove di Sacco). Belonged to the convent of St. An-
                 tony, O.F.M., Padua; items 106 and 107 in the 1449 catalog;
                 106, "Tabula librorum originalium SS. Augustini Ambrosii et
                 aliorum sanctorum cum tabulis copertis coreo albo. Cuius prin-
                 cipium Abiit in agrum cum uno A de azuro et rubeo; 2us quin-
                 ternus incipit neque rogati, finis vero ultimus non auctoritate."
                 Perhaps item 51 in the 1396-1397 catalog: "Primo manipulus
                 florum cum tabulis et corio albo per totum et cum cathena."
                 Edited by K. W. Humphreys, *The Library of the Franciscans of
                 the Convent of St. Antony* (Amsterdam 1966) 29, 85.
                 G. Abate, G. Luisetto, *Codici e manoscritti della Biblioteca An-
                 toniana* 1 (Vicenza 1975) 225-226.

Padova, Biblioteca Universitaria MS 675, s. xv (1402), Italy (Padua)
ff. 1-182   Thomas of Ireland, *Manipulus florum.* f. 1r-v, prologue, beg.
                 (rub.) "Incipit manipulus florum. [text] Abiit in agrum...."
                 ff. 1v-180v, text, ends "... parentes o. Et in hoc est finis huius
                 manipuli florum. Deo gratias eiusque matri virgini gloriose
                 Marie ac toti curie celesti. Amen. Completus scribi [*sic*] per me
                 Arnoldum de Welnis Leodiensis dyocesis 1402, die mercurii
                 viii marcii, Padue commorantem apud Sanctam Margaretam.

Explicit manipulus florum compilatus a magistro Thoma de Ybernia." ff. 181-182, table (in 3 cols.).

Parchment; 2 cols., 44 lines; quires of 10 leaves. Catchwords; signatures. 188 × 140 mm (284 × 215 mm), ruled in lead; one hand, littera textualis. Red initial (8 line) decorated with blue and red. Alternating red and blue initials. Medieval foliation in arabic numerals. Modern binding, leather over old boards incorporating original ex-libris "Iste liber est Sancte Iustine"; old numbers, f. iⱽ, "YY.3.n.44" cancelled; f. iiⱽ, "AC.4"; ff. iiⱽ, 180v, 182, "301.A.14"; 3 fols. of musical fragments from the original binding bound in.

2ndo folio, *habet vinum.* Belonged to S. Giustina of Padua, o.s.b., no. 301.a.14; ex-libris notes, ff. iiV, 1, 180v, 182.

L. A. Ferrai, "La biblioteca di S. Giustina di Padova," in G. Mazzatinti, *Inventario dei manoscritti italiani delle biblioteche di Francia* 2 (Rome 1887) 602.

Padova, Biblioteca Universitaria MS 1007, s. xv, Italy (?)

ff. 1-183v Thomas of Ireland, *Manipulus florum.* f. 1r-v, prologue, beg. (rub.) "Incipit manipulus florum compilatus a magistro Thoma de Hibernia ordinis predicatorum. [text] Abiit in agrum...." ff. 1v-182v, text, ends "... parentes o. Explicit manipulus florum compilatus a magistro Thoma de Hibernia." f. 183r-v, table (in 4 cols.).

Paper; long lines (ff. 1-35) and 2 cols. (ff. 35-182v), 41 lines; quires of 10 leaves. Catchwords; signatures. 133 × 93 mm (210 × 154 mm), ruled in lead; one hand, littera textualis. Blue initial (8 line) decorated in red; floral frame in red. Red initials. Modern leather binding.

2ndo folio, *infirmitatis sue.* f. 2 bottom, "Iste liber est congregationis Casinensis deputatus monasterio Sancti Benedicti de Padoly diocesis Mantuanae signatus."

Padova, Biblioteca Universitaria MS 1243, s. xiv (ca. 1328-1344), Italy (Padua?)

ff. 1-162 Thomas of Ireland, *Manipulus florum.* ff. 1-2v, beginning of an incomplete copy; f. 1r-v, prologue, beg. "Abiit in agrum...."; ff. 1v-2v, text, ends s.v. *Accidia.* f. 4r-v, prologue, beg. (rub.) "Incipit manipulus florum [editus, *expunged*] supra extracciones originalium editus a magistro Thoma de Hybernia quondam socio [de, *expunged*] de Sorbona [de Sorbona, *expunged*]. [text] Abiit in agrum...." ff. 4v-157v, text, ends "... parentes o. Hoc opus compilatum a magistro Thoma de Ybernia quondam socio de Sorbona." In another hand: "sub anno Domini MCCCVI, die veneris post Passionem apostolorum Petri et Pauli." In the text hand again: "Explicit manipulus florum." In red, below: "1344 de mense januarii. 1328 de mense octubris." ff. 157v-158, table (in 4 cols.), ends "Finit anno Domini MCCCVI, die veneris post Passionem apostolorum Petri et Pauli." ff. 158-162, list of authors and works.

Parchment; 2 cols., 46 lines; quires of 12 leaves. Catchwords. 184 × 123 mm (267 × 200 mm), ruled in lead; two or three main hands, littera textualis (i, ff. 4-128v; ii, 129-158; probably a third, 158v-162). Initial (8 line) left blank. Initials in red. Medieval foliation in arabic numerals. Bound in pasteboard (s. xvii-xviii); label on back cover, "Banco x T"; f. iᵛ, "B.25."

2ndo folio, *Quid prodest.* Belonged to the Augustinian Hermits of Padua.

Paris, Bibliothèque de l'Arsenal MS 389, s. xv¹, France

ff. 1-276   Thomas of Ireland, *Manipulus florum.* ff. 1-2, prologue, beg. (rub.) "Incipit manipulus florum sive extractiones originalium a magistro Thoma de Hymbernia quondam scolari de Sorbona. [text] Abiit in agrum...." ff. 2-268v, text, ends "... parentes o. Explicit manipulus florum." ff. 268v-269v, table (in 4 cols.), with folio references added. ff. 269v-276v, list of authors and works.

Parchment; 2 cols., 38 lines; quires of 12 leaves. Occasional catchwords; leaves signed (ia, iia, iiia). 135 × 94 mm (212 × 141 mm), ruled in lead; one hand, littera textualis. Initial (8 line) with filigree and cascade; alternating red and blue initials (with tendrils) and paragraph marks. Running headlines (A, B, C). Authors noted in marg. Late medieval foliation, arabic numerals. Rebound in half leather. Two fore-edge clasp marks, f. 1.

2ndo folio, *quod in se.* Belonged to the Franciscan house at Châlons-sur-Marne: f. 1, "Bibliothecae ff. minorum Catalaunensium."

Catalogue général des manuscrits publiques de France: Paris, Bibliothèque de l'Arsenal 1 (Paris 1885) 251.

MS seen.

Paris, Bibliothèque de l'Arsenal MS 524, s. xv (AD 1402), France

ff. 1-266   Thomas of Ireland, *Manipulus florum.* f. 1r-v, prologue, beg. "Abiit in agrum...." ff. 1v-264v, text, ends "... parentes o. Explicit manipulus florum finitus ac completus per manum Petri van de Leydis anno Domini MCCCCII in vigilia Nativitatis Domini. Deo gratias. Hoc opus est compilatum a magistro Thoma de Hybernia quondam socio de Sorbona Parisis." ff. 265-266, table (in 3 cols.); later hand (s. xv-xvi) adds ascription to John of Wales, and two entries for *Zelus*, beg. "Zelus dupplex est...; Zelum tuum ... Bernardus ... super Cantica."

Parchment; 38-41 long lines; quires of 8 leaves. Catchwords: leaves signed (ai, aii, aiii *and* 1, 2, 3). 178 × 133 mm (287 × 215 mm), ruled in ink (frame only); one hand, littera bastarda. Initial (6 line) parted gold and blue, filigree and tendrils; alternating red and blue initials (with tendrils) and paragraph marks. Running headlines (A, B, C); tituli noted in lower marg. Authors noted in marg. Bound in mottled parchment over pasteboards.

2ndo folio, *pretii maioris.* Written by Petrus van de Leydis, 24 Dec. 1402. f. 266v, "... presbyter emi istum librum ... anno millesimo...." Belonged to Celestines of Paris (no. 356); ff. 1, 264v, 266r-v, "Celestinorum Beate Marie de Parisiis."

Catalogue général des manuscrits publiques de France: Paris, Bibliothèque de l'Arsenal 1 (Paris 1885) 376; C. Samaran and R. Marichal, *Catalogue des manuscrits en écriture latine portant des indications de date, de lieu ou de copiste* 1 (Paris 1959) 95, pl. LXXIII.

MS seen.

Paris, Bibliothèque de l'Université MS 215, s. xiv (before 1315), France (Paris)

f. 1r-v   Patristic extracts added in a cursive hand, possibly from the *Manipulus*; continued on ff. 249-250

ff. 2-248v   Thomas of Ireland, *Manipulus florum.* f. 2r-v, prologue, beg. "Abiit in agrum...." ff. 2v-241, text, ends "Explicit manipulus florum compilatus a magistro Thoma de Hyṣbernia quondam socio de Serbona, et incepit frater Johannes Galensis ordinis fratrum minorum doctor in theologia istam tabulam et magister Thomas finivit." ff. 241-242v, table (in 3 cols.). ff. 243-248v, list of authors and works; final gathering missing, ends "[Tullius] ... O Tyte siquid [*catchword*: ego]."

ff. 249-250   Additional patristic extracts (ff. 249v-250, in same hand as f. 1r-v).

Parchment; 2 cols., 36 lines; quires of 12 leaves. Catchwords in boxes; quires signed ".;. corr per Mᵗ." 215 × 145 mm (290 × 210 mm), ruled in lead; one hand, littera textualis. Initial (6 line) parted with filigree and cascade. Alternating red and blue initials (with tendrils) and paragraph marks. Authors noted in marg. Rebound (s. xix).

2ndo folio, *clari]or omni secreto.* Belonged to the Collège des Cholets (fd. 1295), whose books passed in 1763 to the Collège Louis-le-Grand; f. 1, "De domo Choletorum Parisius" (s. xv). Former nos. 188.1.9, 256, 155.

Catalogue général des manuscrits publiques de France: Université de Paris (Paris 1918) 64-65.

MS seen.

Paris, Bibliothèque Mazarine MS 1031, s. xiv in., France

ff. 1-204   Thomas of Ireland, *Manipulus florum.* f. 1r-v, prologue, beg. (rub.) "Incipit manipulus florum sive extractiones originalium a magistro Thoma de Hymbernia quondam socio de Sorbona. [text] Abiit in agrum...." ff. 2-204, text; incomplete, at end of quire f. 204v, "*Virtus k.* ... careat, qui ergo unam... [*catchword*: habet omnes habet]."

Parchment; 2 cols., 42 lines; quires of 12 leaves. Catchwords in red boxes; leaves signed (ai, aii, aiii) in red. 184 × 122 mm (255 × 176 mm), ruled in lead; one hand, littera textualis. Initial (5 line) parted red and blue with filigree and cascade; alternating red and blue initials and paragraph marks. Running headlines (A, B, C). Authors noted in marg. Rebound in half leather, 1895.

2ndo folio, *sunt non*. At head of prologue, f. 1, "In nomine [...] hoc opus incipio."

A. Molinier, *Catalogue des manuscrits de la Bibliothèque Mazarine* 1 (Paris 1885) 518.

MS seen.

Paris, Bibliothèque Mazarine MS 1032, s. xiv (1306), France (Paris)

ff. 1-296v   Thomas of Ireland, *Manipulus florum*. ff. 1-2, prologue (in lower marg.: "Incipit manipulus florum sive extractiones originalium a magistro Thoma de Hymbernia (!) quondam scolari de Sorbona"), beg. "Abiit in agrum...." ff. 2-289, text, ends "Hoc opus compilatum est a magistro Thoma de Ybernia quondam socio de Sorbona. Explicit manipulus florum." ff. 289-291, table, ends "Finit anno Domini M CCC VI die veneris post Passionem Petri et Pauli." f. 291v, blank. ff. 292-296v, list of authors and works, lacking final quire; ends, f. 296v, "[Bernardus, *De laude nove militie*] ... ad bellum...."

Parchment; 2 cols., 39 lines; quires of 4 leaves. A collection of exemplar *peciae* of the 75-pecia edition. Catchwords; *pecia* numbers (i, ii, iii) at head of gatherings, upper left; gatherings signed ("corr") twice by corrector. 170 × 108 mm (227 × 155 mm), ruled in ink; one hand, littera textualis. Initial (4 line) parted red and blue with filigree and cascade. Alternating red and blue initials and paragraph marks. Running headlines (A, B, C). Authors noted in marg. Rebound in full leather (1974).

2ndo folio, *enim est qui*.

A. Molinier, *Catalogue des manuscrits de la Bibliothèque Mazarine* 1 (Paris 1885) 518.

MS seen; see plate 4.

Paris, Bibliothèque Mazarine MS 1033, s. xiv, France

ff. 1-472   Thomas of Ireland, *Manipulus florum*. ff. 1-2, prologue, beg. "Abiit in agrum...." ff. 2-455v, text, ends "Hoc opus compilatum a magistro Thoma de Ybernia quondam socio de Sorbona." ff. 455v-457v, table (in 3 cols.), ends "Finit anno Domini M CCC VI die veneris post Passionem apostolorum Petri et Pauli." ff. 457v-472, list of authors and works, ends "... dulcior gustus. Explicit, Deo gratias."

Parchment; 33 long lines; quires of 12 leaves. Catchwords in decorated boxes. 123 × 75/80 mm (160 × 112 mm), ruled in lead; one hand, littera textualis. Initial (5 line) parted red and blue with filigree and cascade. Alternating red and blue initials (with filigree and tendrils) and paragraph marks. Authors noted in marg. Medieval foliation in arabics.

2ndo folio, *Jeronimus.* On flyleaf ii, "Precium huius libri vi equites."

A. Molinier, *Catalogue des manuscrits de la Bibliothèque Mazarine* 1 (Paris 1885) 518.

MS seen.

Paris, Bibliothèque Mazarine MS 1034, s. xiv², France

ff. 1-165   Thomas of Ireland, *Manipulus florum.* f. 1r-v, prologue, beg. (rub.) "Incipit manipulus florum sive extractiones originalium edita a magistro Thoma de Hybernia quondam socio de Serbona. [text] Abiit in agrum...." ff. 1v-159v, text. f. 160r-v, table (in 4 cols.), with tituli numbered in arabic numerals. ff. 161-165, list of authors and works.

Parchment; 2 cols., 47 lines; quires mostly of 8 leaves. 208 × 150 mm (251 × 181 mm), ruled in lead; probably two hands, littera textualis: i, ff. 1-6; ii, 6-165. Initial (4 line) parted red and blue, with filigree and cascade. Paragraph marks in red. Running headlines (A, B, C—and tituli with arabic numerals). Authors noted in marg.

2ndo folio, *prelium hostem.* f. 165, "IIII florenos dedit frater Guillelmus de Sancto Jacopo pro isto libro." Belonged to the convent of the Grands-Augustins in Paris, no. 1202.

A. Molinier, *Catalogue des manuscrits de la Bibliothèque Mazarine* 1 (Paris 1885) 518.

MS seen.

Paris, Bibliothèque Mazarine MS 4318, s. xv med.

ff. 1-56v   Thomas à Kempis, Letters

ff. 57-79v   Gregory I, *Super Cantica canticorum* (extracts)

ff. 80-133v   Thomas of Ireland, *Manipulus florum* (extracts). ff. 80-131v, text, beg. "Abstinencia...," ends "[Xpistus] ... sit molestus." ff. 132-133v, table.

ff. 135ff.   Sermons given to the Windesheim Congregation

ff. 198ff.   J. Gerson, *Contra detractores ... ordinis Carthusiensis* (extracts)

ff. 200ff.   Short history of the Carthusian Order

ff. 206ff.   Fr. Gerard, *Regule ordinis Carthusiensis*

ff. 225ff.   Letter by a Carthusian concerning religious duties, signed "Ex domo capelle ordinis Carthusiensis juxta Angiam, per fratrem vestrum Jo. Kuibber in eodem domo curatum quem scitis."

f. 234r-v   Bull of Calixtus II addressed to the monks of Cluny

ff. 235-295   *Gesta beati Johannis evangeliste*

ff. 295v-308   Peter Damian, *Sermo de beato Johanne*

A collection of pieces. Paper and parchment; 2 cols., 37-41 lines. 150/160 × 110 mm (200 × 140 mm), ruled; several hands, littera currens. Modern binding.

2ndo folio, *pauper superbus* (f. 81). f. 1, "Liber domus capelle Beate Marie juxta Angiam"; f. 224, "Detur domino Nychasio Kuibber de Angia, curato Sancti Trudonis juxta Brugis"; f. 308v, "Johannes Ascha."

A. Molinier, *Catalogue des manuscrits de la Bibliothèque Mazarine* 3 (Paris 1890) 300-301.

MS seen.

Paris, Bibliothèque Nationale MS 2615, s. xiv¹, France

ff. 1-194   Thomas of Ireland, *Manipulus florum.* f. 1r-v, prologue, beg. "Abiit in agrum...." ff. 1v-188, text, ends "Hoc opus compilatum a magistro Thoma de Hybernia quondam socio de Sorbona." f. 188r-v, table (in 4 cols.), ends "Finit anno Domini M CCC VI die veneris post Passionem apostolorum Petri et Pauli." ff. 189-194, list of authors and works.

Parchment; 2 cols., 48 lines; quires mostly of 8 leaves. Catchwords; leaves signed (ai, aii, aiii). 181 × 102 mm (225 × 150 mm), ruled in lead; one hand, littera textualis. Initial (15 line) historiated: Magister in black robes, seated in chair, lecturing from book to students; frame with vine leaves. Alternating red and blue initials (with tendrils) and paragraph marks. Running headlines (A, B, C). Authors noted in marg. Bound in red morocco with royal arms (s. xviii); chain mark f. 1 top center.

2ndo folio, *virtutum.* Colbert no. 3728.

P. Lauer, *Catalogue général des manuscrits latins* 2 (Paris 1940) 548.

MS seen.

Paris, Bibliothèque Nationale MS lat. 3336, s. xiv¹, France (Paris)

ff. 2-224v   Thomas of Ireland, *Manipulus florum.* f. 2r-v, prologue, beg. (rub.) "Incipit tabula originalium scilicet Augustini, Ambrosii et sic de aliis qui sunt numero XXXVI auctores secundum ordinem alphabeti qui (!) vocatur manipulus florum edita a magistro Thoma de Ybernia quondam socio [*corr. from* socius] de Sarbona. [text] Abiit in agrum...." ff. 3-223v, text, ends "... Explicit manipulus florum compilatus a magistro Thoma de Ybernia quondam socius (!) de Sarbona. Deo gracias." f. 224r-v, table, with folio references added.

Parchment; 2 cols., 44 lines; quires of 12 leaves. Catchwords (frequently in red boxes), quires signed; leaves signed. 170 × 102 mm (248 × 175 mm), ruled in ink; one hand, littera textualis. Initial (6 line) and frontispiece (L-frame supporting a greyhound chasing a hare, and a bird); alternating red and blue initials (with tendrils) and paragraph marks. Authors noted in marg. Medieval foliation in arabic numerals. Copied from a 24-pecia exemplar. Pecia notes in pink boxes, ff. 70, 79, 106 etc. Bound in red morocco; Colbert arms on covers.

2ndo folio, *luce clarior.* Arms within the initial f. 2, bendy or and azure (unidentified). f. 2 (erased), "Iste liber est ... et post mortem eius...." Belonged to the Benedictine abbey of Montmajour near Arles: f. 223v (effaced and darkened with oak galls), "et est conventu Arelatis ... de Monte Majori" (s. xiv). Colbert no. 4171.

Catalogue général des manuscrits latins 5 (Paris 1966) 214.
MS seen.

Paris, Bibliothèque Nationale MS lat. 7347, s. xiv[1], France

Composite volume made up of fragments of four MSS of disparate origin.

Pt. IV

ff. 17-29

Thomas of Ireland, *Manipulus florum* (fragment). ff. 17-20, text, from "[*Voluntas*] ... quam ipsa sibi et hoc...," ends "Hoc opus est compilatum a magistro Thoma de Hybernia quondam socio de Sorbona." ff. 20-21v, table (in 3 cols.), ends "Finit anno Domini M CCC sexto die veneris post Passionem apostolorum Petri et Pauli." ff. 21v-24v, 27-29, list of authors and works, ends "... dulcior gustus. Explicit iste liber, sit scriptor crimine liber, amen. Nomen scriptoris benedic Deus omnibus horis. Amen."

Part IV: parchment; 2 cols., 42 lines; quires: 1[8], 2[4], 3[1]. Catchwords; leaves signed in red (i, ii, iii). 180 × 120 mm (252 × 182 mm); one hand, littera textualis. Alternating red and blue initials (with tendrils) and paragraph marks. Running headlines (A, B, C). Authors noted in marg.

MS seen.

Paris, Bibliothèque Nationale MS lat. 14990, s. xiv[2], France (Paris)

ff. 2-202

Thomas of Ireland, *Manipulus florum*. f. 1r-v, prologue, beg. "Abiit in agrum...." (rubric, added f. 1 upper marg., "Incipit manipulus florum sive extractiones"). ff. 2-192, text, ends "Hoc opus compilatum a magistro Thoma de Hybernia quondam socio de Serbona. Explicit manipulus florum." ff. 192-194, table. ff. 194-199, list of authors and works, ends "... dulcior gustus. Explicit manipulus florum." ff. 199v-201, extracts *Predestinacio o.-Prelatio x.*, illegible above from poor quality of parchment, rewritten here in a cursive hand of the fourteenth century. f. 202, extracts *Obediencia h.-x.*, rewritten here for the same reason.

ff. 138-141v

Portion of an unidentified text, apparently added in error.

Parchment; 2 cols., 44 lines; quires of 12 leaves. Catchwords; leaves signed (a, aa, aaa, and in arabic numerals). 182 × 125 mm (240 × 170 mm), ruled in lead; one hand, littera textualis. Initial (5 line) parted with filigree and cascade. Alternating red and blue initials and paragraph marks. Running headlines (A, B, C; tituli added occasionally). Authors noted in marg. Foliated by Claude de Grandrue. Bound in parchment over pasteboard with arms of St-Victor.

2ndo folio, *in omelia*. Belonged to the Augustinian canons of St-

Victor, Paris; no. NNN 23 in the catalog of Claude de Grandrue, 1514. f. 1v, table of contents. f. 2 bottom, St-Victor ex
libris and anathema: "Iste liber est Sancti Victoris Parisiensis.
Quicumque eum fueratus fuerit vel celaverit vel titulum istum
deleverit anathema sit. Amen." f. 2v bottom, St-Victor heraldic
device, and "Ihesus—Maria—S. Victor—S. Augustinus."
MS seen.

Paris, Bibliothèque Nationale MS lat. 14991, s. xiv¹, France

ff. 1-186v   Thomas of Ireland, *Manipulus florum.* f. 1r-v, prologue, beg.
                  (rub.) "Incipit tabula originalium sanctorum secundum ordinem
                  alphabeti extracta a libris XXXVI auctorum edita a magistro
                  Thoma Ybernico quondam socio domus scolarium de Sorbona
                  Parisiensis civitate. [text] Abiit in agrum...." ff. 1v-180v, text,
                  ends "Hoc opus est compilatum a magistro Thoma de Ybernia
                  quondam socio de Sorbona. Explicit manipulus florum. Hic
                  liber est scriptus; qui scripsit sit benedictus. Nomen scriptoris
                  est Hugo." ff. 180v-181v, table, ends "Finit anno Domini
                  MCCCVI die veneris post Passionem apostolorum Petri et Pauli."
                  ff. 181v-186v, list of authors and works.
                  Parchment; 2 cols., 46 lines; quires of 8 leaves. Catchwords;
                  quires signed in roman numerals; leaves signed (aⁱ, aⁱⁱ, aⁱⁱⁱ).
                  188 × 130 mm (222 × 165 mm), ruled in lead; one hand, littera
                  textualis. Initial (6 line) parted with filigree and cascade. Alter-
                  nating red and blue initials (with tendrils) and paragraph marks.
                  Running headlines (A, B, C, with tituli at head of columns).
                  Authors noted in marg. Foliated by Claude de Grandrue. Bound
                  in green parchment over boards (s. xv); chainmark, front cover
                  top center; label, "PP 20"; remains of two fore-edge clasps.
                  2ndo folio, *trucidamus et.* Written by "Hugo." Belonged to the
                  Augustinian canons of St-Victor, Paris; no. PP 20 in the
                  catalog of Claude de Grandrue. f. i, St-Victor ex-libris. f. iiᵛ,
                  table of contents (Claude de Grandrue). ff. 1 and 286v,
                  anathema. f. 1v bottom, St-Victor heraldic device and
                  "Ihesus—Maria—S. Victor—S. Augustinus."
                  MS seen.

Paris, Bibliothèque Nationale MS lat. 15985, s. xiv (1306), France (Paris)

ff. 2v-213v   Thomas of Ireland, *Manipulus florum.* ff. 2v-3, prologue, beg.
                  "Abiit in agrum...." ff. 3-206, text, ends "Hoc opus est com-
                  pilatum a magistro Thoma de Ybernia quondam socio de Sar-
                  bona." ff. 206v-207, table, ends "Finit." f. 207v, blank.
                  ff. 208-213v, list of authors and works.
                  Parchment; 2 cols., 45 lines; quires of 12 leaves. Catchwords in
                  red boxes. 230 × 150 mm (290 × 205 mm), ruled in lead; writ-
                  ten by Thomas of Ireland, littera textualis. Initial (4 line) with
                  red and blue cascade. Alternating red and blue paragraph
                  marks. Tituli shadowed in red. Running headlines (tituli).
                  Authors noted in marg. Bound in calf over late medieval

boards; paper label on back cover, "49"; chain marks on boards and flyleaves front top center, back bottom center; title written on front cover, "Manipulus florum."

2ndo folio, *f. Abstinencia.* Written by or for Thomas of Ireland. Given by Nicholas of Bar-le-Duc (d. 1310) to the Sorbonne (nos. 922, 1007): f. 1v, "Iste liber est magistri Nicholai de Barroducis" (s. xiv in.); f. 214v, "Iste liber est pauperum magistrorum de Sarbona ex legato magistri Nicholai de Barro ducis. Precium vi librarum. Inter flores originalium." Does not appear in the Sorbonne catalogs.

MS seen; see plate 3.

Paris, Bibliothèque Nationale MS 15986, s. xiv (1306), France (Paris)

Pt. I

ff. 2-231   Thomas of Ireland, *Manipulus florum.* ff. 2-3, prologue, beg. "Abiit in agrum...." ff. 3-224v, text, ends "Explicit manipulus florum collectus a magistro Thoma de Ybernia. Iste liber est datus collegio magistrorum de Serbona." ff. 225r-v, table. ff. 226-231, list of authors and works.

ff. 231v-233v   blank

Pt. II

ff. 234-259v   Nicholas of Lisieux, *Opera.* Given to the Sorbonne by Robert de Sorbon.

Manuscript in two parts, bound together after 1338. Part I: parchment, 2 cols., 44 lines; quires of 8 leaves. Catchwords in red boxes. 227 × 142 mm (288 × 200 mm), ruled in ink and lead; written by or for Thomas of Ireland, littera textualis. Alternating red and blue paragraph marks. Tituli shadowed in red. Running headlines (tituli). Authors noted in marg. Corrector's signature "corr." to the right of each catchword. Bound in calf over late medieval boards, rebacked; remains of paper label on back cover; chain marks front flyleaf top and bottom center; remains of 2 fore-edge clasps.

Part I: 2ndo folio, *eo magis.* Given on completion by Thomas of Ireland to the Sorbonne; f. 1v, "Manipulus florum quem fecit magister Thomas Hybernicus socius huius domus. Orate pro anima eius. Precium 8to librarum. xix' inter flores." No. xxxix.19 in the 1338 catalog of the Sorbonne; ed. L. Delisle, *Le cabinet des manuscrits* 3 (Paris 1881) 43. Former nos. 923, 1002, 834.

MS seen; see plates 1 and 2.

Paris, Bibliothèque Nationale MS lat. 16532, s. xiv¹, France

ff. 1-262   Thomas of Ireland, *Manipulus florum.* ff. 1-2, prologue, beg. (rub.) "Incipit manipulus florum sive extractiones originalium editus a magister Thoma de Ybernia quondam socio de Sorbona. [text] Abiit in agrum...." ff. 2-253v, text, ends "Hoc opus est compilatum a magistro Thoma de Ybernia quondam socio de Sorbona." ff. 253v-255, table (in 3 cols.). ff. 255-262, list of authors and works.

Parchment; 2 cols., 41 lines; quires mostly of 12 leaves. Catchwords in red boxes. 180 × 115 mm (243 × 170 mm), ruled in
lead; one hand, littera textualis. Initial (6 line) in gold with
white highlights; frame of spiky vine leaves supporting a bird,
and a greyhound chasing a hare. Initial of text (6 line) gold with
vine frame. Alternating red and blue initials (with tendrils) and
paragraph marks. Running headlines (A, B, C). Authors noted in
marg. Copied from a 75-pecia exemplar; pecia marks ff. 45v,
52, 55v, 58v. Half-back green vellum Sorbonne binding; chain
marks, front flyleaves, top and bottom center.

2ndo folio, *scin]tillas nititur calefacere.* f. 262v, "Iste liber est de
... deportaverat ... *[faded].*" Possibly the *Manipulus* left to the
Sorbonne by Guillelmus Jafort Anglicus, d. before 1338 (his
Bible recorded in the 1338 catalog, no. I.38); this is the only
surviving MS of the *Manipulus* at the Sorbonne which fits the
date and for which a donor is not known; cf. L. Delisle, *Cabinet
des manuscrits...* 2 (Paris 1874) 152. f. 262 bottom, added,
"16. liber. Manipulus florum in quo auctores multorum ...iorum
secundum ordinem alphabeti. Item nomina et numeri (?) quasi
omnium doctorum preteritorum et librorum eorundem."

MS seen.

Paris, Bibliothèque Nationale MS lat. 16533, s. xiv med. (after 1347), France

ff. 3-11   Thomas of Ireland, *Manipulus florum.* List of authors and works,
               ends "Thomas Ybernicus socius de Sorbona complevit hoc
               anno Domini 1306."

ff. 12-102v   Notes and extracts from philosophical and theological texts

ff. 103-335   Thomas of Ireland, *Manipulus florum.* ff. 103-323, extracts, beg.
               (rub.) "Aliqua de manipulo florum. [text] Abstinencia est
               quando quis pro amore Dei...," ends "[Xpistus] ... iugum meum
               suave est etc. Explicit de hac compilatione ... Thomas Yber-
               nicus socius domus Sorbone hoc compilavit anno CCC VI post
               Passionem Petri et Pauli...." f. 104, "Magister Thomas Yber-
               nicus socius de Sorbona complevit hoc anno Domini millesimo
               CCCVI." ff. 142-143, table, tituli numbered. f. 323v, ab-
               breviation of prologue. f. 324r-v, table (in 5 cols.). ff. 326-
               335, short extracts from the *Manipulus florum.* Cf. B.N. lat.
               16708.

Paper; varying number of long lines; quires of varying lengths.
Size of written space varies (225 × 150 mm); unruled; one
hand, littera textualis currens, that also wrote B.N. MSS lat.
16408 and 16621. No decoration. Numerous index notes.
ff. 103-323: running headlines. Authors noted in marg.

2ndo folio, *de ordine.* Apparently a fourteenth-century Sorbonne
master's commonplace book. Belonged to the Sorbonne
(nos. 990, 1076).

MS seen.

Paris, Bibliothèque Nationale MS lat. 16708, s. xiv-xv, France (Paris)

Extracts from manuscripts at the Sorbonne:

ff. 1-40   Extracts from various ancient and medieval poets, including Virgil, Ovid, Lucan, Horace, Propertius, Tibullus, Balduinus Cecus, Juvenal, Statius, Alan of Lille, Marcianus, Boethius.

f. 40r-v   Additional extracts

ff. 41-53v   Verse abridgement of the Bible

ff. 54-153v   Thomas of Ireland, *Manipulus florum*. Extracts, beg. "Abstinencia est quando quis pro amore Dei...," ends "[Xpistus] ... iugum meum suave est etc. Explicit de hac compilatione ... Thomas Ybernicus socius domus Sorbone compilavit anno Domini CCCVI post Passionem Petri Pauli [*sic*]." Cf. B.N. lat. 16533.

f. 154r-v   Extracts

ff. 155-296v   Extracts from various ancient and medieval prose writers, including Livy, Cicero, Seneca, Augustine, Petrarch.

ff. 297-310   Florus, Epitome of Livy

Paper and parchment; varying number of long lines; quires of varying lengths. Size of written space varies, ruled by dry point and ink (frame only); largely one hand, littera bastarda. No decoration. Frequent index notes in marg. Halfbacked in green vellum; chain marks front top center.

2ndo folio, *fulmina*. Apparently a late fourteenth or early fifteenth-century Sorbonne master's commonplace book. Belonged to the Sorbonne (nos. 988, 1707).

MS seen.

Paris, Bibliothèque Nationale MS nouv. acq. lat. 708, s. xv, S. France or N. Italy

ff. 1-252v   Thomas of Ireland, *Manipulus florum*. f. 1r-v, prologue, beg. (rub.) "Incipit tabula originalium vocata manipulus florum secundum ordinem alphabeti compilata ex XXXVI libris originalium a magistro Thoma d'Ybernia ordinis fratrum minorum. [text] Abiit in agrum...," reworked. ff. 1v-251, text, ends "Explicit manipulus florum." ff. 251-252v, table (in 3 cols.).

Paper; 38 long lines; quires of 10 or (mostly) 12 leaves. Catchwords; leaves signed (ai, aii, aiii). 146 × 109 mm (213 × 153 mm), ruled in ink; one hand, littera currens. Initial (5 line). Decoration of initials and paragraph marks alternates: one page red, the next page alternating red and blue.

2ndo folio, *valet aut*. f. 1 top, stamp and ink, "D.U.A. no. 3640." Ink stamp f. i, library of the Count Hercule de Silva. Sale 1869, Potier, Paris, no. 176. Given to the Ecole des Chartes by the heirs of B. Hauréau, and by the Ecole to the Bibliothèque Nationale in December 1899.

MS seen.

Paris, Bibliothèque Ste-Geneviève MS 1447, s. xiv², France

ff. 1-244v   Thomas of Ireland, *Manipulus florum*. f. 1 (flyleaf), excerpts from the *Manipulus*. f. 2r-v, prologue, beg. (rub.) "Incipit manipulus florum sive extractiones originalium editus a magistro Thoma de Hybernia. [text] Abiit in agrum...." ff. 2v-239, text, ends "Hoc opus est compilatum a magistro Thoma de Ybernia quondam socio de Sorbona. Explicit manipulus florum." ff. 239v-240, table (in 5 cols.), ends "Fuit (!) anno Domini mcccvi die veneris post Passionem apostolorum Petri et Pauli." ff. 240-244v, list of authors and works.

Parchment; 2 cols., 50 lines; quires of 12 leaves. Catchwords, occasionally in boxes; leaves signed (a i, a ii, a iii). 207 × 116 mm (275 × 183 mm), ruled in ink; one hand, littera textualis. Initial (5 line) parted with filigree and cascade. Alternating red and blue initials (with tendrils) and paragraph marks. Running headlines (A, B, C). Authors noted in marg. Bound in brown calf with rules over pasteboard; chain marks ff. 1, 2 bottom and top center; fore-edge clasp marks.

2ndo folio, *et carni et.* The binding contained (now affixed to the back pastedown) the vow of obedience of Guillebert de Beaumont, 15 October 1489, to the monastery of Ste-Barbe-en-Auge, suggesting that the manuscript may have come from there to Ste-Geneviève, as did a number of volumes such as Ste-Geneviève ms 1646. Belonged to Ste-Geneviève in 1753 (dated ex-libris).

C. Kohler, *Catalogue des manuscrits de la Bibliothèque Sainte-Geneviève* 2 (Paris 1896) 33.

ms seen.

Piacenza, Biblioteca comunale ms Pallastrelli 186, s. xv (4 Nov. 1483), Italy (Padua)

ff. 1-296v   Thomas of Ireland, *Manipulus florum.* f. 1-2, prologue, beg. "Abiit in agrum...." ff. 2-295, text, ends "... parentes o. In monasterio Sancte Iustine Padue, die iiii novembris 1483, hora xxiii, explicit, laus Deo. Maximo labore ac vigiliis per me D. Zacha expletus est." ff. 295v-296v, table (in 2 cols.), folio references added; incomplete, ends with "Pacientia."

Paper; 38 long lines; quires of 10 leaves. Catchwords, bottom center. 145 × 85 mm (200 × 142 mm), ruled in ink; one hand, littera humanistica. Blue initial (8 line) on yellow ground, with 3 small Ps within the initial. Alternating red and blue initials; tituli and author citations in red. Bound in pasteboard (s. xix).

2ndo folio, *securius allegari.* Written at the monastery of S. Giustina in Padua; ex-libris note, cancelled, f. 1.

ms seen on film.

Praha, Knihovna Metropolitní Kapituli ms C.XXXIV.2, s. xv[1] (1425), Bohemia

ff. 2-255   Thomas of Ireland, *Manipulus florum.* ff. 2-3, prologue, beg. "Abiit in agrum...." ff. 3-253v, text. ff. 253v-255, table, with folio nos. in roman numerals added; ends "Explicit liber mani-

pulus florum scriptus per manum Blasconis presbyteri de Dobr-
zano alias de Chwalenicz plebanum, finitusque est feria quarta
ante Beate Agnetis virginis A.D. 1425."

ff. 255v-256   *Quales debeant esse illi clerici qui ad sacros ordines promoventur*
Paper; 2 cols., 44 lines. 222/232 × 155/160 mm (310 × 225
mm), ruled in ink; one hand, littera currens. Initial (10 line)
with filigree. Initials and paragraph marks in red.

2ndo folio, *gut]tas sitim.* Contains notes pertaining to the Council
of Constance 15 June 1416. Written by Blasco priest of
Dobran, who also wrote and/or owned several other manuscripts (catalog nos. 91, 173, 176, 483, 511) that belonged to
Procopius of Cladrub who gave them to the chapter library; ex-
libris note, "Domini Procopii [de Cladrub] plebani de Pomuk."

A. Patera and A. Podlaha, *Soupis Rukopisů knihovny Metropolitní
kapitoly Pražské* 1 (Prague 1910) 258 no. 454.

MS seen on film.

Praha, Knihovna Metropolitní Kapituli MS C.XXXVII.1, s. xiv², Bohemia

ff. 1-3v   *De septem doloribus BMV*
f. 4   *De conversione Pauli*
ff. 4v-7v   blank
ff. 8-159v   Thomas of Ireland, *Manipulus florum.*   f. 8r-v, prologue, beg.
"Abiit in agrum...."   ff. 8v-153v, text, abbreviated, ends
"... parentes o."   ff. 154-155, table, with tituli numbered in
arabic numerals.   ff. 155-159v, additional extracts s.vv.
Meritum, Milicia, Misericordia, Monachus, etc., beg. "*Meritum.
Bona moderatrix omnium rerum...,*" ends s.v. *Superbia,* "...
nequaquam corpus eius elacio deseruit. Gregorius in moralibus."

ff. 160-218v   Nicholas of Lyra, *Super Ecclesiasten*
f. 219r-v   *Sermo de iudicio extremo, sermo de BMV*
Paper; 2 cols., 47 lines. 220/240 × 141/155 mm (295 × 215
mm), ruled in ink; one hand, littera currens. Opening initial
(10 line), secondary initials (with tendrils) and paragraph marks
in red.

2ndo folio, *vel peregrinans* (first quire); *umbracula* (f. 9).

A. Patera and A. Podlaha, *Soupis Rukopisů knihovny Metropolitní
kapitoly Pražské* 1 (Prague 1910) 260-261 no. 458.

MS seen on film.

Praha, Knihovna Metropolitní Kapituli MS C.XXXVII.2, s. xiv ex., Bohemia

ff. 2-242v   Thomas of Ireland, *Manipulus florum.*   f. 2r-v, prologue, beg.
"Abiit in agrum...."   ff. 2v-241v, text.   ff. 241v-242v, table
(in 3 cols.).
Parchment; 40 long lines. 193 × 115 mm (275 × 180 mm), ruled
(frame only); one hand, littera bastarda. Red initials and paragraph marks.

2ndo folio, *sed quia non.* Belonged to the metropolitan chapter
library of Prague.

A. Patera and A. Podlaha, *Soupis Rukopisů knihovny Metropolitní kapitoly Pražské* 1 (Prague 1910) 261 no. 459.
MS seen on film.

Praha, Knihovna Metropolitní Kapituli MS C.CVII, s. xiv[1], France

ff. 1-242v   Thomas of Ireland, *Manipulus florum.* f. 1r-v, prologue, beg. (rub.) "Incipit manipulus florum sive extractiones originalium a magistro Thoma de Hybernia quondam socio de Sorbona. [text] Abiit in agrum...." ff. 1v-235, text, ends "Hoc opus est compilatum a magistro Thoma de Ymbernia quondam socio de Sorbona. Explicit manipulus florum." ff. 235-236, table (in 4 cols.), with folio numbers in arabic numerals (added). ff. 236-242v, list of authors and works.

Parchment; 2 cols., 47 lines. Catchwords in boxes. 174 × 110 mm (245 × 155 mm), ruled in ink; one hand, littera textualis. Initial (8 line) parted, with filigree and cascade. Alternating red and blue initials (with tendrils) and paragraph marks. Running headlines (A, B, C). Authors noted in marg.

2ndo folio, *of]feruntur ut.* Pastedown, "Liber magistri Procopii de Cladrub," professor of theology, dean of the metropolitan chapter, who left a substantial personal library to the cathedral; see MS C.XXXIV.2 above.

A. Patera and A. Podlaha, *Soupis Rukopisů knihovny Metropolitní kapitoly Pražské* 1 (Prague 1910) 307 no. 539.
MS seen on film.

Praha, Narodni Museum MS XII.G.5, s. xiv[2] (ca. 1384), Bohemia

ff. 1-60   Peter of Limoges, *De oculo morali*, ends "... qui sine fine vivit et regnat. Anno Domini millesimo CCC LXXX quarto, Vincencii martiris. Amen."
ff. 60v-61v   blank
ff. 62-104v   *Expositio in Cantica canticorum*, ends "Explicit feria 4[a] post ... a. 1383."
f. 105r-v   *De VII mirabilibus mundi*
ff. 105v-114v Thomas of Ireland, *Manipulus florum.* List of authors and works, ends "... dulcior gustus. Explicit manipulus florum."
ff. 114v-115 List of heretical sects
f. 115r-v   *Examinacio hereticorum*
ff. 116-119v John of Hildesheim, *De tribus regibus* (excerpts)

Paper; 35 long lines; quires of 10 leaves. 155 × 107 mm (209 × 150 mm), ruled in ink; several hands, littera currens. Initials and paragraph marks in red. Medieval foliation, upper right. Bound in half leather over boards; fore-edge clasp mark.

2ndo folio, *ourrus* (?). Given to the church of Český Krumlov by its former chaplain, Matthew; f. 1, "Hunc libellum pro ecclesia Crupnensi legavit dominus Matheus olim capellanus eiusdem ecclesie."

F. M. Bartoš, *Soupis Rukopisů Národního Musea v Praze* 1 (Prague 1926) 244 no. 3251.
MS seen.

Praha, Universitní Knihovna MS IV.C.7, s. xiv-xv, Bohemia

ff. 1-189   Thomas of Ireland, *Manipulus florum.* f. 1r-v, prologue, beg.
             "Abiit in agrum...." ff. 1v-187v, text. ff. 187v-189, table,
             with tituli numbered; ends "Explicit manipulus florum per
             Bundl (?)."
             Paper; 2 cols., 50 lines; quires of 12 leaves. Catchwords in red
             boxes. 202 × 138 mm (296 × 220 mm), ruled in ink (frame
             only); one hand, littera currens. Initials and author citations in
             red. Bound in leather stained pink over boards; front cover:
             5 boss marks, 2 fore-edge clasp marks, 2 labels ("D 13" and
             "Manipulus florum"); back cover: 5 boss marks.
             2ndo folio, *Demetria]dem virginem.* Inside front cover, 2 ex-libris
             notes, erased. Old pressmark and title, f. i: "F 10 Manipulus
             florum."
             J. Truhlář, *Catalogus codicum manu scriptorum latinorum* 1
             (Prague 1905) 255 no. 634.
             MS seen.

Praha, Universitní Knihovna MS V.E.25, s. xv (1411?), Bohemia

ff. 1-104   Thomas of Ireland, *Manipulus florum,* excerpts. ff. 1-102v, text,
             beg. "Abstinencia. Bonum est in cibo...," ends "Expliciunt ex-
             cerpta manipuli florum, sit laus Deo." Followed by 16 lines of
             further extracts. ff. 103-104, table (in 3 cols.), ends "Finitus
             est liber iste sub anno [cut out] xi in die ... sancti Johannis."

ff. 105-238 *Sermones de tempore*
             Paper; 32 long lines; quires of 12 leaves. 155/166 × 99/109 mm
             (212 × 148 mm), ruled in ink (frame only); one hand, littera
             currens. Initials and paragraph marks in red. Bound in paper
             boards.
             2ndo folio, *opprimitur.* f. 1 top, "Hunc librum assignavit olim
             dominus Georgius Anshelmi ecclesie in Waniaw (?) perpetuis
             temporibus permanendum pro predicatore sive predicatoribus
             studendum. Orate pro eo."
             J. Truhlář, *Catalogus codicum manu scriptorum latinorum* 1
             (Prague 1905) 377 no. 919.
             MS seen.

Praha, Universitní Knihovna MS XII.B.18, s. xiv (1385), Bohemia

ff. i-247v   Thomas of Ireland, *Manipulus florum.* f. i, table (in 4 cols.).
             f. 1r-v, prologue, beg. "Abiit in agrum...." ff. 1v-240v, text,
             ends "... parentes. Et sic est finis huius libelli scripti in crastino
             b. Eufemie." ff. 241-247v, list of authors and works, ends
             "... dulcior gustus. Explicit manipulus florum ... Scriptum est
             presens volumen a.d. 1385 in die b. Eufemie virginis per Chil-
             mann (Thilmann?) ... dum e tricorio principatus...," followed
             f. 247vb by a sermon of St. Augustine.
             Paper; 2 cols., 39 lines; quires of 12 leaves. Quires signed on first
             leaf. 235 × 153 mm (296 × 215 mm), ruled in ink (frame only);
             one hand, littera bastarda currens. Initial (9 line). Red initials

and paragraph marks. Additional texts occasionally added in marg. (cf. ff. 7v-8) in a neat round gothic hand. Bound in parchment over boards; title on front cover and label, "Y"; 2 fore-edge clasp marks.

2ndo folio, *congruencia.* Belonged to the monastery of the Holy Crown, O.Cist.; f. 1, "Liber monasterii Sancte Corone sacri ordinis Cisterciensis."

J. Truhlář, *Catalogus codicum manu scriptorum latinorum* 1 (Prague 1905) 180 no. 2123.

MS seen.

Praha, Universitní Knihovna MS XXIII.F.96 (Lobkowitz 521), s. xiv², Germany

ff. 1v-86v Thomas of Ireland, *Manipulus florum* (abridged). f. 1v, prologue, beg. "Abiit in agrum...." ff. 1v-80v, text, ends "Explicit manipulus florum. Hoc opusculum est compilatum a magistro Thoma de Ybernia quondam socio de Sorbona," followed by one column of brief extracts. ff. 81-85, list of authors and works. f. 86r-v, table.

ff. 86v-88 Extracts from the Fathers and Scripture, beg. "Vitam doctorum repentant...."

Parchment; 2 cols., 41 lines; quires of 10 leaves. Quires signed in roman numerals. 127 × 87 mm (178 × 130 mm), ruled in ink; one hand, littera textualis. Red initials and paragraph marks. Weissenau binding (s. xvi), stamped vellum with label on front cover and fore-edge clasp mark.

2ndo folio, *Per abstinenciam.* Belonged to the Premonstratensians of Weissenau near Regensburg.

P. Lehmann, "Handschriften aus Kloster Weissenau in Prag und Berlin," in his *Erforschung des Mittelalters* 4 (Stuttgart 1961) 64.

MS seen.

Reims, Bibliothèque municipale MS 514, s. xiv¹, France

ff. 1-200v Thomas of Ireland, *Manipulus florum.* f. 1r-v, prologue, beg. "Abiit in agrum...." ff. 1v-199v, text (f. 4v blank), ends "Hoc opus est compilatum a magistro Thoma de Ybernia quondam socio de Sorbona. Orate pro eo." ff. 199v-200v, table (in 4 cols.) with folio nos. added in roman numerals, ends "Hic liber est scriptus; qui scripsit [sit] benedictus."

f. 201 Added extracts (s. xv in.) from the chronicle of Peter of Coral, abbot of St-Martin of Limoges.

Parchment; 2 cols., 48 lines; quires of 12 leaves. Catchwords in decorated boxes. 223 × 150 mm (305 × 227 mm), ruled in lead; one hand, littera textualis. Initial (4 line) parted with filigree and cascade. Alternating red and blue initials (with tendrils) and paragraph marks. Running headlines (A, B, C). Authors noted in marg. Medieval foliation in roman numerals. Rheims binding,

CATALOG OF MANUSCRIPTS   385

grey whittawed calf over boards; label on back cover; marks of
two fore-edge clasps.

2ndo folio, *per abstinenciam*. Belonged to the chapter library of
Rheims cathedral (B, ord. 5, no. 99).

*Catalogue général des manuscrits des bibliothèques publiques de
France: Départements* 38 (Paris 1904) 687-689.

MS seen.

Reims, Bibliothèque municipale MS 515, s. xv, France

ff. 1-166   Thomas of Ireland, *Manipulus florum*. Text, beg. "Abstinencia.
Bonum est..."; with one column of added patristic extracts at
end s.v. *Xpistus*, ends "... ut nomen ... et gemis. Hec Josephus."

Paper; 2 cols., 52 lines; quires of 12 leaves. 223×160 mm
(300×216 mm), ruled in dry point (frame only); one hand, littera cursiva. Initials left incomplete. Rheims binding, grey whittawed leather over boards; chain mark back bottom center; with
erroneous label "Valerius" and title "Valerius Facta memo-
rabilia."

2ndo folio, *inobediens*. Probably belonged to the chapter library of
Rheims cathedral, to judge from its binding.

*Catalogue général des manuscrits des bibliothèques publiques de
France: Départements* 38 (Paris 1904) 689.

MS seen.

Rodez, Bibliothèque municipale MS 62, s. xiv med., France

pp. 1-572   Thomas of Ireland, *Manipulus florum*. pp. 3-5, prologue, beg.
(rub.) "Incipit manipulus florum sive extracciones originalium a
magistro Thoma de Hymbernia quondam socius de Sorbona.
[text] Abiit in agrum...." pp. 5-554, text, ends, "Hoc opus
compilavit Thomas de Ybernia quondam socius de Sorbona."
pp. 554-557, table. pp. 557-572, list of authors and works.

Parchment; 2 cols., 36 lines; quires of 12 leaves. 155×97 mm
(210×140 mm). Bound in whittawed leather over boards;
chain and clasp marks, front cover top center; paper label, back
cover.

Belonged to Hugh of Charente, monk of Bonnecombe, O.Cist.;
p. 574, "Iste liber est fratris Hugonis de Carenta monachi
Bonecumbe" (s. xv).

*Catalogue général des manuscrits des bibliothèques publiques de
France: Départements* 9 (Paris 1888) 234.

MS seen.

Rouen, Bibliothèque municipale MS 648, s. xiv², France

Pt. I

ff. 1-138   Thomas of Ireland, *Manipulus florum*. f. 1r-v, prologue, beg.
(rub.) "Incipit tabula librorum originalium scilicet Augustini,
Ambrosii et sic de aliis qui sunt numero xxxvi auctores, secundum ordinem alphabeti qui vocatur manipulus florum edita a
magistro Thoma de Hibernia quondam socio de Sarbona. [text]

Abiit in agrum...." ff. 1v-133, text, ends "... parentes o. Hoc opus compilatum a magistro Thoma de Ybernia quondam socio de Sorbona. Explicit manipulus florum." ff. 133-134, table, ends "Finit anno Domini MCCCVI die veneris post Passionem apostolorum Petri et Pauli." ff. 134v-138, list of authors and works.

Pt. II
ff. 139-218 Petrus Aureoli *Compendium sensus litteralis totius sacre scripture* Probably two manuscripts joined at an early date: Pt. II is written in long lines in a littera bastarda; but the ruling, dimensions of the written space, and decoration are the same as Pt. I.

Pt. I: Parchment; 2 cols., 51 lines; quires of 12 leaves. Catchwords; leaves signed (ai, aii, aiii). 210 × 150 mm (282 × 210 mm), ruled in lead with red ink frame; one hand, littera textualis. Initial (8 line) parted with filigree and cascade. Alternating red and blue initials (with tendrils) and paragraph marks. Running headlines (A, B, C). Authors noted in marg. Foliation (s. xv?) in arabic numerals. Binding, s. xix.

2ndo folio, *ab illicitis.* Belonged to Jumièges, O.S.B.
Catalogue général des manuscrits des bibliothèques publiques de France: Départements 1 (Paris 1886) 166.
MS seen.

Rouen, Bibliothèque municipale MS 649, s. xiv¹, France

ff. 2-211 Thomas of Ireland, *Manipulus florum.* f. 2r-v, prologue, beg. "Abiit in agrum...." ff. 2v-210, text, ends "Explicit manipulus florum. Hoc opus est compilatum a magistro Thoma de Ybernia quondam socio de Sorbona de Sarbona (!)." ff. 210-211, table (in 4 cols.), ends "Finit." f. 211, introductory paragraph (s. xv) to the list of authors and works (list not included).

Parchment; 2 cols., 45 lines; quires of 12 leaves. Catchwords in decorated boxes; leaves signed (ā, ā̄, ā̿). 205 × 135 mm (305 × 230 mm), ruled in lead; one hand, littera textualis. Initial (9 line) parted with filigree and frame of cascades. Alternating red and blue initials (with tendrils and filigree) and paragraph marks. Running headlines (A, B, C). Authors noted in marg. f. 26 bottom, first leaf of quire: "corr. per nobis" and "corr. iterum." Binding, s. xix.

2ndo folio, *etatis periculosa.* f. 1v (flyleaf), table of tituli (s. xv). Belonged to St-Ouen de Rouen, O.S.B. (no. 0.7).
Catalogue général des manuscrits des bibliothèques publiques de France: Départements 1 (Paris 1886) 166.
MS seen.

Saint-Omer, Bibliothèque municipale MS 671, s. xiv¹, France

ff. 1-224v Thomas of Ireland, *Manipulus florum.* f. 1r-v, prologue, beg. (rub.) "Incipit manipulus florum sive extractiones originalium a magistro Thoma de Himbernia quondam socio de Sorbona. [text] Abiit in agrum...." ff. 1v-216, text, ends "Hoc opus est compilatum a magistro Thoma de Ybernia quondam socio de Sorbona. Explicit manipulus florum." ff. 216-218, table, ends "Finit anno Domini MCCC^{mo} sexto die veneris post Passionem Petri et Pauli." ff. 218-224v, list of authors and works, ends "Dextram tamen scribentis benedicat lingua legentis. Amen."

Parchment; 2 cols., 46 lines; quires of 12 leaves. Leaves signed (a, b, c). 188 × 120 mm (244 × 173 mm), ruled; one hand, littera textualis. Initial (3 line) parted with filigree, tendrils and cascade frame. Alternating red and blue initials (with filigree, tendrils and cascades) and paragraph marks. Running headlines (A, B, C). Authors noted in marg. Binding (s. xviii-xix) with arms of Bishop Benedict of Béthune.

2ndo folio, *vermis diviciarum*. Belonged to the abbey of St-Bertin, O.S.B.

Catalogue général des manuscrits des bibliothèques publiques des départements, 4⁰ ser., 3 (Paris 1861) 295.

MS seen.

Salamanca, Biblioteca de la Universidad MS 2702, s. xiv

ff. 1-266   Thomas of Ireland, *Manipulus florum*
Parchment; 2 cols., 40 lines. (235 × 160 mm).
2ndo folio, *et quas.*

Salzburg, Bibliothek der Erzabtei St. Peter MS a.VI.7, s. xv, Germany/Austria

A miscellany (391 folios) of some 39 verses, brief works (including a tract by John Hus), sermons and excerpts, concerning especially the scriptures, canon law, and the monastic life.

ff. 66-89v   Thomas of Ireland, *Manipulus florum.* Extracts from select topics, beg. "*Electio.* Quis ferat si quis...," ends s.v. *Voluntas,* "... meus lingua manus requirantur. Explicit."
Paper; 32 long lines. Dimensions of written space vary, 174/202 × 102/136 mm (223 × 148 mm); one hand, littera currens.
2ndo folio, *in sua.* Belonged to St. Peter of Salzburg, O.S.B.
MS seen on film.

Salzburg, Bibliothek der Erzabtei St. Peter MS a.IX.4, s. xiv med., Germany/Austria

ff. 1-178   Thomas of Ireland, *Manipulus florum.* f. 1r-v, prologue, beg. (rub.) "Incipit tabula originalium sive manipulus florum secundum ordinem alphabeti extracta a libris XXXVI auctorum edita a magistro Thoma de Ybernia quondam socio de Serbona Paris.' civitatis. [text] Abiit in agrum...." ff. 1v-172v, text, ends "Explicit manipulus florum compilatus a magistro Thoma de Hybernia quondam socio de Sorbona et incepit frater Iohannes Galensis ordinis fratrum minorum doctor in theologia istam tabulam et magister Thomas finivit." ff. 172v-173, table (in 4 cols.), folio references added. ff. 173v-178, list of authors and works.

ff. 178v-189   Prosper, *De vera innocencia*
                Parchment; 2 cols., 50 lines; quires of 12 leaves. First folio
                of each quire signed in roman numerals. 237 × 158 mm
                (324 × 233 mm); one hand, littera textualis. Initials left un-
                finished. Running headlines. Medieval foliation in roman
                numerals.
                2ndo folio, *ut fecit.* Belonged to the abbey of St. Peter, Salzburg,
                o.s.b.
                MS seen on film.

Salzburg, Bibliothek der Erzabtei St. Peter MS b.VI.14, s. xv[1], Ger-
        many/Austria

Pt. I

ff. 1-164   *Vocabularium latino-germanicum ... per Andream Pichelsdorfer*
f. 164v   *Arbor consanguinitatis*
f. 165r-v   blank
ff. 166-209   Aristotelian *auctoritates*
ff. 209-211   Seneca, *auctoritates*
ff. 211-214   Boethius, *auctoritates*
ff. 214-217   *Proverbia Salomonis*
ff. 217-221v   Seneca, *Proverbia alphabetica*
ff. 222-225v   Thomas of Ireland, *Manipulus florum*, fragment. f. 222, prologue,
                beg. "Abiit in agrum...." ff. 222-225v, text; manuscript breaks
                off, ends s.v. *Adulacio*, "... Cassiodorus in quadam epistola ...
                [*catchword*: eliminat a p.]."

Pt. II

ff. 226-232   *Notae et questiones de diversis materiis theologicis speciatim exe-
                geticis et dogmaticis*
                Part I: Paper; 33 long lines; quires of 12 leaves. Catchwords.
                Ca. 163 × 95 mm (217 × 143 mm); ruled in ink; two hands, lit-
                tera currens. Initials left unfinished.
                2ndo folio, *Ab inde.* Belonged to St. Peter of Salzburg, o.s.b.
                MS seen on film.

Seitenstetten, Stiftsbibliothek MS 122, s. xv (1419), Germany/Austria

ff. 1-90v   Thomas of Ireland, *Manipulus florum.* f. 1r-v, prologue, beg.
                "Abiit in agrum... [*added i.m.*: Incipit manipulus florum com-
                pilatus a magistro Thoma de Hybernia quondam socio de Sor-
                bona]." ff. 1v-90v, text (abbreviated), ends "Explicit mani-
                pulus florum finitus per manum Mathie decani Katzpechk tunc
                temporis in Mayrhof positi et siti, anno Domini millesimo
                quadringentesimo decimo nono, feria sexta post Conversionem
                sancti Pauli apostoli."
ff. 91-93v   blank
ff. 94-200   Nicholas de Lyra, *Sermones*
ff. 200v-207v   blank
ff. 208-255v   Bede, *Interpretationes nominum hebraeorum*
ff. 256-259   Council of the diocese of Passau, 1419 (Bp. George of Hohen-
                lohe)

ff. 259-268   Council of the province of Salzburg, 1418 (Abp. Eberhard III)
ff. 268-275v Thomas Aquinas, homilies
ff. 276-279   Augustine, *Sermo de dedicatione ecclesiae vel altaris consecratione*
               Paper; 2 cols., 41 lines; quires of 10 leaves. Catchwords. 225 × 150 mm (295 × 210 mm), ruled in ink (frame only); one hand, littera currens. Initials left unfinished.
               2ndo folio, *umbracula*. Belonged to the Benedictine abbey of Seitenstetten.
               MS seen on film.

Sevilla, Biblioteca Colombina MS Vitrina 2.138.27, s. xiv

               Thomas of Ireland, *Manipulus florum*

Siena, Biblioteca comunale MS G.VIII.27, s. xiv

ff. 11-173v   Thomas of Ireland, *Manipulus florum*. Mutilated at beginning and end. f. 11r-v, prologue, beg. "...ta]libus litteris invenientur auctores...." ff. 11v-173v, text, ends s.v. *Xpistus*, "... Gemina dulcedo suavitatis exu[berat...."

Soissons, Bibliothèque municipale MS 112, s. xiv[1], France (Paris)

ff. 1-236   Thomas of Ireland, *Manipulus florum*. f. 1r-v, prologue, beg. (rub.) "Incipit tabula librorum originalium scilicet Augustini, Ambrosii et sic de aliis qui sunt numero xxxvi auctores secundum ordinem alphabeti qui vocatur manipulus florum, edita a magistro Thoma de Ybernia quondam socio de Sarbona. [text] Abiit in agrum...." ff. 1v-235, text. ff. 235v-236, table.
               Parchment; 2 cols., 39 lines. Quires of 12 leaves. 195 × 125 mm (255 × 180 mm), ruled in lead; one hand, littera textualis. Opening initial (7 line) rose with vine stems, on gold and blue background; spiky vine-leaf frame on inner and lower margins. First initial of text (5 line) parted red and blue, with cascade and tendrils. Alternating red and blue initials (with filigree and tendrils) and paragraph marks. Foliated in roman numerals, upper left verso. Authors noted in marg. Bound in half leather over paper (s. xviii-xix).
               2ndo folio, *quid alimentorum*
               Catalogue général des manuscrits des bibliothèques publiques de France: Départements 3 (Paris 1885) 97-98.
               MS seen.

Soissons, Bibliothèque municipale MS 140, s. xiv[1], France (Paris?)

ff. 1-259v   Thomas of Ireland, *Manipulus florum*. f. 1r-v, prologue, beg. "Abiit in agrum...." ff. 1v-250, text, ends "... parentes o. Hoc opus est compilatum a magistro Thoma de Ybernia quondam socio de Sorbona. Explicit manipulus florum." ff. 250-251, table (in 4 cols.). f. 251v, blank. ff. 252-259v, list of authors and works.
               Parchment; 2 cols., 38 lines. Quires of 12 leaves; leaves signed in roman numerals. 155 × 105 mm (200 × 140 mm), ruled in lead; one hand, littera textualis. Opening initial parted gold and blue,

with red and blue cascade, filigree and tendrils. First initial of
each new letter of the alphabet (3 line) parted red and blue, with
tendrils. Alternating red and blue initials and paragraph marks.
Running headlines (A, B, C). Authors noted in marg. Bound in
half leather over boards (s. xviii-xix); bookplate, "Bibliotheca
Praemonstratensis."
2ndo folio, *cum quibus*. Belonged to the Premonstratensians of
Soissons.
*Catalogue général des manuscrits des bibliothèques publiques de
France: Départements* 3 (Paris 1885) 114-115.
MS seen.

Tarazona, Biblioteca de la catedral MS 63

ff. 1-282v   Thomas of Ireland, *Manipulus florum*. Prologue, text, table and list
                  of authors and works.

Tarragona, Biblioteca provincial MS 17, s. xv, Catalonia

ff. 1-257   Thomas of Ireland, *Manipulus florum*. f. 1r-v, prologue, beg.
                  (rub.) "Incipit liber qui manipulus florum dicitur compilatus per
                  fratrem Thomam Anglicum. [text] Abiit in agrum...." ff. 1v-
                  254, text, ends "Explicit liber qui dicitur manipulus florum,
                  Deo gratias." ff. 254v-257, table.
                  Parchment; 25-29 long lines. 140 × 100 mm (198 × 142 mm).
                  Alternating red and blue initials.
                  2ndo folio, *sint appenit* (?). Belonged to the Cistercian monastery
                  of Santa Maria de Poblet y de Santes Creus.
                  J. Dominguez Bordona, *El escritorio y la primitiva biblioteca de
                  Santes Creus*, Instituto de estudios Tarraconenses "Ramón
                  Berenguer IV" (Tarragona 1952) 16. Idem, *Manuscritos de la
                  Biblioteca pública de Tarragona*, Instituto de estudios Tarra-
                  conenses "Ramón Berenguer IV" (Tarragona 1954) 9.

Toledo, Biblioteca del Cabildo MS 10-8, s. xiv, Spain

ff. 1-108   Thomas of Ireland, *Manipulus florum*. f. 1r-v, beg. "Abiit in
                  agrum...." ff. 1v-105v, text, ends "Explicit manipulus florum
                  compilatus a magistro Thoma quondam socio de Sartona (!).
                  Deo gratias, amen." ff. 105v-108, table.
                  This manuscript disappeared from the library in 1934.

Tortosa, Biblioteca del Cabildo MS 75, s. xiv

ff. 1-128   Thomas of Ireland, *Manipulus florum*. Beginning mutilated. ff. 1-
                  124v, text, beg. s.v. *Apostoli*, "... velit ut meus. Optarem...,"
                  ends "Hoc opus est compilatum a magistro Thoma de Ybernia
                  quondam socio de Sorbona. Explicit manipulus florum."
                  ff. 124v-125, table. ff. 125-128, list of authors and works.
                  Parchment; 2 cols. (313 × 214 mm).
                  Belonged to the cathedral library of Tortosa.
                  B. Bertomeu, *Los códices medievales de la catedral de Tortosa*
                  (Barcelona 1962) 220.

Toulouse, Bibliothèque municipale MS 222, s. xiv (1 March 1307 N.S.), France (Paris)

ff. 1-311   Thomas of Ireland, *Manipulus florum.* ff. 1-2, prologue, beg. (rub.) "Incipit manipulus florum sive extractiones originalium a magistro Thoma de Hymbernia quondam scolari de Sorbona. [text] Abiit in agrum...." ff. 2-309, text (with additions, s. xiv-xv, to entry for *Maria*), ends "Hoc opus est compilatum a magistro Thoma de Ybernia condam socio de Sorbona." ff. 309-311, table (with references to folios, added), ends "Iste liber finitur anno Domini millesimo tricentesimo sexto, die mercurii in festo sancti Albani. Explicit Deo gracias." f. 312r-v, blank.

      Parchment; 2 cols., 39 lines; quires of 12 leaves. Catchwords. 155 × 99 mm (210 × 150 mm), ruled in lead; one hand, littera textualis. Initial (5 line) parted with filigree and cascade. Alternating red and blue initials and paragraph marks. Running headlines (A, B, C). Authors noted in marg. Contemporary foliation on the verso. Flyleaves from a s. xii glossed Boethius *De consolatione.* Rebacked leather on boards; chain mark ff. 1, 312, bottom center; remains of fore-edge clasp; label with title on back cover.

      2ndo folio, *Sydonius.* Belonged to the Dominican convent in Toulouse.

      Catalogue général des manuscrits des bibliothèques publiques des départements, 4° ser., 7 (Paris 1885) 141.

      MS seen.

Tours, Bibliothèque municipale MS 35, s. xiv, France

ff. 1-218v Thomas of Ireland, *Manipulus florum.* f. 1r-v, prologue, beg. (rub.) "Incipit manipulus florum sive extractiones originalium a magistro Thoma de Ybernia quondam socio de Sarbona. [text] Abiit in agrum...." ff. 1v-218v, text, ends "Hoc opus est compilatum a magistro Thoma de Ybernia quondam socio de Sarbona. Explicit manipulus florum."

ff. 219-276 *Liber Pharetrae*, rearranged in alphabetical order; beg. "*Acceptio personarum*. Nostri principes cum pauperes delinquentes publice...," ends "*Zelus* ... honoribus totum datur, sanctitati nichil. Explicit opus extractum de pharetra, dimissis originalibus que in manipulo florum reperiuntur." ff. 275-276, table of chapters.

      Parchment; 2 cols., 40 lines; quires of 12 leaves. Catchwords; leaves signed (i, ii, iii). 165 × 110 mm (229 × 160 mm), ruled in lead; one hand, littera textualis. Initial (8 line) parted red and blue, with filigree and cascade. Alternating red and blue initials (with tendrils) and paragraph marks. Authors noted in marg. Bound in leather over boards.

      2ndo folio, *Quam suave mihi.* Belonged to St-Martin of Tours (no. 156).

Catalogue général des manuscrits des bibliothèques publiques de France: Départements 37 (Paris 1900) 23-24.
MS seen on film.

Tours, Bibliothèque municipale MS 36, s. xiv, France

ff. 2-182v
Thomas of Ireland, *Manipulus florum.* ff. 2-177, text, first leaf lacking; beg. "[*Abstinencia*] ... est primus gradus intemperancie. Ieronimus in quadam epistola...," ends "Hoc opus compilatum a magistro Thoma de Ybernia quondam socio de Sorbona. Explicit manipulus florum." f. 178, table. ff. 178-182v, list of authors and works, ends "... dulcior gustus. Explicit, Deo gracias."

Parchment; 2 cols., 48 lines; quires of 10 leaves. Catchwords in boxes. 195 × 138 mm (274 × 196 mm), ruled in lead; one hand, littera textualis. Major initials parted red and blue. Alternating red and blue paragraph marks. Running headlines (A, B, C). Authors noted in marg.

2ndo folio, *est primus.* Given by "Martinus Chaboz divini legis professor prefate ecclesie canonicus et scholasticus" to St-Martin of Tours (no. 146).

Catalogue général des manuscrits des bibliothèques publiques de France: Départements 37 (Paris 1900) 24.
MS seen on film.

Tours, Bibliothèque municipale MS 37, s. xiv, France

ff. 2-196v
Thomas of Ireland, *Manipulus florum.* f. 2r-v, prologue, beg. "Abiit in agrum...." ff. 2v-195, text, ends "Hoc opus compilatum est a magistro Thoma de Ybernia quondam socio de Sarbona Parisiensi." ff. 195-196v, table. f. 196v, beginning of the introductory paragraph to the list of authors and works, "Notandum est quod...," ends "... ad principia et fines ac...," left incomplete. ff. 197-200, blank.

Parchment; 2 cols., 41 lines; quires of 12 leaves. Catchwords. 200 × 135 mm (285 × 213 mm), ruled in lead; one hand, littera textualis. Initial parted red and blue, with filigree and cascade. Alternating red and blue initials (with tendrils) and paragraph marks. Running headlines (tituli). Authors noted in marg. Bound in grey leather over boards.

2ndo folio, *tu vero summa.* Belonged to Yves Mesnager, canon and penitentiary of the cathedral of Tours, who left many books to the chapter library in the fifteenth century; f. 196v, "Iste liber est Yvonis canonici et penitenciarii Turonensis."

Catalogue général des manuscrits des bibliothèques publiques de France: Départements 37 (Paris 1900) 24-25.
MS seen on film.

Trier, Stadtbibliothek MS 91/1075, s. xv², Germany

ff. 1-271   Jordanus of Quedlinburg, *Postillae super Bibliam*
ff. 272-277v Thomas of Ireland, *Manipulus florum.* List of authors and works

ff. 278-294   Caesarius of Arles, *De honestate mulierum*
Paper; 2 cols. 236/243 × 152/156 mm (304 × 208 mm); various hands, littera currens. Bound in brown leather.
2ndo folio, *aromata primo*. Belonged to the house of Poor Clares in Trier (fd. 1453). The manuscript, esp. the list of authors and works, is discussed by P. Bissels, "Wissenschaft und Bibliographie im spätmittelalterlichen Trier," *Kurtrierisches Jahrbuch* 6 (1965) 54-60, who mistakes the list for the catalog of a private library.
M. Keuffer, *Beschreibendes Verzeichnis der Handschriften der Stadtbibliothek zu Trier* 1 (Trier 1888) 66.
MS seen on film.

Troyes, Bibliothèque municipale MS 1261, s. xiv¹, France

ff. 1-2v   Extracts and notes, continued on ff. 285-286 below
ff. 3-284v   Thomas of Ireland, *Manipulus florum*.   f. 3r-v, prologue, beg. "Abiit in agrum...."   ff. 3v-276, text.   ff. 276-277, table. ff. 277-284v, list of authors and works.
ff. 285-286   Notes and extracts continued from ff. 1-2v above
Parchment; 2 cols., 35 lines; quires of 12 leaves. Catchwords; leaves signed. 150 × 100 mm (250 × 143 mm), ruled in lead; one hand, littera textualis. Initial (10 line) gold on blue with white highlights and spiky vine frame. Alternating red and blue initials and paragraph marks. Running headlines. Authors noted in marg. Bound in whittawed leather over boards, rebacked.
2ndo folio, *percipere quicquid*. Belonged to the abbey of Clairvaux, O.Cist. (no. L 63).
Catalogue général des manuscrits des bibliothèques publiques des départements 2 (Paris 1855) 517.
MS seen.

Troyes, Bibliothèque municipale MS 1458, s. xiv, France

ff. 1-475v   Thomas of Ireland, *Manipulus florum*.   ff. 1-2v, prologue, beg. (rub.) "Tabula originalium sive manipulus florum secundum ordinem alphabeti extracta a libris triginta et sex auctorum edita a magistro Thoma de Hybernia quondam socio de Sorbona. [text] Abiit in agrum...."   ff. 2v-474v, text, ends "Explicit manipulus florum compilatus a magistro Thoma de Hybernia quondam socio de Sorbona."   ff. 474v-475v, table (in 4 cols.), final quire lost; ends *"Vita eterna...."*
Parchment; 2 cols., 31 lines; quires of 12 leaves. Catchwords in red boxes; leaves signed (ai, aii, aiii, and 1, 2, 3). 159 × 100 mm (223 × 153 mm), ruled in lead; one hand, littera textualis. Initial (6 line) parted red and blue, with filigree and cascade. Alternating red and blue initials (with filigree and tendrils) and paragraph marks. Back pastedown from a glossed Bible (s. xiii). Bound in whittawed leather over boards; chain mark front cover, bottom center; label on back cover.
2ndo folio, *ideo ne*. Belonged to the abbey of Clairvaux, O.Cist. (no. L 64).

Catalogue général des manuscrits des bibliothèques publiques des départements 2 (Paris 1855) 609-610.

MS seen.

Troyes, Bibliothèque municipale MS 1785, s. xiv (1313 N.s.), France (Paris)

ff. 1-285   Thomas of Ireland, *Manipulus florum*. f. 1 r-v, prologue (space left for rubric), beg. "Abiit in agrum...." ff. 2-283, text, ends "Hoc opus est compilatum a magistro Thoma de Ybernia quondam socio de Serbona." ff. 283-285, table, ends "Finit anno Domini MCCCVI die veneris post Passionem apostolorum Petri et Pauli; et Robertus de Marcelliaco finivit litteram anno MCCCXII die mercurii post Ramos palmarum in villa Parisius," i.e., 11 April 1313 (N.s.).

Parchment; 2 cols., 32-36 lines; quires of 12 leaves. Catchwords occasionally decorated; leaves signed (ai, aii, aiii). 120/122 × 78/80 mm (169 × 104 mm), ruled in lead; two hands (i, ff. 1-109; ii, 109-285), littera textualis. Initial (4 line) parted red and blue with cascade. Alternating red and blue initials (with filigree and tendrils) and paragraph marks. Running headlines added (A, B, C). Authors noted in marg. Bound in whittawed leather; chain mark, front and back cover, bottom; label on back cover.

2ndo folio, *Agellius*. f. 1, at head of prologue, "Ave Maria gracia plena, Dominus tecum." Finished by Robert *de Marcelliaco*. Belonged to Peter Ceffons, monk of Clairvaux who studied at the Cistercian house in Paris; f. 285, "Iste liber est fratris Petri de Ceffons quem fecit scribi Parisius scolaris existens ibidem." He gave it to the abbey of Clairvaux, O.Cist. (no. A 56). C. Samaran and R. Marichal, *Catalogue des manuscrits en écriture latine portant des indications de date, de lieu ou de copiste* 5 (Paris 1965) 517 and pl. XLII. Regarding Ceffons see D. Trapp, "Peter Ceffons of Clairvaux," *Recherches de théologie ancienne et médiévale* 24 (1957) 101-154.

Catalogue général des manuscrits des bibliothèques publiques des départements 2 (Paris 1855) 746.

MS seen.

Uppsala, Universitetsbiblioteket MS C.608, s. xiv, France

ff. 2-204   Thomas of Ireland, *Manipulus florum*. f. 2r-v, prologue, beg. "Abiit in agrum...." ff. 2v-199, text, ends "Hoc opus est compilatum a magistro Thoma de Ybernia quondam socio de Sarbona." f. 199v, table. ff. 199v-204, list of authors and works, ends "Explicit manipulus florum."

Parchment; 2 cols., 48 lines; quires of 12 leaves. Catchwords. 198 × 120 mm (272 × 185 mm), ruled in lead; one hand, littera textualis. Historiated initial (5 line) in blue, red and gold, with tendrils. Alternating red and blue initials with filigree. Running headlines. Bound in leather over boards; 4 ivory bosses, front cover.

2ndo folio, *abstinere et quas.* Belonged to the Brigittines of St. Mary in Vadstena (fd. 1344); f. 1v, "Liber monasterii Sancte Marie in Watzsteno"; Vadstena no., f. 1, "C 2° primus in ordine." On back pastedown, "Constitit xxi florenis."

Valencia, Biblioteca de la catedral MS 266, s. xiv[1]. France

ff. 1-307
Thomas of Ireland, *Manipulus florum.* f. 1r-v, prologue, beg. "Abiit in agrum...." ff. 1v-296, text, ends "Hoc opus est compilatum a magistro Thoma de Ybernia quondam socio de Sorbona. Explicit manipulus florum." ff. 296-298, table; first 24 tituli are numbered, with roman numerals. ff. 298-307, list of authors and works, with additions in the marg. ff. 303v, 305, 305v, 307 (marginalia printed in catalog; see below).

Parchment; 2 cols., 39 lines; quires of 8 leaves. Catchwords. 175 × 108 mm (240 × 158 mm); one hand, littera textualis. Large initial, with text enclosed in frame. Alternating red and blue initials (with tendrils) and paragraph marks. Authors noted in marg.

2ndo folio, *ni]titur calefacere.*

E. Olmos Canalda, *Catálogo descriptivo: Códices de la catedral de Valencia,* ed. 2 (Madrid 1943) 191-192.

MS seen on film.

Vaticano (Città del), Biblioteca apostolica vaticana MS lat. 1169, s. xiv[2], Italy

f. 1r-v
Peter Damian, *Institutio monialis* chap. 6 (added, s. xv-xvi). See f. 176 below.

ff. 2-175v
Thomas of Ireland, *Manipulus florum.* f. 2r-v, prologue, beg. "Abiit in agrum...." ff. 2v-174v, text. f. 175r-v, table (in 4 cols.), with decorated initials.

f. 176
Hymn, *De gloria paradisi*; added in hand on f. 1r-v above

Parchment; 46 long lines; quires of 8 leaves. Catchwords, bottom center. 221 × 134 mm (272 × 198 mm), ruled in ink; one hand, littera textualis rotunda. Initial (14 line) parted red and blue with filigree. Primary initials decorated. Red initials and paragraph marks. Bound in red leather.

2ndo folio, *suscipere.* Notes of various possessors: f. 2 (erased), "Iste liber ... manipulus florum est fratris Nicolai de Nuceria ordinis predicatorum ... die viii aprilis." f. 176 (erased), "Iste liber est magistri Nicolai de Nuceria ordinis predicatorum quem emit per manum dompni [Bu... Bad...] pro xx ducatis et uno carlino, anno Domini MCCCCXXI die viii mensis septembris, xv indictione"; regarding Nicholas see F. Ehrle, *I più antichi statuti della facoltà teologica dell'Università di Bologna* (Bologna 1932) 107 n. 107. f. iᵛ (erased), "De chorreto manipulus ... have[r?] conperato ... per duchati nove de Francescyno Tornaboni ... de Medici, MCCCCLXV." f. iᵛ, "Hier[onymus della Rovere] cardinalis Rancanetensis" (d. 1 Sept. 1507).

M. Laurent, *Codices Vaticani latini, codices 1135-1266* (Vatican City 1958) 44-45.

MS seen.

Vaticano (Città del), Biblioteca apostolica vaticana MS Barberini 458, s. xiv[1], France (Paris)

ff. 1-349v
Thomas of Ireland, *Manipulus florum.* ff. 1-2, prologue, beg. (rub.) "Incipit manipulus florum. [text] Abiit in agrum...." ff. 2-336v, text, ends "... parentes o. Hoc opus est compilatum a magistro Thoma de Ybernia quondam socio de Serbona." ff. 336v-339, table. ff. 339-349v, list of authors and works, ends "... dulcior gustus. Explicit manipulus florum, Deo gracias. Amen."

Parchment; 2 cols., 33 lines; quires of 12 leaves. Catchwords encircled. 145×96 mm (202×140 mm), ruled in lead and ink; one hand, littera textualis. Initial (7 line) parted red and blue with filigree and cascade. Alternating red and blue paragraph marks. Running headlines, ruled (A, B, C). Authors noted in marg. Pecia marks ("pe xxxix" etc.), ff. 75, 102, 115v, 144v, 172v, 177, 186, 195, 227, 241, 332; copied from 75-pecia exemplar. Typically Parisian in hand, layout and color; corrections in a hand similar to if not identical with that which corrected the exemplar pieces in Paris Mazarine MS 1032. Bound in brown leather (s. xvi) rebacked; fore-edge clasps; chain mark, f. 1 bottom center; label back cover, "Manipulus florum."

2ndo folio, *Maximus.* f. 349v, erased (s. xiv), "Iste liber est conventus Sancte Marie super Minervam de urbe, ordinis fratrum predicatorum"; see T. Kaeppeli, "Antiche biblioteche domenicane in Italia," *Archivum Fratrum Praedicatorum* 36 (1966) 60. No. 164 in the inventory (s. xv ex.) of the house; ed. G. Meersseman, *Mélanges Auguste Pelzer* (Louvain 1947) 605-634.

MS seen.

Vaticano (Città del), Biblioteca apostolica vaticana MS Borghese 247, s. xiv (1315), France (Paris)

This is one of the school books of Peter Roger (Clement VI) written when he was at Paris; it is full of notes and extracts from various texts (described by Maier; see below), among which the following from Thomas of Ireland, *Manipulus florum*:

ff. 20-21v
List of authors and works (copied from Paris, Bibl. univ. MS 215)

ff. 189-195v
Extracts from the text, beg. "*Amor* bo. Ames parentem si equus est...," ends "[*Deus* ad.] ... est. Ita dico Lucili." Excerpted from a 24-pecia exemplar; f. 194 (*Correctio* al.), "Hic incipit vi[a] p[a]"; f. 195v (*Deus* ad.), "Hic finitur vi[a] pecia."

Parchment; long lines and 2 cols. (respectively), ca. 127 lines; quire structure varies. Ca. 333×209 mm (368×250 mm), ruled in hard point; written by Peter Roger, notula cursiva.

Initials left incomplete. Authors noted in marg. (ff. 189-195v).

2ndo folio, *Contra in omni.*

A. Maier, "Der literärische Nachlass des Petrus Rogerii (Clemens VI) in der Borghesiana," *Recherches de théologie ancienne et médiévale* 15 (1948) 332-356, 16 (1949) 72-98, esp. 92-96. She did not identify the source of the list of authors and works. A. Maier, *Codices Burghesiani Bibliothecae Vaticanae*, Studi e testi 170 (Vatican City 1952) 295-301.

MS seen.

Vaticano (Città del), Biblioteca apostolica vaticana MS Palat. lat. 226, s. xv (1438-1447), Germany

A compendium or handbook containing a large number of fragmentary texts and notes (described in part in Stevenson; see below), including:

ff. 50v-57v   Thomas of Ireland, *Manipulus florum.* List of authors and works, to Chrysostom; beg. "Nota aliquos libros originalium sanctorum...," ends "... *finis*: cum Sancto Spiritu in secula seculorum.... 1447 in octava Agnetis."

Paper; long lines; quires of 12 leaves. 150 × 99 mm (210 × 151 mm), ruled in ink (frame only); several hands (i, ff. 1-104v; ff. 105-204v, various hands). Bound in velum over paper boards.

2ndo folio, *clama.*

E. Stevenson, *Codices Palatini latini Bibliothecae Vaticanae* 1 (Rome 1886) 50-52.

MS seen.

Vaticano (Città del), Biblioteca apostolica vaticana MS Palat. lat. 233, s. xv[1], Germany

Pt. I

ff. 1-165   Francis de Mayronis, *Flores beati Augustini*; ff. 117-156v, table to works of St. Augustine

Pt. II

ff. 168-296   Thomas of Ireland, *Manipulus florum.* f. 168r-v, prologue, beg. "Abiit in agrum...." ff. 169-291', text, ends "Explicit manipulus florum compilatus a magistro Thoma de Hybernia quondam socio de Sorbona erra parisiensem in verbo Sorbona [*sic*]." ff. 291-292, table, followed by added material for *Adulatio*. ff. 292v-296, list of authors and works.

ff. 296v-297   *Sermo de festivitate conversionis ad vitam monasticam*

f. 297v   Excerpt from St. Bernard, *De Iuda Iscariota*

Part II: paper; 2 cols.; quires of 12 leaves. 237 × 170 mm (288 × 222 mm), ruled in ink (frame only); two hands (i, ff. 168-296; ii, 296v-297v), littera currens. Red initials and paragraph marks. f. i, table of contents to pt. I. Bound in green parchment over paper boards; chain mark f. 298v top center.

2ndo folio, *apud philosophos* (pt. I), *nichil sic* (pt. II). f. 298v, verses in German.

E. Stevenson, *Codices Palatini latini Bibliothecae Vaticanae* 1 (Rome 1886) 54.

MS seen.

Vaticano (Città del), Biblioteca apostolica vaticana MS Palat. lat. 391, s. xv (1458), Germany (Colmberg)

Pt. I
ff. 1-109v   Nicholas Gorran, *Distinctiones*, with table (ff. 1-10).

Pt. II
ff. 110-379v   Thomas of Ireland, *Manipulus florum*. f. 110r-v, prologue, beg. "Abiit in agrum...." ff. 110v-370, text, ends "Et sic explicit totum corpus manipuli florum magistri Thome de Anglia ordinis predicatorum; per manum Nicole Hoffman factum est hoc opus in castro Colmberg, in vi^a Purificationis sub anno Domini MCCCCLVIII etc. Heu male finivi quia non bene scribere scivi. Rex regum Christe tibi sit gratus liber iste. Amen." ff. 370-371v, table. ff. 372-379v, list of authors and works.

f. 380   Fragments of an astronomical table; conjuncts and opposites for 1357. Taken from the binding; perhaps written by the writer of pt. I.

Pt. II: Paper; 2 cols., 44 lines; quires of 16 leaves. 228 × 145 mm (286 × 197 mm), ruled in ink (frame only); written by Nicholas Hoffman, littera currens. Red initials and paragraph marks. Running headlines.

2ndo folio, *clamavi* (pt. I), *facilitate* (pt. II).

E. Stevenson, *Codes Palatini latini Bibliothecae Vaticanae* 1 (Rome 1886) 115.

MS seen.

Vaticano (Città del), Biblioteca apostolica vaticana MS Palat. lat. 616, s. xiv^1, France (Paris)

ff. 1-228   Thomas of Ireland, *Manipulus florum*. f. 1r-v, prologue, beg. (rub.) "Incipit manipulus florum sive extractiones originalium a magistro Thoma de Hybernia quondam socio de Serbona. [text] Abiit in agrum...." ff. 1v-220, text, ends "Hoc opus compilatum a magistro Thoma de Ybernia quondam socio de Sorbona. Explicit manipulus florum." ff. 220-221, table, ends "Finit anno Domini MCCCVI die veneris post Passionem apostolorum Petri et Pauli." ff. 221-228, list of authors and works.

Parchment; 2 cols., 46 lines; quires of 12 leaves. Catchwords in decorated boxes; leaves signed (a-f). 175 × 112 mm (228 × 158 mm), ruled in ink; one hand, littera textualis.

Initial (3 line) with frame. Alternating red and blue initials (with tendrils) and paragraph marks. Running headlines (A, B, C). Authors noted in marg. Tituli (in text and table) numbered in arabic numerals. Bound in red morocco.

2ndo folio, *dominica quarta*. Bought by Bertold of Schönau for the Cistercian abbey of St. Mary in Schönau in 1340; f. iᵛ, "Noverint universi tam presentes quam futuri quod frater Bertholdus de Schon. parisius tempore studii sui sub venerabili in Christo patre et domino ... domino Luddoldo abbate librum istum pro communi usu, utilitate et studio omnium dominorum et fratrum dicte domus comparavit de bursa sibi assignata, anno Domini MCCCXL." Ex-libris of St. Mary of Schönau, ff. 1, 228. Note, f. iᵛ: "Manipulus florum proprie dicitur esse multarum spicarum per manum in unam collectio, sed flores sanctorum et doctorum dicuntur esse ipsorum auctoritates. Hic iste liber dicitur manipulus florum quia collectus est ex omnibus dictis sanctorum et doctorum catholicorum."

E. Stevenson, *Codices Palatini latini Bibliothecae Vaticanae* 1 (Rome 1886) 221.

MS seen.

Vaticano (Città del), Biblioteca apostolica vaticana MS Rossi 217, s. xiv¹, France

ff. 1-175   Thomas of Ireland, *Manipulus florum*. f. 1r-v, prologue, beg. (rub.) "Incipit tabula librorum originalium qui vocatur manipulus florum compilata a magistro Thoma de Ybernia quondam socio de Sarbona. [text] Abiit in agrum...." ff. 1v-169, text, ends "Explicit manipulus florum compilatus a magistro Thoma de Hybernia quondam socio de Sarbona (*corr. to* Serbona)." ff. 169v-170, table. ff. 170-175, list of authors and works, ends "Laus tibi sit, Christe, quem labor explicit iste."

Parchment; 2 cols., 54 lines; quires of 12 leaves. Catchwords in dotted boxes; leaves signed (i-vi). 179 × 116 mm (226 × 146 mm), ruled in lead; one hand, littera textualis. Initial (8 line) cross-hatched gold and blue with fleurs de lys; vine frame supporting greyhound chasing a hare. Alternating red and blue initials (with tendrils) and paragraph marks. Authors noted in marg. Bound in brown morocco (s. xviii-xix).

2ndo folio, *evangelia parte vᵃ*.

MS seen.

Vaticano (Città del), Biblioteca apostolica vaticana MS Rossi 465, s. xiv¹, France

Pt. I

ff. 1-32v   Nicholas of Hanapis, *Exempla sacre scripture*

Pt. II

ff. 33-183v   Thomas of Ireland, *Manipulus florum*. f. 33r-v, prologue, beg. (rub.) "Incipit tabula originalium sive manipulus florum secundum ordinem alphabeti extracta a libris xxxvi auctorum edita a magistro Thoma de Ybernia quondam socio de Serbona parisiis civitate. [text] Abiit in agrum...." ff. 33v-178v, text, ends "Explicit manipulus florum compilatus a magistro Thoma de Hybernia quondam socio de Sorbona. Et incipit Galensis ordinis minorum ista tabula et magister Thomas finivit." ff. 178v-179v, table (in 4 cols.). ff. 179v-183v, list of authors and works.

Two manuscripts of similar date and origin (each 56 lines/col., ruled in similar dimensions), joined together with foliation of the sixteenth century. Pt. II: Parchment; 2 cols., 56 lines; quires of 12 leaves. Catchwords in boxes; leaves signed (a-f). 211 × 125 mm (302 × 195 mm), ruled in lead; one hand, littera textualis. Initial (7 line) parted red and blue, with filigree and cascade. Alternating red and blue initials (with tendrils) and paragraph marks. Running headlines added (A, B, C). Authors noted in marg. Bound in brown morocco (s. xviii-xix).

2ndo folio, *Deus de* (pt. I), *per Simonem* (pt. II).

MS seen.

Vaticano (Città del), Biblioteca apostolica vaticana MS Rossi 646, s. xv², Italy

ff. 1-422   Thomas of Ireland, *Manipulus florum*. f. 1r-v, prologue, beg. (rub.) "Incipit tabula originalium sive manipulus florum secundum ordinem alphabeti extracta a libris viginti trium (!) auctorum edita a magistro Thoma Ybernico quondam socio de Sorbonio Parisius civitate. [text] Abiit in agrum...." ff. 1v-412v, text. ff. 412v-421, list of authors and works. ff. 421v-422, table (in 3 cols.).

Paper; 28 long lines; quires of 14 leaves. Catchwords. 107 × 70 mm (152 × 104 mm), unruled; one hand, littera currens. Red initial (8 line). Red initials and paragraph marks. Stamped leather binding (s. xv ex.), restored.

2ndo folio, *Abstinencia*. f. 423, "Ad usum fratris Christofori de Varisio (?) ordinis minorum."

MS seen.

Vich, Museo episcopal MS 52, s. xiv¹, France

ff. 1-218v   Thomas of Ireland, *Manipulus florum*. f. 1r-v, prologue, beg. (rub.) "Incipit tabula originalium sive manipulus florum secundum ordinem alphabeti extracta a libris xxxvi auctorum edita a magistro Thoma de Hybernia quondam socio de Sarbona. [text] Abiit in agrum...." ff. 1v-212, text, ends "... parentes o. Hoc opus est compilatum a magistro Thoma de

Ybernia quondam socio de Sorbona." ff. 212-213, table. ff. 213-218v, list of authors and works.

Parchment; 2 cols., 40-43 lines; quires of 8 leaves. Catchwords. 203 × 130 mm (255 × 205 mm), ruled in ink; one hand, littera textualis. Initial (9 line) parted gold and blue with red tendrils and filigree. Alternating red and blue initials with tendrils and filigree. Bound in parchment (s. xix¹).

2ndo folio, *consuetudine*. Probably given to the cathedral library of Vich in 1371 by the archdeacon Bernat de Finestres.

R. Beer, *Handschriftenschätze Spaniens* (Vienna 1894) 551 n. 87. MS seen on film.

Wien, Oesterreichische Nationalbibliothek MS lat. 1334, s. xiv¹, Germany

ff. 1-264   Thomas of Ireland, *Manipulus florum*. f. 1r-v, prologue, beg. (rub.) "Incipit manipulus florum sive extractiones originalium editus a magistro Thoma de Ybernia quondam socio de Sorbona. [text] Abiit in agrum...." ff. 1v-255, text, ends "Hoc opus compilatum est a Thoma de Ybernia quondam socio de Sorbona. Explicit manipulus florum." ff. 255-256v, table, ends "Finit anno Domini millesimo tricentesimo sexto, die veneris post Passionem apostolorum Petri et Pauli." ff. 256v-264, list of authors and works.

Parchment; 2 cols., 44 lines; quires of 12 leaves. Leaves signed (a, aa, aaa). 170 × 110 mm (220 × 150 mm), ruled; one hand, littera textualis. Initial (4 line) with cascade. Alternating red and blue initials and paragraph marks. Running headlines (A, B, C).

2ndo folio, *malis sed*. Belonged to the abbey of Melk, o.s.b.; ex-libris note, "Iste manipulus ... Monte Carmeli"; no. C 59 in the 1483 catalog of Melk, ed. T. Gottlieb, *Mittelalterliche Bibliothekskataloge Oesterreichs* 1 (Vienna 1915) 140, 180.

F. Unterkircher, *Katalog der datierten Handschriften in lateinischer Schrift in Oesterreich* 1 (Vienna 1969) 38 pl. 65; *Tabula codicum manuscriptorum ... in Bibliotheca Palatina Vindobonensi asservatorum* 1 (Vienna 1864) 221.

MS seen.

Wien, Oesterreichische Nationalbibliothek MS lat. 1555, s. xiv, Germany

ff. 1-209   Thomas of Ireland, *Manipulus florum*. f. 1r-v, prologue, beg. (rub.) "Incipit manipulus florum sive extractiones originalium a magistro Thoma de Hybernia quondam socio de Sorbona. [text] Abiit in agrum...." ff. 1v-202, text, ends "Hoc opus est compilatum a magistro Thoma de Ybernia quondam socio de Sorbona." ff. 202-203, table, ends "Finit anno Domini MCCCVI die veneris post Passionem apostolorum Petri et Pauli." ff. 203-209, list of authors and works.

Parchment; 2 cols., 45 lines; quires of 12 leaves. Catchwords; leaves signed. 200 × 140 mm (280 × 195 mm), ruled in ink; one hand, littera textualis. Alternating red and blue initials and paragraph marks. Running headlines (A, B, C). Authors noted in marg. Bound in leather over boards (s. xv); chain mark, back cover top center; paper label on front cover.

2ndo folio, *mater sanitatis*. Belonged to the library of Salzburg Cathedral, no. 107; item 307 in the 1443 catalog of Johannes Holveld, ed. G. Möser-Mersky and M. Mihaliuk, *Mittel-alterliche Bibliothekskataloge Oesterreichs* 4 (Graz 1966) 46.

F. Unterkircher, *Katalog der datierten Handschriften in lateini-scher Schrift in Oesterreich* 1 (Vienna 1969) 41 pl. 66; *Tabula codicum manuscriptorum ... in Bibliotheca Palatina Vindobonensi asservatorum* 1 (Vienna 1864) 252.

MS seen.

Wien, Oesterreichische Nationalbibliothek MS lat. 1611, s. xiv med., Germany/Austria

ff. 1-379   Thomas of Ireland, *Manipulus florum*. ff. 1-2, prologue, beg. (rub.) "Incipit manipulus florum sive extractiones originalium edita a magister Thoma de Ybernia quondam socio de Sor-bona. [text] Abiit in agrum...." ff. 2-366, text, ends "Hoc opus est compilatum a magistro Thoma de Ybernia quondam socio de Sorbona." ff. 366-368v, table, with folio references; ends "Finit anno Domini MCCCVI, die veneris post Passionem apostolorum Petri et Pauli." ff. 368v-379, list of authors and works.

Parchment; 2 cols., 36 lines; 165 × 110 mm (233 × 162 mm); one hand, littera textualis. Majuscules slashed in red. Running headlines (A, B, C). Medieval foliation (upper left verso).

2ndo folio, *Ricardus. Hugo*. Ex-libris note, "Collegii Christi."

F. Unterkircher, *Katalog der datierten Handschriften in lateini-scher Schrift in Oesterreich* 1 (Vienna 1969) 42 pl. 67. *Tabulae codicum manuscriptorum ... in Bibliotheca Palatina Vindobonensi asservatorum* 1 (Vienna 1864) 262; M. Denis, *Codices manuscripti theologici Bibliothecae Palatinae Vindo-bonensis* 2 (Vienna 1799) 1056-1058.

MS seen.

Winston-Salem, N.C., Wake Forest University Library MS lat. 1410a, s. xv (ca. 1410), Eastern Europe (Bohemia?)

ff. 1-15   *Ars praedicandi*

ff. 15v-34   Thomas of Ireland, *Manipulus florum*. Extracts, beg. (rub.) "Sequuntur alique auctoritates sanctorum doctorum in materia predicabili necessarie extracte a manipulo florum secundum ordinem litterarum alphabeti. Et primo de [text] Abstinentia. Augustinus in sermone de dominica quarta in Adventu: Qui sic se...," ends s.v. *Votum*, "Ysidorus libro secundo soliloquiorum: ... que sue scelere adimpletur. Ex-pliciunt alique auctoritates sanctorum doctorum in materia predicabili utiliter extracte a manipulo florum."

ff. 35-180v   Bible; N.T. and Proverbs, Ecclesiastes, Canticles, Lamentations, Habakkuk, Malachi. Equipped with a calendar; lectionary *de tempore*, *de sanctis* and *communis*; and prayers for before and after sermons.

Parchment; 42-46 long lines. 85 × 58 mm (107 × 73 mm), ruled in lead; two hands, littera currens (i, ff. 1-178v; ii, 178v-180v). Red and blue initials, ff. 35-180v. Occasional running headlines. Modern red leather binding with gold tooling.

2ndo folio, *ferie quarte*. Inside front cover, "Fr. Gilbertus Vacca minor." On added paper flyleaf, "Ce rare et trés précieux manuscrit ... provient de la bibliothèque de M. de Joursamault (?) d'Autun dont il portait le numéro 22...," followed in pencil by "From the Hospital of Beaune." Bookplate of Solomon R. Guggenheim.

J. B. Allen, "An Unrecorded *Ars Predicandi*," *Wake Forest University Library Newsletter* 1.1 (1969) 2-3.

Worcester, Cathedral Library MS F.153, s. xiv[1], England

ff. 5-134v   Thomas of Ireland, *Manipulus florum*.   f. 5r-v, prologue, beg. (rub.) "Incipit tabula originalium sive manipulus florum secundum ordinem alphabeti extracti a libris xxxvi auctorum. [text] Abiit in agrum...."   ff. 5v-130v, text, ends "Explicit manipulus florum compilatus a magistro Thoma de Hybernia condam socio de Serbona et incepit frater Johannes Galensis ordinis fratrum minorum doctor in theologia istam tabulam et magister Thomas finivit."   ff. 130r-v, table (in 3 cols.), ends "Finit tabula aurea."   ff. 130v-134v, list of authors and works.

Parchment; 2 cols., 63 lines; quires of 12 leaves. Catchwords; leaves signed (Ai, Aii, Aiii). 280 × 155 mm (353 × 218 mm), ruled in ink; one hand, littera textualis. Initial (9 line) parted with English crosshatch and cascade. Blue initials with red tendrils; alternating red and blue paragraph marks. Authors noted in marg. Table marked with fore-edge tab. Early binding, white leather over boards; medieval label on back cover.

2ndo folio, *ieiunare debemus*. ff. 1-4, 136-137, pastedown and flyleaves from a Roman law text with gloss (s. xiv, Italy). Belonged to Worcester Cathedral library, no. 48 in Patrick Young's catalog of 1622-1623; I. Atkins, N. Ker, eds., *Catalogus librorum manuscriptorum Bibliothecae Wigorniensis* (Cambridge 1944) 36.

J. K. Floyer, *Catalogue of Manuscripts Preserved in the Library of Worcester Cathedral*, rev. by S. G. Hamilton (Oxford 1906) 82.

MS seen.

Worcester, Cathedral Library MS Q.23, s. xiv[1], France

ff. 1-313v   Thomas of Ireland, *Manipulus florum*.   ff. 1-2, prologue, beg. (rub.) "Incipit manipulus florum sive extractiones originalium a magistro Thoma de Hibernia quondam [extr]acte (!). [text] Abiit in agrum...." ff. 2-302, text, ends "Hoc opus est compilatum a magistro Thoma de Hybernia quondam socio de Sorbona." ff. 302v-304v, table. ff. 305-313v, list of authors and works, ends "... dulcior gustus. Liber est totus completus, Deo gracias explicit."

Parchment; 2 cols., 38 lines; quires of 12 leaves. Catchwords in boxes. 164×110 mm (218×148 mm), ruled in ink; one hand, littera textualis. Initial (8 line) with gold background; L-frame, supporting greyhound chasing a hare, and an owl. Alternating red and blue paragraph marks. Running headlines (A, B, C). Recently rebound in white leather; ff. i, 1, chain mark top center.

2ndo folio, *fi]nem suum differt.* Belonged to Worcester Cathedral library; f. i, Worcester ex-libris; no. 238 in Patrick Young's catalog of 1622-1623, ed. I. Atkins and N. Ker, *Catalogus librorum manuscriptorum Bibliothecae Wigorniensis* (Cambridge 1944) 50.

J. K. Floyer, *Catalogue of Manuscripts Preserved in the Library of Worcester Cathedral*, rev. by S. G. Hamilton (Oxford 1906) 120.

MS seen.

Wrocław, Biblioteka Uniwersytecka MS I.F.616, s. xiv², Lower Silesia (Breslau)

Contains, among other things:

ff. 193-345   Thomas of Ireland, *Manipulus florum.* f. 193r-v, prologue, beg. (rub.) "Hic incipit liber qui dicitur manipulus florum. [text] Abiit in agrum...." ff. 193v-345, text.

Paper; 2 cols., ca. 42 lines. 229×150 (289×207 mm).

2ndo folio, *mortisque parieter* (!). Belonged to the Dominicans of Breslau.

Wrocław, Biblioteka Uniwersytecka MS I.F.764, s. xiv², Lower Silesia (Głogów?)

ff. 1-230v   Thomas of Ireland, *Manipulus florum.* f. 1r-v, prologue. ff. 1v-224, text. ff. 224-225, table. ff. 225-230v, list of authors and works.

Paper; 2 cols., ca. 41 lines. 214×137 mm (306×220 mm).

2ndo folio, *utantur divites.* Belonged to the collegiate church at Głogów.

Wrocław, Biblioteka Uniwersytecka MS I.F.765, s. xv¹, Lower Silesia (Rauda)

ff. 1-255   Thomas of Ireland, *Manipulus florum.* f. 1r-v, table. f. 2r-v, prologue. ff. 2v-247v, text. ff. 247v-255, list of authors and works.

           Paper and parchment; 2 cols., ca. 44 lines. 228 × 152 mm
           (290 × 203 mm).
           2ndo folio, *Abiit in* (f. 2r), *est carere* (f. 3r). "Ex libris monasterii
           Raudensis."

Wrocław, Biblioteka Uniwersytecka MS I.F.766, s. xv (1452), Lower Silesia
           (Breslau)

ff. 1-248   Thomas of Ireland, *Manipulus florum.* f. 1r-v, prologue. ff. 1v-
           240v, text. ff. 240v-241, table. ff. 241v-248, list of authors
           and works.
           Paper; 2 cols., ca. 40 lines. 242 × 165 mm (303 × 207 mm).
           2ndo folio, *tu quare extolleris.* Belonged to the Church of Corpus
           Christi, Breslau.

Wrocław, Biblioteka Uniwersytecka MS I.Q.455, s. xv (1432), Lower Silesia
           (Żagán)

ff. 1-391   Thomas of Ireland, *Manipulus florum.* ff. 1-3, prologue. ff. 3-
           390, text. ff. 390v-391v, table.
           Paper; ca. 36 long lines. 174 × 94 mm (225 × 145 mm).
           2ndo folio, *quia conversio licet.* Belonged to the canons regular of
           Żagán.

INDEX OF SECOND FOLIO REFERENCES

a licitis caute, Assisi 244

ab illicitis, Rouen 648

ab inde, Salzburg b.VI.14

abiit in, Wrocław I.F.765

abstinencia, Cambridge Peterhouse 164;
   Vatican Rossi 646

abstinencia tua, Clm 14637

abstinere et quas, Uppsala C.608

accipiantur, Linz 117

ad hoc in, London British Library Add.
   15340

ad quod, Cambridge Corpus Christi
   Coll. 518

ad prelium, Kremsmünster 222

Agellius, Troyes 1785

al. Ipsis enim, Firenze Med. Laur. Plut.
   XXXIV sin. 4

aliter non, Nice 29

ante annos, Köln Hist. Arch. G.B. fol.
   168; Nürnberg Cent. III 63

apud philosophos, Vatican Palat. lat.
   233

aromata primo, Trier 91/1075

articulus s[cil.] crede, Bruxelles 3672-
   3690

Augustinus in, Oxford Lincoln Coll. 98

calefacere et, Melun 16

capitulum sextum quod, Lüneburg 77

cere ne collectio, Berlin lat. theol. qu.
   17

cio introducit, Cambridge Peterhouse
   268

clama, Vatican Palat. lat. 226

clamavi, Vatican Palat. lat. 391

cognosci et, Arras 771

congruencia, Praha Univ. Knih.
   XII.B.18

consuetudine, Vich 52

contra in omni, Vatican Borghese 247

corpus non edomat, Kraków Bibl. Jagiel.
   402

corruerunt, Graz 574

ctio ut dicebat, Halle, Quedlinburg 215

cum quibus, Soissons 140

d. Utantur divites, Escorial Q.III.11
da pauperibus, Leipzig 629
de ordine, Paris B.N. lat. 16533
dem virginem, Praha Univ. Knih. IV.C.7
despicias improvidus, Padova Antoniana 208
destruitur, München Universitätsbibl. 2° cod. 22
Deus de, Vatican Rossi 465
doleant se, Basel B.IV.9
dominica quarta, Vatican Palat. lat. 616
dominica vero, Clm 14591
dominus, Fermo 97
duodecim sunt, Graz 888; New Haven Yale 380

edendum precepit, Clm 16463
eisdem alimentis, Clm 3724
enervatur, Graz 1254
enim est, Paris Bibl. Maz. 1032
enim vino et, London British Library Add. 17809
eo magis, Paris B.N. lat. 15986
esse nobiscum, Berlin lat. theol. fol. 131
est carere, Wrocław I.F.765
est primus, Tours 36
est proprius gradus, Berlin lat. theol. fol. 239
et carni et, Paris Bibl. Ste-Geneviève 1447
et quas, Salamanca 2702
etatis periculosa, Rouen 649
etiam satiatus, Alba-Iulia III-32
evangelia parte, Vatican Rossi 217
ex parte, Escorial F.II.18
extenditur, Cambridge Peterhouse 163

f. Abstinencia, Paris B.N. lat. 15985
f. Augustinus in, Klosterneuburg 391
facilitate, Vatican Palat. lat. 391
facilius est, Köln Hist. Arch. G.B. 4° 215
ferie quarte, Winston-Salem, Wake Forest lat. 1410a
feruntur ut, Praha Met. Kap. C.CVII
finis retractare, Budapest Országos Széchényi Könyvtár lat. 196

Fulgentius, Cambrai 242
fulmina, Paris B.N. lat. 16708

gaudiis, London British Library Add. 24129
gaudium est, Augsburg fol. 348
Gregorius m., Lincoln Cathedral 191
guenda sunt, London British Library Egerton 652

habet vinum, Padova Univ. 675
hoc modo, Hamburg Jac. 15

ideo ne, Troyes 1458
ieiunare debemus, Worcester F.153
Ieronimus, Paris Bibl. Maz. 1033
in omelia, Paris B.N. lat. 14990
in prima, Cambridge Univ. Ii.VI.39
in sua, Salzburg a.VI.7
incentiva viciorum, Kraków Bibl. Jagiel. 401
incipiunt, München Universitätsbibl. 2° cod. 107
infirmitatis sue, Lyon 711; Padova Univ. 1007
inobediens, Reims 515
intervalla, Nice 29

libero ad, Chambéry 25
luce clarior, Paris B.N. lat. 3336; Madrid B.N. 234

magna virtus, Arras 305
malis sed, Wien 1334
mater sanitatis, Admont 580; Wien 1555
maximum, Cambridge Univ. Ii.VI.39
Maximus, Vatican Barb. 458
metus fuerat, Milano Bibl. Ambrosiana T.124.sup.
miani pretulit, Köln Hist. Arch. G.B. 4° 152
mior sed non, Hamburg Jacobi 15
misericorditer, Basel Universitätsbibl. B.IX.23
modestia, Admont 81
monachi etiam, Oxford Oriel Coll. 10
mortisque parieter, Wrocław I.F.616

nec penitus, Arras 305
necessariis, Charleville 10
necesse est, London British Library Royal 7.C.III
negocium ut, Basel Universitätsbibl. B.IX.23
nem suum differt, Worcester Q.23
nichil sic, Vatican Palat. lat. 233
nonnulli vitam, Clm 12310
nore sublimior, Oxford Magdalen Coll. 97
nota, Admont 580

o. Hostem, Lincoln Cathedral 48
opprimitur, Praha Univ. Knih. V.E.25
or omni secreto, Paris Bibl. Univ. 215
originalium non, Clm 5345
ourros (?), Praha Narod. Mus. XII.G.5

pauper de, Berlin lat. theol. fol. 150
pauper superbus, Paris Bibl. Maz. 4318
per abstinenciam, Praha Univ. Knih. XXIII.F.96; Reims 514
per mortali, Clm 8954
per Simonem, Marseille 331; Vatican Rossi 465
percipere quicquid, Troyes 1261
petere potest, Graz 746
prelium hostem, Paris Bibl. Maz. 1034
pretii maioris, Paris Bibl. Arsenal 524
proprio nomen, Firenze Naz. Cent. conv. sopp. I.6.12

quam suave, Brugge 171; Tours 35
quare extolleris, Charleville 38
quasdam igitur, Clm 14545
qui amicitiam, Budapest Országos Szé-chényi Könyvtár lat. 74
qui sic, Admont 81
qui sic se, Göttweig 134
quia conversio licet, Wrocław I.Q.455
quia si, Cambridge Gonv.-Caius Coll. 402
quid alimentorum, Soissons 112
quid prodest, Padova Bibl. Univ. 1243
quid vos, Clm 3725
quod in se, Paris Bibl. Arsenal 389
quod sicut, Oxford Merton Coll. 129

rem bonam, Cambridge Univ. Ff.VI.35
Ricardus. Hugo, Wien 1611

scilicet ad, Clm 5404
securius allegari, Piacenza Pallastrel-li 186
sed quia non, Praha Met. Kap. C.XXXVII.2
Seneca malum, Angers 325
sint appenit (?), Tarragona 17
sunt et, Douai 458
sunt non, Paris Bibl. Maz. 1031
suscipere, Vatican lat. 1169
Sydonius, Toulouse 222

tamen ymmo, Köln, Dombibl. 182
tas sitim, Praha Met. Kap. C.XXXIV.2
ticere ne, Arras 580
tilem originalium non, Frankfurt Leonh. 4
tillas nititur, Paris B.N. lat. 16532
titur calefacere, Valencia 266
tribulatio, Clm 3212
trucidamus et, Paris B.N. lat. 14991
tu quare extolleris, Wrocław I.F.766
tu vero, Tours 37

valet aut, Paris B.N. n.a.l. 708
vel necesse, Gdańsk 1984
vel peregrinans, Praha Met. Kap. C.XXXVII.1
vel quantum, Firenze Naz. Cent. conv. sopp. F.III.570
vermis diviciarum, St-Omer 671
29 Claudicare, Frankfurt Praed. 17
virtutem, Paris B.N. lat. 2615
umbracula, Praha Met. Kap. C.XXXVII.1
umbraculum, Seitenstetten 122
vomellis non, Braunschweig 65
ut aliis, Graz 445
ut fecit, Salzburg a.IX.4
ut si VIII, Dublin 312
utantur divites, Escorial Q.III.11; Frankfurt Praed. 143; Wrocław I.F.764

Appendix 8

Index to the *Manipulus florum*

The following is an index of the authors and works that are quoted in the *Manipulus florum*. One of its principal uses will be to help one determine whether or not a given writer of the fourteenth and later centuries has used the *Manipulus* as the intermediate source for his quotations from patristic, medieval and ancient works. We have not attempted to verify or identify Thomas of Ireland's citations nor to correct his misattributions— since any writer who drew upon the *Manipulus florum* will have repeated Thomas' errors.

The word "(prologue)" appended to an author's name identifies those thirty-six authors whom Thomas lists in his prologue as being the most frequently cited. For each work the following information is given: (1) A reference to the appearance of the work in Thomas' bibliography, appended to the *Manipulus florum* and edited in Appendix 6. (2) The number of extracts ostensibly taken from the work, and Thomas' own source for the quotations, if it has been identified. This latter most frequently will be FP (*Flores paradysi*) or LE (*Liber exceptionum*); see above, Ch. 5 section II-A. Since both of these *florilegia* are difficult to search, it is inevitable that we have overlooked many of Thomas' borrowings; therefore, even when we have not found the specific extracts that Thomas includes, we have noted that a given title is cited in the FP and the LE. We have not noted as a probable source "a manuscript of this text," unless there is a specific manuscript to cite. (3) The topic-headings in the *Manipulus florum* under which the work is cited. We have not given the specific reference letters for the quotations, since these vary from one printed edition to another. We have not listed the topic-headings when a work appears in over fifty sections, since this is tantamount to saying *passim*.

A[ulus] Gellius (prologue)
> [Noctes Atticae]; 9 extracts; s.v. *Consolatio, Correctio, Fabula, Loquacitas, Patria, Philosophia, Servitus.*

Alanus (prologue)
> De complanctu nature, De conquisitione nature, De compl. sive de conq. nature (bibliography xv: 9); 19 extracts, probably taken from Thomas of Ireland's manuscript of the *De planctu*, Vatican MS Reg. lat. 1006; s.v. *Adulatio, Advocati, Avaritia, Deus, Fabula, Fama, Gula, Invidia, Sapientia, Superbia.*

Alexander [Nequam]

De naturis rerum; 1 extract; s.v. *Philosophia.*

Alquinus

De immolatione Abrahe; 1 extract; s.v. *Compassio.*

Ambrosius (prologue)

Without title; 3 extracts, 2 of which are taken from FP; s.v. *Discordia, Mansuetudo, Stultitia.*

De Caim et Habel; 6 extracts, 2 of which are taken from FP and 2 from LE; s.v. *Error, Iudex, Libido, Penitentia, Scriptura, Verecundia.*

Contra hereticos; 1 extract; s.v. *Nativitas.*

De David (cf. bibliography III: 15); 4 extracts, taken from LE; s.v. *Mulier, Penitentia, Usura.*

Epistolae (bibliography III: 31); 8 extracts, 2 of which are taken from FP and 1 from LE; s.v. *Conversatio, Delitie, Libido, Peccatum, Sacerdos, Tentatio.*

Epistola ad Constantium; 3 extracts, 2 of which are taken from LE and 1 from FP; s.v. *Conscientia, Sapientia.*

Epistola ad Siagrium; 1 extract, taken from LE; s.v. *Testimonium.*

Ep. ad Simplicianum, 3 extracts, taken from LE; s.v. *Fortitudo, Penitentia, Servitus.*

Ep. ad Theodosium imperatorem (cf. bibliography III: 18); 1 extract, taken from FP; s.v. *Sacerdos.*

Ep. ad Vercellensem ecclesiam (bibliography III: 33); 5 extracts, 3 of which are taken from LE; s.v. *Contemplatio, Ira, Mansuetudo, Ociositas, Superfluitas.*

Exameron (bibliography III: 2); 9 extracts, 3 of which are taken from FP and 2 from LE; s.v. *Innocentia, Malitia, Mors, Oratio, Ornatus, Senectus, Simplicitas, Spes.*

De Excessu fratris (bibliography III: 3); 1 extract, taken from FP; s.v. *Mors.*

De Iacob et vita beata (bibliography III: 27); 2 extracts, taken from LE; s.v. *Ira, Servitus.*

De Immolatione Abrahe; 1 extract; s.v. *Virtus.*

De Interpellatione Iob (bibliography III: 14); 1 extract (work cited, FP); s.v. *Avaritia.*

De Ioseph; 7 extracts, 1 of which is taken from LE; s.v. *Confessio, Consolatio, Homo, Libertas, Natura, Penitentia, Sanctitas.*

De Misterio Pasche, Epistola de m. P. (bibliography III: 21); 1 extract; s.v. *Resurrectio.*

In Natali sancti Eusebii; 1 extract, taken from LE; s.v. *Laus.*

De Noe; 1 extract, taken from LE; s.v. *Tentatio.*

De Obitu Theodosii; 1 extract, taken from FP; s.v. *Venia.*

De Obitu Valentini (bibliography III: 32); 1 extract, taken from FP; s.v. *Lacrima.*

De Officiis (bibliography III: 1); 80 extracts, 9 of which may have come from

LE and 11 from FP, but the remainder and perhaps all 80 from B.N. MS
lat. 15641; s.v. *Adiutorium, Adulatio, Amicitia, Amor, Beatitudo, Bellum,
Beneficia, Conscientia, Consilium, Cupiditas, Divitie, Elemosina, Fabula,
Fides, Fortitudo, Gratia, Honestas, Hospitalitas, Humilitas, Ieiunium,
Iniuria, Ira, Iustitia, Lascivia, Liberalitas, Loquacitas, Mercatio, Misericordia, Modestia, Mulier, Oratio, Ornatus, Parentes, Promissio, Relinquere, Taciturnitas, Temperantia, Verecundia, Victoria, Virginitas, Virtus.*

In Oratione; 1 extract; s.v. *Eucharistia.*

De Paradiso (bibliography III: 29); 3 extracts (work cited in both FP and LE);
s.v. *Detractio, Ira, Iustitia.*

In Pastorali sive de dignitate sacerdotali (bibliography III: 19); 14 extracts; s.v.
Correctio, Gloria mala, Hospitalitas, Prelatio, Simonia.

De Patriarchis (bibliography III: 23); 2 extracts, taken from FP; s.v. *Discordia.*

De Penitentia (cf. bibliography III: 22, 24); 3 extracts (work cited in FP); s.v.
Ebrietas, Oratio.

De Sacramentis (bibliography III: 10); 6 extracts, 4 of which are taken from
LE; s.v. *Eucharistia.*

Sermones; 11 extracts, 2 of which are taken from LE; s.v. *Advocati, Avaritia,
Contemptus, Delitie, Gula, Humilitas, Ipocrisis, Passio, Penitentia, Sacerdos, X̄p̄s.*

Sermo de Advincula Petri; 2 extracts, taken from LE; s.v. *Correctio, Penitentia.*

Sermo Apostolorum Petri et Pauli; 1 extract, taken from LE; s.v. *Apostoli.*

Sermo de Assumptione; 1 extract; s.v. *Amor.*

Sermo de Cathedra sancti Petri; 1 extract, taken from LE; s.v. *Societas.*

Sermo de Helya et ieiunio (bibliography III: 12); 2 extracts; s.v. *Conversio,
Ieiunium.*

Sermo de Ieiunio; 1 extract; s.v. *Gula.*

Sermo de Pascha; 2 extracts; s.v. *Senectus.*

Sermo de Passio; 1 extract; s.v. *Crux.*

Sermo in Quadragesime; 6 extracts, taken from LE; s.v. *Gula, Ieiunium, Verbum, Vita humana presens.*

De Spiritu sancto; 3 extracts (work cited in both FP and LE); s.v. *Apostoli, Peccatum, Testimonium.*

Super illud Apostoli: Non litigiosum; 1 extract; s.v. *Prelatio.*

Super Beati Immaculati; 23 extracts, 5 of which are taken from LE, 5 from FP,
2 from either one; s.v. *Avaritia, Confessio, Desiderium, Dilectio, Doctrina, Elemosina, Exemplum, Fides, Ignorantia, Inimicitia, Iudex, Iuventus, Loquacitas, Pacientia, Passio, Pietas, Secularis, Verbum, Verecundia,
Virtus.*

Super epistola prima ad Corinthios; 7 extracts, 4 of which are taken from LE;
s.v. *Correctio, Iudex, Liberalitas, Munus, Predicatio, Veritas.*

Super ep. ad Galathas; 1 extract, taken from LE; s.v. *Reconciliatio.*

Super illud Iohannis: Attulit ager cuiusdam diuitis etc.; 2 extracts, 1 of which
comes in part from *Decretum*; s.v. *Cupiditas.*

Super Lucam; 39 extracts, at least 19 of which are taken from LE, at least 2 from FP, and at least 2 from either; s.v. *Adventus domini, Ambitio, Apostoli, Beneficia, Correctio, Desperatio, Deus, Diabolus, Divitie, Gratia, Humilitas, Ira, Lacrima, Mansuetudo, Maria, Mercatio, Parentes, Passio, Predicatio, Societas, Studium, Venia, Virtus, Voluptas, X̄p̄us.*

Super Malachiam; 2 extracts; s.v. *Acceptio personarum.*

Super Marcum; 1 extract; s.v. *Desperatio.*

Super Mattheum (including references of the type, Super illud Matth. ...); 6 extracts; s.v. *Correctio, Oratio, Parentes, Passio, Proditio, Venia.*

Super libro de Nabithe (bibliography III: 11); 2 extracts (work cited in LE); s.v. *Avaritia.*

Super Psalmos; 8 extracts (work cited in both FP and LE); s.v. *Anima, Humilitas, Medicina, Mundus, Oratio, Paupertas, Regimen.*

Super illud Thessalonicenses 1: Nisi discensio venerit etc., *or* ... illud: Rapiemur cum illis in nubibus; 3 extracts, taken from LE; s.v. *Adventus domini, Antichristus, Resurrectio.*

Super illud ad Timotheum 4: Pietas ad omnia utilis est, *or* ... illud: Modico vino utere; 2 extracts, at least 1 of which is taken from LE; s.v. *Misericordia, Servitium.*

Super illud ad Titum 1: Hospitalitatem etc.; 1 extract; s.v. *Hospitalitas.*

De Trinitate (bibliography III: 30); 2 extracts (work cited in LE); s.v. *Dilectio, Fides.*

De Viduis (bibliography III: 7); 7 extracts, 3 of which may be taken from LE; s.v. *Coniugium, Eucharistia, Iuventus, Liberalitas, Oratio, Pietas, Virginitas.*

De Virginibus; 1 extract; s.v. *Fraus.*

De Virginitate (bibliography III: 6); 15 extracts, at least 4 of which are taken from FP, 1 from either FP or LE; s.v. *Castitas, Cupiditas, Fides, Loquacitas, Maria, Mundus, Ornatus, Verecundia, Virginitas.*

Anselmus (prologue)

De Casu diaboli (bibliography XII: 4); 1 extract; s.v. *Peccatum.*

Cur deus homo (bibliography XII: 1); 1 extract; s.v. *Iustitia.*

In Meditationibus (bibliography XII: 13); 2 extracts; s.v. *Consideratio,* Mors.

De Similitudinibus (bibliography XII: 16); 1 extract; s.v. *Iudex.*

Apulegius

De Deo Socratis; 1 extract, perhaps taken from Vat. MS Reg. lat. 1572; s.v. *Laus.*

De Dogmate Platonis; 1 extract, perhaps taken from Vat. MS Reg. lat. 1572; s.v. *Electio.*

Aristoteles

Liber Ethicorum; 1 extract; s.v. *Luxuria.*

De Problematibus; 2 extracts, from Hugo de S.V. *De disciplina monachorum* and Seneca *De beneficiis*; s.v. *Conversatio, Liberalitas* (not in printed editions; omitted from ed. princ. *Liberalitas ai.*).

Augustinus (prologue)

Without title; 15 extracts; s.v. *Amor, Ascensio, Heresis, Infernus, Iniuria, Ira, Malitia, Mandatum, Mors, Mundus, Oratio, Ornatus, Voluntas.*

De Agone christiano (bibliography II: 83); 4 extracts, at least 2 of which are taken from LE; s.v. *Ascensio, Venia, Veritas.*

De Baptismo contra Donatistas (bibliography II: 24); 2 extracts, taken from LE; s.v. *Presumptio, Sacramentum.*

De Baptismo parvulorum (bibliography II: 32); 5 extracts, at least 1 of which is taken from FP; s.v. *Coniugium, Gratia, Peccatum, Scriptura.*

De Benedictionibus Esau et Iacob; 1 extract, taken from LE; s.v. *Verbum.*

De Bono coniugali (bibliography II: 79); 2 extracts (work cited in both FP and LE); s.v. *Castitas.*

De Caritate; 4 extracts, at least 1 of which was taken from FP and at least 1 from LE; s.v. *Damnus, Deus, Fides, Spes.*

De Cathetizandis rudibus (bibliography II: 59); 19 extracts, at least 4 of which are taken from LE, and part of 1 from *Decretum* (work cited in FP); s.v. *Amor, Caritas, Contemptus, Senectus, Studium, Superbia, X̄p̄ū̄s.*

De Civitate dei (bibliography II: 1); 55 extracts, at least 14 of which may be taken from FP or LE; s.v. *Amor, Antichristus, Avaritia, Consideratio, Correctio, Creatio, Gloria eterna, Homicidium, Honor, Honestas, Iactantia, Ipocrisis, Iudex, Luxuria, Martirium, Mirabile, Misericordia, Mors, Pax, Pena, Philosophia, Prelatio, Querere deum, Rapina, Sanctitas, Scriptura, Servitus, Societas, Sortilegium, Superbia, Voluntas.*

De Cohabitatione clericorum et mulierum; 2 extracts; s.v. *Mulier.*

De Communi sermone clericorum; 1 extract; s.v. *Fama.*

De Communi vita clericorum; 5 extracts, taken from LE; s.v. *Castitas, Correctio, Religio.*

Confessiones (bibliography II: 4); 38 extracts, 4 of which may be taken from LE, 1 from FP, 1 from either; s.v. *Abstinentia, Adulatio, Amicitia, Amor, Anima, Consideratio, Consolatio, Consuetudo, Conversio, Convitium, Cupiditas, Curiositas, Deus, Fama, Gaudium, Gloria mala, Luxuria, Meritum, Mirabile, Miseria, Mundus, Obstinatio, Pena, Securitas, Servitium, Sortilegium, Tristitia, Venia, Violentia.*

De Conflictu vitiorum et virtutum (bibliography II: 55); 9 extracts, s.v. *Accidia, Crudelitas, Cupiditas, Gaudium, Gloria mala, Gula, Luxuria, Passio, Superbia.*

De Continentia viduali; 1 extract (work cited in LE); s.v. *Castitas.*

Contra academicos (bibliography II: 40); 1 extract, taken from FP; s.v. *Discordia.*

Contra epistolam Parmeniani (bibliography II: 90); 3 extracts, taken from FP; s.v. *Communitas, Pax, Sacramentum.*

Contra Faustum (bibliography II: 68); 5 extracts (work cited in LE); s.v. *Bellum, Heresis, Incarnatio.*

Elemosina, Eloquentia, Error, Gloria eterna, Ira, Laus, Malitia, Mors, Natura, Prosperitas, Sacerdos, Superbia, Tribulatio.

Epistola ad Armentarium et Paulinum; 2 extracts; s.v. *Votum.*

[Ep.] ad Aurelianum; 1 extract; s.v. *Monachus.*

[Ep.] ad Bonifacium (cf. bibliography II: 35); 2 extracts; s.v. *Bellum.*

Ep. ad Casulanum; 1 extract, taken from *Decretum*; s.v. *Consuetudo.*

[Ep.] ad Christinum; 1 extract (extract appears, under different titles, in both FP and LE); s.v. *Veritas.*

Ep. ad Dioscorum; 13 extracts, at least 2 of which are taken from LE (work cited in FP); s.v. *Beatitudo, Curiositas, Gloria eterna, Humilitas, Ira, Laus, Mors, Mundus, Oratio, Superbia.*

Ep. ad Hesicium; 2 extracts; s.v. *Antichristus.*

Ep. ad Hieronimum (cf. bibliography II: 75); 6 extracts (work cited in FP and LE). s.v. *Adiutorium, Amicitia, Correctio, Discere, Fortitudo, Veritas.*

Ep. ad Iponenses; 1 extract; s.v. *Detractio.*

Ep. ad Macedonium; 6 extracts, taken from LE; s.v. *Aduocati, Amor, Correctio, Iustitia, Restitutio, Virtus.*

Ep. ad Marcellinum; 3 extracts, at least 1 of which may be taken from either FP or LE; s.v. *Correctio, Error, Gratitudo.*

Ep. ad Nebridium; 1 extract; s.v. *Ira.*

Ep. ad Paulinam (cf. bibliography II: 64); 2 extracts (work cited in FP and LE); s.v. *Contemplatio, Relinquere.*

Ep. ad Polentium; 1 extract; s.v. *Votum.*

[Ep.] ad Possidonium; 2 extracts; s.v. *Ornatus.*

Ep. ad Probam; 4 extracts, 1 of which is taken from LE and 1 from either LE or FP; s.v. *Beatitudo, Divitie, Oratio, Pacientia.*

Ep. ad Publicellam; 1 extract, taken from LE; s.v. *Excusatio.*

Ep. ad quendam comitem; 9 extracts, at least 6 of which are taken from FP; s.v. *Avaritia, Cupiditas, Ebrietas, Elemosina, Regimen, Residivatio, Spiritus sanctus, Superbia.*

[Ep.] ad sacras uirgines; 20 extracts; s.v. *Ebrietas, Sobrietas, Virginitas.*

Ep. ad Sebastianum; 1 extract, taken from either FP or LE; s.v. *Compassio.*

Ep. ad Simplicianum (bibliography: II: 112); 1 extract (work cited in LE); s.v. *Sortilegium.*

Ep. ad Vincentium Donatistam (cf. bibliography II: 31); 2 extracts (work cited in LE); s.v. *Correctio, Religio.*

Ep. ad Volusianum; 8 extracts (work cited in LE); s.v. *Apostoli, Incarnatio, Laus, Resurrectio, Scriptura.*

Exhortationes; 1 extract; s.v. *Mors.*

De Fide ad Petrum (bibliography II: 84); 5 extracts, 1 of which may be taken from FP; s.v. *Coniugium, Ecclesia, Infernus, Libido, Peccatum.*

De Fide et operibus (bibliography II: 65); 1 extract (work cited in FP); s.v. *Gloria eterna.*

De Fide et simbolo (bibliography II: 109); 1 extract, taken from LE; s.v. *Ascensio.*

De Genesi; 2 extracts (work cited in FP); s.v. *Infernus, Scriptura.*

De Genesi contra Manicheos (bibliography II: 42); 5 extracts, at least 3 of which are taken from LE; s.v. *Amicitia, Consuetudo, Curiositas.*

De Genesi/Super Genesim ad literam (bibliography II: 3, II: 86); 3 extracts (work cited in both FP and LE); s.v. *Anima, Laus, Scriptura.*

De Gratia Novi Testamenti (bibliography II: 58); 1 extract, taken from LE; s.v. *Mors.*

De Heresibus (bibliography II: 71); 1 extract; s.v. *Religio.*

Homilia; 1 extract; s.v. *Relinquere.*

Homilia de divite; 1 extract; s.v. *Divitie.*

Homilia XII; 1 extract; s.v. *Iudex.*

Ad Ianuarium; 4 extracts, taken from LE; s.v. *Consuetudo, Eucharistia.*

De Incarnatione domini contra Iudeos; 2 extracts, taken from LE; s.v. *Incarnatio.*

Ad Inquisitores Ianuarii (bibliography II: 85); 1 extract; s.v. *Libertas.*

De Laude caritatis; 4 extracts (work cited in LE); s.v. *Caritas, Dilectio.*

De Libero arbitrio (bibliography II: 5); 19 extracts, at least 7 of which are taken from LE, at least 3 from FP, at least 1 from *Decretum*; s.v. *Avaritia, Bonum, Meritum, Miseria, Peccatum, Pena, Predestinatio, Sapientia, Securitas, Veritas, Voluntas.*

De Mirabilibus sacre scripture (bibliography II: 9); 1 extract; s.v. *Penitentia.*

De Moribus ecclesie, De mor. ecc. contra Manicheos (cf. bibliography II: 43); 7 extracts, at least 2 of which may be taken from LE (work cited in FP); s.v. *Amor, Curiositas, Gloria eterna, Proximus, Providentia, Temperantia.*

De Musica (bibliography II: 107); 1 extract, taken from FP; s.v. *Consuetudo.*

De Natura demonum; 2 extracts, 1 of which and at least part of the other are taken from *Decretum*; s.v. *Sortilegium.*

De Natura et gratia (bibliography II: 69); 2 extracts, taken from LE; s.v. *Maria, Superbia.*

De Novo cantico (bibliography II: 137); 1 extract, taken from LE; s.v. *Odium.*

De Octoginta tria questionum (bibliography II: 22); 9 extracts (work cited in FP and LE); s.v. *Amicitia, Fortitudo, Mirabile, Suffragium.*

De Opere monachorum (bibliography II: 19); 8 extracts, at least 1 of which may be taken from FP and 1 from LE; s.v. *Excusatio, Infirmitas, Ipocrisis, Labor, Misericordia, Obedientia, Religio.*

De Ovibus (bibliography II: 50); 3 extracts, taken from LE; s.v. *Exemplum, Fides, Prelatio.*

De Paradiso; 2 extracts; s.v. *Mandatum.*

De Pastoribus (bibliography II: 49); 3 extracts, taken from LE; s.v. *Exemplum, Prelatio.*

De Patientia (bibliography II: 56); 1 extract (work cited in FP); s.v. *Pacientia.*

De Peccatorum meritis et remissione; 1 extract (work cited in FP and LE); s.v. *Instabilitas*.

De Penitentia (bibliography II: 48); 4 extracts (work cited in FP); s.v. *Confessio, Penitentia*.

De Perfectione iustitie, De p. ius. hominis (bibliography II: 67); 2 extracts (work cited in FP); s.v. *Perfectio*.

De Predestinatione et gratia (cf. bibliography II: 6); 1 extract (work cited in FP and LE); s.v. *Scriptura*.

De Predestinatione sanctorum (bibliography II: 10); 4 extracts (work cited in FP and LE); s.v. *Error, Predestinatio*.

De Quantitate anime (bibliography II: 60); 1 extract, taken from LE; s.v. *Anima*.

De Quattuor virtutibus caritatis (bibliography II: 136); 1 extract, taken from LE; s.v. *Passio*.

De Questionibus evangelii, Liber questionum (bibliography II: 88); 3 extracts (work cited in FP); s.v. *Abstinentia, Bellum*.

Regula (bibliography II: 46); 5 extracts, at least 3 of which are taken from LE; s.v. *Modestia, Religio, Superbia*.

Retractationes (bibliography II: 82); 1 extract (work cited in FP and LE); s.v. *Loquacitas*.

De Sancta viduitate (bibliography II: 78); 2 extracts, s.v. *Amor, Virginitas*.

Sententie Prosperi; 3 extracts, 2 of which are taken from FP and 1 perhaps from the *Gloss*; s.v. *Electio, Oratio, Pena*.

In quadam Sermone (bibliography II: 148); 52 extracts (sermons are cited extensively in FP and LE); s.v. *Acceptio personarum, Adiutorium, Advocati, Amicitia, Anima, Avaritia, Castitas, Conscientia, Consideratio, Conversio, Delitie, Ebrietas, Electio, Excusatio, Gratia, Ingenium, Invidia, Magister, Medicina, Mors, Mundus, Odium, Oratio, Parentes, Passio, Peccatum, Pena, Pietas, Prelatio, Senectus, Solemnitas, Tempus, Verbum, Virtus, Vita humana presens*.

Sermones 22, 29, 31; 5 extracts, taken from LE; s.v. *Divitie, Fides, Superbia*.

Sermo 36; 3 extracts, perhaps from *Decretum* (not verified); s.v. *Penitentia*.

Sermo 54 super Mattheum; 1 extract; s.v. *Castitas*.

Sermo de Apostolis; 2 extracts; s.v. *Apostoli*.

Sermo Apostolorum Petri et Pauli; 2 extracts, taken from LE; s.v. *Apostoli*.

Sermo de Ascensione; 4 extracts, at least 1 of which may be taken from LE; s.v. *Ascensio, Sapientia*.

Sermo de Assumptione; 2 extracts, at least 1 of which is taken from LE; s.v. *Amor, Maria*.

Sermo de Caritate; 2 extracts, at least 1 of which is taken from LE; s.v. *Correctio, Excusatio*.

Sermo de Decimis; 1 extract; s.v. *Decima*.

Sermo de Decollatione sancti Iohannis baptiste; 2 extracts, taken from LE; s.v. *Iuramentum*.

Sermo de Divite; 1 extract; s.v. *Elemosina.*

Sermo de Dominica ivᵃ in Adventu; 2 extracts, at least 1 of which is taken from LE; s.v. *Abstinentia, Consuetudo.*

Sermo de Eclipsi solis; 1 extract; s.v. *Curiositas.*

Sermo de Epiphania; 1 extract; s.v. *Nativitas.*

Sermo de Ieiunio; 2 extracts; s.v. *Ieiunium.*

Sermo de Igne purgatorio; 1 extract, taken from the *Decretum*; s.v. *Pena.*

Sermo super Mattheum; 3 extracts; s.v. *Caritas, Consideratio, Prosperitas.*

Sermo de Natali domini; 1 extract, taken from LE; s.v. *Passio.*

Sermo de Nativitate beate Marie; 2 extracts; s.v. *Maria.*

Sermo de Parasceve; 2 extracts; s.v. *Crux.*

Sermo de Pascha; 4 extracts, at least 1 of which may be taken from LE; s.v. *Beatitudo, Resurrectio.*

Sermo de Puero centurionis; 1 extract; s.v. *Bellum.*

Sermo de Quadragesima; 4 extracts, at least 1 of which may be taken from LE; s.v. *Excommunicatio, Oratio, Passio, Venia.*

Sermo in Quarta dominica quadragesime; 1 extract; s.v. *Rapina.*

Sermo de Resurrectione; 1 extract, taken from LE; s.v. *Ascensio.*

Sermo de sancto Stephano; 1 extract, taken from LE; s.v. *Damnum.*

Sermo de sancto Vincentio; 2 extracts, taken from LE; s.v. *Confidentia, Tentatio.*

De Sermone domini in monte (bibliography ii: 87); 10 extracts, at least 3 of which may be taken from LE; s.v. *Adiutorium, Correctio, Iactantia, Ipocrisis, Iudex, Laus, Liberalitas, Mansuetudo, Peccatum, Providentia.*

De Sermone domini (cf. bibliography ii: 87); 4 extracts, at least 2 of which may be taken from LE; s.v. *Concupiscentia, Correctio, Misericordia, Ornatus.*

De Simbolo (cf. bibliography ii: 142); 4 extracts, 2 of which are taken from FP and 2 from LE; s.v. *Desperatio, Gloria eterna, Iudex, Passio.*

De Singularitate clericorum; 15 extracts, at least 7 of which may be taken from LE; s.v. *Clericus, Confidentia, Luxuria, Mulier, Periculum, Potestas, Providentia, Sacerdos, Solitudo, Tentatio, Voluptas.*

Soliloquia (bibliography ii: 28); 4 extracts (work cited in LE); s.v. *Deus, Mulier, Penitentia, Satisfactio.*

De Spiritu et anima (bibliography ii: 103); 4 extracts; s.v. *Anima, Dilectio, Gloria eterna.*

De Spiritu et littera; 8 extracts, 7 of which are taken from FP and 1 from LE; s.v. *Beatitudo, Concupiscentia, Fides, Gratia, Lex, Mirabile, Spes.*

Super illud Actuum; Elevatus est in celum; 1 extract, probably taken from the *Gloss*; s.v. *Ascensio.*

Super illud I Corinthios 6: Secularia iudicia etc.; 1 extract, probably taken from the *Gloss*; s.v. *Iudex.*

Super illud Ecclesiastici 7: Non te iustifices ante deum quoniam agnitor cordis est; 1 extract, probably taken from the *Gloss*; s.v. *Presumptio.*

Super ep. ad Galatas (bibliography II: 145); 5 extracts, at least 4 of which are taken from LE; s.v. *Correctio, Mendacium, Misericordia.*

Super illud Galatas 6: Michi absit gloriari nisi in cruce domini nostri; 1 extract, probably taken from the *Gloss*; s.v. *Crux.*

[Super illud Iacobi, i.e.,] In originali tractans illud Iacobi: Que enim est vita nostra; 1 extract; s.v. *Vita humana presens.*

Super illud Iob 27: Que est spes, ypocrite; 1 extract, probably taken from the *Gloss*; s.v. *Ipocrisis.*

Super Iohannem (bibliography II: 25); 57 extracts (work cited in LE); s.v. *Adventus domini, Auditor, Baptismus, Beatitudo, Beneficia, Caro, Confessio, Consolatio, Cor, Creatio, Crux, Desiderium, Deus, Devotio, Doctrina, Fides, Gaudium, Gloria eterna, Gratia, Homicidium, Humilitas, Ieiunium, Invidia, Laus, Mendacium, Mors, Murmur, Nativitas, Nocumentum, Opus, Passio, Peccatum, Petitio, Predestinatio, Predicatio, Querere deum, Regimen, Servitium, Simplicitas, Tribulatio, Veritas, Vita humana presens, Voluntas, X$\overline{pu}$s.*

Super ep. Iohannis (bibliography II: 106); 5 extracts, at least 4 of which are taken from LE; s.v. *Caritas, Consideratio, Mors, Mundus.*

Super illud I^e [ep.] Iohannis: In hoc manifesti sunt filii dei et filii diaboli; 1 extract, probably taken from the *Gloss*; s.v. *Dilectio.*

Super Mattheum; 8 extracts; s.v. *Consuetudo, Divitie, Ecclesia, Meritum, Odium, X$\overline{pu}$s.*

Super, *or* Tractans, illud Matthei [etc.]; 8 extracts, probably taken from the *Gloss*; s.v. *Blasphemia, Eucharistia, Intentio, Ipocrisis, Laus, Reconciliatio, Venia.*

Super illud: Pater noster qui es in celis etc.; 1 extract, probably taken from the *Gloss*; s.v. *Deus.*

Super Psalmos; 86 extracts, at least 3 of which may be taken from LE, 1 from FP, 1 from either; s.v. *Adulatio, Ambitio, Amor, Beatitudo, Confessio, Consuetudo, Conversio, Desiderium, Deus, Devotio, Diabolus, Divitie, Elemosina, Gaudium, Gloria mala, Gloria eterna, Innocentia, Ipocrisis, Ira, Laus, Mandatum, Martirium, Mendacium, Mercatio, Misericordia, Mundus, Obedientia, Opus, Oratio, Paciencia, Patria, Paupertas, Pax, Peccatum, Penitentia, Profectus, Prosperitas, Querere deum, Regimen, Sapientia, Senectus, Spes, Tentatio, Timor, Tribulatio, Virginitas, Vita humana presens, Voluntas, X$\overline{pi}$anus.*

Super illud Psalmorum [etc.]; 6 extracts, probably taken from the *Gloss*; s.v. *Angelus, Gratitudo, Patria, Superbia, Verbum.*

Super epistolam ad Romanos (bibliography II: 144); 1 extract, taken from LE; s.v. *Gratia.*

De Trinitate (bibliography II: 2); 17 extracts, at least 5 of which may be taken from LE (work cited in FP); s.v. *Adulatio, Consideratio, Contemplatio, Creatio, Fides, Miseria, Peccatum, Potestas, Proximus, Sapientia, Studium, Trinitas, Veritas, Voluntas.*

De Unico baptismo (bibliography II: 11); 2 extracts, 1 of which is taken from LE and 1 from *Decretum*; s.v. *Baptismus, Error.*

De Utilitate credendi (bibliography II: 57); 1 extract, taken from LE; s.v. *Amor.*

De Utilitate penitentie agende; 6 extracts, at least 3 of which may be taken from LE; s.v. *Desperatio, Gloria eterna, Pena, Penitentia.*

De Vera religione (bibliography II: 17); 15 extracts, at least 1 of which may be taken from LE (work cited in FP); s.v. *Adiutorium, Amicitia, Curiositas, Damnum, Iustitia, Libertas, Odium, Peccatum, Philosophia, Sacramentum, Sapientia, Scriptura, Voluntas, Xp̄us.*

De Verbis apostoli; 20 extracts, at least 8 of which may be taken from LE and 1 probably taken from the *Gloss;* s.v. *Adiutorium, Bellum, Divitie, Gratia, Ignorantia, Incarnatio, Ira, Iuramentum, Iustitia, Martirium, Mendacium, Passio, Paupertas, Profectus, Restitutio, Voluntas.*

De Verbis domini; 44 extracts, at least 2 of which may be taken from LE; s.v. *Abstinentia, Amissio rerum, Avaritia, Bellum, Conversio, Cor, Correctio, Elemosina, Fides, Humilitas, Inimicitia, Invidia, Iuramentum, Militia, Miseria, Passio, Paupertas, Pax, Petitio, Prelatio, Presumptio, Prosperitas, Rapina, Resurrectio, Superbia, Tentatio, Timor, Trinitas, Venia, Voluntas.*

De Viduis; 1 extract; s.v. *Devotio.*

De Virginitate, De sancte virginitate (bibliography II: 77); 5 extracts (De sancte virginitate cited in FP and LE); s.v. *Devotio, Gratitudo, Labor, Maria, Passio.*

De Vita christiana (bibliography II: 30); 4 extracts, taken from LE; s.v. *Dilectio, Mors, Xp̄ianus.*

De Vita clericorum; 6 extracts (work cited in LE); s.v. *Ira, Predicatio, Relinquere, Superbia, Venia.*

De Vita eterna; 1 extract; s.v. *Gloria eterna.*

Avicenna

Metaphysica; 1 extract; s.v. *Iustitia.*

Basilius (prologue)

Exameron; 8 extracts, at least 4 of which are taken from LE; s.v. *Amor, Consideratio, Humilitas, Oratio.*

Homiliae; 2 extracts, at least 1 of which is taken from LE; s.v. *Cupiditas, Elemosina.*

In sua Regula; 1 extract, taken from LE; s.v. *Consuetudo.*

[Super, i.e.] Tractans, illud Matthei 5: Vos estis lux mundi; 1 extract, probably taken from the *Gloss;* s.v. *Apostoli.*

Beda (prologue)

Without title; 1 extract; s.v. *Honor.*

Super Actus apostolorum; 1 extract; s.v. *Sortilegium.*

Super Cantica; 2 extracts, at least 1 of which is taken from LE; s.v. *Adventus domini, Amor.*

Super Esdra; 3 extracts, taken from LE; s.v. *Castitas, Divitie, Error.*

[Super, i.e.] Tractans, illud Iohannis 3: Erat homo ex phariseis; 1 extract, taken from LE; s.v. *Ascensio.*

Super Lucam; 10 extracts, at least 6 of which are taken from LE; s.v. *Adulatio, Amor, Baptismus, Contemplatio, Nativitas, Patria, Relinquere, Sanctitas, Spiritus sanctus, Tentatio.*

Super illud Matthei 17: Ecce mater tua; 1 extract, probably taken from the *Gloss*; s.v. *Parentes.*

Super Parabolas; 3 extracts, taken from LE; s.v. *Ira, Simplicitas.*

Super Proverbia; 5 extracts, 3 of which are taken from LE and 2 from the *Gloss*; s.v. *Accidia, Consuetudo, Gratia, Iudex.*

De Templo Salomonis, De tabernaculo S.; 7 extracts, at least 6 of which are taken from LE; s.v. *Consuetudo, Doctrina, Luxuria, Oratio, Simplicitas, X$\overline{pu}$s.*

Bernardus (prologue)

Without title; 13 extracts; s.v. *Gloria eterna, Ipocrisis, Mors, Mundus, Obedientia, Ociositas, Oratio, X$\overline{pu}$s.*

De Amore dei (bibliography VI: 10); 1 extract; s.v. *Amor.*

Apologia; 14 extracts, at least 6 of which may be taken from FP; s.v. *Abusio, Cor, Ecclesia, Gula, Ingenium, Medicina, Monachus, Ornatus, Prelatio.*

Colloquium Simonis ad Petrum (bibliography VI: 11); 3 extracts; s.v. *Relinquere.*

De Consideratione, Ad Eugenium papam (bibliography VI: 1); 36 extracts, 9 of which may be taken from FP; s.v. *Advocati, Ambitio, Amor, Clericus, Compassio, Conscientia, Consideratio, Contemplatio, Cor, Correctio, Detractio, Deus, Divitie, Fides, Fortitudo, Intentio, Maria, Modestia, Murmur, Ociositas, Paciencia, Pena, Prelatio, Prosperitas, Societas.*

De Contemptu mundi; 1 extract; s.v. *Lacrima.*

De Diligendo deo (bibliography VI: 9); 8 extracts, 3 of which may be taken from FP; s.v. *Adiutorium, Amor, Creatio, Excusatio, Ingratitudo, Querere deum, Superbia.*

De Duodecim gradibus humilitatis (bibliography VI: 6); 13 extracts, 1 of which may be taken from FP; s.v. *Confessio, Excusatio, Fides, Humilitas, Ignorantia, Miseria, Presumptio, Querere deum, Superbia, Veritas.*

Epistolae; 64 extracts (work cited in FP); s.v. *Abusio, Accidia, Auditor, Beatitudo, Caritas, Castitas, Clericus, Confessio, Contemplatio, Delitie, Devotio, Disciplina, Doctrina, Eucharistia, Exemplum, Fides, Gloria bona, Gloria eterna, Humilitas, Ignorantia, Incarnatio, Ira, Iudex, Iustitia, Medicina, Monachus, Mors, Nobilitas, Ociositas, Pax, Pena, Penitentia, Perfectio, Perseverantia, Pietas, Prelatio, Religio, Sacerdos, Sapientia, Scandalum, Victoria, Voluntas, Votum, X$\overline{pu}$s.*

Epistola ad Fulconem; 1 extract; s.v. *Timor.*

Ep. ad Henricum archiepiscopum Senonensem; 2 extracts; s.v. *Ambitio, Prelatio.*

[Ep.] ad Imericum cancellarium; 1 extract; s.v. *Gratitudo.*

[Ep.] ad Sophiam virginem; 1 extract; s.v. *Solitudo.*

Ep. ad Theobaldum comitem; 2 extracts; s.v. *Iuventus, Prelatio.*

Expositio regule b. Benedicti pt. 3 c. 7, tractans illud Proverbiorum 25: Celum sursum et terram deorsum (cf. bibliography vi: 13); 1 extract; s.v. *Prelatio*.

De Libero arbitrio (cf. bibliography vi: 5); 8 extracts (work cited in FP); s.v. *Gratia, Libertas, Peccatum, Voluntas*.

Meditationes (bibliography vi: 14); 1 extract; s.v. *Anima*.

Ad Milites templi, De Nova militia (bibliography vi: 8); 8 extracts, at least 5 of which are taken from FP; s.v. *Bellum, Confessio, Incarnatio, Mors, Nativitas, Obedientia, Securitas, Xp̄us*.

De Precepto/Preceptis et dispensatione (bibliography vi: 3); 17 extracts, 4 of which may be taken from FP, and the remainder, if not all 17, may be taken from B.N. ms lat. 16371; s.v. *Amor, Intentio, Mandatum, Monachus, Obedientia, Religio, Scandalum, Votum*.

Sermones; 165 extracts (work cited in FP); under 78 topic-headings.

Sermo de Adventu; 1 extract; s.v. *Adventus domini*.

Sermo de Angelis; 4 extracts; s.v. *Angelus*.

Sermones super Cantica canticorum (bibliography vi: 2); 130 extracts, probably taken from B.N. ms lat. 16371; under 71 topic-headings.

Sermo dedicationis; 1 extract; s.v. *Anima*.

Sermo de Epiphania; 1 extract; s.v. *Nativitas*.

Sermo Omnium sanctorum; 1 extract; s.v. *Tentatio*.

Sermo in Quadragesime; 1 extract; s.v. *Ambitio*.

Sermo ad scholares; 2 extracts; s.v. *Tempus*.

Sermo de Trinitate; 2 extracts; s.v. *Trinitas*.

Sermo Petri et Pauli; 2 extracts; s.v. *Apostoli*.

Super illud I Cor. 8: Scientia inflat, caritas edificat; 1 extract, probably taken from the *Gloss*; s.v. *Caritas*.

[Super, i.e.] Tractans, illud Matth. 22: Duces ceci excolantes culicem camelum aut glutientes; 1 extract, probably taken from the *Gloss*; s.v. *Correctio*.

Super Missus est (bibliography vi: 4); 8 extracts, 5 of which may be taken from FP; s.v. *Humilitas, Maria, Ornatus, Religio, Superbia*.

Super illud Psalmorum [etc.]; 3 extracts, probably taken from the *Gloss*; s.v. *Ascensio, Clericus, Dilectio*.

Boetius (prologue)

Without title; 1 extract; s.v. *Gloria eterna*.

De consolatione (bibliography xviii: 3); 24 extracts, 12 of which may be taken from LE; s.v. *Beatitudo, Caro, Consideratio, Divitie, Fama, Gloria mala, Inimicitia, Liberalitas, Miseria, Odium, Pax, Potestas, Prosperitas, Regimen, Remuneratio, Reverentia, Sobrietas, Studium, Voluptas*.

De disciplina scholarium (bibliography xviii: 4); 5 extracts; s.v. *Exercitatio, Magister, Negligentia*.

Cassianus (prologue)

Without title; 2 extracts, taken from LE; s.v. *Monachus*.

Collationes patrum; 34 extracts, at least 24 of which may be taken from LE;

s.v. *Castitas, Cogitatio, Devotio, Discere, Discretio, Fraternitas, Humilitas, Ieiunium, Luxuria, Monachus, Negligentia, Obedientia, Oratio, Perfectio, Presumptio, Relinquere, Senectus, Sobrietas, Voluntas.*

In quadam Epistola; 1 extract; s.v. *Parentes.*

De Institutis monachorum; 12 extracts, at least 9 of which are taken from LE; s.v. *Abstinentia, Accidia, Caro, Gula, Instabilitas, Relinquere, Solitudo, Timor.*

De Spiritu accidie; 1 extract, taken from LE; s.v. *Ociositas.*

De Spiritu superbie; 1 extract, taken from LE; s.v. *Humilitas.*

Cassiodorus (prologue)

Without title; 14 extracts; s.v. *Apostoli, Eloquentia, Lex, Meritum, Votum.*

Epistolae; 111 extracts; under 58 topic-headings.

Super Beati immaculati; 2 extracts; s.v. *Mors, Testimonium.*

Super illud: Beati quorum; 1 extract; s.v. *Confessio.*

Super Psalmis; 141 extracts, at least 7 of which may be taken from FP (work cited in LE); under 81 topic-headings.

Cato

Without title; 1 extract, probably taken from *Proverbia philosophorum*; s.v. *Fides.*

Cesarius (prologue)

In Amonitione; 10 extracts, at least 9 of which are taken from LE; s.v. *Elemosina, Exemplum, Gaudium, Ieiunium, Mors, Religio, Venia.*

Chrisostomus (prologue)

Without title; 3 extracts; s.v. *Humilitas, Martirium, Sobrietas.*

De Compunctione cordis; 9 extracts, at least 7 of which are taken from LE; s.v. *Contemplatio, Contritio, Delitie, Doctrina, Inimicitia, Meritum, Potestas, Reconciliatio.*

In suo Dialogo (bibliography IX: 3); 8 extracts, at least 6 of which are taken from LE; s.v. *Correctio, Potestas, Prelatio, Sacerdos, Violentia.*

De Dignitate sacerdotali (bibliography IX: 3); 5 extracts; s.v. *Sacerdos.*

Epistola ad Heliodorum monachum; 1 extract; s.v. *Penitentia.*

Homiliae (cf. bibliography IX: 2); 13 extracts (work cited in LE); s.v. *Gloria bona, Gloria mala, Incarnatio, Infernus, Meritum, Odium, Residivatio, X̄pīanus.*

Homilia de Ascensione; 1 extract, taken from LE; s.v. *Homo.*

Homilia hodierna; 1 extract, taken from LE; s.v. *Ascensio.*

De Laudibus Pauli homilia (bibliography IX: 5); 7 extracts, at least 2 of which may be taken from FP and 2 from LE; s.v. *Apostoli, Ira, Laus, Predicatio, Veritas.*

In Policratico, P. de nugis curialium, De vestigiis philosophorum, etc.; 15 extracts, taken from FP, which is also the source of this misattribution; s.v. *Adulatio, Amicitia, Conversatio, Discretio, Doctrina, Humilitas, Philosophia, Potestas, Prosperitas, Regimen, Sapientia, Studium.*

Quod nemo leditur nisi a semetipso (bibliography ix: 4); 1 extract, taken from
  LE; s.v. *Divitie.*

De Reparatione lapsi; 11 extracts, at least 5 of which may be taken from LE
  and 2 from FP; s.v. *Anima, Delitie, Desperatio, Gloria eterna, Honor,*
  Meritum, Nocumentum, Penitentia.

In quodam Sermone; 3 extracts (sermons cited in FP and LE); s.v. *Correctio,*
  Lacrima, Penitentia.

Sermo de confessoribus; 1 extract, taken from LE; s.v. *Sanctitas.*

Sermo super epistola ad Hebreos; 12 extracts, 10 of which are taken from LE
  and 2 from FP; s.v. *Abstinentia, Auditor, Caro, Compassio, Contemptus,*
  Divitie, Gratia, Monachus, Pacientia, Paupertas, Senectus, Virtus.

Sermo de Iohanne baptista (bibliography ix: 2); 2 extracts, taken from LE; s.v.
  Sanctitas, Timor.

De Simbolo; 9 extracts, at least 4 of which may be taken from FP; s.v. *Ascen-*
  sio, Consideratio, Fides, Gratitudo, Intentio, Munus, Regimen.

[Super] Iª ad Corinthios 15; 1 extract, probably taken from the *Gloss*; s.v.
  Iudex.

Super Iohannem; 1 extract; s.v. *Gloria mala.*

Super Mattheum (bibliography ix: 1); 182 extracts (work cited in FP and LE);
  under 88 topic-headings.

Super illud: Mulier ecce filius tuus etc.; 1 extract, probably taken from the
  Gloss; s.v. *Parentes.*

Super illud: Sic deus dilexit mundum; 1 extract, probably taken from the
  Gloss; s.v. *Amor.*

Ciprianus (prologue)

De Duodecim abusionibus: 9 extracts, taken from LE; s.v. *Abusio, Castitas,*
  Iustitia, Iuventus, Senectus, X̄p̄ianus.

In quadam Epistola; 4 extracts (letters are cited in LE); s.v. *Diabolus, Fraus,*
  Martirium, Murmur.

Epistola 2ª de Disciplina et habitu virginum; 4 extracts, at least 3 of which are
  taken from LE; s.v. *Conversatio, Disciplina, Ornatus.*

Epistola 6ª de Mortalitate; 1 extract, taken from LE; s.v. *Gloria eterna.*

Epistola 5ª de Oratione dominica; 2 extracts, at least 1 of which is taken from
  LE; s.v. *Oratio, Perfectio.*

De Laudibus penitentie; 1 extract; s.v. *Penitentia.*

In Sermone; 1 extract, probably taken from *Decretum*; s.v. *Consuetudo.*

De Virginitate; 2 extracts; s.v. *Virginitas.*

Damascenus (prologue)

Without title (bibliography xi: 3); 3 extracts (cited without title in FP); s.v.
  Angelus, Crux, Resurrectio.

Tractans illud Matthei 16: Tu es Christus filius dei vivi; 1 extract, probably
  taken from the *Gloss*; s.v. *X̄p̄us.*

Decretum

> 28 extracts, 25 of which have been located in *Decretum*; s.v. *Baptismus, Bellum, Caritas, Clericus, Compassio, Consuetudo, Contemptus, Conversatio, Cupiditas, Decima, Electio, Peccatum, Penitentia, Securitas, Simonia, Sortilegium, Tribulatio, Voluntas.*

Diogenes

> Without title; 5 extracts, probably taken from *Proverbia philosophorum*; s.v. *Adulatio, Amicitia, Coniugium.*

Dionisius

> Epistola ad Timotheum (bibliography I: 5.9); 2 extracts; s.v. *Apostoli.*

Effrem

> Without title; 3 extracts, taken from LE; s.v. *Antichristus, Mundus, Presumptio.*

Eusebius

> Sermo; 1 extract; s.v. *Religio.*

Fulgentius (prologue)

> Ad Probam; 2 extracts, taken from LE; s.v. *Ieiunium, Nativitas.*
> In quodam Sermone; 1 extract; s.v. *Dilectio.*
> Sermo de sancto Stephano; 1 extract, taken from LE; s.v. *Sanctitas.*
> Tractans illud Matthei: Omnis arbor etc.; 1 extract, probably taken from *Gloss*; s.v. *Rapina.*

Gilbertus

> Without title; 1 extract; s.v. *Abusio.*

Glosa

> 56 extracts; s.v. *Acceptio personarum, Adventus domini, Antichristus, Ascensio, Consideratio, Consuetudo, Curiositas, Decima, Detractio, Dilectio, Discordia, Divitie, Doctrina, Electio, Elemosina, Exemplum, Gratia, Gula, Honor, Ieiunium, Ingenium, Ipocrisis, Iudex, Iuramentum, Loquacitas, Mansuetudo, Oratio, Predicatio, Promissio, Rapina, Regimen, Relinquere, Residivatio, Resurrectio, Reverentia, Sacerdos, Sapientia, Tribulatio, Veritas, Virginitas.*

Gregorius (prologue)

> Without title; 4 extracts; s.v. *Humilitas, Mendacium, Spiritus sanctus, Timor.*
> Dialogorum libri (bibliography V: 3); 15 extracts, 1 of which may be taken from LE and the remainder, or all 15, from B.N. MS lat. 15309 (work cited in FP); s.v. *Anima, Eucharistia, Exemplum, Gloria eterna, Infernus, Mors, Nobilitas, Pena, Perfectio, Predestinatio, Prelatio, Reconciliatio.*
> In quadam Epistola; 2 extracts; s.v. *Contemplatio, Liberalitas.*
> Epistola ad Iesanum; 1 extract; s.v. *Ecclesia.*
> Homiliae (super Evang.?); 135 extracts, at least 4 of which and probably many more are taken from LE; under 68 topic-headings.

Homilia 29 tractans illud Canticorum 2°: Ecce iste venit saliens in montibus; 2 extracts, probably taken from *Gloss*; s.v. *Ascensio, Incarnatio.*

Homiliae super Evangelia, 36 extracts, at least 7 of which may be taken from LE (work cited in FP); s.v. *Abstinentia, Adulatio, Amor, Angelus, Ascensio, Avaritia, Auditor, Consuetudo, Conversio, Correctio, Desiderium, Exemplum, Fides, Martirium, Oratio, Pacientia, Parentes, Pena, Penitentia, Predicatio, Solemnitas, Verbum, Voluntas.*

Homiliae super Ezechielem (bibliography v: 4); 76 extracts, probably taken from B.N. lat. 15309 (work cited in LE); s.v. *Adulatio, Advocati, Amor, Auditor, Conscientia, Contemplatio, Correctio, Debitum, Detractio, Deus, Ecclesia, Exemplum, Gloria eterna, Homicidium, Humilitas, Ira, Labor, Lacrima, Malitia, Miseria, Pacientia, Paupertas, Peccatum, Predicatio, Prelatio, Prosperitas, Religio, Relinquere, Reverentia, Sacerdos, Salus, Scandalum, Scriptura, Servitium, Societas, Spiritus sanctus, Taciturnitas, Temperantia, Verecundia, Vicium, Virginitas, Virtus.*

[Homiliae] super Mattheum; 11 extracts; s.v. *Conversio, Infernus, Ingenium, Iudex, Iuramentum, Mors, Odium, Penitentia, Resurrectio, Spiritus sanctus.*

Moralia (bibliography v: 1); 493 extracts, probably taken from B.N. MS lat. 15674 (work cited in LE); under 143 topic-headings.

Pastorale (bibliography v: 2); 74 extracts, probably taken from B.N. MS lat. 15310 (work cited in FP and LE); s.v. *Abstinentia, Ambitio, Amicitia, Auditor, Caritas, Cogitatio, Confessio, Correctio, Detractio, Dilectio, Discordia, Elemosina, Excusatio, Exemplum, Gula, Ieiunium, Inimicitia, Lacrima, Laus, Loquacitas, Medicina, Oratio, Pacientia, Paupertas, Pax, Penitentia, Petitio, Predicatio, Prelatio, Prosperitas, Regimen, Sapientia, Satisfactio, Securitas, Subiectio, Taciturnitas, Tentatio, Timor, Venia.*

Registrum; 26 extracts, 8 of which may be taken from LE; s.v. *Adiutorium, Ambitio, Consolatio, Contemptus, Correctio, Dilectio, Ecclesia, Elemosina, Honor, Ipocrisis, Ira, Iustitia, Lacrima, Ordo, Potestas, Prelatio, Sacerdos, Simonia, Solemnitas, Subiectio.*

Super illud Genesis 19: In montem te salvam fac; 1 extract, probably taken from the *Gloss*; s.v. *Perfectio.*

Super illud Proverbiorum 25: Doctrina viri per patientiam noscitur; 1 extract, probably taken from the *Gloss*; s.v. *Doctrina.*

Gregorius Nazianzenus

Apologeticus; 10 extracts, 5 of which are taken from LE, 4 from FP, and 1 from either LE or FP; s.v. *Discere, Doctrina, Malitia, Pax, Predicatio, Regimen, Sapientia.*

Haymo

Without title; 1 extract, taken from the *Gloss*; s.v. *Antichristus.*

Hieronimus (prologue)

Without title; 9 extracts; s.v. *Gloria eterna, Heresis, Maria, Opus, Ornatus, Superbia.*

In prologo Biblie; 1 extract; s.v. *Scriptura.*

De Cohabitatione clericorum et mulierum (bibliography IV: 8); 1 extract; s.v. *Securitas.*

Contra Iovinianum (bibliography IV: 13); 6 extracts (cited as "Epistola ad I." in LE); s.v. *Electio, Gula, Mulier, Solitudo.*

Contra Vigilantium; 2 extracts; s.v. *Contemplatio, Oratio.*

Epistolae (bibliography IV: 18); 91 extracts (letters cited in FP and LE); under 64 topics-headings.

Epistola ad Augustinum; 1 extract; s.v. *Excusatio.*

Epistola ad Celantium; 13 extracts, at least 4 of which may be taken from LE and 1 from FP; s.v. *Abstinentia, Adulatio, Consuetudo, Detractio, Humilitas, Ieiunium, Laus, Nobilitas, Nocumentum, Veritas.*

Epistola ad Cyprianum; 2 extracts, at least 1 of which may be taken from LE; s.v. *Mors, Tribulatio.*

Ep. ad Damasum papam; 3 extracts, at least 1 of which may be taken from FP and 1 from LE; s.v. *Iudex, Scriptura, Voluptas.*

Ep. ad Demetriadem; 32 extracts (work cited in FP); s.v. *Abstinentia, Adulatio, Amicitia, Amor, Cogitatio, Conversatio, Doctrina, Ieiunium, Innocentia, Invidia, Ira, Iustitia, Ociositas, Oratio, Scriptura, Studium, Vicium, Virginitas, Voluntas.*

Ep. de duobus filiis; 2 extracts (work cited in FP); s.v. *Curiositas.*

[Ep.] ad Eustochium; 3 extracts (work cited in FP); s.v. *Ornatus, Solemnitas, Virginitas.*

[Ep.] ad Evandrum presbiterum; 1 extract; s.v. *Ecclesia.*

Ep. ad Exuberantium; 1 extract; s.v. *Apostoli.*

Ep. ad Fabiolum/Fabiolam; 2 extracts, taken from LE; s.v. *Acceptio personarum, Superfluitas.*

Ep. ad Furiam; 1 extract (work cited in FP); s.v. *Abstinentia.*

Ep. ad Genitiam; 1 extract; s.v. *Virginitas.*

[Ep.] ad Heliodorum/Eliodorum; 15 extracts, at least 3 of which may be taken from FP and 4 from LE; s.v. *Consolatio, Electio, Exemplum, Iudex, Monachus, Mors, Parentes, Religio, Relinquere, Resurrectio, Solitudo.*

[Ep.] ad Letam; 3 extracts, taken from LE; s.v. *Abstinentia, Contemptus, Conversio.*

Ep. ad Marcellam; 3 extracts (work cited in FP); s.v. *Correctio, Munus, Pietas.*

Ep. ad Marcum; 1 extract (work cited in FP); s.v. *Religio.*

Ep. ad matrem et filiam; 2 extracts (work cited in FP); s.v. *Luxuria, Mulier.*

Ep. ad Nepotianum; 23 extracts, at least 4 of which may be taken from FP, 1 from LE, and 3 from either; s.v. *Amor, Clericus, Detractio, Excusatio, Gloria mala, Ieiunium, Labor, Laus, Loquacitas, Misericordia, Mulier, Ornatus, Paupertas, Predicatio, Religio, Sacerdos, Sanctitas, Senectus.*

Ep. ad Occeanum; 3 extracts, at least 1 of which may be taken from FP; s.v. *Correctio, Ebrietas, Electio.*

[Ep.] ad Pammachium (bibliography IV: 11); 6 extracts, at least 1 of which may be taken from FP and 1 from either FP or LE; s.v. *Acceptio personarum, Contemptus, Monachus, Predicatio, Verecundia.*

Ep. ad Paulinam; 8 extracts, at least 1 of which may be taken from FP; s.v. *Amicitia, Avaritia, Gula, Liberalitas, Monachus, Pietas, Sanctitas, Xp̄us.*

Ep. ad Riparium presbiterum; 2 extracts (work cited in FP); s.v. *Correctio, Iniuria.*

Ep. ad Rufinum (cf. bibliography IV: 9); 2 extracts, taken from FP; s.v. *Amicitia, Coniugium.*

[Ep.] ad Rusticum monachum; 16 extracts, at least 1 of which may be taken from FP and 1 from LE; s.v. *Abstinentia, Adulatio, Avaritia, Communitas, Detractio, Excusatio, Monachus, Mulier, Proditio, Religio, Solitudo.*

Ep. 121 ad Sabinianum; 1 extract, taken from LE; s.v. *Adulatio.*

Ep. ad Salvinam; 2 extracts, at least 1 of which is taken from LE; s.v. *Divitie, Libido.*

Ep. ad Sardanianum; 1 extract; s.v. *Laus.*

Ep. ad Susannam; 1 extract, taken from FP; s.v. *Penitentia.*

Ep. ad Thesifontem; 1 extract, taken from FP; s.v. *Perfectio.*

Ep. ad Theodorum monachum; 3 extracts; s.v. *Militia, Perfectio.*

De Homine perfecto; 1 extract, taken from LE; s.v. *Providentia.*

Sermones; 6 extracts, at least 2 of which may be taken from LE; s.v. *Amor, Gula, Ociositas, Passio, Penitentia.*

Sermo de Assumptione; 3 extracts, at least 1 of which may be taken from FP; s.v. *Maria.*

Super Exodum; 1 extract; s.v. *Prelatio.*

[Super, i.e.] Tractans illud Iudicum 11: Votum vovit etc.; 1 extract, probably taken from the *Gloss*; s.v. *Votum.*

Super Psalmos; 10 extracts, at least 6 of which are taken from LE and 1 from FP; s.v. *Adulatio, Gloria eterna, Monachus, Pax, Peccatum, Scriptura.*

Super illud Psal. [etc.]; 2 extracts, probably taken from the *Gloss*; s.v. *Ascensio, Beatitudo.*

Super illud Ecclesiastici: Non est dicere hoc nequius illo, omnia enim in tempore suo comprobantur; 1 extract, probably taken from the *Gloss*; s.v. *Tempus.*

Super Isaiam; 9 extracts, at least 4 of which may be taken from LE: s.v. *Adulatio, Electio, Fortitudo, Gaudium, Ipocrisis, Lacrima, Prosperitas, Scriptura.*

Super Isaiam lib. 1 super illud: Vinum tuum mixtum est aqua; 1 extract, probably taken from the *Gloss*; s.v. *Predicatio.*

Super Hieremiam; 3 extracts (work cited in FP and LE); s.v. *Medicina, Mendacium, Tempus.*

Super Hier. lib. 1 super illud: In tempore afflictionis dicet surge etc.; 1 extract, taken from LE; s.v. *Adiutorium.*

Super Ezechielem; 6 extracts, 4 of which are taken from FP and 2 from LE; s.v. *Pena, Predicatio, Providentia, Sacerdos, Veritas.*

Super Danielem; 1 extract (work cited in LE); s.v. *Philosophia.*

Super illud Danielis: Beatus qui expectat et pervenit usque ad dies MCCCXXXV; 1 extract, taken from LE; s.v. *Antichristus.*

Super Hosee; 2 extracts, taken from FP; s.v. *Detractio, Simplicitas.*

Super duodecim prophetas lib. 2 super illud Ezechielis 3: Filii hominis etc.; 1 extract, taken from LE; s.v. *Conversatio.*

Super Ioel; 3 extracts, taken from LE; s.v. *Fortitudo, Ira, Tristitia.*

Super Hamos; 3 extracts, 2 of which are taken from LE; s.v. *Acceptio personarum, Fortitudo, Peccatum.*

Super Ionam; 2 extracts, at least 1 of which may be taken from LE; s.v. *Mors, Sortilegium.*

Super Micheam prophetam; 3 extracts, at least 1 of which may be taken from LE; s.v. *Amicitia, Odium.*

Super Habaccuch; 1 extract, taken from LE; s.v. *Oratio.*

Super Ageum prophetam; 1 extract, taken from LE; s.v. *Sacerdos.*

Super Mattheum; 18 extracts, at least 2 of which may be taken from LE; s.v. *Adventus domini, Angelus, Apostoli, Concupiscentia, Divitie, Hospitalitas, Humilitas, Iniuria, Iudex, Ociositas, Passio, Religio, Relinquere, Timor, Venia, Xp̄us.*

Super illud Matthei [etc.]; 20 extracts, probably taken from the *Gloss*; s.v. *Apostoli, Cor, Fama, Innocentia, Ipocrisis, Magister, Mansuetudo, Mirabile, Parentes, Passio, Prosperitas, Relinquere, Scandalum, Superfluitas, Venia.*

Super Marcum; 6 extracts, at least 2 of which are taken from LE; 1 from FP, and 1 from either; s.v. *Ieiunium, Oratio, Penitentia, Spiritus sanctus, Superbia.*

Super Lucam; 3 extracts, s.v. *Eucharistia.*

Super Epistolam ad Romanos; 2 extracts (work cited in LE); s.v. *Discordia.*

Super Ep. ad Galathas; 2 extracts (work cited in FP and LE); s.v. *Scriptura, Veritas.*

Super Ep. ad Ephesios; 3 extracts, at least 2 of which are taken from LE and 1 probably from the *Gloss*; s.v. *Correctio, Scriptura, Vita humana.*

Super Ep. ad Titum; 4 extracts, at least 1 of which may be taken from LE; s.v. *Clericus, Correctio, Ebrietas, Mansuetudo.*

Super illud: Dimitte mortuos sepelire; 1 extract, probably taken from the *Gloss*; s.v. *Parentes.*

Super illud: Si quis episcopatum desiderat; 1 extract, probably taken from the *Gloss*; s.v. *Prelatio.*

De Viduis; 1 extract, possibly taken from FP (correctly attrib. to Ambrose there); s.v. *Liberalitas.*

Hilarius (prologue)

Super Mattheum; 3 extracts, taken from LE; s.v. *Pax, Penitentia, Xp̄us.*

De Trinitate (bibliography VII: 1); 7 extracts, at least 5 of which are taken from LE; s.v. *Ascensio, Detractio, Doctrina, Ecclesia, Heresis, Magister.*

Hugo de Sancto Victore (prologue)

Without title; 44 extracts; s.v. *Abstinentia, Acceptio personarum, Adulatio, Blasphemia, Cogitatio, Contritio, Curiositas, Detractio, Devotio, Divitie, Ebrietas, Ecclesia, Fides, Heresis, Homo, Honor, Humilitas, Ignorantia, Ingratitudo, Innocentia, Instabilitas, Ira, Luxuria, Mansuetudo, Misericordia, Modestia, Murmur, Natura, Negligentia, Oratio, Petitio, Religio, Superbia, Tentatio, Tribulatio, Vicium.*

De Anima (bibliography xiv: 10); 34 extracts; s.v. *Anima, Conscientia, Consideratio, Cor, Gloria mala, Infernus, Infirmitas, Loquacitas, Malitia, Monachus, Paciencia, Pena, Scriptura, Securitas, Societas, Superbia, Timor, Tristitia.*

De Arca mistica, De a. Noe (bibliography xiv: 14); 2 extracts; s.v. *Contemplatio, Scriptura.*

De Claustro anime (bibliography xiv: 11); 44 extracts, probably taken from B.N. ms lat. 15315; s.v. *Abusio, Avaritia, Caro, Compassio, Conversio, Deus, Ecclesia, Exemplum, Gula, Humilitas, Martirium, Monachus, Paciencia, Paupertas, Pax, Pietas, Predicatio, Prelatio, Religio, Sacerdos, Sapientia, Superbia, Tentatio.*

Didascalicon (bibliography xiv: 15); 26 extracts; s.v. *Auditor, Confidentia, Discere, Doctrina, Homo, Magister, Patria, Philosophia, Sapientia, Studium, Taciturnitas.*

De Disciplina monachorum (bibliography xiv: 18); 18 extracts, taken from B.N. ms lat. 15315; s.v. *Conversatio.*

De Duodecim abusionibus; 16 extracts; s.v. *Monachus, Obedientia, Obstinatio, Prelatio, Religio, Sacerdos.*

De Institutione novitiorum (bibliography xiv: 17); 4 extracts, taken from ms 15315; s.v. *Correctio, Disciplina, Exercitatio, Verecundia.*

De Laude caritatis (bibliography xiv: 21); 1 extract, probably taken from ms 15315; s.v. *Caritas.*

In Meditationibus, De meditatione (bibliography xiv: 3); 3 extracts, taken from B.N. ms lat. 15693; s.v. *Contemplatio, Ipocrisis.*

De Misteriis ecclesie (cf. bibliography xiv: 29, xiv: 35); 1 extract; s.v. *Penitentia.*

De Operationibus trium dierum (bibliography xiv: 9); 3 extracts, taken from ms 15693; s.v. *Mirabile.*

De Sacramentis (bibliography xiv: 1); 3 extracts, taken from ms 15693; s.v. *Incarnatio, Salus, Simonia.*

De Scripturis sacris (bibliography xiv: 26); 1 extract, taken from ms 15315; s.v. *Virtus.*

Ad Socium volentem nubere (bibliography xiv: 12); 7 extracts, probably taken from ms 15315; s.v. *Coniugium, Mulier.*

De Substantia dilectionis (bibliography xiv: 8); 1 extract, probably taken from ms 15693; s.v. *Dilectio.*

De Tribus voluntatibus in Christo (bibliography xiv: 5); 1 extract, probably
   taken from ms 15693; s.v. *Compassio.*

De Vanitate mundi (bibliography xiv: 20); 2 extracts, probably taken from ms
   15315; s.v. *Gloria mala, Sapientia.*

De Vera sapientia (bibliography xiv: 7); 1 extract, possibly taken from ms
   15693 (ff. 143-145, "De sapientia Christi"); s.v. *Desperatio.*

Huguccio

Without title; 7 extracts; s.v. *Detractio, Gula, Invidia, Studium.*

Innocentius

De vilitate conditionis humane; 38 extracts; s.v. *Acceptio personarum, Advocati, Ambitio, Avaritia, Compassio, Contritio, Cupiditas, Divitie, Ebrietas, Gula, Luxuria, Miseria, Ornatus, Paupertas, Prelatio, Prosperitas,
   Senectus, Servitus, Superbia, Tribulatio.*

Iohannes Saresberiensis

Policraticus: *see* Chrisostomus.

Isidorus (prologue)

De Conflictu viciorum et virtutum; 2 extracts, taken from le; s.v. *Iactantia,
   Mendacium:*

Ethimologiae (bibliography viii: 2); 26 extracts, 12 of which may be taken
   from le; s.v. *Anima, Antichristus, Avaritia, Beatitudo, Confessio, Consuetudo, Discordia, Divitie, Doctrina, Ebrietas, Fabula, Ipocrisis, Lex,
   Medicina, Philosophia, Providentia, Sanctitas, Sanitas, Sapientia, Solici-
   tudo, Stultitia, Superbia.*

De Sinodis; 2 extracts; s.v. *Discretio, Religio.*

In Sinonimis; 9 extracts; s.v. *Consuetudo, Discretio, Doctrina, Fraus, Iniuria,
   Magister, Voluptas.*

Soliloquia; 13 extracts, taken from le; s.v. *Abstinentia, Conscientia, Consuetudo, Conversatio, Excusatio, Ira, Loquacitas, Mansuetudo, Societas,
   Votum.*

De Summo bono (bibliography viii: 1); 116 extracts, probably taken from
   B.N. ms lat. 15734 (work cited in fp and, as "Sententiae," in le); under
   59 topic-headings.

Super Hamos propheta; 2 extracts; s.v. *Abstinentia, Vita humana presens.*

Super Mattheum; 1 extract; s.v. *Coniugium.*

Leo papa (prologue)

Without title; 2 extracts; s.v. *Lex.*

In quadam Epistola; 1 extract, taken from *Decretum;* s.v. *Potestas.*

Sermones; 20 extracts, 3 of which are probably taken from *Decretum* and the
   rest probably from fp; s.v. *Avaritia, Communitas, Confessio, Conversatio,
   Cupiditas, Desperatio, Divitie, Electio, Incarnatio, Ociositas, Opus, Pax,
   Tentatio.*

Sermo de Apparitione; 8 extracts, at least 4 of which are taken from le; s.v.
   Accidia, Liberalitas, Mandatum, Misericordia, Nativitas.

Sermo Hodiernus; 2 extracts; s.v. *Ascensio.*

Sermo de Ieiunio; 3 extracts, at least 1 of which may be taken from LE; s.v. *Elemosina, Exemplum, Satisfactio.*

Sermo de Ieiunio septimi mensis; 4 extracts, at least 1 of which may be taken from LE; s.v. *Caritas, Ieiunium, Passio.*

Sermo de Ieiunio decimi mensis; 1 extract, taken from LE; s.v. *Abstinentia.*

Sermo de Pentecoste; 2 extracts, taken from LE; s.v. *Modestia, Spiritus sanctus.*

Sermo Petri et Pauli; 1 extract; s.v. *Apostoli.*

Sermo 4ª de Quadragesima; 1 extract, taken from LE; s.v. *Paupertas.*

Super illud: Date inquit et dabitur vobis; 1 extract, probably taken from the *Gloss*; s.v. *Elemosina.*

Tractans illud: Beati qui lugent; 1 extract, probably taken from the *Gloss*; s.v. *Compassio.*

Lucanus

Without title; 1 extract, probably taken from *Proverbia philosophorum*; s.v. *Exactio.*

Maximus (prologue)

In quodam Sermone; 1 extract ("Omeliae" cited in LE); s.v. *Favor.*

Sermo Apostolorum Petri et Pauli; 1 extract, taken from LE; s.v. *Apostoli.*

Sermo de Iohanne baptista; 1 extract, taken from LE; s.v. *Consuetudo.*

Sermo de Martiribus; 1 extract, taken from LE; s.v. *Crux.*

[Sermo] in Natali domini; 3 extracts, taken from LE; s.v. *Ieiunium, Nativitas, Xp̄ianus.*

Sermo de Pascha; 1 extract; s.v. *Resurrectio.*

Origenes (prologue)

Epistola apologetica; 1 extract; s.v. *Error.*

Super Exodum homiliae; 4 extracts, at least 3 of which are taken from LE; s.v. *Correctio, Solemnitas, Spes, Studium.*

Super illud Exodi 8: Percutiam omnes terminos tuos ranis; 1 extract (work cited in LE); s.v. *Advocati.*

Super Leviticum homiliae; 11 extracts, taken from LE; s.v. *Correctio, Cupiditas, Doctrina, Electio, Excommunicatio, Ordo, Predicatio, Restitutio, Sanctitas, Sobrietas, Solitudo, Testimonium.*

Super librum Numerorum homiliae; 12 extracts, at least 5 of which are taken from LE; s.v. *Angeli, Correctio, Electio, Fortitudo, Predestinatio, Tentatio.*

Super Iudicum hom. 2; 1 extract, taken from FP; s.v. *Deus.*

Super Ezechielem homiliae; 5 extracts, taken from LE; s.v. *Adulatio, Paciencia, Superbia.*

Super Mattheum; 3 extracts (work cited in LE); s.v. *Iuramentum, Maria, Perfectio.*

Super epistolam ad Romanos; 1 extract, taken from LE; s.v. *Ambitio.*

Paulinus

Epistola ad Augustinum; 1 extract; s.v. *Sanctitas.*

Petrus Blesensis

Without title; 7 extracts, probably taken from B.N. MS lat. 16714; s.v. *Doctrina, Iudex, Lacrima, Mendacium, Mundus, Munus, Ociositas.*

De Amicitia; 9 extracts, taken from FP; s.v. *Amicitia.*

Epistolae; 17 extracts, taken from B.N. MS lat. 16714; s.v. *Doctrina, Medicina, Militia.*

Petrus Ravennensis (prologue)

Without title; 10 extracts; s.v. *Consilium, Ecclesia, Invidia, Patria, Providentia, Pusillanimitas, Secularis, Societas, Votum.*

Epistolae; 31 extracts; s.v. *Adulatio, Consilium, Conversio, Correctio, Dilectio, Electio, Elemosina, Exactio, Fama, Fraus, Gloria mala, Infirmitas, Ingenium, Ingratitudo, Iudex, Prelatio, Promissio, Pusillanimitas, Sapientia, Simonia, Tentatio, Tribulatio.*

Sermones; 41 extracts, 6 of which may be taken from LE; s.v. *Adulatio, Ambitio, Amor, Avaritia, Bellum, Beneficia, Conversio, Correctio, Cupiditas, Curiositas, Discretio, Divitie, Ebrietas, Elemosina, Fides, Ieiunium, Ipocrisis, Misericordia, Parentes, Penitentia, Potestas, Prelatio, Prosperitas, Religio, Resurrectio, Venia.*

Sermo de Iohanne baptista; 1 extract; s.v. *Sanctitas.*

Sermo exponens illud Matthei 25: Esurivi et de etc.; 1 extract, probably taken from the *Gloss*; s.v. *Misericordia.*

Super illud: Arborem fici quidam plantatam habebat etc.; 1 extract, probably taken from the *Gloss*; s.v. *Homo.*

Super illud: Diliges dominum deum tuum etc.; 1 extract, probably taken from the *Gloss*; s.v. *Amor.*

Tractans illud Matthei [etc.]; 3 extracts, probably taken from the *Gloss*; s.v. *Diabolus, Xp̄us.*

Pitagoras philosophus

Without title; 2 extracts, taken from *Proverbia philosophorum*; s.v. *Avaritia, Coniugium.*

In suis Preceptis; 3 extracts; s.v. *Disciplina, Loquacitas, Providentia.*

Plato

Without title; 1 extract, perhaps taken from *Proverbia philosophorum* (Plato cited in FP); s.v. *Eloquentia.*

Plinius (prologue)

Historiae mundi (cf. bibliography XVI: 1); 7 extracts, probably taken from B.N. MS lat. 6803; s.v. *Homo, Mirabile, Mors, Prosperitas.*

Prologus de Naturali historia (bibliography XVI: 1); 1 extract, probably taken from MS 6803; s.v. *Ingratitudo.*

Prosper (prologue)

Sententiae (bibliography XI: 2); 2 extracts; s.v. *Prosperitas, Regimen.*

De Vita contemplativa (bibliography xi: 1); 28 extracts, 4 of which may be taken from LE; s.v. *Abstinentia, Clericus, Consideratio, Contemplatio, Correctio, Dilectio, Ecclesia, Excusatio, Gloria eterna, Ociositas, Perfectio, Predicatio, Prelatio, Religio, Sacerdos, Sanctitas, Temperantia, Virtus.*

De Viciis et virtutibus; 1 extract, taken from LE; s.v. *Invidia.*

De Vocatione gentium; 4 extracts, taken from LE; s.v. *Curiositas, Tentatio.*

Proverbia philosophorum

6 extracts, without name of author; s.v. *Coniugium, Discere, Paciencia, Sollicitudo.*

See also: Cato, Diogenes, Lucanus, Pitagoras, Plato, Socrates, Solon, Theophrastes.

Quidam sanctus

Without title; 1 extract; s.v. *Anima.*

Rabanus (prologue)

De institutione clericorum; 1 extract, taken from *Decretum*; s.v. *Baptismus.*
Sermones; 2 extracts; s.v. *Amor.*
Super Mattheum (bibliography x: 5); 21 extracts; s.v. *Avaritia, Blasphemia, Correctio, Divitie, Ecclesia, Elemosina, Fraternitas, Gloria eterna, Iniuria, Ira, Misericordia, Mulier, Pax, Rapina, Relinquere, Resurrectio.*

Raby Moyses (prologue)

Without title (= Dux dubiorum, bibliography xvi: 2); 2 extracts, taken from B.N. MS lat. 15973; s.v. *Discere, Scriptura.*

Ricardus de Sancto Victore (prologue)

Without title; 2 extracts; s.v. *Amor, Sollicitudo.*
De Contemplatione (bibliography xiii: 11); 3 extracts; s.v. *Caro, Iustitia, Sapientia.*
De Differentia mortalis et venialis (bibliography xiii: 7); 1 extract; s.v. *Peccatum.*
De Potestate ligandi (bibliography xiii: 2); 1 extract; s.v. *Baptismus.*
In quodam Sermone; 1 extract; s.v. *Curiositas.*
De Trinitate (bibliography xiii: 1); 1 extract; s.v. *Fides.*
De Verbis apostoli tractans illud: Non fermento malitie et nequitie etc. (cf. bibliography xiii: 5, 8); 1 extract; s.v. *Malitia.*

Salustius

Without title; 1 extract (Sallust cited in FP); s.v. *Honor.*

Seneca (prologue)

Without title; 15 extracts; s.v. *Consilium, Crudelitas, Electio, Gloria bona, Hospitalitas, Lascivia, Ociositas, Odium, Patria, Pusillanimitas, Solitudo, Spes, Virtus.*
De Beneficiis (bibliography xix: 3); 57 extracts, probably taken from B.N. MS lat. 15730, though 2 may be taken from LE; s.v. *Adiutorium, Ambitio,*

Beneficia, Contemptus, Curiositas, Gratitudo, Ingratitudo, Liberalitas, Petitio, Servitus, Servitium, Studium.

De Clementia ad Neronem (bibliography xix: 4); 10 extracts, 1 of which may be taken from FP, but most of which probably are taken from MS 15730; s.v. *Correctio, Crudelitas, Ipocrisis, Mansuetudo, Misericordia, Potestas, Regimen.*

De Contemptu mortis; 4 extracts; s.v. *Mors.*

Epistolae ad Lucilium (bibliography xix: 2); 503 extracts, at least 8 of which are taken from LE, but most of which are taken from MS 15730 (work cited, without epistle numbers, in FP); under 124 topic-headings.

Epistolae ad Paulum (bibliography xix: 1); 6 extracts, probably taken from MS 15730; s.v. *Apostoli, Pacientia.*

De Ira (bibliography xix: 19); 4 extracts, s.v. *Consideratio, Consilium, Ira.*

De Moribus (bibliography xix: 14); 63 extracts; s.v. *Adiutorium, Amicitia, Amor, Avaritia, Conscientia, Consuetudo, Contemptus, Convitium, Correctio, Crudelitas, Desperatio, Disciplina, Fama, Gloria mala, Inimicitia, Intentio, Invidia, Laus, Libido, Loquacitas, Magnanimitas, Mors, Nobilitas, Ornatus, Pacientia, Paupertas, Pax, Peccatum, Potestas, Predicatio, Promissio, Providentia, Reconciliatio, Senectus, Servitus, Solitudo, Suspitio, Taciturnitas, Tristitia, Venia.*

De Naturalibus questionibus (bibliography xix: 20); 3 extracts, taken from FP; s.v. *Mors.*

Proverbia; 123 extracts (work cited in FP); under 79 topic-headings.

De Quattuor virtutibus (bibliography xix: 5); 18 extracts, at least 11 of which are taken from LE and the rest probably from MS 15370; s.v. *Castitas, Cogitatio, Conversatio, Doctrina, Iustitia, Lascivia, Laus, Magnanimitas, Providentia.*

De Remediis fortune/fortuitorum (bibliography xix: 15); 15 extracts (work cited in LE and, as "De fortuitis," in FP); s.v. *Amissio rerum, Damnum, Dolor, Fama, Miseria, Patria, Paupertas.*

Rhetorica sua (bibliography xix: 6); 11 extracts; s.v. *Consuetudo, Curiositas, Eloquentia, Exemplum, Gula, Honestas, Libertas, Prosperitas, Regimen, Studium.*

De Senectute; 3 extracts, at least 2 of which may be taken from FP (s.n. Cicero); s.v. *Mors.*

De Sententiis oratorum (bibliography xix: 8); 16 extracts; s.v. *Convitium, Eloquentia, Exemplum, Nobilitas, Prosperitas, Servitium, Superbia, Taciturnitas, Timor, Tristitia.*

De Tranquillitate animi (bibliography xix: 11); 3 extracts; s.v. *Ingenium, Prosperitas.*

De Tusculanis questionibus; 1 extract (work cited, s.n. Cicero, in FP); s.v. *Adulatio.*

Sidonius (prologue)

Epistolae; 13 extracts; s.v. *Advocati, Bellum, Convitium, Doctrina, Eloquentia, Loquacitas, Regimen, Studium, Taciturnitas.*

Socrates

Without title; 4 extracts, taken from *Proverbia philosophorum*; s.v. *Avaritia, Parentes.*

Exhortationes; 4 extracts; s.v. *Prosperitas, Regimen, Vita humana presens.*
Sententie; 1 extract; s.v. *Providentia.*

Solinus (prologue)

De Mirabilibus mundi; 5 extracts; s.v. *Electio, Fama, Pietas, Verecundia.*

Solon

Without title; 1 extract, taken from *Proverbia philosophorum*; s.v. *Amicitia.*

Taurus

Commentum Platonis; 1 extract, taken from Aulus Gellius; s.v. *Correctio.*

Theofrastus

Without title; 3 extracts, taken from *Proverbia philosophorum*; s.v. *Amicitia.*
Liber de nuptiis; 1 extract, taken from Jerome *Ad Iovinianum*; s.v. *Mulier.*

Tullius (prologue)

Without title; 18 extracts; s.v. *Amicitia, Anima, Castitas, Confidentia, Detractio, Gloria bona, Gloria mala, Instabilitas, Malitia, Mendacium, Mercatio, Obedientia, Obstinatio, Ornatus, Testimonium.*

De Amicitia (bibliography xvii: 4); 22 extracts (work cited in FP); s.v. *Adiutorium, Amicitia, Iniuria, Pena, Prosperitas, Societas, Utilitas.*

In quadam Epistola (bibliography xvii: 13); 1 extract; s.v. *Sapientia.*

De Natura deorum (bibliography xvii: 8); 1 extract; s.v. *Religio.*

De Naturalibus questionibus; 2 extracts; s.v. *Anima, Natura.*

De Officiis (bibliography xvii: 5); 20 extracts (work cited in FP); s.v. *Amicitia, Discretio, Favor, Honestas, Ingratitudo, Iniuria, Innocentia, Iudex, Iustitia, Lascivia, Magnanimitas, Mansuetudo, Sobrietas, Voluptas.*

De Paradoxis (bibliography xvii: 10); 1 extract (work cited in FP); s.v. *Delitie.*

Rhetorica (bibliography xvii: 1-2); 54 extracts; s.v. *Advocati, Ambitio, Amicitia, Consilium, Correctio, Doctrina, Eloquentia, Exercitatio, Exemplum, Fides, Fortitudo, Homo, Iniuria, Invidia, Ira, Lascivia, Libertas, Libido, Mansuetudo, Modestia, Mulier, Pacientia, Pietas, Potestas, Prelatio, Prosperitas, Providentia, Rapina, Reverentia, Sapientia, Securitas, Vita humana presens.*

De Senectute (bibliography xvii: 6); 1 extract, taken from FP; s.v. *Consilium.*

De Tusculanis questionibus; 4 extracts (work cited in FP); s.v. *Accidia, Bellum, Timor.*

De Universalitate (= Timaeus, bibliography xvii: 9); 2 extracts; s.v. *Philosophia.*

Valerius [episcopus]

Sermones; 22 extracts, taken from FP; s.v. *Adiutorium, Confessio, Convitium, Desperatio, Divitie, Elemosina, Humilitas, Iniuria, Liberalitas, Meritum, Misericordia, Potestas, Presumptio, Sollicitudo, Taciturnitas.*

Valerius [Walter Map]

Epistola ad Rufinum (bibliography XVI: 4); 11 extracts, taken from B.N. MS lat. 16359; s.v. *Coniugium, Mulier.*

Valerius Maximus (prologue)

Without title (= De mem. dict., bibliography XVI: 3); 32 extracts, at least 1 of which may be taken from FP, but most if not all of which are taken from B.N. MS lat. 5839; s.v. *Ambitio, Amicitia, Amissio rerum, Avaritia, Convitium, Correctio, Detractio, Doctrina, Fraus, Gloria bona, Iactantia, Invidia, Ipocrisis, Ira, Iudex, Luxuria, Militia, Ociositas, Oratio, Parentes, Patria, Paupertas, Presumptio, Proditio, Rapina, Solitudo, Verecundia, Violentia.*

De Memorabilibus dictis (bibliography XVI: 3); 18 extracts, taken from MS 5839; s.v. *Bellum, Coniugium, Consolatio, Consuetudo, Conversatio, Ebrietas, Gloria mala, Lex, Pacientia, Pena, Presumptio, Reverentia, Taciturnitas, Vita humana presens.*

De Moderatione romana; 1 extract; s.v. *Adulatio.*

Vegetius (prologue)

De Re militari; 33 extracts; s.v. *Bellum, Consilium, Exercitatio, Militia, Presumptio, Venia.*

Victorinus

Without title; 2 extracts; s.v. *Desperatio, Lacrima.*

Bibliography

Abate, Giuseppe, and Giovanni Luisetto. *Codici e manoscritti della Biblioteca Antoniana*. Fonte e studi per la storia del santo a Padova 1. 2 vols. Vicenza 1975.

Abbott, Thomas K. *Catalogue of the Manuscripts in the Library of Trinity College, Dublin*. Dublin 1900.

Achery, Luc d', ed. *Spicilegium*, 3 vols. Paris 1723.

Alberigo, Giuseppe, et al., eds. *Conciliorum oecumenicorum decreta*. Rev. ed. Basel 1962.

Albertus Magnus. *Opera omnia*. Ed. A. Borgnet. 38 vols. Paris 1890-1899.

Allen, Judson B. "An Unrecorded *Ars Predicandi*." *Wake Forest University Library Newsletter* 1.1 (1969) 2-3.

Alverny, Marie-Thérèse d'. *Alain de Lille: Textes inédits*. Études de philosophie médiévale 52. Paris 1965.

Ambrose. *De officiis*. Ed. J. G. Krabinger. Tübingen 1857.

——. *De virginibus libri tres*. Ed. E. Cazzaniga. Torino 1948.

——. *De virginitate*. Ed. E. Cazzaniga. Torino 1954.

Anselm. *Opera omnia*. Ed. F. S. Schmitt. 6 vols. Edinburgh 1946-1961.

Antolín, G. *Catálogo de los códices latinos de la Real biblioteca del Escorial*. 5 vols. Madrid 1910-1923.

Atkins, Ivor, and N. R. Ker, eds. *Catalogus librorum manuscriptorum Bibliothecae Wigorniensis, made in 1622-1623 by Patrick Young*. Cambridge 1944.

Auer, Albert. *Johannes von Dambach und die Trostbücher vom 11. bis zum 16. Jahrhundert*. Beiträge zur Geschichte der Philosophie und Theologie des Mittelalters 27. Münster 1928.

Augustine. *Confessiones*. Ed. M. Skutella. Leipzig 1934.

——. *De fide rerum quae non videntur*. Ed. and trans. M. F. McDonald. Washington 1950.

——. *Enchiridion*. Rev. ed. Otto Scheel. Tübingen 1930.

Pseudo-Augustine. *De xii gradibus abusionis*. Ed. S. Hellman. Texte und Untersuchungen 34.1, pp. 32-60. Leipzig 1909.

Autrand, Françoise. "Les librairies des gens du Parlement au temps de Charles vi." *Annales: Économies, Sociétés, Civilisations* 28 (1973) 1219-1244.

Auvray, Lucien, ed. *Les registres de Grégoire ix*. 4 vols. Bibliothèque des Écoles françaises d'Athènes et de Rome 9, ser. 2. Paris 1890-1955.

Bale, John. *Scriptorum illustrium maioris Brytannie ... catalogus*. 2 pts. Basel 1557-1559.

Balić, P. C. "De auctore operis quod 'Ars fidei catholicae' inscribitur." In *Mélanges Joseph de Ghellinck, S.J.* 2 (1951) 793-814.

Bandini, Angelo. *Catalogus codicum latinorum Bibliotheca Mediceae Laurentianae.* 5 vols. Florence 1774-1778.

Barlow, Claude W., ed. *Epistolae Senecae ad Paulum et Pauli ad Senecam.* Papers and Monographs of the American Academy in Rome 10. 1938.

Baron, Roger, ed. "Hugonis de Sancto Victore Epitome Dindimi in philosophiam." *Traditio* 11 (1955) 91-148.

———. "Hugues de Saint-Victor: Contribution à un nouvel examen de son œuvre." *Traditio* 15 (1959) 223-297.

Bartholomew of Pisa. *Liber conformitatum.* Milan 1510.

Bartoniek, Emma. *Codices latini medii aevi.* Budapest 1940.

Bartoš, F. M. *Soupis Rukopisů Národního Musea v Praze.* 2 vols. Prague 1926-1927.

Basler Chroniken. 7 vols. Leipzig 1872-1915.

Baudrier, H. L. *Bibliographie lyonnaise.* 12 vols. Lyon 1895-1921.

Bavel, Tarsicius van. "Parallèles, vocabulaire et citations bibliques de la 'Regula sancti Augustini'." *Augustiniana* 9 (1959) 12-77.

Becker, Gustav, ed. *Catalogi bibliothecarum antiqui.* Bonn 1885.

Beer, Rudolf. *Handschriftenschätze Spaniens.* Vienna 1894.

Benzing, Josef. *Die Buchdrucker des 16. und 17. Jahrhunderts im deutschen Sprachgebiet.* Wiesbaden 1963.

Bernard. *Opera.* Ed. J. Leclercq et al. Vols. 1- . Rome 1957- .

Bertling, A., and O. Günther. *Katalog der Danziger Stadtbibliothek.* 6 vols. in 5. Gdańsk 1892-1921.

Bertola, Ermenegildo. "Di alcuni trattati psicologici attribuiti ad Ugo da S. Vittore." *Rivista di filosofia neo-scolastica* 51 (1959) 436-455.

Bertomeu, B. *Los códices medievales de la catedral de Tortosa.* Barcelona 1962.

Bissells, Paul. "Wissenschaft und Bibliographie im spätmittelalterlichen Trier." *Kurtrierisches Jahrbuch* 6 (1965) 54-60.

Blench, J. W. *Preaching in England.* Oxford 1964.

Blic, J. de. "Walafrid Strabon et la Glossa ordinaria." *Recherches de théologie ancienne et médiévale* 16 (1949) 1-28.

Blumenkranz, Bernhard, ed. *Gisleberti Crispini Disputatio Iudei et Christiani....* Stromata 3. Utrecht 1956.

Boethius. *Opuscula sacra.* Ed. H. F. Stewart and E. K. Rand. London 1918.

Bonaventure. *Opera.* 7 vols. Rome 1588-1596.

———. *Opera omnia.* Ed. A. C. Peltier. 15 vols. Paris 1864-1871.

———. *Opera omnia.* 11 vols. Quaracchi 1882-1902.

Bonnes, J. P. "Un des plus grands prédicateurs du XIIᵉ siècle: Geoffroy du Louroux, dit Geoffroy Babion." *Revue bénédictine* 56 (1945-1946) 174-215.

Bougerol, Jacques-Guy. *Introduction à l'étude de saint Bonaventure.* Bibliothèque de théologie, ser. 1, 2. Tournai 1961.

Boyle, Leonard E. "The *Compilatio quinta* and the Registers of Honorius III." In *Scritti in onore di Giulio Battelli* (forthcoming).

——. "The *Oculus sacerdotis* and Some Other Works of William of Pagula." *Transactions of the Royal Historical Society*, ser. 5, 5 (1955) 81-100.

——. "A Study of the Works Attributed to William of Pagula with Special Reference to the *Oculus sacerdotis* and *Summa summarum*." 2 vols. D.Phil. diss. Oxford 1956.

——. "The *Summa confessorum* of John of Freiburg and the Popularization of the Moral Teaching of St. Thomas...." In *St. Thomas Aquinas 1274-1974: Commemorative Studies* 2: 245-268. Toronto 1974.

——. "The *Summa summarum* and Some Other English Works of Canon Law." In *Proceedings of the Second International Congress of Medieval Canon Law*, ed. Stephan Kuttner and J. J. Ryan, pp. 415-456. Monumenta iuris canonici, ser. C, 1. Vatican City 1965.

Bozon, Nicholas. *Contes moralisées*. ed. Lucy Toulmin Smith and Paul Meyer. Paris 1889.

——. *Metaphors of Brother Bozon*. Trans. "J.R." London 1913.

Bradley, John W. *A Dictionary of Miniaturists, Illuminators, Calligraphers and Copyists*. 3 vols. London 1887-1889.

Brady, Ignatius. "The Rubrics of Peter Lombard's Sentences." *Pier Lombardo* 6 (1962) 5-25.

Brandis, Tilo, and H. Maehler. *Katalog der Handschriften der Staats- und Universitätsbibliothek Hamburg* 4. Hamburg 1967.

Braun, Placidus. *Notitia historico-literaria de codicibus manuscriptis in bibliotheca ... ad SS. Udalricum et Afram Augustae extantibus*. 2 vols. Augsburg 1791-1796.

Bremme, Hans J. *Buchdrucker und Buchhandler zur Zeit der Glaubenkampfe*. Geneva 1969.

Brincken, Anna-Dorothee von den. "*Tabula alphabetica* von den Anfängen alphabetischer Registerarbeiten zu Geschichtswerken." In *Festschrift für Hermann Heimpel* 2: 900-923. Göttingen 1972.

Bryan, William F., and G. Dempster, eds. *Sources and Analogues of Chaucer's Canterbury Tales*. Chicago 1941.

Bühler, Curt F., ed. *The Epistle of Othea*. Trans. Stephen Scrope. Early English Text Society 264. London 1970.

——. "The *Fleurs de toutes vertus*." PMLA 64 (1949) 600-601.

——. "The *Fleurs de toutes vertus* and Christine de Pisan's *L'épître d'Othéa*." PMLA 62 (1947) 32-44.

——. "The Two Issues of the First Edition of the *Manipulus florum*." *Gutenberg Jahrbuch* 28 (1953) 69-72.

Callus, Daniel A. "The Contribution to the Study of the Fathers Made by the Thirteenth-Century Oxford Schools." *Journal of Ecclesiastical History* 5 (1954) 139-148.

——. "New Manuscripts of Kilwardby's 'Tabulae super originalia patrum'."
    Dominican Studies 2 (1949) 38-45.

——. "The 'Tabulae super originalia patrum' of Robert Kilwardby O.P." In
    Studia medievalia in honorem ... Raymundi Josephi Martin, pp. 85-112.
    Bruges 1948.

Campbell, P. G. C. *L'épitre d'Othéa: Étude sur les sources de Christine de Pisan.*
    Paris 1924.

Catalogue des ouvrages mis à l'Index. Paris 1826.

Catalogue général des manuscrits des bibliothèques publiques de France: Départe-
    ments. 8° ser. 51 vols. Paris 1886-1956.

Catalogue général des manuscrits des bibliothèques publiques de France: Paris,
    Bibliothèque de l'Arsenal. 9 vols. Paris 1885-1892.

Catalogue général des manuscrits des bibliothèques publiques de France: Université
    de Paris et universités des départements. Paris 1918.

Catalogue général des manuscrits des bibliothèques publiques des départements.
    4° ser. 7 vols. Paris 1849-1885.

Catalogue of Additions to the Manuscripts in the British Museum in the Years
    MDCCCXLI-MDCCCXLV. London 1850.

—— *in the Years* MDCCCXLVIII-MDCCCLIII. London 1868.

—— *in the Years* MDCCCLIV-MDCCCLXXV. 3 vols. London 1875-1880.

Catalogue of Books Printed in the XVth *Century now in the British Museum.* 9 pts.
    to date. London 1908-

A Catalogue of the Manuscripts Preserved in the Library of the University of
    Cambridge. 6 vols. Cambridge 1856-1867.

Cazzaniga, E. *Incerti auctoris "De lapsu Suzannae."* Torino 1948.

Chaix, Paul. *Recherches sur l'imprimerie à Genève de 1550 à 1564.* Geneva 1954.

Charland, Th.-M. *Artes praedicandi: Contribution à l'histoire de la rhétorique au*
    moyen âge. Publications de l'Institut d'études médiévales d'Ottawa 7. Paris
    1936.

Chartier, Roger, et al. *Nouvelles études lyonnaises.* Histoire et civilisation du
    livre 2. Paris 1969.

Châtillon, Jean. "L'héritage littéraire de Richard de Saint-Laurent." *Revue du*
    moyen âge latin 2 (1946) 149-166.

Chenu, Marie-Dominique. *Introduction à l'étude de S. Thomas d'Aquin.* Paris
    1951.

Chevallier, Philippe. *Dionysiaca: Recueil donnant l'ensemble des traductions latines*
    des ouvrages attribués au Denys de l'Aréopage. Bruges 1937.

Christine de Pisan. *Livres des Fais....* Ed. S. Solente. 2 vols. Paris 1936-1940.

Cicero. *De amicitia, De senectute.* Ed. C. F. W. Mueller. Leipzig 1898.

——. *Epistulae ad familiares.* Ed. H. Sjögren. Leipzig 1925.

——. *De finibus bonorum et malorum.* Ed. Th. Schiche. Leipzig 1915.

——. *De inventione.* Ed. E. Stroebel. Leipzig 1915.

——. *De natura deorum.* Ed. W. Ax. Leipzig 1961.

——. *De officiis.* Ed. C. Atzert. Leipzig 1963.

——. *Orationes in L. Catelinam quattuor.* Ed. Peter Reis. Leipzig 1933.

——. *Orationes in M. Antonium Philippicae.* Ed. A. Klotz and F. Schoell. Leipzig 1918.

——. *De paradoxis.* Ed. O. Plasberg. Leipzig 1908.

——. *De divinatione, De fato, Timaeus.* Ed. W. Ax. Leipzig 1938.

Pseudo-Cicero. *De ratione dicendi ad C. Herennium.* Ed. F. Marx (Leipzig 1894).

Cincuenta años de la antigua Biblioteca de Cataluña. Barcelona 1968.

Cocchia, Enrico. "Magistri Iohannis de Hysdinio Invectiva contra Fr. Petrarcham et Fr. Petrarchae contra cuiusdam Galli calumnias Apologia." *Atti della Reale accademia di archeologia ... di Napoli,* n.s. 7.1 (1920) 91-202.

Cockshaw, Pierre. "Une source d'information codicologique: Les protocoles de notaires conservés aux Archives de la Côte-d'Or." *Scriptorium* 25 (1971) 67-70.

Congar, Yves. "Henri de Marcy, abbé de Clairvaux, cardinal-évêque d'Albano et légat pontifical." *Analecta monastica* 5/*Studia Anselmiana* 43 (1958) 1-90.

Corpus christianorum series latina. Vols. 1- . Turnhout 1953-

Corpus scriptorum ecclesiasticorum latinorum. Vols. 1- . Vienna 1866- .

Coulton, George G. *Five Centuries of Religion.* 4 vols. Cambridge Studies in Medieval Life and Thought. Cambridge 1923-1950.

Coxe, H. O. *Catalogus codicum manuscriptorum qui in collegiis aulisque Oxoniensibus hodie adservantur.* 2 vols. in 19 pts. Oxford 1852.

Daly, Lloyd W. *Contributions to a History of Alphabetization in Antiquity and the Middle Ages.* Collection Latomus 90. Brussels 1967.

—— and B. A. Daly. "Some Techniques in Mediaeval Latin Lexicography." *Speculum* 39 (1964) 229-239.

Daniel, Natalia, et al. *Die lateinischen mittelalterlichen Handschriften der Universitätsbibliothek München.* Vols. 1- . Wiesbaden 1974- .

Davis, Natalie. "Publisher Guillaume Rouillé, Businessman and Humanist." In *Editing Sixteenth-Century Texts,* ed. Richard J. Schoeck, pp. 72-112. Toronto 1966.

Davy, Marie-Madeleine. *Les sermons universitaires parisiens de 1230-1231.* Études de philosophie médiévale 15. Paris 1931.

Dekkers, Eligius. *Clavis patrum latinorum.* Ed. 2. Sacris erudiri 3. Bruges 1961.

Delalain, Paul. *Étude sur la librairie parisienne du xiiie au xive siècle.* Paris 1891.

De la Mare, Albinia C. *Catalogue of the Medieval Manuscripts bequeathed to the Bodleian Library, Oxford, by James R. Lyell.* Oxford 1971.

Delaruelle, Étienne. "L'état actuel des études sur le Catharisme." In *Cathares en Languedoc: Cahiers de Fanjeaux* 3: 19-41. 1968.

Delisle, Léopold. *Le cabinet des manuscrits de la Bibliothèque nationale.* 3 vols. Paris 1868-1881.

Denis, Michael. *Codices manuscripti theologici bibliothecae palatinae Vindobonensis latini aliarumque occidentis linguarum.* 2 vols. in 6 pts. Vienna 1793-1802.

Destrez, Jean. "L'outillage des copistes du xiiie et du xive siècle." In *Aus der*

Geisteswelt des Mittelalters, ed. Albert Lang, et al., pp. 19-34. Beiträge zur Geschichte der Philosophie und Theologie des Mittelalters, Texte und Untersuchungen Suppl. 3. 2 vols. Münster 1935.

——. *La pecia dans les manuscrits universitaires du XIIIe et du XIVe siècle*. Paris 1935.

—— and M. D. Chenu. "*Exemplaria* universitaires des XIIIe et XIVe siècles." *Scriptorium* 7 (1953) 68-80.

—— and G. Fink-Errera. "Des manuscrits apparemment datés." *Scriptorium* 12 (1958) 56-93.

Dobson, Eric J. *Moralities on the Gospels*. Oxford 1975.

Domenichelli, Theophilus, et al., eds. "Compendium chronicarum fratrum minorum scriptum a patro Mariano de Florentia." *Archivum franciscanum historicum* 2 (1909) 92-107, 305-318, 457-472, 626-641.

Domínguez Bordona, Jesús. *El escritorio y la primitiva biblioteca de Santes Creus*. Instituto de estudios Tarraconenses "Ramón Berenguer IV." Tarragona 1952.

——. *Manuscritos de la Biblioteca pública de Tarragona*. Instituto de estudios Tarraconenses "Ramón Berenguer IV." Tarragona 1954.

Dondaine, Antoine. "Apparat critique de l'édition d'un texte universitaire." In *L'homme et son destin*, pp. 211-220. Actes du premier congrès international de philosophie médiévale. Louvain 1960.

——. "Guillaume Peyraut, vie et œuvres." *Archivum fratrum praedicatorum* 18 (1948) 162-236.

——. *Secrétaires de saint Thomas*. 2 vols. Rome 1956.

Dondaine, Hyacinthe François. *Le corpus dionysien de l'Université de Paris au XIIIe siècle*. Rome 1953.

Douglass, E. Jane Dempsey. *Justification in Late Medieval Preaching*. Studies in Medieval and Reformation Thought 1. Leiden 1966.

Dudik, Beda. *Statuten des ersten Prager Provincial-Concils vom 11. und 12. November 1349*. Brno 1872.

Duin, Johannes Josef. "La bibliothèque philosophique de Godefroid de Fontaines." *Estudios Lullianos* 3 (1959) 21-36, 137-160.

Durliat, Marcel. "Le rôle des ordres mendiants dans la création de l'architecture gothique méridionale." In *La naissace et l'essor du gothique méridional au XIIIe siècle: Cahiers de Fanjeaux* 9 (1974) 71-85.

Emden, Alfred B. *A Biographical Register of the University of Oxford to A.D. 1500*. (BRUO). 3 vols. Oxford 1957-1959.

Evans, Robert F. "Pelagius, Fastidius and the Ps. Augustinian *De vita christiana*." *Journal of Theological Studies*, n.s. 13 (1962) 72-98.

Faider, Paul. *Catalogue des manuscrits conservés à Namur*. Gembloux 1934.

Faye, Christopher U., and William H. Bond. *Supplement to the Census of Medieval and Renaissance Manuscripts in the United States and Canada*. New York 1962.

Fédou, René, et al. *Cinq études lyonnaises.* Histoire et civilisation du livre 1. Paris 1966.

Feret, Pierre. *La faculté de théologie de Paris.* 7 vols. Paris 1900-1910.

Ferrai, Luigi A. "La biblioteca di S. Giustina di Padova." In *Inventario dei manoscritti italiani delle biblioteche di Francia,* ed. Giuseppe Mazzatinti, 2: 579-661. Rome 1887.

Fink-Errera, Guy. "De l'édition universitaire." In *L'homme et son destin,* pp. 221-228. Actes du premier congrès international de philosophie médiévale. Louvain 1960.

———. "Une institution du monde médiéval: La 'pecia'." *Revue philosophique de Louvain* 60 (1962) 184-243.

Fischer, Imgard. *Handschriften der Ratsbücherei Lüneburg* 2: *Die theologischen Handschriften.* Wiesbaden 1969.

Flahiff, G. B. "Ralph Niger: An Introduction to His Life and Works." *Mediaeval Studies* 2 (1940) 104-126.

Floyer, John K. *Catalogue of Manuscripts Preserved in the Chapter Library of Worcester Cathedral.* Rev. by Sidney G. Hamilton. Oxford 1906.

Fournier, Paul, and G. LeBras. *Histoire des collections canoniques en Occident.* 2 vols. Paris 1931-1932.

Fowler, David C. "John of Trevisa and the English Bible." *Modern Philology* 58 (1960) 81-98.

Fowler, George B. "Additional Notes on Manuscripts of Engelbert of Admont." *Recherches de théologie ancienne et médiévale* 28 (1961) 269-282.

———. *The Intellectual Interests of Engelbert of Admont.* New York 1947.

Franklin, Alfred. *La Sorbonne: Ses origines, sa bibliothèque.* Ed. 2. Paris 1875.

Frenken, Goswin. *Die Exempla des Jacob von Vitry.* Quellen und Untersuchungen zur lateinischen Philologie des Mittelalters 5.1. Munich 1914.

Friend, A. C. "The Life and Unprinted Works of Master Odo of Cheriton." D.Phil. diss. Oxford 1936.

Gabriel, Astrik L. *A Summary Catalogue of Microfilms of 1000 Scientific Manuscripts in the Ambrosian Library, Milan.* Notre Dame, Ind. 1968.

Gagnér, Anders. *Florilegium Gallicum.* Skrifter utgivna av Vetenskaps-Societeten i Lund 18. Lund 1936.

Garand, Monique-Cécile. "Les copistes de Jean Budé (1430-1502)." *Bulletin de l'Institut de recherche et d'histoire des textes* 15 (1969) 293-332.

Gervase of Canterbury. *Chronicle.* Ed. William Stubbs. Rolls Series 73.1. London 1879.

Ghellinck, Joseph de. "A propos d'un catalogue des œuvres de Hugues de Saint-Victor." *Revue néo-scolastique de philosophie* 21 (1914) 86-88.

———. "Un catalogue des œuvres de Hugues de Saint-Victor." *Revue néo-scolastique de philosophie* 20 (1913) 226-232.

———. "Une édition ou une collection médiévale des *opera omnia* de saint

Augustin." In *Liber Floridus: Mittellateinische Studien P. Lehmann...*, ed. Bernhard Bischoff, pp. 63-82. St. Ottilien 1950.

——. *"Originale* et *originalia."* *Archivum latinitatis medii aevi* (*Bulletin Du Cange*) 14 (1939) 95-105.

——. "Patristique et argument de tradition au bas moyen âge." In *Aus der Geisteswelt des Mittelalters*, ed. Albert Lang, et al., pp. 403-426. Beiträge zur Geschichte der Philosophie und Theologie des Mittelalters, Texte und Untersuchungen Suppl. 3. 2 vols. Münster 1935.

Giancotti, Francesco. *Ricerchi sulla tradizione manoscritta delle sentenze di Publilio Siro.* Messina 1963.

Gilson, Étienne. *Les idées et les lettres.* Paris 1932.

Glorieux, Palémon. *Aux origines de la Sorbonne.* 2 vols. Études de philosophie médiévale 53-54. Paris 1965-1966.

——. "Pour jalonner l'histoire littéraire du xiiie siècle." In *Aus der Geisteswelt des Mittelalters*, ed. Albert Lang, et al., pp. 482-502. Beiträge zur Geschichte der Philosophie und Theologie des Mittelalters, Texte und Untersuchungen Suppl. 3. 2 vols. Münster 1935.

——. *Répertoire des maîtres en théologie de Paris au xiiie siècle.* 2 vols. Études de philosophie médiévale 17-18. Paris 1933-1934.

——. "Sermons universitaires parisiens de 1267-1268." *Recherches de théologie ancienne et médiévale* 16 (1949) 40-71.

Grabmann, Martin. *Methoden und Hilfsmittel des Aristotelesstudiums im Mittelalter.* Sitzungsberichte der Bayerischen Akademie der Wissenschaft, phil.-hist. Abt. 5. Munich 1939.

——. *Mittelalterliches Geistesleben.* 3 vols. Munich 1926-1956.

Grand, Philippe. "Le quodlibet xiv de Gérard d'Abbeville." *Archives d'histoire doctrinale et littéraire du moyen âge* 31 (1964) 207-269.

Green, William, ed. *Aurelii Augustini Contra academicos....* Stromata 2. Utrecht 1955.

——. "Mediaeval Recensions of Augustine." *Speculum* 29 (1954) 531-534.

Grosseteste, Robert. *Epistolae.* Ed. H. R. Luard. Rolls Series 25. London 1861.

Gruijs, Albert. "Jean de Schoonhoven...." *Archivum latinitatis medii aevi* (*Bulletin Du Cange*) 32 (1962) 135-187 and 33 (1963) 35-97.

——. *Jean de Schoonhoven (1356-1432) ... De contemptu huius mundi: Textes et études.* 3 vols. Thèse de doctorat du 3e cycle. Nijmegen 1967.

Gwynn, Aubrey. "The Sermon-Diary of Richard Fitzralph, Archbishop of Armagh." *Proceedings of the Royal Irish Academy* 44 (1937-1938) sect. C, 1-57.

Hain, Ludwig F. T. *Repertorium bibliographicum....* 2 vols. Stuttgart 1826-1938. *Supplement....* By W. A. Copinger. 2 pts. London 1895-1902.

Hainisch, Erwin, ed. *Die Kunstdenkmäler des Gerichtsbezirkes Lambach.* Oesterreichische Kunsttopographie 34. Vienna 1959.

Hall, George D. G. *The Treatise on the Laws and Customs of the Realm of England Commonly Called Glanvill.* Medieval Texts. London 1965.

Halm, Karl, et al. *Catalogus codicum latinorum Bibliothecae Regiae Monacensis.* 2 vols. in 7 pts. Munich 1868-1881. Ed. 2 of vol. 1 pts. 1-2. Munich 1892-1894.

Hamacher, Johannes. *Florilegium Gallicum: Prolegomena und Edition der Exzerpte von Petron bis Cicero De oratore.* Lateinische Sprache und Literatur des Mittelalters 5. Frankfurt a.M. 1975.

Häring, Nikolaus M. "The Liberal Arts in the Sermons of Garnier of Rochefort." *Mediaeval Studies* 30 (1968) 47-77.

———. "Notes on the Council and Consistory of Rheims (1148)." *Mediaeval Studies* 28 (1966) 39-59.

Hartel, Wilhelm von. *Bibliotheca patrum latinorum hispaniensis.* 6 vols. Vienna 1886.

Haskins, Charles H. *Studies in Medieval Science.* Ed. 2. Cambridge, Mass. 1927.

Hatch, William H. P. *Facsimiles and Descriptions of the Minuscule Manuscripts of the New Testament.* Cambridge 1951.

———. *The Principal Uncial Manuscripts of the New Testament.* Chicago 1939.

Hauréau, Barthélemy. *Hugues de Saint-Victor: Nouvel examen de l'édition de ses œuvres.* Paris 1859.

———. "Thomas d'Irlande." *Histoire littéraire de la France* 30 (1888) 398-408.

Hayes, Richard J., ed. *Manuscript Sources for the History of Irish Civilization.* 11 vols. Boston 1965.

Heathcote, Sheila J. "The Letter Collections Attributed to Master Transmundus." *Analecta Cisterciansia* 21 (1965) 35-109, 167-238.

Heiric of Auxerre. *I collectanea di Eirico di Auxerre.* Ed. Riccardo Quadri. Spicilegium Friburgense 11. Fribourg 1966.

Higonnet, Ethel C. "Spiritual Ideas in the Letters of Peter of Blois." *Speculum* 50 (1975) 218-244.

Hingeston-Randolph, Francis C., ed. *The Register of Walter de Stapeldon, Bishop of Exeter.* London 1892.

Holmberg, John, ed. *Das "Moralium dogma philosophorum" des Guillaume de Conchis.* Uppsala 1929.

Hudson, Anne. "A Lollard Compilation and the Dissemination of Wycliffite Thought." *Journal of Theological Studies*, n.s. 23 (1972) 65-81.

———. "A Lollard Compilation in England and Bohemia." *Journal of Theological Studies* n.s. 25 (1974) 129-140.

Hugh of Saint-Victor. *Didascalion.* Ed. Charles H. Buttimer. Washington 1939.

Humbert of Romans. *Opera de vita regulari.* Ed. J. J. Berthier, 2 vols. Rome 1888-1889.

Hümpfner, Tiburtius. "Archivum et bibliotheca Cistercii et quatuor primarum filiarum ejus." *Analecta sacri ordinis Cisterciensis* 2 (1946) 119-145.

Humphreys, K. W. *The Library of the Franciscans of the Convent of St. Antony.* Amsterdam 1966.

Hunt, Richard W. "Chapter Headings of Augustine *De Trinitate* Ascribed to Adam Marsh." *Bodleian Library Record* 5 (1954) 63-68.

———, ed. *The Coming of the Friars: A Commemorative Exhibition.* Oxford 1974.

———. "Manuscripts Containing the Indexing Symbols of Robert Grosseteste." *Bodleian Library Record* 4 (1953-1954) 241-255.

Der Index der verbotenen Bücher. Ed. Joseph Hilgers. Freiburg i. Breisgau 1904.

Index librorum prohibitorum. Rome 1900.

Isidore. *Etymologiarum sive originum libri xx.* Ed. W. Lindsay. Oxford 1911.

Jaffé, Philippe, and G. Wattenbach. *Ecclesiae metropolitanae Coloniensis codices manuscripti.* Berlin 1874.

James, Montague Rhodes. "The Catalogue of the Library of the Augustinian Friars at York." In *Fasciculus Joanni Willis Clark dicatus*, pp. 2-96. Cambridge 1909.

———. *A Descriptive Catalogue of the Manuscripts in the Library of Corpus Christi College, Cambridge.* 2 vols. Cambridge 1909-1913.

———. *A Descriptive Catalogue of the Manuscripts in the Library of Gonville and Caius College.* 2 vols. Cambridge 1907-1908.

———. *A Descriptive Catalogue of the Manuscripts in the Library of Peterhouse.* Cambridge 1899.

———. "The List of Libraries Prefixed to the Catalogue of John Boston and the Kindred Documents." *Collectanea franciscana* 2 (1922) 37-60.

———, ed. *Walter Map: De nugis curialium.* Oxford 1914.

Pseudo-Jerome. *De fide simboli apud Niceam expositio.* Ed. Cuthbert Turner, in *Ecclesiae occidentalis monumenta iuris antiquissima* 1: 355-363. Oxford 1913.

John Chrysostom. *Opera omnia.* Ed. Fronton du Duc. 12 vols. Antwerp 1614.

John of Damascus. *De fide orthodoxa.* Ed. E. M. Buytaert. Franciscan Institute Publications, Text Series 8. New York 1955.

Jordanus of Quedlinburg. *Liber vitasfratrum.* Ed. R. Arbesmann and W. Hümpfner. New York 1943.

Kaeppeli, Thomas. "Antiche biblioteche domenicane in Italia." *Archivum Fratrum Praedicatorum* 36 (1966) 5-80.

———. "Le *Campus floretum* de Thomas Waleys." *Archivum Fratrum Praedicatorum* 35 (1965) 85-92.

———. "Praedicator Monoculus: Sermons parisiens de la fin du xiiie siècle." *Archivum Fratrum Praedicatorum* 27 (1957) 120-167.

———. *Le procès contre Thomas Waleys, O.P.* Institutum hist. Fratrum Praedicatorum Romae ad S. Sabinae, Dissertationes historicae 6. Rome 1936.

———. *Scriptores ordinis Praedicatorum medii aevi.* 2 vols. to date. Rome 1970- .

Ker, Neil R. "The English Manuscripts of the *Moralia* of Gregory the Great." In *Kunsthistorische Forschungen Otto Pächt zu seinem 70. Geburtstag*, ed. Artur Rosenauer and Gerold Weber, pp. 77-89. Salzburg 1972.

——. *Fragments of Medieval Manuscripts Used as Pastedowns in Oxford Bindings.* Oxford Bibliographical Society Publ. n.s. 5. Oxford 1954.

Kern, Anton, ed. *Verzeichnis der Handschriften im deutschen Reich 2: Die Handschriften der Universitätsbibliothek Graz.* Leipzig 1939.

Keuffer, Max, et al. *Beschreibendes Verzeichnis der Handschriften der Stadtbibliothek zu Trier.* 10pts. Trier 1888-1931.

Kleinhans, Arduinus. "De concordantiis biblicis S. Antonio Patavino aliisque Fratribus Minoribus saeculi xiii attributis." *Antonianum* 6 (1931) 273-326.

Klenke, M. Amelia. "Nicholas Bozon." *Modern Language Notes* 69 (1954) 256-260.

Kluxen, Wolfgang. "Die Geschichte des Maimonides im lateinischen Abendland als Beispiel einer christlich-judischen Begegnung." *Miscellanea medievalia* 4: *Judentum im Mittelalter*, pp. 146-166. Berlin 1966.

——. "Literargeschichtliches zum lateinischen Moses Maimonides." *Recherches de théologie ancienne et médiévale* 21 (1954) 23-50.

Knaus, Hermann. "Ein rheinischer Gesamtkatalog des 15. Jahrhunderts." *Gutenberg Jahrbuch* (1976) 509-518.

Kohler, Charles. *Catalogue des manuscrits de la Bibliothèque Sainte-Geneviève.* 2 vols. Paris 1893-1896.

Krämer, Sigrid. "Neue Nachrichten über die ehemalige Pfarrbibliothek von Ebern." *Mainfränkisches Jahrbuch für Geschichte und Kunst* 28 (1976) 36-47.

Lacombe, George. *La vie et les œuvres de Prévostin.* Bibliothèque thomiste 11, Section historique 10. Le Saulchoir 1927.

—— and Beryl Smalley. "Studies on the Commentaries of Cardinal Stephen Langton." *Archives d'histoire doctrinale et littéraire du moyen âge* 5 (1931) 5-220.

Lang, Albert, et al., eds. *Aus der Geisteswelt des Mittelalters.* Beiträge zur Geschichte der Philosophie und Theologie des Mittelalters, Texte und Untersuchungen Suppl. 3. 2 vols. Münster 1935.

Lauer, Ph., et al. *Catalogue général des manuscrits latins.* Vols. 1- . Paris 1939- .

Laurent, Marie H. *Codices Vaticani latini, codices 1135-1266.* Vatican City 1958.

Lebon, Joseph. "Sur la doctrine eucharistique de Hériger de Lobbes." In *Studia medievalia in honorem ... Raymundi Josephi Martin*, pp. 61-84. Bruges 1948.

Leclercq, Jean. "Inédits bernardins dans un manuscrit d'Orval." *Analecta monastica* 1/*Studia Anselmiana* 20 (1948) 142-166.

——. *The Love of Learning and the Desire for God.* Trans. C. Misrahi. Ed. 2 rev. New York 1974.

——. "Le magistère du prédicateur au xiiie siècle." *Archives d'histoire doctrinale et littéraire du moyen âge* 15 (1946) 105-147.

——. "Les manuscrits de l'abbaye de Liessies." *Scriptorium* 6 (1952) 51-62.

Lecoy de la Marche, Richard-Albert. *La chaire française au moyen âge.* Paris 1868.

Lehmann, Paul. *Erforschung des Mittelalters.* 5 vols. Stuttgart 1959-1962.

Levens, Peter. *Manipulus vocabulorum.* Ed. H. B. Wheatley. Camden Society 95, 1867.

Lieftinck, Gerard I. *De Librijen en scriptoria der Westvlaamse Cisterciënserabdijen Ter Duinen en Ter Doest in de 12ᵉ en 13ᵉ Eeuw....* Mededelingen van de koninklijke vlaamse Academie voor Wetenschappen, Letteren en schone Kunsten van België, Kl. der Let. 15 no. 2. Brussels 1953.

List of Additions to the Manuscripts in the British Museum, MDCCCXXXVI- MDCCCXL. London 1843.

Little, Andrew, and F. Pelster. *Oxford Theology and Theologians.* Oxford 1934.

Lohr, Charles H. "Medieval Latin Aristotle Commentaries." *Traditio* 26 (1970) 135-216.

Longpré, Ephrem, ed. *Tractatus de pace auctore fr. Gilberto de Tornaco.* Quaracchi 1925.

Lub, Jacques, ed. *Hantboec.* 2 vols. Assen 1962.

Lull, Raymond. *Opera latina.* Ed. Friedrich Stegmüller. 5 vols. Palma 1959-1967.

Mabille, Madeleine. "Les manuscrits de Gérard d'Utrecht." *Bibliothèque de l'École des chartes* 129 (1971) 5-25.

——. "Pierre de Limoges, copiste de manuscrits." *Scriptorium* 24 (1970) 45-47.

——. "Pierre de Limoges et ses méthodes de travail." *Collection Latomus* 145 (1976) 244-251.

McCulloch; Florence. *Medieval Latin and French Bestiaries.* Chapel Hill 1960.

Mackinney, Loren C. "Medieval Medical Dictionaries and Glossaries." In *Medieval and Historiographical Essays in Honor of James Westfall Thompson,* ed. James Lea Cate and E. N. Anderson, pp. 240-268. Chicago 1938.

Macrobius. *In somnium Scipionis Commentarii.* Ed. I. Willis. Leipzig 1963.

Maier, Anneliese. *Codices Burghesiani Bibliothecae Vaticanae.* Studi e testi 170. Vatican City 1952.

——. "Der literarische Nachlass des Petrus Rogerii (Clemens VI) in der Borghesiana." *Recherches de théologie ancienne et médiévale* 15 (1948) 332-356, 16 (1949) 72-98.

Mandonnet, Pierre, et al. *Saint Dominique.* 2 vols. Paris 1938.

Mangenot, Eugène. "Concordance de la Bible." *Dictionnaire de la Bible* 2 (1926) 892-905.

Mansi, Joannes D., ed. *Sacrorum conciliorum nova ... collectio.* 53 vols. Venice, etc. 1758-1927.

Marks, Richard B. *The Medieval Manuscript Library of the Charterhouse of St. Barbara in Cologne.* Analecta Carthusiana 21. Salzburg 1974.

Martène, Edmond, and U. Durand. *Veterum scriptorum et monumentorum ... collectio.* 9 vols. Paris 1724-1733.

Martin of Braga. *Opera omnia.* Ed. Claude W. Barlow. New Haven 1950.

Maxima bibliotheca veterum patrum. 27 vols. Lyons 1677.

Mazzatinti, Giuseppe, and A. Sorbelli. *Inventari dei manoscritti delle biblioteche d'Italia* 4. Forli 1894.

Meersseman, Gilles-Gérard. "L'architecture dominicaine au XIIIe siècle: Législation et pratique." *Archivum Fratrum Praedicatorum* 16 (1946) 136-190.
———. "La bibliothèque des frères de la Minerve à la fin du XVe siècle." In *Mélanges Auguste Pelzer*, pp. 605-634. Louvain 1947.
———. "Eremitismo e predicazione itinerante dei secoli XI e XII." In *L'Eremitismo in occidente nei secoli XI e XII*, pp. 164-181. Atti della seconda Settimana internazionale di Studio, Mendola ... 1962. Miscellanea del Centro di studi medioevali 4. Milan 1965.
Meyer, Gustav, and M. Burckhardt. *Die mittelalterlichen Handschriften der Universitätsbibliothek Basel.* 3 vols. Basel 1960-1975.
Meyer, Wilhelm. *Die Sammlungen der Spruchverse des Publilius Syrus.* Leipzig 1877.
Mezey, László. *Codices latini medii aevi Bibliothecae Universitatis Budapestinensis.* Budapest 1961.
Michaud-Quantin, Pierre. "Guy d'Évreux, OP, technicien du sermonnaire médiéval." *Archivum Fratrum Praedicatorum* 20 (1950) 213-233.
Migne, Jacques P., ed. *Patrologiae cursus completus ... series latina*(PL). 221 vols. Paris 1844-1864.
Mittelalterliche Bibliothekskataloge Deutschlands und der Schweiz. Ed. Paul Lehmann, et al. Vols. 1- . Munich 1918- .
Mittelalterliche Bibliothekskataloge Oesterreichs. Ed. Theodor Gottlieb, et al. Vols. 1- . Vienna 1915- .
Molinier, Auguste. *Catalogue des manuscrits de la Bibliothèque Mazarine.* 4 vols. Paris 1885-1898.
Moore, Philip S. *The Works of Peter of Poitiers.* Publications in Medieval Studies 1. Notre Dame, Ind. 1936.
Müller, Karl, ed. *Soliloquium de arrha animae und De vanitate mundi.* Bonn 1913.
Muratori, Lodovico A. *Rerum italicarum scriptores,* 25 vols. Milan 1723-1751.
Mynors, Roger A. B. *Durham Cathedral Manuscripts to the End of the Twelfth Century.* Oxford 1939.
———. "The Latin Classics Known to Boston of Bury." In *Fritz Saxl 1890-1948: A Volume of Memorial Essays from his Friends in England*, ed. D. J. Gordon, pp. 199-217. London 1957.

Nentwig, Heinrich. *Die mittelalterlichen Handschriften in der Stadtbibliothek zu Braunschweig.* Wolfenbüttel 1893.
Newton, Francis. "Tibullus in Two Grammatical *Florilegia* of the Middle Ages." *Transactions and Proceedings of the American Philological Association* 93 (1962) 253-286.
Nolhac, Pierre de. *Pétrarque et l'humanisme.* 2 vols. Paris 1907.
Norton, Frederick J. *Italian Printers 1501-1520.* London 1958.

Olmos Canalda, Elias. *Catálogo descriptivo, códices de la catedral de Valencia.* Ed. 2. Madrid 1943.

Ong, Walter. *The Presence of the Word.* New Haven 1967.
———. *Rhetoric, Romance and Technology.* Ithaca 1971.
Orlandi, Stefano. *La biblioteca di S. Maria Novella in Firenze dal sec. xiv al sec. xix.* Florence 1952.
Ott, Ludwig. *Untersuchungen zur theologischen Briefliteratur der Frühscholastik.* Beiträge zur Geschichte der Philosophie und Theologie des Mittelalters, Texte und Untersuchungen 34. Münster 1937.

Pantin, William A. "John of Wales and Medieval Humanism." In *Medieval Studies Presented to Aubrey Gwynn S.J.*, ed. J. A. Watt et al., pp. 297-319. Dublin 1961.
Parkes, Malcolm B. "The Influence of the Concepts of *Ordinatio* and *Compilatio* on the Development of the Book." In *Medieval Learning and Literature: Essays Presented to R. W. Hunt*, ed. J. J. G. Alexander and M. T. Gibson, pp. 115-141. Oxford 1976.
Patera, Adolf, and A. Podlaha. *Soupis Rukopisů knihovny Metropolitní kapitoly Pražké.* 2 vols. Prague 1910-1922.
Paulus, Nicolaus. *Geschichte des Ablasses im Mittelalter.* Paderborn 1922-1923.
Pauly, August, and G. Wissowa. *Paulys Real-Encyclopädie der classischen Altertumswissenschaft.* 34 vols. in 2 ser. Stuttgart 1894-1972.
Pelster, Franz. "Das Leben und die Schriften des Oxforder Dominikanerlehrers Richard Fishacre (1248)." *Zeitschrift für katholische Theologie* 54 (1930) 517-553.
Peter Lombard. *Sententiae in iv libris distinctae.* Ed. Ignatius Brady. Vols. 1- . Spicilegium Bonaventurianum 4. Grottaferrata 1971- .
Pez, Bernard. *Thesaurus anecdotorum novissimus.* 6 vols. Augsburg 1721-1729.
Pfeiffer, Hermann, and B. Cernik. *Catalogus codicum manu scriptorum qui in bibliotheca canonicorum regularium S. Augustini Claustroneoburgi asservantur.* 2 vols. Klosterneuburg 1922-1931.
Pliny the Elder. *Naturalis historiae libri xxxvii.* Ed. Ludwig von Jan and C. Mayhoff. 5 vols. Leipzig 1892-1933.
Pliny the Younger. *Epistularum libri decem.* Ed. R. A. B. Mynors. Oxford 1963.
Pinborg, Jan. *Die Entwicklung der Sprachtheorie im Mittelalter.* Beiträge zur Geschichte der Philosophie und Theologie des Mittelalters 42.2. Münster i.W. 1967.
Podlaha, Antonin. *Die Bibliothek des Metropolitankapitels.* Prague 1904.
Poorter, Alphonse de. *Catalogue général des manuscrits des bibliothèques de Belgique* 2: *Catalogue des manuscrits de la Bibliothèque publique de la ville de Bruges.* Gembloux 1934.
Porcher, Jean. "Le 'De disciplina scholarium', traité du xiiie siècle faussement attribué à Boèce." *École nationale des chartes: Positions des thèses* (Paris 1921) 91-93.
Potthast, August. *Bibliotheca historica medii aevi.* 2 vols. Berlin 1895-1896.

Powicke, Frederick M. *The Medieval Books of Merton College.* Oxford 1931.

—— and C. R. Cheney. *Councils and Synods.* Vols. 1- . Oxford 1964- .

Powitz, Gerhardt. *Kataloge der Stadt- und Universitätsbibliothek Frankfurt a.M.* 2 and 3: *Die Handschriften der Stadt- und Universitätsbibliothek Frankfurt a.M.* Frankfurt 1968-1974.

Pozzi, Giovanni. "Roberto de' Bardi e S. Agostino." *Italia medioevale e umanistica* 1 (1958) 141-153.

——. "La 'Tabula' di Jean de Fayt al 'Collectorium' di Roberto de' Bardi." In *Miscellanea G. G. Meersseman,* pp. 257-311. Italia sacra 15. Padua 1970.

Pratt, Robert A. "Jankyn's Book of Wikked Wyves: Medieval Antimatrimonial Propaganda in the Universities." *Annuale mediaevale* 3 (1962) 5-27.

Prete, Serafino. *I codici della Biblioteca comunale di Fermo.* Florence 1960.

Quétif, Jacques, and J. Échard. *Scriptores ordinis Praedicatorum.* 2 vols. Paris 1719-1723.

Raciti, Gaetano. "L'autore del 'De spiritu et anima'." *Rivista di filosofia neo-scolastica* 53 (1961) 385-401.

Randstrand, Gunnar. *Querolusstudien.* Stockholm 1951.

Richard of Saint-Victor. *De Trinitate.* Ed. Jean Ribaillier. Textes philosophiques du moyen âge 6. Paris 1958.

Roberts, Phyllis B. *Stephanus de Lingua-Tonante: Studies in the Sermons of Stephen Langton.* Pontifical Institute of Mediaeval Studies, Studies and Texts 16. Toronto 1968.

Robertson, Durant W., Jr. "Frequency of Preaching in Thirteenth-Century England." *Speculum* 24 (1949) 376-388.

Robson, Charles A. *Maurice de Sully and the Medieval Vernacular Homily.* Oxford 1952.

——. "The Pecia of the Twelfth-Century Paris School." *Dominican Studies* 2 (1949) 267-279.

Rochais, Henri M. "Contribution à l'histoire des florilèges ascétiques du haut moyen âge latin: Le 'Liber scintillarum'." *Revue bénédictine* 63 (1953) 246-291.

——. "Florilèges spirituels." In *Dictionnaire de spiritualité* 5 (1964).

Rose, Valentin. *Verzeichniss der lateinischen Handschriften der kgl. Bibliothek zu Berlin.* 3 vols. Berlin 1893-1919.

Ross, Braxton. "*Audi Thoma ... Henriciani nota*: A French Scholar appeals to Thomas Becket?" *English Historical Review* 89 (1974) 333-338.

Roth, Benno. *Aus mittelalterlichen Bibliotheken der Seckauer Bischöfe.* N.p. 1960.

Rouse, Richard H. "The *A* Text of Seneca's Tragedies in the Thirteenth Century." *Revue d'histoire des textes* 1 (1971) 93-121.

——. "Bostonus Buriensis and the Author of the *Catalogus scriptorum ecclesiae*." *Speculum* 41 (1966) 471-499.

——. "Cistercian Aids to Study in the Thirteenth Century." *Studies in Medieval Cistercian History* 2 (1976) 123-134.

——. *The Development of Aids to Study in the Thirteenth Century.* Rosenbach Lectures in Bibliography, University of Pennsylvania (forthcoming).

——. "The Early Library of the Sorbonne." *Scriptorium* 21 (1967) 42-71, 227-251.

——. "*Florilegia* and Latin Classical Authors in Twelfth- and Thirteenth-Century Orléans." *Viator* 10 (1979) (forthcoming).

——. "The List of Authorities Appended to the *Manipulus florum.*" *Archives d'histoire doctrinale et littéraire du moyen âge* 32 (1965) 243-250.

——. "Manuscripts Belonging to Richard de Fournival." *Revue d'histoire des textes* 3 (1973) 253-269.

—— and Mary A. Rouse. "Biblical Distinctions in the Thirteenth Century." *Archives d'histoire doctrinale et littéraire du moyen âge* 41 (1974) 27-37.

—— ——. "The *Florilegium Angelicum*: Its Origin, Content and Influence." In *Medieval Learning and Literature: Essays Presented to R. W. Hunt,* ed. J. J. G. Alexander and M. T. Gibson, pp. 66-114. Oxford 1976.

—— ——. "The Texts Called *Lumen anime.*" *Archivum Fratrum Praedicatorum* 41 (1971) 5-113.

—— ——. "The Verbal Concordance to the Scripture." *Archivum Fratrum Praedicatorum* 44 (1974) 5-30.

Rouzet, Anne. *Dictionnaire des imprimeurs, libraires et éditeurs des xve et xvf^e siècles dans les limites géographiques de la Belgique actuelle.* Nieuwkoop 1975.

Ruf, Paul. "Eine altbayerische Gelehrtenbibliothek des 15. Jahrhunderts und ihr Stifter Bernhard von Kraiburg." In *Festschrift Eugen Strollreither,* ed. Fritz Redenbacher, pp. 219-239. Erlangen 1950.

Russo, Carlo F. "Studi sulla divi Claudii Apokolokintosis." *La parola del pasato: Rivista di studi classici* 2 (1946) 241-259.

Salimbene de Adam. *Cronica.* 2 vols. Ed. F. Bernini. Scrittori d'Italia 187-188. Bari 1942.

Samaran, Charles, and R. Marichal. *Catalogue des manuscrits en écriture latine portant des indications de date, de lieu ou de copiste.* Vols. 1- . Paris 1959- .

Sarton, George. *Introduction to the History of Science.* 3 vols. Baltimore 1927-1948.

Savage, Ernest A. "Notes on the Early Monastic Libraries of Scotland with an Account of the *Registrum librorum Anglie* and of the *Catalogus scriptorum ecclesiae* of John Boston of the Abbey of Bury St. Edmunds." *Edinburgh Bibliographical Society* 14 (1930) 1-46.

Schäfer, Karl H. *Die Ausgaben der apostolischen Kammer unter Johann xxii.* Paderborn 1911.

Schmaus, Michael. "Das Fortwirken der Augustinischen Trinitätspsychologie...." In *Vitae et Veritati: Festgabe für Karl Adam*, pp. 44-56. Düsseldorf 1956.

Schmidt, Adolf. "Mittelalterliche Lesezeichen." *Zeitschrift für Bücherfreunde* 2.1 (1898-1899) 213-215.

Schneider, Karin. *Die Handschriften der Stadtbibliothek Nürnberg*. 2 vols. Wiesbaden 1965-1967.

Schneyer, Johannes B. *Repertorium der lateinischen Sermones des Mittelalters.* 6 vols. Beiträge zur Geschichte der Philosophie und Theologie des Mittelalters, Texte und Untersuchungen 43. Münster 1969-1975.

Schöpf, Friedrich G., ed. *De laude caritatis libellus*. Dresden 1857.

Schreiber, Heinrich. "Drehbare mittelalterliche Lesezeichnen." *Zentralblatt für Bibliothekswesen* 56 (1939) 281-293.

Schuermans, Henri. "Bibliothèque de l'abbaye de Villers." *Société archéologique de l'arrondissement de Nivelles* 6 (1898) 193-236.

Schulte, Johann F. von. *Die canonistischen Handschriften*. Prague 1868.

——. *Die Geschichte der Quellen und Literatur des canonischen Rechts.* 3 vols. Stuttgart 1875-1880.

Seneca. *De beneficiis, De clementia*. Ed. C. Hosius. Leipzig 1914.

——. *Dialogorum libri XII*. Ed. E. Hermes. Leipzig 1905.

——. *Epistulae ad Lucilium*. Ed. Otto Hense. Leipzig 1914. Ed. Leighton D. Reynolds. Oxford 1965.

——. *Naturales quaestiones*. Ed. A. Gercke. Leipzig 1907.

Pseudo-Seneca. *Epistolae Senecae ad Paulum apostolum et Pauli apostoli ad Senecam*. Ed. Friedrich Haase. Leipzig 1897.

——. *Ludus de morte Claudii*. Ed. Friedrich Haase. Leipzig 1898.

Seneca Rhetor. *Sententiae, Divisiones, Colores*. Ed. A. Kiessling. Leipzig 1872.

Smalley, Beryl. *English Friars and Antiquity in the Early Fourteenth Century.* Oxford 1960.

——. "*Exempla* in the Commentaries of Stephen Langton." *Bulletin of the John Rylands Library* 17 (1933) 121-129.

——. "Jean de Hesdin O.Hosp.S.Ioh." *Recherches de théologie ancienne et médiévale* 28 (1961) 283-330.

——. *The Study of the Bible in the Middle Ages*. Ed. 2 rev. Oxford 1952.

——. "Thomas Waleys O.P." *Archivum Fratrum Praedicatorum* 24 (1954) 50-107.

Southern, Richard W. *Western Society and the Church in the Middle Ages*. Pelican History of the Church 2. Harmondsworth 1971.

Stangl, Thomas, ed. *Tulliana et Mario-Victoriana*. Munich 1888.

Stegmüller, Friedrich. "Die *Consolatio theologiae* des Papstes Pedro de Luna (Benedikt XIII)." In *Gesammelte Aufsätze zur Kulturgeschichte Spaniens* 21: 209-215. Münster 1963.

——. *Repertorium biblicum medii aevi*. 7 vols. Madrid 1950-1961.

Steiner, Arpad. "The Authorship of 'De disciplina scholarium'." *Speculum* 12 (1937) 81-84.

Stevenson, Enrico, and I. B. de Rossi. *Codices Palatini latini Bibliothecae Vaticanae* 1. Rome 1886.

Szentiványi, Robertus. *Catalogus concinnus librorum manuscriptorum Bibliothecae Batthyányanae.* Szeged 1958.

Tabulae codicum manu scriptorum praeter graecos et orientales in Bibliotheca Palatina Vindobonensi asservatorum. 11 vols. Vienna 1864-1912.

Tanner, Thomas. *Bibliotheca Britannico-Hibernica...*. London 1748.

Théry, Gabriel. "Catalogue des manuscrits dionysiens des bibliothèques d'Autriche." *Archives d'histoire doctrinale et littéraire du moyen âge* 10 (1936) 163-209.

———. "Thomas Gallus et les concordances bibliques." In *Aus der Geisteswelt des Mittelalters*, ed. Albert Lang, et al., pp. 427-446. Beiträge zur Geschichte der Philosophie und Theologie des Mittelalters, Texte und Untersuchungen Suppl. 3. 2 vols. Münster 1935.

Thomas Aquinas. *Opera omnia iussu impensaque Leonis XIII. P. M. edita.* 48 vols. projected. Rome 1882- . Includes the following *inter alia*:

22.1-2. *Quaestiones disputatae de veritate.* Ed. A. Dondaine. Rome 1970-1972.

26. *Expositio super Iob ad litteram.* Ed. A. Dondaine. Rome 1965.

41, pts. B and C. *De perfectione spiritualis vitae* and *Contra doctrinam retrahentium a religione.* Ed. H. F. Dondaine. Rome 1969.

47.1-2. *Sententia libri ethicorum.* Ed. R. A. Gautier. Rome 1969.

———. *Super librum de causis expositio.* Ed. H. D. Saffrey. Textus philosophici friburgenses 4-5. Fribourg 1954.

Thomson, S. Harrison. "Grosseteste's Concordantial Signs." *Mediaevalia et humanistica* 9 (1955) 39-53.

———. "Grosseteste's Topical Concordance of the Bible and the Fathers." *Speculum* 9 (1934) 139-144.

———. "Learning at the Court of Charles IV." *Speculum* 25 (1950) 1-20.

Thouzellier, Christine. *Catharisme et Valdéisme en Languedoc.* Ed. 2 rev. Paris 1969.

Trapp, Damasus. "Peter Ceffons of Clairvaux." *Recherches de théologie ancienne et médiévale* 24 (1957) 101-154.

Truhlář, Josef. *Catalogus codicum manu scriptorum latinorum qui in C.R. Bibliotheca Publica atque Universitatis Pragensis asservantur.* 2 vols. Prague 1905-1906.

Ullman, Berthold L. "Classical Authors in Certain Mediaeval *Florilegia*." *Classical Philology* 27 (1932) 1-42.

———. "Joseph Lang and his Anthologies." In *Middle Ages, Reformation, Volkskunde: Festschrift for John G. Kunstmann*, pp. 186-200. University of North Carolina Studies in Germanic Languages and Literatures 26. Chapel Hill 1959.

———. "Petronius in the Mediaeval *Florilegia*." *Classical Philology* 25 (1930) 11-21.

———. *Studies in the Italian Renaissance*. Rome 1955.

———. "The Text of Petronius in the Sixteenth Century." *Classical Philology* 25 (1930) 128-154.

———. "The Text Tradition and Authorship of the *Laus Pisonis*." *Classical Philology* 24 (1929) 109-132.

———. "Tibullus in Mediaeval *Florilegia*." *Classical Philology* 23 (1928) 128-174.

———. "Valerius Flaccus in the Mediaeval *Florilegia*." *Classical Philology* 26 (1931) 21-30.

——— and Philip Stadter. *The Public Library of Renaissance Florence*. Medioevo e umanesimo 10. Padua 1972.

Unterkircher, Franz. *Die datierten Handschriften der Oesterreichischen National-bibliothek*. 2 vols. Vienna 1969-1971.

Valerius Maximus. *Factorum et dictorum memorabilium libri novem*. Ed. C. Kempf. Leipzig 1888.

Valois, Noël. *Guillaume d'Auvergne*. Paris 1880.

Van den Gheyn, J., et al. *Catalogue des manuscrits de la Bibliothèque royale de Belgique*. 13 vols. Brussels 1901-1948.

Vaudois languedociens et Pauvres catholiques: Cahiers de Fanjeaux 2. 1967.

Vega, Ángel C. *De la Santa Iglesia Apostólica de Eliberri-Granada*. 2 vols. España sagrada 55-56. Madrid 1957.

Vennebusch, J. *Die theologischen Handschriften des Stadtarchivs Köln*. 1 vol. to date. Cologne 1976- .

Vernet, André. "Un abbé de Clairvaux bibliophile." *Scriptorium* 6 (1952) 76-88.

Von Nolken, Christina. "An Edition of Selected Parts of the Middle English Translation of the *Rosarium theologie*." D.Phil. diss. Oxford 1976.

Wadding, Lucas. *Annales Minorum seu trium ordinum a S. Francisco institutorum*. 8 vols. Lyons 1625-1654.

———, ed. *Concordantiae morales S. Antonii de Padua*. Rome 1624.

———. *Scriptores ordinis Minorum*. Rome 1650.

Walker, Alice. "The Reading of an Elizabethan." *Review of English Studies* 8 (1932) 264-281.

Walter, Johannes von. *Die ersten Wanderprediger Frankreichs*. 2 vols. Leipzig 1903-1906.

Ware, James. *De scriptoribus Hiberniae*. Dublin 1639.

Warner, George F., and J. P. Gilson. *Catalogue of Western Manuscripts in the Old Royal and King's Collections*. 4 vols. London 1921.

Weiss, Roberto. "The Earliest Catalogues of the Library of Lincoln College." *Bodleian Quarterly Record* 8 (1935-1937) 343-359.

Welter, Jean-Thiébaut. *L'exemplum dans la littérature religieuse et didactique du moyen âge*. Paris 1927.

Werner, Ernst. *Pauperes Christi.* Leipzig 1956.

Wilkins, Ernest H. "Early Alphabetical Indexes." In *The Manly Anniversary Studies in Language and Literature,* pp. 315-322. Chicago 1928.

Williman, Daniel. "The Books of the Avignonese Popes and Clergy: A Repertory and Edition of the Book-Notices in the Vatican Archives, 1287-1420." Ph.D. diss. University of Toronto 1973.

Wilmart, André. "Les allégories sur l'écriture attribués à Raban Maur." *Revue bénédictine* 32 (1920) 47-56.

——. "L'ancienne bibliothèque de Clairvaux." *Collectanea ordinis Cisterciensium reformatorum* 11 (1949) 101-127, 301-319. Repr. from *Mémoires de la Société académique de l'Aube,* ser. 3, 54 (1917) 125-190.

——. *Auteurs spirituels et textes dévots du moyen âge latin.* Paris 1932.

——. "La collection des 38 homélies latines de S. Jean Chrysostome." *Journal of Theological Studies* 19 (1918) 305-327.

——. "Le dialogue apologétique du moine Guillaume, biographe de Suger." *Revue Mabillon* 32 (1942) 80-118.

Winandy, Jacques. "L'œuvre littéraire d'Ambroise Autpert." *Revue bénédictine* 60 (1950) 93-119.

Wisłocki, Władysław. *Katalog rękopisów Biblioteki Uniwersytetu Jagiellońskiego.* 2 vols. Cracow 1877-1881.

Witty, Francis J. "The Beginnings of Indexing and Abstracting: Some Notes towards a History of Indexing and Abstracting in Antiquity and the Middle Ages." *The Indexer* 8 (1973) 193-198.

——. "Early Indexing Techniques: A Study of Several Book Indexes of the Fourteenth, Fifteenth and Early Sixteenth Centuries." *The Library Quarterly* 35 (1965) 141-148.

Wölfflin, Eduard von. *Caecilii Balbi De nugis philosophorum.* Basel 1855.

——. *Publilii Syri sententiae.* Leipzig 1869.

Wolf von Glanvell, Victor. *Die Kanonessammlung des Kardinals Deusdedit* 1. Paderborn 1905.

Wooley, Reginald M. *Catalogue of the Manuscripts of Lincoln Cathedral Chapter Library.* Oxford 1927.

Index of Manuscripts

Major references are in bold face.

Index of Previous Owners

General Index